FIGHTER ACES
OF THE U.S.A.

Other Books by the Authors

FIGHTER ACES
HORRIDO! FIGHTER ACES OF THE LUFTWAFFE
  German edition: DAS WAREN DIE
  DEUTSCHEN JAGDFLIEGER ASSE 1939-1945

BLOND KNIGHT OF GERMANY
  German edition: HOLT HARTMANN VOM HIMMEL

By Constable:
  HIDDEN HEROES
  COSMIC PULSE OF LIFE

By Toliver:
  THE INTERROGATOR

FIGHTER ACES OF THE U.S.A.

By
Raymond F. Toliver
and
Trevor J. Constable

AERO PUBLISHERS, INC.
329 West Aviation Road, Fallbrook, CA 92028

ISBN 0-8168-5792-X

Library of Congress Catalog Card Number 79-53300

Dedicated to:

ALL THE FIGHTER PILOTS
of all the nations and all the wars
who lost their lives in the struggle
for the skies.

Acknowledgments

The authors gratefully acknowledge the assistance they have received from others in the preparation of this book. Research and writing began in 1950. More than two thousand persons have since contributed in many ways. The authors wish that every person involved could be personally mentioned. Countless aces or their survivors and relatives gave unstintingly of their time and treasured historical material. We are in the debt of all these unnamed aides.

Special thanks are due Cletus J. Cattoor of Overland, Missouri, who helped so much in researching the victory credit records for us back in 1951-1955. These labors culminated in the establishment of the first complete USAF World War II ace list. Similar special thanks are due the late Patrick J. Cassidy; the American Fighter Aces Association and its Secretary, William N. Hess; Dr. Mauer Mauer, James N. Eastman, Jr. and the Air University's Albert F. Simpson Historical Research Center at Maxwell AFB, Alabama; the USAF, USN and USMC photo archives; David Schoem, and Janet T. Moskal.

The late Hans Otto Boehm, Historian of the German Fighter Pilots Association, made possible the authoritative treatment of the German aces in this book. Boehm also introduced authors Toliver and Constable to each other, for which we are eternally grateful. Hans Ring and Ernst Obermaier also provided invaluable data on the careers of the leading German aces, as did such individuals as Adolf Galland, Dieter Hrabak, Eduard Neumann, Johannes Steinhoff, Erich Hartmann and countless others.

The first real insight into the feats of Japanese aces in World War II — heretofore shrouded in mystery — has been made possible by Japanese historians Yasuho Izawa and Ikuhiko Hata who have spent years digging into the records of the Japanese fighter units. Their cooperation with the authors was most helpful.

We have sought to contribute a unique and definitive work to American aviation history. Without our legions of helpers through the years, this book would not have been possible. To all who have aided us, therefore, we extend our heartfelt thanks.

Raymond F. Toliver

Trevor J. Constable

Los Angeles, California 1979

Introduction

This book is the first comprehensive volume ever published dealing with American fighter pilot aces over the entire period of U.S. engagement in aerial warfare—from World War I through Vietnam. Even Americans who fought with the Allies before American entry into World War I have been finally "brought home" as American aces in this book. Changes in aerial tactics and technology are described technically, but are given a living dimension in accounts of the aces themselves—dynamic participants in the most deadly scoring game of all time.

Statistics are an integral part of acedom. No effort has been spared over many decades to ensure that the ace lists in this book are the most complete and authentic compilations of American ace statistics ever publicly offered. Research actually began during the boyhoods of the authors, with collection of all available material on the aces of World War I. Concentrated research began in 1951, and by 1960 Colonel Toliver had compiled a list of American aces sufficient to serve as eligibility documentation for membership in the then newly-formed American Fighter Aces Association. Honorary membership was awarded to co-author Toliver for this work, together with an appointment as permanent historian for the Association.

Every available official and quasi-official list of American aces—including the massive statistics of the U.S. armed services with their periodic revisions—has been embodied in the ace lists in this book. Despite this effort, there may still be unintentional or anomalous omissions. The book deals with more than 1300 aces in five separate wars. For any such omissions, the authors apologize. They are indebted to the U.S. Navy, U.S. Marine Corps and U.S. Air Force for outstanding cooperation through the years.

Aces are a military elite. Large additions to this fraternity are now highly unlikely, given technological trends and realities. America has trained over 100,000 military pilots since the dawn of aviation, but only one percent became aces—pilots credited with five or more aerial victories. This book attempts to set down the reasons for the rarity of fighter aces among all those who have flown in combat. By reliving the evolution and background of aerial warfare in the aces' own words, and setting this against an unfolding tactical, technical and statistical backdrop, the authors hope that they have fashioned some kind of monument to these men. This monument should be in the reader's consequent perspective on why the aces are the most elite of all military brotherhoods.

DAREDEVIL AND TOP SCORER

Captain Edward V. Rickenbacker is seen here in the cockpit of his Nieuport 28 fighter. He wrote an immortal record as America's ace of aces in WWI, and lived to become one of the major architects of U.S. civil aviation. Rickenbacker was the most famous American pilot of his time, a daredevil who believed that he wouldn't leave the earth before his time. He passed away in 1977, a giant of the air age.

(USAF)

WWII TOP FIGHTER ACE

Captain Richard Ira Bong, top scoring American ace of all wars. His score of 40 Japanese airplanes shot down in aerial combat is unchallenged by other American aces. From Poplar, Wisconsin, Bong flew combat with the 49th Fighter Group, SWPA. He lost his life while transitioning to P-80 jet fighters at Burbank, California 6 August 1945.

(USN)

Lt. Randall H. Cunningham
Mira Mesa, California. First American ace of the Vietnam War (10 May 1972).

America's Top Fighter Aces

TOP AMERICAN ACE OF THE KOREAN WAR

Joseph M. McConnell, flying with the 39th Fighter-Interceptor Squadron in Korea, became the 27th American USAF pilot to become a MiG ace on 16 February 1953. By 18 May he had scored his fifteenth victory to become the first "triple ace" of the Korean War. Later the same day he scored his sixteenth and final victory and became the top fighter ace of the Korean War.

Captain Richard "Steve" Ritchie, TOP USAF ACE OF VIETNAM WAR: Air Force Academy graduate Steve Ritchie shot down five MiG-21 aircraft in Vietnam between May 10 and August 28, 1972. He is tied with the U.S. Navy's Randall "Duke" Cunningham for top fighter pilot ace honors of the Vietnam War as each pilot has five victories. Ritchie, from Reidsville, North Carolina, now lives in Golden, Colorado.

Ace Lists

TABLE OF CONTENTS

Chapters

The Beginning of Military Aviation

(USAF)

A Wright airplane is trucked to Fort Meyer, Virginia, for evaluation and testing in 1908. Note the solid-wheeled cart on which the machine was transported. Yes, only yesterday, this was the acme of aerial technology.

1

THE MAKING OF A FIGHTER ACE

The clashing dynamism of the medieval joust was reborn in this century in the form of aerial combat. While faceless millions were mowed down in the 1914-18 war to moulder into the mud of Flanders, high above these scenes of unprecedented mass slaughter, individual combat was having its renaissance. The dull butcheries of trench warfare were a moral and military obscenity divested of all glory, but in the clean and open struggle for the sky man flew against man in skilled combat. This kind of fighting was easy to comprehend and even easier to glorify against the inhuman tapestry of the ground war. The result was the emergence of the fighter ace as this century's most glamorous warrior.

Amid the sputtering of primitive engines and the whine of the wind in struts and wires, all the lineaments of the knightly joust reappeared in the infant art of aerial combat. While divisions were often decimated in the mud below, and masked troops seared and suffocated each other with poison gas, chivalry and sportsmanship ruled the fighting in the skies. Mighty artillery barrages, mass attacks and storms of machine gun fire sundered every human bond between enemies on the ground, but aloft the opposing flyers waved to each other and even saluted. Sporting rules grew up around aerial combat as though by formal agreement. A new heraldry blossomed in wildly colored and patterned airplanes, often decorated with mascot devices of the pilot's own design.

The kind of war these airmen fought bore little relationship to the mass effects of modern armies and navies. Their individualistic type of fighting was an echo from the past, before the juggernaut of technology intruded upon the settlement of disputes. Many of the characteristics and much of the spirit of a *game* were present in aerial combat in World War I and have continued in an attenuated form down to the present day. As a consequence, the men who flew fighter planes, regardless of the uniform they wore, are joined by a common bond of almost mystical quality. Among the thousands so joined there is an inner and elite brotherhood—the fighter aces.

Just as the fighter pilots literally rose above the impersonal nature of modern warfare, so did the fighter aces rise above their fellow fighter pilots. The factors that make a fighter ace are so variable, so elusive of analysis and so far beyond the reach of the ordinary fighter pilot that the United States has been able to produce only 1400 fighter aces in this century. In the nearly twenty years of warfare involving America since 1917, over 60,000 fighter pilots have taken to the air for Uncle Sam. *Less than three percent of these men became aces.*

Wartime publicity, novels and motion pictures have etched an archetypal fighter ace in the public mind. He is often depicted as a devil-may-care girl-chaser, a hard-drinking, glamorous hedonist who flies, fights or loves on a prodigious scale. Late-night orgies are supposed to be his stock in trade. Despite these exertions, he is always first into the air as the Dawn Patrol goes bucketing up to challenge the hated Black Baron.

If this fictional fighter ace ever existed in the world of reality, few authentic aces ever knew him. There have always been aces who were drinking men, and plenty of playboys and ladies' men—that is all part of the ace image—but these frivolous aspects of behavior invariably concealed sterner qualities. Without these qualities, few could survive in aerial combat, let alone become aces.

The real fighter ace is likely to be a man of above average intelligence and education, but even this is not universal. There are many men who were woefully short on academic training whose character, will power and natural ability enabled them to win through to the coveted title of "ace." Drive, persistence and fighting spirit could and did make up for educational deficiencies.

The ace is more than likely to be a direct and plain-spoken man, often forceful of manner. The overwhelming majority of aces are individualists. This might be expected, for no other individual fighting man in any era, dependent in the end entirely on his own abilities, has wielded the deadly powers conferred on a pilot by a fighter plane.

America's aces include many professional aviators, men who made aerial combat and the preparation for it their life's work. Most aces have nevertheless come from other occupations, or even direct from school and college in wartime. All shared a common attraction to the magnificent adventure of flying. War brought this adventure within the reach of many who otherwise would never have known its magic.

Combat flying developed in many men personal capacities and skills that would otherwise have lain dormant. The awakening and sharpening of these qualities have always been central to the making of a fighter ace. Skill, dash, courage and judgment have all

been required in an exceptional degree—all qualities drawn from the individual's inner resources. These qualities cannot actually be taught. Blending, balancing and controlling these qualities is achieved through both training and experience.

These inner resources in aerial combat meet and mingle with such uncontrollable external factors as luck and opportunity. Interwoven with these in turn, and exerting a decisive influence on the success of the individual pilot, has been that special plexus of powers and skills that makes a man a *good shot*.

Contrary to popular ideas, shooting ability and not flying ability has always been the fighter pilot's most important asset, and the asset most likely to make him a fighter ace. Air-to-air shooting ability with machine-guns and cannons is a highly esoteric skill, and few indeed are the fighter pilots ever to master this skill completely. Those blessed with the native ability to shoot at a moving target from

(U.S. Army)

BILLY MITCHELL, 1898
Standing at the extreme left is William "Billy" Mitchell, photographed with fellow officers of the U.S. Signal Corps at Jacksonville, Florida in 1898. The airplane had yet to be invented, but the slender young man on the left would have his name indelibly associated with America's aerial destiny. Mitchell was posthumously awarded the Medal of Honor for his services to U.S. military aviation.

**THE WRIGHT AIRPLANE
CIRCA 1909**
The fighter aircraft in which
more than 1300 Americans became aces had their roots
in the aeronautical science
founded by the Wright
Brothers. There are human
beings still living who were
around when this aircraft
was the finest flying
machine in the world.

(Erickson Collection)

a moving platform, the movement of both being in three dimensions, were almost certain
to become aces—even if they were not exceptional pilots.

This book contains a number of interesting
and highly revelatory observations on air-to-
air shooting from the aces themselves. Strange
as it may seem, it was all too often the
smooth-as-silk pilot who went to his doom under the enemy's guns, while cruder pilots of
lesser experience repeatedly escaped. This was
because the slick pilot's reactions in the air
were predictable to an enemy pilot of similar
skills. When the smooth pilot took evasive action, his enemy could sometimes predict these
maneuvers in advance, and the evading pilot
would make a lethal rendezvous with a well-
aimed stream of bullets or cannon shells.

The ham-fisted rough pilot, on the other
hand, often reacted unpredictably when
bounced. His salvation lay in his sheer crudity
as an airman. He might wrench his aircraft
into turns an experienced pilot would never
have attempted out of elegant concern for the
airplane, or plunge himself into a negative-G
maneuver that would throw off a pursuing
enemy. Whether he was rough or smooth,
however, the fighter pilot who could shoot was
likely to become an ace if given adequate opportunity.

Good eyesight was important to the pilots of
World War I, but not as crucial as it became
in World War II, Korea and Vietnam. At 150
mph in the 1914-18 conflict it would be difficult to close a target that could be seen easily
miles away. In World War II, with straight
and level fighter speeds of around 350 mph, a

target could be attacked if it could be seen at
any distance under most conditions. The same
was true in jet combat in Korea and Vietnam.

The pilot with good eyes, able to pick out
the tiny speck in the heavens that an aircraft
becomes at five miles, had another of the attributes of an ace. Spotting the enemy at great
distances permitted the pilot to place himself
in an attacking position and get the enemy
machine on the defensive. In the words of the
greatest fighter ace of all time and all the nations, Erich Hartmann of Germany, "He who
sees the enemy first already has half the victory." This kind of visual skill, combined with
a shooting eye, resulted in many a victory and
many an ace.

Physical toughness has always been essential in the making of an ace. With the evolution of aerial combat and aircraft, the physical
requirements have undergone a
metamorphosis, with World War I, World
War II, Korea and Vietnam, each requiring a
different kind of toughness. All four conflicts
demanded the highest qualities of physical
and mental endurance.

The aces of World War I had to be able to
take direct physical punishment on a scale
never subsequently repeated or equaled. Mer-
cilessly buffeted by the elements before they
fought for their lives, physical discomfort for
the 1914-18 pilots was a heavy burden. The
roar of the wind, the blasting of their machine
guns a few feet from their faces and the
thunder of their crude engines frequently left
them deaf for days. Descending half-frozen
from open cockpit combat, they often couldn't
stand up when they clambered stiffly to the

ground. Many World War I pilots carried circulatory ailments with them throughout the rest of their lives.

The pioneers shared with their World War II, Korean War and Vietnam War counterparts the fierce demands made on the human structure when a man fights literally for his life. The World War I pilot was additionally haunted by the possibility that his machine might shed its wings, especially after a few hits. The inflammable nature of these early fighting planes made a fiery death in the heavens an ever-present likelihood, from which the only possible deliverance was a horrifying death leap—without a parachute.

Improved aircraft design in World War II brought a measure of pilot comfort, but with improved performance came a new set of physical demands. Combat now took place in the 300-400 mph bracket. The controls of the airplanes at these speeds became extremely heavy. Fifteen minutes of combat would test the physical strength of an Atlas, and pilots often fought soaked with sweat from these exertions.

A fighter pilot could not hope to become an ace in World War II without strong arms and shoulders, and a powerful back. Leading aces on both sides could always sense any physical weakening of an opponent in the air. If a pilot's strength began to fail, his experienced enemy would probably notice the decline as soon as did the fatigued pilot. In gladiatorial fashion, such a combatant was actually physically overpowered—by an enemy who had never laid a hand on him. All this went on while they pirouetted thousands of feet above the earth.

The same physical rigors were not required of the jet pilots. Hydraulically operated controls were just being designed into aircraft at the end of World War II. America's jet aces, mounted on the F-80 Shooting Star and F-86 Sabrejet in Korea, had hydraulically operated flight controls and flew well-insulated against the high altitude cold. These jets could be maneuvered at speeds approaching that of sound with no more physical strength required than that of the proverbial "97-pound weakling."

The jet aces nevertheless landed after combat in an exhausted condition, known as being "clanked." The direct demands made on their bodies were less than those of the two world wars. The nerve-draining ordeal of fighting for

their lives was the same as ever. Added to this was a new and formidable dimension to aerial fighting—the exacting mental and psychological demands of feather-touch flying and teamwork at near the speed of sound. The physical demands may have been diminished, but the psychological strain had risen steeply as aircraft became more complex and flew higher and faster than ever before. Only a strong man—mentally and physically—could make it to acedom in the jets.

Technical progress continued after Korea. The fighter pilots in Vietnam flew jet aircraft of mind-boggling complexity and staggering size and weight. In the workhorse F-4 Phantom II, a second crew member had been added to share the burdens of complex avionics and sophisticated weapons systems that were beyond the capacity of a lone pilot to operate and tend.

Vietnam fighter pilots faced new challenges arising from technical advancement. Supersonic speeds meant crushing G-forces in turning battles or evasive maneuvers, from which the pilots were delivered only by the merciless wringing action of their G-suits. They had to be super athletes to meet these punishing physical demands.

In the mental and psychological sphere new specters bedeviled the fighter pilots. At supersonic speeds, aerial combat acquired a flashing, mercurial quality. The enemy could be behind you in an instant, and the haunting advent of air-to-air and ground-to-air missiles was a constant source of anxiety. Death could come with thunderclap swiftness any time, to any pilot, no matter what his expertise and combat acumen.

In Vietnam, his conqueror might not even be a pilot at all. The American fighter pilot could be snuffed out by a small Oriental in spectacles miles away on the ground. He would have no more reality to this foe than the bright spot his Phantom jet made on the glowing phosphors of a Russian-built radar scope. Aerial combat had changed since the days of the Red Baron.

The ace of World War I had a 1,500-pound aircraft of wood and fabric to fly. The engine boasted perhaps 350 hp in the later days of the conflict. Top speeds in a dive of 200 mph were the zenith of aircraft performance. The first aces won their laurels in fighters that flew in combat at speeds considerably less than the stalling speed of the jets flown by the aces of

Korea and Vietnam. This well-nigh incredible spectrum of aircraft performance, more than 1,500 mph wide, was developed within the lifetimes of many World War I aces.

Knowledge of the enemy's strengths and weaknesses has always played a substantial role in the making of an ace. While it is generally true that the machine imposes limits on the man, the great aces have always been able to stretch those limits. In all the wars, there is a high probability that every fighter plane flown by the combatants had some kind of flaw or weakness—either innately or by combat comparison with enemy aircraft they were encountering. If he was to become an ace therefore, a pilot had to know those things about his own machine that might kill *him* rather than the enemy.

The P-47 was a case in point. Affectionately known as the "Jug" by those who flew it, the P-47 Thunderbolt could dive as fast as anything in the air prior to the German Me-262 jet. The Thunderbolt nevertheless had one serious aerodynamic fault, connected with this combat asset of high diving speed, that claimed the lives of a number of its pilots.

The P-47's control stick would freeze in a dive from high altitude at high speed. No amount of human strength could budge the stick. What did the pilots do? By instinct and training they rolled back on the trim tab in an effort to raise the nose. No luck. The heavy machine kept going headlong for the deck. Desperately the pilot would roll in more trim tab and pull with all his strength on the stick.

Reaching heavier air at about 18,000 feet, the pilot of the plummeting Jug would find his strength and the trim beginning to take effect. In a few seconds the effect became violent! Hitting between 500 and 600 mph in its dive, the P-47 was hurtling downward at better than 800 feet per second. The tail of the aircraft was simply torn off in the resulting fifteen to thirty-G pullout. Seldom was the pilot able to recover his senses in time to bail out.

Even the beautiful "pilot's aircraft," the German Focke-Wulfe 190, was cursed with a mach limitation that caused it literally to fall out of control. This flaw was quickly spotted by Allied pilots and exploited to the full. The ingenious manipulation of technical strengths and weaknesses brought many an American pilot into the fraternity of aces.

The Me-262 twin-engined jet that the Germans made operational in World War II enjoyed a substantial performance margin over the best Allied fighters, and also packed the devastating punch of four 30mm cannons. The Me-262 could easily outdistance pursuing Allied fighters, provided both of its jet engines were functioning. The weakness of the Me-262 was its fuel limitation, and American pilots exploited this weakness.

A favorite tactic in countering the Me-262 jet was for the American Mustangs to set up patrols near known Me-262 bases. When the jet fighters appeared on return from operations the tactical balance was tipped against them, by virtue of their being short on fuel and possibly also slowed by battle damage. The German pilots were also put at a psychological disadvantage by the swarms of enemy fighters awaiting them and the fuel warning light glowing on their own instrument panels. Many Me-262's were downed under these circumstances, which were an exploitation of a weakness by the long range American fighters.

Knowing the enemy's capabilities, and respecting them, was a firm step toward becoming a living ace. In World War I, German aircraft were generally superior in performance, except for range. German superiority in climb, speed, maneuverability and firepower governed the tactics used by the Allied pilots, with the range disparity compelling most combat over German-held territory.

In World War II, the German fighters were again a tough proposition, especially in the defense of Germany. American pilots who fought them did so at the end of a long flight from British bases, or from makeshift strips behind advancing Allied armies in the late months of the war. Technical superiority over the famed Me-109 in Germany proved to be a tall order, long in the filling. Only with the advent of the equally famed P-51 Mustang was the technical superiority of the Me-109 in its own skies finally overcome.

The Japanese Zero was the dogfighting master of the Pacific skies in the early months of the conflict. The leading aces of the Pacific Theater were American pilots who exploited intelligently the superior technical aspects of aircraft like the P-38 Lightning, and avoided the close dogfighting so favorable to the Japanese. This meant deserting traditional, World War I-derived methods of aerial fighting.

In a turning battle—the major legacy of

(USAF)

EARLY AERIAL ARMAMENT TESTS
Military men of foresight were not long in figuring out how to carry armament aboard airplanes. With Lieutenant Selfridge piloting on the right, General Dargue mans a Lewis gun in early tests. Lieutenant Selfridge was later killed in test flight with Orville Wright.

World War I being the dogfight—the Japanese Zero was outstanding. 20mm cannons as armament enabled the Japanese pilots to exploit their turning superiority with great hitting power. When the Americans avoided the dogfight and confined their attacks to rapid firing passes, the odds tilted sharply in their favor—even when flying the older Curtiss P-40.

These American "hit and run" tactics exposed a serious technical flaw of the Zero—vulnerability to gunfire. This weakness was not alone technical, for it also gave the hard-pressed Americans of the early battles a psychological lift. Flamers often resulted from a few hits. The American fighters by contrast proved to be far more robust than the Japanese. The enemy needed many hits to down an American fighter unless they happened to kill or wound its pilot.

The aggressive competitive spirit essential to the making of an ace had to be constantly tempered by technical awareness. As the decades passed, the need for such technical awareness increased along with the complexity of fighter aircraft. In this respect, the thundering rush of the brave medieval knight, with its all-or-nothing outcome, disappeared from the aerial joust. Aloft the thrusts were coldly calculated as well as deadly.

Tactics in aerial combat developed erratically, and were modified mainly by technical innovations, and the see-saw changes of fortune they offered to each of the combatants in turn. Before the First World War, in the pioneer days of military aviation, there was no accepted concept of *aerial combat* accompanying military adoption of the airplane. Many eminent military leaders refused to take aviation seriously. "The aeroplane is good sport, but worthless for use by the Army" said the famous French soldier Ferdinand Foch in 1911. A few years later he was the Allied *generalissimo,* with hundreds of aircraft overhead.

Prior to 1914 the military took a limited view of aircraft, seeing them primarily as mobile observation platforms—an improvement, as it were, on the observation balloon. Aircraft were not looked upon as new weapons in their own right. This was true on both the German and Allied sides. The brilliant Giuilio Douhet of Italy, who foresaw accurately the rise of airpower as the primary tactical and strategic factor in future warfare, was rewarded for his views with jail.

Douhet became the Clausewitz of airpower much later, but in his own time military conservatives considered him a joke. His apostles and devotees in America, who included "Billy" Mitchell, did not have sufficient influence to get the air weapon the attention and support that it deserved. In France, Britain and Germany the same situation applied. Only in Russia, where Igor Sikorsky was building huge four-engined aircraft with enclosed cabins for the military, did there seem to be any comprehension by military authorities that a new dimension to warfare was imminent.

Early military aircraft in World War I were slow machines. Their operational purpose was to fly over the battlefield and its environs and report on the progress of the ground war. Generals ensconced in chateaux miles behind the front with maps and cognac found aircraft a handy innovation.

These reconnaissance pilots—German on one side, British and French on the other—frequently spotted each other while making their aerial rounds of the battlefield. Often they waved to each other, or saluted, as they flew close. Their ability to get off the ground and stay precariously airborne united them in a grateful and chivalrous brotherhood. Aggressive acts soon followed nevertheless, and aerial combat was on its way out of the womb of ideas and into the world of reality.

One daring English pilot, Lieutenant Norman Spratt, made such hostile moves toward a German two-seater that the enemy pilot did the World War I version of "hitting the panic button." Landing quickly and jumping out, he set his plane afire with a signal pistol, whereupon he went scurrying back to the German lines on foot. This is believed to be the first aerial combat victory on record, although neither aircraft was armed. Weapons were not long in coming.

Observation planes began carrying bags of bricks, hand grenades and other lethal objects. Originally the intention was to drop this material on enemy troops in the trenches. Soon the possibilities of a new mode of warfare began to dawn on the airmen. Dumping their loads on each other's aircraft started the new epoch. Pistols, rifles and eventually machine guns were added to the aerial arsenal. Potshots at the enemy became standard operating procedure.

More than one of these early crates was sent plummeting to earth by an avalanche of bricks released from a machine flying above. Another cunning tactic was to drop lead pellets by the bagful into an enemy's propeller arc. Tiny though these pellets were, they were sufficient to shatter the wooden props of the day and destroy an aircraft.

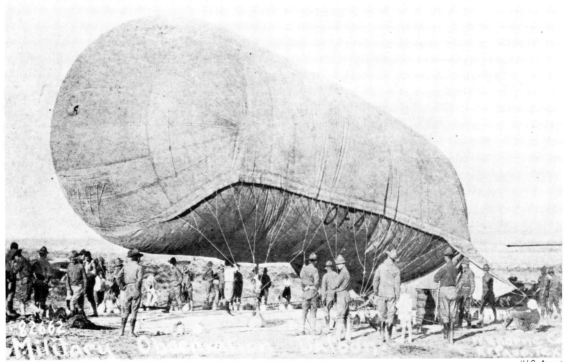

(U.S. Army)

THE OBSERVATION BALLOON OF WWI:
Second Lt. Frank Luke shot down 14 German observation balloons between the 12th and the 29th of September, 1918. This is a balloon of the Ohio National Guard in 1917. Field artillery observers were undergoing training at El Paso, Texas when this photo was taken.

The space age has provided an echo of the pellet tactic, heretofore seemingly a half-forgotten historical curiosity. Research has shown that millions of tiny BB-sized pellets might bring down a satellite or an ICBM. Where the World War I pellet bombers had to drop their missiles down on the enemy flying below, their space age descendants ponder methods of boosting the pellets up into the path of the satellite, missile or other object that they wish to bring down.

In the early aerial combats, long before the term "ace" had ever been applied to airmen, the ideal tactic was to fly formation with the German and knock him down with pot-shots to the engine, propeller, fuel tank or pilot. Advantage was soon sought by the pilots in these encounters, and this gave birth to the first tactical maneuvering of aerial combat. All aerial tactics have evolved from this initial search for advantage.

To gain advantage on a German pilot, the Allied flyer with a rear observer-gunner would try to get in front of the German machine. Vulnerable in this position to the Allied gunner, the German pilot was prevented from returning the fire, lest he blow off his own propeller. This same maneuver gave protection to a pilot who had run out of ammunition while his opponent had not.

By staying in front of the pursuing enemy machine, a fleeing pilot could avoid being sprayed with lead. A tactical response to this early situation was the appearance of "pusher" type aircraft like the British FE-2B and Vickers "Gunbus," which put a gunner in a front nacelle with an enormous field of fire in the forward direction. Tactics born of these early encounters underwent a decisive change due to the brainchild of a determined Frenchman named Roland Garros.

Famous as a speed and stunt pilot before the war, Garros set aerial combat on the path it was to follow right down to the days of the heat-seeking air-to-air missile. Garros could see what the consequences would be if pilots could fire machine guns directly through the propeller arc. His approach to the problem was terrifyingly direct.

The Frenchman attached heavy steel deflector plates to the propeller blades of his plane. He then mounted a machine gun on the upper forward fuselage so that it fired directly through the propeller arc. A percentage of the bullets hit the deflector plates and ricocheted.

Most of the bullets sped on through the propeller arc to the target.

Garros could now aim his gun by aiming his whole aircraft, something that was previously impossible. The days of formation flying with a foe—the epoch of lateral air-to-air pot-shots—had come to an abrupt end. Instead of avoiding a tail-chase of a German aircraft, Garros now did everything possible to promote this maneuver, and in the beginning the Germans fell readily into the trap. Enemy pilots felt they were gaining the advantage of Garros when he finished up on their tail.

Certainly the Frenchman's early victims must have been among history's most surprised pilots. Serene in their assurance that they had outmaneuvered the French *schweinhund*, and that their observer-gunner would riddle him in due course, they suddenly found themselves absorbing a storm of machine gun fire. Seconds later they had become statistics in a deadly scoring game.

Garros scored five kills in two weeks with his forward-firing gun. Then the ingenious Frenchman, who diced with death every time he pulled his gun trigger, fell victim to the law of averages. Opening fire with a German machine in his sights, he blew off his own propeller despite the deflector plates. The resulting vibration caused a joint in his fuel system to separate, and Garros made a forced landing—behind the German lines.

Reacting with typical energy to their good luck in capturing Garros and his deadly scout plane, the Germans brought the innovation to the attention of Anthony Fokker. The Dutch builder of Germany's greatest warplanes took the Garros idea and added a crucial innovation. Fokker designed the interrupter cam, a simple device that prevented the machine gun from firing when a propeller blade was in front of the gun muzzle. Fully synchronized machine guns in pairs quickly followed, the Germans had the advantage, and the way was opened to a new kind of aerial jousting.

Tactics changed radically. The ideal attack with the new device was to steal up silently behind an enemy and get as close as possible before opening fire. Accuracy diminished with distance, and the pioneers established the practice of closing in before striking. Even as late as the Korean War there was one American ace who said: "The hell with gunsights. Stick some chewing gum on the windshield, shove the gum up the other guy's tailpipe and let drive!"

Advantage passed immediately to the Germans with the advent of forward-firing synchronized machine guns, but did not long endure. German aircraft were shot down, the interruptor cam was copied by the British and French and the tactical struggle continued, settling into more or less classic patterns. The dogfight was born.

As the World War I pilot closed in, if his opponent spotted him and turned quickly then the attacker would try to turn even more sharply and get behind his quarry. With both aircraft in a vertical bank, the pursuer had to be able to pull his nose far enough ahead of his quarry to fire and have the rapidly moving enemy aircraft *fly into the stream of bullets.* He had to be able to "pull lead" on his foe.

This action of two fast-turning aircraft chasing each other closely resembled two dogs trying to nip each other's hindquarters. Allied pilots soon began to refer to actions of this kind as "dogfights." The Germans called such battles "rhubarbs." The term and the tactical essentials have remained the same down to this day.

Forward-firing machine guns were responsible for the emergence of the First World War's most popular fighter tactic—the dive out of the sun. With the sun at his back and as much altitude advantage as possible, the attacking pilot bounced his foe. The enemy in turn was blinded by the sun when he searched the sky, and could be taken unawares from this quarter. Douglas Bader, the RAF's legless ace in World War II, insisted on return to this tactical essential and it paid off against the Germans in the Battle of Britain.

In all the wars in which America's fighter aces were made, the bounce out of the sun was a fundamental. Pounded into four generations of fighter pilots in their training, it served them well in combat, including the epoch of sophisticated avionics and supersonic fighters. Failure to remember the importance of altitude and sun usually resulted in dead pilots. To attack with the advantage of sun and altitude has remained the first principle of aerial warfare. Living aces continue to emphasize the value of these fundamentals. Modifications appropriate to the Vietnam era are dealt with in the relevant chapter, but sun and altitude rule on as the gods of air-to-air combat.

Another enduring maneuver developed in World War I after the advent of the forward-firing machine gun was the "inverted vertical reversement." This maneuver was intended to remove an enemy aircraft from a position of advantage astern. Two aircraft in aerial combat eventually wound up in a vertical bank, each trying to close the circle, get on the enemy's tail and open fire.

The winner in such an encounter was usually the pilot who could slowly close the gap between the planes, thereby putting himself in position to shoot. Right at this moment, when the pursued pilot was about to feel the full force of his enemy's guns, he would execute the dramatic "inverted vertical reversement."

The pursued pilot would suddenly increase his bank so that his machine would roll 180 degrees under. Simultaneously slapping the stick back into the full rear position, including the full bank, the pursued pilot would snap-roll through the inverted position. He would then stop the roll in a vertical bank going in the opposite direction.

Since the other pilot in the firing position had to have his quarry under his nose in order to gain the necessary firing lead angle, he was usually unable to see his target make the reversement—until it was too late. In a split second the maneuver was completed. The hunted suddenly became the hunter, lining up his adversary for a lethal burst.

A tricky maneuver to perform, the inverted vertical reversement was deadly when pulled off by a good pilot. Used in different ways World Wars I and II and in Korea, the inverted vertical reversement brought many aerial victories to America's aces. Some aces are alive today thanks to their skilled use of this maneuver in evasion.

In World War II, aircraft like the P-51, P-47, Me-109 and Spitfire were too fast and heavy to execute the snap portion of the inverted vertical reversement if the speeds exceeded 300 mph. The maneuver was also a fantastic speed killer, and tactics usually demanded that most combat be fought at full throttle. Under these conditions, the classic maneuver was modified simply to a high-speed reversement, with no attempt to make it a snap maneuver.

The Royal Air Force called this modification a "three-quarter underneath roll" and used it to advantage with the Spitfire and Hurricane when attacked by Me-109's and

FW-109's. The Germans used the maneuver also, and several leading Luftwaffe aces were masters of this tactic. The speed killing element acted like a massive and effective air brake and could be tactically exploited in the right circumstances.

In the Korean War, the inverted high-speed reversement was used in classic fashion by F-86 pilots battling the MiG-15's. As the Soviet-built jets had a higher ceiling than the American Sabres, the MiG's would dive from their superior altitudes to open combat. The Sabre pilots would wait until the MiG's opened fire, and then break violently into the attacking jets.

Hurtling down in their dives with superior speed, the MiG's would overshoot and pass behind the Sabres. The American pilots would then execute an inverted, or perhaps an overhead high-speed reversement on the tail of the fast-departing MiG's, immediately opening fire. A hit that holed the MiG's canopy or damaged its engine in this situation made it relatively simple for the Sabre pilot to close on the damaged machine and shoot it down. In this way, the basic tactic of the reversement has endured.

As mentioned above, the speed-killing properties of the snap maneuver were also applied to definite tactical purpose. A snap roll at 275 mph in a P-51 would kill 75 mph of speed in less than two seconds. Two snap rolls would kill nearly 180 mph. Some pilots used the snap roll against a fast-closing enemy. Others used it to prevent overshooting a target. The maneuver could kill so much speed so quickly that a skilled pilot could often place himself suddenly and squarely behind his enemy. The well-timed use of this aerial brake could put an able pilot in perfect shooting position against a foe who only seconds earlier was in the role of aerial executioner.

Most of America's top surviving aces believe that overtaking and passing—overshooting— was one of the cardinal sins of aerial combat. Why? Because if the pilot on his firing run missed or only damaged his enemy, and then overshot the hostile aircraft, all the enemy pilot had to do was put his gunsight on his erstwhile attacker and press the triggers. Pilots who overshot were actually shooting themselves down. Untold dozens of pilots on both sides nevertheless met their doom through this example of a fatal mistake.

There are some American aces very much alive today, despite the foregoing remarks on overshooting, who often overshot and can talk about it now in the land of the living. These aces are men who believed that speed should seldom be slackened in aerial combat, since it is the only thing that can be traded for altitude. Planning their attacks on full speed and with absolute confidence in their marksmanship, they always had a plan for the breakoff. This usually consisted of a break underneath the enemy pilot in his blind spot before he could discover where his attacker had gone. During this brief and crucial period, the Americans would put all possible distance between themselves and the enemy plane. Without such a planned overshoot, which depended on a high rate of closure, overshooting was likely to be fatal, no matter how brilliant the pilot.

In the light of these explanations, it seems incredible that any combat pilot would have been stupid enough—in breaking off from his overshoot—to *pull up in a zoom directly in front of and above the enemy he had just attacked.* This scenario was nevertheless enacted all too often. Almost every experienced fighter pilot has at least one recollection from his combat days of someone doing this Hollywood-style zoom. Even a mortally wounded enemy pilot could not fail to riddle such a sitting duck. The hot-shots who tried this maneuver never lived to join the circle of aces.

As aerial combat began to take definite shape in World War I, teamwork and tactics with large formations of planes gradually ousted the aerial lone wolf. The highly individualistic plane against plane, pilot against pilot way of fighting with all its correspondences to duelling and jousting, began to disappear. An occasional lone wolf like America's Frank Luke would blast his way to glory, but such pilots were exceptions and usually were quickly killed. The lone wolf simply could not prevail against well-led formations.

Pilots who were gifted as aerial commanders, with a flair and instinct for leading formations, found the road to immortality open. The last year of World War I belonged to such pilots. The Royal Air Force's Major James T. McCudden and Major Edward "Mick" Mannock were probably the outstanding Allied tacticians, and their counterparts were Oswald Boelcke and the immortal "Red Knight of Germany," Baron Manfred von Richthofen. They were the forebears of the famous fighter leaders of World War II, Korea and Vietnam.

Richthofen's "Circus" and the tactics he had developed gave America's first fighter aces a hard row to hoe, and influenced the air war long after the Baron had gone to Valhallah. Almost uncannily, Richthofen grasped the mechanics of teamwork, which he introduced on the German side. The Baron could see that a two-, three-, or four-plane formation could quickly box in a lone plane, making maneuver impossible for the Allied pilot.

Psychology was also a weapon in such encounters. Often by its very presence the larger German formation terrified the lone Allied pilots into making errors. No one knew better than von Richthofen how easy it is to shoot down a pilot who is rattled.

As formation flying developed on both sides, Richthofen's strategy was to dive out of the sun into the Allied formations, hoping to break them up and scatter them into individual elements that could be easily downed. His victory record is a testament to his tactical expertise.

Richthofen has often been criticized in retrospect for his tendency to pick on inexperienced pilots, which he shot down while his formation provided protection. Such views cannot be accorded much value when aerial combat is considered realistically. The name of the game is shoot the other man down. All great aces have had the capacity to perceive lack of aggressiveness in the air.

Richthofen had this capacity in high measure, combined with outstanding flying, gunnery and leadership talents. To all this must be added a hunter's nose. At the moment of his death, Richthofen was hotly pursuing the aircraft of Lt. Wilfred May of the RAF, who that morning was on his very first combat sortie.

Personality traits of the Baron may have made him an unpleasant man to serve with, but his reputation amongst Allied flyers was awesome. Richthofen was both respected and feared. His presence at the front created a climate of terror, and his morale value to the Germans was inestimable. Richthofen's leadership, tactical skill and the technical

(National Archives)

CURTISS JN-4D "JENNY"

"An apology for an airplane" was how American ace Fred Libby described the Jenny, but it did yeoman service as a trainer for U.S. Air Service fighter pilots. After the war, the Jenny was extremely popular as a barnstorming aircraft.

superiority of German aircraft made him a legend in his own lifetime. He dominated the air war until his death. His 80 aerial victories—the highest score by any ace in World War I—became a landmark and the coveted goal of a later generation of German pilots. No Allied pilot in any war would ever reach 80 kills.

Richthofen's dictum laid out the fundamentals of aerial fighting for all time: *"Find the enemy and shoot him down. Anything else is nonsense."* Half a century and three wars later in Vietnam, the supersonic super-athletes flying America's jets were still hewing to this primal dictum. Radar and electronic counter measures greatly complicated the searching process, but MIGCAP patrols were still finding the enemy so he could be shot down. The Defense Department financed *Project Red Baron* to evaluate air-to-air encounters in Southeast Asia. If downward glimpses are permitted from Valhallah, the Red Baron must have smiled smugly at the enduring quality of his tactical legacy.

Fortunately for the Americans of World War I, Baron Richthofen was killed before the U.S. Air Service became active on the Western Front. His demise has long been controversial, the popular records of World War I crediting the downing of Richthofen to Canadian Captain Roy Brown. Contemporary claims from the army that the Baron had been machine-gunned from the ground were lost in the numerous glamorized versions of the affair.

Gunner Donald Buie of Australia claimed in 1959 to have shot down Richthofen with a machine gun, using a homemade sight that he had designed in the trenches to give him the proper firing lead angle. Violent controversy thereupon erupted. An exhaustive investigation of the whole matter was initiated by the eminent and internationally respected British aviation historian, Mr. D. A. Russell.

Mr. Russell's conclusion was that it was impossible in view of the facts he uncovered to credit the victory to Captain Brown. The British investigator also declined to assign the coveted honor to Donald Buie, whose claim he considered as implausible as that of Captain Brown. Mr. Russell attributed the Baron's death to ground fire, and held there to be no doubt of this fact. Investigation proved that several machine-gunners fired on Richthofen from the ground, Buie being ruled out because of his position relative to the Baron at the fatal moment. Richthofen's death has been called "the dogfight that will never end," and that is the truth of the matter.

The lesson of Richthofen's demise is the mortal danger to which even the most formidable aerial fighter exposes himself when he flies close to the ground. The Red Baron had become contemptuous of this danger in his final months. Warned by concerned fellow pilots not to press his luck, the greatest aerial fighter of World War I undid himself by flying low over the trenches.

AERIAL WORKHORSE
The two-place DH-4 with a Liberty engine was built in the U.S. and sent to France as an all-purpose aircraft. The machine proved a good one.

The air-to-ground role for the fighter pilot always reeked with danger. The highest qualities of courage, mind and skill were called upon in the tactical fighter pilot. Combat with other aircraft was rare. Tactical fighters acted more like artillery, supporting infantry and armor, and beating up enemy concentrations, supply dumps, trains and road convoys.

Acedom was not granted any fighter pilot for demolishing these important enemy facilities. Nevertheless it would be unfair in a work dealing with fighter aces not to acknowledge the massive contribution to victory made by the fighter pilots who were almost entirely confined to the air-to-ground role. With only rare opportunities to try their wings in air-to-air combat, they succeeded in earning the admiration of the aces.

Fighter pilots in all wars, with the possible exception of Richthofen, have disliked flying low over ground targets. The possibility of becoming a statistic in strafing operations mounted rapidly as flak weapons multiplied in numbers and efficiency. Flying low allowed the enemy to concentrate his lethal hails of fire and steel. Ground troops joined in with every available weapon wherever possible, to help in clawing down their aerial tormentors. An ace might be unconquerable in the sky, but if he flew close to the ground in the combat zone long enough, his chances of survival diminished to zero.

Aces like Duane Beeson and the seemingly invincible Francis Gabreski, tops in aerial combat, were shot down and taken prisoner as the result of ground-strafing operations. To fly in the ground-support role month in and month out, as did so many unknown American fighter pilots in World War II, Korea and Vietnam, took immense and sustained courage. No one knows this better than the aces who tasted close-support fighter piloting at various times during their careers.

In the making of a fighter ace, a crucial role is played by statistics. Everything else that goes into making an ace finishes up as numbers—the pilot's victory tally. Statistics may be fairly characterized as the villain in the "drama of the aces," because statistics always stand between the hero and his goal of acedom.

Long after the shooting wars have ceased, the war of statistics has continued. There has been almost as much vocal and paper fighting over victory credits and official scores as there was in the air during wartime. A major element in sustaining this virtually perpetual controversy is the completely *nonofficial* nature of the "ace" title. The U.S. military establishment stresses that acedom is unofficial. That same establishment nevertheless officially plunges into reviews and revisions of fighter pilots' scores often enough to add official statistical confusion to the status of those bearing the unofficial title. What is needed is a firm, permanent official decision on these statistical matters.

Officialdom blew hot and cold on the ace idea from the early days of the U.S. Air Service, the precursor of today's USAF. The question of aces, the qualifications for an ace and how these qualifications were to be assessed and recorded were all matters for considerable official flim-flam. The French were the first to recognize that the *chasse* (pursuit) pilot of outstanding achievement should have some unique and distinctive title. The French coined the term "ace," and were the first to refer to their top scoring fighter pilots as aces.

The British and the Germans followed the French lead, although the British, like the Americans, have never accepted the title officially within their military establishment. The term was also slow in gaining general currency during World War I. The late Captain Frederick Libby of Sterling, Colorado, an American who served in the RFC in 1916 and 1917 and became an ace, recalled that it was mid-1917 before he ever heard the term used.

Libby was serving under the command of British ace Sholto Douglas at the time, and a French pilot made a forced landing at their field. When the Frenchman clambered out he was resplendently attired and heavily beribboned. He announced to the British pilots that he, the Frenchman, was an ace. Libby recalls the Frenchman's chagrin at finding that most of the British pilots had more kills than he did, but had never heard the term "ace" used before. After the Frenchman's departure they kidded each other about how they were "aces."

The French, British and Germans set ten confirmed aerial victories as the standard qualification for an ace. Since the warring powers between 1914 and 1917 did not include the United States, there were already dozens of Allied and German aces at the time of America's entry into the war. The only

American aces were expatriates flying in the service of Britain and France.

American development of the air weapon had been extremely slow. The possibility of there not being a single American ace in an American unit became very real. When American air units had still not gone into action at the beginning of 1918, the likelihood of any American pilot in a U.S. unit scoring ten kills before Germany's collapse became increasingly remote. From no victories to ten victories seemed a long road.

American qualification for aces was accordingly reduced to five victories rather than the ten recognized by the other Allied powers and Germany. The value of aces for morale purposes was not underrated, especially in isolationist areas of the United States where a certain antipathy towards the war existed. The ace was to become an easily comprehended symbol for the American public, one that would enable Americans to say, "We're really in it."

With characteristic dash, a number of American fighter pilots in World War I exceeded ten aerial victories, despite America's late entry into the air war. This original departure of the U.S. ace standard from ten to five victories has nevertheless applied from World War I down to the present day. The "five down" standard applies in this book and in all the lists in the Appendix. The same standard of five victories now applies generally throughout the world and is even given in dictionaries.

The war of statistics has been going on ever since World War I, and only the Korean and Vietnam aces seem immune from continual reviews of their scores by official and quasi-official historians. The changing standards of victory confirmation, the various means of recognizing and documenting aerial victories once scored and the matted tangle of different procedures in different commands have all united to create a historian's nightmare.

Typical of the problems presented to any researcher in this field seeking to follow official guidelines is the explanation given in this extract from a letter written by the Director of Air Service, U.S. Army, and dated 5 January 1920:

"The U.S. Air Service does not use the title 'ace' in referring to those who are credited officially with five or more aerial victories over enemy aircraft. It is not the policy of the Air Service to glorify one particular branch of aeronautics, aviation or aerostation at the expense of another . . .

. . . the work of observation and bombardment is considered equally as hazardous as that of pursuit, but due to the fact that observation and bombardment pilots are not called upon merely to destroy enemy aircraft, it should not be allowed to aid in establishing a popular comparison of results merely by relative victories."

In this letter may be detected the germinal sentiments from which the "bombardment vs. pursuit" controversy came to dominate American military aviation until World War II. The order accompanying the letter, in addition to being a masterpiece of jabberwocky, drops the following statistical bombshell:

"An addition of the victories listed herein does not furnish the number of enemy aircraft destroyed, due to the fact that the Air Service method of crediting gave each person who participated in the combat one victory. Thus, if three were concerned in one fight to the destruction of one enemy airplane, each U.S. combatant would be credited with one victory, if properly confirmed, but the enemy loss would still be but one airplane."

A few of the World War I pilots whose names are published in the Ace List of this book are not statistically entitled to membership in the elite fraternity. Under the rules of World War II, Korea and Vietnam they would have received fractional credits, and this would have reduced their victory totals below five. The problem thus becomes not only one of statistics, but also one of ethics. Most of these men are now dead, but were regarded as aces without question during their lifetimes and until 1969, when the USAF published its Historical Study #133.

Dated 7 June 1969, this study broke down the tacitly confirmed whole kills into the appropriate shared kills. The victory totals are significantly lower as a consequence. The authors have chosen to show the Study #133 confirmations in a separate column for two reasons:

1. The shared kills were generally counted as full kills when the lists were first compiled after World War I, and were also generally accepted. The honored "ace" title was generally accorded. Cancelling this honor half a century later is a misuse of statistics, even when their accuracy is

not in dispute.

2. Study #133 deals only with credits won by U.S. Air Service personnel, not with the credits won while flying with the British or French forces.

The list published by the Director of Air Service in 1920 actually contains, therefore, the names of flyers who really did not shoot down an enemy aircraft. Historically and statistically they received one full victory credit, a practice which has since been attributed erroneously to the World War II Luftwaffe.

To make everything from the beginning completely accurate and consistent is a research task that borders on the impossible. Officialdom will also speedily render such an undertaking futile. No sooner does the historian taking this picayune approach to ac-

curacy strip American combat pilots of an ace standing accorded them for half a century, than he must confront a modern, recently created counterpart of the same problem— Vietnam.

Phantom jets operating against the MiG-17's and MiG-21's over Vietnam carried two pilots, the GIBS (Guy In the Back Seat) serving mainly as radar operator, navigator and special weapons man. Fresh from getting everything straight over those World War I scores, the USAF now decided that each MiG downed would result in a full victory credit for *each of the two pilots.* Five MiG's downed created *two* American aces! Whatever the merits of the USAF decision to extend the ace honor in this way, the statistical war was on once again after the guns were stilled.

Such historical probings as have been made

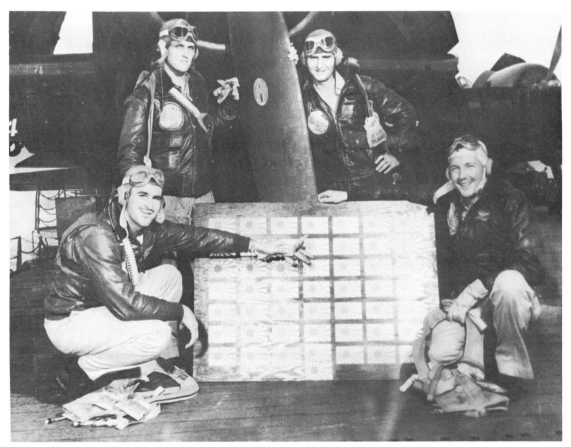

(USN-French)

TEAMWORK! VALENCIA AND HIS "MOWING MACHINE"
The latter stages of WWI were the proving grounds of teamwork and cooperation as the key to successful aerial combat. In the Pacific Theater in WWII, the U.S. Navy fighter division led by Lt. Eugene A. Valencia served as one of the best examples. These four, in a very short time, scored 50 kills against the acrobatically superior Japanese Zeros. Valencia kneels at left and Lt. James B. French kneels at right. Lt. Clinton L. Smith stands at left while Lt. Harris E. Mitchell steadies the propeller for the photographer.

of the ace issue by official U.S. sources are unable, by the nature of things, to extend any proper credit to American aces who flew in the service of foreign nations. The authors believe that if an American citizen became a fighter ace, then he is entitled to be considered an American fighter ace regardless of the uniform he wore while winning his spurs in the air.

These men included such luminaries of early American combat flying as Major Raoul Lufbery, 17 victories; Second Lieutenant Frank L. Baylies, 12 victories; Captain G. DeFreest Larner, 8 victories; and Lt. Colonel William Thaw, 5 victories. These men all fought with the famed Lafayette Escadrille. They go to their rightful places as American aces in this book.

For the purposes of this book, an ace is considered to be the *pilot* of a fighter-type aircraft credited with five or more confirmed aerial victories. Aerial victories are considered to be against *piloted* enemy aircraft, with observation balloons included for the period of World War I.

While there have been gunners on aircraft who have been credited with five aerial victories or more, they have not been considered as fighter aces for the purposes of this book. Some pilots of bomber-type aircraft made the Ace Lists where they were at the controls and did the firing. Gunners are credited with assists.

Worthy of mention here, among many quite irreconcilable anomalies from the early days of aerial warfare, is the role played by observer-gunners in the epoch prior to the advent of the forward-firing synchronized machine gun. There were many aircraft types that put the observer-gunner in a forward nacelle. In the early days, the observer was often an officer, the pilot an NCO.

Survivors of this era emphasized that victory in aerial combat depended then upon the observer-gunner rather than the pilot. In the brief training given to RFC observers it was pounded into these men that they had their pilot's life in their hands. RFC practice in this period was to credit the victory to the observer who actually did the shooting.

The only American to be concerned with this transitional period was Frederick Libby of Sterling, Colorado. In his special case, it is not necessary to make an exception to the essential "pilots only" rule for acedom. Observer Libby later became a pilot and made his ace

rating as a pilot. His career is exhaustively covered in the next chapter.

Confining the ace title to pilots is not intended to take anything away from the aerial gunners for their feats. To be considered a fighter ace, however, a flyer must have been in control of the aircraft he flew in and to have directed its firepower against manned enemy aircraft. This is the broad, general interpretation of a fighter ace preferred by the American Fighter Aces Association. One of its aims is to exclude credits toward ace standing for aircraft destroyed on the ground.

Wherever possible, the lists compiled by the authors are based on the records. During the period of World War II each air force and theater of operations had its own methods of formally acknowledging aerial victories. For this reason, the facts concerning all aerial victories will never be finally determined. Victory statistics for World War II have already been revised by the USAF Historical Division.*

U.S. confirmation rules required not only firm evidence of the destruction of an enemy aircraft, but acceptance of that evidence by higher HQ and formal notification to the pilot by higher authority of his victory credit. In the World War I epoch, another pilot could confirm destruction of an enemy aircraft. Observers on the ground, watching combat over the trenches and around the front lines, frequently provided documentation of aerial victories. Wherever possible, air commanders worked in close cooperation with the army to ensure this kind of evidential backing for victory claims.

World War II saw aerial combat move on to a much broader canvas. Aerial battles mainly took place out of sight of the ground forces, and often hundreds of miles from ground combat. Gun cameras proved to be a highly efficacious method of confirming aerial kills. When film taken from a claiming pilot's gun camera documented his verbal report with objective evidence, the crediting of the kill was certain. These combat films also provided some graphic records of the right and wrong way to bring down another airplane in combat.

Erich Hartmann of Germany, the all-time world champion fighter pilot, always advocated closing in to the shortest possible range before firing. In Arizona during his jet

*USAF Historical Study No. 85 Office of Air Force History published July 1978.

training days, Hartmann got great satisfaction out of numerous American gun camera films that were available to the young American pilots also training on the base. The close-in attacks almost invariably showed the enemy plane disintegrating with a blast.

Some forty percent of American kills in World War II and Korea were confirmed by gun cameras. Fifty percent were confirmed by eye witnesses to the battle, a wingman or other pilot in a position to see the outcome, or a witness on the ground to the final destruction of the enemy machine. Ten percent of American victories were confirmed by other means, such as discovery of wreckage and from interception of enemy radio traffic by Allied monitors. This is the broad basis upon which the statistics have been created—confirmation of victories.

In World War II, divergent views existed in every theater of operations, as well as in each branch of the service, regarding aircraft destroyed on the ground. Most fighter pilots considered that an aircraft destroyed on the ground included those destroyed while rolling their wheels during takeoff or landing, as well as taxiing, hangared or parked aircraft. Some pilots had high personal standards entirely their own in these matters. 2nd Lieutenant James L. Brooks of the 15th Air Force, a 13-victory ace, once shot down a Fieseler Storch observation plane more or less in passing, like swatting a fly. He made no claim because he considered the victory "too easy." The Storch was airborne, but it just wasn't a worthy victory to Brooks.

"On the ground" kills were dubious for many reasons. The attacking pilot could not always tell whether the aircraft was actually destroyed, unless it blew up. If it blew up, it was difficult to know whether it was a real aircraft or a dummy loaded with inflammables. Japanese talent with dummies in the Pacific became legendary. When an enemy aircraft exploded *in the air* there was no doubt of the authenticity of either the machine or the victory.

Another reason for excluding ground kills from credit toward an ace standing is an anomalous scoring situation created in Europe in 1945 by the 8th Fighter Command. The Germans began to refuse aerial combat. The Luftwaffe would not always take off to challenge Allied aircraft, sometimes because they lacked fuel and parts, and sometimes

because waning German air strength was being conserved for the ground support role. 8th Fighter Command of the USAAF took emergency countermeasures.

Full victory credits were suddenly announced for aircraft destroyed on the ground. Aimed at inducing fighter pilots to abandon the relative safety of air-to-air combat for the low-level hell of the strafer, this order was to open a new chapter in the statistical war. Incentive was nevertheless needed to get the fighters down into the undiminished hails of flak that protected surviving Luftwaffe airfields. Granting full victory credits for on-the-ground kills was the 8th Fighter Command's way of further eroding enemy air power.

Pilots hated low-level strafing mainly because they surrendered most of the advantages of being airborne. Their piloting skill and aerial combat experience meant little. If their aircraft were badly hit or they were hit themselves, the deck came up to meet them in a hurry. No limping back to base or bailing out was open to them. A forced landing was the best they could hope for, and much more likely was a fiery death crash.

All fighter units everywhere faced these facts, but the 8th Fighter Command was the only unit of the U.S. forces in World War II that ever gave and confirmed full victory credits for ground kills. The Navy, Marine Corps and the rest of the Army Air Force kept track of ground kills only haphazardly, mainly because the essential nature of the operations precluded any exact tallying.

Some outstanding pilots of the 9th Air Force in Europe destroyed dozens of enemy aircraft on the ground, but never received credit towards an ace title for any of them. The anomalous nature of the ground-kill credits given by 8th Fighter Command is dramatically illustrated by the twenty ground kills attributed to the Navy's top ace, Captain David McCampbell. Added to his thirty-four aerial victories, these ground kills would boost his official score to fifty-four—had McCampbell been serving with the 8th Air Force in the 1945 emergency.

Many American fighter pilots will look in vain for their names in this book and its appended ace lists. These lists are based on the records, but do not necessarily duplicate them. Where the records say four aerial victories and two on-the-ground kills, then that individual is not an ace under the definitions

AMERICAN FIGHTER ACES ASSOCIATION INITIAL MEETING: Sixty-three of America's aces met for the first time after foundation of the Aces Association on September 23, 1960 at San Francisco. By 1978 the number of member aces has swelled to over 400.

(AFAA)

applying in this book.

In compiling lists involving over 1400 men and a period of more than six decades, there may well be unintentional omissions. For these the authors offer their apologies, while standing firmly by the "five aerial victories" criterion. This standard is strictly observed, despite any 8th Air Force orders that may have been published naming a particular pilot an ace after one or more ground kills built his victory total to five or more.

Kills shared in the air count as fractions. The method of assessment has been straightforward. If two pilots attacked an enemy machine and successfully shot it down, with neither pilot able to claim individual credit for the kill, the victory was split. Each pilot was given half a victory credit. All fractional credits have been similarly determined. These are the statistical factors that go into the making of an ace, and in leaving the statistics it is worth observing that statistical anomalies have as often kept pilots from entering the elite fraternity, as they have admitted others who do not rightly belong to the fraternity.

In the making of an ace there is the scientifically indefinable force conveyed by the word *drive*. The overwhelming majority of aces, and virtually all the top aces, were men who strongly desired combat and would fight to get into combat. The aces were men who would go to sometimes incredible lengths to circumvent or surmount barriers that arose between them and aerial fighting. A considerable list could be compiled for example, of pilots who were washed out by USAAF instructors, but who just would not accept such a verdict. They packed their bags, went to Canada and joined the RCAF, trained as pilots and later became aces flying out of England. They literally forced their way into aerial combat. Nobody could block men powered by such drive, and they realized their goal—they became aces.

Studies by the USAF have revealed from extensive personal histories that the aces had been strong and aggressive competitors since boyhood. They were limit testers, rule

benders, risk takers and precedent breakers all their lives, and these qualities made them excel in the grimmest contest of all—aerial combat. Their value in terms of their contribution to victory was out of proportion to their numbers. Less than 3 percent of all fighter pilots to take the air for Uncle Sam, they accounted for some *forty percent of all enemy aircraft downed by fighters.*

In the specific instance of the 8th Fighter Command in Europe in World War II, 5.2 percent of its 5,000 fighter pilots became aces. These 261 men brought down 40 percent of all the aerial kills scored by the 8th Air Force fighters. Similar results came out of fighter combat in Korea, where 4.8 percent of the pilots became aces and accounted for over 38 percent of the kills.

Decades after these facts, the Defense Advanced Research Projects Agency commissioned a feasibility study to predict the combat effectiveness of fighter pilots. The military wanted to find out if ace potential could be predicted, and ineffective pilots weeded out by our own side instead of being eliminated by the enemy. McDonnell Douglas completed this study in 1977, and it weighs almost as much as Eddie Rickenbacker's Nieuport. The essence of the report is that through various established techniques, only a few of which are currently in use by the USAF, America should be able to produce much more effective fighter pilots overall than it does now or has in the past.

The arcane blend of shooting and flying ability, intuition and eyesight, physical coordination and endurance, instinct and technology, luck and opportunity—all welded together by the drive and lust for combat—will probably always elude precise scientific analysis. What is certain is that the medieval knight never needed to bring such formidable powers to the joust, nor required such a host of seconds and supporters to make the joust possible and record its outcome for posterity. Now let's meet some of America's knights of the air.

VICTIM OF ARCHIE

"Archie" (the World War I term for antiaircraft fire) brought this 5-man German AEG G-105 to earth on June 2, 1918. First Division of the AEF was credited with the kill near Catillon, France.

(Erickson Collection)

The Way it Was — WWI

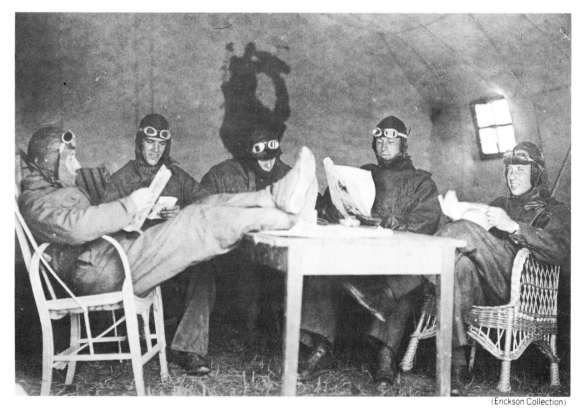

(Erickson Collection)

Tours, France, 1918. American pilots pass the time with magazines and newspapers from home while on alert. Oldtimers who were there say it was hard to tell which pilots were standing alert and which were just trying to keep warm.

2

ACES OF
WORLD WAR I

When World War I began in 1914, there were no eager hordes of dashing young pilots waiting to fly themselves to glory as aces. On the contrary, there was only the dimmest apprehension by military thinkers of the potential and significance of aircraft. Aviation advocates within the military were few, and were regarded stonily by high commanders rooted in the cavalry epoch—an era that was about to end under the withering fire of massed machine guns. Nineteenth century minds ruled in military circles, and in the eleven years between the first powered flight of the Wright brothers and the outbreak of World War I, aviation technology developed at a snail's pace.

Under inexorable war pressures between 1914 and 1918, the airplane was transformed from an invention of dubious military value into a revolutionary new fundamental of war. The die was cast. Aircraft were not decisive in World War I, but the speed with which they added a dynamic new dimension to military science showed that they would dominate the future. Symbolic of this new military epoch was the new warrior to whom it gave both birth and scope—the fighter ace.

The foundations of American military aviation on outbreak of World War I appear in retrospect as pathetically inadequate. Almost five years were allowed to slip by after the invention of the airplane in 1903 before trials were conducted on the first U.S. Army aircraft. These trials killed Lieutenant T. E. Selfridge and injured Orville Wright. Pressure was applied high in the Army to abandon the airplane. The new invention and the germinal conceptions for its military employment fortunately proved bigger than its opponents.

The U.S. Army took delivery of its first airplane on 2 August 1909. By June the following year, the service boasted one officer, nine enlisted men, one Wright airplane, one Baldwin airship and three captive balloons. The mighty USAF of today is the direct descendant of this organization. A more rapid

development in the five years prior to World War I might have been expected. Subsequent employment and rapid development of the airplane by the warring powers prior to America's involvement, certainly provided a major incentive to the U.S. military to press forward with aeronautical expansion and training. Surprisingly little was actually done.

By 6 April 1917, when America entered the war, the Aviation Section of the U.S. Army had increased only slightly. The service boasted only 65 officers, of whom a sparse 35 were flying officers. *With only 35 pilots available, the U.S. was plunging into a world conflict*—an almost incredible situation from today's perspective. Fifty-five aircraft and 1,087 enlisted men completed the inventory of American aerial strength. History now fairly characterizes this as a deplorable record for the land of the airplane's birth. America's aerial tardiness was to have far-reaching consequences.

Flying schools were in operation in four centers—Memphis, Tenn., Mineola, N.Y., Essington, Pa., and San Diego, Calif. The foundation for the production of large numbers of fighter pilots was thus insufficient for a major warring power. Many additional schools were subsequently opened, but the lack of facilities *in being* upon America's entry into the conflict meant that it was well into 1918 before U.S. fighter pilots went seriously into action.* This largely accounts for the relatively small number of American aces in World War I, and for their limited victory totals compared with Allied and German aces.

A bright spot in this period was the appointment of Lieutenant Colonel William "Billy" Mitchell as Army Aviation Officer. Destined to become one of the world's dominant aviation prophets, as well as America's most controversial aviation advocate, Mitchell's exertions played a leading part in getting

* Lack of sufficient fighter pilot training facilities in being also hampered the German Luftwaffe in WWII, when it became necessary to train hundreds of fighter pilots.

American airpower off the ground. Strong impetus was given to U.S. Air Service expansion by General Pershing's call for a minimum of sixty-nine Balloon Companies in France by the autumn of 1918.

The 29th Provisional Squadron left the United States for Europe in July 1917. This unit went first to England, and redesignated the 1st Aero Squadron, landed in France on 1 September 1917 to enter the fray. The first official U.S. aviation unit to go overseas, the men of the 1st Aero Squadron had some illustrious unofficial predecessors.

The adventure of flying, the challenge of a new form of combat in the air, and a hatred for the Kaiser's imperialism brought a number of Americans into the fight well ahead of their countrymen. Impatient for action, these Americans volunteered to serve with the French and British forces, and many of them made history. Little has been published about the Americans who flew with the British, but most of those who volunteered for the French Army finished up in Nieuport 124, a unit specially formed for them by the French Air Department.

Activated on 21 March 1916, Nieuport 124 was initially known as Escadrille Americaine, and subsequently became the immortal Lafayette Escadrille. This unique force probably received more publicity during and following World War I than any other combat unit involving Americans. Stories about the Lafayette Escadrille, both fact and fiction, are being written and filmed to this day. The names of the Lafayette's leading personalities are household words among America's aviation buffs.

Strong emotional factors swirled around the Lafayette Escadrille. The unit epitomized and further perpetuated the tradition of kinship and help in times of deep trouble that has existed between France and the United States since the American Revolution. Considerable glamor and an aura of colorful adventure suffused itself through everything reported or written about the expatriate Americans in their dashing French uniforms. All these elements united to virtually obliterate historically the large contribution to Allied victory made by the Americans who served with the British forces.

These expatriate Americans were not integrated into units of their own, and thus there was no point of focus, such as existed through the Lafayette Escadrille, to illuminate their deeds. They nevertheless served with great distinction in the Royal Flying Corps, Royal Air Force and Royal Navy. Scattered through more than a dozen units of the British forces, little is known of these Americans today, and they have always been in the shadow of the glorious Lafayette Escadrille. To the extent that historical research allows, this book gives all due credit to these men by listing their victory totals in the Appendix, and they are welcomed home half a century later as American aces.

DEVOTED HIS LIFE TO AIR POWER

Brigadier General William "Billy" Mitchell was America's most outspoken and forceful air power advocate in WWI and in the doldrum years of the 1920's and 1930's. He devoted his life and career to making his nation supreme in the air. Controversial throughout his life, he was awarded the Medal of Honor posthumously for his pioneer foresight in the service of American military aviation.

(Erickson Collection)

34

Typical of this long lost and elite corps of American aces is Captain Frederick Libby of Sterling, Colorado. Because it was possible to locate Libby in Los Angeles, California, in the nineteen sixties, he will be dealt with at some length. This section of the book will then be representative of the numerous American aces who served with the British in World War I without receiving any historical credit or recognition. Fred Libby passed away in Los Angeles on 9 January 1970, but he will prove to be as immortal as any American ace when the quality of his deeds becomes more widely known.

Raised as a Colorado cowboy, Fred Libby had just turned twenty-two when World War I broke out. In Canada at the time, he immediately joined the Canadian Army, and was shipped to France the following year. Life in the trenches in the rainy spring of 1916 was more than he could stand. When the Royal Flying Corps sent out a call for observers by circulating bulletins in the trenches, Libby jumped at the chance to get out of the rain, mud and muck.

The enticing possibility was broached in the bulletin that successful applicants would be made second lieutenants in the RFC, after a probationary period. To Private Libby this was a substantial upward leap and a strong inducement. The RFC did not mention in the bulletin, of course, that the life expectancy of an observer was *ten operational hours,* which meant that only a handful survived to become officers!

Here is Fred Libby's own story of his first day in the RFC:

"On arrival at HQ, 23rd Squadron RFC, I was questioned by the C.O., Major Ross Hume, concerning my military experience. I had to tell him point-blank that I had never touched a machine gun or an aeroplane in my life. He sent me immediately for half an hour's instruction on the gun range, after which I was to go up on a training flight with Lieutenant Price.

"Coaching with the Lewis gun came easy. At that time the standard armament on most British aircraft, the Lewis used a drum of forty-seven rounds. This doesn't seem like much by modern standards, but in 1916 and to a cowboy who'd been used to making every shot count, forty-seven rounds seemed like a hell of a lot of firepower.

"When I came back from the range, Lieu-

tenant Price's plane was being wheeled out. It was an FE-2B, a pusher type of machine in which the observer sat in front of the pilot in an open nacelle. When you stood up to shoot, all of you from the knees up was exposed to the elements. There was no belt of any kind to hold you. Only your grip on the gun and the side of the nacelle stood between you and eternity.

"Toward the front of the nacelle was a hollow steel rod with a swivel mount to which the gun was anchored. This gun covered a huge field of fire forward. Between the observer and the pilot a second gun was mounted, for firing over the FE-2B's upper wing to protect the aircraft from rear attack. This second gun was at least as dangerous to the observer as it was to the enemy.

"Adjusting and shooting this gun required that you stand right up out of the nacelle— *with your feet on the nacelle coaming! You had nothing to worry about except being blown out of the aircraft by the blast of air, or tossed out bodily if the pilot made a wrong move. There were no parachutes and no belts.* No wonder they needed observers!

"I was to fire at a petrol tin on the ground as Price whizzed over the field at low altitude. I was instructed to fire bursts. The three firing passes proved my amateurism. On the first pass, after being hurled to the floor of the nacelle on takeoff, my unprotected eyes filled with tears and I couldn't even see the tin, let alone shoot at it. On the second pass I had wiped away the tears, and pointing the gun where I thought the tin would show up, I waited tensely. When it slid into view, I pressed the trigger and let all 47 bullets go in one big burst. The can leaped in the air. I'd hit it!

"Now I had to change drums for the return pass. I was so flustered that when I released the clip that held the empty drum in place, it flew out of my hand. Whipped back by the blast of air, the magazine cannoned off the instrument board and narrowly missed first the pilot's head and then the propeller. Lieutenant Price looked daggers at me.

"On the next pass I tried to make up for my amateurish conduct. The contents of the entire drum again blurted off in one burst, but this time the can really rolled and went springing into the air. We landed and taxied up to the can. The thing looked as though someone had hit it a few times with a pickaxe.

"Major Hume congratulated me with a typically British 'good show' when we climbed out of the aircraft. I went to lunch in the sergeant's mess, and afterwards stretched out on a cot in a pup tent in anticipation of a nap. The farewell binge my Canadian buddies had given me in the trenches was having its consequences. My head felt like a gourd full of dried peas. Things were looking better. I was chatting about aerial gunnery with a sergeant pilot who was my tentmate, when an orderly ap-

peared staggering under a load of flying gear—heavy coat, gloves, helmet, boots and goggles. Dumping them in the tent he said, 'These are yours. You're flying at three this afternoon. You're to be on the field ready by 2:30.'

"At first, I assumed it would be a further training mission, but my veteran tentmate soon disillusioned me. I was going up on an operational flight over enemy territory, less than six hours after my arrival at Le Hameau.

After Fred Libby's clumsy morning perfor-

Captain Frederick Libby, RFC, WWI (14.00): Captain Libby won the British Military Cross fighting with the RFC 25th Squadron. He was from Sterling, Colorado.

(Imperial War Museum)

(Constable Collection)

BRITISH FIGHTER — AMERICAN GUNNER

In this rare official Royal Flying Corps photograph, the FE-2B fighter in which Colorado cowboy Fred Libby was gunner-observer is seen returning from German territory on September 23, 1916. The right wing of Libby's machine, which shows in dark tones here and with only part of the roundel visible, had been replaced after battle damage the previous day. No Man's Land and the trenches near the Somme can be seen far below. Libby became first American to down five aircraft in aerial combat as RFC gunner, and then later became a pilot ace in his own right.

mance, particularly in letting the empty ammunition drum fly back in his face, Lieutenant Stephen Price was in no doubt that the American newcomer needed more training before he would be of any use on operations. Price knew what heavy demands were placed on observer-gunners. His last observer, a seasoned veteran of the South African War, had suffered a nervous breakdown from the strain of operational flying. Two and three sorties a day had been too much for him, and he was now grounded. Price added an additional perspective for the authors on this same epic day in Fred Libby's life.

"Fred Libby came to us as a Canadian private—an American from Colorado, stocky, slightly bandy, with reddish coloring and unblinking eyes. I am sure one would have traced a Red Indian pedigree if one had gone very far. He was quiet, serious and unassuming—and inexperienced. When our 42 year-old Eurasian C.O.—whom we called Chu Chin Chow—told me that afternoon that I must take Fred on an over-the-line operation, I objected strongly. Our whole formation could have been endangered by having an observer who had never before in his life been in an aeroplane. I took someone else. Chu Chin Chow assigned Fred to Lt. Hicks, whose observer had just been killed."

Fred Libby again takes up his narrative:

"At 2:30 I was out on the field, assigned to Lt. Hicks. He congratulated me on my morning's shooting and said he was glad to have me aboard. When I mumbled my doubts about being able to identify enemy planes, especially if I didn't see the insignia, he gave me a thumbnail course on aerial tactics—1916 style. 'It's very simple. If he's friendly, he'll show you his colors. If he doesn't show his colors, let him have it.'

"The machine in which I was observer would be the upper back escort, which put us behind and above the other five aircraft in our formation. This was the roughest and most vulnerable spot of all. As we lurched into the air, my mind was reacting as though this was my last operational flight as well as my first. In the way things are supposed to happen to a drowning man, all the scenes of my childhood came swimming back to mind—my family and home in Sterling, my favorite horses and pet dogs. I wondered if I'd ever feel Mother Earth underfoot again.

"These visions evaporated as the formation assembled and we set off for enemy territory. Looking down, I could see the trench systems of both sides, irregular black lines etched in the pockmarked plain of mud where I was floundering around only yesterday. Shuffling on my knees in the nacelle, I was consumed by the realization that my life and my pilot's life depended on my vigilance.

"I had just scanned the rest of our formation below us when out of the blue and to our right came an enemy ship. He was slightly higher than us. Telltale bluish puffs of tracer ammunition were spitting from the German plane, and I immediately grabbed for the Lewis gun, which was resting in a clip on the left side of the nacelle.

"I meant to throw the gun over to the clip on the front of the nacelle, so I could get into action. I was overeager, and all thumbs. Missing the clip completely, I fell back in the nacelle with the heavy gun on top of me. Furious with myself, I kicked the gun off my chest and struggled it into shooting position.

"The German machine passed in front of us and went into a vertical bank. The iron crosses on his wings looked huge and menacing. Still off balance, I squeezed the trigger of the Lewis and again committed the same error as in the morning's training flight. The whole forty-seven rounds went spurting off into the sky, leaving me there with an empty gun and the German still as large as life.

"To my immense relief, the German slipped from view below us, going about his business. I put another drum on the Lewis in case he came back, and crouching in the nacelle on my knees, I prayed he wouldn't. Looking up, I could see that the German's bullets had riddled our upper wing. Little tatters of fabric fluttered from the holes. I got comfort thinking the German was as green as me.

"When Hicks slapped me on the head with his glove to signify that the operation was over, I turned to find him holding out his hand to shake. I shook it. When we touched down at Le Hameau, I noticed that there was a big bunch of officers milling about by the hangars. I glimpsed the red tabs that went with high British rank, but it meant nothing else to me.

"As I swung down out of the plane, I was confronted by a highly agitated sergeant major. Colonel Shephard, C.O. of our wing, was on the field and wanted to see me immediately. The colonel was beaming when I walked over to him. As I went to salute he grabbed my

hand and pumped it furiously.

"'First flight, first fight . . . wonderful, wonderful. When they go down in flames Libby, by God, they don't come back up again.'

"I must have looked as though a mine had gone off under me. I didn't even know I had hit the German machine, let alone sent it down in flames. My brief aerial battle and the blazing demise of the German had been observed and reported back to our squadron by artillery observers as soon as it had occurred. This was why the elated colonel was on the field waiting for me.

"On my first day in the RFC I had my first contact with both aircraft and machine guns. I had my first day's training, my first operational flight and scored my first aerial victory. All this took place between ten in the morning and four in the afternoon. There were to be many more aerial battles before I left the RFC, and many other victories, but if ever an aviator had luck for his angel, it was me on that unforgettable day."

Fred Libby holds a unique place among American fighter pilots. He was the first American to shoot down five enemy aircraft in aerial combat. Only the achievement of this tally as an observer, instead of as a pilot, prevents his occupying the historic spot of first American ace. He shot down his fifth confirmed German plane on 27 August 1916.

Assigned permanently to Lt. Stephen Price after his first victory, Libby and the English pilot became one of the RFC's more notable fighting partnerships in the FE-2B. An elegant, intuitive pilot, Steve Price and the stocky American cowboy came to read each other's minds like all great combat teams have done. Further operations soon verified that hitting the can on the field and downing his first German fighter were not flukes, but the results of an uncanny, instinctive marksmanship.

Fifty years later, Fred Libby said, "I never actually *aimed* a gun in my life. As far as I am concerned, aerial gunnery was 90 percent instinct and 10 percent aim. Since boyhood, I had been used to shooting snakes, rabbits and vermin with a pistol, and what I wanted to hit I knew I would hit. Sights were of little value to a man who had shot accurately all his life by sheer instinct."

This talent was to have lethal consequences for the Germans. Libby drilled in his off-duty hours until he could dismantle the Lewis blindfolded. He drilled himself in the cockpit of the grounded FE-2B until he could set and align his gun in the nacelle with machine-like precision. He designed and had built a special butt stock for the dangerous upper gun. This enabled him, standing right up out of the cockpit, to make his shoulder and the pistol grip a unity—to brace and steady himself for attacks from the rear.

Any German fighter coming around for an attack from what he figured was the poorly defended rear of the FE-2B, would find himself running into a stream of tracer, and rarely did the unblinking American ever miss. Steve Price wrote the authors of this time:

"Fred was a deadly and economical gunman, and his length of vision was fantastic. Having hit his target, he would at once move over to his camera so as to bring back evidence. I was always glad I sat behind his gun."

The dauntless pair fought on through the bitter struggle on the Somme, always in the air, always in fights and always over enemy territory. Two and three sorties were a normal day's operations whenever weather permitted. They flew fighter cover for history's first tank attack. In those early days, the counting of aerial victories had not achieved the importance that it assumed in later years, and there were many German planes that fell to Libby's gunnery far behind enemy lines and were never confirmed. By November 1916, however, he had knocked down ten confirmed and been awarded Britain's Military Cross for conspicuous gallantry. Steve Price was similarly decorated, and both officers received their awards personally from King George V at Buckingham Palace on 13 December 1916.

Replacements at 11 Squadron RFC had totalled more than four times the total flying personnel of the unit during the Libby-Price partnership, and now it was over. Fred Libby was chosen for pilot training. Commissioned a pilot on 4 March 1917, he was assigned to 43 Squadron, then under the command of Major Sholto Douglas, later Lord Douglas of Kirtleside and Air Chief Marshal of the RAF in World War II. As has been previously related, Libby repeated his 1916 "one day wonder" feat by shooting down an Albatros fighter on his first operational flight as a pilot on his first day with 43 Squadron.

Another thirteen kills were confirmed during the ensuing months as Fred Libby flew scores of sorties against the Germans. His British comrades-in-arms treated the young American with respect and affection. He had thrown his energies into their war, flown beside them, and made a record of which any flyer alive could be proud. There was about him then, and there remained until the end of his days, a natural gentlemanly quality that reached the hearts of his English squadron mates.

Symbolizing these accords, a fellow pilot in 43 Squadron presented him with a beautiful American flag on 28 May 1917, shortly after the U.S. entered the war. A token of friendship, the flag was to become an historic piece of bunting. Major Stanley Dore, who had replaced the injured Sholto Douglas as squadron commander, offered a suggestion that was to help make history.

"You're a flight commander now, Libby. Why don't you cut the flag into strips and use it as streamers on the wings of your plane? That way, you can fly your country's flag in Fritz's face every time you go up. Let him know that America's in the war. Carry your flag right into his territory. That'll give the bastards something to think about."

Libby caught the magic of the idea and it was done. All through that spring, summer and autumn of 1917, Old Glory was flown in Fritz's face on hundreds of missions that took the American pilot into German territory. The Stars and Stripes of Fred Libby was the first American flag to be flown over enemy territory in World War I. A symbol of defiance and challenge, the flag stayed flying, for the skillful and formidable Libby was never shot down.

In September of 1917, Billy Mitchell requested the transfer to the U.S. forces of Captain Frederick Libby. His experience and capabilities were abundantly evident to Mitchell when the two men spent an evening together at the 43 Squadron base in France. Libby agreed to the transfer, and taking his precious and now tattered and stained flag with him, returned to the USA.

For months he had been bothered by impaired circulation, so much so that upon landing after flights, his ground crew would have to hold him up until circulation came back into his legs. He was bone-tired and war weary—on the ragged edge of all his reserves of endurance. He concealed his condition, and was given command of 22 Squadron, which he

eventually found down in Texas at Hicks Field.

Gone were the niceties of an RFC officers' mess. Recruits, sergeants and officers all messed together in a huge tent, stampeding for seats at the clang of a dinner bell. 22 Squadron had one Jenny biplane—its total equipment. Fred Libby felt as though his world was collapsing, as indeed it soon would.

A few days after arriving at Hicks Field, he took up the Jenny. After the Bristol Fighter, the Sopwith 1½-strutter and the DH-4 he had flown overseas, it was a rackety apology for an airplane. He thought it was the deadest ship he had ever flown—or so it seemed. The controls were oddly, strangely unresponsive. As he brought the Jenny in for a landing, he realized that his muscles were not obeying his will. *Paralysis was gripping him!*

Superhuman effort enabled him to land the Jenny and taxi to the hangar, but he couldn't get out of the cockpit. From the waist down, he felt like a lump of stone. This time wasn't like the others, when the circulation was merely slowed from cold. His heart began thudding with alarm. His men hauled him out of the plane and lowered him to the ground. His legs wouldn't hold him. He flopped on his back beside the machine, panting, desperate, stricken, his arms beating on the grass like the fluttering wings of a stunned bird—a war bird who would fly no more. For Fred Libby there had been too much war. He was finished.

After months of varied therapy in the finest medical institutions of the day, the eminent New York specialist Dr. Joseph Franken pronounced him totally and permanently disabled. He would never fly another plane. Successive attacks could be expected through the years, and his spine would become progressively ankylosed. He was to pay in heavy installments for over fifty years for his relentless gallantry. The sturdy body of the cowboy would never be the same. He was a cripple.

His war career was to be crowned with one of those supernal moments that any man is lucky to have just once in his life. As 1918 progressed, he could move around fairly well, although he was permanently unfit for flying duty. He was the central figure in a Liberty Loan promotion in New York City in October 1918, under the auspices of the Aero Club of America. Fred Libby's tattered flag, the first American flag to fly over enemy territory in World War I, was put up for auction at

Carnegie Hall.

Alan Hawley and Augustus Post of the Aero Club prevailed on Libby to appear personally with the flag, the morning after the auction, which had brought a stunning $3,250,000 in to the Liberty Loan. The officials hoped to bring in even more subscriptions. What they brought to New York instead was a moment of indescribable emotion, centered on the crippled Libby and his flag.

The New York Tribune of 18 October 1918 couches the events in the language and tone of those times:

"THRONG IN TEARS GREETS TATTERED FLAG FROM FRONT"

"A timid young officer with a tattered thing in his hands mounted the Liberty Theater platform yesterday, and while he stood there, cheeks burning with embarrassed red and eyes looking straight down his nose, a crowd that had a moment before gaped and grinned and jostled, after one slow stare and with a sudden passion stormed toward him. They rolled forward in a tumult of noise, men and women with welcome in their voices and tears in their eyes. Not sightseers cheering a show, but a people greeting their own hero. Then a girl reached out, and over the crowd caught the tattered thing, held it hard and with swimming eyes raised it to her lips.

"The voices stopped and the air was silent as a prayer. The first American flag to fly over the German lines, in the hands of the aviator who had carried it there had come back to New York to be baptized with the tears and kisses of a motley New York throng. Those hundreds sought to grasp the precious strips of red and white and shake the hand of Captain Frederick Libby.

"This torn old thing amid all the bright flags of Fifth Avenue was a Holy Banner. The procession passed along clutching its rags as though performing a sacrament. Some touched it lightly, some shook it as if it were a paw, the women kissed it, soldiers saluted it, while Captain Libby still tried to hide behind it, with the shame that every real hero seems to have for his own valor."

The war was over three weeks later, but it was to be a torturing presence for Fred Libby all the rest of his days. He fought a running battle for the health he had lost in the war. The spinal attacks came as predicted, and

were progressively more crippling. Libby never stopped fighting.

He married, and raised two fine step-daughters. He plunged into the oil business and was a successful wildcatter, alternating handsome strikes with cash-consuming dry holes. Major outfits like Union Oil and Richfield were often partners with "Cap" Libby, and along the way, the ex-aviator was one of the founders of what is now Western Airlines. Thirty years after a 1917 forced landing had done the initial damage, he finally lost his left eye. Still there remained one more climactic peak to the flying career that had begun that dismal day in 1916 at Le Hameau.

On the fiftieth anniversary of the U.S. Air Force, Fred Libby was invited to take part in the Los Angeles celebrations of the event. The media were on hand as the old ace clambered first into a modern flying suit and then into the rear seat of a jet fighter. These were two ordeals for the heavily crippled Libby, but he got aboard and found Captain Iven Kincheloe, the Korean War jet ace and test pilot, at the controls.

The jet was warm and unbelievably quiet. As they soared aloft above the parched soil of Southern California, time stood still. Looking down, it wasn't hard for Libby to imagine in the curving scars of the Los Angeles freeways far below the front line trenches in the France of his youth. The past was coming even closer. Kincheloe was on the intercom.

"You want to take her for a while, Fred?"

"Sure I'll take her. Thanks."

"Just remember the controls are real light to the touch. Everything else should be just about the same."

The sure, well-shaped hands that had nursed aloft the flimsy fighting crates of 1917 and flown them to glory, reached out now to the feather-touch stick of the jet. The bandy legs settled on the rudder. Fifty years had passed, but his gift for flying had not left him.

He rolled and dived and soared and banked, dropping his years and the burden of his twisted spine like a cloak. Time stood still, and then for those few magic minutes rolled backward down through the decades. In that sublime echo of the past, the old Colorado eagle flew once more.

When the jet landed after the historic flight, a beaming Iven Kincheloe told newsmen, "The old boy is as good as he ever was." For

American aviation history, it was quite a moment.

When the authors resurrected Fred Libby in their book *Fighter Aces** the old war bird was inundated with fan mail. This flood of appreciation, right from the American heart, continued to reach him until his death in January 1970. The eulogy at his funeral was appropriately delivered by co-author Colonel Raymond F. Toliver, who had himself grown up in Libby's Colorado listening to legends of the mysterious fighter ace from Sterling, and who later was able to bring him out of the historical shadows.

Beside Colonel Toliver as he delivered the eulogy were the remnants of that sacred flag, stained with the castor oil of World War I. Fred Libby never let go of the treasured relic, and his brave life ended without a single loose end. His memory is held in high honor by America's fighter aces, who have a strong affinity for the quality of courage.

Libby's story and career exemplify much of the color, mystery and exciting early history that surround these early expatriate pilots who flew with the British and French. Those who flew with the British suffered at least a temporary loss of their U.S. citizenship, an indignity that was not visited upon members of the Lafayette Escadrille.

On 31 August 1916, just four days after Fred Libby shot down his fifth German plane as an observer-gunner, an American flying as a pilot with the Royal Flying Corps downed his fifth German plane and became the first American fighter ace. He was Captain Alan M. Wilkinson, twenty-five years old and already a veteran of a year's aerial combat. He was commissioned on 14 June 1915.

By war's end, Wilkinson was a major with nineteen aerial victories to his credit. He was certainly among the first Americans to fly in combat in World War I, and may even have been the first. Wilkinson never transferred to the AEF from the RFC, and is therefore almost unknown to most aerial combat buffs. The factual record of this expatriate ace's career puts him among the top American combat pilots of the conflict.

Wilkinson flew with 24th Squadron RFC from 16 January 1916, until 13 October 1916.

* Fred Libby's complete story is told under the chapter heading "Horses Don't Fly" in Trevor J. Constable's *"Hidden Heroes,"* published by Arthur Barker Ltd., London 1971.

(Constable Collection)

Trevor J. Constable and Captain Frederick Libby, RFC (14.00): Constable, left, is co-author of this book and lives in San Pedro, California. Libby, the "Colorado Cowboy," scored 10 victories as a gunner in the RFC's 25th Squadron, then returned as a pilot and scored 14 in fighters. He suffered from crippling arthritis. This photo was taken a year before his death.

This means that he was in what many regard as the hardest fighting of the air war for the British. He scored his first five kills between 16 May 1916 and 31 August 1916. In the same period, he is credited with four probables. Most action at this time was taking place behind the German lines, and confirmation of many downings was impossible.

Setting the seal on Wilkinson's war career, and also hearing high testament to his bravery, was his double award in 1916 of the British Distinguished Service Order. The DSO is the highest decoration that an officer of the British services can win—other than the coveted and rarely awarded Victoria Cross. To win the DSO twice is a considerable distinction.

Serving with the Lafayette Escadrille from the days of its foundation was the man more generally accepted as America's first fighter ace—Raoul Lufbery. He was flying during the same period as Wilkinson, and under the same difficult conditions. Lufbery was a fitting figure to enrich Franco-American traditions. French-born, he was taken to the United States by his immigrant parents, and was naturalized in 1910. In his personality, citizenship status and deeds, Lufbery united the two great nations of which he was a part.

Aged twenty-nine in 1914, Raoul Lufbery returned to France and enlisted as an airplane mechanic in the French Army. His background for this was excellent. For several years before the war he had barnstormed around the world with famed French pioneer aviator Marc Pourpé. Both men returned to France to fight on the outbreak of war.

When Pourpé was killed shortly after the Battle of the Marne, Lufbery suffered a deep personal blow. He set out to avenge Pourpé's death, and applied immediately for pilot training. He flew in action for the first time on 7 October 1915, as the pilot of a Voisin bomber.

Despite some earlier difficulties with his training, Lufbery proved to be an exceptional combat pilot with a talent for improvising tactics. As has been pointed out earlier, aerial tactics evolved rapidly in the crucible of war, without any initial theoretical underpinning. Lufbery came into his own with the machines and armament of his day when he transferred to fighters in 1916.

Scoring his first victory on 30 July 1916, Lufbery had six kills by Christmas Day of the same year. Although not yet an ace by the French standard of ten aerial victories, America had its first ace when Lufbery was released reluctantly to the U.S. Army by the Lafayette Escadrille. His transfer took place on 21 January 1918.

Assigned to the 94th Aero Squadron, First Pursuit Group, Lufbery proceeded to add to his Lafayette Escadrille glories.* Because of his foreign birth and service with the French, his final status was not formally decided until many years after the war. His score has been the subject of numerous disputes, and is generally acknowledged to have been far higher than the seventeen kills with which he is officially credited.

Since most fighter combat took place in 1916 and early 1917 behind the German lines, the majority of Allied fighter pilots active during this period probably shot down at least twice the number of aircraft with which they are officially credited. Confirmation of these kills was usually impossible. Until the "ace" concept became firmly associated with aerial victories, furthermore, there was no special urgency or significance attached to the confirmation of kills.

When Lufbery on occasion confided to some of his contemporaries that he had downed as

*The U.S. Air Service, however, does not credit him with a single victory after his transfer to the American service.

many as fifty German planes—with the bulk of them unconfirmed due to their being far behind enemy lines—he was probably talking fact and not fiction. His demonstrated abilities in front of his fellow pilots were sufficient proof that he could have amassed a large number of unconfirmed downings. History has not clothed him in the transparent raiment of the boaster.

Lufbery's place among the immortals of the air is assured by his development of the "Lufbery Circle"—a useful and enduring aerial tactic that saved the lives of many Allied pilots in two world wars. When Richthofen's Circus was at the height of its power, the Baron's uncanny grasp of the essentials of aerial fighting enabled him to inflict terrible losses on his foes. The "Lufbery Circle" was devised to offset partially the technical disparity between German and Allied aircraft—which added to von Richthofen's assets.

Lufbery and his pilots would fight until the Germans, mounted on superior aircraft, began to gain the advantage. Lufbery would then enter a tight turn or circle, with the other members of his squadron following close behind him. Friend was behind friend, so that if any German machine entered the circle in an effort to get into firing position behind any of Lufbery's planes, the German would come immediately under the guns of the following American pilot.

The German might shoot down his intended victim, but would himself certainly be shot down. The odds against successfully penetrating a Lufbery Circle were high, and discouraged most German pilots from tackling the Americans when they went into this formation. Continuing this circle, Lufbery would gradually work the formation back to the Allied side of the lines. Once the circle reached Allied territory, the Germans usually gave up the chase and flew away.

On 19 May 1918, while serving with the 14th Pursuit Squadron, Raoul Lufbery tackled a massive German photo-reconnaissance aircraft near Toul airfield. The German machine was armored, and on Lufbery's first pass his numerous hits had no effect. As the ace made a second firing pass, the German rear gunner threw a burst into Lufbery's engine. The little Nieuport was soon a flying ball of fire. Jumping in midair from this inferno, Lufbery came cartwheeling down with his flying suit smoldering. There were no parachutes for fighter pilots in those days, and the ace plummeted into a small stream, there to be crushed by the impact. His death was a heavy blow to the Americans.

Lufbery was the third-ranking AEF ace of World War I, and is credited with seventeen victories. If Alan Wilkinson is excluded because of his British service, Lufbery was the first American ace. In musings with his fighter pilot companions, Lufbery once said, "There will be no 'after the war' for fighter pilots." His death in combat fulfilled the prophecy of the dark-haired Franco-American in his own case, but the Lufbery Circle kept his name before America's fighter pilots for years after his passing. "Luf's" historical niche is secure, and he lives on as a dominant pioneer figure.

Among Lufbery's fellow Americans in the Lafayette Escadrille was Major Charles J. Biddle, who came to the elite formation from Escadrille 73. Biddle was also later transferred to the U.S. Air Service, and he spent the remainder of his flying career with the 13th Aero Squadron, 4th Pursuit Group. He was credited with seven aerial victories until the USAF made its 1969 revisions of World War I scores as explained in Chapter One. He is now credited with 3.16 aerial victories with the AEF, plus one with the Lafayette Escadrille.

Charles Biddle's 1919 book, *Way of the Eagle*, contains a number of letters written by the American ace during wartime. These missives provide absorbing insight into the thinking of a World War I pilot. They have an immediacy usually missing from retrospective writing. Just like Lufbery, Biddle came out second best in a battle with an armored German plane, less than a week after Lufbery was killed.

The possibility exists that Biddle battled the identical machine that downed Lufbery, for the German gunner was evidently an exceedingly good snap shot in much the same way as was Fred Libby. Biddle tells the story of this fight, and its sequel, in a letter written 25 May 1918 from the Ocean Hospital at La Panne in Belgium:

"... Ten minutes after the first fight we were flying along inside our own lines, when I noticed a peculiar two-seater circling very low down between the trenches. He could not have been more than six hundred metres up. I took him for an English infantry liaison machine, which he very much resembled, but then noticed that he seemed to circle into the Boche lines with remarkable impunity considering his low altitude, so I decided to investigate.

"Sure enough, there were the old black crosses on him showing plainly as he swung almost under me in making a turn over our lines ... It was the first Boche machine of the kind that I had ever seen, and, indeed, I have never heard of anyone that I know running into one like it. He had a rounded body like some French machines, the tail was square and the lower wing much shorter than the upper, like many of the English two-seater observation planes. All the Hun two-seaters that I have ever seen or heard of before have both the upper and lower wings approximately the same length. In addition, it was the slowest bus you ever saw, and I think I could go two miles to his one.

"All this leads me to believe that it was a new type of German armored plane which they call 'Junkers' and which I have read about in the aviation reports. They are built especially for this low infantry liaison work, and are heavily armored about the fuselage to protect them from fire from the ground. In consequence of their great weight, they cannot go very high and are extremely slow.

"This fellow must have been a squadron leader or something, for he had four big streamers attached to his wings, one on the top and another on the lower plane on each side ... it is very common for patrol leaders to carry streamers so that their pilots may easily distinguish them from the other machines in the patrol.

"Whether or not this fellow was what I think he was, I hope that when I am flying again, I may see him and have another go at him. He certainly got the best of me, and I don't feel at all vindictive about it, as it was a fair fight. But just the same, it would give me more satisfaction to bring that boy down than any five others. It would also be interesting to see whether his hide is thick enough to stand a good dose of armor-piercing bullets at short range. An incendiary bullet in his gas tank might also make his old boiler factory a warm place to fly in.

"As soon as I was sure that the machine was really a Hun, I dove down on him and made up my mind this time to get at good close range. I did, and ended up fifty yards directly behind his tail and just below, but I had one bad mistake, a real beginner's trick which was the cause of all my troubles.

"I was not far enough below him, and I had not fired more than one or two shots when I got caught in the back draught from his propeller, which joggled my machine about so accurate shooting became an impossibility. I saw one tracer go to one side of him, and another several feet on the other side, so stopped shooting for a second to get in better position. Anyone with a little experience should know better than to get himself caught like this, especially myself, for I had the same thing happen with the first Hun I ever brought down.

"That time I dove down a little before shooting at all, and then fired from a good position a little lower down. I tried to remedy the situation in the same way this time, but in doing so I entirely failed, for the instant, to ap-

preciate the very slow speed of the Hun. I was already close to him, and when I dove down and then pulled up to shoot, I found that I had overshot and was almost directly under him— so much so that it was impossible to get my gun on him.

"He started swerving from side to side to get me out from under him, so that the machine-gunner could shoot, and I tried to stay under him, swerving as he did and at the same time slowing down my motor to the limit so as to let him get ahead of me enough to allow me to start shooting again. The Boche and I were at this time about twenty yards apart, and if he had only had a trap door in his bottom he might have brought me down by dropping a brick on my head. However, he did not need it.

"The Hun gave a twist which took me for an

(National Archives)

A CONFIRMED VICTORY

Captain Charles J. Biddle, C.O. of the 13th Aero Squadron and formerly with the Lafayette Escadrille, brought down this German two-seater on August 14, 1918, near Nancy, France. The German pilot survived the downing, although his observer was killed. The aircraft was placed on display in the town square at Toul. Captain Biddle came out of WWI with 7 victories to his credit, but USAF historical statisticians dropped him to 3.16 kills fifty years later.

44

instant beyond the protection of his fuselage. It was only for a second or two, but it was sufficient for the observer, who proceeded to do the quickest and most accurate bit of shooting that I have yet run up against. As a rule in such a situation, you see the observer look over the side of his machine at you, and then swing his gun around on its pivot and point it in your direction. While he is doing this, you have time to duck.

"In this case, I saw a black-helmeted head appear over the edge of the Hun machine and almost at the same instant he fired, as quickly as you could snap-shoot with a pistol. In trying to slow down as much as possible, I had gotten into almost a loss of speed, so that my machine did not perhaps answer to the controls as quickly as it otherwise would have.

"This, however, made no difference for he was as accurate as he was quick, and his very first shot came smashing through the front of my machine above the motor, and caught me just on top of the left knee. How many bullets hit the machine I don't know, and never had a chance to find out, but my motor went dead at once, so that knocked out all chance of any further shots at the Boche.

"I dove under him out of his line of fire, and then twisting sharply around, planed back for our own lines, trying to make the most of what little height I had . . . I kept working away till the last minute, trying to get the motor going, for anyone who knows this country knows that it is utterly impossible to land any machine in it without crashing, let alone a Spad, which requires at least as great speed for landing as any other type.

"All my efforts were useless, however, and I saw that there was nother for it but to smash up as gracefully as possible. The thing that bothered me most was not the smash, for that would probably result only in a little shaking up, but I thought I was further in the Hun lines than I was, and had most unpleasant visions of spending the rest of the war in Germany . . .

"Just at the last moment I veered the plane a little to avoid landing in the middle of a barbed-wire entanglement, and then the instant my wheels touched the ground, over my machine went in the middle of its back with a loud crash . . . Scrambling out, I lost no time in rolling into a nearby shellhole."

Diving from shell hole to shell hole, Biddle began avoiding by turns the strafing runs made on him by his late adversary, German artillery fire and the combined small-arms efforts of several hundred German infantrymen. Wallowing through mud and stagnant water, with his sodden flying suit adding an almost intolerable burden of extra weight to his wounded leg, Biddle eventually stumbled to safety in a position occupied by the Royal Irish Rifles. He survived World War I.

The Americans of the Lafayette Escadrille had learned the essentials of air fighting as they had developed. This know-how was passed on to the inexperienced American pilots coming from the United States after America's entry into the war. Since aerial combat was a dynamic art, only a participant could learn its lessons and provide authentic guidance and leadership to green pilots. In this respect, the American fighter pilots of the Lafayette Escadrille made an invaluable contribution to the success of the fledgling U.S. Air Service.

The U.S. Air Service's first aerial combat did not take place until 5 February 1918, almost a year after America's declaration of war. Reconnaissance planes of the 1st Squadron were attacked by German fighters and a brisk battle ensued. 2nd Lieutenant Stephen W. Thompson and his French pilot shot down a German plane and they shared the victory.

Over a month later an American pilot flying in the AEF scored the first actual victory. 1st Lt. Paul F. Baer of the 103rd Pursuit Squadron shot down an enemy plane on 11 March and then repeated the act on the 16th of March. Baer went from one distinction to another, getting his third tally on 6 April and his fourth on the 12th of April. He added a shared kill for ½ victory credit on 23 April and finally became the first American ace in the AEF on 8 May 1918 when he shot down another German plane. He celebrated by shooting down a second one the same day, bringing his total to 6½. This accounting does not include a balloon he was reported to have destroyed. No one saw it go down! Baer survived the war and Baer Field at his home town of Fort Wayne, Indiana, is named in his memory. Baer died on 12 September 1930.

Meanwhile, other AEF pilots began to score. On 27 April 1918 James Norman Hall scored his first kill, and three officers shared another the same day. They were Chris W. Ford, William Thaw and James Norman Hall again. Charles J. Biddle, Douglas Campbell, Alan F. Winslow, George E. Turnure, Charles H. Wilcox and Edward V. Rickenbacker followed suit in short succession before the end of April.

The experienced German opposition was a tremendous challenge, but in a short time the Americans developed the skills and acumen that only actual war can provide. Before long, they had redressed to a great degree the technical disadvantages under which they flew. As the final year of the war progressed, tactics became more and more important. Daylight fighter operations built up from two- and three-machine formations to mass flights and battles involving thirty to forty aircraft on both sides. American squadrons played a leading role in these events as strength from the USA flowed into the conflict.

The second AEF pilot to win acedom in an American uniform was Captain Edward V. Rickenbacker.* He became in due course the American "Ace of Aces" in World War I. By every measure, Rickenbacker was the most famous pilot of his time, and right down to this day he probably enjoys a "recognition factor" among the general public of the USA exceeding that of any other fighter ace America has produced.

A man of energy, daring and imagination, Rickenbacker was already a nationally famous auto-racing driver at the time of American entry into World War I. His later achievements as an ace pilot and as a businessman have overshadowed this earlier phase of his career, but his racing experience was largely responsible for the development of Rickenbacker's fantastic mechanical sense and coordination.

The 1977 Defense Advanced Research Projects Agency's *Feasibility Study to Predict Combat Effectiveness for Selected Military Roles: Fighter Pilot Effectiveness,* has a great deal to say about ideal fighter pilot types. This massive compendium of scientific and quasi-scientific material demonstrates how modern psychological testing, flight simulator workouts and similar techniques can be used to improve fighter pilot effectiveness and largely predict such effectiveness. If all this dedicated labor could somehow be embodied in one individual, there's little doubt he'd be a facsimile of Eddie Rickenbacker.

*30 May 1918

He was from boyhood a record breaker, a thrill-seeker, a fierce competitor and a limit tester. He was ingenious, energetic, resourceful and technically competent. Given what we now know about the qualities that make up a fighter ace, his joining the Signal Enlisted Reserve Corps in New York City in May of 1917, seems like a pedestrian act. He was assigned to the Aviation Section, however, and three days later was on his way to France. The famous race driver served as a chauffeur with Aviation Headquarters of the AEF. As we would expect from the modern studies, Eddie soon started pushing. He came into contact with Billy Mitchell and impressed the pioneer leader with his determination to fly combat.

Since Rickenbacker was considered "too old" at twenty-eight for a fighter pilot, it took the intervention of someone like Mitchell to pave the way for Rickenbacker's flying training. The future fighter ace, the modern studies tell us, either hurdles or bursts through all such barriers. Rickenbacker was in the classic mold.

He trained at Tours, and found his way eventually into the 94th Aero Squadron as a pilot. This was the famous "Hat in the Ring" squadron, which found immortality due to the deeds of Rickenbacker and others who served with the 94th. Surely it was a stellar formation.

In command of the 94th when Rickenbacker joined was the sagacious air fighter Raoul Lufbery. Under "Luf's" experienced eye, Rickenbacker broke in and began his spectacular climb to the top scoring spot. He scored his first kill on 29 April 1918, and on 30 May scored his fifth aerial victory, which made him an ace. For a man who was too old to be a fighter pilot, he had made a brilliant beginning.

Rickenbacker went on to score 19 victories that were exclusively his, plus two shared with another pilot, and one shared with two other pilots for a total of 20.33 kills. He was additionally credited with destroying four balloons for a victory total of 24.33. A fifth balloon, supposedly confirmed thirty years after the war, failed to survive the scrutiny of the 1969 Victory Credits Board.

History does not confine such anomalies solely to the famous, as another American pilot of World War I could testify. Captain Charles R. D'Olive was credited with a World

46

War I score of four victories, and spent forty-five years outside the elite fraternity of aces. On 18 June 1963, to D'Olive's great satisfaction, one of his two additional victory claims was confirmed by the USAF. Captain Charles D'Olive, late of the 93rd Aero Squadron became an ace. Acedom was nice while it lasted.

What the USAF gives, it may also take away, with every statistical study representing some kind of threat to some ace, somewhere—including those who are completely out of this world and beyond caring. Six years after D'Olive was granted the great honor of his life, USAF Historical Study #133 (June 1969), shows him with but four kills.* He had scored three kills on 13 September 1918, but shared two of these with another pilot. In 1918, pilots were given full credits,

*Rickenbacker is also a victim of the "new method" of counting victories. For years he was known to have 26 kills, but closer scrutiny by Study #133 reveals that he counted *shared* kills as full credit. In reality, he has $23 + .50 + .50 + .33 = 24.33$.

but under the scoring rules of Study #133, D'Olive has only four credits.

From August to September 1918, Eddie Rickenbacker was in the hospital. He made his stellar fighting record in a scant three months of combat, and no other American pilot surpassed his 24.33 victories until well into World War II. Billy Mitchell is reputed to have said, "If the war had lasted a few more weeks, Eddie Rickenbacker would have been a general." His later career certainly proved that he had all the qualities of a great general.

Rickenbacker was an exponent of the classic bounce out of the sun. He believed in the fundamental value of altitude to the attacking pilot, and this, combined with his natural aggressiveness, outstanding piloting skill and superlative shooting, placed him among the greatest combat pilots produced by the United States.

A legend in his own lifetime, Rickenbacker's philosphy was born of the incredible physical disasters he survived. He once turned end over end in a race car at Indianapolis. A

(USAF)

RICKENBACKER AND BLESSE

Edward V. Rickenbacker, Eastern Airlines president and top American ace of WWI with 26 victories, chats with Korean War ace Major Fredrick C. Blesse (10 victories). The Spad and the F-86 "Sabre" in the background show the giant strides made in 35 years of fighter development.

devastating airline crash near Atlanta, Georgia in February 1941, broke his hip, elbow and nose and scooped his left eye out of its socket. The following year, he almost died of exposure after a crash in the South Pacific. Rickenbacker's indomitable courage kept both him and his younger companions alive until rescue.

What did the "Ace of Aces" himself say about these numerous flirtations with death? "The thought I had held since boyhood never deserted me. I was a dynamic part of progress and life. Some Power was taking care of me, keeping me alive for some purpose, some fulfillment."

His fulfillments included a major role in the development of modern civil aviation in the USA. He was the dominant force in Eastern Airlines for decades. In these days of mass jet travel, we do well to remember that it took some tough, independent, never-say-die men to create this particular miracle, and Eddie Rickenbacker was one of them. His autobiography was published by Prentice Hall Inc. of N.Y. in 1967. When Eddie Rickenbacker died on 23 July 1977, a giant's work lay behind him, and he had become an honored part of both acedom and Americana.

Behind Rickenbacker among the aces of the AEF is Frank Luke of Arizona. He holds a special niche among American aces because fourteen of his victories were balloons. He shot down only four airplanes. The fury and success with which he hurled himself on the gasbags earned him the immortal nickname of the "Arizona Balloon Buster."

Luke's career was as brilliant as it was brief. To term his career "meteoric" is to do final justice to an overworked word. Lieutenant Luke shot down his first aircraft, and confirmed this victory on 12 September 1918. Seventeen days later, Luke's score had risen to fourteen German observation balloons and four aircraft,* and Lieutenant Luke was dead. He was killed on the ground by German infantry while standing amid the wreckage of his crashed fighter, in an episode that epitomized his phenomenal courage.

The best-known biographical study of Frank Luke comes from the files of the USAF:

"Frank Luke (World War Ace). Born Phoenix, Arizona, May 19, 1897, son of Mr.

*USAF Historical Study #133 of June 1969 credits 11.83 balloons to Luke as he shared 3 kills with one other pilot and a fourth with two other pilots.

and Mrs. Frank Luke, Sr.

"Frank Luke, the most spectacular air fighter of the World War, enlisted in the Signal Corps, U.S. Army, on September 25, 1917, as a private.

"He was then sent for flying training to Rockwell Field, San Diego, California, on January 23, 1918, and was subsequently commissioned a Second Lieutenant in the Aviation Section, Signal Officers Reserve Corps.

Arriving overseas for advanced flying training, he was stationed at the 3rd Aviation Instruction Center, Issoudon, France, where he remained until May 30, 1918, leaving for Caziaux. On July 26, 1918, he was ordered to active duty at the front with the 27th Aero Squadron, 1st Pursuit Group, in the Aisne-Marne salient. Three weeks later he engaged in his first aerial combat and shot down an enemy airplane, the beginning of a long list of victories. During his active flying at the front he was officially credited with the destruction of eighteen enemy craft—four airplanes and fourteen balloons."

Luke stood out among his contemporaries because at a time when formation flying and team tactics were beginning to dominate aerial warfare, he was the archetypical lone wolf. He was a throwback to the spirit that held sway in the air war's earlier years. An iron will and fierce determination were coupled to his lone wolf nature. He drove home these savage solo attacks even against the repeated orders of his commanding officer. Like any talented artist, Luke resented controls on his work, and he was courageous almost to a fault.

Balloons were not easy targets. Protected by bristling batteries of antiaircraft and machine guns, they were a great temptation because of their bulk and immobility, but any would-be balloon buster had first to run a terrifying gauntlet of fire and steel before he could shoot at the gasbag. As soon as he had finished his firing pass he would again be taken under fire from the ground—often by hundreds of soldiers. Fighter squadrons were often assigned to protect balloons, the eyes of the artillery. For a lone fighter plane to tackle a balloon was by 1918 little more than heroic madness.

Luke ignored these risks. He made observation balloons his specialty, and he elevated their destruction to the stature of art. In one week of September 1918, two days of which he

**Lt. Frank Luke,
USAEF, WWI (18.00)**

Luke, known as the "Arizona Balloon Buster," shot down 3 German aircraft and 2 German balloons on the 18th of September, 1918. Here he poses with the wreckage of one of his victims, a German Pfalz. He flew with the 27th Aero Squadron and lost his life eleven days after this photo was taken.

(Erickson Collection)

did not fly, Lieutenant Frank Luke sent down no fewer than thirteen of the gasbags in flaming tatters.

His only departure from his lone wolf ventures was his brief fighting partnership with a kindred spirit in the 27th Squadron, Lieutenant Joseph F. Wehner, who was killed in action 18 September 1918. Wehner was also a balloon buster, and his five victories were all balloons—downgraded to 3.5 aerial victories by USAF Historical Study #133. During the St. Mihiel offensive, the two aces downed five gasbags between them. Returning from one of these encounters Luke and Wehner were separated, and while returning alone to his airfield, Luke downed three German aircraft.

Lieutenant Luke absented himself from his squadron on 28 September 1918 without permission. The young Arizonan was hauled before his C.O. and severely reprimanded. He was also grounded. Telling a born combat pilot that he could not fly while the war thundered all around him was like ordering the tide to stay out.

Without permission Luke took off in his plane and landed at a neighboring field. Orders for his arrest were issued, then countermanded from higher up before they could be carried out. Luke took off again, his target three German balloons in the Meuse regions.

Luke destroyed two of the balloons. In the second strike, the law of averages caught up with the balloon busting young ace. The hail of protective fire found its mark and he was wounded severely. Ignoring his wounds, Luke pressed home his attack on the third balloon, sent it down in flames and turned for home.

Grinding along at 150 feet, fighting to retain consciousness, Luke spotted German troops on the road near Murvaux. He promptly made several strafing runs on the road, killing six Germans and wounding many more. More hits were made by the enemy on his riddled aircraft, and he was forced to land, rolling to a stop in the middle of the German positions.

Surrounding the American pilot, the German infantry called on him to surrender. No dishonor lay in that course for the Arizona Balloon Buster, but the idea of surrender never entered the ace's mind. Standing in the wreckage of his riddled ship, he bravely drew his pistol and began firing at the German infantry. A crash of rifle fire on a roadway near Murvaux closed the incredible career of America's most spectacular World War I ace.

Captain Alfred A. Grant, Luke's C.O., who had opposed the ace's unruly conduct as a matter of discipline, was the first to urge the award of the Congressional Medal of Honor. This decoration was approved and added to the Distinguished Service Cross and Oak Leaf Cluster awarded Luke for earlier bravery. The decorations were presented later to his father, Frank Luke, Sr.

Aged only twenty-one at the time of his death, Frank Luke had blazed a glorious chapter in the history of American aviation. He set a standard of courage and boldness that no pilot would ever surpass. More than any other American pilot, Luke epitomized the classically heroic aspects of the fighter

49

FOKKER D-VIII: Redoubtable German Air Service fighter was the Fokker D-VIII, one of a large collection of successful fighting airplanes designed by Anthony Fokker for Germany.

ace. His story was told and retold hundreds of times through the years. A statue of him was erected in the Capitol grounds at Phoenix, and the USAF has a permanent commemorative link with the Balloon Buster through Arizona's Luke AFB.

Ranked for scoring laurels between Rickenbacker and Luke are a number of Americans who served exclusively with the British, never transferring to the U.S. forces. These Americans were:

Captain Stanley Rosevear, RFC, 23
William C. Lambert, RFC, 22
Captain F. W. Gillette, RAF, 20
Sub-Lieutenant John J. Malone, RNAS, 20
Major Alan M. Wilkinson, RFC, 19

There is also the anomalous figure of Captain Frederick Libby to bear in mind, with ten kills as an observer and fourteen as a pilot—all of them airplanes—more airplanes downed in aerial combat in World War I than any other American aviator.

Lieutenants Frank Hale and Paul T. Iaccaci, both of the RAF and both with eighteen kills, rank in the overall American scoring in World War I with Lieutenant Frank Luke of the AEF. Many of the expatriate American aces received high British awards for bravery, Wilkinson's double award of the DSO probably being the greatest distinction earned by these men, but Sub-Lieutenant John J. Malone of the Royal Naval Air Service also won the DSO. He was killed in action in May 1917.

Ranked behind Rickenbacker, Luke and Lufbery among the AEF aces is Lieutenant George A. Vaughn of Brooklyn, N.Y., who flew with the 17th Pursuit Squadron. A superlative shot with an instinct for combat tactics, Vaughn downed twelve German planes and one observation balloon for a total of thirteen victories in World War I.

Enlisting directly from Princeton University in 1917, Vaughn trained in England and Scotland, and was then assigned to 84th

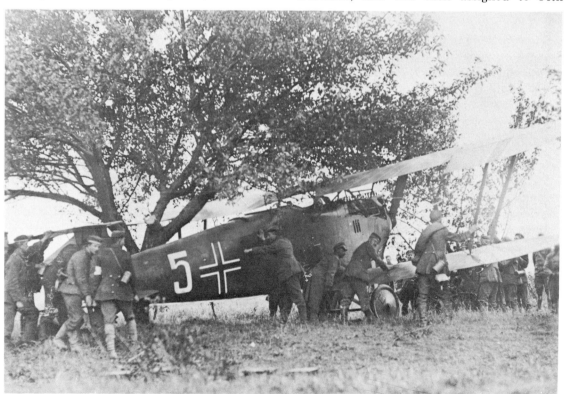

Squadron, RAF. While with this British outfit, Vaughn shot down five planes and a balloon. Seven aircraft were actually downed, together with the balloon, but four of these were shared with other pilots. This gave Vaughn five credits upon transfer to the AEF in August 1918.

Assigned to the 17th Pursuit Squadron as a flight commander, Vaughn put his experience to work. He downed another four and a half German aircraft, which gave him thirteen kills by the old standards but only 9.5 according to the 1969 USAF Historical Study #133.

An extract from George Vaughn's Distinguished Service Cross citation gives insight to his qualities as a fighting pilot:

"For extraordinary herosim in action near Cambrai, France, September 22, 1918. Lieutenant Vaughn, while leading an offensive flight patrol, sighted eighteen enemy Fokkers about to attack a group of five Allied planes flying at low level. Although outnumbered nearly five to one, he attacked the enemy group, personally shot down two enemy planes, the remaining three planes of his group shooting down two more. His courage and daring enabled the group of Allied planes to escape. Again, on September 28, 1918, he alone attacked an enemy advance plane, which was supported by seven Fokkers, and shot the advance plane down in flames."

Vaughn maintained his enthusiasm for aviation after the war. For many years he was a partner in the Casey Jones Academy of Aeronautics at LaGuardia Field in New York.

With twelve aerial victories, one less than Vaughn, Captain Elliott White Springs is usually ranked fifth among AEF aces, a distinction he shares with Captain Field E. Kindley of the 148th Aero Squadron. Historical Study #133, however, credits Springs with 10.75 victories—putting him ahead of Vaughn—and the same study credits Kindley with 11 victories—putting him ahead of Springs. In terms of fame, however, Springs ranks second only to Rickenbacker among the aces of World War I. His is an unusual case.

Elliott White Springs' books on aerial combat made him a far more famous flyer in the postwar period than he had been as a war ace. A whole new generation of American boys was introduced to aerial warfare through his books. He glamorized the fighter pilot more than any other American writer. His books could easily lead the reader of the nineteen twenties and thirties to believe that the fighter pilot had the most glamorous of all war jobs.

Another notable American ace credited with twelve victories is Frank L. Baylies, who flew in the Lafayette Escadrille with Raoul Lufbery. One of the best combat pilots in the French unit, Baylies' victory tally suffered in

SHELTER FOR A VALUED BIRD

Left: German personnel struggling with a Hanover observation and bombing airplane in 1918 on the Western Front. The aircraft is being concealed under the trees.

FOKKER D-VII

Right: German ground crew jockeys a Fokker D-VII outside a canvas hangar somewhere on the Western Front. Note the man hanging on to the tailskid.

(National Archives)

the same way as Lufbery's from inability to confirm. Both pilots had numerous kills behind the German lines, and like Lufbery, Baylies probably had around twice the kills that the records show. He was killed in aerial combat in 1918.

Also unable to confirm a number of kills was Arthur Raymond Brooks, an MIT graduate of 1917, who joined the Aviation Section immediately after winning his degree. Trained in Canada at Toronto, Brooks went overseas early in 1918 and downed ten German aircraft. The Army at that time credited him with only six, and when USAF Historical Study reviewed the situation in 1969, Brooks was reduced to 2.33 kills due to credits shared with other pilots.

Brooks contributed a vivid account of World War I aerial combat set down in December 1918, while the events were fresh in his mind and not embellished by time and memory.

"On the 14th of September 1918, with a section composed of six Spads, we attempted to clear the area for a reconnaissance plane. Three Fokker groups composed of five, six and twelve planes were observed, and our leader and squadron commander, whom I call 'big fellow' for more reason than his stature, headed for the center group of six. Intent as we were on the center group, the last formation of twelve Fokkers got around on our right rear and jumped us. I saw them as they neared us, but had no time to warn the leader of our flight, other than by just nosing down, gaining speed, and then turning to the right over his head and into the Fokkers.

"Before a second or two I had penetrated the Boche formation, and from that time on I never saw another of my mates. But I was treated to a fine display of daytime pyrotechnics. We were at 5,000 meters (about 15,000 ft.), the 'we' in this case referring to

(National Archives)

SOPWITH CAMEL

The renowned Sopwith Camel F-1, was one of the most famous fighters of World War I. American ace Fred Libby characterized it as "a hell of a good airplane, but you had to be on your toes with it all the time."

(Erickson Collection)

SPADS AND SOPWITHS, 1918: Spad XIII's in the rear rank, and Sopwith A-2 observation and photo aircraft, line up in front of a camouflaged canvas hangar at Colombey-les-Belles, France, 1918.

SPAD XIII IN THE SNOW

This was a standard pursuit plane of WWI. Powered by a 235 hp Hispano engine, the Spad XIII had a top speed of 135 mph. This particular Spad, number 15, was flown by Captain Jacques M. Swaab of Philadelphia, Pennsylvania. Swaab ended the war with 10 kills. Later analysis by USAF historians reduced his tally to 8.5 victories. The aircraft belongs to the 22nd Aero Squadron, AEF.

(National Archives)

myself and at least eight red-nosed Richthofen Circus Fokkers bent on an eight-to-one shot. We were about ten miles on the German side of the front line. My chances of escape were so slight that I figured I had come to my end.

"I was scared, but in spite of much high tension and yelling at the top of my voice, I calculated, by the nature of my training, I suppose, that I would get as many Fokkers as possible before the inevitable. For ten minutes from our three-mile height down to a few hundred feet, and through that distance behind the lines to our own side, I passed through rather a mystery.

"I side-slipped continuously, and whenever a Fokker would get on my tail, I would go through the most absurd gyrations as quickly as possible. Twice I tried to ram Fokkers. One red-nosed nightmare came in from right, endeavoring to draw me under . . . I had just time to dip enough to see his features before I fired incendiaries, and he was aflame.

"I turned immediately on another, feeling that a vigorous offense was the best defense. After a short burst from very close quarters I was satisfied that the second Fokker was out of the fight, although he did not catch fire. It was being surrounded that saved me thus far. The Germans could not shoot at me without being in their own way most of the time, or bringing one of their own aircraft into the line of fire.

"White tracer ribbons would cut through between my wings often, so close that if I reached out my hand the stream of bullets would have cut it off. My engine worried me because the pressure in my gas tank failed in certain positions of the airplane. My gravity

(National Archives)

OBSERVATION AIRCRAFT, WWI: Salmson 2A2 observation plane flies over the Western Front in WWI. Fighter pilots hunted such aircraft, which were major source of intelligence on enemy movements.

feed was so low that I had to preserve it.

"Once my prop stopped dead before I could switch over to the gravity tank. I stared at the stationary blade, and instinctively nosed down just as an enemy burst swept in front of my forehead, shattering my windshield and clattering into my right gun, rendering it useless except for single shots. Two more Boche planes, in their tactical work, happened to get in the way of my now single gun line of fire, and down they went. My spirits soared as the odds diminished.

"I now had a better feeling that came with finding myself over Lake Lachausee, with a good two thousand metres of altitude and only four German planes still paying me attention. This was still too much attention to suit me. I figured the danger was greater for me now than with the whole swarm, because there was less chance of the Germans getting in their own way.

53

U.S. Air Service, Colombey-les-Belles, Spad XIII's ready for action at an airdrome near the front in September 1918.

READY FOR FRONT LINE SERVICE

American Spad XIII's and DH-4's lined up at the AEF's 1st Air Depot ready for transfer to squadrons at the front. Scene is at Colombey-les-Belles, France, July 28, 1918.

"A 220 hp Spad can outdive a Fokker D-7, and for 1,500 metres with full motor I spun, nose-dived and then slithered toward the ground, flattening out just over rolling country with a fair chance over the four Germans. Two of these, and then one finally, kept up the chase for a short distance. They retreated to my glad astonishment before crossing the lines.

"I don't know how I got back. One incendiary bullet had burned itself out in the main spar of my upper wing. Five bullets went through the fuselage within four inches of my back. Holes were scattered all over my poor Spad. The aircraft had to be salvaged."

Had gun cameras been installed in Brooks' aircraft, he may well have been the first American ace ever to score a quadruple kill. His last three kills in this encounter were never confirmed under the victory rules of the day. By such vivid interplays of luck, skill, courage and aggressive determination were fighter aces made in World War I.

Captain Brooks not only survived the war, he remained in the Air Service until December of 1922. Returning to the USAAF at the begin-

ning of World War II, Brooks was determined to again take a fighter plane into combat. Fate decreed otherwise. A series of spinal operations denied Brooks the fulfillment of his courageous dream. He was for many years Publications Manager of Bell Telephone Laboratories at Whippany, New Jersey,

Lieutenant David Sinton Ingalls was the U.S. Navy's first and only fighter ace in World War I—an historic distinction. He joined the First Yale Unit and went to France for training with the French at Claremont Forand. Further training followed with the British at Gosport, Turnbury and Ayr. Ingalls flew fighters while assigned to the U.S. Naval Air Station at Dunkirk. During this period he downed a Rumpler observation plane, and tells the story in his own words:

"On 24 September 1918, Hobson and I went out at about 5:30 PM in our Camels. We flew along the lines at 15,000 feet for some time, got disgusted and started home as it was getting dark. Saw some Archie off La Paune, and also a German Rumpler. I caught up with him between Newport and Ostend, but he was so slow I overshot. So I dove again. He would

54

turn one way to give his observer a good shot at me, and I would try to keep under him, making a bigger circle so his observer could not shoot.

"I came up underneath him, again overshooting, but succeeded in firing a few rounds. Nothing happened, so I dropped and worked for a good position. On a turn he almost got me, for before I could make the out-side circle, his observer fired about ten shots, the tracers going between the struts on my left side. We were only ten yards off at the time, and I could see the two Huns in their black helmets.

"All the time we were getting further behind their lines . . . and I was getting madder. Finally, I gave up the cautious, careful tactics, got straight behind him and kept firing for probably one hundred rounds. At last a big puff of smoke came up like an explosion. I felt fine. It was a long way over, so I had to contour-chase (hedgehop) and was shot up by ground fire from a machine gun. My Camel had to be scrapped and I was given a new one."

After the war, Ingalls left the Navy and entered the publishing business. His distinguished career between the wars included service as Undersecretary for Air, on the staff of the Secretary of the Navy. Ingalls entered the Navy again in World War II, this time on the staff of Pacific Air Command. He later became Executive Officer of the Air Central Coordination Group, Forward Area, and also served on the staff of ComAir South Pacific.

A successful businessman, David Ingalls was for many years President and Publisher of the Cincinatti *Times-Star*. In terms of long

(USAF)

NIEUPORT 28: American units flew this Gnome-powered biplane until it was replaced with the Spad XIII. The Nieuport's 170 hp engine gave it a top speed of 124 mph.

service to his country, he has few rivals. His five aerial victories in World War I include an observation balloon shot down in combat. His numerous decorations included the Distinguished Service Medal from his own country, the Legion of Honor from the French, and the British Distinguished Flying Cross.

By 11 November 1918 there were 70 Americans who had earned the ace distinction. Possibly another fifty actually did down the required number of German aircraft without being able to confirm these kills. America's late entry into the war held down the number of aces, and considering the extremely short time that AEF pilots were actually in combat with the enemy, the American record is a good one. Approximately forty Americans earned acedom in British or French service, and only thirty made ace in the AEF according to USAF Historical Study #133.

Using the contemporary crediting practices of World War I, however, the conflict ended with 111 American fighter aces. The unofficial status of the ace title permits any student or enthusiast to accept whichever approach suits his or her concepts of acedom. The authors do not believe that the standards of World War I should be revised a half century later, or that such projects are warranted, with their constant injections of new official statistics into a matter that officialdom considers unofficial.

Incontrovertible by any standards was the phenomenal expansion undergone by U.S. military aviation by the end of the war. Few military leaders in 1914 could possibly have foreseen the rise of American airpower between 1917 and 1918. From its skeleton status in April of 1917, the U.S. Air Service ex-

(National Archives)

THE FAMOUS SE-5: Royal Aircraft Factory product powered with a Hispano 210 hp engine and capable of a top speed of 121 mph. The SE-5 saw considerable combat, but in the latter stage of World War I was used extensively as a pursuit trainer.

READY FOR ACTION

The tension and high activity of a WWI airfield are brilliantly captured in this "moving still" from Signal Corps archives, 1918. Pilots are aboard their Nieuport 28 fighters ready for takeoff. Several have already been started and mechanics can be seen swinging the propellers on two more. Canvas hangars appear in the foreground and left background.

(Erickson Collection)

OPEN AIR REPAIRS

American mechanics work on a Nieuport 28, left, and a Breguet two-seater at an open air repair facility in France, 1918.

TEST AND REPAIR FACILITY 1918

Liberty and other engines were rebuilt and repaired at this facility at Romorantin, Loire et Cher, France. Testing of repaired or rebuilt engines involved several hours hard running with heavy metal propeller. Americans set up their facilities rapidly, were ready for an immense air effort in 1919 had war lasted.

(Erickson Collection)

AMERICAN AIRPLANE FACTORY IN FRANCE: By 1918 the U.S. Air Service had elaborate, American-manned facilities to support its efforts. Fuselage assembly is being carried out here at the U.S. Air Service production and maintenance center at Romorantin, France.

panded to 45 squadrons and 767 pilots in the AEF. There were 491 observers, 23 gunners and 740 aircraft assigned to the various armies in the field.

American aviators had flown more than 35,000 hours over the enemy lines in 13,000 pursuit flights. In 1,100 bombing missions, American pilots dropped more than 275,000 pounds of bombs, and America's airmen had shot down 781 enemy aircraft confirmed, while losing 289 machines to the enemy in combat. Impressive as these statistics were at the time, they veiled the immeasurably greater power that had not had time to uncoil.

The sleeping giant of American productive power had been stirred into reluctant wakefulness. Had World War I lasted another six months, there would have been a fulfillment of the politicians' assertions that American aircraft would darken Europe's skies with their huge numbers. A wise man studying the aerial power that would have

been in America's grasp by early 1919 could only have concluded that under no circumstances should the sleeping giant again be provoked. Wise men were not to prevail after the "war to end all wars."

By the middle nineteen-thirties, war clouds once more were gathering in Europe. The Spanish Civil War provided a trial ground for new weapons, tactics and military techniques. Modern tactical airpower had its birth in the Spanish crucible. The significance of this conflict, and what it portended for the future of airpower in warfare, was largely lost on the onlooking and generally isolationist U.S.A.

American pilots nevertheless entered the Spanish Civil War, and three of them became aces under the "five down" standard. About thirty Americans volunteered for service with the Loyalist forces, but only about seventeen actually flew combat, the remainder being turned down for lack of experience or because of medical problems. Those who got into the

(A. H. Landis/H. Allen Herr)

LACALLE SQUADRON,
Spanish Civil War
Ace Frank G. Tinker, from DeWitt, Arkansas, stands at extreme left. Harold Evans "Whitey" Dahl, Sidney, Illinois, is kneeling second from the left.

Lt. Frank G. Tinker,
Spanish Civil War (8.00)
Tinker was schooled at the U.S. Naval Academy and graduated in 1933. He took his flight training at Randolph Field, Texas and Pensacola, Florida. This photo taken after returning from Spain and rejoining the USN.

(Lucille Tinker/H. Allen Herr)

58

air flew against German and Italian-flown aircraft in the service of Franco's rebels.

The most successful American ace of the Spanish Civil War was Lieutenant Frank Tinker of the U.S. Navy. Most sources credit Tinker with eight victories, two of these being the then-new Me-109 fighters supplied by Germany. Tinker is the first American ace to shoot down an Me-109. He survived the Spanish conflict, in which the opposing side was led in the air by such luminaries as Adolf Galland, Werner Moelders and Guenther Luetzow. Tinker committed suicide in 1939.

Other American aces of the Spanish conflict were Harold E. Dahl*, with five victories and Albert J. "Ajax" Baumler whose victory tally has been variously reported from five to eight kills, five and a half victories being most likely. Ajax Baumler survived the Spanish War, and ran up five more victories as a major with the 10th U.S. Air Force in World War II. He was the first American to become an ace in each of two separate wars, and died in August 1973 from injuries sustained in an automobile accident.

The participation of American pilots in the Spanish conflict was an adventurer's attempt to stay in tune with the times. They did more to meet in a practical fashion the dominant menace of the nineteen thirties than most Americans of their time. Their effort—as aces and pilots—stands in vivid contrast to the stagnation of official American airpower at the same period.

The best military minds had failed to grasp fully the future significance of airpower. Like the tank, airpower was regarded more as a novelty—an embellishment—than as a new and decisive dimension to warfare. Only sacrificial efforts like those of Billy Mitchell and the devotion of a hard core of less famous airpower advocates stood between the United States and disaster.

What the best-trained professional experts could not grasp with certainty and completeness went far beyond the lay public's ken. Working upon the lay public, however, was the powerful imagery of fighter pilot books, fighter aviation motion pictures, and shoals of pulp magazines in the tradition of *Flying*

---

* Harold Evans "Whitey" Dahl claimed only 4 victories but Spanish leaders insist Dahl had five. The authors, however, have been unable to document a single victory for Dahl. He was in actual combat for less than a month at the front.

(USAF)

Captain Albert J. "Ajax" Baumler, USAF (13:00): An ace of the Spanish Civil War (8:00 victories), Baumler returned to the USAAF, flew with the 23rd Fighter Group in the CBI and scored five more kills, bringing his total to 13. His home was in Denison, Texas, and he passed away in 1968. Baumler was the first American to become an ace in two wars.

Aces. What Mitchell and de Seversky and others had to say about airpower could not really reach people who weren't directly involved in these technical matters. The blizzard of fighter ace adventure fiction and books about the real-life World War I aces, made people air-minded through their sense of adventure and their imagination.

All this kept aircraft and the men who flew them in the public mind. Certainly the ace was over-glorified, but American boys steeped in and teethed on the glamorous treatment of the fighter ace were inspired to emulate these figures. Most American aces of World War II confess to being inspired through the books about aces that they devoured in their youth.

The ace was a bold, new and valiant figure in modern combat. He had won his spurs in World War I. He was also the bearer of a message from the future, for behind him loomed the unknown terrors held for posterity by the new air weapon—the flail that the aces of

59

World War I had wielded in its primal form.

The statistics tell the dry facts of American aviation's baptism of fire, but the facts were made by men—111 or 70 of them depending on whose statistics you prefer—who were a classic cross-section of American manhood. Raoul Lufbery, the immigrant boy straddling Old Country and New World; Frederick Libby, the Colorado cowboy and expatriate soldier-of-fortune; Eddie Rickenbacker, the all-American mechanical genius soaring from the humblest beginnings to immortality; David Sinton Ingalls, the gentleman patriot; Frank Luke, heroism incarnate and a throw-back to the Age of Valor; and the dozens of less colorful but courageous Americans who found their way into World War I's fraternity of aces.

Their ranks have thinned away now almost to nothing, but they symbolized for over twenty years a new and vital kind of military prowess. What they won so arduously in blood and conflict was almost cast away in the years that followed the winning of their glory. Then came the new generation of fighter pilots—the young men they had inspired—to snatch back the fortunes of their country from the locust years between the wars.

The Aces of World War I

(National Archives)

First Lt. Paul Frank Baer, U.S. Army Air Service WWI (9.0): Baer, from Fort Wayne, Indiana, joined the Lafayette Escadrille of the French Flying Corps and later transferred to the AEF 103rd Pursuit Squadron. He was killed December 9, 1930 when his aircraft struck the mast of a Chinese junk near Shanghai, China. USAF Study No. 133, June 1969, credited Baer with 7.75 victories. Lt. Baer was the first fighter pilot in the AEF to become an ace.

(National Archives)

Lt. Frank Leaman Baylies, FFC WWI (12.0): Enlisted in the French Flying Corps in May 1917. Baylies was shot down twice. The first time he escaped from his German captors, but the second time, June 17, 1918, he was shot down in flames over Rollet, Oise, France. No AEF service. He was born in New Bedford, Massachusetts on September 23, 1895.

(National Archives)

Major Charles John Biddle, USAAS WWI (8.0): Biddle, from Andalusia, Pennsylvania, joined the French Foreign Legion in 1917, transferring to the FFC Lafayette Escadrille soon afterwards. After the U.S. entered the war, he was assigned to the 103rd Pursuit Group and then to the 13th Pursuit Group. He scored 2 with the FFC and 6 with USAAS(AEF).

(National Archives)

Captain Thomas G. Cassady, FFC/AEF (9.0): Cassady, from Freedom, Indiana, joined the French Flying Corps and was assigned to Escadrille 157, transferring to the AEF in April 1918. His first five victories were with the FFC and his last four with the AEF. However, three of the last four kills were shared victories and the USAF Study 133 gave him just 1.63 credits (1.0+.16+.14+.33) so officially, after nearly 60 years, Cassady's total becomes **6.63**!! He's still an ace! His duty with the AEF was with the 28th Pursuit Group.

**Captain James A. Connelly,
FFC WWI (6.0)**
Connelly, from Philadelphia,
Pennsylvania, fought with
the Lafayette Escadrille
in the French Flying Corps.

**Lt. Arthur R. Brooks,
USAEF, WWI (6.00)**
Framingham, Massachusetts
and Short Hills, New Jersey.
Brooks scored one kill with
the 139th Pursuit Sqdn.
and claimed five more while
assigned to the 22nd Sqdn.

(National Archives)

WWI ACE WHO MADE GENERAL RANK

Captain Everett R. Cook of Germantown, Tennessee, downed 5 German aircraft with the 91st Aero Squadron in France. Seen here in 1919 with a captured German fighter, Cook stayed in the service, rose to Brigadier General, USAF. A distinguished WWII career culminated with his appointment as Deputy Chief of Staff, U.S. Strategic Air Force. USAF historians in 1969 reduced his WWI score to 1.23 victories because of shared kills. Neither general officers nor mere lieutenants escaped the statistical axe.

(National Archives)

(d'Olive Collection)

First Lt. Charles R. d'Olive, (5.00)WWI
Cedar Falls, Iowa
93rd Pursuit Squadron AEF
Picture taken November 11, 1918
at Toul, France.

(National Archives)

Captain John Owen Donaldson, RFC WWI (8.00): Though an American AEF officer, Donaldson was an exchange pilot attached to the Royal Flying Corps 85th Squadron. All his combat victories were with that unit. He was from Washington, D.C.

SERVICE IN TWO WARS

Captain Harvey W. Cook of Wilkinson, Indiana had a colorful career. An ambulance driver in France before U.S. entry into the war, he transferred to the U.S. Air Service in September 1917, and flew with the 94th Pursuit Squadron, the famed "Hat in the Ring" unit, on the Western Front. He downed 7 enemy aircraft, consisting of 3 airplanes and 4 balloons, to make ace. Cook was a pioneer airmail pilot in 1920, and was with the Army Air Corps until 1928. Uncle Sam recalled him to active duty in 1942. As Colonel Cook he was killed in the South Pacific in March 1943. His acedom survived USAF statistical scrutiny in 1969, although his 7 victories were reduced to 5.66.

(National Archives)

(USAF)

Lt. Lloyd A. Hamilton, RFC/AEF WWI (9.00)

Hamilton, from Burlington, Vermont, scored 3 combat victories over German planes plus getting ½ credit for a balloon while flying with the British RFC. After he joined the AEF in France, he scored 2.33 more kills over aircraft plus shooting down a balloon. USAF Study 133 credits him with 6.83 victories. KIA over France in 1918.

(USN)

Cdr. David Sinton Ingalls, USN, WWI, (5.00)
The only American Navy ace of WWI! Ingalls
was sent to France with the first Yale Unit
and attached to the Royal Navy Air Service
Squadron 213 for combat duty. He shot down 4
German aircraft and one German balloon to
make it five and acedom. After the war, he
served as Undersecretary of the USNavy for
a stint, then became president and publisher
of the Cincinnati TIMES STAR. He was
born in Cleveland, Ohio.

(USAF)

First Lt. Frank O'D. Hunter, AEF WWI (8.00)
Hunter, who is shown here in England as a
Brigadier General, rose to the rank of Major
General in WWII. In WWI he flew with the
AEF's 103rd Pursuit Group. USAF Study 133
credits him with 6.50 kills in WWI. General Hunter
is from Savannah, Georgia.

(Libby Collection)

WWI ACE FLIES A JET
Two USAF officers flank WWI ace
Fred Libby just after Libby
had flown in the T-33 jet with
Iven Kincheloe. Though suffer-
ing in the final stages of
deformative arthritis most
obvious here, Libby demonstrated he still had the touch
for flying fighters. At left
is London, Kincheloe at right.

First Lt. Field E. Kindley, AEF (12.00) WWI
Kindley, from Pea Ridge, Arkansas, joined the RFC in England and scored one victory before coming over to the USAEF's 148th Pursuit Squadron. The USAF Study of 1969 reduced his official credits to 11.00. Kindley was killed in an aircraft crash at Kelly Field, Texas on February 1, 1920.

(National Archives)

(National Archives)

First Lt. Reed G. Landis, RFC/AEF WWI (10.00):
Landis shot down 9 German aircraft and one balloon for his ten victories with the 40th Squadron of the RFC. He joined the USAEF, serving with the 20th Aero Squadron but claimed no victories. Landis is the son of Kenesaw Mountain Landis.

(National Archives)

Captain Gorman DeFreest Larner, FFC/AEF (8.00)
This New York City native joined the Lafayette Escadrille of the French Flying Corps, scoring three kills with them before transferring to the USAEF. He claimed five more victories with the US 103th Pursuit Squadron.

Captain Frederick C. Libby, of Sterling, Colorado, photographed in France in May 1917 as a Flight Commander with No. 43 Squadron Royal Flying Corps. Libby is credited with 10 aerial victories as an RFC observer and 14 aerial victories as a pilot. It is reliably estimated that he flew more than 1,000 operational sorties against the Germans, probably more than any other American airman in either of the two world wars.

(National Archives)

Lt. Frank Luke, USAEF, WWI, (18.00)
Luke, from Phoenix, Arizona, was credited with four German aircraft shot down and 14 enemy observation balloons destroyed. The USAF Historical Study of 1969, however, credits him with 4 planes and only 11.83 balloons, as many were "shared" victories, for a total of 15.83. Luke was killed in action on September 29, 1918.

(Toliver Collection)

"LUF" French-born Major Raoul Lufbery became a U.S. citizen in 1909. With 17 victories, Lufbery is the third-ranked American ace of WWI. He was a Lafayette Escadrille luminary before transferring to the AEF, gave valuable advice and guidance to green American pilots. A self-educated and remote man, he told contemporaries he didn't believe he would survive the war. A horrifying death leap from a blazing fighter confirmed this intuition.

(Erikson Collection)

Major John W. F. M. Huffer and Major Raoul Lufbery, WWI AEF (17.0)
Huffer (not an ace and number of victories unknown) and Lufbery talk near a Nieuport 28 of the 94th Aero Squadron at Toul, France on April 18, 1918. All of Lufbery's victories were with the Lafayette Escadrille of the FFC.

(National Archives)

Lt. William T. Ponder, FFC/USAEF WWI (5.00): Mangum, Oklahoma. FFC, Lafayette Escadrille, 3.0 victories. AEF 103rd Pursuit Squadron, 2.0 victories. Total 5.00.

(National Archives)

Captain David McKelvy Peterson, FFC/USAEF (5.00): Honesdale, Pennsylvania. FFC Lafayette Escadrille, 1.0 victory. AEF 94th Pursuit Squadron, 3.0 victories. 95th Pursuit Squadron, 1.0 victory. Total 5.00.

Captain Edwin C. Parsons, FFC, WWI (8.00)
From Osprey, Florida, Parsons joined the Lafayette Escadrille of the French Flying Corps in April of 1916.

Lt. David E. Putnam, FFC/USAEF (6.00)
Brookline, Massachusetts. Lafayette Escadrille French Flying Corps, 2 victories. 139th Pursuit Squadron, AEF, 4 victories. 6.0 total.

(Parsons Collection)

(National Archives)

(Erikson Collection)

October 18, 1918.
Original 94th Pursuit Squadron survivors in France:
These are the only 94th pilots left in France of the original complement, the others killed in action, transferred to other units, POWs in Germany, or sent back to the States. L. to R.: Lt. Joseph H. Eastman, Captain James A. Meissner (8.0), Lt. Edward V. Rickenbacker (26.0), Lt. Reed M. Chambers (7.00), and Lt. Thorne C. Taylor (2.0).

"TOO OLD"
At 28 years of age, Eddie Rickenbacker was considered "too old" for fighter piloting. Through Colonel Billy Mitchell's intervention, Rickenbacker got into pilot training, qualified rapidly and became the top-scoring ace of WWI. Credited with 26 kills in WWI, even the eminent and immortal Captain Eddie did not escape the 1969 USAF historical scythe. His score was reduced to 24.33 because of shared kills.

(Toliver Collection)

(USAAS)

THE PIONEERS!!!
It's a long way to Tipperary!
First Lt. Edward V. Rickenbacker, left, and two other members of the 94th Pursuit Squadron, First Lt. Douglas Campbell and Captain Kenneth Marr, pose at Toul, France with a fighter plane of the era. Rickenbacker eventually became America's top ace with 26 victories. Campbell was considered the first AEF ace until the statistics proved that Lt. Paul F. Baer beat him to number five a few days earlier. Captain Marr, right, made several claims but all failed to be confirmed by witnesses.

(National Archives)

(National Archives)

Lt. Elliott White Springs, RFC/USAEF WWI (12.00): Lancaster, South Carolina. Springs scored one victory with the British RFC and 11.0 with the 148th AEF Pursuit Squadron. USAF Study 133 gives him credit for only 9.75 AEF plus 1.0 RFC.

Lt. Jacques M. Swaab, USAEF, WWI (10.00): Philadelphia, Pennsylvania. 22nd Pursuit Squadron, AEF.

(Combat Pilots Association)

(Todd Collection)

THREE ACES — THREE WARS

Robert M. Todd (left), one of the surviving American aces of World War I with 5 victories, trades flying yarns with General Felix Rogers, USAF, a 9th Air Force ace of World War II with 7 victories over the Germans, and with Colonel Francis Gabreski, who made ace in both WWII and the Korean War with a lifetime tally of 34.5 victories. Their experience spans combat aviation from WWI biplanes to the jets of Korea.

Second Lt. Robert M. Todd, USAEF (5.00): San Diego, California. 17th Pursuit Squadron. Scored three confirmed victories and shared two others.

69

**First Lt. Jerry C. Vasconcells,
WWI USAEF (6.00)**
Lyons, Kansas and
Denver, Colorado.
AEF, 27th Pursuit Squadron.

(National Archives)

First Lt. George A. Vaughn, WWI RFC/AEF (13.00)
Dongan Hills, New York.
RFC, 85th Squadron. 6.0 aircraft plus 1 balloon.
AEF, 17th Pursuit Squadron, 6.0 aircraft.

(National Archives)

(National Archives)

Major William Thaw, FFC/USAEF (5.83):
Pittsburgh, Pennsylvania. Thaw was the fourth American to join
the FFC when he signed up on December 24, 1914. While Immelmann,
Boelcke and Osterreicher were developing the details of aerial
jousting for the Germans, Thaw, Lufbery and Prince were the
Americans doing the same thing for the Allies. 4.0 victories
with the Lafayette Escadrille, 1.83 victories with the
103rd Pursuit Squadron, USAEF.

(Toliver Collection)

FIRST AEF VICTORY
Lieutenant Alan F. Winslow was the first AEF fighter pilot in an American unit to down a German aircraft in World War I. He flew with the 94th Aero Squadron, and scored his historic victory on February 7, 1918.

(Zistell Collection)

Lt. Errol H. Zistell, RFC/USAEF WWI (6.00)
Bay Village, Ohio. Zistell fought with the 42nd Squadron of the Royal Flying Corps and scored 3 aerial victories. Transferring to the AEF's 148th Pursuit Squadron, Zistell added three more to make it six. He also served in WWII and rose to the rank of Major General.

(Signal Corps U.S. Army)

WAR BIRDS AT THE ARMISTICE, 1918
This rare Signal Corps photograph shows some of America's war aces and pilots on Armistice Day, 1918. From left, they are: Captain J. D. Este, 13th Pursuit Squadron, 4 victories; Captain E. V. Rickenbacker, 94th Pursuit Squadron, 26 victories; Captain Sellers; Lt. Hugh Brewster, 49th Pursuit Squadron, 2 kills; Lt. Charles R. d'Olive, 93rd Pursuit Squadron, 5 kills; Lt. Bradley J. Gaylord, 96th Bomber Squadron, 1 victory; Lt. James Knowles, 95th Pursuit Squadron, 5 victories; Lt. Howard G. Rath, 96th Bomber Squadron, 2 victories; Lt. L. C. Simon, 147th Pursuit Squadron, 2 victories. Photograph was taken at Rembercourt, France. Victory tallies are those of the First World War accrediting system, not later revisions.

Between WWI and WWII:

Development of fighter aircraft for the U.S. military was woefully inadequate between the wars. Defense higher-ups had convinced themselves that fighters were obsolete, that the new bombers were so fast and heavily armed that they could neither be caught nor shot down. This is the first-line fighter of the U.S. Army Air Corps in the late 1920's and early 1930's, the Curtiss P-6E powered by an in-line D-12 Conqueror engine.

The Boeing P-12, successor to The Curtiss P-6E "Hawk"
In the early 1930's, Boeing supplied the USAAC with this agile fighter which was a pilot's dream to fly. When WWII began in 1939, Air Corps squadrons were phasing these out in favor of P-35 and P-36 airplanes. In Europe, the English were phasing in Hurricanes and Spitfires, while the Germans were fully equipped with the Me-109 (often called the Bf-109).

3

USAAF ACES OF WORLD WAR II PACIFIC THEATER

The European war in the early morning of 7 December 1941 was little more than newspaper reports to the residents of Hawaii. There were no American combat units involved or located anywhere near the conflict. The few adventurous Americans who had donned foreign uniforms to enter the struggle fought in anonymity. Stunning change came at 7:56 A.M. on that unforgettable Sunday, as Japanese naval aircraft attacked Pearl Harbor. The attack was a shocking fulfillment of the prophecy of America's General William "Billy" Mitchell.

By 0830 the same morning, An American fighter pilot flying in an American unit and wearing the uniform of the United States had shot down the first Japanese aircraft of the war. History has given no final verdict yet on who scored this first aerial kill. Lieutenants George S. Welch, Harry M. Brown, John J. Webster, John L. Dairns, Kenneth A. Taylor and Robert J. Rogers of the Army Air Corps all got airborne and made contact with the raiders.

Several Japanese planes were shot down. Welch* claimed four kills. Since each of the pilots mentioned claimed at least one Japanese aircraft, the only certainty is that one of these six men drew first blood. In the heat of battle, and under the shocking circumstances of the attack, every pilot forgot to note the time of his first kill, an omission for which they could hardly be blamed.

Sudden and devastating, the Pearl Harbor attack was over in a few hours. Hawaii went on its way, shaken up and injured, but destined to stay out of Japanese reach for the rest of the war. Six hours after Pearl Harbor, the Japanese began raining blows on the Philippines. They attacked and subsequently took Clark Field on Luzon, sixty miles north of Manila.

In the Philippines, the Army Air Corps and the Philippine Air Force were pathetically unprepared for war. Although Japanese "Nell" reconnaissance aircraft had been regularly overflying Manila and other American bases in the Pacific, preparations for the conflict by the Americans were meager. The world situation had impelled no special vigilance or precautions, because America thus far was untouched.

A few new P-40E fighters had arrived for the Army Air Corps, but many of these were not actually in commission. The machines had not been processed through the Manila Air Depot. On the day the war began in the Philippines, the 24th American Pursuit Group gave a status report showing ninety aircraft in commission. This group's task was to defend the Philippine Islands from air attack.

The 24th had fifty-four P-40E's, eighteen P-40B's and eighteen P-35's on the base. Only the P-40E's could be considered firstline aircraft by the standards then prevailing. More

(U.S. Army Air Corps)

* George S. Welch gained sixteen confirmed victories in World War II.

73

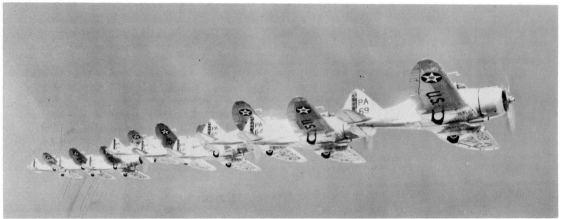

(U.S. Army Air Corps)

The Seversky P-35: In the mid-1930's, Alexander deSeversky produced this promising fighter. Underpowered and easy to ground-loop, it did not fare well and was soon replaced by the Curtiss P-36. This plane, the P-35, was the forerunner of the Republic Thunderbolt, the P-47.

EASY PREY
Curtiss P-36 fighters were flown by the French in the early days of WWII. They were much inferior to the German Me-109, and many now-famous German fighter aces scored their first aerial kills over these aircraft during the Battle for France.

(Toliver Collection)

than one pilot considered even the P-40E to be obsolescent and a stopgap at best.

The Americans in the Philippines, no less than at Pearl Harbor, were "caught with their pants down." When the first Japanese bombs fell on Iba Field, four American fighters of the 3rd Pursuit Squadron were caught landing on the runway. Five minutes after the blow at Iba, the Japanese poured the punishment on Clark Field. An American staff meeting was in progress, and the field was loaded with ninety B-17 Fortresses and some twenty P-40 fighters.

As the attack went in, four of the 24th Pursuit Group fighters were taking off. These four machines were the only ones to survive this devastating early stroke by Japanese airpower. All the other aircraft were pulverized on the ground as the Japanese bomb pattern made a shambles of Clark Field. The big base was immobilized, but the four fighters that were airborne made their presence felt against the Japanese enemy.

Lieutenant Joseph H. Moore, commander of the 20th Squadron and of the surviving flight, took his small but angry force thundering up toward the Japanese, driving for the bombers. The covering Japanese fighters quickly spotted the Americans, dove on them, and the first aerial battle over the Philippines began.

Second Lieutenant Randall Keaton whipped his P-40 into a stern chase on an enemy fighter. Winding the P-40 into as tight a turn as he dared, Keaton gained a firing lead angle on the enemy machine. He let drive with his guns and the Japanese fighter exploded and plunged earthward. Looking around for more targets, Keaton saw his flight commander, Lieutenant Moore, flame two more Zeros in quick succession.

The four Americans were so heavily outnumbered that they could do little more than maneuver defensively once the Zeros swarmed in on them. They learned quickly that the P-40 and P-35 were no match for the Zero in close dogfighting. Since all fighter pilots up to that time had been trained to dogfight in the tradition of World War I, the Zero forced some hurried reeducation.

The maneuverability of the Zero and the lethal punch of its twin cannon made meeting with the Japanese on their own terms something akin to suicide for the American pilots. The Japanese pilots at this time were already masters of their craft, with extensive combat exerperience over China. As Japan's "first team," they knew how to exploit the Zero's qualities. They also knew the weaknesses of the American fighters, and were therefore among the most formidable opponents faced in the air by American pilots at any time in history.

These early days in the Philippines served to verify with special force the warnings concerning the Zero issued to the USAAF from China by General Chennault. In one desperate encounter after another, the American fighter pilots learned the limitations of the P-40 in combat with the Zero and how best to use their machines against the elusive, fast-turning Japanese aircraft.

Tactics meant hitting the Nip at top speed, and then making a run for it. The pilots who learned this lesson often went through the agony of watching other Americans die who would not learn. The slick Japanese pilots took pride in shooting their enemies out of the top of a loop. Picking their moment to strike, they showed all the cool aplomb of a surgeon making an incision.

Lieutenant Boyd D. "Buzz" Wagner became the first American ace of World War II in the Pacific area. The same Lieutenant Joseph Moore who led the four lucky fighters in their escape from embattled Clark Field remembers Wagner's efforts in those dark days. Writes Moore:

"Buzz shot down three Jap I-97's (single-place, fixed-gear aircraft) over Appari on one flight. He also burned ten-plus on the ground while strafing a field near San Fernando on the coast of Lingayen Gulf. Later, out of New Guinea, he led a flight of P-40's to Lae and Salamaua and was bounced by a larger number of Zeros. Buzz got two on that flight.

"He was subsequently ordered to cease participation in aerial combat and concentrate on directing air operations out of New Guinea. Shortly afterwards, he returned to the United States and was killed in the crash of a P-40

after departure from Eglin AFB in the early months of 1943."

Moore retired a Major General in the USAF. He was erroneously listed in the records at one time as an ace with five kills. Moore himself has always denied most emphatically his right to belong to the exclusive club. He wrote to the authors:

"I have three confirmed Nips, all in the air, but the balance of the action in the Philippines was one-sided and obscure. I am sorry that I am not eligible to be among the aces."

A review of the official records agrees with General Moore, although many quasi-official lists include him as an ace. He earned himself a niche in history nonetheless as a fighter pilot who survived American airpower's grimmest days.

The second of the Pacific aces was Lieutenant Ed Dyess. He fought to the end in the Philippines, was captured and took part in the infamous Bataan Death March. Dyess later escaped from his pesthole prison in April, 1943. He got back to the United States, only to be killed in a P-38 crash near Burbank, California. He is usually credited with five aerial victories, although the records of this period are understandably indefinite. The official USAF study does not credit him with five.

The Pacific Theater produced the two top American aces of World War II, Richard Bong and Thomas B. McGuire. Both were majors and both flew the P-38, an aircraft generally considered by pilots to be third best of the P-51, P-47 and P-38. Bong's forty victories make him the greatest American ace of all the wars, and McGuire's thirty-eight kills make him second only to Bong.

Major Dick Bong has become one of the immortal American heroes. His legendary career as a fighter ace has been extensively recorded, and there is little that can be said about him that has not been said a hundred times before.

He was an expert at teamwork. A firm believer in having a strong, aggressive protector of his flanks, he usually flew with the most capable and battle-tested wingman available. Bong was a master tactician and an outstanding shot. His special experience with his marksmanship serves to endorse what has been said earlier in this book concerning shooting skill in the making of an ace.

Already an ace at the end of his first tour of combat duty, Bong was returned to the United

(U.S. Army Air Corps)

Bell XFM-1 Fighter, Multi-place: In 1937 the U.S. Army Air Corps tried to procure a long-range bomber-escort fighter. This was the approach made in the early days of the program. The design proved unwieldy in the air so was dropped in favor of the XP-38. The Bell "Airacuda" weighed nearly 18,000 pounds, was crewed by 5 men, powered by early V-1710 Allison water-cooled engines mounted to provide "pusher" power. The two nacelles carried a forward firing 37mm cannon. Rear-firing .30 cal. machine guns were mounted in the side blisters. The Airacuda's top speed was only 270 mph!

P-40 at KUNMING
Carrying distinctive shark's mouth nose pattern, a P-40 comes in for a landing at Kunming, China, an airbase used by AVG fighters.
Date: September 15, 1942.

(USAF)

States for rest and recuperation. After this, he went to the Air Force Gunnery School. Major Bong said many times, after his return to the Pacific:

"If I had only known as much about aerial gunnery on my first tour as I did when I came out of gunnery school, I might easily have scored eighty kills."

Since Bong was not a boastful man, why did he make such a statement? He was rough on himself with his answer.

"The Jap fighters I failed to down escaped mainly because I just did not know enough about the mechanics and art of air-to-air shooting."

Coming from a pilot who was already considered a top-notch deflection shot in combat, this surely indicates that the art of air-to-air shooting can be improved by diligent study of the mechanics involved, like all arts. Bong's statement serves to confirm and support the postwar statement of Saburo Sakai, the greatest living Japanese fighter pilot. He said that many times American fighters had him cold, and yet their shooting was so poor that he escaped from what he considered to be certain death at the hands of the Americans.

Bong always told the story of one of his missions a little ruefully, since he was no neophyte at the time it occurred. With twenty kills to his credit, Bong intercepted a Japanese formation escorted by fighters and made ready to hack some of them down. Bong suddenly realized that the aircraft on his wing was not that of his usual wingman. He glanced at the machine. The vivid red meatballs of Japan glared back at him. His wingman was a Zero!

Bong slapped his left throttle closed and flipped the P-38 into a split-ess and a vertical dive. Unable to locate the Zero in his mirror, he leveled off at fifteen thousand feet to see if he had actually lost the Jap. Once in level flight, the Zero popped into his mirror again. The Jap was still behind him, just a little too far away for accurate shooting.

Bong flipped quickly to the right, split-essed once again and drove the P-38 wide open to the deck. Leveling off just a few feet above the waters of Oro Bay in New Guinea, he had gained a few hundred yards on the Zero. The Japanese machine could not dive with the P-38. As Bong now pulled away to about a mile lead over his pursuer, both engines wide open, he whipped the P-38 into a tight left-hand turn.

This maneuver zoomed him into the middle of an unobserved formation of nine Zeros—all of them suddenly intent on the demise of Richard Ira Bong.

Like Captain Arthur Brooks of World War I fame, who landed in a similar mess with a covey of Fokkers, Bong decided there was only one course of action—aggression. Like the ace he was, Bong tore at the Zeros, gaining an immediate psychological advantage as he flew head-on at the lead Zero and exploded it with a short burst.

The other eight Zeros, higher and diving to the attack, seemed unnerved by the sudden, dramatic loss of their leader. Wavering in pur-

pose, their fire went wild. Bong exploited their confusion. Picking out another Zero and exploding it, he went twisting upwards at full throttle and threw a snap shot from his vertical climb squarely into a third Zero. This machine did not explode, but it slowed, smoldered and went waffling out of the fight.

Pulling every ounce out of the P-38's screaming engines, Bong went streaking away from the scene. He outdistanced the disorganized and shaken remnants of the Japanese formation, and returned successfully to base.

The great ace frequently told this story on himself to fledgling pilots under his command and to others he later trained. The melee that almost cost him his life illustrated in classic fashion why a fighter pilot must know everything going on around him in combat. Many pilots have flown similarly into enemy formations never to emerge. In Bong's words, "There is nothing more frightening in this world than to look off your wingtip and see a long line of enemy propeller spinners lining up *for a pass at you.*"

Fifth Air Force pilots who flew with Dick Bong have often said that they believe the Dick Bong-Thomas J. Lynch team to have been the hottest fighter combination in the Pacific. Certainly it was the hottest Army team in the theatre. Lynch was an exceptional leader in his own right and, with a final score of twenty kills in World War II, proved himself to be among America's best fighter pilots. When he teamed with Bong, it was a formidable alliance, as numerous Japanese pilots discovered.

Bong and Lynch would trade the leadership position during a rhubarb with perfection and precision, as though each of them was intuitively flying the other's aircraft as well as his own. They were like two men constantly able to read each other's thoughts. In battle, one was always in firing position on the enemy, while the other kept the shooting aircraft's tail clear.

Bong, Lynch, Lieutenant Delman Moore and another pilot became involved in a fracas with Japanese fighters one day and Lt. Moore's P-38 had one engine hit by enemy gunfire. They were 200 miles from home base and at the time Moore's plane was crippled the four Americans were literally surrounded by Japanese fighters. Seeing Moore's plight, Bong ordered him to head for home. Then

FORK TAILED DEVIL

(USAF)

German fighter pilots called the P-38 Lightning built by Lockheed the "fork tailed devil," but top German aces considered the P-38 relatively easy to shoot down. Top-scoring American aces of all time, Bong and McGuire, both flew this fighter to glory in the Pacific. The Japanese found the P-38 an easy kill, too, until USAAF pilots developed high-speed tactics. The P-40 and P-38, with a few P-39's here and there, bore the brunt of USAAF combat in the PTO until the P-47 and P-51 came out rather late in the war.

Bong and Lynch acted as "rear guard" and kept the aggressive Japanese from attacking the cripple as the four American planes edged homewards at single-engine speed. Delbert Moore probably owed his life to his flight buddies who were more concerned with protecting him than with trying to score more kills for themselves.

Like so many top aces who survived innumerable contacts with the enemy in the air, Bong lost his life in an aircraft accident after the war. A glorious fighter, immortalized by his deeds and already a part of American folklore, Bong crashed to his death in a P-80 jet at Burbank, California, on 6 August 1945. He was decorated profusely, his awards including the Congressional Medal of Honor, the DSC, two Silver Stars, seven DFC's and 15 Air Medals.

In twenty months of combat, Major Thomas B. McGuire scored thirty-eight aerial victories. Hailing from Ridgewood, New Jersey, McGuire was a brilliant combat pilot as well as a splendid comrade-in-arms to inexperienced pilots. Blessed with a knack for guiding fledgling pilots, he fed newly arrived pilots the fruits of his experience. He gave freely of the lessons he had learned the hard way.

This deep concern for his fellow pilots, which in no way prevented McGuire's own prolific scoring, was probably responsible for his untimely death in combat. On 7 January 1945, McGuire and another experienced fighter pilot were taking two newly arrived Air Corps captains on a sweep over Los Negros Island when they were bounced by a single Japanese Hamp—an audacious foe.

The Hamp made a perfect run on the American formation and sent the leader of the second flight down in flames before being spotted. McGuire saw the Hamp almost in firing position on one of the inexperienced pilots, and made an extremely sharp turn in order to rescue this man. McGuire was famous for the tight turns he was able to wring out of the P-38, but on this occasion he turned a little too tightly.

The twin-boomed fighter entered a high-speed stall, followed by a spin. At fifteen hundred feet altitude, McGuire had no chance to recover control. His fighter plunged into the ocean while the Hamp escaped unharmed. Superb as an air fighter, McGuire's sacrificial death in an aerial accident rather than the enemy prevented his going on to even greater glories.

Postwar research has indicated strongly that McGuire and his formation were shot down by Shoichi Sugita, Naval Air Pilot First Class, of the Imperial Japanese Navy. Sugita was a brilliant pilot with eighty kills to his credit when he met his end three months after the battle involving Major McGuire. Sugita's career is dealt with in Chapter Nine, devoted to the enemy aces.

Lt. Colonel John R. Alison got his first five aerial victories while flying with the 75th Fighter Squadron. Promoted to Lt. Col. after the third kill, he moved up to the 23rd Group Hq and raised his score to six. His last victory came on 31 May 1943.

"Flying a P-40 over Henyang, China, twelve thousand feet at night, I picked up the exhaust of three Jap bombers at fifteen thousand feet. I had closed to within two hundred feet when a Jap gunner in a turret position on the bomber hit my P-40 broadside. He

(USAF)

WORKHORSE OF THE EARLY DAYS

This Curtiss P-40, christened "Sue," heads for its home base in India after dropping its 500-lb. bomb on the Japanese supply dump at Kamaing, Burma, in 1943. The P-40 did yeoman service in many roles until later and better U.S. aircraft appeared to take vengeance on the Japanese. This aircraft belongs to the 51st Fighter Group.

stitched a line of holes from the prop to the tail.

"I started firing at very close range. The first bomber I hit pulled up into a steep climb, badly hit but not burning. I moved from one to the other of the remaining two bombers, and they exploded one after the other. The concussions shook my aircraft.

"I tried to get down to a friendly field just below, but as I started a landing approach, my aircraft caught fire. I had to ditch quickly— and into the river I went. I emerged wet and wounded, but had two confirmed victories plus one probable."

Alison lives in Washington, D.C. today, where he is an executive in the aviation industry. He is also a lively figure in the affairs of the American Fighter Aces' Association.

Blind flying is one thing, but blind shooting is quite another, as Captain Ernie J. Ambort of Little Rock, Arkansas, can testify. Sometimes fighter pilots have taken long odds when the chips were down. Ernie Ambort is one of them.

"We had just relieved the first flight and started to orbit at 8,000 feet to cover a destroyer evacuating wounded from the Philippines. Out of a 3,500-foot lower broken-cloud layer came two Jap fighters in a dive-bombing attack or Kamikaze on the destroyer.

"In the ensuing near-vertical dive at full throttle to intercept these Japs, I knew that in order to properly lead the Jap for a full deflection shot I would not be able to see him. My wingman, Lieutenant H. A. Hammett of Boston, Massachusetts, would get a better sighting on the number two Jap.

"I hastily calculated that my P-38 was probably worth more than any destroyer, but due to the number of people involved, and all those sick and wounded boys, I decided I'd ram this Jap if necessary. On the open channel I called the destroyer's fire control officer and asked him to hold their fire and watch for me if I bailed.

"Trusting in luck rather than ability, I put in lead, held my triggers full down and waited. When I flew through billows of black smoke and saw pieces of the Jap aircraft lodge in mine, I knew he had blown up just before our flight paths crossed. I pulled up in time to see Hammett's hits blow up the second Jap, who crashed into the ocean one hundred feet astern of the destroyer.

"Sometime later, when things had quieted down, Hammett and I buzzed the destroyer before returning to base. The gratifying waves of crutches, bandages and plaster casts told me that this had truly been my most thrilling aerial victory."

Ernie Ambort survived the war. He served with the 49th Fighter Group and is credited with five aerial victories.

Getting personal stories from some of the

79

aces was very much like asking these men to pull out a good front tooth. Colonel William M. Banks of Raleigh, West Virginia, proved to be one of these. Bill Banks would much rather talk about other pilots at length, praising and admiring their skills. Banks' own nine aerial victories in the Pacific give him plenty to talk about. His wingman probably saved his life in this incident:

"During combat with some Japanese fighters, I found myself in the embarrassing position of having lost my airspeed at very low altitude. At this time, I spotted a Jap fighter closing in on my tail for the kill."

The attacking Japanese pilot had committed one of the cardinal errors of aerial combat—he had forgotten or failed to observe his opponent's wingman. Lieutenant Malcolm Rand of Mexico, Maine, was intent on protecting Banks, and provides the rest of the story:

"I was in range astern and closed on the Zeke to about fifty yards before firing. The first few shots burst on the right elevator. I corrected a little and there were shots bursting all over his wings and fuselage. I fired until flames shot out from all parts of his plane. I pulled up and saw him crash in the water. The action took place from one thousand feet on down. Captain Banks saw the plane crash. The enemy pilot appeared skilled and eager for combat, but I don't believe he saw me protecting Captain Banks' tail."

Lieutenant Rand was later killed in action in a fighter strike against Bobo Airfield, Dutch New Guinea. His memory is safe with Colonel Banks who says of Rand today: "He was one of our most outstanding pilots. At least three other pilots in our squadron owed their lives to his skill, courage and devotion to duty. His death was a great loss to his country." Many aces feel similarly towards gallant wingmen who failed to survive the conflict or make ace themselves. Rand did score two victories.

Still flying with the Air National Guard at Savannah, Georgia, is Captain Philip E. Colman, a fighter pilot officially credited with nine kills gained in two wars. Colman fought first with the 5th Fighter Group of the 14th Air Force in the Pacific from 1942 to 1944. He fought again in Korea with the 4th Fighter Interceptor Group in 1952, where he came within one frame of 16mm gun-camera film of confirming his fifth MiG-15 kill. This victory would have put him into the ultraexclusive in-

ner circle of aces who scored five kills in each of two wars.

Phil Colman recalled his most memorable combat experience with frank words: "Every damned one of them was exciting."

Captain Robert Marshall De Haven is an ace who maintained his connection with aircraft following World War II. He knocked down fourteen Japanese aircraft while flying with the 14th Air Force in the Pacific. De Haven is currently with Hughes Aircraft Corporation in California, and is married to singer Connie Haines.

De Haven's first six victories were gained in the P-40, an aircraft that could excel its mediocre qualities in the hands of a pilot who knew his stuff. A number of skilled American pilots learned how best to use the obsolescent machine against Japanese aircraft, and did well with the P-40. De Haven flew also in flights with Dick Bong, Thomas McGuire and Gerald R. Johnson during the Philippine campaign. This incident sticks in his mind:

"On 2 November 1944, I was leading a squadron flight of fourteen P-38's out of Tacloban airstrip on a dive-bombing strike against Jap shipping in Ormac Bay, on the west side of Leyte. Intelligence reported a concentration of troop transports, with destroyer and cruiser escorts, landing troops in the area.

"Our strategy was to take the first six aircraft across the bay at low level, drawing naval ack-ack. This would permit the remaining eight aircraft, carrying 500-pound bombs, to make their attacks with minimum opposition. Although reports of enemy aircraft in sizable numbers came in, we went unmolested during the first portion of the attack, and one of our pilots got a direct hit with a 500-pounder on a troopship.

"About the time decoy flights were pulling up at the far end of the bay and the dive-bombing runs were almost over, enemy aircraft were spotted in several directions by our pilots. One was sighted at six o'clock to me.

"I went into a tight climbing turn to meet the enemy head-on. Since my wingman stayed glued to me during the turn, the enemy pilot lost his enthusiasm and broke off into a climbing turn. My position was better now, and the chase was continued.

"Gradually I gained on the Jap, climbing in the process to 16,000 feet. He was identifiable now as one of the new Jack fighters. For some reason, he elected now to enter a shallow dive,

which against the P-38 was decidedly unwise. I needed full power for quite awhile to catch him, but at 10,000 feet and indicating 400 mph he was in front of me at point-blank range.

"Two short bursts produced no apparent effect. But on the third burst, the Jap disintegrated with a violent blast. Flying debris thundered against my P-38. My windshield was smothered in Japanese engine oil, and I had to use side vision and the careful directions of my wingman to get back to base.

"During the disassembly of my P-38, in one of the oil cooler scoops, a large portion of one of the Japanese pilot's maps was found. This memento is today a prized possession. Another memento of this combat is a copy of orders sending me Stateside from the Philippines after twenty-two months overseas. They are dated 1 November 1944. My most memorable mission had been unknowingly 'on my own time'."

Warren D. Curton of Spring City, Tennessee, was a young Second Lieutenant flying with the 49th Fighter Group in the Pacific when plain old fighter pilot's savvy brought him a spectacular aerial victory. Curton is a jet pilot now, but he was mounted on a P-38 on 5 December 1944. With three other P-38's, he was flying cover for a Navy convoy off the Leyte coast:

"Suddenly my number four pilot reported that an Oscar had come out of the clouds and was closing on our tail. We immediately turned into the enemy plane, whereupon he broke off his attack and raced westward, climbing into the sun.

"I closed in, but I couldn't see the Oscar because I was looking directly into the sun. By using my tinted goggles, I could see everything except within the diameter of the sun itself. Knowing I was in range, I fired directly into the disc of the sun. My wingman, over to one side, reported that I was getting hits on this Jap I couldn't even see.

"The Oscar now turned right. As he did so, I fired a 30-45-degree deflection shot, getting hits in the wing root and cockpit area. He started flaming and tried a crash dive into a nearby landing craft. He missed and plunged into the ocean."

Warren Curton ended World War II with five aerial kills credited during his service with the 5th Air Force.

Colonel William D. Dunham of Nez Perce,

Idaho, scored sixteen aerial victories over the Japanese. He flew with the 5th Air Force. "Dinghy" Dunham also sank two Japanese troopships estimated at ten thousand tons apiece. Pressed for a story, he recollects best a melee in which aggressive American action demoralized a superior Japanese force.

"While flying cover for skip-bombing attacks on Jap shipping, my eleven-plane squadron attacked thirteen Jap fighters. I shot down two on the first pass, and in the next ten minutes shot down two more. We completely routed the attacking Japs."[*]

The four quick kills Dunham passes off so modestly conceal a talent that ranks him high on the aces' own list. He is recognized as one of the most formidable deflection-shooting artists among America's aces. Dunham demonstrated this skill in an aerial battle that cost the life of one of America's outstanding pilots, Colonel Neel E. Kearby, who is credited with twenty-two aerial victories.

Intent on a Nip kill Kearby did not know that his wingman had been taken out of position in the fight. An alert Japanese pilot promptly latched on to Kearby's tail. Seeing this disastrous turn of luck, Dinghy Dunham swung quickly in an attempt to scare the Jap off, and began firing at one thousand yards from ninety degrees deflection.

Disintegrating amid a gout of orange flame the Japanese plane was doomed, but its pilot had already held his triggers down on Major Kearby. The famed pilot, ace and Medal of Honor winner, crashed to his death. Pilots who flew with Dunham speak in awe of his shooting skill, which is belied by his relatively modest sixteen kills. In Dunham's case, opportunity to use his skills did not come as often as it might have done, something that is true of a number of other superb American marksmen. Dunham retired from the USAF as a Brigadier General.

There is no more vigorous advocate of the art of aerial gunnery than Major Nelson DeCoursey Flack, Jr., whose views on the subject were gleaned from the hard school of experience. An erstwhile member of the 49th Fighter Group in the Pacific, Flack tells this story on himself:

"Arriving in combat with fifty hours of P-40 experience and negligible fixed-gunnery training, like all the others I concentrated on back-

*[*] 7 Dec. 1944

OSCAR PURSUES B-25
Japanese Oscar fighter is intent on demise of an American B-25 bomber at Hansa Bay in New Guinea. Fire was exchanged both ways but nobody went down in this particular encounter.

breaking acrobatics as the sine qua non of successful combat flying. For a year I scattered ammunition profusely at several dozen Japs, primarily from large deflection angles and maximum to minimum range, but without success.

"Then I decided on serious application of gunnery principles, and I really studied the 100-mil sight. Shortly afterward, I ran into a Jap fighter at 10,000 feet. With deflection 120 degrees, and range about 2,000 feet, I estimated his speed at about 300 mph.

"Just as though I were operating a slide rule, I slowly eased in exactly three radii with the P-38, and then began firing at about 1,000 feet and 90-degree deflection. Instantly the center wing section exploded violently. The shattered Jap fighter tumbled down in fragments. I was convinced. A combat pilot is a gunner, not an aerial acrobat."

Major Flack successfully applied these same principles on four other occasions against the Japanese, and thereby gained admission to the fraternity of fighter aces. He is also credited with five probables.

Three versus twenty-four are long odds in aerial combat, but time and again the power of aggressive pilots to reduce such odds has been demonstrated. Psychological factors, and especially an aggressive spirit, bulk large in aerial combat. Captain Richard H. Fleischer of Quincy, Massachusetts, took part in an aerial battle in which big dividends came from a bold assault.

"With two other pilots, I engaged approximately ten enemy dive-bombers and fourteen fighters which we had caught bombing and strafing U.S. PT-boats. In just a few minutes we had destroyed seven. When the rest of our squadron arrived, we knocked down another seven. The U.S. Navy confirmed sixteen kills, although we only claimed fourteen, without loss to ourselves. The action took place in December, 1943, south of New Britain. I received credit for one fighter and one dive-bomber."

Captain Fleischer flew with the 248th Fighter Group in the Pacific Theater and is credited with six aerial victories.

Known in the Air Force as the "Kankakee Kid" after his home town in Illinois, William Kenneth Giroux shot down ten Japanese aircraft in the Pacific Theater. One of his combat reports gives insight into the aerial pyrotechnics of this colorful ace.

"A. Mission number 6-385, 2 November 1944, 12 P-38's.

"B. Cover for B-24 to Mindanao Sea Area.

"C. Time and altitude of attack: 1215/L at 8,000 feet.

"D. We were escorting B-24's to look for a task force in the Mindanao Sea. We found quite a few ships in Ormac Bay. I could not say just what type they were or how many because we were climbing, and I saw an enemy fighter right after we got to the target. The ack-ack was very heavy from the ships as our *bombers neared target on their bombing runs. I saw the first fighter going in on the bombers just as they were over the target. He did not seem to mind his own ack-ack, so I followed him in.*

"I shot at ninety degrees deflection just as he started to fire on the bombers, and he broke away. He was smoking a little, and I figured he might go down. But he kept going, and as I pulled up into the sun, I waited for him to start for the bombers again. He did, and I dove, coming up under him. I closed in to twenty-five yards, gave him a short burst, and he blew up. This was a Hamp-type fighter.

"Up until this action I had been alone, but as the Hamp was going down, Lieutenant Loh joined me. By this time the bombers had made their run and were on course for home. They were about twenty-five miles west of the Camotes Islands. Lieutenant Loh and I started back for the bombers, and I saw one enemy fighter drop a phosphorous bomb. I overtook this fighter and got three shots at it, all ninety to forty-degree deflection. On the third shot we were about a hundred feet above the water. I got a short burst in the wing root and he also blew up, splashing into the water. He too was a Hamp.

"Another enemy fighter had joined the flight by then, and I noticed him about five hundred feet above me and to my left. I started a fast climb and turned into him, but he only got a very short burst. He then did a wing-over, and Lieutenant Loh got on his tail. Lieutenant Loh fired a few shots and the enemy fighter turned left. As Lieutenant Loh pulled up I got in a forty-degree deflection shot. This third Hamp burst into flames and crashed on Pacijan Island just south of a small lake."

For this action the Kankakee Kid got the Silver Star. He shot down four other Japanese planes with similar applications of the deflection shooter's art, but these machines were not seen to crash by others and are credited to Giroux only as probables. He also sank a 10,000-ton tanker by pressing home a determined attack, and for this action he was awarded the DFC. Giroux still lives in Kankakee.

An air show at San Diego on Independence Day, 1947, saw the tragic end of Colonel John C. Herbst, one of the outstanding Air Corps aces of the Pacific Theater. He crashed while piloting a Lockheed F-80 Shooting Star. His death was a deep loss to the Air Force and to his country.

Although not among America's top-scoring aces, Herbst is revered and remembered today not only as a brilliant pilot and top marksman, but also as a man of outstanding leadership talent. Few doubt that Herbst could have easily joined America's top scoring aces had he been given adequate rein by his superiors. Still, he had 18 official kills!

General Claire Chennault grounded Herbst after his eleventh victory ordering him to "plan operations instead of taking part in them." Herbst complied, like the good soldier he was, but he managed nevertheless to shoot down another seven Japanese planes during "training and indoctrination flights"—no mean feat.

Herbst's first victory was with the 76th Squadron of the 23rd Group but the remaining 17 were with the 74th Squadron. All 18 victories were scored between 17 June 1944 **and** 17 January 1945, and he rose in rank from Captain to Major to Lt. Colonel in that time period.

General Bruce K. Holloway USAF was among the professional aviators who became aces in World War II. He graduated from West Point in June, 1937, and from the West Point of the Air at Kelly and Randolph Fields in Texas in October, 1938. His most memorable combat experience came in May of 1943:

I was on a lone visual reconnaissance over Formosa, in a P-40 out of Henyang, China, with staging out of five-gallon cans at Kienow. I saw many large Japanese training formations, and avoided detection by ducking in and out of a thousand-foot overcast. I encountered a single bomber offshore, and closed to ten yards range. I shot the bomber down using about fifteen rounds of ammunition."

Four-star General Holloway's distinguished service in China won him the coveted Chinese Order of the Sacred Tripod from Generalissimo Chiang Kai-shek. He is officially credited with 13 aerial victories.

The P-40 built by Curtiss, and used by General Holloway in the mission he describes, was the aircraft type that bore the brunt of the early Pacific aerial fighting. There were a few older and earlier types of aircraft battling the Japanese in the first days, including a handful of Boeing P-26's, but the P-40 was all America had to begin the war in the Far East in numbers sufficient to hurt the enemy.

The pilots of the American Volunteer Group used the P-40 for fighting, bombing, reconnaissance and for hauling cargo. As one ebullient Flying Tiger said, "If we only had a periscope for it, we could use it for a submarine, too." Considering that the P-40 was well below the standard required for fighter combat in the European Theater, the airplane's record in the Pacific must rank it historically as among the great fighter aircraft of World War II.

In three years of combat in China, where it was the mainstay of the 23rd Fighter Group, 941 Japanese aircraft went down under its guns. This was a ratio of fifteen Japanese losses for every loss by the 23rd, and it is doubtful if any other Pacific unit could claim such a record.

The American Volunteer Group under Chennault made their P-40's count in the struggle. They gained official confirmation for 297 Japanese aircraft destroyed during the AVG's relatively short life. Every fighter pilot who flew the P-40 in combat recalls with affection and gratitude the machine's incredible ability to absorb the punishment of cannon fire from the Zero and still keep flying.

The P-38 Lockheed Lightning was introduced into the Pacific fighting primarily to extend combat range and to give American pilots twin-engined safety while flying over long stretches of open ocean. The P-38 was greeted with soaring enthusiasm. This became somewhat dampened when the Japanese pilots began shooting the Lightnings down with alarming ease and in large numbers.

No small element in these early failures was a certain tactical ineptitude on the part of the Americans. As they learned how to exploit the Lightning's strong points, and as improved versions of the P-38 came forward from the United States, the aircraft did well. As American teamwork evolved the Lightning did even better.

In a turning dogfight, the Zero could usually take the measure of the P-38, and unfortunately there was a tendency on the part of many American pilots to get into this kind of battle. Most of them had spent their early years reading about World War I dogfights, and prewar training tended to follow in the World War I groove. Reeducation was quickly forced when the turning ability of the Zero proved to be so formidable.

Aces like Bong, Lynch and McGuire soon turned the tables on the best of the Japanese pilots. The high altitude, speed and dive superiority of the P-38, intelligently translated into tactics, permitted many Pacific aces to run up strings of kills in the sleek, twin-boomed fighter. For one thing, the superior altitude capability of the Lightning permitted the American pilots to choose combat as they wished. The inferior ceiling of the Zero, like the inferior Japanese teamwork, proved to be something that Japanese skill, courage or fanaticism could not overcome.

The P-51 Mustang, which appeared somewhat later in the Pacific war, became the top-notch all-around fighter there even as it proved to be the best all-purpose fighter in Europe. Old P-47 and P-38 pilots often rise to dispute this, but the statistical record, as well as the postwar testimony of the Japanese pilots, leaves little doubt that the P-51 was the superior aircraft of the three.

Major John Alden Tilly USAF, of Mill Valley, California, flew with Major Thomas McGuire in the 431st Fighter Squadron. He recalls an incident in flying the P-38 that reveals how much depended on the man rather than the machine:

My second victory provided particular satisfaction, because it was a classic example of the P-38's little-known but nevertheless excellent maneuverability. At first glance, the aircraft seemed large and ungainly. But in this combat, I was able to stay behind and inside the enemy's turn at approximately 1,000 feet above the water and 100 mph. That P-38 shook and shuddered, but never snapped a spin. The hits from my guns finally turned the Jap plane into a ball of flames. I was close to this Jap while firing—so close that oil from his stricken engine completely covered my windshield. When I got back home, I had to slow down just above stalling speed, roll down the side window and wipe a clear spot on the windshield with my handkerchief before I could land."

Tilly flew 159 missions in the P-38 and is credited with five aerial victories. He is extremely proud to have flown with McGuire,

(USAF)

P-61 "Black Widow": The USAF and U.S. Navy and Marines were slow to develop a night fighter capability in WWII. The need was not recognized until mid-war so ingenuity took over and day fighters were modified for the task, but could only function perfunctorily. Off the drawing boards did come one designed for the mission, the P-61 Black Widow, but it did not get into the war until the last few months of hostilities in the Pacific area. This photo was taken at Wright-Patterson AFB, Ohio, where the aircraft was undergoing tests in 1944. The three Air Force officers are W/O Harold Marshall, Major Ray Toliver, and Major Sidney T. Smith.

(Toliver Collection)

BUSINESS END OF A P-38
Captain Kenneth G. Ladd's P-38, "Windy City Ruthie," boasted only 10 Rising Sun flags at the time this photograph was made. Ladd added two more for a WWII total of 12 Japanese aircraft downed. Photo was made in New Guinea where Ladd served with the 8th Fighter Group.

whom he considers to have been the complete master of the P-38. "He knew of the P-38's surprising maneuverability," recalls Tilly, "and more than a few of his thirty-eight kills were due to his willingness to turn with the Jap fighters—something most of our boys thought impossible."

Despite the performance disparity between the P-38 and the P-51, the Lightning had its devoted advocates. There can be no doubt that the faith and ability of a P-38 pilot, wherever he plied his trade, could wring from the Lightning superior and often surprising performance. For the run-of-the-mill fighter pilot, such attainments were impossible. For the exceptional pilot, who loved, studied and flew the P-38 with everything that was in him, the enemy held no terrors.

Such a P-38 devotee was, and is, Colonel John H. Lowell of Denver, Colorado. Lowell served in the ETO, and on one occasion, with his whole group watching and a beer bust riding on the outcome, he took on an RAF Spitfire Mark XI in mock combat.

The encounter took place over Lowell's home base of Honington, in East Anglia, and Lowell administered a sound thrashing to the fabled British fighter. Lowell believed that the P-38L was able to fight anything that flew, and in this instance, with him at the controls, the P-38L proved superior even to Britain's great thoroughbred.

Lowell is credited with 7.5 aerial kills in Europe, but few other pilots in the USAAF could make the P-38 perform as he did. For the most part, the journeymen pilots who forsook the Lightning for the Mustang as the newer machine flowed out to the squadrons were rarely sorry to say goodbye to the P-38. Lowell lives near Golden, Colorado.

Colonel John S. Stewart was in command of the 76th Squadron of the 23rd Fighter Group, 14th Air Force, when the fabulous and long-awaited P-51 arrived in the China-Burma-India Theater. The impact of this superb machine on pilot morale forms Colonel Stewart's outstanding memory of aerial combat:

"In early 1944 the 176th Squadron received its first P-51B's, and for the first time in nearly two years, we had an aircraft that could perform with or exceed the capabilities of the best Japanese fighter planes. Their Tojo had been able to out-dive, out-turn, out-run and generally out-perform our P-38's and P-40's.

"These wily Japs had developed their deadly "high-low" tactics, and were giving us fits. Then in came the P-51B's. One of our squadrons took off in P-38's, and we followed with two flights of Mustangs. At 21,000 feet, a flight of twelve Tojos bounced the P-38's, but for the first time, we had aircraft above them. Our Mustangs were at 30,000 and 32,000 feet.

"I led my element down on a Tojo which had shot one engine out of a P-38 and was circling to finish him off. The Jap saw us coming, and started a sharp turn. He was visibly shaken when we out-turned him, so he dove for the deck. We found that we could out-run him too, for when he leveled off at a hundred feet above the deck, we steadily closed in on him.

"He tried evasive action, but it was to no avail. I got to close range, gave him about seventy rounds, and he exploded violently. One Tojo was eliminated, but best of all, we all knew that we were flying a better fighter than the Japanese."

Colonel Stewart is credited with nine aerial victories, all of them gained in the Pacific Theater. He now lives in Monument, Colorado.

Lieutenant Colonel Gerald Richard Johnson of the USAAF in World War II has frequently been confused with two namesakes among America's aces—Gerald W. Johnson of Owenton, Kentucky, and Robert S. Johnson of Garden City, New York, both of whom won fame in the ETO as fighter aces.

Gerald R. Johnson called Eugene, Oregon his home town, although he was born in Kenmore, Ohio. He enlisted in the Air Corps in 1941, and in May of 1942 was sent to Alaska. Over the Aleutians he had his first aerial combat, downing two Japanese planes, but without confirmation of his victories. Later assigned to the 49th Fighter Group in the Pacific, in fighter pilot's parlance Johnson "got hot." He ran up a string of eleven confirmed kills and eleven probables before being sent to the United States for rest and recuperation. On his return to the Pacific in late 1944, Johnson got hot again and ran up another eleven kills and eight more probables by war's end.

With twenty-two aerial victories, the DSC, Silver Star and Legion of Merit among other awards, Johnson was commander of the Atsugi Air Base near Tokyo right after the end of the Second World War. On 7 October 1945, he was acting as pilot of a B-17 Fortress that became hopelessly lost in a typhoon. The aircraft's radio was knocked out, and under these grim conditions, Johnson gave his parachute to a passenger who had come aboard without one. All on board the B-17 who jumped were picked up, but Johnson and his copilot were killed in the crash of the aircraft.

Because he did not survive this postwar incident, Gerald R. Johnson's career has been confused with those of the other Johnsons. Pilots who knew Gerald R. are warm in their praise of his gallantry, and his admirers include General George Kenney, wartime commander of the Far East Air Force. General Kenney told Johnson's father: "You are the father of the bravest man I ever knew, and the bravest thing he ever did was the last thing, and when he did not need to be brave."

When the Japanese attacked Pearl Harbor, Verl E. Jett of Belle, Missouri, was based at Wheeler Field in Hawaii. He managed to get an *unarmed* fighter into the air during the attack. This probably made him the most frustrated fighter pilot in history. All he could do was save the aircraft from certain destruction while he witnessed the fury of the attack from a fighter plane's cockpit, powerless to intervene.

Subsequently, Jett was sent to Australia, where he qualified on P-39's. He joined combat with the Japanese in the New Guinea area, this time with his guns loaded and ready. One incident made a special impression on him:

"While leading a flight of P-39's, I spotted a Norma-type bomber at ten thousand feet. I made a 180-degree turn and got on his tail for an attack. The sky was full of cumulus clouds, and breaking in and out of this stuff as I tried to stay on this Jap's tail, I nearly collided with him four or five times. Each time I managed to recover position and give him a full burst of all guns. Then both of the Jap's engines burst into flames. By this time, I had pulled excessive manifold pressure, causing the rocker-arm bolts to break. Two cylinders would not fire. With the engine missing, I turned back to Milne Bay, a 150-mile flight over an ocean teeming with sharks. I wondered if I was going to become a victory myself.

"My wingman saw the Norma crash into the sea and sink fifteen miles north of Watutu Point on Goodenough Island. When I landed, I was assigned another aircraft and ordered to return to the scene of the Norma's crash and search for survivors. The bomber was supposed to have been carrying Jap VIP's, but at the spot where the Norma went in there was only an oil slick."

Lieutenant Colonel Jett ended the war with seven aerial victories confirmed, and with the unforgettable experience of having watched the Pearl Harbor attack from the air. Jett lives in Twain Harte, California.

The top living ace of the USAAF in the Pacific is Colonel Charles Henry MacDonald, credited with twenty-seven aerial victories over the Japanese. Pennsylvania-born MacDonald was commissioned into the regular USAAF in 1939 and was a fighter pilot stationed at Hawaii's Wheeler Field when the blow fell on Pearl Harbor.

The din of the Japanese attack woke him up, and it was a somewhat bewildered young Lieutenant MacDonald who made his way to Wheeler through the rubble and smoke. He set up an alert system with the remaining serviceable P-36's and P-40's, and flew patrol along the west coast of Oahu until it was determined that the Japanese were not going to send in a second attack.

After an apprehensive hour and a half aloft, MacDonald and his fellow pilots flew back to Honolulu, and there ran into a veritable hornet's nest. The trouble came not from the long-gone Japanese flyers, but from the jittery American gunners on the ground. A fierce hail of flak rose to meet the friendly fighters. With gas low, MacDonald had no option but to run the gauntlet, landing back safely at Wheeler Field in spite of stiff American opposition.

A thorough professional, MacDonald's later career included command of the famed "Satan's Angels," the 475th Fighter Group whose alumni included Thomas B. McGuire. Only Bong, McGuire, the Navy's McCampbell (thirty-four kills) and the Marines' "Pappy" Boyington (twenty-eight kills) topped MacDonald's score in the Pacific. He retired from the USAF in the middle nineteen sixties after a distinguished postwar career.

The American fighter pilots in the Pacific had many "characters" in their ranks, and numerous funny stories have found their way into legend concerning these men. A typical character is Captain Richard L. West of Chillicothe, Missouri, a comrade-in-arms of the "Kankakee Kid" mentioned earlier.

West became the "Samson of the South

(Toliver Collection)

BRINGING THE WAR HOME TO JAPAN
Japanese aircraft heads down in flames to impact on the home islands, after being riddled by an American fighter in January of 1945. Photographs like this, in conjunction with full sequences showing the chase, the hits and the exploding, made confirmation of victories certain.

Pacific" when he swore he would not cut his hair until he had downed his first Japanese plane. His hair had reached an oppressive length under the tropical conditions of the South Pacific when he finally splashed a Zero.

West was then seized by the dread that if he now cut his hair, he would never get another Jap. He fought over Australia, New Guinea, the Celebes, Borneo and the Philippines, racking up 14 aerial kills and needing a haircut so badly he was afraid it would shatter the shears. West survived both the war and his first haircut, and lives today in his native Chillicothe. His first aerial action is the one he remembers best. Why? Because, in West's own words, "I was near immobility with fear."

In the middle nineteen-fifties, the Air Research and Development Command made a study of the personality traits of fighter pilots, and concluded that practically all aces are "characters" in some degree or another. The ARDC Study indicated that aces generally are those who set their hearts and minds on becoming aces. Those who made the grade strongly desired further aerial combat, which is generally the opposite of the nonaces.

Studies of this kind can only deal in broad generalities, for there are surviving aces who take a dim view of personal glory and of special recognition for aerial victories gained in battle for their country. This substantial but nevertheless minority faction has an elo-

quent spokesman in a U.S. Navy ace, Lieutenant Commander Edward Overton, Jr., of Washington, D.C. Overton puts his views this way; not long before his passing:

"Most men fight because they have to. A few, perhaps, find glory beyond their wildest dreams. Most develop an understanding of teamwork, comraderie and give-and-take, which will always be helpful to them. But one's perspective concerning awards and aces becomes significantly altered when one considers the "unknown" ones. Victories and awards, I suppose, are part of the game, but each individual knows in his heart whether his "well done" was deserved or not . . . the records really belong to those who are not listed."

Among the personality traits of aces, a disregard for or obliviousness to danger is frequently found. It is this kind of character who can recall, almost conversationally, the petrifying experience of flying head-on into the hail of fire put up by a formation of bombers. Colonel Franklin Nichols, of Wewoka, Oklahoma, is a typical instance. With three accompanying P-40's, Nichols tackled a flight of eighteen Jap Betty bombers near Buna, New Guinea, on the first anniversary of Pearl Harbor.

"We bounced them and broke up the bomb run before a single bomb was dropped. We knocked two of the Bettys down and I got credit for one of them."

This laconic description conceals the special kind of courage it takes to fly into a storm of bullets pumped out by upwards of eighty guns, turned on four lonely fighter planes. Colonel Nichols ended World War II with five aerial victories confirmed.*

Major Sammy A. Pierce of Ayden, North Carolina, scored seven aerial kills with the 49th Group of the 5th Air Force. He remembers a melee that took place while he

*Colonel Nichols was another member of "Satan's Angels," the 475th Fighter Group. He retired from the USAF in the rank of Major General.

was flying out of Dobodura, New Guinea, in March of 1943:

"We were scrambled for an intercept mission. I was flying the number two position on the third flight leader. Right after takeoff, the number four man in the flight had to return with propeller trouble, making it a three-ship flight. Due to sketchy radar facilities, the controller could give us only approximate locations, so the four flights split into patrol formations to sweep the whole area. My flight sighted the Japs at 25,000 feet—headed for the harbor under construction at Oro Bay. The enemy formation was still about fifty miles out at sea.

"Our flight climbed to the right-hand side above the bomber formation, which consisted of twenty-seven Bettys with a top cover of sixty Zekes. The flight leader rolled into an overhead 180-degree pass, picking out the lead ship in the first element of the bomber formation. I followed him in, picking up the lead ship in the second element of the Jap formation. I was firing from a position relatively straight down, and my windshield began to fog. I tried to clear it off, and as a consequence, my pullout was a little late. I damned near rammed the Jap wingman in the outside element of the formation.

(USAF)

Captain Dick Bong's P-38: This photo of Bong's P-38 was taken a few days after he had scored his 27th victory on a raid to Hollandia. Bong also had credit for a "probable" which later became a confirmed 28th. After an "R & R" trip home, Bong returned to the Pacific Theater and ran his total up to 40. Bong lost his life the day after Hiroshima was atom bombed, while flying a P-80 jet at Burbank, Calif.

(USAF)

80th Fighter Group pilots at Dinjan, India: All these pilots had two or more Japanese planes to their credit but only the fourth man from the left scored enough to make acedom. They are: Lt. Ralph E. Ward, Lt. Gale H. Lyon, Lt. J. B. Patton, Flight Officer Sam E. Hammer (ace), Lt. R. D. Bell, Lt. P. A. Marshall and Lt. H. H. Doughty. August 15, 1944. Note skull-head squadron insignia.

"I cleaned my windshield of fog and moisture. While rejoining, I spotted a Jap fighter making a pass on the number three man in our flight. The Jap was slightly above and forty-five degrees to my right. I pulled the nose far enough in front of his line of flight to at least shoot in front of him. It was all I could do to take him off the number three man. When I fired, I saw hits on the Zeke around the wing root and just forward of the wing in the fuselage. He fell off to the left in a steep diving attitude. I followed him, and fired one more burst into him until he hit the water.

"Climbing back up, I found I'd been separated from the flight leader and number three man. I climbed above the bombers, which by this time had jettisoned their bombs and were hightailing it for New Britain. I made my next pass on the third element of the bombers, and knocked one engine out of a bomber which lost altitude. As he dropped, I made three more passes at him until I ran out of ammo.

"Now the Zekes were on me. A three-ship element came down after me. It was my turn to run. Heading for home and nosing down, I managed to outrun my three pursuers. I was just congratulating myself when I ran into a single additional Zeke—head-on.

"He had about three thousand feet of altitude on me. He rolled over and started a diving pass. I held my heading until I thought he was just about in range, then I pulled up into a direct line with him. He broke off and pulled up to my right. I made a diving turn to the left and held her wide open all the way to Dobodura. Although I only got two credits out of this, our three-ship flight got seven Japanese aircraft and caused the bombers to jettison bombs and bolt before reaching the target."

Sammy Pierce himself later became a victim of Japanese aerial gunnery in October, 1943. After being shot down, he landed near the Japanese lines. He managed to evade capture, and by a turn of good luck stumbled across some Australian Infantrymen. The Aussies got Pierce back to his unit, and he survived World War II to become a career USAF officer.

Another victim of the Japanese fighter pilots was Captain John E. Purdy of Wyandotte, Michigan. He had seven aerial victories to his credit when he was shot down over Luzon in the Philippines. After more than two weeks with the guerrillas, Purdy was finally picked up by an Air Corps PBY. On the flight back to his unit, he had time to reflect on the naive newspaper stories published in the United States, which told of Japanese pilots with two-dimensional eyesight who could neither shoot nor fly well. Purdy lives today in Kettering, Ohio.

Purdy remembers another incident in the same area:

"I was leading a flight of four P-38's on patrol over the West coast of Leyte, when I spotted six Jap Vals heading toward Cebu Island. I closed on a Val from dead astern at 500 feet altitude, and found we were directly over the Jap airbase at Cebu City. I fired a short burst and hit the Val's port engine. It smoked, exploded and crashed north of Cebu City. I tackled another Val at the same altitude, but as I approached it from behind, the Jap plane banked to the right. I closed to 250 yards, fired a short burst at forty-degree deflection. Hits and explosions peppered the Val, and he rolled over and plunged straight into the ground.

"Everything had been going my way up to now, but suddenly all hell broke loose. My wingman, Lieutenant John A. Nelson, called and said he'd been hit by flak. The shell had exploded in his parachute, injuring his legs. At the same time, Lieutenant Ettien, the other wingman in my flight, called that a group of Jap fighters was directly over our heads.

"It was impossible to try and race out from under these Japs, and each time they would close in on us, we would have to go into a Lufbery Circle for mutual protection. We couldn't get back home that way. Strangely enough, the Jap fighters broke away after awhile, and we made it home. Whatever caused that breakaway—fuel shortage, fear of other P-38's or what, saved our skins, because our fuel was very low.

*"The payoff came at home base. Captain William Grady, my tentmate, who had a flight of Lightnings in the area at the time, accused me of trying to shoot down all the Jap planes myself. It seems he could hear our flight conversations on the radio, but we could not hear his urgent pleas to let him know where the fun was. I doubt if he'll ever believe I couldn't hear him."**

Credited with twenty-two aerial victories,

* Grady just missed becoming an ace. He scored four confirmed victories.

Colonel Jay Thorpe Robbins of Coolidge, Texas, emerged from World War II as the tenth-ranking ace of the PTO. Most of these victories were gained in the P-38, although Robbins also flew the P-40 and P-39. He once lived a lifetime in a few seconds, in a combat experience he is unlikely ever to forget:

"I was leading the 80th Squadron in a low level escort for B-25's attacking Rabaul, New Britain, in October, 1943. While the B-25's went in for the attack, we fought a dogfight with Zeros, lasting about twenty-five minutes. I shot down three of them for sure, and another one I wasn't sure about. The Zeros withdrew, and with almost all my ammo gone I climbed to 24,000 and started home. Then I spotted one lone Jap fighter, who had already seen me and was making a suicidal head-on attack. There was no doubt he intended to ram.

"He opened fire at 800 yards, and though our rate of closure was very rapid, he gave no indication of intent to break. I held my fire until range was 250 yards, then aimed at his wing root and pulled the trigger. Only two of my guns responded. They fired about twenty rounds and then quit. I was out of ammunition, but the Jap's left wing flashed and sheared at that same instant. I broke hard right, barely missing the Zero and flying through a shower of debris that damaged my Lightning. The firing of that twenty rounds seemed like an eternity."

Robbins retired as a Lt. General and now lives in San Antonio, Texas.

Throughout the Pacific air war, the American urge for competition, so much a part of the national heritage, had to be disciplined in dealing with the tricky and highly maneuverable Zeros. Although the abler American pilots often won victories by dogfighting with the light Japanese aircraft, the surest way for the average pilot to survive was to avoid close dogfighting.

These tactical truths were strongly impressed on tyro pilots during their training but there still came to the squadrons in the Pacific a steady stream of hotheads who had to be shown, often at the cost of their own lives, that the Zero was a superior aircraft for this kind of close action.

Teamwork and the right tactics eventually demoralized the Japanese fighter pilots, but to the very end it was a sort of aerial picnic for a skilled Japanese pilot if he could inveigle an American into a dogfight with him. One audacious and able Japanese pilot, whose feats are dealt with in the chapter on the enemy aces, made a specialty of taking on and defeating even the greatly superior Mustang in this kind of combat.

The Japanese were never short of tricks, lures and decoy gimmicks, even though their teamwork and communications never approached that of the Americans they flew against. Japanese tactics of this kind form the outstanding combat memory of Major Leonard Randall Reeves of Texas. Since the incident almost cost "Randy" Reeves his life, it is well etched in his mind and he recalls it thus:

"In March, 1945, our squadron was supposed to hit Nanking in order to keep the Japs busy there and prevent their concentration on the Okinawa landings. Eight hit the airfields to strafe parked bombers, and the other eight were to engage the Jap airborne patrols.

"The Jap radar was working, and better than thirty Jap fighters were waiting for us as we bored in. They were the new Jacks, not as maneuverable as the Zekes, but faster and much more rugged. They were above us, and some were level with us as we came in at 27,000 feet.

"The Japs would send out their usual decoy, a guy simulating a novice pilot flubbing around and not knowing what to do. When you concentrated on this decoy, the rest of the Japs would bounce you. In this case, the 'professional novice' got too far from his flock. I shot him down before his pals could get to us.

"Right after this contact, the air was jumping with enemy planes. My wingman, Lieutenant Beck, and I spotted a 'squirrel cage' of Japs. It wasn't a vertical one, but one halfway between a Lufbery and a loop, with eight Jap planes in it. One Jap had closed up too tightly on the man ahead of him, so we snuck in, shot him down and snuck out again before the Jap astern of us could close the distance and save his overeager comrade.

"Soon all my ammo had gone, and I called to Beck to join up and we would go home. He came in, but instead of joining up, he seemed to be taking lead on me. I immediately thought he must be mistaking me for a Jap. I was so concerned I yelled, 'Don't shoot, Beck, this is ole Randy!' Then blam—*I was hit by gunfire.*

"I realized instantly that a Jap had closed

The famous ZERO, Type 21, A6M2
This picture was made in early 1942 in the Celebes Islands. Acrobatically and in the turning dogfight, this aircraft had no peer during WWII on either side.

(Toliver Collection)

on me while I was watching Beck. Out of control, my ship rolled over, buffeting like hell and throwing the stick back in my guts. I chopped the power and rolled in full tail down trim. The nose started to come up—slowly. Finally on an even keel, I found myself completely alone, with no Beck or anyone else in sight and the weather closing in.

"An hour and a half from home, I managed to join up with two of my flight. They checked my plane and reported part of my tail planes shot away. I landed without flaps, and when I got out and saw the damage, I wondered how in hell she flew at all."

Randy Reeves came through World War II with six aerial victories officially credited. These kills were gained in ten months of service with the 10th Air Force in India, and a further nine months with the 14th Air Force in China. He was a member of the famed 530th Squadron, known to the Japanese as the "Yellow Scorpions" because of the yellow noses and tails on their aircraft.

A single wild aerial battle elevated William A. Shomo to the fraternity of aces, won him immortality among combat pilots and gained him the Congressional Medal of Honor. Shomo was flying with the 82nd Tactical Reconnaissance Squadron in the Pacific at the time of his epic encounter. Time: January 11, 1945. Place: Over Luzon, P.I. Shomo modestly makes light of it:

"As flight leader of two P-51 Mustangs on an armed reconnaissance mission over Northern Luzon, I sighted twelve Tony fighters escorting a Jap Betty bomber near Tuetubaro in the Cagayen Valley. My wingman, Lieutenant Paul Lipscomb, and I

attacked the formation. Lipscomb shot down three fighters, while I shot down six and the bomber as well. The remaining three fighters fled. A ranking Japanese air marshal was later confirmed as killed in the bomber, hence the heavy fighter escort."

Bill Shomo's seven kills in this encounter have earned him a special place among American fighter pilots. He finished the Second World War with eight victories, and now lives in Pittsburgh, Pennsylvania.

An outstanding fighter pilot may not necessarily be a high-scoring pilot. Leading, guiding and planning fighter operations has called for exceptional talent and has not always led to large tallies of aerial kills. The capacity to function in the sphere of leadership rather than in individual brilliance has been given to very few men. Fighter leaders of this kind who also made ace are extremely rare.

Epitomizing this breed was Brigadier General Clinton D. Vincent, affectionately known in the USAAF as "Casey" Vincent. He downed six Japanese aircraft himself, but his leadership paved the way to many kills by others. As long as the enemy's planes went down, and plenty of them, "Casey" felt that his job was well done.

A vigorous and dedicated missionary for fighter aviation, which always seems to fall on hard times when America is not at war, "Casey" Vincent's death in 1955 was a heavy blow to all who knew and followed him. He believed the fighter arm should continue to develop to that ultimate point where missiles would completely replace manned fighters for aerial defense. The fighter arm and fighter aviation were first in Vincent's heart. He

(Toliver Collection)

SPECTACULAR NEAR-MISS

Japanese "Nick" fighter slashes by under the starboard wing of American B-29, causing consternation among bomber pilots. Formation may be seen to be disrupted by this maneuver, often mistaken by American pilots as kamikaze attacks. In actual fact, Japanese fighter pilots tried to force individual B-29's out of formation by near-miss, head-on passes, so that separated B-29 could be set upon by Japanese fighters. Massed firepower of formation was usually a strong deterrent to fighter attack.

devoted his life's energies to this goal, and rightly belongs among America's most dedicated airmen.

Born in Gale, Texas, in 1914, General Vincent called Natchez, Mississippi, and San Antonio, Texas, his home towns. He saw his first aerial combat with the 35th Pursuit Group in the China-Burma-India Theater. He was Chief of Staff of the China Air Task Force and of the 14th Air Force. He later commanded the 68th Composite Wing in the CBI.

He became a brigadier general in 1944, aged twenty-nine. His most exciting combat experience was recorded for the authors shortly before his death:

"We were escorting B-24's over Hong Kong, and ran into a new type of Jap fighter, later called the Hamp, which gave us a start. I shot down one just as he slid into position fifteen yards from a B-24. It was a great feeling of elation to see him explode and know that the bomber boys had been saved. Low on gas, I almost landed in the river on the way home, and barely made it to an abandoned air strip near our base."

Only 34 American fighter aces in the history

of aerial combat were able to shoot down 20 or more foes in aerial combat. Only a few of these experts failed to survive and return home. Perhaps the greatest single loss among them was Lieutenant Colonel Robert B. Westbrook, whose 20 aerial victories in the Pacific set the seal on a remarkable and unforgettable personality.

Westbrook's home town was Hollywood, California, and in appearance he could have passed as a member of the Barrymore family with his classically handsome face and profile. As a pilot and leader, however, Westbrook in today's parlance "had his act together." His flying skill was backed up with comprehensive mechanical knowledge and practical expertise. His father's carburetor shop in Los Angeles was his early training ground in developing these skills.

An ROTC cadet captain at Hollywood High School, he was in the California National Guard when it went into Federal service before the war. He won his commission at Officer Candidate School, and applied for flight training. He showed outstanding leadership quality from his ROTC days onwards, and rose to become one of the top scoring fighter pilots of the PTO.

"Westy," as he was nicknamed, was not only a pilot's pilot, but was also a ground crewman's pilot. Westbrook logged many hours working on the line alongside mechanics, finding more efficient ways to keep the P-38's flying. This showed up in record numbers of fighters in commission in his units.

Westbrook flew 367 combat missions totaling 554 hours, and had 20 aerial victories to his credit by 22 November 1944. With months of Pacific war still ahead, "Westy" was in a good position to move up among America's best ever. Like many another ace unconquered in the air, he was brought down by ground fire.

Strafing a gunboat in an effort to take the heat off two of his fellow P-38 pilots who were attacking a freighter in the Macassar Strait, "Westy" ran into a hail of lead. His right engine burst into flame and the P-38 went in hard from 700 feet, breaking up on impact. His comrades flew low over the spot but found no trace of the 13th Air Force hero. He had won the Silver Star, the DSC, the DFC and the Air Medal with 15 clusters. "Westy" is warmly remembered to this day.

The overwhelming majority of fighter operations in the Pacific were conducted by the U.S. Navy and Marine Corps, working hand in glove in their island-hopping progress towards Japan. The Army Air Force produced only 165 fighter aces in the Pacific Theater of Opertions, against more than twice that number of Navy and Marine aces.

The USAAF was in action in the Pacific from the opening explosions to the final victory. The few stories and combat sketches here are only a sampling of the kind of fighter activity USAAF pilots undertook in this theater. The Army and the PTO produced the two top American aces of all time, Richard Bong and Thomas McGuire.

Ground down by the initial Japanese assault almost to nothing early in 1942, USAAF fighters made a dramatic comeback in the next three years to help the Navy and Marines drive the Japanese from the skies. Army P-38's were responsible for what was probably the sweetest moment of American revenge in World War II—the interception and destruction in the air of the transport aircraft that was bringing Japanese Admiral Yamamoto to Bougaineville. The planner of the Pearl Harbor attack went to his death under the guns of Lieutenant Thomas Lanphier or Lieutenant Rex T. Barber. Each of these two aces shot down a Betty bomber apiece and it is uncertain which Betty the admiral was in at the time.*

The Pacific USAAF aces flew combat with the added hazard of long over water distances. Carrier landings were not for them. Navigational aids were minimal, the possibility of ditching in the ocean an ever-present backdrop to all combat, and despite a vigilant rescue system many Army pilots survived combat only to die by drowning.

In the European Theater of Operations the USAAF had the lion's share of the fighter combat, against an equally rugged foe, mounted on far better aircraft than the Japanese. The ETO aces fought a different war from the Pacific struggle, and also had much the better of the wartime publicity. The contribution of the Pacific aces to victory was considerable nevertheless, and their glory second to none.

*Lanphier scored 5½ victories during the war and Barber had 5.

AMERICA'S AVENGER

Captain Thomas G. Lanphier receives the DFC and the Silver Star from Brigadier General Dean C. Strother for outstanding services in the PTO. Lanphier is credited with five aerial victories, including what was probably the most satisfying downing of all time — the destruction of Admiral Isoroku Yamamoto's personal transport over Kahili, near Bougainville, on April 18, 1943. Admiral Yamamoto was the conceiver of the Pearl Harbor attack, and Tommy Lanphier put "PAID" to that account on behalf of Uncle Sam. There is much doubt, however, as to whether Lanphier or Rex Barber actually shot down Yamamoto's plane.

(USAF)

(Toliver Collection)

HISTORIC GROUP

There are six aces in this rare photograph who accounted for 127 Japanese aircraft between them. Major Dick Bong, the top-scoring American ace of all the wars, 40 victories, is third from right. From left, the officers are: Lt. Col. George Walker, C.O. 49th Fighter Group; Col. Bob Morrisey, A-3, 5th Fighter Command; Lt. Col. Gerald R. Johnson, third-ranking ace of the Pacific, 24 kills; First Lt. Milton Mathre, 5 kills; Major Wally Jordan, 6 kills; Major Dick Bong, 40 kills; Major Thomas McGuire, second-ranking Pacific ace, 38 kills; Captain Robert De Haven, 14 kills. The group was assembled in commemoration of the 49th Fighter Group's 500th air-to-air victory, achieved by Lt. Mathre. Scene is at Tacloban on Leyte, November 2, 1944.

TOUGH YOUNG TIGER
Major John R. Alison flew with the Flying Tigers in China before transferring to the USAAF, for service with the 14th, 10th, and 5th Air Forces before the end of hostilities. This photograph shows Alison with a shark-nosed P-40 at a base in China. Credited with six aerial victories, Alison had a successful peacetime career in the aerospace industry as a top executive.

(Toliver Collection)

The USAAF Aces of World War II Pacific Theater

(Toliver Collection)

Lt. Ernest J. Ambort, USAF (5.00): Little Rock, Arkansas. 9th Squadron, 49th Fighter Group, SWPA. Scoring his first victory on October 31, 1944, it took Ambort just 37 days to become an ace, his fifth coming on December 7, 1944.

(Aschenbrener)

Major Robert W. Aschenbrener, USAF (10.00): Chatsworth, California. Aschenbrener (left)flew with the 8th Squadron, 49th Fighter Group, SWPA, to score his ten victories. Other 8th Squadron pilots are William M. Elliott from Texas, David Winternitz from Colorado, and Charles A. Peterson from Iowa. This photo taken in New Guinea.

(USAF)

Captain Abner M. Aust, USAF (5.00): Bartow, Florida. Aust flew Mustangs from Iwo Jima to Japan and back, eight-hour flights, with the 457th Fighter Squadron, 506th Group.

Captain John W. Bolyard, USAAF (5.00)
From Panama City, Florida, Bolyard scored his five victories in the CBI with the 74th Squadron, 23rd Fighter Group during the last two months of 1944. The first two kills, scored 3 November 1944 over Amoy, China, included a victory over Japanese ace W.O. Takeo Tanimizu who had thirty-two victories.

(USAF)

(Toliver Collection)

Major Walter G. Benz, Jr., USAF (8.00)
New Braunfels, Texas. In two tours with the 342nd Squadron of the 348th Fighter Group, Benz made his acedom. He scored his last four victories within nine days in December 1944.

Major William M. Banks, USAF (9.00)
Banks, now residing in Lewisburg, West Virginia, fought in the Southwest Pacific with the 348th Fighter Group. A regular officer, Banks retired as a colonel.

(USAF)

Richard Ira Bong, USAF (40)
From Poplar, Wisconsin, Dick Bong was the top American fighter ace in the Pacific Theater of Operations (PTO). Bong scored his 5th victory on January 8, 1943 and General Kenney, commander of the Allied Air Forces in the SWPA, sent him to Australia for some rest. When Bong returned to New Guinea he scored his sixth kill on March 3rd. This photo was made of him on March 6, 1943. His rank at the time was first lieutenant.

(USAF)

97

PILOT BROWN IN AIR FORCE
At least twelve aces named Brown went into the WWII records. Here is Captain Harry W. Brown of Alamo, California, who downed six Japanese aircraft during service in the PTO. This shot shows him aboard a P-36 in Hawaii in 1941.

AVG ACE, CHINA
Captain George T. Burgard was among the more successful American aces with the Flying Tigers in China. He is credited with 10.75 victories. The Selinsgrove, Pennsylvania man is seen here with his P-40, while flying with the Loi Wing in China in April 1942.

Major Harry C. Crim, USAF (6.00): Atlanta, Georgia. Leading the 531st Squadron of the 21st Fighter Group in the Central Pacific from Iwo Jima to Tokyo, Crim scored his six kills between April 7 and July 6, 1945.

Captain Dallas A. Clinger, USAF (5.0): Clinger, who hails from Etna and Alpine, Wyoming, faced his combat destiny in the CBI. Flying with the 23rd Group, he shot down four Japanese planes while assigned to the 16th Fighter Squadron and his fifth with the 74th Squadron. His fighter pilot friends called him "the Wyoming Cowboy."

Lt. Colonel George A. Davis, USAF CMH (21.00)

Colonel Davis, from Hale Center and Lubbock, Texas, shot down seven Japanese aircraft in the Southwest Pacific flying with the 348th Fighter Group in WWII. In the Korean War, Davis shot down 14 North Korean planes to bring his total to 21 victories. Davis was shot down February 10, 1952 on his 60th Korean combat mission and was awarded the Congressional Medal of Honor posthumously.

(USAF)

(Toliver Collection)

FORMER AERIAL ENEMIES MEET IN PEACE

Captain Robert M. DeHaven, formerly of the 49th Fighter Group of the 5th Air Force in the PTO, shares war reminiscences with Japan's top living fighter ace, Saburo Sakai, credited with 64 victories. Sakai lost one eye in South Pacific action, but continued to fly combat to the end. DeHaven is credited with 14 victories and resides in Encino, California.

(Toliver Collection)

STRING OF KILLS

Captain Robert M. DeHaven ran up 14 kills against the Japanese in his P-38, as the rising sun flags testify. DeHaven flew with the 49th Fighter Group of the 5th Air Force. This photograph was made at Lingayen, Luzon in the Philippines in June of 1945. DeHaven made it through the war safely, became a successful executive in peacetime.

(Mo. ANG)

Lt. Colonel Charles H. DuBois, Jr., USAF (5.00)

As a first lieutenant, DuBois fought with the 76th Squadron of the 23rd Fighter Group. He retired as a major general and lives in Chesterfield, Missouri.

Captains William K. Giroux (10.0) and Richard L. West (14.00) These two 8th Fighter Group pilots fought in the SWP area. Giroux hails from Kankakee, Illinois and West from Chillicothe, Missouri. (Hinman-Miami)

USAF)

Colonel William D. "Dinghy" Dunham, USAF (16.00) Dunham flew combat in the SWP with the 348th Fighter Group. Besides the 16 Japanese planes shot down, Dunham was credited with sinking two Japanese transport ships of an estimated 10,000 tons each. He retired as a brigadier general and lives in Spokane, Washington.

(USAF)

Major Maxwell H. Glenn, USAF (7.50): Glenn, from Winnfield, Louisiana, flew with the 459th FS, 80th Fighter Group in the CBI theatre.

(USAF)

Captain Richard Henry Fleischer, USAF (6.00): Fleischer was with the 340th Squadron, 348th Fighter Group in the SWP. He is from Quincy, Massachusetts, but lives in Altadena, California.

SEVEN JAPANESE AIRCRAFT DOWNED
Major Marvin E. Grant of Racine, Wisconsin flew 189 combat missions in the PTO against the Japanese. He is credited with seven victories while flying with the 348th Fighter Group.

(Toliver Collection)

(USAF)

(USAF)

Major Joseph Henry Griffin, USAF (7.00): Okalahoma City, Oklahoma. Three victories with the 75th Squadron, 23rd Fighter Group in the CBI and four more in the ETO with the 367th Fighter Group.

Major Samuel E. Hammer, USAF (5.00) Hammer scored his victories flying with the 90th Squadron of the 80th Fighter Group in the CBI. He was from Neal, Kansas and lost his life in an auto accident at San Marcos, Texas on January 18, 1953.

(Toliver Collection)

Lt. Cheatham W. Gupton, USAF (5.00): Durham, North Carolina. Gupton, flying with the 9th Squadron of the 49th Fighter Group in the SWPA, scored all five of his victories during the month of November 1944.

(Toliver Collection)

13 VICTORIES, PTO
The higher the score, the fewer the pilots who made them, but Oregonian John F. Hampshire downed 13 Japanese aircraft in WWII. He ended the war as a captain with the 23rd Fighter Group.

101

Colonel Bruce Keener Holloway, USAF (13.00)
Lt. Colonel Holloway, shown here being decorated at Kunming, China on February 16, 1943 by General Claire L. Chennault, rose to four-star general. In WWII, Holloway flew with the 76th Squadron and the 23rd Fighter Group in the CBI to score his 13 victories. Knoxville, Tennessee.

(USAF)

TEXAN TIGER
David Lee "Tex" Hill was an outstanding performer with Chennault's AVG, racking up 11.25 kills during his service in China. He made ace a second time with the USAAF, downing 6 more Japanese aircraft with the 23rd Fighter Group in the Pacific. His lifetime score: 17.25 aerial victories. He ended the war as a colonel.

(USAF)

(USAF)

Lt. Cyril F. Homer, USAF (15.00)
Homer, who was promoted to captain during his combat successes, calls Sacramento, California his hometown. He flew with the 80th Squadron of the 8th Fighter Group in the 5th Air Force in the SWP. In this photo he had just received the Silver Star award.

Lt. Colonel John C. Herbst, USAF (18.00)
Col. Herbst flew in the 14th Air Force, 23rd Fighter Group, 74th Fighter Squadron. His home was Pala, California. Herbst was killed in the crash of a Lockheed P-80 jet fighter on July 4, 1946 near San Diego during an aerial demonstration.

(USAF)

(USAF)

Lt. Colonel Gerald Richard Johnson, USAF (22.00)
Flying with the 49th Fighter Group, 5th AF in the SWP, Johnson scored 22 victories to add to two unconfirmed victories in the Aleutians in September of 1942. He was born in Kenmore, Ohio but his hometown was Eugene, Oregon. Gerald R. Johnson lost his life in the disappearance of a B-17 he was piloting in Japan on October 7th, 1945. Lost due to a typhoon, Johnson gave his parachute to a passenger and went down with his plane.

(Toliver Collection)

(USAF)

Captain Verl E. Jett,   USAF (7.00): Twain Harte, California. After scoring his first victory with the 36th Squadron in December 1942, Jett returned to the SWPA with the 475th Fighter Group and scored six more in late '43 and early '44.

Captain Kenneth A. Jernstedt, AVG (10.50): Hood River, Oregon. Jernstedt was the fifth-ranking ace of the original Flying Tigers, the American Volunteer Group.

"PERFECT!"
So indicates Flying Tiger ace James H. Howard, who downed 7.33 aircraft with the AVG. After transfer to the USAAF and the 354th Fighter Group he made ace a second time, won the Congressional Medal of Honor and ended WWII as Colonel James H. Howard with 13.33 victories as his career score. He retired as a brigadier general.

(Toliver Collection)

(King Collection)

AN ACE NAMED KING

As Major Charles W. King, this pilot won acedom with the 35th Fighter Group of the 5th Air Force. He is seen here later in his flying career as Colonel King, USAF. King is credited with five victories.

(Toliver Collection)

Major Gerald R. Johnson, USAF (22.00): Eugene, Oregon. Johnson scored four victories on 12 December 1944, bringing his total to 21 and winning him promotion to lieutenant colonel a few days after this photo was taken. He returned to combat on 2 March 1945, shot down another Japanese plane to make it 22.00 for him.

(USAF)

Captain Curran L. "Jack" Jones, USAF (5.00): Salado, Texas. This ace of the SWPA flew with the 35th Fighter Group.

Major Wallace R. Jordan, USAF (6.00): Long Beach, California. 9th Squadron, 49th Fighter Group, 5th Air Force, SWPA. Jordan led the 49th Group on both its long-range attacks on Balikpapan, Borneo, bagging three of his six victories on these eight-hour sorties.

(Toliver Collection)

Major John S. Loisel, USAF (11.00)
West Point, Nebraska and now Richardson, Texas. Loisel flew with the 36th Fighter Squadron and with the 475th Fighter Group, both in the SWPA.

(USAF)

(USAF)

Colonel Neel E. Kearby, USAF (22.00)
Colonel Kearby became a legend in the USAF early in 1944. From San Antonio, Texas, Kearby flew with the 348th Fighter Group and 5th Fighter Command. Between 4 September 1943 and 5 March 1944 he scored all his victories under most difficult conditions. He was lost in action on 5 April 1944 and was awarded the Congressional Medal of Honor for his feats.

(USAF)

Lt. Colonel Joseph J. Kruzel, USAF (6.50)
Shalimar, Florida. As a first lieutenant with the 17th Provisional Squadron in the SWPA, Kruzel scored his first three victories over Japanese. As a lieutenant colonel he went to the ETO and flying with the 361st Fighter Group scored 3.50 more over German pilots. He retired as a major general.

(Toliver Collection)

Lt. Francis J. Lent, USAF (11.00): Lt. Lent, from Minneapolis, Minnesota, flew with the 475th Fighter Group, SWPA.

SAW WWII START FOR THE U.S.
Colonel George Edward Kiser was a young pilot in the Philippines when WWII came in like a thunderclap there on 8 December 1941. He returned to the U.S. in 1943, and was assigned to the 9th Air Force in the ETO. Nine aerial victories credited with the 49th Fighter Group, PTO.

(USAF)

105

(Smithsonian)

Captain Donald S. Lopez, USAF (5.00)
Alexandria, Virginia. Lopez saw his
action in the 23rd Fighter Group, 14th AF,
in the China-Burma-India (CBI) theater of
war. USAF officially credits Lopez with
only three victories because no one saw
his fifth and his guncamera film did
not record the kill . . . a mid-air collision
with a Jap fighter which tore a wing off
the Zero. Lopez managed to nurse his
fighter to an American base and landed
safely. His fourth claim was lost in
the paper shuffle.

Colonel Charles H. MacDonald, USAF (27.00): MacDonald
was born in Dubois, Pennsylvania but presently lives in
Costa Rica. He was leader of the 475th Fighter Group,
"Satan's Angels," and is the 7th ranking American fighter
ace. This photo was taken while he was a flying cadet.

(USAF)

(USAF/Charpentier)

(Toliver Collection)

Captain Marvin W. Lubner, USAF (6.00): Brussels,
Belgium. 76th Squadron, 23rd Fighter Group. CBI. Lubner
flew two tours with the 23rd Group, scoring two victories
the first tour in late 1942. Lubner, in cockpit of Mustang, is
attended by his crew chief Staff Sergeant H. R. Wilk.

14 KILLS — 14TH AIR FORCE
Colonel Edward O. McComas of Winfield, Kansas
destroyed 14 Japanese aircraft during his
Pacific service with the 14th Air Force.
His record includes one day with five kills.

106

Major Thomas B. McGuire, USAF CMH (38.00)

No. 2 American ace. From Paterson, New Jersey, McGuire flew with the 431st Squadron, 475th Fighter Group in the SWPA. He scored a triple for his first victories on 18 August 1943. He ended his tally with another triple on Christmas Day, 1944, and a foursome on the 26th of December, 1944, bringing his total to 38. He lost his life in action 7 January 1945.

(National Archives)

(USAF)

First Lt. James Bruce Morehead, USAF (7.00):

Morehead's first two victories were with the 17th Provisional Squadron and the remainder with the 8th Squadron, 49th Group in the SWPA. He claimed one German plane shot down while with the 1st Fighter Group in the MTO but it is unconfirmed. He lives in Petaluma, California.

Lt. Colonel John L. McGinn, USAF

(5.00): Los Angeles, California. 347th Fighter Group, SWPA 3.0, 55th Fighter Group, ETO 2.0; total 5.00. Commander 335th Fighter Squadron, 55th Group.

(USAF)

(USAF)

Lt. Colonel John W. Mitchell, USAF (15.00)

San Anselmo, California. Eight victories with the 339th Squadron, 347th Group in the SWPA and three more with the 15th Fighter Group in the Central Pacific, for a total of 11.00 in WWII. During the Korean War, Mitchell added four MiGs to his tally for a total of 15.00 in two wars.

Capt. Paul C. Murphey, USAF (6.00)

Meridian, Texas. All six of his victories were with the 80th Squadron, 8th Fighter Group in the SWPA.

(USAF)

(Toliver Collection)

Lt. Colonel Charles H. Older, USAAF (18.50): Los Angeles, California. Older, now a California Supreme Court judge, fought with the AVG's under Chennault, scoring ten victories, ranking in seventh place among the AVG aces. Joining the USAAF 23rd Fighter Group in the CBI, Older added 8.5 more kills, making it a total of 18.50. (USAF Study 85 credits him with only seven USAF kills, so his total may be 17.00.)

(Toliver Collection)

Major Edward S. Popek, USAF (7.00): Tacoma, Washington. Flying with the 342nd Squadron of the 348th Fighter Group in the SWPA, Popek got his last two kills on 1 August 1945. He retired as a colonel.

Captain Joel B. Paris, USAF (9.00): 7th Squadron, 49th Fighter Group, SWPA. Roswell, Georgia.
(USAF)

(Toliver Collection)

Major Franklin A. Nichols, USAF (5.00) El Paso, Texas. Four victories with the 7th Squadron, 49th Fighter Group and his fifth with the 431st Squadron, 475th Fighter Group, SWPA.

Lt. Sammy A. Pierce, USAF (7.00): Ayden, North Carolina. As a flight officer with the 8th Squadron, 49th Fighter Group in the SWPA, Pierce scored on 11 April 1943, following up with a double on May 14th. Nineteen months later, again with the 8th Squadron, but a first lieutenant this time, Pierce demonstrated he had been honing his skills by shooting down four Japanese planes on 26 December 1944.

(USAF)

(USAF)

Lt. Col. Edward F. Rector, AVG/USAF (10.50): Alexandria, Virginia. AVG 6.50, USAF 14th AF, 23rd Group 4.00. Total 10.50.

(Flying Tiger Line)

FLYING TIGER IN CHINA

Captain Robert W. Prescott downed 5.25 Japanese aircraft with the AVG in China. A Texan from Fort Worth, Prescott survived the war to enter civil aviation as the founder of the Flying Tiger Line, of which he was president and chief executive officer. Prescott is seen here with his P-40 fighter during WWII. He died on 3 March 1978.

(Toliver Collection)

Lt. John A. Purdy and Major Warren R. Lewis: Lewis, from Superior, Iowa, had seven victories when this photo was taken in the SWPA in 1944. Lt. Purdy was a newcomer, but he too had seven kills by December. He is from Kettering, Ohio. Both flew with the 433rd Squadron, 475th Fighter Group, SWPA.

(Toliver Collection)

Lt. C. B. Ray, USAF (5.00): Bakersfield, California. Another of the 80th Squadron, 8th Fighter Group, SWPA fighter aces.

Lt. Robert J. Stone, Tracy, Minnesota: (7.0)
At full speed just above the ground over Nittagahara air field, southern Kyushu on 10 June 1945, Stone zoomed to evade a Betty bomber just taking off. Two of the 25 Zeke fighters queued up behind Stone's Mustang collided and crashed into the airborne Betty, all three splattering to the ground. USAF Study 85 does not credit Stone with these three kills, leaving him officially with only 4.0 victories.

Colonel Andrew J. Reynolds, USAF (10.00)
Seminole, Oklahoma. 49th Fighter Group, SWPA.
Won the Silver Star three times, the first time for combat
over Darwin where he destroyed two Japanese fighters
and a bomber on a single pass.   (USAF)

(USAF)

NEW GUINEA CEREMONY

Captain Daniel T. Roberts receives the Air Medal from Brigadier General Paul B. Wurtsmith in New Guinea.
Roberts downed 14 Japanese aircraft during service with the 475th Fighter Group in WWII. Many of
Roberts' flying buddies believe Roberts was the best combat pilot in the SWPA.

**First Lt. Leonard Randolph
Reeves, USAF (6.00):** Lan-
caster, Texas. 530th
Squadron, "Yellow Scor-
pions," 311th Fighter
Group in the CBI.   (USAF)

(USAF)
Brigadier General Robert R. Rowland, USAF (8.00):
As a colonel, commanded the 348th Fighter Group in the SWPA. Now
retired as a major general and living in Virginia Beach, Virginia.
Originally from Lodi, Ohio.

110

HEAVIER THAN AIR—AND HOW!

Colonel Jay T. Robbins USAF tries his hand at piloting another kind of heavier-than-air machine than those in which he flew to WWII glory. Robbins downed 22 aircraft in the Pacific, flying with the 8th Fighter Group of the 5th Air Force. He made the Air Force his career, and retired as a lieutenant general. (Toliver Collection)

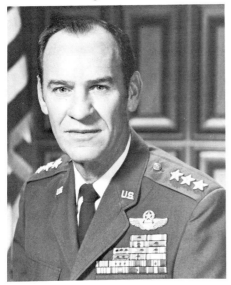

(USAF)

Lt. General Jay Thorpe Robbins, USAF (22.00)
Cooledge and San Antonio, Texas. One of the top American fighter aces, Robbins flew with the 8th Fighter Group in the SWPA. Co-author Toliver, when serving as commander of the 20th Tactical Fighter Wing (1957-1959) at Wethersfield, England, was fortunate to have this most capable and effective officer as deputy commander.

(Rossi)

Squadron Leader John R. Rossi, AVG (6.25):
Fallbrook, California. Rossi, shown here shining his boots at Mingladon Airport, Rangoon in February 1942, Has worked for Flying Tiger Airlines since the war.

Major Jay T. Robbins, USAF (22.00)
Cooledge, Texas. 80th Squadron, 8th Fighter Group, 5th AF, SWPA. One of the finest USAF commanders, Robbins rose to the rank of lieutenant general. Retired now, he lives in San Antonio, Texas. (USAF)

"GOD IS MY CO-PILOT"

Colonel Robert L. Scott's inspiring wartime best seller on fighter piloting in the Far East made his name a household word in the USA. A 23 F. Gp. pilot, he became an ace with the USAAF in the Far East and is credited with ten victories. Scott is seen here in Germany, where he served after the war and in the jet age as C.O. of the 36th Fighter Bomber Wing, based at Furstenfeldbruck. He retired as a brigadier general from the USAF. The tiger on the fuselage of his F-84 Thunderjet is a reminder of his Flying Tigers service. (USAF)

Major William Arthur Shomo, USAF (8.00) CMH
Shomo, from Pittsburgh, Pennsylvania. Flying with the 82nd Tactical Reconnaissance Squadron, 5th AF, SWPA, Shomo scored his first victory on 10 January 1945. The next day, in a 15-minute battle, he shot down six Japanese fighters and a bomber over Northern Luzon to win the Congressional Medal of Honor.

(USAF)

(USAF)
First Lt. John A. Tilley, USAF (5.00): Homestead, Florida. 431st Squadron, 475th Fighter Group, 5th AF, SWPA.

(U.S. Army)

LIGHTNING ACE

Lt. Murray J. Shubin was a lightning ace for more reasons than just the P-38 he flew, the giant bulk of which dwarfs him in this wartime photo. Shubin became an ace in 45 minutes in one blistering engagement over Guadalcanal. He flew with the 347th Fighter Group of the 13th Air Force, and ended the war with 13 kills credited. His P-38 is named "Oriole" for his Australian fiancee.

112

(USAF)

Major Arland Stanton, USAF (8.00)
New Milford, Pennsylvania.
7th Squadron, 49th Group, SWPA.

(USAF)

Captain Cornelius M. Smith, Jr., USAF (11.00) Captain Smith, shown here as a lieutenant colonel, lives in Tavares, Florida. 80th Squadron, 8th Fighter Group, SWPA.

Colonel Robert Lee Scott, USAF (10.00)
Sun City, Arizona. This photo made of the ace in his heyday in the CBI. Scott flew with the 23rd Fighter Group for all of his victories. He is the author of several excellent books.   (USAF)

(USAF)

Colonel John S. Stewart, USAF (9.00):
Monument, Colorado. 76th Squadron, 23rd Fighter Group, CBI.

Major James B. Tapp, USAF (8.00)
7th AF, 15th Fighter Group, Central Pacific. Lompoc, California.

113

Lt. Colonel Sidney S. Woods, USAF (7.00)
Yuma, Arizona. Woods had two victories with
the 9th Squadron, 49th Group in the SWPA, then
added five more with the 4th Fighter Group
in the ETO.

(USAF)

(USAF)

Captain Richard L. West, USAF (14.00):
Chillicothe, Missouri. 35th Squadron, 8th
Group, SWPA.

(Watts)

Captain Oran Stanley Watts, USAF (5.00)
Tulare, California.
118th Reconnaissance Squadron
attached to the 23rd
Fighter Group in the CBI.

Lt. Colonel Robert B. Westbrook, USAF (20.00)
Hollywood, California.
Westbrook's first 15 victories were
with the 44th Squadron, 18th Fighter Group.
He added the last five fighting with
the 347th Fighter Group. SWPA. He
was KIA on 22 November 1944. This photo
in the cockpit of a P-38 taken in
Dutch New Guinea. (USAF)

THREE AIR FORCE GENERALS
OF FIGHTER RENOWN

Brigadier General Clinton "Casey" D. Vincent (left) and Brigadier General Bruce K. Holloway (right) — both colonels at the time of this rare photograph — flank the immortal General Claire L. Chennault of the Flying Tigers in China. Vincent destroyed six Japanese aircraft in combat, Holloway destroyed 13, and General Chennault may have been an ace but never admitted it. These three were the masterminds of the air war in China in WWII.

(Toliver Collection

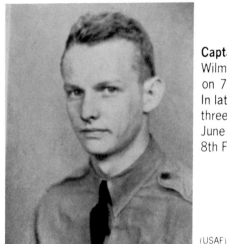

(USAF)

Captain George S. Welch, USAF (16.00)

Wilmington, Delaware. Welch scored four victories at Pearl Harbor on 7 December 1941, flying with the 47th Pursuit Squadron. In late 1942, in the SWPA with the 36th Fighter Squadron, he added three more. Back to the PTO for a third combat tour in June of 1943, Welch flew with the 80th Squadron of the 8th Fighter Group and raised his tally to 16.00 confirmed kills.

(National Archives)

(American Fighter Aces Association)

FROM HOLE-IN-ONE TO HOLE-IN-ONE!

Four outstanding aces try their hands (and eyes) at the links. Good golfers all, they were good fighter pilots all some 30 years ago. Billy Hovde, ETO 355th Group; James K. Johnson, Korea 4th Wing; Gerald A. Brown, ETO 55th Group; Sidney S. Woods, 49th Group, SWPA, and 4th Group ETO, rehash shots and strokes. 33.5 victories between them.

Major Boyd D. Wagner, USAF (8.00)

Johnstown, Pennsylvania. 17th Pursuit Squadron in the Philippines when WWII started, Wagner scored four victories on 13 December 1941 and his 5th to become an ace on the 16th of December. First USAAF ace of WWII.

Three Top Aces of the 56th:

The WOLFPACK, under the leadership of Hub Zemke and Dave Schilling, produced the 1st, 2nd, 5th and 7th ranking American aces of the ETO. These three accounted for 68¼ aerial victories over Luftwaffe airplanes. Zemke (17.75), Schilling (22.50) and Gabreski (28.00). (Conger Collection)

The Americans who made their way to England to fight with the RAF and RCAF between 1939 and 1941 were Uncle Sam's only representatives in the European air war at the time of Pearl Harbor. Their presence was unofficial, but nevertheless welcome. There were no USAAF combat units deployed anywhere in the European area, in contrast with the Pacific, where the USAAF was widely deployed and presumably ready for war.

As a consequence of these dispositions, the first American bomber raid on the Continent did not take place until 12 June 1942*, with the first attack by B-24 aircraft on the Ploesti oil refineries in Rumania. The next American raids came on 4 July 1942, when four airfields in the Netherlands were attacked by twelve RAF Bostons (American-built A-20's), six of these machines being manned by American pilots and crews as a familiarization operation.

Not until 14 August 1942 did a fighter plane manned by an American pilot in a USAAF unit make its first kill against the Germans. Flying a P-39 fighter, Lieutenant Shaffer shot down a Focke-Wolfe "Kurier" over Iceland* when the lumbering German reconnaissance plane came under his guns. On 19 August 1942, the first German machine to be shot down over Europe by a USAAF unit was claimed following an aerial battle over Dieppe. Lt. Samuel F. Junkin was one of the two pilots credited with a victory that day.

During the first six months following Pearl Harbor, U.S. airpower was fighting with its back to the wall in the Pacific. This immediate and urgent involvement prevented any rapid build-up of U.S. air strength in the European Theater of Operations. There were other consequences that upset many of the best-laid schemes of American war planners.

The planners had concluded that by producing large numbers of bombers with high speed, good defensive firepower and high-altitude capability, unescorted deep penetrations could be made into Germany by daylight. The tragic experience of the RAF experiments with the B-17 in this type of operation compelled a modification of the plan. The first bomber missions would henceforth be heavily escorted by fighters until they proved factually that they could defend themselves against enemy fighters.

General Henry "Hap" Arnold wanted to hold off all commitments of the B-17's and B-24's against the Luftwaffe until he could send them in great numbers. In this way, the awesome firepower of the formations could take the starch out of the German fighter opposition. General Arnold was not to realize this goal.

Due to war circumstances beyond Arnold's control, the B-17's and B-24's had to be committed virtually piecemeal. An urgent demand developed for swarms of American fighters as a result. Heretofore played down in the officially adopted American aerial policies, fighters now came into their own as the hard realities of war swept away the superficialities of war theory. Until American fighters were provided, the burden of defending the bombers fell to the RAF.

Fighter aircraft were ferried from the United States to units in England. Initially, the 31st Fighter Group (P-39's) had to leave its aircraft in America because the B-17's assigned to lead them across the Atlantic were diverted to the Pacific. The pressure was on and the Fortresses were needed at Midway Island.

The 31st therefore went to England by sea, minus aircraft, and was equipped with RAF

*Thirteen USAAF B-24's, en route from the USA to China under the command of Col. H. A. Halverson, took off from Fayid, Egypt. Twelve bombed the Ploesti oil fields. Damage was slight and opposition was light.

*Lt. Joseph D. Shaffer, Jr., of the Iceland Fighter Command, and a transient 8th AF pilot, Lt. Elza E. Shahan, each received ½ credit for shooting down an FW200 this date.

Spitfires. The 52nd Fighter Group followed the same procedure. Hence these American units saw their first fighter combat in the ETO in British aircraft bearing U.S. insignia.

American fighter pilots entered the ETO with well-founded misgivings about the experienced German pilots they were to face. American bomber losses were already high. Fighter losses rose sharply when they began escorting the bombers. German pilot quality in 1942 was very good, although it went into decline in the period 1943-45. The top Germans were always formidable.

The German aircraft were rugged and could take punishment. Unlike the Japanese planes, of which reports had already flashed through USAAF units, the Luftwaffe's sturdy Me-109's did not burst into flame from a few hits and explode like the Japanese Zero. The top German pilots, some with experience dating back to the Spanish Civil War, often turned the tables on green American pilots. Neophyte Americans were sometimes shot down by those habile Germans even when the latter were themselves flying seriously damaged machines. This kind of German pilot talent caused considerable tremor in the USAAF units in England. More will be said concerning the Germans in the chapter devoted to the enemy aces.

American fighter pilots lost many a battle in these early days because they failed to learn the value and the theories of the high-angle deflection shot. The enemy was hard to surprise. He was wily. Getting into a good stern chase position on him was difficult.

A good high-deflection artist could often damage the Me-109's oil coolers, disable the hydraulic system that allowed the landing gear to drop in midair, set a gas tank alight or create an engine malfunction. Any such damaging blow could dramatically swing the odds in the deflection shooter's favor, often forcing the German to make a wrong move or straighten out—just long enough for the classic final kill from dead astern.

New gunsights, designed in 1942 and produced in 1944 and 1945, were intended to solve the problem of trajectory for American pilots, but the war ended before more than minor results could be attained. Even at the time of the Korean War, American fighter pilots were still not sold on new-fangled sights. Many of them opposed radar sights. "Kentucky windage" was employed, or in the clas-

(Conger Collection)

JUG! THUNDERBOLT! LEAD SLED! P-47: This photo of a P-47 fighter will give the reader an idea of why the famed combat machine enjoyed all those nicknames.

sic expression of one of America's leading aces—"stick some gum on the windshield, then ram the gum up their tailpipe and let go." Soviet pilots in World War II actually used hand-painted circles on their windshields as gun sights.

As the bomber sorties into Germany mounted, it was soon evident that the major threat to this offensive was the German fighter force. Bomber raids with fighter escort were much less costly in casualties and aircraft than were unescorted raids. The long-range escort fighter became the *sine qua non* of successful daylight bomber operations. The clamor for its rapid development found a response in the production of the Republic P-47 Thunderbolt.

The P-47 was the first USAAF fighter to provide the badly needed long-range protection to the bomber streams. The 4th Fighter Group, based at Debden RAF Station near Saffron Walden, Essex, was the first unit to receive the new aircraft. A better unit to blood the P-47 could not be found.

The 4th Fighter Group had been formed in September, 1942, from the 71st, 121st, and

133rd Eagle Squadrons of the RAF. These tough, combat tested pilots were a valuable cadre around which to form a new unit. Under the command of Colonel Edward W. Anderson, they said goodbye to their slender, greatly esteemed Spitfires in March of 1943 and mounted the massive Thunderbolt with considerable misgivings.

At 14,000 pounds, the Thunderbolt weighed almost three times as much as the Spitfire. Many of the American pilots, accustomed to the heavyweight punch of the Spitfire's four 20mm cannons, did not like resigning themselves to the Thunderbolt's eight .50-caliber machine guns. Despite the experience of the pilots flying with the 4th Fighter Group, enemy kills came slowly. The P-47 scored its first kill south of Dieppe on 15 April 1943.

Other new squadrons were being equipped with the P-51 Mustang, destined to prove itself the outstanding single-engined fighter of World War II. Colonel Hubert "Hub" Zemke's 56th Fighter Group, dubbed the "Wolf Pack," had clawed down 300 German aircraft by the time the 4th had racked up its 150th kill with the P-47. When the 4th Fighter Group was re-equipped with Mustangs on 26 February 1944, the American race for high scoring Group honors started in earnest.

By war's end, the initially laggard 4th Fighter Group claimed to be the best, with 549 enemy aircraft destroyed in the air and 466 destroyed on the ground for a total of 1,015. However, two other groups reported more air-to-air kills. Zemke's Wolfpack claimed 665.5 aerial victories and the 357th Group claimed 595.5 aerial kills. For the purposes of this book, which is devoted to aces and counts aerial victories only, Zemke's Wolfpack is the top USAAF Group of the ETO.

By comparison, the most successful German fighter unit on the Western front was JG-26 "Schlageter," known to the Allied pilots as the "Abbeville Boys." In more than five years of aerial combat, the "Abbeville Boys" claimed over 2,700* Allied aircraft shot down. Worth noting is that the German unit had almost three full years of combat before the first USAAF Fighter Group in Europe was formed. The German record is nevertheless impressive.

The ETO is deemed to include all aerial ac-

*JG-52 on the Russian front shot down over 10,000 aircraft.

tivity over Europe proper, as well as such areas as Italy and North Africa. One top American ace of the ETO is Colonel Francis S. Gabreski, with a total of twenty-eight confirmed kills. Blonde, blue-eyed and sharp-featured Gabreski hails from Oil City, Pennsylvania. Of Polish descent, he is possessed of all the traditional charm of his ancestors. Greying now, but still a compact dynamo of a man, "Gabby," as he is known in the fraternity of American aces, is America's top living ace.

Gabreski was going great guns at the time of his World War II downing. Like many other seemingly invincible combat pilots, he was

(USAF)

Lt. General Carl A. Spaatz and Major James A. Goodson: General Spaatz decorates Major Goodson with the DSC in this photo. Goodson scored 14.00 aerial victories with the USAAF 4th Group in the ETO. Today, Goodson lives in Brussels, Belgium.

either nailed by flak or bent his propeller against a rise in the terrain during ground-attack operations. He was taken prisoner. He is one of seven American pilots to win acedom in both World War II and Korea.

Gabreski took to jets easily. Six and one-half communist jet fighters fell to his guns in Korea, bringing his all time victory total to

(Toliver Collection)

8th FIGHTER COMMAND LEADER AND LEADING ACE: Major General William Ellsworth Kepner, commander of 8th Fighter Command in the ETO, and pioneer balloonist, poses with Captain Robert S. Johnson, first USAAF ETO ace to surpass Rickenbacker's WWI record of 26 victories. Kepner retired as a lieutenant general. Johnson became top test pilot for Republic Aviation Corp. and is now an insurance executive in New York City.

34.5 kills. Only Bong and McGuire, with 40 and 38 victories respectively, surpass Gabreski, and both died in crashes.

Robert S. Johnson of Lawton, Oklahoma, tied for top honors, first place among America's ETO aces as a member of Hub Zemke's Wolfpack—the 56th Fighter Group. Johnson shot down his first German aircraft in June, 1943 and went on to become the leading ace of the ETO. He held this distinction until Gabreski caught him in April, 1944. He is credited with twenty-eight aerial victories. The recently published "official" USAF study on WWII aces credits Johnson with only 27 victories.

Johnson is another of the many aces who are of shortish stature. Five feet seven inches tall, he has to a marked degree the cold blue eyes attributed to aces so often in fiction. Notwithstanding this striking physical feature, he is a friendly man with a fine sense of humor and is extremely modest. Even in bull sessions he never exaggerates. Johnson always gives the impression of poise, confidence and a razor-sharp intelligence. He was undoubtedly one of the deadliest American aces of World War II.

Bob Johnson flew his last combat mission on 8 May 1944 and returned to the United States to finish his career in the service. Johnson's removal from combat flying while at the zenith of his career typifies a practice that was prevalent in the Allied air forces. When a man had run up a good score of kills, higher commanders showed a readiness to remove such a pilot from combat flying.

The reason was not only the likelihood of losing the man eventually if he went on flying combat, but the very real need to exploit the experience and prestige of such fliers in training new recruits. This Allied practice was not followed on the German side, where, in the words of General Adolf Galland, "our aces flew until they were killed."

In their *Fighter Aces of the Luftwaffe,* a companion volume to this one, the authors have presented a statistical comparison between the victory record of Bob Johnson and German ace Werner Moelders, the first fighter pilot in history to score 100 aerial victories. Although Johnson's combat career was much shorter, when all factors are taken into account by appropriate adjustment he emerges impressively from this comparison with one of the greatest fighter pilots Germany ever produced. The Americans were rotated out of the combat zone for long periods to training and other duties connected with national morale, while the Germans were kept unremittingly in combat save for brief home leaves.

Bob Johnson was released from active duty on 1 January 1946, a well-decorated and distinguished airman. He holds the DSC, Silver Star, ten DFC's, the British DFC and four Air Medals. He required only thirteen months to amass his score of twenty-eight aerial victories. Johnson was the first member of the Wolfpack to break Captain Eddie Rickenbacker's World War I record. Very much alive today, Johnson is an insurance executive in New York City and he lives in Woodbury, Long Island.

Johnson's advice to fellow pilots and fledglings alike was a telegraphic distillate of common sense: "It's better to come home tired with a sore neck from looking constantly in every direction than it is to leave the thing you

AERIAL VICTORY	(GERMAN) MOLDERS	(GERMAN) HARTMANN	(US) JOHNSON
1	6th sortie	19th sortie	11th sortie
5 (Ace)	53rd sortie	68th sortie	43rd sortie
10	78th sortie	120th sortie	54th sortie
20	116th sortie	184th sortie	73rd sortie
28	142nd sortie	194th sortie	91st sortie
50	204th sortie	251st sortie	
100		309th sortie	

An interesting comparison of sorties vs. victories. Hartmann went on to fly 1425 sorties and scored 352 confirmed victories. Captain Robert S. Johnson was withdrawn from combat after his 100th sortie.

sit on back in enemy territory."

He was a firm believer in teamwork, and made this generous salute to the wingman and his vital but unspectacular job:

"Any time you lose your wingman, you've lost 75 percent of your eyes and fighting strength. Jerries will shoot at anyone. Never think you're a favorite to them. Anyone can get it, some of the best have gotten it, so keep your eyes open."

When asked to recount for this book his most memorable combat experience, Bob Johnson said: "The victories were not nearly as impressive or as memorable to me as was keeping from being a victory."

The third-ranking American ace in the ETO was Major George Earl Preddy, Jr., of Greensboro, North Carolina. He was killed in action on Christmas Day in 1944, aged 25, after flying in combat in both the Pacific and European Theaters. He is credited with 26.83 victories against the Germans. He won another victory in 1942 while flying fighters out of Australia against the Japanese but this one was never confirmed.

Preddy's death was one of Fate's more ironic twists. On 25 December 1944, Preddy bounced a formation of four German aircraft, shooting down one of them on the first surprise pass. In the ensuing dogfight, Preddy exploded a second Me-109. The two remaining Germans split up and fled, one racing eastward, the other diving for the deck with Preddy in hot pursuit.

Allied ground troops, watching the aerial battle after the fashion of soldiers in the trenches in the First World War, sent up a stream of flak and small-arms fire in an effort to hit the Me-109. The ground gunners failed to lead the diving Me-109 far enough. The hail of fire struck the pursuing Preddy's Mustang instead, and he crashed almost on top of the

Major George Earl Preddy, Jr., USAF (26.83)
22 victories with the 487th Squadron and four with the 328th Squadron, 352nd Fighter Group in the ETO's 8th AF. Preddy, from Greensboro, North Carolina, shot down six Luftwaffe aircraft on the 6th of August 1944. KIA 25 December 1944 by Allied fire from the ground while chasing a German fighter. Preddy was considered one of the finest all-around American fighter pilots.

(USAF)

friendly troops who had killed him.*

The less famous fighter aces of the ETO came from all walks of civilian life, and the talents of some of them were by no means confined to flying. Gerald Lynn Rounds, an ace with 97th Fighter Squadron of the 82nd Fighter Group, is a man with several strings to his bow.

Today Rounds is a research chemist with the Kaiser Steel Corporation at Fontana, California. His experiences while flying with the famed "Forked Tailed Devils" Squadron at the controls of a P-38 provided him with the raw material to exhibit an unusual talent for narrative writing. Rounds' description of operations with the P-38 is a lively classic of the feelings, apprehensions and emotions of a World War II fighter pilot:

The 'Forked Tailed Devils' stood cold and gaunt at the 9 A.M. briefing on 8 February 1943. The target is to be Gabes, two hundred miles south of Tunis in North Africa, being used as an evacuation port for Rommel's army as Montgomery presses in from the south. We're escorting B-25 Mitchells. We're told to expect a little fighter opposition, 109's and 190's.

"*Escorting the B-25 has been expensive, one pilot and one plane per mission on the average. Some of our best men have got the hammer. We are green and are up against an experienced enemy in good aircraft. Our boys are scared, but they're learning.*

"*We are all thinking about this as we walk out to our P-38's. The sky is overcast, and the air is cold and wet. Spam and powdered eggs for breakfast sit in a stagnant ball in the stomach. The crew chief meets us and the tension eases a little as we slide into the familiar cockpit of the P-38. She's a dream, an honest aircraft, she always warns you of immediate trouble.*

"*The engines are warm, thanks to the crew chief, and catch easily with a heavy blurp through the turbosuperchargers, then run smoothly and solidly. You check each engine instrument as you watch the first flight taxi out from its dispersal point. Then the other flights are moving.*

"*You release the toe-pedal brakes and glide ahead off the smooth dispersal pad on to the*

rough, waterlogged taxiway. You are one of two spares for this mission. The flights are getting off in good shape, and your engines check clean at forty-five inches of mercury as you sit on the end of the runway.

"*Number four flight is off and you clear the two Allisons and give her loose reins. The counter-rotating props cause no torque, and the takeoff is easy except for the drag caused by the soft spots in the wet dirt runway. The belly tank necessitates a little trim after the wheels are up into their wells.*

"*A quick count of the four flights looks discouraging. All sixteen planes are forming up. After sweating out the mission the night before, then thorough briefing, and takeoff, you expect at least one of the boys to have some trouble . . . so it won't all have been in vain.*

"*Radios are being checked at low altitude, so the enemy won't pick them up. You listen anxiously as all the boys check in with their code and number 'Meatball 2-2' . . . 'Meatball 2-3' . . . 'Meatball 2-4' . . . then Major Whittliff flattens out on course and the flights assume escort position at his side and to the rear.*

"*In five minutes, our rendezvous course will bring us to the circling bombers. Already in the distance you can see the small swarm of bee-like objects milling in slow motion against the mountain backdrop. Then you get a break. A man in number three flight peels off sharply from formation and chandelles over you and the other waiting spare P-38. Oil streaks from the left oil cooler to the empennage tell you why.*

"*As you look over your shoulder you see his left engine slowly feather up and the prop blades stand motionless as he cuts it off. You hope he makes the tricky one-engined landing okay. The other spare closes in to the vacated position just as the number two man in the second flight glides slowly out of formation. There's no visible reason, but you know that an instrument is telling the pilot that his plane is not fit for combat.*

"*You increase your manifold pressure to forty inches, and close up rapidly into the 2-2 position. As you slide into tight formation to get the attention of the leader, letting him know that he has a new wingman, you remember that Captain Petersen is in this 2-1 position. He recognizes you. There's a friendly hand gesture, and you slip out into the loose,*

* *Wings God Gave My Soul*, written by Joseph W. Noah and published by Charles Baptie Studios, Annandale, Va. in 1974, gives an excellent account of Preddy's combat career.

flexible combat formation.

"You drank green French beer with your element leader after the mission the night before last. You've flown a lot with him, and are confident of his judgment. You're proud to be his wingman and feel an added sense of responsibility because of it.

"On course for Gabes, you begin the slow tactical weave back and forth over the B-25's. This weave will increase in tempo as the target and danger of attack approach, until it is violent but coordinated shifting of each four-ship flight from one side of the bombers to the other, all the while covering their most vulnerable area—to the rear and above.

"The thought runs through your mind that this is an odd place to be sitting—you're 5,000 feet up, in a comfortably warm cockpit, moving at 225 mph toward someone who wants to kill you. This prompts a look over your gondola nose at the top two gun barrels jutting into the slipstream. You know there are two more below those, and nestled in the center of the four fifties is a cannon. One explosive shell from that cannon will down an aircraft.

"You jump. No gunsight! A quick twist of the rheostat shows it to have been turned too

dim to show up in the daylight. Now it stands out well, a solid orange circle with a pipper in the center. Good! A water pistol would be as good in aerial combat as a plane without a gunsight.

"You are reminded to flick on the small switch on the panel marked 'guns.' The two black buttons under your right thumb and forefinger are now 'hot.' Better watch how you hold the column with your right hand.

"You burn every landmark below into your memory. You might get caught alone and have to come back 'on the deck' where navigation is much more difficult. You might even have to walk back—or maybe die of thirst in that waste down there.

"Your mind goes back to the dirty Arab woman who does your laundry. Will she have it by tomorrow? Wait! Where's the fourth plane in number three flight? Didn't see him leave. Watch yourself and be careful, he could have been a Kraut coming in instead of a friend leaving.

"At noon the Tebessa Mountains are falling behind, and with them the dismal cloud that cloaks their environs. The warm sun sparkles through the plexiglass canopy, and for a mo-

(USAF)

Captain Richard A. Peterson, USAF (15.50): Captain Peterson, kneeling second from the left in the front row, flew with the 364th Squadron of the 357th Fighter Group in the ETO. He is from Alexandria, Minnesota. In this photo he was visiting with a B-17 bomber crew shortly after an escorted bombing mission to the Ruhr Valley.

ment you forget that this marvelous thing in which you sit enjoying the beauties of the world below can also be a greased runway to hell.

"You check your map. There's the Gulf of Gabes ahead. The map goes back into your knee pocket and you pull the zipper shut. Everything must be secure for combat.

"The tempo of the weave is increasing. You're twisting your neck as far as it will go. The sun is at nine o'clock high, and you squint at it through your spread fingers. No 'bogies.' Captain Pete is wrapping in tighter on the outside of the weaves now and you have to be on the ball to stick with him.

"The coast is under your nose. You look down and see streaks of dust below the formation, and another batch of these streaks over to the north. Airfields. Those are fighters taking off in abreast formation.

"The bombers are turning on the bomb run. You're losing Captain Pete—manifold pressure forty-five inches—you increase the rpm from 2,200 to 2,600—now you close up nicely on your leader. Perspiration pours down your ribs from under your arms, the shirt, dress shirt, flying suit and leather jacket are soaking wet in the middle of your back and armpits. Both your thin pigskin gloves are sodden, but your experience has shown that this hide hangs to the wheel well when wet.

"You're cranking your head 'round for a glimpse of the fighters who'll soon be up to try and nail you. You glimpse bombs drifting down from a trio of B-25's. Good! Now the formation can pick up some speed. The oil temperature's too high now. You flick the oil cooler flap switch to side open and jam the coolant valves forward.

"You're headed homeward, but why don't the damned bombers put their noses down? Let's have a little more speed. Let's get the hell out of here before we're jumped.

" 'Eight o'clock high!' blasts in your ears from the phones. Your head yanks around to left and right. Damn it, there they are . . . little sharpened sucker sticks with an afterthought wing. 109's, eight of them. They're climbing hard, will be going like hell when they come through.

"You reach down and snap the two fuel selector valves to 'reserve.' Up goes the tank release switch. You push the button, and there's a surge upward as you lose 500 pounds of tank and gasoline. The sleek, teardrop

tanks tumble awkwardly earthward in a shower underneath the whole P-38 formation.

" 'Here they come' hits you from both sides of the head. You see them, you're on the other side of the formation from the attack. The 109's have their pencil noses pointed down in a steep dive. Our left flight breaks into them.

" 'Timber—four o'clock high!' Hell. That's my side of the formation. Pete slams in full right rudder and aileron. His plane snaps over into a vertical bank. He hauls the column into his stomach and the 38's tail sinks into a blackout turn. Then you're right behind him, and as you sneak a glance through the top of your canopy you glimpse three 109's with the leading edges of their wings winking flame from their guns. Two of them are winking at you. The 109's whip through and under like comets, and you complete your turn just short of a high-speed stall.

"Your turn puts you and Pete behind the formation. You're now tail-end Charlies and you both hasten to catch up. Rpm levers are jammed to the stops. Throttles are shoved through the stops. Manifold pressure climbs to an engine-torturing sixty-five inches. The engines are way beyond their limits, but you have to have the power.

"Garbled warnings pour through your radio. Three 109's come drilling down from four o'clock high. You press your mike button to warn Pete. He doesn't answer. You yell to him to break right as the 109's come in. You feed in right rudder and aileron fast and suck the stick back. You know that Pete hasn't heard you and this is the only reason for abandoning your element leader. One 109 is ahead of you, firing at Pete and about to cross your bow. You clinch both buttons. The first belch of the four fifties and the 20mm cannon seems to stop your thirty-eight dead in the air. Then the guns settle down to a steady hammering.

"The 109 slips through your lethal stream and disappears below your nose. You continue turning tightly until the Germans behind you slide over the top. You reverse your turn rapidly on the top to prevent being left too far behind. You're on your back and hauling your nose down hard. Through your canopy top, looking down at the ground now, you don't see Pete. Maybe he broke with you and completed the turn. No, no, you argue with yourself, he wouldn't do that, he'd know better.

"You keep her nose down to pick up speed as you flash above the desert. You're all alone.

'What in hell do I do if I'm jumped now?' you think. You roll your head and eyes, checking the whole sky. There's another 38 below you. Must be Pete! Both his engines are smoking.

"You dump your column forward and the nose plunges down. You slam up into your belt and your head thumps against a rib in the canopy. A clump of dried mud from the floor floats oddly up in front of your face. As you dive, you get a good view of the ground 8,000 feet below and of the whole battle. Two pillars of black smoke billow up from the desert brush. You wonder if they are 38's.

"The main part of the squadron is a mile ahead, and still beating off the 109 attacks. You see one 38 half a mile ahead and well below the rest. He's going down, with the white smoke from the prestone system streaming behind him. The wings are turning slowly one over the other and the tail is washing around sloppily. You think of the boy slumped over the column.

"As you roll up behind Pete he snaps into a left bank. You see that a 109 has tried a long-range cannon shot on the rear of the formation far ahead. Pete closes in and the German pilot doesn't see him until it is too late. Pete comes in behind him and the German makes a mistake. He tries a tight climbing turn to shake you and Pete. The German hasn't learned that a 38 will turn inside him at any speed.

"Pete's guns start pumping and his withering fire takes its toll. The 109 pilot tries to squeeze a little more out of the turn and snaps uncontrollably. One and a quarter turns later the German recovers on his back, dives out in a split arse and Pete ceases fire.

"You watch the 109 as he begins his pullout. There's a livid yellow flash, and all that's left of him is a black ball of smoke, like a flak burst.

"Pete slams tight right and loses you. Just as you get tipped into the turn, a 109 shoots over the top of Pete and one streaks past your tail in a steep dive. Pete reverses his turn and banks back toward course. This is your chance to catch up on him by 'cutting across the pie,' but as your tired right arm forces the wheel up, you catch a glimpse of something disappearing under your right wing. You reverse the bank, and there's a 109 closing behind Pete and leaving a trail of black powder behind. Perfect! He's lined up for an eighty-degree deflection shot for you.

"You've got to hurry, or the Kraut will have Pete bored in. The radio's clogged, so you can't warn Pete. You go into a left bank and find the 109 in your gunsight ring. Back on the stick and the pipper pulls ahead of the German. He's following the pipper nicely. But

HARD TO SPOT
Mottle camouflage on this Me-109 fighter from JG-27 in North Africa makes the aircraft difficult to spot against the desert floor. Empennage and underside of wings were usually painted light blue to make aircraft equally hard to see against the African sky from below.

(Constable Collection)

(Combat Pilots Asso.)

TRIO OF ACE AMERICANS

General Felix M. Rogers (center), himself a 9th Air Force ace in Europe in WWII with seven victories, is flanked by two other distinguished aces. On the left is Colonel Frances S. Gabreski, America's top-scoring living ace with 34.5 victories in WWII and Korea. On the right, the USAF's first and only pilot ace of the Vietnam conflict, Captain Steve Ritchie with five victories over the MiG-21. All three are now retired from the USAF.

whoa! The pipper is sitting right on Pete's canopy. You'll be shooting directly at Pete.

"You won't hit Pete because there's no 'lead' on him. You hesitate a moment to quickly query the laws of motion and relativity in your head. And hope they're still in force as you clamp both black buttons. Again the initial burst jars the 38's whole airframe.

"You follow the 109 round the bend as the guns hammer. He sits in position as though you have him chained to the pipper. Flashes pepper along the upper surface of the 109's wing. The flashes sparkle and crackle all over the German's canopy as the incendiaries appear to explode on contact. Shrouded in white smoke, the 109 falls off your pipper, and you release the buttons and fall in behind Pete.

"The 109 goes into a steep spin, belching thick black smoke. You can't follow him down, or even watch him, you've been too long already without sweeping the sky with your eyes. Unless Pete happens to see the German crash, it will go into the books as a 'probable.'

"Magically, the 109's have gone and the sky is clearing up. Everyone is weaving over the bombers protectively. The radio is silent and you wonder if it is out of commission. You count the 38's. There are five missing.

"You settle down to escort the bombers, your mouth feeling like one of those dry wooden paddles that the doctors use. You snap the right side of the mask off the helmet and fish out your pipe from the knee pocket.

Tobacco? Damn it, it's in your shirt pocket under the chute buckle, under the flight suit. Five minutes later, when you are half undressed and finally have fished out the tobacco, it's sodden with sweat.

"You stuff it in the bowl and light up anyway. It doesn't burn worth a damn, but it tastes good. You're tired and time drones easily away. When the bombers split off for their field, you begin looking for the half-green slush hole that your aircraft calls home. The peeloffs look tired as you moan over the strip at 300 mph.

"On the pad, the crew chief is waiting. He spots you in, the engines are cleared and the props suddenly transform themselves from shimmering discs into sharp knife blades. You heave yourself out, and while you walk to the interrogation center a lone 38 roars over the field, a jagged hole gaping in his horizontal stabilizer. 'Lucky boy,' you think to yourself as you realize what the 20mm cannon might have done to him and his machine.

"Then Captain Pete grabs you and all but kisses you with excitement because you knocked the 109 off his tail. 'But I thought sure as hell you were going to shoot me down,' he says. The formal scoring sobers you a little. Four bombers and a 38 are gone, maybe more.

"Then the tension slowly ebbs. By evening the adrenal pit in your stomach is gone and your hand is steady again. Steady enough at least to hold another glass of green beer with Captain Pete."

Gerald Rounds was born in Imlay City, Michigan, on 26 April 1921, and shot down five German aircraft while flying eighty-two combat missions in P-38 aircraft. He saw action from December 1942 until September 1943, engaging in combat over Africa, Sicily and Italy, with the 12th Air Force.

If young fighter pilots in World War II had a common dream, it was to be an ace overnight. Eighth Air Force Captain William H. Allen USAF, of Los Angeles and Long Beach, California, made this dream a staggering reality in one of the most unusual feats in the history of fighter aviation. He became an ace in *one mission,* with five victories in just a few minutes on 5 September 1944.

Modest in the manner of many of the aces, Captain Allen provides a terse explanation for his success.

"I got into the middle of a large group of German aircraft, and was able to chase them at will. I believe the pilots were relatively inexperienced, because their evasive action was ineffective." With those few words, Captain Allen dismisses his rare distinction among America's fighter aces. Allen currently lives in Oklahoma City, Oklahoma.

As any veteran combat pilot will testify, one of the cardinal sins of aerial combat is to forget about the enemy's friends. "Just as you have a wingman, so has the enemy. Just as you have squadron mates who are never far away if you keep your wits about you, so has the enemy. Just as you can turn toward these mates and have them take the leech off your tail, so can you be sucked into a similar trap by the enemy you are pursuing." So might any fighter leader of World War II have lectured his fledglings.

In the dynamic rough and tumble of aerial combat, the fighter pilot was often lucky enough to find an enemy who had forgotten everything except his target. Such an enemy was vulnerable. Major Robert M. Becker of Shattuck, Oklahoma, and Los Angeles, California, tells a story of such an incident in

DEFEAT IN THE AIR

This FW-190 fighter runs afoul of machine gun fire from the 8th Air Force fighter near Kassel, Germany in WWII. The sequence of gun camera frames shows the German machine being lined up, taking hits and then spouting flame prior to heading down to final impact. —

(USAF)

his combat career, where target fixation seemed to be an epidemic amongst his foes.

"On Memorial Day, 1944, I was on a sweep deep in the heart of Germany when we met a large formation of fighters that were picking away at a group of Fortresses. Luckily, I found myself in good position to attack a twin-engined Me-410, whose pilot was really intent on the B-17 in front of him.

"The job took only a matter of seconds. As I pulled off him there was another Me-410 in my sights, also oblivious to everything but the 20mm cannon fire he was pouring to the Fortress in front of him. A quick burst and he was aflame. With two down I felt it was time to pull up and get the sweat out of my eyes, but there was number three up ahead. Once again the German pilot was hammering the Forts and not watching his tail. It seemed incredible.

"Lest I commit the same error as my victims, I took a quick look to clear my own tail. Then I got as close to this German as I could and let go with all six fifties. That put an end to him and to my own perfect day."

Major Becker is credited with seven victories over the Germans while fighting with the USAAF's 362nd Fighter Squadron in the ETO.

Some emphasis has been laid in this book on the importance to a fighter pilot of the knack of shooting at a moving target from a moving platform, all movement being in three dimensions. Some American pilots mastered this knack, although they were few in number. If they were also great pilots, they were almost certainly headed for big scores, unless they themselves were shot down, perhaps by one of the many outstanding German pilots who had made themselves masters of the difficult art of air-to-air shooting.

Colonel Walter C. Beckham of De Funiak Springs, Florida, was one of the American aces with outstanding shooting skill. He shot down eighteen German aircraft in less than six months of combat with the 353rd Fighter Group. Beckham was undoubtedly on his way to new records for American aces when misfortune struck on 22 February 1944.

"We were returning to base after fuel shortage had forced us to terminate our bomber escort mission. Our great 353rd Group Commander, Glenn Duncan, was leading the Group, and leading my 351st Squadron in do-

ing so. I followed him, leading the second section of eight planes.

"He spotted an airplane landing at a field that I later learned was Ostheim. In typical style he immediately dived down and hit the now taxiing FW-190. He made what was for me a fatal remark—'There are lots of them down here.' I had circled at maybe 15,000 feet, and had seen six or seven planes on the ground, but figured they were probably dummies. I had been 'had' before this way, diving down to shoot planes on the ground, only to see as I passed a few feet above that their canvas wings were drooping.

"This time I was convinced that Glenn would be close enough to spot dummies, and I decided that these must be the real McCoy. They were. On diving down to attack with wingman George Perpente and element leader Frank Emory, I was hit by something when I was still at 4-5,000 feet altitude—long before I began firing.

"In firing at ground targets, one always began at long ranges, conversely to chasing a flying aircraft. I felt and heard this hit. I sprayed the several planes on the ground, which I'm pretty sure were FW-190's, while the field lit up with tracer, muzzle flashes and shellbursts as the German flak lashed back. I could see the 190 that Glenn had hit now burning on the runway. A white-suited gent was spraying the blazing wreck. I tried for a moment to bend my plane around and hit it again—and perhaps the fireman who might be needed elsewhere. I couldn't turn sharply enough.

"Smoke is belching from my engine. But it still runs. I cut off the fuel—coasting—no help. Woods are northward, England is westward. I am in no trouble if my engine keeps running, and I ask my friends to proceed on home. They can't help me with my fire, they ought to be heading for England, not to that forest country to the north.

"I unfasten the seat and shoulder belts and run the canopy back. I'm hoping for the smoke to go away, while ready to bail out fast. Where there's smoke there's fire? Whoever said that is damned right. Here comes flame popping up between the rudder pedals.

"I'm down well under a thousand feet. There's no question about what to do. Let's do it. I stand up in the seat and try to dive out of the left side of the cockpit. I'm stuck! What the hell is holding me? Parachute strap, belt

tangled, what? Where? I tug and feel around but I can't budge. Time to do a little thinking.

"I sit back down. I jam the stick forward with my right foot. Departing the cockpit as she plunges down I feel a bump, but it doesn't hurt. I make a joke that I have 'ejected' myself—this before ejection seats were invented!

" 'Lucky, lucky, lucky,' I say to myself as I pull the ripcord on my parachute. 'Worry about it opening? Why should I?' I tell myself. You just got out of a scorching cockpit, face pink from the heat, eyelashes and eyebrows singed. My chute blossoms. I jar upright. 'No Purple Heart,' I tell myself. My 'Little Demon' hits the ground below me with a gout of fire. I could have been aboard.

"I slip the chute just once, intending to miss landing in a line of trees beside a roadway. This action is just enough to land me in a tree top. More luck follows as I miss any branches with my body and go slipping through unharmed. The chute catches and suspends me nicely about two to three feet above the ground. Perhaps now my troubles are just beginning.

"A German civilian crowd assembles. I catch the word 'schweinhund' often. One of them has a long switchblade knife. Before hostilities open, the police from nearby Opladen arrive and take me to their pokey."

Colonel Beckham spent the rest of the war in Stalag Luft III at Sagan, and at Moosburg. He was liberated by Patton's 14th Armored Division on 29 April 1945. Beckham would prefer to forget the mission on which he was downed, but there is one he does remember, a case of lightning inspiration under stress.

"I was attacking an Me-109. On overshooting him, it suddenly occurred to me that a barrel roll would put me back in firing position. It did. The puzzle to me has always been why this idea should suddenly occur in the excitement of a fight, and not during leisurely thought on the ground."

Walt Beckham lives today in Albuquerque, New Mexico.

Another of the top-notch aces of the ETO was Lieutenant Colonel Duane Willard Beeson of Boise, Idaho. Filled with a great sense of adventure, Beeson enlisted in the RCAF in 1940 when he was only nineteen years old. He later transferred to the 71st Eagle Squadron in April of 1942 and to the USAAF in September of 1942.

Beeson flew Hurricanes, Spitfires, Thunderbolts and Mustangs in combat, which represented a fair range of fighter aircraft types. He shot down 17.33 aircraft, but was himself another victim of German flak in a low-level mission. He crashed and was taken prisoner, spending the final thirteen months of the war in Stalag Luft I at Barth, Germany.* At the time he was shot down, Beeson was in a neck-and-neck race with Captain Don Gentile for the ETO fighter pilot top score.

Neat and meticulous in his dress, clean-cut, dark-haired and handsome, he epitomized the fighter pilot hero of World War II. He was a Lieutenant Colonel at twenty-six years of age. The Citation to his Distinguished Service Cross gives insight into his qualities and skill.

"For extraordinary heroism in action with the enemy, 29 January 1944. Captain Beeson, while leading a flight of P-47 aircraft escorting bombers attacking Frankfurt, Germany, led his flight and his squadron down to engage enemy fighters harassing a formation of heavy bombers. As his squadron dived to the attack, Captain Beeson observed six enemy aircraft coming down on his squadron from above. Aware of the immediate danger to his squadron, accompanied only by his wingman, he turned into the oncoming aircraft. During the turn, an enemy fighter scored strikes on his tail-plane, impairing the operational efficiency of the aircraft. Despite this, and an unfavorable tactical position, he pressed home his attack against odds of three to one. The daring and vigor of his action scattered the opposing aircraft and permitted his squadron to proceed to the aid of the bombers. In combat ranging from 15,000 feet to 200 feet, Captain Beeson succeeded in destroying two of the enemy, and his heroism no doubt saved many fighters and bombers from damage and possible destruction. The unselfish bravery of Captain Beeson reflects great credit upon himself and the Armed Forces of the United States."

Beeson's tactical methods were along classic lines. Like the RAF's Douglas Bader, he had carefully studied the tactics of the great World

---

*Detailed accounts of Colonel Beckham's and Colonel Beeson's adventures from shootdown and capture, through interrogation and incarceration in a Stalag Luft, will be found in author Toliver's book, *The Interrogator* (Aero Publishers, 1978), the full story of Germany's Master Interrogator of the fallen American fighter pilots in the ETO, Hanns-Joachim Scharff.

War I pilots. He believed in keeping plenty of speed in his bounces. "The aircraft with speed has the initiative, because speed can be converted into altitude," said Beeson. He also had his own ideas about overshooting an enemy. "I think it's a good thing," he said. "Hold your fire until within range and clobber him in the last instant before you must break away. It's sorta like sneaking up behind and hitting him with a baseball bat." This same tactical approach was the key to the success of Germany's Erich Hartmann, the greatest fighter pilot of all time.

A brilliant officer and pilot, Lieutenant Colonel Beeson remained in the USAF after World War II. In one of those strange quirks of destiny, Beeson passed away on 13 February 1947, from a brain tumor while on the way to Walter Reed Hospital. He is buried in Arlington National Cemetery. His unfortunate loss was typical in a way of many fighter pilots who, surviving several years of imminent death in the skies, returned to die in the United States in automobile accidents, falls, freak aircraft crashes or from ill-health.

Lieutenant Colonel Louis Benne of Harrison, Pennsylvania, flew P-38's with the 49th Squadron of the 14th Fighter Group in the Mediterranean area, and is credited with five aerial victories. Benne thought he "had it made"when he was scheduled for what appeared to be a milk run on his 52nd mission. Due for rotation, he felt sure it would be his last mission. It was. The only problem was that Benne did not rotate back to the United States.

"Although it was to be a milk run, we were awakened early and there was the usual rush to dress, get breakfast and get to briefing. My tour was actually over, as the rule was fifty missions and you went home.

"We were providing close escort for heavies attacking Petfurdo, Hungary. Numerous groups would attack from different directions, dispersing the Luftwaffe's counter effort.

"We were to cover the area north of the target, the most likely place for enemy action, and I felt uneasy at the briefing. I was leading the squadron and my own flight was very low on experience. The other three pilots had less than ten missions between them.

"Over the target aircraft were called out at

Anxious moments at Debden:
Standing on the control tower balcony at RAF Station Debden in England, the British Minister of War Production, Honorable Donald Nelson (civilian clothes) watches as heavily laden USAAF P-47 Thunderbolts take off on an escort mission to Germany. At left is Lt. Colonel Chesley G. Peterson (7.0) and on the right is Brigadier General Frederick L. Anderson.   (USAF)

*nine o'clock and six o'clock positions, and I
radioed the squadron to drop belly tanks. The
enemy consisted of about fifty Me-109's and
FW-190's. 'This'll be interesting,' I thought to
myself. 'Fifty against fifteen P-38's.'*

"*We were soon in the thickest battle I had
experienced. I found myself firing at an Me-
109, got some hits and continued on around. I
then noticed I was alone. Later I found out my
number two man had trouble dropping his
tanks and kept going down 11,000 feet before
getting rid of them. Number three and four
followed him, leaving me at 22,000 feet attempting to join the rest of the squadron.*

"*I saw an Me-109 making a pass at another
flight. I dove down and commenced firing
from approximately five hundred yards to one
hundred yards, and from thirty degrees to
dead astern. I registered fatal hits and saw the
enemy burst into flames. I turned toward the
squadron again and found myself on the tail of
another 109. I fired short bursts, and began to
get angry at myself for not registering a fatal
hit. Pieces of the canopy flew off the 109 when
I myself was hit by another Me-109 behind
me.*

"*My right engine was shot out, the instrument panel shattered and the left engine was
burning. I was also hit in the shoulder by fragments of a 20mm shell which exploded in the
cockpit.*

"*I snapped my airplane into a spin and had
to leave it due to the fire. I bailed out and was
captured by the enemy shortly afterward. The
pilot who shot me down buzzed me a few times
on the ground and later visited me in the
hospital in Budapest. Through an interpreter
he told me that I was not as fortunate as the
pilot I was shooting at when he shot me down.
He had bailed out and was flying again. He
also told me that I was his thirteenth
American victory, and that he had been flying
Me-109's for six years.*"

Almost a year in prisons left Colonel Benne
with the impression that his 52nd mission was
the morning he should have "stood in bed."*

Historians have little doubt that the almost
incredible bungling of the Me-262 jet decisively assisted the Allies in winning the air war
over Europe. The appearance of this
revolutionary machine caused consternation
among the Allied pilots. With a top speed of
well over 500 mph and armed with the lethal
punch of four 30mm cannon, the Me-262 was
the kind of weapon that has turned the tide in

wars of the past.

A comparable example of a lost military opportunity is hard to find. When these magnificent aircraft were placed in the hands of Germany's great aces, they were a devastating
weapon. Tangling with the Me-262 in the
greatly inferior Mustang and Thunderbolt
called for exceptional skill from the American
pilots, many of whom were able to shoot down
the jets.

Colonel George F. Ceuleers of Georgetown,
Colorado, is among the pilots who downed an
Me-262 while flying a Mustang. Colonel
Ceuleers served with the 364th Fighter Group
in the ETO and shot down 10.5 German aircraft. Like many of America's airmen, Colonel
Ceuleers is not reluctant to discuss his experiences, and he is naturally proud of his
triumph over the Me-262. The authors pieced
the story together from combat reports, newspaper accounts and German versions of the
incident.

Colonel Ceuleers had already flown a successful mission protecting a B-17 strike
against Hamburg. His formation was
homebound when Ceuleers spotted a formation of Liberators going in to hammer
Hanover. Flying above an overcast, the Libs
were having a rough time with eight German
jets, which were slashing back and forth
through the slow-moving American bombers
with little opposition.

While Ceuleers watched, one of the German
jets knocked down two of the Liberators on
one pass with deadly bursts of its four 30mm
cannon. Ceuleers immediately decided to go
to the aid of the embattled bombers.
Disregarding the speed advantage of approximately 150 mph which the jet had over the
Mustang, the American flight leader took his
four P-51's into position for a head-on attack
at 29,000 feet.

After the first successful attack, the victorious 262 broke off the action. The German
pilot "poured the coal" to his machine,
slanting his fast fighter downward for a hole in
the clouds. Ceuleers saw he was being outdistanced, and decided not to try to beat the
German for the cloud opening. Instead, he
shoved the Mustang's stick forward and led
his flight down through the overcast to intercept the jet. The race for the kill was on.

* Colonel Benne lives in Scottsdale, Arizona, as this is
written.

For 250 miles the German and the American raced over the German countryside, the jet marginally faster but the Mustang in the hands of a very determined pilot. The Mustang's manifold pressure shot up to seventy inches, nine inches in excess of the maximum allowed for war emergency power. Ceuleers kept going down. In level flight, he would have done nothing more than inhale the jet's exhaust fumes, but because of the overcast, the German pilot was loath to fly instruments. He played into Ceuleer's hands, for diving combat suited the American perfectly against the sleek German jet.

Because of its laminar flow wing, the Mustang could dive with almost any aircraft. Most World War II wings reached compressibility more quickly than the Mustang's, at which time a bubble developed in the air flowing over the wings. The aircraft would then become unstable and fall out of control.

For twenty minutes the two pilots raced, with Ceuleers slowly gaining. Little did Ceuleers know of the problem facing the German pilot. One of his Jumo 004 engines had failed and now the Mustang had a slight edge in speed and maneuverability. By now the Mustang's Merlin engine was almost leaping off its mountings, but as the chance for the kill came, Ceuleers poured even more power to the tortured engine. Screaming and howling with seventy-five inches of manifold pressure, the Mustang excelled itself for a few brief moments according to Ceuleers.

At five hundred feet over Leipzig, Ceuleers closed the gap. In full view of the startled and bolting citizenry below, the American poured six hundred rounds of heavy machine-gun fire into the jet. Fire belched from the German's right engine. Then the canopy flew off. The enemy pilot pulled his dying aircraft up sharply and released his safety belt, leveling out so that inertia would pop him clear and let him use his chute. Seconds later the Me-262 dived into the ground and exploded in a gout of flame.

Ceuleers eased back on his throttle and gratefully watched the manifold pressure subside. Expecting to find himself alone in enemy territory, he took a quick look around. Right behind him were the Mustangs of his own flight. They had clung to him throughout the long chase at speeds he believes approached 500 miles per hour.

Colonel Ceuleers flew 103 combat missions.

(USAF)

Squadron Leader Michael Gladych, Pol (10.00): A Polish Air Force pilot who fought in the Battle of Britain, Gladych was assigned to instruct American fighter pilots in combat operations. Attached to the 56th Wolfpack, Gladych soon raised his aerial claimed kills to eighteen, plus eight destroyed on the ground. USAF confirmed ten aerial victories. The RAF reportedly has confirmed 12.0 victories for Gladych prior to his service with the USAAF. If so, he may have 22.0 kills or more to his credit. Today, Gladych lives in the United States and is an American citizen. This photo shows Gladych being decorated at the 56th base of Debden by Brigadier General Auton.

He was awarded the DSC, four DFC's, eleven Air Medals and the French Croix de Guerre. Although his victory over the jet was a classic, on another occasion he destroyed four Me-109's in one mission, a notable feat.

Lieutenant Colonel Donald H. Bochkay USAF is another of the American aces who brought down the Me-262 while flying the Mustang. With 13.83 victories (13 plus .5 plus .33), Bochkay brought down two of the fabulous German jets. He is a pilot who believes in the right amount of confidence as a factor vital to success in aerial combat. "Overconfidence is as destructive as no confidence at all" is the way he summarizes his views.

Bochkay evidently brought the right amount of everything into the air on 18 April 1945, when he ran into an Me-262.

"We flew deep in enemy territory, our mission being a fighter sweep into Prague, Czechoslovakia. Leaving the Blue Section, I spied an Me-262 climbing up toward the bomber track. I was at 32,000 feet with two flights of P-51D's. The German jet was about 12,000 feet under me, flying at a 90-degree angle when he passed me. I called him out and gave the command to drop tanks. I rolled over and firewalled everything I had, 3,000 rpm and around 70 inches of manifold pressure.

"I leveled out on his tail indicating around 500. That would give me a good 150 mph speed edge over him. I ranged him on my K-14 and held off until I was 300 yards behind him. In perfect range, I pulled the trigger. All my shots hit his left jet engine, and about knocked it out of its frame. He split-essed as soon as I hit him and poured full kob to his good engine. Still having speed over the jet, I split-essed right after him. At 18,000 feet we were going straight down when my ship started to porpoise . . . it was hitting terminal velocity, and this was the fastest I'd ever traveled in an aircraft.

"The Me-262 didn't leave me, and as we pulled out on the deck, still going flat out, he blew his canopy and started to get out. As he put his hands on the back of his seat, I let him have another full burst of API. The pilot disappeared into the cockpit and at the same time pushed full left rudder. At the speed we were going, his ship couldn't take it. The right wing snapped off, and then the whole tail. The jet exploded in the air before it hit the ground. I flew over the wreckage, rocked my wings and set course for home base."

Lieutenant Colonel Bochkay flew with the 363rd Fighter Squadron, 357th Group in the ETO. He flew 123 combat missions and his victories include Me-109's, Me-110's, FW-190's and two Me-262 jets. Bochkay retired from the USAF and lives today on Fisher Street in Highland, California.

Wartime letters from fighter pilots to their families are often revelatory of fighter-pilot thinking and attitudes. Lieutenant Grant M. Turley of Aripine, Arizona, served with the 78th Fighter Group at Duxford, and shot down six German aircraft before his death in combat. The following excerpts are from a letter Turley wrote to his mother, Mrs. Wilma F. Turley, and his wife, Katherine Ballard Turley, just twenty-five days before the young ace's final mission:

"February 10, 1944

"I am quite excited, for I finally fired my guns, have been bounced and have done some bouncing all in the same day. The final story was two Me-109's for Lieutenant Turley! We were bounced at 26,000 feet, and I broke (I'm an element leader now) with my wingman and managed to get on the tail of two Me-109's as they made a climbing turn away. They saw us coming and broke for the deck, with us on their tails. I shot one of them going down and then got a couple of short bursts into the other and he crash-landed burning."

Ten days later Turley became Arizona's first World War II ace, and he wrote:

"I am tired—had a mission today and shot down my fifth Hun. I am an 'ace,' so they say. A lot of it has been luck, maybe a little skill. I have dreamed of being an ace, but now that I have succeeded it doesn't seem important any more."

On 6 March 1944, while participating in one of the first daylight missions over Berlin, Turley shot down his seventh German aircraft, only to fall victim to a German airman seconds later. He is buried in the U.S. Military Cemetery, Neuville-en-Condroz, nine miles southwest of Liege, Belgium.

The outstanding combat team of the ETO was undoubtedly the classic Godfrey-Gentile combination, which evoked much historic comment, both Allied and enemy. Captains Don S. Gentile and John T. Godfrey made their historic rendezvous as fighting partners after both had served as fighter pilots with the British forces.

Ohio-born Gentile got into the fray first by joining the RAF in July, 1941. By Pearl Harbor time, he was a Pilot Officer flying combat missions out of England. Transferred to the USAAF in August, 1942, he made his historic connection with Godfrey in the 336th Squadron, 4th Fighter Group.

Canadian-born Godfrey was raised in the United States, and after completing his high school education in Rhode Island, tried to join the USAAF as an aviation cadet. He was rejected. Like many other American aces who were originally rejected by the American forces, or who were washed out during training by inexpert instructors, Godfrey headed for Canada. He was commissioned in the RCAF in October of 1942 and was sent to England. Godfrey transferred to the USAAF in April,

1943, and was an ace before his twenty-first birthday.

Like Bong and Lynch of Pacific fame, Gentile and Godfrey would change positions during a battle, taking it in turns to assault the enemy and protect each other's tails. Winston Churchill called them the "Damon and Pythias of the twentieth century," General H. H. "Hap" Arnold praised them as the greatest combat team of the war, and Herman Goering is alleged to have said that he would gladly give two squadrons for their capture.

The two aces were withdrawn from combat just when they were really getting hot, and sent home to stress the value of teamwork to the American people. The two pilots sold war bonds and were separated when Gentile was assigned to Wright-Patterson Air Force Base as a test pilot.

Godfrey returned to Europe, but things were no longer the same. He was shot down and captured by the Germans, an event which purportedly delighted Goering. Gentile was

not allowed to return to combat, and was kept testing aircraft until well after the end of the war in which he had scored 19.83 aerial victories.

Called "Captain Courageous" by President Roosevelt, the dark-haired Gentile won the DSC, Silver Star and numerous other American decorations. His foreign awards include Britain's DFC. Like his Pacific counterpart, Richard Bong, Don Gentile was killed in a postwar aircraft accident while testing a Lockheed F-80 Shooting Star.

John Godfrey survived his internment by the Germans and two abortive attempts at escape, in either of which he might easily have been killed. He tried a third time. On this occasion, he made his way to the American lines near Nuremburg in April, 1945. As Major Godfrey he was placed on inactive status in January, 1946, and became a Rhode Island lace manufacturer and breeder of racehorses. He is credited with 16.33 aerial victories.

Before the twin financial charms of oil and

(USAF)

TOP USAAF ACES OF PTO AND ETO MEET WITH TOP LEADER

USAAF Commander-in-Chief General H. H. "Hap" Arnold is flanked by ETO top ace Captain Robert S. Johnson (left) and Major Richard Ira Bong, top Pacific Theater ace of the USAAF. Bong had 40 victories, Johnson had 28. Bong flew 200 combat missions and Johnson flew 100. In 1978, Johnson's official tally was reduced to 27 by the USAF, his 26th claim being moved to the "probable" status lacking positive confirmation.

ranching captured Lieutenant Colonel Richard E. Turner of Estes Park, Colorado,* he was a successful fighter pilot with the 354th Fighter Group. He scored eleven victories over the Germans, but almost became a victory in the first fighter escort to Berlin on 16 March 1944:

"The bombers aborted due to weather and a mid-air collision while still short of the target. A gaggle of sixty Me-109's jumped us from five o'clock high, out of the sun, hitting my squadron first. I called for the squadron to break into the Germans and I dropped my combat tanks. My engine quit before I could switch to the main tanks, and as I reached down for the switch, my wingman and the rest of the element thought I had been hit. They left me as my plane dived.

"The engine recovered but my speed was low. As I looked around there was no squadron—but there were four Messerschmitts diving at me from five o'clock high. I chopped the throttle, dropped flaps, skidded to the left and almost stalled. The 109's flashed past, barely missing me. I cleaned up the flaps, opened the throttle and dove after them. I caught up with the Germans and as two winged over and split-essed away, I took the nearest of the remaining two and fired from about three hundred yards.

"Hits sparkled behind his cockpit and at the left wing root. His ammunition in the left wing exploded and the wing snapped off. Canopy and pilot left the German machine right after the wing.

"The second 109 had disappeared—behind me! I broke left, but he stuck, with height, speed and position. Feeling futile, I hesitated, waiting to dive and skid out of his line of fire when he opened up. He must have been out of ammo, because he did a quick wing-over and dove for home without firing. I felt real lucky.

"After the war, commanding the 405th Fighter Group at Regensburg, Germany, I met one Kurt Mueller, who believes, as do I after comparing all the records, that he was the

(Conger Collection)

121st EAGLE SQUADRON INSIGNIA
This insignia of 121st Eagle Squadron was approved personally by King George of England. The 4th Fighter Group inherited the Eagle Squadrons when the USAAF came into the war.

pilot I shot down on that 16th day of March, 1944."

The top American fighter pilot of the Mediterranean Theater was Major John J. Voll of Goshen, Ohio. With twenty-one aerial kills to his credit it is likely that he could have become America's leading ace with a little additional opportunity. He ran up his twenty-one victories in just fifty-seven missions and seven months — an exceptional record for American combat pilots.

Voll shot down his first enemy plane on 23 June 1944, over Ploesti. A scant five months later, with twenty-one aerial victories, he was on his way back to the United States. He well remembers his last mission on 16 November 1944:

"I chased a Ju-88 into a formation of Hun fighters in the Udine area. I got him okay and after five minutes or so of pitched battle, I had shot down two FW-190's, one Me-109, with a 109 and a 190 as probables and two more as damaged. I had all thirteen of them to myself. The confirmed victories gave me the lead in the theater with twenty-one."

To be called "The Whiz" was not an unexpected thing for Major William T. Whisner of the 352nd Group of the 8th Air Force, as it is a nickname he has had most of his life. The

---

*Today, Turner lives in Scottsdale, Arizona. On July 31st, 1976, his son, Drew Turner, heroically sacrificed his own life while warning residents and tourists in the Big Thompson River canyon in Colorado, of an impending flash flood. 139 persons are known to have perished in the flood, but countless others owe their lives to the actions of Drew Turner and a Colorado State Patrolman named Purdy.

truth is, however, that he proved himself to be an absolute whiz, worthy to rank among the all-time great American fighter pilots.

Whisner ran up a string of 15.5 aerial victories in the ETO, and followed these up with 5.5 victories over the MiG-15's in Korea, giving him a total of 21 aerial victories in two wars. He is one of the "magic 7" to become an ace in two separate wars.

Whisner is America's seventh jet ace and is unique among airmen in that he holds three DSC's. From his long combat career, the Whiz best remembers an incident over Belgium in January, 1945:

"As we taxied out on the ice-covered strip for a New Year's dawn patrol, we became involved in Goering's last big air effort. As we neared takeoff position swarms of FW-190's came out of the east with Me-109 top cover. We leapt off right in the face of the 190's, which were flying at about five hundred feet. The commander, Colonel J. C. Meyer, was firing at one of them before his gear was retracted. He subsequently attributed this feat to me, but since he was first off and first to fire, I am crediting this feat to the right man.

"Twelve in number (P-51's), we were soon in a deck-level fight with about fifty enemy aircraft. Thirty seconds after takeoff I was firing into a 190 at one hundred yards range, altitude two hundred feet.

"The 190 fell off on the left wing, hit the ground and exploded. I watched this a split second too long, for a 190 put six 20mm cannon shells into me, temporarily spoiling the fun. I shook loose from him and discovered that my only problem was a little oil on my

windscreen. There were plenty of Jerries left to shoot at, and in the next half hour I managed to knock down another 190 and two 109's.

"All the action took place right over the strip, and the low altitude made the confirmations quick and simple, making the action a fighter pilot's dream. When the action was over, the twelve of us had destroyed twenty-three enemy machines, without loss to ourselves. This was probably one of history's finest dogfights, and it is one that I will never forget."

Successor to Colonel Hubert Zemke in command of the 56th Fighter Group in August, 1944, was Lieutenant Colonel David C. Schilling, America's twelfth-ranking ace with a total of 22.5 German aircraft shot down. During the war, along with pilots like Don Gentile, Bud Mahurin and J. C. Meyer, Schilling got the full glare of publicity.

Worth recording here is that Colonel Schilling is one of the most decorated American fighter pilots, with a full range of awards, both domestic and foreign. The United States awarded him the DSC and one Oak Leaf

*Clusters are awarded in lieu of receiving the medal again. It is called an "oak-leaf cluster" and represents an additional award or awards of the same medal.

Major Charles E. Yeager, USAF (11.50) Cedar Ridge, California. 363rd Squadron, 357th Fighter Group. Five confirmed on 12 October 1944 and four on 27 December 1944. Shown here with the Bell X-1A, Yeager was first man to exceed speed of sound.

(USAF)

(NAA)

The North American P-51 "Mustang"

The German Messerschmitt 109 was considered by most to be the best fighter in the air until the Mustang came along. This is a P-51H model.

Cluster*, the Silver Star and two Oak Leaf Clusters, the DFC with ten Oak Leaf Clusters, and the Air Medal with nineteen Oak Leaf Clusters. The British DFC, the Belgian Croix de Guerre with Palm, the French Croix de Guerre and the Chilean El Merito are just a few of his foreign awards. He was killed in England in 1956 in an auto accident.

A distinguished American fighter ace who epitomized perhaps more than any other American airman the wartime accords between Britain and the United States was Wing Commander Lance Wade of the Royal Air Force. He was a Texan who exuded the fighting spirit for which his home state is justly famed.

Wade joined the RAF in Canada in April, 1941, and was commissioned Pilot Officer on 23 May 1941. Assigned to the 33rd Fighter Squadron in August of 1941, he entered combat with the Desert Air Force in North Africa shortly afterward.

He shot down twenty-five enemy aircraft in aerial combat and destroyed numerous aircraft on the ground. He was awarded the Distinguished Service Order and the DFC with two bars. Wade has passed into history as one of the leading RAF fighter pilots of World War II with an honored place in RAF annals although he is virtually unknown today in the United States. His qualities are best summarized in the citation to his DSO, supplied through the courtesy of the Imperial War Museum:

"Since being awarded a second bar to the Distinguished Flying Cross, this officer has continued to lead his squadron in operations against the enemy in the North African campaign and during the invasion of Sicily and the campaign in Italy. He has destroyed a further five enemy aircraft bringing his total victories to at least twenty-five enemy aircraft destroyed, and others damaged. An outstanding leader and fighter pilot, W/Cdr. Wade's great skill, courage and devotion to

137

31st FIGHTER GROUP STRATEGY

Colonel Charles M. McCorkle, commander of the USAAF 31st Group in the Mediterranean Theater (11.0 victories) and some of his fighter pilots. Left to right: Lt. Robert E. Little, Lt. Walter J. Goehausen (10.0), Captain Leland P. Molland (11.0), Colonel McCorkle, Captain Murray D. McLaughlin (7.0), and Major John J. Voll (21.0).

duty have largely contributed to the high efficiency attained by his squadron."

Wing Commander Wade lost his life over an Allied air base at Amendola, Italy, in the accidental crash of his Spitfire. He was buried in the military cemetery at Termoli on 15 January 1944.

Only eleven Americans in the history of aerial warfare shot down more enemy aircraft than Wade. Like many Americans of World War I who became aces in the service of the British or French, he never transferred to the U.S. forces and is consequently omitted from all official mention in America. Like many other Americans who ran up substantial scores while in the service of the British or French, John Malone, Stanley Rosevear and Frederick Libby being typical examples, Lance Wade ran nowhere in the publicity sweepstakes. This book should help rectify this and other unfortunate historical oversights.

(Toliver Collection)

CRACK SHOT

Colonel Walter C. Beckham, seen here as a captain in this wartime photograph, shot down 18 German aircraft in less than six months of combat with the 353rd Fighter Group.

USAAF Aces of the European Theater of Operations (I)

Lt. Colonel Robert L. Baseler, USAF (6.00)
Westminster, California. Shown here flanked by his P-51 crew chief, S/Sgt. Clement Eckert (left) and his armorer S/Sgt. John Rounds (right), Baseler flew with the 325th Fighter Group in the MTO.

(Baseler Collection)

(Toliver Collection)

Lt. Col. Donald A. Baccus, USAF (5.00): Carmichael, California. 359th and 360th Squadrons, 356th Fighter Group, ETO.

(USAF)

(USAF)

Lt. Louis Benne, USAAF (5.00): Phoenix, Arizona. 49th Squadron, 14th Fighter Group in the MTO. Benne scored a double on 7 April 1944, got a single 24 May and ended his string with another double on 14 June. He was shot down 14 June and resided in Budapest until 5 September, then went to Stalag Luft 3 at Sagan. Later he was moved to Stalag Luft 7 at Moosburg. Benne passed away in 1978.

Capt. Duane Willard Beeson, USAAF (19.33)
The "Boise Bee" from Boise, Idaho flew with the RAF Eagle Squadrons (two victories), then with the USAAF 4th Fighter Group where he added 17.33 additional kills before being knocked down and captured by the Germans. He spent the remainder of the war as a POW at Stalag Luft I. Beeson died of a brain tumor in 1947.

Colonel Donald J. M. Blakeslee, RAF/USAAF (15.50)

Blakeslee scored four victories with the Eagle Squadrons, then added 11.50 more while commanding the famed 4th Fighter Group of the USAAF. Blakeslee came from Fairport Harbor, Ohio, and was one of the finest combat leaders in the USAAF during the early days of WWII.

(USAF)

(USAF)

Major Donald Harlow Bochkay, USAAF (13.83)

Fighting with the 357th Group in the ETO, Bochkay claimed 14.83 victories (14 + .50 + .33) but USAF Study 85 failed to confirm one victory. Born in Ashtabula, Ohio, Bochkay now lives in Highland, California. Two of his victories were over the speedy Me-262 German jets.

Lt. Robert J. Booth, USAF (8.00): Visalia, California. 369th Squadron, 359th Fighter Group. Best day: Three victories on 8 May 1944 over Germany.

(Toliver Collection)

Major John L. Bradley, USAAF (5.00): Shreveport, Louisiana. First two victories with the 59th Squadron and last three with the 58th Squadron, 33rd Fighter Group, MTO.

(Toliver Collection)

(USAF)

Lt. Colonel Lowell K. Brueland, USAF (12.5 WWII + 2.00 Korea = 14.50): Brueland, from Callendar, Iowa, fought with the 354th Fighter Group in the ETO in WWII and with the 51st Fighter Wing in Korea.

(USAF)

Lt. Bruce W. Carr, USAAF (14.00): Satellite Beach, Florida. 353rd Squadron, 354th Fighter Group, 9th AF, ETO. A triple on 12 September 1944, followed by five on 2 April 1945!

(USAF)

Major William E. Bryan, USAAF (7.50)
Ocean Springs, Mississippi.
503rd Squadron, 339th Fighter Group, ETO.
Now retired as a Major General.

(Toliver Collection)

THE SMILE THAT DISAPPEARED

Lieutenant Richard G. Candelaria shot down six German aircraft in the ETO to become an ace, which may account for his smiling visage in this wartime photograph. Flying with the 479th Fighter Squadron, Candelaria wasn't smiling when he was shot down by flak near Rostock in East Prussia, on 13 April 1945. He survived the food in POW camp and after the war became a restaurant owner in California — serving better food than the Germans.

(USAF)

Captain Fred J. Christensen, USAF (21.50): From Watertown, Massachusetts, Captain Christensen cut a wide swath across enemy territory and scored 21.5 to become the third ranking ace of the 56th Fighter Group, the WOLFPACK. S/Sgt. Carl Conner from Wolf Creek, West Virginia, shortly after the pilot had scored six victories on 7 July 1944, congratulates Captain Christensen.

Captain Raymond Charles Care, USAF (6.00): Born at Angola, Indiana but now residing in San Antonio, Texas. Captain Care flew and fought with the RAF 71 Eagle Squadron and the 4th USAAF Fighter Group, flying 104 combat missions. He was shot down on 15 April 1944 and as a POW passed through the Luftwaffe Intelligence and Evaluation Center at Oberursel, interrogated by the famed master quizzer Hanns-Joachim Scharff. Care says that all his combat sorties were routine until that last one on 15 April 1944. In the Korean War, Lt. Colonel Care flew 50 missions as pilot in a B-26 Night Intruder.

(USAF)

(USAF)

Lt. Colonel George Ferdinand Ceuleers, USAF (10.50): The 364th Fighter Group in the ETO boasted eight aces. Top man is Lt. Colonel Ceuleers from Bridgeton, New Jersey and Black Hawk, Colorado. Shown in the cockpit of a Mustang, Ceuleers bagged four enemy fighters on a single sortie on 23 December 1944.

Captain Gordon B. Compton, USAF (5.50): Born in New Orleans, calls Dallas his hometown, but presently lives in Wichita, Kansas. Compton flew with the 351st Squadron of the 353rd Fighter Group to score all his victories.

(USAF)

FIVE DOWN, WWII, ETO

Colonel Merle M. Coons, USAF, of Fountain Valley, California made the service his career after WWII. He downed five enemy aircraft while flying with the 55th Fighter Group, 8th Air Force.

(Toliver Collection)

DAHLBERG, 14 Victories

Wilson, Wisconsin was the hometown of Captain Kenneth Dahlberg, who flew with the 354th Fighter Group in the 9th Air Force in Europe.

(Toliver Collection)

Colonel William Allen Daniel, USAF (5.00)
Daniel, born in Birmingham, Alabama and now living in Alexandria, Louisiana, flew with the 307th and 308th Squadrons of the 31st Fighter Group in the MTO. He eventually became the group commander (4 December 1944 to end of the war). His last victory, on 24 March 1945, was over a Luftwaffe Me-262 jet.

(USAF)

(USAF)

ACE IN TWO WARS

Lt. Colonel George A. Davis was an aggressive and highly capable Texan from Lubbock, who became an ace in both WWII and the Korean War. His seven victories in the ETO gave him priceless early experience of aerial combat. He downed 14 enemy aircraft in Korea for a lifetime tally of 21 victories. He was shot down in a fighter battle where the odds were six to one against him. Davis was awarded the Congressional Medal of Honor posthumously. His WWII combat was with the 364th Squadron, 348th Fighter Group.

(USAF)

Captain James E. Duffy, USAF (5.20)
Duffy, who lives in North Caldwell,
New Jersey, scored his victories in the
ETO flying with the 354th Squadron of the
355th Fighter Group.

(USAF)

First Lt. Urban L. Drew, USAF (6.00)
Lt. Drew was the first American to score
a "double" against the German Me-262 jets.
He caught up with them on 7 October 1977.
He was assigned to the 375th Squadron,
361st Fighter Group in the ETO. Originally
from Detroit, Drew now lives at
Datchet-Slough, England.

Captain Ernest C. Fiebelkorn, USAF (9.00): Lake Orion, Michigan. 77th Squadron, 20th Fighter Group, 8th AF, ETO. He was the top ace of the 20th Group. He was, perhaps, the first pilot to lose his life in the Korean War. USAF records show that he shot down Luftwaffe jet ace Walter Nowotny (258 victories) on 8 November 1944. (USAF)

144

(USAF)

Major Benjamin H. Emmert, Jr., USAF (7.00): In WWII Emmert flew with the 318th Squadron of the 325th Fighter Group and scored six aerial victories before he was shot down by small arms fire at Debrecen, Hungary, 1 September 1944. On bailout, he hit the tail of his plane and spent many months in hospitals in Debrecen, Budapest and Meiningen, Germany. In Korea with the 4th Fighter Wing, Emmert added a MiG-15 to his tally, making it 7.00. He lives in Tempe, Arizona, but was born in Erwin, Tennessee.

(Toliver Collection)

Captain Harry E. Fisk, USAF (5.00)
Colorado Springs, Colorado. 356th Squadron, 354th Fighter Group, 9th AF, ETO. The 356th shot down 156 enemy aircraft. Fisk helped by getting a triple on 29 October 1944.

(USAF)

Captain Norman J. Fortier, USAF (5.83): This Barrington, New Hampshire pilot flew with the 355th Fighter Group.

Colonel Glenn E. Duncan, USAF (19.00)
Duncan, from Houston, Texas, scored his kills fighting with the 353rd Fighter Group. Some time prior to D-Day, Duncan formed a special strafing unit called "The Buzz Boys" which was extremely effective against military targets on the Continent. Shot down on one of these sorties, Duncan was an evadee in Germany, Holland and Belgium but returned safely to England.

(USAF)

(Toliver Collection)

ROW OF CROSSES

Captain Robert J. Goebel was a dashing young ace in WWII with eleven aerial victories. Goebel is seen here perched on his fighter with the victory marks of a double ace, during his service with the 15th Air Force.

(National Archives)

Major John B. England, USAF (17.50)

Whatever John England was listening to in this photo taken while he was a Flying Cadet in 1943, he must have liked to hear. He learned a lot, too, and became one of the most brilliant of the USAF fighter aces. His combat was with the 362nd Squadron of the 357th Fighter Group. Pre-destined to become one of the top USAF officers, England crashed tragically to his death in the mid-1950's. He was from Caruthersville, Missouri.

Major Robert William Foy, USAF (15.00)

Pictured here while still a Flying Cadet, Foy flew with the 357th Fighter Group. He is from Oswego, New York.

(USAF)

(National Archives)

Colonel Andrew J. Evans, Jr., USAF (6.00): Evans was a major and a lieutenant colonel during his WWII combat days with the 357th Fighter Group in the ETO. In the Korean War, Colonel Evans was deputy wing commander of the 49th Fighter-Bomber Wing and was shot down by small arms gunfire on 27 March 1953. He was a POW of the North Koreans only six months but was systematically starved and threatened with execution periodically, losing 60 pounds from his normal weight of 148 pounds. He was born in Charleston, South Carolina.

(USAF)

Captain Walter J. Goehausen, USAF (10.00): Issaquah, Washington. 308th Squadron, 31st Fighter Group, 15th AF, MTO.

(USAF)

Colonel Gordon M. Graham, USAF (7.00)
Taft, California.
Colonel Graham, who retired in the rank of major general, fought with the 355th Fighter Group to gain his victories. Today he is an executive with the McDonnell Douglas Corp.

(Toliver Collection)

"CAPTAIN COURAGEOUS"

Captain Don S. Gentile is credited with 19.83 aerial victories in Europe, and was called "Captain Courageous" by President Franklin D. Roosevelt. With John Godfrey, he formed one of the stellar fighting elements of the entire USAAF, rose to major and ended the war covered in glory. He was killed in a flying accident shortly after WWII. Like Godfrey, Gentile was also first an RAF fighter pilot, as indicated by the RAF pilot's wings worn on the right breast of his USAAF uniform. He transferred to the USAAF in September 1942, and was assigned to the 336th Squadron of the 4th Fighter Group.

REJECT WHO MADE GOOD

The USAAF rejected John T. Godfrey as pilot material, so the Canadian-born Godfrey joined the RCAF, was commissioned and went to England as a fighter pilot. Transferring to the USAAF in 1943, he became Don Gentile's wingman and the two cut a swathe through the Luftwaffe, in one of the USAAF's great fighter teams. The onetime reject rose to major in the USAAF before being shot down and interned as a POW. He had 16.33 victories in World War II—not bad for a man evaluated as unsuited to pilot training.

(USAF)

IN ACTION EARLY — 3 September 1939
Lt. Colonel James A. Goodson, USAF, was aboard the British
liner Athena when it was torpedoed off the Irish coast
on 3 September 1939. Goodson joined the RAF in 1940,
and transferred to the USAAF in September of 1942.
He downed fourteen German aircraft before being shot down
over Germany in 1944. Goodson served with the famous
4th Fighter Group in Europe.

(Toliver Collection)

(Toliver Collection)

"HERKY"

Nicknamed "Herky," Major Herschel H. Green is credited with
18 victories over the Luftwaffe, while flying with 325th Fighter
Group of the 15th Air Force. In this wartime photograph,
Green holds an obviously happy canine mascot.

(USAF)

Captain Clayton K. Gross, USAF (5.00): 354th Group. Now
lives in Portland, Oregon.

(USAF)

**Captain Raymond Frederick Harmeyer,
USAF (6.00):** 309th Squadron, 31st Fighter
Group in the MTO. From New Orleans,
Louisiana.

148

(Toliver Collection)

SWASTIKAS AND RISING SUNS

Colonel James H. Howard's colorful war career included acedom with the Flying Tigers (7.33 kills) and with the 354th Fighter Group of the USAAF (6 kills). The aggressive Texan flew in both the big leagues — the Pacific and the ETO — and won the Congressional Medal of Honor.

(USAF-20FBW)

Major James E. Hill, USAF (5.00)
Hill, from Stillwater, Oklahoma, scored his acedom while flying with the 388th Squadron, 365th Fighter Group in the 9th Air Force in the ETO. He has advanced to four star general and is presently commander of NORAD in Colorado Springs.

(USAF)

Captain John H. Hoefker, USAF (8.50)
Captain Hoefker lives in Taylor Mill, Kentucky now. In WWII he flew with the 10 Tac-Recce Group, 15th RCN Squadron in the ETO. He was the first 9th AF reconnaissance pilot to become an ace.

(Toliver Collection)

Lt. Colonel Thomas L. Hayes, USAF (8.50)
Annandale, Virginia. 364th Squadron, 357th Fighter Group, ETO. Hayes retired as a Brigadier General.

(USAF)

Captain Maurice G. Long, USAF (5.50)
Apple Valley, California.
Long flew an early war tour with the 17th Provisional Squadron, 49th Group in the SWPA but scored all his victories late in the war in the ETO flying with the 361st Fighter Group, 8th AF.

(Hess Collection)

Captain Walter J. Koraleski, USAF (5.53): Detroit, Michigan. 354th Squadron, 355th Fighter Group, 8th AF, ETO.

(Letzter)

Second Lt. Otto D. Jenkins, USAF (8.50): Lt. Jenkins, from Kermit, Texas, fought with the 362nd Squadron, 357th Fighter Group in the ETO.

(Toliver Collection)

KIENHOLZ — SIX KILLS

Captain Donald D. Kienholz served in both the ETO and PTO in WWII. He is credited with six victories. Service was with the 1st Fighter Group of the 15th Air Force in Europe, and with 508th Fighter Group of the 20th Air Force in the Pacific.

First Lt. David Wayne Howe, USAF (6.00): Howe, from East Hickory, Pennsylvania, fought with the 334th Squadron, 4th Fighter Group. He joined the RCAF in 1941 and transferred to the USAAF in June 1943.

(Bell Aircraft Corp.)

150

(USAF)

Captain Charles P. London, USAF (5.00): Captain London, now living in Huntington Beach, California, flew with the 78th Fighter Group in the ETO.

(Toliver Collection)

Lt. Colonel Joseph J. Kruzel, USAAF (6.50)
Shalimar, Florida.
Kruzel, shown here in June 1944 briefing the 361st Fighter Group, 8th AF, ETO, scored three victories with the 17th Provisional Squadron in the SWPA, then was sent to the ETO where he added 3.50 more to his tally. He retired in the rank of major general.

(USAF)

Colonel Morton D. Magoffin, USAF (5.00)
Magoffin, originally from Deerwood, Minnesota but now living in Pleasanton, California, flew in the 9th Air Force, ETO, with the 362nd Fighter-Bomber Group. He spent some time in German hospitals in Evreux and L'Hospital de la Pitie', Paris in August 1944.

LIKED THE SPITFIRE
Captain J. Barry Lawler downed eleven enemy aircraft while flying with the 52nd Fighter Group in the 15th Air Force. All his kills were gained in the Mustang but Lawler said his happiest days were flying Spitfires out of Corsica with the British, "strafing up and down the west coast of Italy."

(Toliver Collection)

151

(USAF)

Captain Nicholas Megura, USAF (11.84):
Bridgeport, Connecticut. 334th Squadron, 4th Fighter
Group, 8th AF, ETO.

(USAF)

General Carroll W McColpin, RAF/USAF (8.00): Navato,
California. McColpin was a squadron leader with 71st
and 121st Eagle Squadrons in the RAF, then transferred
to the USAAF and flew with the 404th Fighter Group. He
scored 8.0 with the RAF. He retired as a major general.

Captain Virgil K. Meroney, USAF (9.00)
Pine Bluff, Arkansas. 487th Squadron, 352nd Fighter
Group, 8th AF, ETO. Starting his record with a double on
1 December 1943, Meroney scored another double the next
time out, on 4 December 1944. (Toliver Collection)

(USAF)

Colonel Arthur F. Jeffrey, USAF (14.00): Jeffrey flew in the ETO
with the 434th Squadron, 479th Fighter Group. His hometown
was Picher, Oklahoma, but today he lives in San Jose, California.

NOW A LIEUTENANT GENERAL
Captain George G. Loving made ace with the 31st Fighter Group
of the 15th Air Force in WWII. He is credited with five aerial
victories. The Lynchburg, Virginia man stayed in the USAF,
rose to lieutenant general and presently commands Far East
Air Forces in Japan. (Toliver Collection)

Lt. Colonel John C. Meyer, USAF (26.00): Meyer, from Forest Hills, New York, shot down twenty-four German aircraft flying with the 352nd Group. He added two more to his tally in the Korean War, making it 26. Meyer advanced to four star general and the position of vice chief of staff of the USAF. He died 2 December 1975.

(USAF)

General William W. Momyer, USAF (8.00)
Momyer, from Seattle, Washington, was commander of the 33rd Fighter Group in the MTO. He rose to four star general and was commander of Tactical Air Command. (USAF)

(Toliver Collection)

FIVE KILLS, ETO

Lt. Colonel Jack Oberhansly in a pensive moment at Duxford, England, during his service with the 4th Fighter Group of the 8th Air Force. Oberhansly is credited with five victories, all with the 82nd Squadron of the 78th Fighter Group.

(D.C./ANG)

Colonel Willard Wesley Millikan, USAF (13.00)
Millikan, who advanced to major general, flew with the RAF Eagle Squadron in 1942, then with 334th and 336th Squadrons of the 4th Fighter Group in the ETO. He was a POW of the Germans in Stalag Luft II at Sagan from May 1944 to January 1945 and in Stalag Luft VIIA at Moosburg until May 1945. He died 19 October 1978.

153

Colonel Chesley G. Peterson, RAF/USAF (7.00)

A squadron leader with RAF Eagle Squadron 71, Peterson shot down six German planes. After transferring to the USAAF, he shot down one more plane with the 4th Fighter Group to make it 7.00. Peterson retired as a brigadier general. His hometown was Santaquin, Utah.

(USAF)

(USAF)

Capt. Robert G. Schimanski, USAF (6.00)

Spokane, Washington. 364th Squadron, 357th Fighter Group, 8th AF, ETO.

(USAF)

First Lt. Peter E. Pompetti, USAF (5.50):

Fort Worth, Texas. 84 Squadron, 78th Fighter Group, 8th AF, ETO. Shot down 17 March 1944, POW.

(Toliver Collection)

BRILLIANT

(National Archives)

Captain Harry A. Parker, USAF (13.00):

15th AF, 325th Fighter Group. Parker was killed in action in April 1945. His home was Milford, New Hampshire.

Major George E. Preddy, Jr., flew in the Pacific and in Europe, gaining his greatest fame against the Luftwaffe, flying with the 352nd Fighter Group out of England. One of the quickest and deadliest American aces, Preddy was tragically downed by the ground fire of American troops who were trying to bring down a German plane he was pursuing. Preddy is credited with 26.83 aerial victories. In five minutes on 6 August 1944, Preddy shot down six German aircraft.

Lt. Gerald E. Tyler, USAF (7.00): Sarasota, Florida. 364th Squadron, 357th Fighter Group, ETO. Tyler scored a triple on 18 September 1944.

(USAF)

(Toliver Collection)

FIGHTER ACE TO FOUR STAR GENERAL

Major Felix Michael Rogers, "Mike" to his friends, wrote a great war record in Europe in WWII. He was C.O. of 353rd Fighter Squadron, 354th Fighter Group, 8th Air Force, and is credited with seven kills over the Luftwaffe. After the war, Rogers rose to four star general before his retirement.

Lt. Colonel Dale E. Shafer, USAF (7.00): Shafer, from Waynesville, Ohio, scored his first four victories in the MTO with the 309th Fighter Squadron, 31st Fighter Group. On his second combat tour, he scored three victories in the ETO with the 503rd Squadron of the 339th Fighter Group, 8th AF. One of the finest acrobatic and combat pilots in the entire USAF. Retired as a major general.

(USAF)

(Toliver Collection)

Lt. William J. Schildt, USAF (6.00): San Diego, California. 95th Squadron, 82nd Fighter Group, 12th AF, MTO. Schildt scored a triple on 11 April 1943 which qualified him for acedom.

"They went thataway!" Lt. William R. Perkins (2.00) and Lt. Robert L. Shoup (5.50) of Port Arthur, Texas. They flew with the 356th Squadron, 354th Fighter Group, 9th AF, ETO.

(Toliver Collection)

155

Major William T. Whisner, Jr., USAF WWII/Korea (21.00): Shreveport, Louisiana and Tampa, Florida. WWII, 8th AF, 487th Squadron, 352nd Group (15.50); Korea, 4th and 51st Wings (5.50).

(USAF)

(USAF)

Brigadier General John W. Vogt, USAF (8.00): Annapolis, Maryland. Originally with the 63rd Squadron, 56th Fighter Group, Vogt scored 5.0. With the 360th Squadron, 356th Group, he added 3.0 more to his tally. Rank at that time was major.

(Toliver Collection)

Major John M. Simmons, USAF (7.00) Gadsden, Alabama. 317th Squadron, 325th Fighter Group, MTO. Scored all his victories while still a lieutenant.

(Toliver Collection)

Captain John L. Sublett, USAF (8.00): Midland, Texas. Sublette, flying with the 362nd Squadron, 357th Fighter Group, 8th AF, ETO, started off with a flair on 27 November 1944 when he shot down three Luftwaffe aircraft. He scored two more on the 14th of January, 1945 to make ace, then added two more on the 2nd of March. One more on 20 March made it 8.0 and finis.

Lt. Robert D. Welden, USAF (6.25) Aspen, Colorado. A double on 5 January 1944 and a triple on 25 February and Welden was an ace! 356th Squadron, 354th Group, 9th AF, ETO.

(USAF)

Major Richard E. Turner, USAF (11.00): Scottsdale, Arizona. 356th Squadron, 354th Fighter Group, 9th AF, ETO. Turner was one of the USAF's ablest and most promising fighter leaders, but crippling arthritis forced him to quit flying.

(USAF)

(Toliver Collection)

ACE AND AEROSPACE PIONEER

Lieutenant Colonel Charles E. Yeager became an ace in WWII while flying with the 357th Fighter Group in the 8th Air Force in Europe. He is credited with 11.5 aerial victories. "Chuck" Yeager remained in the service after WWII, became the first man to break the sound barrier and wrote a distinguished record in aerospace pioneering.

(USAF)

Colonel Reade F. Tilley, RAF/USAF (7.00)

Colorado Springs, Colorado. All victories scored while flying with RAF Squadrons 121, 601 and 126. Currently president of Eagle Squadrons Assoc., he has been the motivating force behind a book titled THE EAGLE SQUADRONS— YANKS IN THE RAF, (Ziff-Davis Publishers) authored by Vern Haugland and due out in August 1979.

(Toliver Collection)

RAF AND USAF, WWII

Captain Frederick O. Trafton, Jr., joined the RAF as a fighter pilot in January of 1942, and flew for nine months with the British. Transferring to the USAF, he flew with both the 8th and 15th Air Forces. He shot down five enemy aircraft, and his war adventures include being downed in Yugoslavia. He spent three months evading the Germans before returning to the 31st Fighter Group in Italy.

Wing Commander Lance C. Wade, RAF (25.00)

Broaddus, San Augustine, Texas. Top American ace while flying with the RAF in WWII, Wade commanded 145 Squadron. He was killed in the crash of his Spitfire at Amendola, Italy on 12 January 1944. Wade became an ace flying Hurricanes the first week he was in combat. His 25 victories made him the leading ace of the RAF in the Desert Air Force at the time of his death.

(Imperial War Museum)

157

Some live,
Some die!

Major Paul A. Conger lived to tell about it!
On the first strafing mission over Hamburg, Major Conger took several hits from what appeared to be German 20mm shells. One shot entered the cockpit on left rear of the canopy (top photo). Shrapnel from this hit wounded Conger in the shoulder. Almost simultaneously, another shell holed his right rudder pedal (middle photo), knocking his right foot off pedal. A third hit smashed part of the instrument panel. Squadron-mate Mike Gladych escorted Conger on the 1½-hour flight back to England although Conger never did see Gladych. Bottom photo shows Conger in base hospital awaiting medical care. He was hospitalized three months. Conger is an ace with 11½ victories.

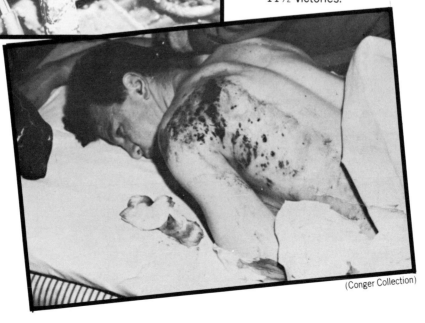

(Conger Collection)

5

USAAF ACES OF THE EUROPEAN THEATER OF OPERATIONS (2)

Amid the grimness and tension of war in the air, there was still room for humor and comradeship. Without the contrast and relief provided by these qualities, life in a World War II fighter squadron would have been too taut even for the strongest men. Sometimes when humor came, it was as riotous as the combat had been grim.

Lieutenant Colonel Henry W. Brown of Dallas, Texas, was the leading actor in a humorous chapter of accidents involving himself and his own squadron commander. Brown was the leading ace in the ETO with 14.20 victories when he was shot down over Germany. He made a forced landing in his crippled P-51 in a pasture. What followed was like a scene out of an Elliott White Springs novel or *The Dawn Patrol*.

Brown's squadron commander, Colonel Charles W. Lenfest of Boise, Idaho, himself an ace with 5½ victories, landed his P-51 in the pasture close to Brown's machine. Lenfest's intention was to throw his parachute away, take Brown on his lap and fly the crowded Mustang back to safety. Lady Luck was unfortunately "out to lunch."

Lenfest's Mustang dug a wheel deep in the pasture mud while making a turn. Realizing his aircraft was hopelessly mired, Lenfest switched off, jumped out and shook hands with the mortified Brown. Arm in arm the two pilots swaggered off down a lane, waving farewell to the rest of the squadron milling helplessly overhead.

As they left the clearing, the two pilots failed to see Lieutenant Al White coming in low over the treetops, flaps and wheels down and ready for a landing. White landed and turned around at the end of the pasture, looking for his CO and flight leader, now long gone from the scene.

The rest of the squadron was now busily buzzing Lenfest and Brown in an effort to get them to turn back down the lane to the pasture. The two pilots failed to get the mes-sage, and Lenfest, infuriated, kept vigorously waving "go home" to his buzzing flock.

Over Al White's radio came the depressed conclusion of his squadron mates. "They don't see you, Al."

Concerned lest he, too, be captured, White gunned his P-51 and joined his buddies overhead for the flight home. Brown and Lenfest walked into internment.

The two-in-one Mustang trick was successfully used when Major Pierce W. McKennon of Clarksville, Arkansas, was shot down near Berlin in March, 1944. McKennon's wingman, Lieutenant George Green of Whittier, California, landed near him. Green dumped out his parachute and dinghy, let McKennon get in first, and then, using him for a cushion, sat in the major's lap and took off. They made it safely home, escorted by the entire 335th Fighter Squadron, and there was a hot time in the unit's Debden mess that night.*

Major McKennon was an ace with twelve aerial victories, and was considered to be one of the best pilots in Colonel Blakeslee's 4th Fighter Group. He was a man determined to

---

*Another Greene, a Captain George B. Greene who became a Major General in the USAF and was stationed at HQ USAF in the Pentagon, Washington, D.C., tells a story of piggyback tests with the P-39 (Bell) in the Southwest Pacific. During the Coral Sea battles, it appeared the USAAF troops stationed in New Guinea might have to abandon their fields at a moment's notice, so every mode of possible transportation was investigated. Benny Greene made a test flight with a P-39. Tiny as the craft was, he squeezed a small mechanic into the area just behind the pilot's seat, took another pilot on his lap, and the three took off on a local excursion just to see if it could be done. Of course, all three were sans parachutes, and there wasn't an inch of spare room in the cockpit of that rear-engined pursuit plane. No doubt, Greene's outfit was extremely happy that they did not have to resort to such extreme measures at that time. There is no doubt, however, that the piggyback rescue or evacuation was accomplished in many types of aircraft during World War II. The Germans and the Japanese also resorted to the extreme of carrying two or more people in a single-seater fighter. On two separate occasions, two Japanese were seen to bail out from Zero aircraft during combat.

be a fighter pilot, despite being washed out at Randolph Field in 1941. He joined the RCAF and switched over to the USAAF in September of 1942. McKennon survived World War II but was killed in 1947 while training a student pilot.

In all there were eleven other Browns beside Henry W. Brown who became American fighter aces in the Second World War. The "Brown Air Force" included a Marine Corps Captain, a Navy Commander, an RCAF Squadron-Leader, and nine USAAF types including Samuel J., who was the top-scoring Brown with his 15.5 victories.

Major Sam J. Brown of Tulsa, Oklahoma, was just ahead of Henry Brown with an ETO score of 15.5 aerial victories. Sam Brown flew with the 31st Fighter Group, which boasted thirty-three aces in its ranks and a total of 571 aircraft destroyed. In such distinguished company, Sam Brown won free acknowledgement as the best all-around fighter pilot in the 15th Air Force. He is remembered to this day by those who flew with him for his standout ability to recognize enemy formations. One of his wingmen says of him: "Sam Brown could recognize the Luftwaffe's outfits and formations better than the Germans' own Adolf Galland."

Another highly successful Brown was Major Quince L. Brown of Bristow, Oklahoma. He is credited with 12.33 aerial victories in the ETO, and late in May, 1944, Quince Brown told pilot friends and newspapermen of one of his sorties in these words:

"We were flying into the sun when I spotted an aircraft quite a distance away that looked like a Mustang. I pulled up ahead just to make sure, and by golly, I got a big surprise as I sailed close over him. It was a 109. I pulled up in a steep chandelle, ran back down on the 109 from behind and gave him a few short bursts from about three hundred yards. As I pulled in closer he still didn't try to evade, and I could see my tracer banging into his wings and tail. Suddenly his nose went down and my shots splashed into the cockpit. He spun and burnt fiercely."

When asked what makes a good fighter pilot, Quince Brown was quick with his answer. "Teamwork! Plenty of teamwork!" He was another of the many outstanding combat pilots who was shot down while groundstrafing over Germany. Irate German civilians who captured this officer killed him a few minutes

(USAF)

LT. HENRY W. BROWN AND LT. GENERAL JAMES H. DOOLITTLE: Lt. Brown, from Dallas, Texas but now calling Sumter, South Carolina his home, talks with General Doolittle following his triple victory over German aircraft on 11 September 1944. Brown spent the last seven months of the war in Europe languishing in Stalag Luft III. Brown is officially credited with 14.2 aerial victories.

after taking him prisoner. His was a sad end, but rage knows no reason.

As a final statistical factor concerning America's World War II fighter aces named Brown, the twelve men accounted for 103.03 enemy aircraft in aerial combat. There were in addition many ground-destroyed machines.

Philosophers are fond of saying that in life things are not always what they seem. For fighter ace John Carder of Red Oak, Iowa, this proved to be the case when he downed what he thought was a Focke-Wulfe 190 over Germany on 23 February 1944. The aircraft was correctly marked with Luftwaffe insignia, and after some aerial hijinks, Carder triumphed over the 190. Later in the day when his camera-gun film was processed and evaluated, Carder was shocked to learn from Intelligence that he had shot down not a FW-190 but a Republic P-47 Thunderbolt. Apparently it was a captured U.S. machine that the Germans were trying out in combat.

While it might surprise any World War II combat pilot to learn he had mistaken the sleek, slender FW-190 for the portly Thunderbolt, Carder's efficiency was not impaired by the incident. He shot down seven German aircraft before being downed himself on 12 May 1944. On his second try, Carder escaped from prison camp in April of 1945.

Colonel Frank J. "Spot" Collins of Breckenridge, Texas, is among the aces who flew in both the Pacific and European Theaters in World War II. A stocky 190-pounder, Collins is a square-jawed, handsome man who has preserved into middle life the quick-thinking toughness that made him an ace. His nickname derives from a white spot about three inches in diameter in his otherwise greying black hair. All nine of his aerial victories were scored in the Mediterranean Theater of Operations. Collins could not isolate any one World War II combat incident in his career as standing out above the others. A combat report of Collins, however, written on 27 May 1943, yields the following excerpt:

"I turned into an Me-109 and became separated from the rest of my flight in doing so. Just then, four 109's jumped me, but I managed to break under and evade them. I saw an Me-109 on one of the P-40's tails, so I turned onto the German's tail. He saw me, turned into me and as we passed head-on, I was so close above him I could see the Heine sitting in his cockpit looking up at me. He had been shooting at me and me at him. As he went by, I turned sharply onto his tail. For some reason, he did not evade. I gave him a long burst and he arched over slowly into a dive and hit the water."

This was Colonel Collins' third aerial victory. After eighty-two combat missions with the 15th Air Force in the Mediterranean area, Collins was sent to the Pacific, where he served with a P-47 outfit near Okinawa.

During a strafing mission, Colonel Collins' Thunderbolt took a Japanese flak hit while howling along just a few feet above the water. Without knowing exactly how it happened, "Spot" recovered consciousness floating in the drink a few hundred yards from the coast of Kyushu. He hid behind a buoy in an attempt to avoid capture by the Japanese, but this effort was to no avail. The Japanese plucked the wounded pilot from the sea and incarcerated him in a bomb shelter without medical attention.

Emaciated and sick, he barely survived to the end of the war. When freed he gradually regained his strength, and in the postwar USAF became Commander of the Tactical Air Command's 31st Fighter Wing in Florida. He retired as a Brigadier General and lives in Tampa, Florida.

Colonel Glendon V. Davis of Parma, Idaho, shot down 7.5 German aircraft while flying with the 357th Fighter Group in England. Shot down himself on 29 April 1944, he managed a grand tour of the underground escape route, finally returning to the 357th on 6 September 1944. Colonel Davis tells a story that intimately involves another unknown American pilot. Thousands of instances exist of one pilot saving the life of another, with the two men going their separate ways and never knowing each other's identity. This story is typical of this timely pilot-to-pilot aid.

"In escorting bombers on a mission to Munich in March of 1944, a box of our bombers some half a mile from my four-ship flight of P-51's called out that they were under attack by a large number of German fighters. Upon reaching them, I saw a P-51 from another group dive down from the bombers, followed closely by two Me-109's who were firing and scoring hits on the American machine.

"With my flight I dove after them, calling to the P-51 to break, break, break, but he continued his near-vertical dive. At this time my entire flight was diving at full throttle. The last glimpse I got of my airspeed indicator showed 475 mph. We drew up on our quarry at approximately 8,000 feet, having started from about 25,000. By firing and scoring hits at extreme range, I diverted one of the Me-109's from the hard-pressed P-51.

"The pursued American aircraft reached deck level and started a circle to the left, followed closely by the remaining Me-109. The other German was holding close above. I joined the circle in the opposite direction, so as to get a head-on shot at the 109, whereupon he broke and with his buddy started to retire.

"Upon straightening out on their tails, I found my four-ship flight in perfect formation on me. As I was preparing to fire on the nearer 109, he wobbled, winged over and went into the ground, evidently as a result of previous hits. I gave the remaining 109 to my wingman, and after a full-throttle chase of some five miles over the treetops, he shot him down.

"This encounter stuck in my mind not just because we got two enemy aircraft and saved one of our own, but because of the perfect teamwork of my entire flight. We went through a full-throttle, near-vertical dive followed by violent maneuvering on the deck, but were still perfectly in formation at the end."

Colonel (then Captain) Davis was one of the P-51's most enthusiastic admirers, as well he might be after this incident which he relates:

"*We were climbing back to the bombers after an attack when I saw five Me-109's coming down through a break in the clouds. We let them get below us and then bounced them from above. On our turn into them, my second element cut inside me and went after the lead three 109's. I singled out the last one and he went for the deck.*

"*While he was looking back at me, his aircraft actually touched the snow-covered ground, but he pulled it back up and kept going. I gave him a burst from three hundred yards, and saw strikes. He cut his engine and began gliding for an open, snow-covered field.*

"*I closed on him, firing all the way, and my bullets riddled his aircraft. Just as I pulled off to avoid colliding, he exploded. Pieces of his machine hit the top and leading edge of my right wing,* smashing it flat.

"*I struggled back up to 29,000 feet and came home by myself. I owe my life to the excellence of American materials and workmanship, as the P-51 was a rugged aircraft. When it first was introduced into World War II it was fast and agile, but its maximum altitude left much to be desired. The P-51B model, however, could really make height and this factor meant we finally had an aircraft that could match either the Me-109 or the FW-190.*"

Courage is rightly esteemed a cardinal quality in the making of a fighter ace. A classic instance of a courageous bluff proving as effective as a battery of machine guns comes from the combat experiences of Lieutenant Colonel George A. Doersch of Seymour, Wisconsin.

After 148 combat missions with the 359th Fighter Group flying Thunderbolts, the then Lieutenant Doersch transitioned to the newly arrived Mustangs in May, 1944:

"*I was at a rest home for a week while the transition was under way, and consequently had flown the Mustang only twice when I went on my first mission in the new aircraft. Escorting 'big friends,' we spotted eighteen FW-190's making a formation pass at a box of the bombers, so we positioned ourselves to be on their tails as they came off the first pass.*

"*As we closed on their tails, I hit a 190 and he went down burning. The remaining Germans split-essed to the deck. I attempted to follow, but as I still had some fuel in my fuselage tank (a critical weight and balance factor in the P-51), my aircraft refused to hold my line of sight properly.*

"*I finally closed and damaged another FW-190 and found in firing at him that all my guns except one had jammed. I lost my quarry trying to clear my guns. Being on the deck and now alone, I began looking for my outfit when I saw an Me-109 coming down nearby in a steep dive.*

"*I pulled in on his tail, lined up closely as he leveled out on the deck and pulled my trigger—all my guns were dead. I overshot him, and as I pulled up beside him he saw me and broke away. I pulled up in a gunnery pass at him and made a photographic pass, then another. After the second photographic pass, for some unaccountable reason the German released his canopy and bailed out.*

"*I went home full of my story, eager to tell the boys of two victories, one with guns and one with bluff. But they turned the tables on me when they told me that when I had lined up the first 190, the rest of my flight had broken into another gaggle of fighters. I had unknowingly engaged all eighteen FW-190's alone. The Germans, not realizing the limited nature of my attack, had turned and fled.*"

Doersch is credited with 10.5 aerial victories. He flew 410 combat hours in World War II, and served with the postwar USAF. He is retired from the USAF, now works with the aerospace industry and lives in Thousand Oaks, California.

The 9th Air Force in Europe produced far fewer aces than the 8th Air Force, but it must be remembered that the 9th was the Tactical Air Force in Europe, and its pilots probably had more effect in hastening the war's end than those of any other U.S. command. The fighter pilots of the 9th lost out in the publicity sweepstakes, but the deadly hazards of low-level flying were their daily business for years. The troops on the ground are among those who will not forget the pilots of the 9th Air Force, who busily busted up trucks, locomotives, tanks, weapons carriers, armored cars, infantry strongpoints or anything else that needed the attention of their guns, rockets and bombs.

Pilots of the 9th Air Force usually did their work with top cover provided by high-flying Spitfires of the RAF or USAAF P-51's. The 9th Air Force proved to be the spawning ground for some of America's most accomplished pilots of fighter aircraft. Some of these men became aces, others did not. A typical case is Lieutenant Colonel John J. Kropenick of Newark, New Jersey.

"Krop" has over seven thousand hours of single-engine jet flying time, about four hundred hours more than his nearest rival and best friend, Lieutenant Colonel Robert C. Tomlinson. He cut his combat teeth with the 9th Air Force, but has only *one* enemy plane to his credit, an Me-109 he caught up with over Europe. Untold hundreds of trucks, parked guns and tanks fell before his guns, but the aerial targets simply did not come his way.

One 9th Air Force luminary who did make his ace ranking is Colonel Paul P. Douglas Jr. of Paragould, Arkansas. Douglas destroyed twenty-seven German planes on the ground and inflicted heavy damage on other ground targets. He proved he could also work "upstairs" by downing seven German aircraft.

Colonel Douglas wears decorations which adequately testify to his success in both major spheres of fighter piloting. He is one of the few Air Force officers to have been awarded the DSC twice. He has to wear two Air Medal rib-

bons on his tunic to accommodate his six silver Oak Leaf Clusters, each Cluster representing the award of five Air Medals. The British awarded Douglas their DFC in recognition of his services.

Reticent about his bold career, Colonel Douglas would only say: "All the aerial victories were exciting, but even more exciting were the close support missions we flew with the American First and Third Armies and with the British Army."

Notable among 9th Air Force pilots and holding a unique place among American aces is Lieutenant Colonel William R. Dunn of Minneapolis, Minnesota. Dunn flew with the 71st (Eagle) Squadron of the RAF before U.S. entry into World War II, and became the first American ace of that conflict during his RAF service.

Seriously wounded in July of 1941 during his seventieth operation with the RAF, Dunn was overlooked in the heavy publicity that surrounded the Eagle Squadrons. He was in hospital and out of sight. His aerial victories with the RAF were confirmed after the war and his right to the distinction of being the

REPUBLIC AVIATION CORPORATION "THUNDERBOLT" REUNION

At a reunion, which is held annually, old cronies get together for convivial nostalgia. Here three erstwhile members of the famous "Zemke Wolfpack," the 56th Fighter Group, recall more than just some battles over Europe. Ralph A. Johnson scored three victories, not enough for acedom. Gerald W. Johnson scored seventeen kills and retired in 1974 as a lieutenant general. Robert S. Johnson scored twenty-eight victories, left the service and served as a test pilot for Republic Aviation and is now an insurance executive in New York City. USAF Study 85 lists the general with 16.50 and Robert S. with 27.00. (Republic Aviation Corp.)

first American ace of World War II was unequivocally established.

Dunn did not transfer to the USAAF until June of 1943, and flew successively with the 53rd Fighter Group and the 406th Fighter Bomber Group. He added 1.0 victory during his USAAF service for a lifetime score of 6 victories. The colorful career of Bill Dunn is comprehensively described in Trevor J. Constable's *Hidden Heroes,* published by Arthur Barker of London in 1971. Suffice it to say here that Dunn's career puts to shame the wildest fiction, involving service in four different military uniforms plus that of the USAF, in which he ended his military career with retirement in 1974.

Another American ace who cut his combat teeth in the Eagle Squadrons of the RAF is Richard L. "Dixie" Alexander of Grant Park, Illinois, who couldn't wait for Uncle Sam to get into the Big War. Dixie Alexander headed north of the border in October of 1940, and enlisted in the RCAF at Windsor, Ontario. The Canadians trained him and he was sent to England in due course, being assigned to 133 (Eagle) Squadron RAF on 8 February 1942.

Alexander flew 62 missions with the RAF, including fighter cover for the Dieppe raid. In this action he was credited with two kills by the RAF. He transferred to the USAAF in London on 23 September 1942, but did not score another aerial kill until 6 February 1944.

"On this occasion I was leading a flight of 8 aircraft when we spotted a couple of Fiesler Storch aircraft and two trainers towing gliders. This was just inland from the west coast of Italy. Our instructions at this time were to shoot anything that moved other than by sail and horse-drawn, so we immediately pounced on them. I was able to destroy the lead Storch with three bursts of cannon and machine-gun fire while he was cutting loose from his glider, and then went back upstairs to oversee the wild melee that followed while we destroyed them all."

Two weeks later on 19 February 1944, Dixie Alexander experienced one of the fighter pilot's starkest nightmares—a wingman who has gone off hunting on his own leaving his element leader unguarded. Thirty Me-109's jumped the twelve fighters Alexander was leading on a sweep over Paglia, Italy. Slashing down from great height, the Germans bounced the Americans in elements of four, firing on the way through and hardly staying to engage beyond the first pass.

Alexander watched their numerical advantage lessen and then sent elements to engage the German fighters as they came down on his formation from above until only Dixie and his wingman were left for top cover. Alexander takes up the narrative.

"There were at this time four 109's still left above us, and I was horrified when I saw that my wingman—whose name I will not mention—had apparently deserted me and gone hunting on his own. For some strange reason, I was not bounced by the Germans. Three of them suddenly peeled off and flew inland, with the fourth heading off in a northwesterly direction. I was at 12,000 feet and the German at 15-16,000.

"I must never have been spotted. They must have thought the entire engagement had gone to the deck, where things were pretty wild. The lone 109 took off in much the same direction as I wanted to go. Using full throttle I kept up with him as he let down to my altitude and then on down to the deck. He must have been heading for Grosseto where the Luftwaffe had based some 109's as well as at Viareggio.

"He now flew up a mountain pass. Closing in to about 75 yards without being observed, my burst of cannon and machine gun fire caught him squarely in the cockpit. He must have fallen over on the stick. The 109 simply nosed down, went straight into the ground and exploded."

Dixie Alexander scored his last aerial victory on his last day of combat flying, 30 May 1944.

"We were escorting B-24's to Wiener-neustadt, giving cover to the bombers who were flying at about 16,000 feet. They were attacked head-on by three 109's who flew directly through the formation, pulled up, half-rolled and started back down at the bombers. I gave the call to Blue section to drop belly tanks and switch on the mains, and we immediately went down after the 109's.

"The Germans made their pass from the rear, and went under the bombers and down, heading for the deck, with us in close pursuit. Singling out one of the 109's, I followed him through seven spirals, waiting for him to level out, meantime dropping 15 degrees of flap and throttling back to keep from overshooting him. Leveling out as we reached the deck, we started up the Danube Valley. Throttled back

still, I was able to shoot from about 200 yards. Pieces flew off the 109 in three good, successive bursts. Belching smoke, the 109 half turned and flew into the side of a hill.

"Now it was my turn. Starting to pull up, I gave the engine more throttle, whereupon it started to sputter. A quick glance confirmed that I was on main tanks, and inasmuch as I was practically on the deck, I had no time to seek ready solutions. Neither could I get enough altitude to risk a bailout. Letting the nose down, I aimed for a couple of small clearings ahead of me—little mountain pastures separated by a small creek.

"Hitting in the pasture, I bounced twice, hurdling the creek and coming to rest in a group of small pines at the far end of the second pasture. These two small areas were of not more than 150 yards diameter each, and they must have been the only level ground in that part of Austria. Other than banging my head on the gunsight and hurting my knee, I was not in bad shape, and immediately got out of the aircraft with my maps, escape pack and pistol.

"Removing the fire-bomb canister that was used to ignite the plane by placing on the wing tanks, I stepped down to the ground. I smelled petrol and noticed a line of four or five holes running just below the cowling. Stray bullets must have nicked a fuel line. The wind was rushing through the pine trees, and after the roar of the engine and the steady chatter on the radio it seemed incredibly quiet.

"I was placing the fire-bomb canister on the wing when I thought I heard a noise. Turning I saw one of the wildest-looking men I have ever seen come charging over the hill. His skin was copper-colored and he had dark hair and a long moustache. He was barefoot and wore only a pair of tattered shorts. He was brandishing a long, curved knife like a scimitar. I thought 'My God! I've landed in Turkey!'

"I pulled my 45 from my boot and hurriedly slid a round into the chamber . . . a good equalizer for the scimitar. The oncoming wild figure, bearing down on me by then, came to a prompt halt, and started waving his arms and yelling, 'Ami! Ami!' To further show his goodwill, he threw down the knife. In English that was as broken as his teeth he told me he was a French forced-laborer and had seen the air action. The knife he carried was for harvesting.

"Pointing to smoke on the horizon, he told

me that it came from the 109 I had downed. He told me that there was a company of German troops just over the hill, and urged me to run for it. He thrust a grubby sandwich into my hand. I put it in my pocket, told him to run, pulled the pin on the fire-bomb canister and took off myself, running down a gully into a new world. For me the war was over, and I was soon a p.o.w."

Captivity for Dixie Alexander was brightened one day six months later when he learned that Varnell, his element leader in that final action and Lampe, his own wingman, had confirmed his downing of the Me-109. He is credited with 6 aerial victories in WWII, 2 while flying with an RAF unit, 2 while in the 12th Air Force and 2 with the 15th Air Force.

Colonel Glenn T. Eagleston, who was born at Farmington, Utah, and calls Davis Creek, California, his present home, was successful as a fighter pilot in two wars. In World War II he became one of the USAAF's most famous aces in the ETO with a score of 18.5 German aircraft destroyed in ninety-six missions. In nine months of jet combat over Korea, Eagleston shot down two MiG-15's to bring his total to 20.5 enemy aircraft destroyed in aerial combat.

Modest and friendly, "Eagle"—as he is known to his pilot friends—is exasperatingly modest about his combat career. His best day was 29 October 1944, when he shot down three Me-109's when leading the 35th Fighter Group across the Rhine. His account of the action epitomizes his modesty:

"We were jumped by one hundred enemy fighters. We shot down twenty-three of them. We lost two Mustangs and only one pilot was killed. I got three 109's that day, which was my best day."

Eagleston takes an active part in the affairs of the American Fighter Aces' Association, ably assisted in the social side of his duties by his attractive wife, known to the aces' fraternity as "Mrs. Eagle."

At meetings and various social affairs of today's American Fighter Aces Association, the typical scene usually includes a compact, wiry Virginian who bears a better than passing resemblance to movie actor Lloyd Bridges. He is James L. Brooks, a man who never seems to stand still. Remarkably youthful in his evening,* Jim Brooks made his mark as an extremely young, sharp 2nd Lieutenant with the

15th Air Force in World War II. He ran up 13 aerial victories against the Luftwaffe. Roanoke, Virginia, is his home town, but he has adopted Southern California as his home for many years.

Brooks was with the 31st Fighter Group during the time that this unit operated from a Russian base against the retreating Germans. Flying out of Piryatin, Russia, with the 307th Squadron, Brooks was assigned to providing top cover for some 82nd Fighter Group P-38's on a special strafing mission. The P-38's were to destroy American aircraft on the ground. This bizarre operation aimed at eliminating a number of captured and flyable U.S. aircraft that were purported by intelligence to be assembled at a Polish airfield. The intelligence proved false, and Jim Brooks and his fellow pilots turned back towards their base in Russia. He takes up the narrative of this experience:

"At this particular time, the German army was in full retreat from Russia into Poland— an unbelievable sight from my vantage point—vehicles of all sorts bumper to bumper on what seemed to be the only highway west available to the Germans.

"East of the Polish city of Lvov, I was leading Blue Section of the 307th Squadron

and Sam Brown, leading Red; the other two squadrons were dogging it somewhere else. To my knowledge, Col. Porky Tarrant, Group Commander, was not on this mission. I called out the targets and gave my section permission to begin strafing. During one of my strafing runs, I shot down a JU-52 transport, presumably full of troops. A few minutes later I shot down a Storch observation plane, which I did not claim because it was too easy. After we worked over the area pretty good, I called for Blue Section to form up over a steel bridge a little west of the action. At this time, Sam with the Red Section formed up on my section. After being on course for Piryatin, Russia, for about 5 to 10 minutes, I saw in a distance large numbers of aircraft circling, and in a sort of traffic pattern. As we drew closer, I recognized them to be the famous Stuka dive bombers, JU-87's taking off from a nearby base and bombing the Russian trenches— World War I type warfare that startled me since they were flying at 500 feet or less. I ordered all flights to attack the Stukas. The boys needed little prodding, but I cautioned them to keep an eye on several Me-109's above us about 3,000 feet.

"During this engagement, the 307th Squadron shot down 24 Stukas and probably destroyed 6 more. I got one. This action was later mentioned in Hans-Ulrich Rudel's book, Stuka Pilot . We could have easily destroyed more, but I thought it prudent to reform and set course because the country was unfamiliar, as well as the base and its location in Russia.

*A fighter pilot's "evening" usually ranges between the ages of 50 and 97 years of age. Jim Brooks is the type to pass from the old age of youth at 87 and the youth of old age at 90, so the authors are a bit presumptuous to say that he is in his evening. We apologize.

1960 AMERICAN FIGHTER ACES ASSOCIATION MEETING: San Francisco provided facilities for the first meeting of the Aces Association. These four aces were among the 63 aces who attended: Vermont Garrison, USAF 4th Gp. WWII, 4 Wg. Korea, 17.33 Glenn Eagleston, USAF 354th Gp. WWII, 4 Wg. Korea, 20.50 Frances Gabreski, USAF 56th Gp. WWII, 51 Wg. Korea 34.50 James Jabara, USAF 355th Gp. WWII, 51 Wg. Korea 16.50

(AFAA)

September 1960 at San Francisco:
Fifteen years after WWII came
to an end, the American Fighter
Aces Association was formed and
held their first meeting. There were
serious moments, as this picture
indicates. Left to right: Frank L.
Gailer, USAF (357th Gp. 5.5);
Spiros N. "Steve" Pisanos, USAF
(4th Gp. 6.00); Eugene W.
O'Neill, USAF (56th Gp. 5.00);
Gerald W. Johnson, USAF
(56th Gp. 16.50).

(AFAA)

Navigation was not easy due to our maps be-
ing somewhat unreliable. En route we were
bounced by Russian Stormoviks, but when I
broke into them they moved off. No one was
lost on this mission, which was incredible.

"Back at base I was interviewed by the
American press that had been flown in from
Moscow and I was introduced to several Rus-
sian generals who congratulated me on the
mission. Several days later en route back to
Italy, I shot down a Me-109, and a bit of
humor can be injected here. Brig. General
'Doc' Strother, Commander of the 206th
Wing, had flown with us to Russia acting for
General Nathan Twining, C. O. of the 15th
AF. I had been told by Colonel Tarrant to
keep an eye on the General to ensure his

safety. We engaged the enemy over Ploesti
and everyone forgot about the General—it
was an overcast day, sort of dark and
foreboding. As I left the target with my sec-
tion, I heard Red Two calling Red One rather
frantically, I may add. After a few such calls,
it dawned on me that General Strother had
become separated from Red flight. Mincing no
words, I told him to set course for home, and I
would try to pick him up. Due to poor
visibility and weather, I never caught sight of
him. I assured him I was close by and to just
hold course for Italy. Needless to say I feared
for his safety. My fears were really groundless.
The General made it back in fine spirits as a
good fighter pilot would always do. This fine
officer and fighter pilot eventually became a

GATHERING OF EAGLES
Aces Association meeting
provides an opportunity for old
teammates to get together. Here
are: Jack T. Bradley, USAF
354th Group, 15.0 victories;
James L. Brooks, USAF 31st
Group, 13.0; Willard W. Millikan,
USAF 4th Group, 5.0; Eugene
A. Valencia, USN VF-9, 23.0.

(AFAA)

four star general.

"After our return, Major Sam Brown, my squadron commander and roommate, recommended me for a cluster to the Distinguished Flying Cross. The decoration panel at HQ 15th Air Force thought a little more highly of my role, and awarded me the Silver Star instead. My name was never mentioned in the dispatches—someone saw to that. I was much too young at the time, and too inexperienced to play the game of politics, being completely dedicated to the high morals and standards that were expected of an officer. This event was a good indication of what life was going to be all about, but the smooth and the rough go together. Brigadier General Strother at a private ceremony in his office pinned the Silver Star on me—a memorable moment."

Multiple scores in a single aerial battle were not uncommon by 1945, but destroying four enemy machines in one encounter is an exceptional feat for any fighter pilot. Among the few who accomplished it was Lieutenant Colonel Francis R. Gerard of Lyndhurst, New Jersey, to whom it brought the award of the Silver Star. The action is recounted in a wartime letter written by Colonel Gerard:

"Magdeburg—the great railway junction southwest of Berlin—has been a prime target for our heavy bombers lately. It's one of the main supply gates for the defense of Berlin.

"Every time I read about Magdeburg being bombed again, I think about the mission I flew there. It was back in September, before the Russians began the big drive that has taken them so close to the German capital. Even then . . . long before Berlin was being threatened . . . we were hammering away at this strategic center.

"On 11 September 1944, I was one of an escort of fourteen fighters flying protection for a formation of heavy bombers. Just before we reached the initial point of the bomb run, we saw two German fighters below us. We figured they were decoys, sent to draw us away from the bombers, so we ignored them.

"Then we saw a formation of a hundred bandits . . . which is what we call German fighters. We dropped our external gas tanks and climbed for the sun.

"The German fighters were in perfect formation. They made a wide turn and started to make a dead astern attack on the bombers. I was the first one in and started to spray them, but they wouldn't break formation. I con-

centrated on one of the 109's and blew him up with one burst. Then another 109 started to peel off toward the bombers, and I gave him a burst—and he went down, too.

"About that time we were all in the middle of the bomber formation. They scored heavily on that one pass, shooting down fourteen bombers. In all there were about two hundred heavies in the formation. It was our job to try and keep the Germans from getting any more of them.

"The Germans started to re-form for another attack, but we now broke them up. I got in the center and started shooting, but two of them got on my tail. I pulled a high, tight turn and a snap . . . and ended up on their tails. I closed on one and gave him two or three bursts. He blew up in my face. Then I gave the other one a short burst and he blew up, too.

"In all, we shot down fifteen of them, and didn't lose any of our fighters."

Gerard is credited with eight aerial victories, all gained in the ETO in World War II. He currently lives in Sea Girt, New Jersey.

The history of the air war is full of incidents where tragedy and comedy have played leading roles in matters of aircraft recognition. Captain George F. Hall of Greenfield, Missouri, and West Palm Beach, Florida, shot down six German aircraft in World War II, but most vividly remembers joining a Luftwaffe fighter formation by mistake:

"Lieutenant Lloyd M. Langdon* and I were watching a flight of what appeared to be friendly Spitfires. We saw the flight join up with another formation to make a gaggle of fifteen or so. Langdon and I were the only P-47 pilots around, and as we had been warned that Spits were in the area, we surmised that these must be the RAF aircraft.

"I closed up on the right-hand corner man, however, and flew close formation on his right wing—for just a few seconds—just long enough to see that big black swastika on his fuselage!

"I pulled back and slid in behind him and let him have it. Hits exploded all over him and pieces flew off in all directions. Down he went in flames as I slid over and got the next German in my sights. I pulled the trigger and he pulled up sharply and fell off to the left. Then I fired on another plane and it went

---

*Lt. Langdon scored two confirmed victories during the war with the 63rd Squadron, 56th Group.

down like a falling leaf with smoke pouring out of it.

"I fired on a third and a fourth 109 before running out of ammunition, and got strikes on both of them. Langdon was doing okay, too, as he got one which exploded and I saw an object falling off another which he had hit. The object was either the canopy or the pilot bailing out. As we broke away, a flight of P-47's from another group came in."

For several years the Me-109 was the scourge of the skies over Europe. Before the advent of the P-51 Mustang there was no aircraft made which could hold its own against Professor Willy Messerschmitt's remarkable product *functioning in its own home skies.* As a result, Allied pilots had to develop tactics which could compensate for technical disparities. Cool common sense was often the best tactic of all, as illustrated in this story by Major Michael J. Jackson of Plainfield, New Jersey:

"On Christmas Day, 1944, Jerry was making every effort to support the Battle of the Bulge. I had my squadron up on a sweep between Bonn and Frankfurt. Ground controller vectored us to a bogie, and while flying at 30,000 near Bonn we spotted numerous Me-109's at about 24,000. I maneuvered to get into the sun, and looking them over, saw they were flying the same battle formation we were flying, three flights of four aircraft each, almost line abreast.

"I gave the order to drop tanks, and in a diving turn onto their rear gave instructions that I would take the man on the far end and each of my squadron was to 'cue up' on the 109 corresponding to his own position. It was the prettiest sight a fighter pilot could ever wish to see.

"Those poor German pilots never knew what hit them. My target blew up in front of me at 150 yards range. My wingman got his, and so right down that beautiful line. All twelve Me-109's went down in pieces or flames on that one spectacular pass. After having been at the 109's mercy for so long during the war, it was a wonderful feeling to have been able to pull this off."

Major Jackson* himself shot down eight German aircraft while flying with the 56th Fighter Group (Zemke's Wolfpack) in the

---

*Jackson is now a B/G and lives in Grand Forks, North Dakota.

ETO.

Youngest American ace in the ETO was Lieutenant Dale E. Karger of McKees Rock, Pennsylvania, who shot down 7.5 enemy aircraft. five of them before his twentieth birthday on 14 February 1945. Lieutenant Karger entered flying school in April 1943, at eighteen years of age. He tells a memorable story of a brush with an ME-262 jet:

"In 1944 after chasing an Me-262 for about fifty miles across Munich, he was leaving me far, far behind with his speed advantage. I was about to lose sight of him when, apparently thinking me long gone, he started a gradual turn to the left. I cut inside the circle, and when still not in range as far as my gunsight was concerned, I fired far ahead of his flight path. I was surprised to see immediate hits. The jet simply rolled over and crashed into some woods. Beside the thrill of downing a jet, this victory was also my fifth, which qualified me as an ace."

Major Wayne L. Lowry of Mason City, Nebraska, an ace credited with eleven aerial victories in the ETO, best recalls his encounter with "Germany's most uncomprehending pilot," whom he whimsically dubs "Mueller" in his story:

"I sighted Mueller over Yugoslavia. As usual he was flying with his head up and locked, approximately a mile ahead of a large formation of American planes. (He was probably pacing the formation, giving speed and altitude information to flak units—Authors' note.) He had been there quite a while when I decided to investigate any Jerry who would be so stupid as to continue flying such a suicidal position for so long. I flew up alongside, half expecting it to be an American P-47 or P-51. The pilot looked right at me, not over thirty yards away. It was an Me-109, with the biggest swastika I have ever seen painted on its sides. I dropped back into position about a hundred yards astern, sighted my guns from dead behind and blew plane and pilot out of the sky."

"Mueller" was certainly determined, but he became one of the eleven German aircraft downed by Major Lowry during his service in the ETO with the 325th Fighter Group of the 15th Air Force.

Top-ranking ace of the State of Missouri in World War II was Captain Raymond H. Littge of Altenburge, with 10.5 aerial victories over the Germans. Littge fought with the 352nd

Fighter Group of the 8th Air Force, flying 391 combat hours in 91 missions.

Littge named one of his sons George Preddy Littge after the famous ace George Preddy of the ETO, whose unfortunate end has been recounted earlier in this volume. One of America's best fighter pilots, admired for skills and abilities that were not adequately reflected in his official victory credit total, Littge lost his life on 20 May 1949, near Maupin, Oregon, while flying an F-84 jet.

Prior to his death, Littge had hoped to write a book on his experiences as a fighter pilot. From his notes for this book the following narratives of aerial combat have been excerpted. The first concerns Littge's victory over an Me-262 jet.

"We had finished a pass through the bomber formation. There was nothing funny about these jet jobs, but this one was having trouble with his landing gear. It kept dropping down and reminded me of a kid who was running away from someone, and whose pants kept dropping down. He was trying to fight, fly and at the same time keep working his gear up. This factor decreased his speed, and I was able to close and clobber him."

The Littge papers also include this account of a battle with the redoubtable Me-109's:

"The tracers that lanced over my left wing told me that I had been singled out by one of the enemy pilots as his opponent. A quick glance at the 109 showed American flags on his canopy, and I quickly went into action—I wasn't about to be the next one to his credit. Sucking the stick back hard into my lap, I turned right. My turn was so tight I blacked out immediately. I gained a thousand feet after rolling out of my turn, and I had lost the Hun that had shot at me.

"A Jerry came flashing down in front of me about five hundred yards away. He was in my line of flight, so I gave him a two-second burst. I didn't see any strikes. He'd been almost ninety degrees to me, so the two radii lead I had given him had not been enough.

"As I swung again wide, looking for a Hun, I got the biggest thrill of my life. I had a ringside seat at the biggest dogfight I'd ever seen. Aircraft were everywhere. German and American both, spinning, rolling, diving, turning—and flashing where bullets and shells were striking home. A 109 was going down and another one was getting clobbered. One of our Mustangs was hit also and was spiralling earthward with smoke pouring out.

"Tracers attracted my attention off to the left. A 109 was on the tail of a Mustang, with another Mustang on the tail of the 109 but with no possible chance of shooting him. The 109's 20mm shells were exploding behind the Mustang's tail, just a little out of range. A few more seconds and he would be in range. By the letters on the aircraft I recognized Captain 'Tex' Sears and Lieutenant Ross as the pilots of the two Mustangs. Ross was in the one being shot at.

"I made a diving pass at the Hun, hoping he would see me and break. He did! My pass was ninety degrees to him. We had him boxed in. If he broke left, I'd be sitting on his tail, and if he broke right, Tex would be on him in a minute.

"The German decided to break into Tex and away from me. With altitude on him, I had no trouble in getting behind him. I let go a burst. Just before I fired he broke left and my bullets missed. His turn was very tight, and due to my higher speed he was off for home before I had turned around. His getaway was short-lived.

"Tex and Ross were after him and behind him in nothing flat. He pulled the same tactics against them as he had against me and succeeded in getting away for a second time, but momentarily. In getting away from them, he flew directly in front of me. I slid down from above him and stayed there.

"Closing on him, I commenced firing in earnest, although a little excited from the previous engagement. My three-second burst clobbered him and started coolant streaming out of his right wing. He decided to hit the deck. I hung on like a leach, firing occasional bursts but not seeing any hits as the chase led down to the deck.

"The German pilot was determined to get home, judging by his evasive action. He kicked his aircraft first from one side, then to the other, skidding and sliding like a block of ice on a tin roof. The end came suddenly, as suddenly as the pursuit had begun. After three or four minutes we were eight miles west of Locker Lake. Here he started climbing for all he was worth.

"With my higher rate of climb, I found myself directly below, which was not the place to be. He was badly hurt, so he probably never saw this advantageous position offered to him two or three times. Together we climbed to

about six thousand, where he suddenly leveled off, and his canopy then flew off and came hurtling by my right wing. Then the pilot himself began bailing out. I fired again, holding the trigger down for a long burst. Strikes registered on the prop, fuselage and the wings. His aircraft started spinning and the fight was over. I watched the machine spin downward until it crashed into a railroad marshaling yard in a giant flash of flame and smoke. The pilot and his opened chute were not to be seen. He had no doubt been killed by the rain of bullets that surrounded his ship just before it started to spin."

The 56th Fighter Group shot down 665.5 aircraft in the ETO to lead all American units in this department. The group fought from 13 April 1943, until 25 April 1945, flying 19,391 sorties in this period. They lost 145 aircraft and suffered 150 casualties. The group produced a covey of aces, many of them among the ETO's most famous pilots. Gabreski, Schilling, Zemke, Robert S. Johnson, Gerald W. Johnson, Donovan Smith and "Bud" Mahurin were among the stellar performers passing through the 56th at one time or another.

The "name" value of these pilots and the publicity they commanded often tended to obscure the sometimes brilliant flying feats of other pilots in the 56th with only five, six or seven aerial victories to their credit. One such overlooked ace was Major Robert A. Lamb of

(Conger Collection)

62nd Squadron, 56th Group "Jugs": This photo taken from a Consolidated B-24 Liberator, shows six P-47 "Jugs" in formation. Later, a 63rd Squadron ace, Bud Mahurin, while making practice attacks on this B-24, zoomed up in front of the bomber, too close, and a propeller of the B-24 cut the tail off Mahurin's P-47. A good 'chute saved Mahurin.

Waldrick, New Jersey, who downed seven German aircraft and eventually rose to command the 63rd Squadron of the 56th Group in the ETO. Major Lamb contributes a narrative dealing with the protection of the bomber streams striking at Festung Europa. The scene is the sky above Emden, where, with eight Thunderbolts, Major Lamb's task is to protect a formation of B-17's and B-24's.

(Toliver Collection)

Cave Tonitrum! Beware of the Thunderbolt!: That's the motto of the 56th Fighter Group, Zemke's "Wolfpack." This P-47 Thunderbolt carries the U N marking of the 63rd Fighter Squadron.

"*The bombers were in serious trouble when we made our rendezvous over Emden. About fifty Me-110's, Me-210's and Ju-88's were sitting behind them, out of range of the 50-caliber tail guns firing rockets into the bomber formations. At first glance it seemed that there were bombers going down everywhere. And sitting above us was a top cover of FW-190's and Me-109's—about 150 aircraft.*

"*I called for an attack on the twin-engined jobs, and in crossing over for the attack, two of my men collided in midair and exploded, reducing us to six. The moment we attacked the German twin-engined aircraft, the German's entire top cover came down on us. We attacked in a rough six-abreast formation, and you could see the crisscross fire from the tail guns of the bombers streaking back past us.*

"*The enemy twin-engined aircraft were in flights of five abreast and they all turned away from our bombers as we came in. I pulled up behind an Me-110 and opened fire at about three hundred yards, seeing hits primarily in the belly and wings. I saw flame break out of the belly as I crossed under. That one was finished.*

"I then saw a flight of five Me-210's at about eleven o'clock and slightly below. I pulled up gradually and opened up on the center ship. I saw his right engine explode and the right wing crumple. Two crewmen bailed out. Number two was gone.

"The remaining four were diving at a steep angle now and it took a little time to get in range. I got another one in my sights and opened up. He veered away and increased his dive angle. I followed. I fired again and as I saw minor hits I ran out of ammunition. At the same instant I noticed we were very low over the water and as I started to pull out the Me-210 dove into the sea. I don't know whether I hit him in a critical spot or whether the pilot failed to see how low he was. In any event, number three was gone.

"On return I learned that not only had we pulled the enemy away from our bombers, but also that the six of us had shot down fourteen and all of us got back. That day I was given confirmation of three enemy aircraft destroyed and was awarded the Silver Star."

To be credited with an aerial kill while the defeated enemy pilot was still firing at him is the unusual experience of William H. Lewis of Oxnard, California, now retired from the USAF. He was flying with the 55th Fighter Group at the time of the incident.

The time is December of 1944, with Lewis leading a flight of four P-51's on an escort mission to Berlin.:

"Enemy aircraft were sighted approaching from south to north at 33,000 feet. There were thirty to forty Me-109's in the formation. I turned my flight to the south to engage the enemy with head-on passes. After the initial pass was made and the enemy formation had broken, I picked one Me-109 which was closest to me and pressed the attack so I could get into firing position.

"After a series of turns the Me-109 split-essed and dove for the deck. As my aircraft was closing rapidly, I was able to roll and dive with such speed that upon completion of the roll I was directly behind the German by not more than twenty feet. The dive angle was close to eighty degress. I fired.

"The enemy pilot then reduced all his power with an abrupt throttle movement, and maintained his attitude in the dive. This forced me to choose between breaking off the attack or attempting to regain position by a similar reduction of power and lowering of

flaps. I chopped the throttle, at the same time forcing the stick forward to maintain a steep dive attitude.

"This maneuver evidently surprised the German, as he continued in front of me at very close range. Thinking I'd outsmarted him, I attempted to pull my nose up slightly to get into position for firing. Just as I did this, he repeated his previous maneuver, and before I could recover from overrunning, he was again behind me.

"With air speed close to 500 mph and at an attitude of 75 degrees, I elected to break off the engagement. A severe loss of altitude had occurred, and I thought I was going to have difficulty pulling out of the dive. There was buffeting and severe vibrations, caused mostly by compressibility but helped by his shots hitting my wings and fuselage.

"I pulled hard on the stick and noticed that I was blacking out at about 8.5 G's. My wingman called that I had gotten the enemy, so I released pressure and went into a steep turn. I saw the 109 spinning to the ground minus a wing. I believe it is unusual to receive credit for an aerial victory while being shot at by the pilot you defeated."

Colonel Lewis is credited with 7.0 aerial victories in the ETO where he saw his Second World War service.

Colonel John H. Lowell, whose faith in the P-38 was dealt with earlier in this book, became an ace while flying with the 67th Wing's 364th Fighter Group. Colonel Lowell flew his first mission against the Germans on 6 March 1944, on the first fighter escort mission to Germany. He flew two combat tours and is officially credited with 7.5 victories. Now a roofing contractor in Golden, Colorado, Colonel Lowell best remembers a tussle with the redoubtable FW-190's:

"Over Berlin we spotted a large gaggle of 190's about to attack. We dropped external tanks and turned into them. I was the first to fire, as I was in the lead, and the lead 190, my target, blew up. All hell broke loose then and every man in my group fired at the enemy that day. I lost two men but we got thirty-three confirmed. My third victory was a long-nosed 190 who took me down to the deck, although I was long ago ready to go home. I ran out of ammo. He was still going strong, and then in a very low pass at me he ran into a tree and blew up. This occurred 5 December 1944."

Colonel Walker M. "Bud" Mahurin of

Fort Wayne, Indiana, is considered by the aces themselves to be one of the best combat pilots America has ever produced. No small part of his success is due to his outstanding ability as an air-to-air shot. He is credited with 19.75 aerial victories in the ETO and one in the SWPA. He added 3.5 MiG-15 jets in Korea, bringing his lifetime score to 24.25 kills in two wars.

Mahurin's career has been extensively publicized in the magazines, and during the war years in the popular press. A dashing, handsome man who epitomizes the hell-for-leather pilot of movies, Mahurin could probably have made it in Hollywood as a romantic star had he not been successful as an aerial warrior.

He is an extremely intelligent man, with sharp, clear eyes that had much to do with his career as an ace. He could spot the enemy long before most other pilots, and he was an ardent advocate of tactical surprise in aerial warfare. "Hit 'em before they even know you're there" was one of his combat credos.

One story about Mahurin concerns his eagerness for kills during his race with another leading ace for top scoring honors in the ETO. The two outstanding pilots were flying together, with Mahurin flying as wingman to the other ace. Mahurin spotted a bandit, waited a few seconds and then dove after the German. After waiting several seconds more, an inordinate time lapse under the circumstances, Mahurin called out the sighting. By this time, he was almost within range of the German and shot the enemy plane down immediately afterwards.

Incensed at Mahurin's infraction of the team rules, his CO was going to try Mahurin by court martial. They both went before a famous USAAF general the next day. The general greeted Mahurin with open arms.

A chill fell over proceedings when the general was informed of the pending trial of the overeager wingman. There was an awkward pause.

"OK, go ahead and try him," said the general to Mahurin's CO. "But you're going to look damned silly, as I just recommended him for the DSC."

As this incident shows, competition for scoring honors was often fierce, but it also served to maintain aggressiveness in the air, a factor that boded no good for the enemy.

Mahurin survived two wars and carved

himself a permanent niche in the history of aerial warfare. In recent years, he has devoted much time to writing. His book *Honest John* is an account of his experiences as a prisoner of the North Korean Reds. He also turned his writing talents to good use as the first Publicity Director of the American Fighter Aces' Association.

Major Gilbert M. O'Brien of Charleston, South Carolina, flew sixty-nine combat missions with the 357th Fighter Group out of Boxted, England, and downed seven German aircraft. His most vivid recollection of aerial combat is of himself as the angriest fighter pilot in the ETO for a few brief minutes he will never forget. Escorting bombers, O'Brien's formation was jumped and a number of B-17's were shot down by a gaggle of perhaps thirty 109's and 190's.

"Many B-17 crewmen had bailed out and at least three Me-109's were gunning our bomber crewmen while they were hanging in parachutes. This angered me beyond words. I got behind one of these Germans, pulled up to extremely close range and fired a short burst. The German pilot, hit and bleeding profusely, bailed out almost instantly and whipped past a few feet under my starboard wing. The Me-109 blew up in my face.

"I immediately executed a wingover, fully intending to shoot the German pilot in his parachute, but instead I spiraled his falling body to the ground. His chute never opened. After seeing this guy actually shooting our people while hanging in parachutes, I felt this was my most satisfying victory."

This is one of the extremely rare instances where German pilots have been accused of shooting parachuting crewmen. In the first place, German orders and policy forbade the action, and in the second place, the parachuters were dropping into captivity anyway so it was unnecessary as well as a dangerous pastime when enemy fighters were present.

Norton AFB in San Bernardino, California, was the scene of Lt. Colonel John F. Thornell's retirement from the USAF in August 1971, and yet another of the great aces of the ETO passed from active duty. Veteran fighter pilots who served in Europe will long remember Thornell's outstanding performance of 17.25 victories in a six-month period from New Year's Day 1944 until 21 June 1944—the end of his tour of duty. Although he was in the

(Conger Collection)

SUNSHINE ON A CLOUDY DAY

The British Isles are renowned for low clouds, foggy days and instrument-flying days on end, so a Petty Girl in a magazine is a brighter moment for all, including the Brass. Major General Jimmy Doolittle and Lt. General Touhey Spaatz (seated) look her over while aces David C. Schilling and Hubert Zemke, Major General William E. Kepner, and Brigadier General Jesse Auton register various reactions.

ETO six months before opening his scoring account, when Thornell's shooting eye came in he rose rapidly to top-scoring spot in the 352nd Fighter Group, leading even the redoubtable J. C. Meyer.

Thornell's most vivid memory of his combat flying days does not pertain to any of his aerial victories. Burned indelibly into his mind is a low-level attack on submarine pens, airfields and strongpoints in the Pas de Calais on 11 March 1944. Led by Colonel Joe Mason, C.O. of the 352nd Fighter Group, the 36 Thunderbolts ran through a hideous three-mile hail of fire and steel hurled at them by flak batteries, hundreds of 20mm flak cannons, machine guns and small arms fire from every German in range.

The attack was pressed home despite the nightmare defensive gauntlet run by the American fighters, and the targets were well

hammered. "Softening up" the defenses for the D-Day invasion resulted in some softening up of the 352nd on this occasion. Two Thunderbolts were lost, including John Thornell's wingman, Lt. Bill Schwenke, and eight others were damaged. Thornell came out of it with a whole skin, and will spend the rest of his life wondering how he ever made it, accompanied always by the unforgettable memory of those moments.

Thornell was awarded the DSC, Silver Star with one Oak Leaf Cluster, DFC and Air Medal each with five clusters and numerous other awards. Just as J. C. Meyer took over the scoring lead of the 352nd Fighter Group from him in 1944, racking up 24 victories ETO, so did Thornell on his retirement leave his friend "J.C." to carry on as a four star general, and vice chief of staff of the USAF.

Colonel Robin Olds, USAF, describes himself as an "Air Force Brat," being the son of the late Major General Robert Olds. With his father in the service, Olds grew up without a real home town. He became a fighter ace in World War II with 12.0 victories over the Germans. Colonel Olds is married to movie star Ella Raines. Excitement ran high for Olds on 25 August 1944 when, as a member of Zemke's group, he took part in a wild melee over Germany. In breaking up a formation of 109's, Olds' flight scattered the German aircraft deckward:

"I continued down after the gaggle and potted one from behind. Then a Mustang passed under me with one of Hermann's (Hermann Goering's - Aus.) boys hot behind him, so I rolled over to lend a hand. I forgot I was already on the verge of compressibility and didn't have that much altitude left. I rolled back level and started to pull out, with the nose shuddering and trying to go steeper. Next my canopy flew off, and I really thought the war was over.

"Using trim I managed to pull out right on the deck over a wheat field southwest of Rostock. That took all the starch out of one slightly clanked fighter pilot. I headed home. Looking round to check for damage, I saw the war wasn't over yet. There was an Me-109 about two hundred feet back and fifteen degrees off, and Hermann sure had the bit in his teeth.

"That prop spinner looked like the 4th of July and as large as a barrel. I horsed my P-38 into a resemblance of a left break, and im-

mediately high-speed stalled. *The thing just didn't want to fly with the canopy and a side panel gone. Hermann immediately overshot, and all I had to do was roll level and squeeze the trigger. It was his turn, and as the pieces flew off his ship, he jumped. This victory was confirmed by a latecomer from the rest of our group and made it three for the day for me."**

Major MacArthur Powers of Inwood, Long Island, New York, served with the famed 11th Fighter Group of the RAF and gained 2.5 victories with the British. To these he added 5 more Germans after transfer to the USAAF's 324th Fighter Group of the 9th Air Force. His experiences include being shot down behind German lines in North Africa, with subsequent escape "thanks to one native and three camels."

Major Powers' most memorable experience has tragic overtones:

"Over Cape Bon, North Africa, on Palm Sunday, 1943, we jumped some seventy-five enemy aircraft. Within the next five minutes I shot four Ju-52's into the water and added an Me-109 that tried to interrupt my party. We did not know that the Germans were evacuating their families from North Africa, although we subsequently had to assist in burial details, which made it a very hollow victory at best."

Long combat experience and intimate knowledge of the comparative strengths and weaknesses of one's own machine and that of the enemy often provided fighter pilots with exciting experiences. Colonel Carl W. Payne of Columbus, Ohio, flew Spitfires out of England in 1942. He was in the Dieppe raid and the escorting of the first American bombing raids in the ETO. Flying subsequently in the Mediterranean Theater he had many more encounters with the Focke-Wulfe 190, Professor Kurt Tank's answer to the Spitfire. He best remembers the invasion of Sicily:

"While patrolling Gila Beach I spotted an FW-190 a few thousand feet above me. We had recently converted to Spitfire VIII's, and I knew that I had him trapped above me. There was no possible way for him to get away as I could out-climb him, out-run him and catch him if he tried to dive through. With this

knowledge I caught him and shot him out of the first turn he made, and then watched him spin 14,000 feet and crash. The tables had turned since Dieppe (19 August 1942) when the FW-190's hammered us and our Spitfires unmercifully, and always from above."

Colonel Payne flew 257 combat missions in World War II, over Europe proper, the Mediterranean area and in the Pacific in 1945. He is credited with seven aerial victories.

Colonel Donovan Smith of Niles, Michigan, was one of the best-known American aces of the ETO and the 56th "Wolfpack" Fighter Group. He was a far finer fighter pilot than his 5.5 victories might suggest, functioning more in the role of leader than spectacular scorer. His most memorable experience conveys something of the whirlwind activity of aerial combat:

"We were over Emden on 11 December 1943, with Gabreski leading the 61st Squadron (sixteen P-47's). I was leading Blue Flight. We spotted twenty German fighters down around 28,000 feet, more than a mile below us, maneuvering to attack the bomber streams. As Gabby set the squadron up for the attack, two of the Jugs in my flight collided in a crossover turn. The flash of flame and loud explosion, together with the falling debris, was interpreted by Gabby as an attack by unseen enemy fighters and away we went.

"We were in a near-vertical dive, and the sky seemed full of enemy aircraft in seconds. My wingman and I nailed two Me-110's carrying rockets and we damaged a Ju-88 in less time than it takes to tell about it. Aircraft were falling all over the sky.

"As I attacked a single Me-110 I glanced over my right shoulder to see all the cylinders in the radial engine of an FW-190. I broke off my attack, gave my Jug full throttle and water injection, and after three climbing left-near-vertical spirals was convinced I had Baron Richthofen on my tail. Two more turns upward and I had gained enough to hammerhead back on him and I started head-on firing passes.

"Two more vertical turns and I'd gained another ten degrees or more, and this time as we passed nearly head-on he kept firing as he passed me—which was confusing. I thought I'd lost my wingman in the violent pull-ups. However, on what proved to be the final pass, I tied the trigger down and saw hits on the 'Baron's' cowling. Then I saw tracers zip past

---

*Robin Olds added four more scores to his total during the Vietnam war, bringing his tally to 16. He retired from the USAF in the rank of Brigadier General and now resides in Steamboat Springs, Colorado. His Vietnam adventures are described in the appropriate chapter.

my wingtip and I whirled to see my wingman pull out from under my tail, where he'd been all the time. The 190 exploded in midair."

Lt. General Donovan F. Smith passed away in 1974 shortly after retirement. He was one of the most respected and revered fighter pilots in the USAF.

Colonel Everett W. Stewart is acknowledged freely by ex-subordinates still serving with the USAF as one of America's greatest fighter leaders. Hailing from Abilene, Kansas, Colonel Stewart commanded the 4th Fighter Group at the end of World War II, and his record includes 7.83 aerial victories gained while fighting with the 352nd, 355th and 4th Fighter Groups. He flew also in the Pacific with the 18th Fighter Group in the dark days of 1941-1942.

In a letter to his father written from England on 20 March 1944, he had this to say:

"Last Saturday I finally achieved a goal I've had ever since I was a kid. You probably remember when I used to read a lot of flying aces magazine stories, etc.? Well, I've always wanted to be a fighter pilot since then, and if I had to go to war, to be an ace. Saturday I got my fifth one, an Me-109.

"On Thursday I got my fourth, over the target area when four of us scattered about thirty Me-109's before they could hit the bombers. We were fighting for almost the next two hours. I must have been in at least ten fights myself, firing at six or more of them. They were all fairly hard shots and I spent a lot of time watching my tail. Several times I'd fire at one and then turn around to get at one coming in from the rear, without seeing what happened to the first one. I chased the last one

all over the foothills and valleys, dodging houses, trees and light lines. I hit him a few times and then ran him through a high-tension line. . . Finis!"

Colonel Ev Stewart and his wife "Sunny" now live in Dallas, Texas.

(Conger Collection)

56th Group Heyday!: Three aces of the "Wolfpack" at Boxted, England. First Lt. John H. Truluck, pilot of "Lucky" P-47, with seven victories. Colonel Hub Zemke with 17.75 and Walker M. Mahurin with 19.75 at the time.

(Toliver Collection)

COVEY OF ACES ON THE PERIMETER ROAD: The leader of the 56th "Wolfpack," Hubert Zemke (left) is escorted by Dave Schilling, Francis S. Gabreski and Fred J. Christensen. When Gabreski was captured by the Germans, this photo graced the wall of Hanns Scharff, the Luftwaffe's master fighter interrogator, much to the consternation of Gabby. Two months later Zemke joined the POWs and saw the photo, too.

(Conger Collection)

IN A STATE OF SHOCK!: Debriefing time for the 56th Group after a harrowing mission against the Luftwaffe. Dog tired but glad to be alive, pilots drink coffee just before debriefing. Left to right: Captain Paul A. Conger, Major Gabreski, Captain Barnum, Captain Morganzello, Colonel Dave Schilling. Profile at extreme right is Norman J. Brooks.

(USAF)

Four of the best of the 56th!
Captain Fred J. Christensen (in cockpit. 21.50), Lt. Colonel David Schilling (22.50), Major Francis S. Gabreski (28.00) and the 56th mentor and leader, Colonel Hub Zemke (17.75). Guess what they are talking about.

THE BRASS VISITS THE WOLFPACK: Wolfpack commander Colonel Hub Zemke (left) listens intently as Lt. General Spaatz (front center) and Major General Jimmy Doolittle (peering over Spaatz' shoulder) talk to Major General William E. Kepner.

(Conger Collection)

15 Pilots, 56 German planes shot down in one day!
These 15 pilots of the 56th Fighter Group matched numbers and shot down 56 Luftwaffe planes during a sortie over Germany in 1944.

(Conger Collection)

FOR MEDICINAL PURPOSES ONLY
Three 56th Group aces relax after a hard day in their office at 30,000
feet over Germany. Left to right: Captain Joe H. Powers (14.50); Captain Robert S.
Johnson (28.00); and Major Gerald W. Johnson (17.00). Lt. General Donavon F.
Smith (deceased) paid this tribute to Joe Powers, who was killed during
the Korean War: "Joe was one of the best fighter pilots I ever knew. He
was one of those unforgettable characters that half the ETO knew!"

**56th Group
Chaplain and part of his flock:**
The chaplain (left) poses with
Major Paul Conger (11½), Major
Leslie C. Smith (7), Major Michael
Jackson (8), Captain Felix Williamson
(13), Major George E. Bostwick (8)
and Lt. Norman D. Gould (4).

No account of ETO fighter aces would be complete without a word concerning "The Hub"—Colonel Hubert Zemke, originally of Missoula, Montana.* His name has already appeared many times in this book as the leader of the 56th Group, which has gone into history and legend as the "Wolfpack."

Zemke was the senior Allied officer at Stalag-Luft One at Barth, Germany, when "they stopped the fight" in 1945. He was shot

down on 16 December 1944, with 17.75 victories to his credit and an unexcelled record as a leader of fighter formations.

"The Hub" was a professional airman, and attended the U.S. Army's flying school in 1936-1937 at Randolph and Kelly Fields. For two years he commanded his Wolfpack before being assigned in August, 1944, to command of the 479th Fighter Group. Four months later "The Hub" became the unwilling guest of the Germans. In p.o.w. camp he again proved to be an inspiring leader.

The years have mellowed the erstwhile

*Today, Colonel Hubert Zemke is retired from the USAF and owns and operates the ZZ Almond Ranch near Oroville, California.

(Conger Collection)

CELEBRATING THE 56TH'S 800TH VICTORY
These seven pilots contributed 60½ of the 800 victories. From left: J. R. Carter (6), Donavon F. Smith (5.5), H. E. Comstock (5.0), David Schilling (22.5), Lucian A. Dade (3), L. C. Smith (7), and P. A. Conger (11.5).

ramrod of the Wolfpack. Today he speaks of aerial combat as something that seems very far away. "They were all easy," he says, "once I hit them." Usually, a little conversation with old fighter pilots soon finds "The Hub" making wings out of his hands and banking steeply above the bar with the best of them. At these times, something of the fierce energy of the World War II fighter leader reappears, a glimpse of the boldly determined man who used to talk like this:

"A fighter pilot must possess an inner urge to do combat. The will at all times to be offensive will develop into his own tactics. If your enemy is above, never let your speed drop and don't climb, because you'll lose too much speed. If you're attacked on the same level, just remember you can outclimb him. Beware of thin cirrus clouds—the enemy can look down through them but you can't look up through them. Don't go weaving through valleys of cumulus clouds, either with a squadron or by yourself. The enemy can be on your tail before you know it.

"When popping down out of a cloud, or up, always do a quick turn and look back. You may have jumped out directly in front of a gun barrel. When attacked by large numbers of enemy aircraft, meet them head-on. In most cases half of them will break and go down. Handle all those remaining in an all-out fight until you're down to one—then take him on.

"Well, it was like this . . .!"
Wolfpack fighters Gabreski (28), Eugene E. Barnum (2), and Justus D. Foster (2) (far right) listen to Frank W. Klibbe (7) tell just how the cow ate the cabbage.

(Toliver Collection)

179

"If there are twenty aircraft down below, go screaming down with full force to pick out the most logical target at the point of firing. Then pull up to a good altitude and develop an attack on one of those remaining enemy pilots who had been shaken out of his helmet by your sudden onslaught.

"I stay with the enemy until he is destroyed, I'm out of ammunition, he evades into the clouds, or I'm too low on gas and ammo to continue. When you have your squadron with you and the enemy has so much altitude you never would get up to him, stay below and to the rear of him—he'll be down.

"Learn to break at the proper time to make a head-on attack—the enemy doesn't like it. Don't run. That's just what he wants you to do. When caught by the enemy in large force, the best policy is to fight like hell until you can decide what to do . . ."

With those few words from a 1944 peptalk to American pilots under his command, it is time to leave Zemke and the ETO. The skies over Europe provided the bulk of the opportunities in World War II for American fighter pilots to join the fraternity of aces. In those days, the Air Force was part of the Army, and there were those who said that the greatest enemy of the Army was the Navy, and vice versa. It is time to look at the different aerial war fought by the U.S. Navy's fighter aces of World War II.

(Conger Collection)

TWO RELAXED FIGHTER PILOTS
Lt. Colonel Lucian A. Dade and Major Donavon F. Smith share a joke about the way Schilling drinks champagne from a punch bowl at his own farewell party.

(USAF/Giuliano)

The archives of men are their memories: Lt. Colonel Walter Krupinski, 197-victory Luftwaffe ace, and Lt. Colonel Erich Hartmann, top ace of the world with 352 aerial victories, listen to the erstwhile leader of the "Zemke Wolfpack," Hub Zemke, at a German airbase in 1961. Krupinski is world's fifteenth ranking ace. Hartmann is number one. Zemke is the twenty-first ranking ace of the USAAF.

(Conger Collection)

Farewell Party for Schilling of the "Wolfpack": This photo, taken before the punch bowl and champagne arrived, shows: (front row) Colonel Mohler, Colonel Schilling, Major Conger and a Polish officer; (back row) Captain Williamson, Lt. Colonel Dade, Major Carter, Major L. C. Smith, and another unidentified Polish officer.

(Conger Collection)

FAREWELL PARTY FOR THE CHIEF:
On 12 August 1944, Colonel David C. Schilling replaced Colonel Hubert Zemke as commander of the 56th Group. Schilling held the job until his tour was completed 27 January 1945 and was succeeded by Lt. Colonel Lucian A. Dade. This photo taken at a 56th farewell party for Schilling. Left to right: Colonel Mohler, Major Jim Carter, Schilling (holding punch bowl filled with champagne) and Lt. Colonel Dade. The two persons at the right are unidentified.

USAF Aces of the European Theater of Operations (II)

Sixteen years after WWII, in May 1961, members of the German Fighter Pilots Association invited members of the American Fighter Pilots Association to come to Geisenheim and participate in dedication ceremonies of a memorial monument to the Fallen Fighter Pilots of WWII. This photo was taken at Hahn Airbase shortly after the arrival of the American contingent. Left to right: Walker Mahurin, James L. Brooks, Werner Andres, Jack S. Jenkins, Adolf Galland, Eugene A. Valencia, Dr. Erich Mix, Gerhard Gobert, Erich Hohagen, Hubert Zemke, Arthur Thorsen, unidentified, and Raymond F. Toliver.

(USAF/Giuliano)

(USAAF)

Captain Joseph H. Bennett (8.50): Captain Bennett, Morton, Texas, flew with both the 56th Group (61st Squadron) and the 4th Group (336th Squadron) to score his 8.5 aerial victories.

(Toliver Collection)

WINGS ON EACH BREAST—5 VICTORIES

Captain Richard L. Alexander in USAAF uniform after transfer from service as a flying officer with the Royal Air Force. RAF wings are worn on his right breast. Alexander downed two German aircraft with the RAF, three more with the USAAF to become an ace.

182

Major Quince L. Brown, USAF (12.33): Shown here while a first lieutenant, Major Brown was shot down on 6 September 1944 and killed by angry civilians. Brown scored all his victories while fighting with the 78th Fighter Group in the ETO. Brown's hometown was Bristow, Oklahoma, hence the OKIE insignia. Fifty-three USAAF fighter pilots named "Brown" scored one or more aerial victories in WWII. (USAF)

(USAF)

Captain Henry William Brown, USAF (14.20): Brown, who retired as a colonel in mid-1970s, has been recognized as having 17.20 victories but the USAF Study #85 lists him with 14.20. He served two tours with the 355th Fighter Group in the ETO, flying both P-47s and P-51s. Shot down in October 1944, Brown's squadron C.O. landed in a pasture to rescue him but when the C.O.'s Mustang got mired in mud, both were captured and sent to POW camps in Germany.

(AF)

Major Sam J. Brown, USAF (15.50): Brown, from Tulsa, Oklahoma became the C.O. of the 307th Fighter Squadron, 31st Group in the MTO. Over Vienna on 26 June 1944, Major Sam Brown shot down four German fighters plus two more as probables, his biggest day of the war. Today he resides in Oklahoma City.

(USAAF)

First Lt. John B. Carder, USAF (7.0):
This young fighter pilot from Corning Street in Red Oak, Iowa, lost his life in an airplane crash in the early 1960s.
In WWII he flew with the 357th Fighter Group in the ETO. April 24, 1944 over Munich, he scored a kill when a Luftwaffe pilot who had fought him dead-even for twenty minutes entered a high-speed stall which gave Carder the break he needed.

(USAF)

Captain James Richard Carter, USAF (6.0)
Shown here as a lieutenant colonel, Carter is from Spokane, Washington but lives today in Las Cruces, New Mexico. His combat was with the 61st Squadron, 56th Fighter Group in the ETO. "18 November 1944, while strafing an oil storage area, our top cover beetled off to strafe a nearby airfield. Top cover was replaced by 16 FW-190s who had us cold! Our youngsters performed beautifully, though, and we got thirteen for the loss of two!"

(Toliver Collection)

WOLFPACK ACE
Major Harold E. Comstock flew with "Hub" Zemke's 56th Fighter Group in the 8th Air Force in WWII. He is credited with five victories. His nickname is "Bunny."

(USAF)

Major Paul A. Conger, USAF (11.50): Sherman Oaks, California. 61st and 63rd Squadron. 56th Fighter Group, 8th AF, ETO.

(USAF)

Lt. Colonel George A. Doersch, USAF (10.50): Doersch scored ten of his victories while a first lieutenant and captain flying with the 370th Squadron of the 359th Fighter Group. He added half a kill with the 368th Squadron. When all his guns quit firing during a battle in May 1944, Doersch continued making "dry run" passes at a German who was so frightened he bailed out. Doersch lives in Thousand Oaks, California.

(USAF)

Lt. Colonel Paul P. Douglas, USAF (7.00): Douglas, who retired as a brigadier general, now lives in Conway, Arkansas. He scored all his victories with the 395th and 396th Squadrons of the 368th Fighter Group, 9th Air Force in the ETO. He is one of the most highly decorated officers of WWII, winning the DSC twice and the Silver Star three times, plus the DFC and 30+ Air Medals.

(USAF)

Major Glendon V. Davis, USAF (7.50): Davis was a captain when he scored his 7½ aerial victories while fighting with the 364th Squadron of the 357th Fighter Group in the ETO. Davis is from Cambridge and Parma, Idaho. He was shot down over occupied France on 29 April 1944 and was an evadee until 6 September, returning to combat as commander of the 409th Squadron.

Major Frank Junior "Spot" Collins, USAF (9.0): Collins, from Breckenridge, Texas originally, now lives in Tampa, Florida. He flew his combat in the MTO flying with the 319th Squadron of the 325th Fighter Group. After the end of hostilities in Europe, Collins flew against the Japanese, but was shot down by flak and held as a POW until the end of the war.

(USAF)

(USAF)

Colonel Glenn T. Eagleston, USAF (20.50): "Eagle" scored all 18.50 victories in WWII flying with the 9th AF's 354th Group, 353rd Squadron. In the Korean War, he added two MiG-15s to his skein, bringing the grand total to 20½ aerial victories. Originally from Farmington, Utah and Alhambra, California, Eagleston has retired to a ranch at Davis Creek, California.

(Toliver Collection)

GABRESKI — THE MAN WHO FLEW TOO LOW

Colonel Francis Gabreski flew 193 combat missions before a low-level strafing mission delivered him to German custody. With 28 victories in the ETO, "Gabby" was a prize to the Luftwaffe. He returned to combat in Korea, downed 6.5 more enemy planes to become one of the "inner seven" American aces to win acedom in each of two wars. Gabreski is enjoying his evening at press time as the top-scoring living American ace, 34.5 victories.

(NJANG)

Captain Francis R. Gerard, USAF (8.0): Gerard, shown in his present rank of major general in the New Jersey Air National Guard, fought with the 339th Fighter Group, 8th AF, ETO.

Pilot Officer William R. Dunn, RAF/USAF (6.00) A 71st Eagle Squadron pilot, Dunn scored 5.0 victories to qualify as the first American to make ace in WWII. Later in the war, Dunn transferred to the USAAF and flying with the 9th AF's 406th Fighter Group, scored another victory to bring his total to 6.0. He is from Arlington, Texas.   (RAF)

186

(Conger Collection)

Boleslaw Michael Gladych, POL/USAF (10.00)
Mike Gladych, shown here with the crew chief of his P-47 in the 61st Squadron of the 56th Fighter Group, ETO, scored ten victories while attached to the USAAF unit. How many he had with the RAF, Polish Air Force or French Air Force is uncertain, but it can be estimated that he has over 20 aerial victories to his credit.

5.5 KILLS, EUROPE
Captain Frances W. Horne was born in Florida and thought often of its balmy charms during combat service with the 352nd Fighter Group of the 8th Air Force in the ETO. Horne became a pharmacist in Tampa, Florida after the war. (Toliver Collection)

(USAF)

Lt. Colonel William J. Hovde, USAF (11.50): Colonel Hovde, San Antonio, Texas, flew with the 358th Squadron, 355th Fighter Group in WWII (ETO) and scored 10.5 aerial victories. In the Korean War, while with the 4th Wing, he knocked down one MiG-15 to raise his overall total to 11.50. On 5 December 1944 over Berlin Hovde shot down 5½ German aircraft.

(USAF)

Captain Jack M. Ilfrey, USAF (8.0)
Ilfrey, from Houston and San Antonio Texas, shot down six German aircraft while flying his first combat tour with the 1st Fighter Group, and added two more with the 79th Squadron, 20th Group two years later. He has recently published his own memoirs "Happy Jack's Go-buggy."

(USAF)

Captain Robert S. Johnson, USAF (28.00)
Johnson, of the 56th Fighter Group, ETO, was the first USAAF pilot to rack up 28 kills. However, one of the victories remained unconfirmed until after Gabreski scored his 28th. USAF Study 85, dated 1978, gives Johnson only twenty-seven victories. Johnson is from Lawton, Oklahoma but has lived in Woodbury, New York for the past thirty years or more.

Captain Robert A. Lamb, USAF (7.00):
Waldwick, New Jersey. Lamb flew with the 56th Fighter Group, 61st Squadron.

(Conger Collection)

SEVENTEEN KILLS, ETO

Lt. Colonel Gerald W. Johnson of Owenton, Kentucky, was among the successful aces of the 56th Fighter Group, flying in Europe with the 8th Air Force. Often confused with other American aces named Johnson, Gerald W. downed seventeen German aircraft. He retired as a lieutenant general and now lives in Little Rock, Arkansas. (USAF)

(Toliver Collection)

EIGHT LUFTWAFFE VICTORIES

Major Michael Jackson downed eight German aircraft in the ETO during his service with the 56th Fighter Group, 8th Air Force. He called Plainfield, New Jersey his hometown, but now resides in Edison, New Jersey.

188

Captain Raymond H. Littge, USAF (10.50)
Captain Littge, from Altenburg, Missouri, scored
10.50 kills in the air plus destroying another thirteen
on the ground while fighting with the 487th Squadron
of the 352nd Fighter Group in the ETO. Littge
died in the crash of an F-84 jet on May 20th, 1949.

Major Bert Wilder Marshall, USAF (7.00):
Marshall, from Greenville, Texas, now
lives in Dallas. Flying with the 355th
Group in the ETO, on 18 August 1944
Marshall was forced to land his P-51 in
German territory, but was rescued by a
very brave squadron mate Royce Priest.

Lt. Colonel William H. Lewis, USAF (7.00)
Lewis, as a captain with the 343rd Squadron,
55th Fighter Group in the ETO, chalked up seven
aerial victories and up to twenty ground-destroyed
credits. He lives in Oxnard, California.

P-38 LIGHTNING LOVER
Lt. Colonel John H. Lowell, seen here during WWII service with the 364th Fighter
Group of the 8th Air Force, was an ace who could really fly the P-38.
Credited with 7.5 victories in Europe, Lowell believed the P-38 was the equal
of any fighter in the air if it were properly flown. He once whipped an
RAF Spitfire in mock aerial combat on a bet.

189

(USAF)

Lt. Frank W. Klibbe, USAF (7.00): Aurora, Colorado. Klibbe flew with the 61st Squadron, 56th Fighter Group, 8th AF, ETO.

(USAF)

"DAWN PATROL" RESCUE ATTEMPT

Colonel Charles W. Lenfest, USAF, of Boise, Idaho, made a valiant attempt to pick up Lt. Colonel Henry W. Brown in Germany when the latter was forced down. Lenfest's Mustang got mired and the two pilots became POWs. Lenfest is credited with five victories. He was C.O. of the 354th Fighter Squadron, 355th Fighter Group, 8th Air Force at the time he became a guest of the Germans—October 1944. Retired as a brigadier general.

(Conger Collection)

Lt. Frank E. McCauley, USAF (5.50)
Hicksville, Ohio.
61st Squadron, 56th Fighter Group,
8th AF, ETO.

(USAF)

Major Walker Melville "Bud" Mahurin, USAF (24.25)
Mahurin, from Ft. Wayne, Indiana but now living at Newport Beach, California, is shown here while with the 56th Group in the ETO. 19.75 victories with the 56th plus 1.0 with the 3rd Commandos, SWPA, plus 3.50 in the Korean War. Mahurin is the only ace with German, Japanese and Korean victories. POW in North Korea from 13 May 1952 until 6 September 1953. America's 14th ranking ace.

(USAF)

Major Pierce W. McKennon, RAF/USAF (12.00)
McKennon joined the RCAF and flew with the Eagle
Squadron scoring one victory. He scored 11.00 more
victories after he transferred to the USAAF 4th Fighter Group
in September 1942. He was from Ft. Smith, Arkansas.
McKennon was killed in an aircraft accident June 18, 1947.

(USAF)

Colonel Robin Olds, USAF (12.00 WWII + 4.00 Vietnam)
Steamboat Springs, Colorado. Olds scored twelve
victories with the 434th Squadron, 479th Fighter Group,
the last to join the 8th AF in the ETO in WWII. He flew
in the Vietnam War and added four more kills, making his
total for both wars 16.00.

(Toliver Collection)

How Close Can You Get?
Captain Eugene W. O'Neill, of Coral Gables, Florida,
fought with the Zemke "Wolfpack" in the ETO and
was credited with 5.0 aerial kills. However, thirty-
three years later USAF Study 85 downgraded his
score and officially credits him with just 4.50 victories. Historians do have their problems! O'Neill, in
the cockpit of a Thunderbolt, is flanked by the plane's
crew.

(Toliver Collection)

Colonel Joseph L. Mason, USAF (5.00):
Columbus, Ohio. Red Mason commanded the 352nd Fighter Group
from 17 May 1943 until 17 November 1944. He scored his last three victories
on 13 May 1944. Joe was a classmate of author Toliver in Class 38C at Randolph and Kelley Fields,
in Texas. He is shown here (center) with his crew. Mason passed away in 1970.

(USAF)

Captain Frank Q. O'Connor, USAF (10.75):
From Oregon City, Oregon, Captain O'Connor shot down 10.75 German aircraft while flying with the 9th AF's 354th Group.

(LTV)

MARSHALL AND PRIEST SHOW HOW IT WAS DONE!
Bert Marshall (right, bottom man) was forced to land his Mustang in enemy territory and his friend Royce W. Priest landed beside him, shucked his parachute, let Marshall get in the Mustang first, then sat on his lap and flew safely back to England. Marshall has seven victories and Priest has five. They both flew with the 354th Squadron, 355th Fighter Group, 8th AF, ETO.

(Toliver Collection)

Captain James M. Morris, USAF (7.33)
Tampa, Florida. The number two ace of the 20th Fighter Group, 8th AF, ETO. Morris flew all his sorties with the 77th Squadron. On 8 February 1944 he shot down four Luftwaffe aircraft.

Brigadier General Glennon T. Moran, USAF (13.0)
General Moran fought his combat tour as a first lieutenant with the 487th Squadron, 352nd Fighter Group in the ETO. He lives in St. Louis, Missouri.

(Mo. ANG)

192

(USAF)

Lt. Colonel Carl W. Payne, USAF (5.00): 12th AF, MTO, 31st Fighter Group. Lower Salem, Ohio.

(National Archives)

Captain Joe. H. Powers, USAF (14.50) The number eight ace of the 56th Fighter Group in the ETO, Powers came from Tulas, Oklahoma.

(USAF)

(Conger Collection)

Captain Michael J. Quirk, USAF (11.00)
Born in Port Henry, New York but now living near Gulf Breeze, Florida, Quirk flew with the 62nd Squadron, 56th "Wolfpack" Group. He was a POW in Germany from 11 September 1944 until May 1945.

First Lt. Robert J. Rankin, USAF (10.00): From Washington, D.C., but now living in Petersburg, Virginia, Rankin flew to acedom with the famed 56th Group "Wolfpack." "On 12 May 1944, Zemke, my wingman, and I attacked approximately fifty German fighters. In a 45-minute engagement I shot down five enemy planes, the last one shot off the tail of Zemke. Got the DSC and promoted to captain!"

Major LeRoy A. Schreiber, USAF (12.00): Plymouth, Massachusetts. Schreiber flew with the 61st and 62nd Squadrons, 56th Fighter Group, 8th AF, ETO.

(National Archives)

(USAF)

Lt. Colonel Donald J. Strait, USAF (13.50): 361st Squadron, 356th Group, ETO. Retired as major general and lives at Shalimar, Florida.

(USAF)

Colonel David C. Schilling, USAF (22.50) Leavenworth, Kansas and Kansas City, Missouri. Schilling, shown here beside an F-80A jet, scored all his victories flying with the Zemke "Wolfpack" 56th Fighter Group. He lost his life in an automobile accident in England in 1955.

(USAF)

Major Leslie C. Smith, USAF (7.00): Smith, shown here as a brigadier general, is from Caruthers, California. Flew with 61st and 62nd Squadrons of the famous Zemke "Wolfpack," the 56th Fighter Group, ETO. "At the time each successive victory was the most exciting. Now they all seem alike!"

Lt. Colonel Everett W. Stewart, USAF (7.83): Dallas, Texas. Stewart first flew a tour in the PTO in 7th AF with the 18th Fighter Group, then a tour in the ETO as commander of the 328th Squadron of the 352nd Group, and later as commander of the 355th Group and the 4th Group.

(USAF)

(Toliver Collection)

IN NORTH AFRICA

This dashing young American fighter pilot in North Africa with his P-40 fighter is Ralph G. "Zack" Taylor, who downed six enemy aircraft in WWII. His unit was the 325th Fighter Group of the 12th Air Force. Captain Taylor of war days remained in the USAF, rose to major general before retirement, and is now board chairman of First Western Savings, Las Vegas, Nevada.

(Vaughn Collection)

Major Harley C. Vaughn, USAF (7.00): Corpus Christi, Texas. 96th Squadron, 82nd Fighter Group, MTO.

(Toliver Collection)
Captain Charles E. Weaver, USAF (8.00): Atlanta, Georgia. 362nd Squadron, 357th Fighter Group, 8th AF, ETO.

(USAF)

Major Samuel James Wicker, USAF (7.00): Sanford, North Carolina. "I was a much wiser fighter pilot!" said Wicker after returning from an all-out battle over Hamburg on 31 December 1944. It was the last mission of his combat tour and he had shot down four enemy planes, bringing his total to seven. He flew with the 383rd Squadron, 364th Group, 8th AF, ETO.

Colonel Oliver B. Taylor, USAF (5.00)
Sausalito, California. 15th AF, 14th Fighter Group, MTO. Taylor was Group C.O. when he scored his victories. This photo taken May 1944 at Triolo Field, Foggia #7, Italy. Taylor, left, stands with his crew chief, assistant crew chief and armorer.

(Taylor Collection)

(USAF)

Captain John F. Thornell, USAF (17.25): Highland, California. 328th Squadron, 352nd Fighter Group, 8th AF, ETO.

(Conger Collection)

Major James C. Stewart, USAF (11.50)
Sacramento, California. 61st Squadron, 56th Fighter Group, 8th AF, ETO. Stewart ended his combat tour with doubles on the 6th, 8th and 20th of March 1944.

(USAF)

Captain Felix D. Williamson, USAF (13.00): Cordelia, Georgia. 62nd Squadron, 56th Fighter Group, 8th AF, ETO.

196

(Toliver Collection)

SIX DOWN IN EUROPE

Major Robert E. Welch downed six German aircraft while serving with the 55th Fighter Group in the ETO. He stayed in the USAF and lost his life in a flying accident at Luke AFB on 23 March 1951. His hometown was Brown City, Michigan.

(USAF)

Captain Ray S. Wetmore, USAF (21.25)
Kerman, California. Originally recognized as having 22.6 victories, Wetmore flew with the 370th Squadron, 359th Group, 8th AF, ETO. Killed in fighter accident at Dow AFB, Maine on 14 February 1951.

(USAF)
Major Victor E. Warford, USAF (8.00)
Chickasha, Oklahoma. 309th Squadron, 31st Fighter Group, 15th AF, MTO. POW at Sagan and Moosburg, Germany 11 October 1944-29 April 1945.

"THEY WERE ALL EASY—ONCE I HIT THEM!"

Colonel Hubert "Hub" Zemke studies the guns with which he hit them while commanding his famous "Wolf Pack" — the 56th Fighter Group of the 8th Air Force in Europe. Credited with 17.75 aerial victories in WWII, Zemke was shot down late in 1944. As senior Allied officer at Stalag Luft I, Zemke did a monumental job of leadership in POW camp that proved his outstanding character and capabilities. He survived WWII and is an almond rancher in California today. (Toliver Collection)

"I'd Rather Be an Ace Than a Four Star General"

(USAF)

So said General Laurence S. Kuter (right), C-in-C, North American Air Defense Command, to Jim Brooks (left) upon his election as president of the American Fighter Aces Association.

Brooks downed thirteen enemy aircraft as a first lieutenant with the 31st Fighter Group in the ETO in World War II.

In the center is the late Commander Eugene Valencia of the U.S. Navy, vice president of the American Fighter Aces Association at that time. Valencia's career included twenty-three aerial victories in World War II, and is fully dealt with in the text.

U.S. NAVY ACES OF WORLD WAR II
(1)

6

The paralyzing tactical and strategic blow struck by Japan at Pearl Harbor had as its objective the destruction of the U.S. Pacific Fleet, or its temporary reduction to impotence. Never in naval history had a fleet traveled such a vast distance from home waters to attempt the surprise strangulation of enemy naval power at a single stroke. As revolutionary as it was bold, the Pearl Harbor attack saw the Japanese Navy desert classical gunfire in favor of carrier-based aerial bombardment. A new epoch had begun.

The shattering surprise, power and force of this large-scale use of naval air power shocked the opponents of American carrier aviation into embarrassed silence. Events of staggering importance and unpredictable consequences had suddenly elevated naval aviation to a position of primacy in the Pacific war. Principles of war doctrines heretofore a source of political and military argument had been devastatingly defined in Hawaii. The Pacific conflict appeared immediately as largely an aircraft carriers' war. Without command of the air over the sea, land power could not be brought to bear. The total outcome would hinge on the building and sinking of aircraft carriers.

The stroke that almost drove America to its knees also gave tremendous stimulus to naval aviation. Positive and rapid developments took place in American naval affairs in the six months following Pearl Harbor, changes and progress that would have required twenty years of peacetime bumbling and wrangling. Politicians who had condemned aircraft carriers and hacked at naval budgets, now began insisting that they had always believed in the aircraft carrier. Party lines and old dogmas evaporated, as Congress voted huge appropriations for new carriers that were to be built immediately.

Development of naval fighter planes was concomitantly seen as essential to sweeping the Japanese from the Pacific. The ensuing months reinforced this development drive, when it was found that the existing Grumman Wildcat fighters were not adequate to cope with the Zero. Top priority was given by the naval authorities to development and production of superior fighters. The magnificent Grumman Hellcat, which first saw action in the Marcus Island area in 1943, was one result of these exertions. The rugged and durable Vought Corsair soon followed.

Fighter aviation in the Navy had little tradition on which to draw. Until the Battle of Balikpapan in 1942, the U.S. Navy had not fought even one surface action in the twentieth century, let alone established any combat tradition or experience for its fighter pilots. David Ingalls of World War I was the only U.S. Navy fighter ace at the time of the Pearl Harbor attack, although several other Americans had become aces in the Royal Naval Air Service in the 1914-18 war.

By war's end in 1945, after three and a half years of phenomenal growth and technical development, the U.S. Navy had 329 new fighter aces to relieve David Ingalls of his solitude. What Japan started, Uncle Sam finished. The oceans of the world had never seen such power as that contained in the mighty U.S. task forces that dominated the Pacific, relentlessly hunting down the last vestiges of Japan's naval power.

Navy aces fought a different kind of war to their army counterparts. Functioning mainly from aircraft carriers, and operating for the most part over the ocean, they faced the problems of exacting navigation and the always-tricky carrier landings in addition to the hazards of fighting the enemy. Engine failure or combat damage usually meant ditching in the sea, and if the pilots survived that hazard, they faced sharks and exposure.

The U.S. Navy pilots faced in their Japanese foes some of the most experienced fighter pilots in the world. The Japanese had been at their trade—with live ammunition—

HELLCATS IN FULL CRY

This Grumman F-6F Hellcat is part of large fighter formation over the Western Pacific in 1944. Navy fighters came back from Pearl Harbor debacle to conduct massive sweeps over Japanese home islands in 1945.

(Toliver Collection)

long enough to develop the vital combat acumen that hones fighting skills even as it keeps a fighter pilot alive. Thoroughly trained and highly skilled, many of Japan's airmen had years of combat experience over China. They had flown against Chinese pilots, and against Soviet pilots in border battles. The Japanese had also fought many soldier-of-fortune pilots from Western countries who flew as mercenaries for China.

The Zero fighter outclassed the equipment initially available to the Americans. Japanese fighter pilot experience accentuated this technical superiority. Americans accustomed to thinking of Japanese technology in terms of cheap pre-war trade goods got a strong psychological shock from the Zero. The nimble, heavily-armed enemy machine was front-line proof that the U.S. Navy faced a redoubtable enemy.

Further aiding the Japanese pilots in the early months was the flood tide of victory on which they rode. Japanese power had sprawled across the Pacific, crushing all resistance. Total victory seemed certain. The brunt of the battle in these grim early days of the air war at sea was borne by a relatively small group of U.S. Navy professionals. From their ranks came the greatest U.S. Navy fighter ace of all time—Captain David McCampbell.

An Annapolis-trained Navy professional (class of '33), McCampbell spent a brief time out of the service in the middle thirties due to Navy budget strictures. Recalled to line duty in 1934, he had to fight his way into naval

aviation, passing out of Pensacola in 1938. He served from first to last with the carrier forces in both the Atlantic and Pacific Fleets. He was aboard the U.S.S. *Wasp* when she made her daring runs to carry Spitfires to Malta, and he survived the sinking of *Wasp* in the Pacific in 1942. McCampbell also served aboard *Hornet* and *Essex*, his great glory days coming while in the latter ship.

Most of McCambell's combat was with Air Group 15. His personal score of thirty-four enemy aircraft shot down is not only remarkable as the outstanding naval record of World War II, but also as the achievement of an "old man" fighter pilot. McCampbell was thirty-four years old when he began cutting a swathe through the Japanese formations!

No other American naval fighter ace came near his score. A brilliant leader, superb shot and top tactician, David McCampbell also holds the all-time American record for the largest number of kills on a single mission: nine confirmed and two probables on 24 October 1944. He is the leading Navy ace of all the wars, the top living Navy ace (1978), and the number two living American ace, but McCampbell's nine confirmed kills on one mission is a feat unequalled by any other American pilot, living or dead, Army, Navy or Air Force.

This spectacular mission is also the most memorable combat experience of the distinguished Captain McCampbell:

"Indubitably, the most exciting action I had in combat occurred during the battles of Leyte

Gulf in the Pacific. On my first flight on the morning of 24 October 1944, I was launched from the U.S.S. Essex *with a group of seven Grumman Hellcats to intercept an incoming raid of a hundred-odd Japs. This was the second and last time I was to take part in a 'fighter scramble,' primarily because my job as Air Group Commander did not normally demand that I engage in this type of combat. Also, after the action, our Admiral said to me, 'It's all right this time, but don't let it happen again.'*

"We intercepted the raid at a distance of about twenty miles from the task group. This incident met the highest expectations of my fondest hopes and dreams of favorable combat conditions. Due to my experience in the previous four months of combat, plus the luck of the Irish, I was able to exploit the situation. Without attempting to explain the action in detail, suffice it to say that I just did what came naturally to one who had spent many years training for just such an occasion.

"My wingman and I accounted for fifteen definitely destroyed. I was credited with nine shot down and two probables. Not a single enemy plane got through to attack our ships.

"After following the decimated formation nearly all the way to Manila, we returned to the vicinity of the task group, exhausted of ammunition and near fuel-exhaustion, to witness the agonized maneuvering of our ships under attack by a second raid, which caused mortal damage to U.S.S.* Princeton. *I landed aboard the* Langley, *since it had the only clear deck in the task group that could take me, and barely had sufficient gas to taxi out of the arresting gear.

"When the final tally was in, the small flight of seven planes I had led were credited with twenty-seven enemy planes destroyed, and an additional eight planes probably destroyed. We had only superficial damage, largely as a result of flying through the debris of exploding enemy planes."*

In addition to the Congressional Medal of Honor, David McCampbell was awarded the Navy Cross, the Silver Star, the Legion of Merit and the Air Medal. As this is written, McCampbell is residing at Lake Worth, Florida.

Just as there were some differences in the various theaters and commands of the USAAF in the awarding of victory credits, so did the U.S. Navy procedures include some non-standard elements. Some Navy units did not split or share victory credits—to the joy of statisticians and historians decades later. Through a gentlemen's agreement, the victory was credited to the pilot among those destroying the enemy machine who had the least number of kills. These Navy units thus more or less followed the Luftwaffe idea of one-pilot-one-kill, which disposed of the confusing half and quarter airplane victory credits.*

A leader and his wingman in combat would frequently both fire at a target. As in the case of David McCampbell on several occasions, there was doubt as to who actually knocked the enemy plane down. McCampbell often gave the victory credit to his wingman, and

---

*USAAF 5th Air Force and 13th Air Force units, also operating in the Pacific, followed the Navy lead in this regard. If more than one fighter participated in the downing of an enemy plane, the decision as to who got the credit was determined by the cut of a card, the roll of a die, or the judgment of the Intelligence Officer, Operations Officer, or unit commander.

(USN)

THIRTY-FOUR RISING SUNS THAT SET EARLY
Thirty-four Rising Suns on the fuselage of his Hellcat fighter attest to the historic record of Captain David McCampbell, top-scoring ace of the U.S. Navy, and top-scoring naval fighter pilot of all the nations and all the wars. McCampbell also holds the American record for the most downings in one engagement — nine — for which feat he received the Congressional Medal of Honor. He served most successfully with VF-15.

bore a reputation for generosity and fairness in this regard. Conjectural though it may be, certainly it is worth observing that a selfish David McCampbell might well have become the all-time top scoring American ace, since he stands only six kills behind Richard Bong.

Lieutenant Commander Edward H. "Butch" O'Hare became the U.S. Navy's first fighter ace with a stunning performance near Rabaul on 20 February 1942. Operating from U.S.S. *Lexington* as a section leader in VF-3, O'Hare was aloft with five other fighters as a wave of Japanese bombers lunged towards the American carrier force. At this critical juncture, O'Hare's wingman reported his guns were jammed. Widely separated from the other four available fighters, O'Hare had to play a lone hand.

Aggression was the only course. Firing into two aircraft in the rear enemy formation, O'Hare sent them down blazing and smoking. Crossing immediately to the other side of the vee-formation, his guns roared again and down went two more enemy bombers. This action had carried the formation close to their bomb release point above the American ships—a situation calling for instant action. O'Hare bored in firing. Another bomber went down. Four more lurched away in obvious distress as O'Hare's ammunition ran out.

An ace in this one standout engagement, Butch O'Hare won the Congressional Medal of Honor and a special niche in Navy tradition. A great coach and teacher of green pilots, he still managed to run up twelve kills of his own before his death in combat. The gunner of a Japanese bomber shot him down at night—a severe loss to America and the U.S. Navy.

Another of the pre-war Navy professionals who held the line for America in the early days of the Pacific war was Captain James H. Flatley, Jr. Almost thirty-six years old when he entered aerial combat for the first time, Jim Flatley was an "old man" as fighter pilots are reckoned. The years between his 1929 Annapolis graduation and World War II put a patina on his skills, and he shot down 6.5 planes in the Pacific—no doubt flown by men much younger than himself.

Like many other Navy pilots who lived through the grim first months of the Pacific war, his most unforgettable experience of combat is connected with the surprise impact of the Zero. Extensive service with VF-2, VF-42 and VF-10 did nothing to diminish this

particular memory of the former Green Bay, Wisconsin man:

"My most unforgettable combat experience was shooting down a Zero in the Battle of the Coral Sea on 7 May 1942. It was my first encounter. I attacked three by myself, having had absolutely no intelligence about them. I was astounded by the performance of the Zero. They outclimbed and out maneuvered my Grumman F4F3, but they could not stay with me in a dive with an aileron turn."

Strong warnings about the formidable performance of the Zero had been sent from China by General Claire Chennault, as mentioned earlier. These warnings were based on actual combat with the Japanese machine by American pilots who were, in most instances, trained professionals from the U.S. armed services flying for China as volunteers. This crucial intelligence never found its way to the USAAF and Navy pilots who had to face the Zero in the first months of the Pacific war.

Navy pilots later discovered a deficiency in the Zero that had an important influence on tactics. Captain Flatley has already referred to this deficiency in his combat account. At high speeds, the controls of the Zero became so heavy that the pilot could not match the turn rate of the F4U, F6F or Army P-38. The U.S. escape tactic was to dive to speeds exceeding 300 mph, start a roll to the left, then reverse the roll to the right and pull out. The Zero could not follow this maneuver due to high control forces.

The steadily increasing technical superiority of the U.S. Navy fighters was also enhanced by improved training. Lessons from the early battles with the Zero were incorporated in this training. The unmatchable resources and industrial power of the U.S. quickly eroded the initial combat edge of the Japanese, of which the Zero became a symbol.

Commanding VF-16 aboard the U.S.S. *Lexington* was Captain Paul D. Buie of Nashville, Georgia, an ace with nine confirmed victories and the following standout memory of combat against the Zekes:

"On 23 and 24 November 194 , the Lexington *was part of a carrier task group covering the invasion of Tarawa in the Gilbert Islands. The* Lexington *was operating between Tarawa and Mille to prevent Japanese air interference with landing operations.*

"About noon on the 23rd, the Lexington *radar controller vectored my twelve-plane*

Combat Air Patrol to a fighter pilot's dream position, 4,000 feet up-sun of a 21-plane parade formation of Zekes. The position was perfect for coordinated high-side and overhead attack. We are sure we got seventeen Zekes, and we think we got all twenty-one of them.

"Action was initiated at 23,000 feet and carried down to 5,000 feet chasing stragglers. In this action, Ralph Hanks bagged five Zekes.

"Same time, same place, next day the twenty-fourth, my twelve-plane formation was again on CAP and vectored to intercept another Jap flight of twenty Zekes and two Bettys. This time the CIC misjudged the altitude of the enemy, and action was begun with Jap fighters having an advantage of 2,000 feet. We met, but could not prevent the Japs' first firing pass, but they never got another chance.

"Action began at 23,000 feet, carried up to 28,000 and then worked down to about 5,000. In this action we got thirteen for sure and think we bagged nineteen. We lost no planes on the twenty-third, and one on the Japs' first firing pass on the twenty-fourth for a certain ratio of thirty to one in the two days of fighting."

Lieutenant Richard L. Bertelson called the U.S.S. *Cabot* home in 1944-1945 while reaching his ace ranking with five aerial victories. Hailing from Minneapolis, Minnesota, Bertelson has one special recollection of aerial combat:

"Ten of us were striking an airfield on a small island north of Okinawa in April 1945. We had just recovered from a run, and as my leader and I were top cover, I looked back and then up into the sun. There must have been at least thirty Zeros pouring down on us. The lead Zero was opening up on my section leader, so I swung into him, fired, blew him up and the dogfight started.

"After a wild melee in which I was lucky enough to shoot down two more, the Nips had all been shot down or had made off."

Lieutenant Bertelson flew eighty-eight missions in World War II. He calls Eden Prairie, Minnesota, his home today.

The Pacific war had its share of oddities, among them a novel kill scored by Lieutenant Commander Roger A. Wolf of Fort Collins, Colorado. He recorded a notable first for the Navy by using his hulking Coronado patrol bomber as a fighter.

Returning from a mission, Wolf looked down and spotted a Jap Betty bomber cruising serenely along about two hundred feet above the ocean. Wolf eased his lumbering machine into a stern chase position on the Betty. The Coronado's guns roared and the Betty, aflame from wingtip to wingtip, cartwheeled into the ocean in a spectacular kaleidoscope of steam, spray, smoke and debris.

Commander Wolf survived World War II, but was killed on 1 October 1955 in the crash of a jet fighter while taking off at El Paso, Texas.

Commander Hugh N. Batten of Huntington, West Virginia, is credited with seven aerial victories in World War II. His most vivid combat memory is of chasing Zeros in the murk near Okinawa, during his service aboard U.S.S. *Essex:*

"On 16 April 1945, near Okinawa, while on CAP we intercepted nine Zeros in low visibility. After the lead section of our flight attacked, I took my section in and my wingman and I each knocked down a Zeke. First section lost contact due to the restricted weather, but they could see planes burning and falling eerily through the murk. By the time they would reach the spot, we would then be far enough away that they could not see us. The first section confirmed seven kills for us.

"My plane was shot up a little, and badly damaged when I flew through the blast of an exploding Zeke. I had four victories and my wingman three. Then on the way home we spotted a Zeke down low. Diving down I pulled the trigger, only to find I had just two shots left. I pulled aside and my wingman made the kill to even the score to four Zekes each. All the victories were further confirmed by my gun-camera film. My wingman was Lieutenant Commander Samuel J. Brocato and we both got the Navy Cross for this mission."

The Sam Brocato referred to in Hugh Batten's battle story also ended the war with seven confirmed victories. The same encounter that stuck in Batten's mind also is the outstanding combat recollection of Sam Brocato:

"We were intercepting a nine-plane flight of Zeros, each of which was carrying a 500-lb bomb externally. We approached undetected from astern and splashed the four trailing Zekes before the others knew we were there. The remaining Zekes then jettisoned their bombs and joined battle.

"The section maintained its integrity during the chase that followed through flipper turns, loops and Immelmanns and in and out of the overcast. During one maneuver we looped up into the overcast to find ourselves on the tails of the Zekes. The Japanese pilots had unintentionally pulled their loop tighter and inside ours. By shifting from offensive to defensive tactics as the situation demanded, and containing the dogfight within a localized area, we were able to destroy four more Zeros. The ninth Zeke either escaped into the clouds or fell victim to a large flight of Corsairs that came on the scene. Batten and I each destroyed four Zeros."

Brocato hails from Baltimore, Maryland, and Hugh Batten lives at Tanneytown, Md.

In numerous experiences related already in this book, aggressiveness proved to be one of the fighter ace's greatest psychological weapons. An aggressive, determined response has been repeatedly demonstrated in aerial combat as a means of turning defeat into victory. Every experienced aerial fighter knows the importance of an aggressive spirit—especially when the odds seem impossibly long.

Lieutenant Eugene Valencia, USN, dramatically turned the tables on his foes in a classic demonstration of this principle. Combat with Japanese fighters resulted in Valencia being separated from other American fighters, and six Zeros descended on him like angry hornets. Firewalling his throttle, Valencia took off in the direction of his carrier, *Yorktown*, the six Zekes hot on his tail.

Howling along for untold miles, pulling the last ounce out of his Hellcat, Valencia was able to maintain a short lead on the pursuing Japanese fighters. The Japanese pilots couldn't overtake the lone American and they couldn't hit him with their guns. Crouched in the Hellcat's cockpit, Valencia suddenly realized that the chase could eventually end only one way, since he was within maximum range of the Japanese guns and he could not coax enough speed out of his F6F to extend his lead. The alternative was to turn and face his foes.

Reefing his Hellcat around as tightly as he could, Valencia hurled himself furiously on Japanese pursuers. From cold turkey the American had turned into a hot aggressor and his guns ripped into the startled enemy planes. Three Zekes exploded in quick succession, the fireballs and smoke registering on the remaining enemy like lethal scoring lights. The game had a completely new aspect now. Demoralized and shocked, the three remaining Zekes turned and took off at full throttle, with Valencia now in pursuit. He chased them as far as he dared, without further result, before returning to his carrier. His gun-camera film confirmed the kills.

Gene Valencia came out of World War II as an ace with twenty-three victories. Only three Navy aces in history were able to record more than twenty victories—David McCampbell, Cecil Harris with twenty-four, and Valencia. A tall, dark and handsome man, Valencia was one of the founding fathers of the American Fighter Aces' Association in 1960. He worked actively in the affairs of the association until his untimely death from a heart attack in 1972.

Valencia led the most successful fighter division in the Navy in World War II. Part of VF-9 aboard U.S.S. *Yorktown*, Valencia's division was famous throughout the Pacific Fleet as "Valencia's Flying Circus." Also known as the "mowing machine," Valencia's division operated in combat with one section engaging and the other section waiting aloft. As the first section broke off combat, the second would descend immediately to re-engage the enemy, and this alternating strike-and-withdraw tactic resembled mower blades.

The dark-haired ace assembled his elite unit in the U.S. after returning as an ace from his first tour. He sought outstanding marksmen and pilots who could enthusiastically give their all to his tactical ideas and to the teamwork essential to their success. With James French, Harris Mitchell and Clinton Smith,* Valencia wrote his success saga in the Pacific. All four men ended the war as aces and with a special place in Navy annals.

The former Lieutenant James B. French kept flying after the war—as a crop duster in Bakersfield, California. Perhaps the harvesting machinery on which he looked down while pursuing this hazardous trade put him in mind of the "mowing machine" from his glory days in the Pacific. Jim French retains one outstanding memory from the stirring times when he scored eleven victories and became a Navy ace:

"*I was leading the section on 17 April 1945, with Gene Valencia leading the division when we engaged about forty Jap fighters at 15,000 feet. We shot down six of them before they got out of auto-lean* (Mixture control setting usually goes to full rich when you go into combat—Aus.) *After that it was tough going for ten to fifteen minutes and the four of us began to realize we could not keep them all cornered for long. We called for assistance— which came—and the Japs bolted. We were low on gas and could not chase them. Valencia*

Smith hails from Jackson, Mississippi, and Mitchell lives in Hutchinson, Kansas.

(USN/French)

VALENCIA'S MOWING MACHINE OF VF-9
This division of fighters of VF-9 accounted for fifty Japanese aircraft shot down. Left to right: Lt. Clinton L. Smith (6); Lt. James B. French (11); Lt. Harris E. Mitchell (10) and Lt. Eugene A. Valencia (23). They flew off USS LEXINGTON and USS YORKTOWN.

had shot down six for sure with one probable and one damaged. His wingman, Lieutenant Harris Mitchell, had clobbered three. I shot down four and my wingman, Lieutenant Clinton O. Smith, had three."

The same action of the "mowing machine" stuck firmly in the memory of Valencia's wingman, Harris Mitchell. Here is his account of the same battle:

"*Date: 17 April 1945*
"*Time: Approximately 0900*
"*Place: East of Okinawa*
"*While flying CAP with two divisions, whose calls were Ruler 4-1,-2,-3,-4 and Ruler 6-1,-2,-3,-4, over a destroyer that was called*

Bright Boy, we received the following message:

"'Ruler 4-1 and 6-1, this is Bright Boy—vector 320 degrees, angels 20, Buster.'

"This is self explanatory except for Buster, which designated a power setting for fast cruise.

"We were at the time circling the destroyer at 5,000 feet and immediately started to climb toward 20,000 and on a heading of 320 degrees. Approximately three minutes later, Bright Boy called us and told us to orbit, because he'd lost the Bogie from his radar screen. A few seconds later, Bright Boy called again, and the message was a little disappointing for 6-1:

"'Ruler 4-1 resume vector 320 degrees, angels 20, Buster, small Bogie ahead sixty miles. Ruler 6-1 return to Bright Boy, orbit angels 10.'

"With this information, we assumed that one or two enemy planes were trying to sneak through our radar screen for a Kamikaze attack. With our division of four planes, we had them outnumbered two to one, which would make it comparatively easy for us to destroy them if we ever made contact.

"Eager for the kill, we climbed steadily to 20,000 feet and settled down to a fast cruise of about 250 knots. Ten minutes elapsed and off in the distance, barely visible, we spotted what we thought was a small bunch of planes. A contact report was made:

"'Tallyho! Ruler 4-1, small bogie ahead 12 o'clock, down thirty miles.'

"We closed our formation a little and all eyes were glued on the enemy formation. As we approached them, they blossomed out from a small speck into something bigger. Another sighting report:

"'Bright Boy, this is Ruler 4-1. Change my tallyho. Ten planes.'

"The odds were no longer in our favor, yet we were still confident, though more concerned than we had been at first. You could tell by the stern expressions on the other pilots' faces that each had gone over his check list and that all was in readiness.

"As the distance kept closing, the enemy formation grew and grew. This time, another sighting report, tinged with urgency:

"'Bright Boy, this is Ruler 4-1. Change my tallyho to twenty-five. Send help.'

"That was the last tallyho before the attack, which we carried out as we had always

planned, trained and hoped for, and which we never in our hearts really expected ever to be able to use.

"We came in high with the sun to our backs and the green and brown camouflaged Japanese fighters with their big, bright meatballs were clearly visible. They weren't even aware of our presence until the first two of them, in the midst of their formation, exploded violently.

"Immediately they all seemed to jettison their bombs simultaneously, the black blobs pouring down out of the formation, the planes leaping and shifting from the diminished weight. We picked the top planes first. As soon as one would burst into flames, we would have another in our sights. For ten minutes or so we zoomed in and out of that formation, wreaking havoc.

"We kept on the offensive continually, protecting each other when necessary. We were beginning to have trouble with our four aircraft keeping the swarms of Jap planes in check, when Ruler 6-1, the second divison, arrived on the scene.

"We rendezvoused, and before departing for our home base on the Yorktown we counted eight parachutes still coming down. Our total score was fourteen Jap fighters destroyed, nine Jap fighters probably destroyed and six damaged. The total was reckoned at thirty-eight, and remarkable as it may seem, not one enemy bullet pierced any of our planes in this action.

The famous "mowing machine," Valencia's Flying Circus, ended the war with fifty kills credited to its pilots, an all-time Navy record for a division. The unit will be part of Navy lore and tradition for generations to come.

Mutually mistaken identity in the air, humorous sometimes in retrospect, proved to be a petrifying experience for a surprising number of America's fighter aces. Lieutenant Commander Robert W. Shackford of Medford, Massachusetts* had this experience and will carry the stark memory of it all his days. He calls it "my most fortunate victory" one of six with which he is credited:

On 19 June 1944, while on a search mission for the Jap fleet, I flew about two hundred miles—almost a solid hour—with a plane about a thousand feet above me that I thought was one of ours. While searching the sea, I

*Since retiring from the Navy, Bob Shackford now lives in Coronado, California.

took a long look up at this aircraft, and got a real jolt to find it was Japanese. I shot the plane down, and it was a case of mutually mistaken identity. I was fortunate, for he was above me and could have shot me down any time during the hour that I cruised with him overhead."

There are other examples in this book of American aces inadvertently flying with German wingmen, and vice versa. All the pilots involved, as well as many other aces whose experiences are not recounted in this book, consider the sudden discovery of an "enemy wingman" to be a superlative recipe for grey hair—getting it, that is, not getting rid of it. The shock effect in these encounters burns their memory indelibly into the mind.

When Lieutenant Johnnie J. Bridges of Shelby, North Carolina, took his gear aboard U.S.S. *Saratoga*, he little realized that he would return from the Pacific war as a Navy ace with six confirmed victories. Bridges best remembers an air battle on 15 December 1944, when his division was flying high cover for an attack on Manila harbor:

"We were at 17,000 feet when sixteen Oscars came out of the sun. For several passes, during which the advantage was with the Japs, we held our own, but we expected the division below us to come and help. They'd lost us. We were operating in sections and were executing a big Lufbery circle for defense, working our way toward a big cloud east of Manila.

One Oscar got anxious and joined the circle

to get in a shot, but was quickly hit himself and dropped away belching smoke. We were too busy to confirm whether he crashed or not. Slowly we inched out way to the cover of the cloud. We made it."

An elite inner cadre of Japanese fighter pilots were superior air-to-air shots, as was the case also with a similar group in the Luftwaffe. Some of these pilots are described in the chapter on enemy aces. A favorite tactic of these Japanese flyers was to get any American machine to enter either a loop or a Lufbery circle, and try to out-turn it. This situation was made to order for the light Japanese machines, and they were often able to lure green American pilots into this trap.

The favorite grandstand shot of the Japanese experts was to shoot an American plane down precisely from the top of the loop. Japanese pilots were seen to enter a vertical Lufbery, sometimes known as a squirrel-cage loop, passing up several shooting opportunities until the precise moment when their enemy was pulling through the top of the loop. Then—blast!

The Japanese pilots of the early Pacific days had few equals in aerobatic flying. Their numerical and technical superiority at that time allowed them to indulge in fancy feats of this kind. As the war progressed and the balance tipped steeply against the Japanese in the air, their main task became staying alive amid the blizzard of U.S. carrier-borne fighters.

JUST ANOTHER HAZARD OF CARRIER OPERATIONS! Quite naturally there is much competition between U.S. Navy and U.S. Air Force pilots, but it is seldom argued if a Navy pilot claims his training is better. Landing on a moving carrier takes exacting skill. This Hellcat was damaged and when landing, the hook caught okay but the entire empennage of the fighter was torn off. Pilot survived.

(USN)

For numerous aces, the most memorable combat experience proves to be not a victory of their own, but rather an occasion on which they were the subject of an enemy victory. Commander James S. Swope of Killeen, Texas, falls into this category. He is credited with ten aerial victories, but none of them stayed in his memory as vividly as his narrow escape from Japanese guns:

"On 16 June 1943, over Henderson Field on Guadalcanal, we engaged an estimated 105 Jap aircraft. While working on some Aichi dive-bombers, I had the misfortune to become engaged singly with a Zero. The F4F is certainly no match for the Zero, but I found it could take a hell of a lot of punishment and still fly.

"I couldn't get a single lick in at the Zeke, but my F4F took two explosive 20mm cannon shells and close to forty 7.7mm bullets. Three cylinders were blown off the radial engine, but I evaded the Jap and still flew that battered F4F 20 miles back to Fighter One strip and the scrap heap."

Pride in a job well done still fills Commander John Carlos Cleves Symmes despite the passage of the years. A longtime resident of Lima, Peru, he is credited with 10.5 aerial victories in the Pacific. He summarizes his memories of the conflict in these terms:

"The record that I like best is that no Navy fighter squadron I was ever with lost a bomber or torpedo-bomber pilot escorted by us to enemy fighters. I am proud to share that good feeling with all the men of those squadrons. For those fighter pilots who did not get back, it represents something concrete and well worth fighting for, since it was one of the primary missions of the fighter pilot to see bombers safely through. In spite of all the baloney written about fighter pilots, the kind of achievement that gives me such pride is indicative of the teamwork without which the war could not have been won.

"On the combat side, my best victory was over Guam one day when my division got away from me chasing enemy fighters after my water injection failed. (Water injection is the mechanical injection of water into the cylinders of an airplane engine, which allows an engine to produce considerably more power without breaking down due to detonation— Aus.) I had detailed the lead as I had no radio.

"I was completely alone and lagging badly when I was jumped by an element of Japs from above. I was able to hold my nerve until they were committed by their speed, then pulled up into them. As the first Jap overshot and dove below me, I flipped over into a dive behind him, figuring that I would at least get him before his wingman got me.

"I shot into him, and although he didn't burn or explode, I undoubtedly shot out his hydraulic system, because a wheel dropped and eventually his engine quit. All the while, we were in a twisting, vertical descent tail chase. The Jap finally went in on Orote Peninsula, and I leveled off on the deck, dodging as best I could through light ack-ack fire. To my surprise, because I was expecting his attack, the Jap number two man had gone, probably scared off by his own side's flak."

Control of the air was not easily wrested from the Japanese in the early months of the Pacific war. Hard-flying, persistent and dogged Navy pilots had their hands full. There were agonizing and bitter moments, in addition to the combat, as recalled by Navy ace Commander Stanley W. Vejtasa of Circle, Montana. He writes of nine and a quarter hours of Combat Air Patrol during the Battle of Santa Cruz on 26 October 1942:

Flying F4F's from Enterprise, *we were in a savage battle when our Task Force, consisting of* Enterprise, Hornet, South Dakota *and escorting cruisers and destroyers, was attacked by hordes of enemy fighters, dive-bombers and torpedo planes. I succeeded in shooting down seven enemy planes in one flight, which is a good indicator of the number of targets available to our fighters.*

"Then came the bitterness. Enterprise *was hit, and our own surface ships had to sink the heavily damaged and helpless* Hornet. *They were grim days."*

Commander Vejtasa is credited with eleven aerial victories in World War II. His first three victories were gained at the controls of a dive-bomber—a Douglas SBD from the *Yorktown* in the Battle of the Coral Sea. The majority of Navy pilots didn't do this well in Hellcats, so Vejtasa's conversion to fighters portended even greater success.

The sneak attack on Pearl Harbor rankled more within the American breast than any other single event of the war. Commander John M. Wesolowski of Detroit, Michigan, got a chance to return the sneak punch against two unsuspecting Japanese. His experience shows how luck and shooting skill can unite to bring aerial victories. Wesolowski is credited with seven kills, but the two of which he writes are those best remembered:

"At Guadalcanal early in the battle, I took off for dusk alert. I got separated from my flight in the overcast at 20,000 feet, so I let down by myself when the alert was over, and found myself just behind eighteen Jap fighters at 5,000 feet.

"Making one pass at the last two planes in the formation, I destroyed them both with about seventy-five rounds of ammo fired. I ducked back into the overcast and returned to Guadalcanal unscathed. I thought about Pearl Harbor, too."

From the pre-war professional ranks of naval aviators came Captain Robert A. Winston, U.S.N. (Ret.), who commanded VF-31 aboard U.S.S. *Cabot* in World War II. While under Winston's command, this squadron shot down sixty-four enemy machines without loss—either operationally or in combat. A Pensacola graduate from the class of '35, Bob Winston saw sixteen of his original thirty-two pilots in VF-31 become fighter aces. Considering how few aces there have been, relative to the total number of pilots trained, this is a truly stellar record. Winston himself best remembers a remarkable triple that came his way near the Palau Archipelago:

"At sunset on 31 March, as Task Force 58 returned from mining the Palau Archipelago, I was flying CAP and was sent by radar to an unidentified bogey seventy-five miles west of the task force.

"It was a formation of twelve Judys in the dusk, and I attacked, leading my four Hellcat division. I got the leader and both his wingmen in one pass—less than ten seconds. My wingmen destroyed the remaining nine enemy aircraft for a grand slam. The Japanese machines proved to be the first Judy kamikaze dive-bombers ever contacted in combat."

Captain Winston died on 3 June 1974, a distinguished career behind him. He was also a noted aviation author. His best-known books were *Dive Bomber* (1939), *Aces Wild* (1941) and *Fighting Squadron* (1946).

That a Pennsylvania mountain boy can make good as a fighter pilot is attested to by the career of Lieutenant Commander Foster J. Blair of Stroudsburg, Pennsylvania. Blair downed five Japanese planes while fighting

with numerous units, including VF-5 and VC-39, aboard such famous carriers as the *Saratoga, Independence, Belleau Wood* and others.

Commander Blair best recalls from his combat career an encounter with high potential to keep other Americans alive:

"As leader of a section of four Wildcats during the invasion of Attu in May of 1943, we sank a Jap landing barge on one pass with our 50-caliber guns. Loaded with about ninety Japanese soldiers, the barge was carrying them to a landing spot behind our troops on the east arm of Holtz Bay. Those enemy troops never made that landing. I feel this contributed to the saving of American lives—troops fighting a rugged war in the jungle. On this account, our strike against that barge was more memorable to me than any of my individual victories."

Lieutenant Commander John W. Dear, an ace with 7.5 aerial victories to his credit, is more noted in ace circles for his unusual ability at destroying Japanese aircraft on the ground. Records of this activity are unofficial, and were never systematically maintained. Nevertheless the unofficial records attribute fifty-two ground kills to Dear. His most memorable combat experience came in the arcane art of nightfighting, where are found the rarest birds in Navy acedom:

"On 4 July 1944 at 0030, I was part of a five-pilot nightfighter unit attached to U.S.S. Hornet, which had just participated in the occupation of the Marianas. Admiral Marc Mitscher ordered Carrier Division Five, which included Hornet, to go north and make a sneak attack on Chi Chi Jima, a sister island to Iwo Jima in the Bonin Group. Admiral "Jocko" Clark relished this assignment, because the islands had been untouched up to this time.

"Two nightfighters, Lieutenant F. L. Dungan and myself, were assigned the job of going in on the islands the night before for the purpose of drawing fire and locating gun positions, keeping the Japs awake and nervous, and locating and identifying any ships there for the bombers to strike shortly after dawn. Planes were not thought to be stationed on the Japanese-held island.

"Buck Dungan and I were launched by catapult at 0030 and flew blacked out formation until we were near the target. Then we separated to make sector search with radar for

ships that might be in the vicinity. There were none.

"Buck beat me back to the island, and had already started on his run to draw fire . . . and did he draw fire! I never saw more tracer ammunition erupt from one concentrated spot before or since. Fortunately, those Japs had no electronic aiming devices, so they were firing in a pattern hoping that we would fly into a projectile. We made scores of runs, but were not touched.

In the predawn light around 0430 I spotted ships streaming out of the harbor by the dozens. One of these was a destroyer, off to one side of the main force and somewhat isolated. I decided to use the last of my two 500-lb bombs on this warship.

"I made a glide-run from about 8,000 feet, pulling up at about two hundred feet . . . and missed by about fifty feet. As I pulled up, Buck let out a yell for help. He had three planes on his tail. After spotting him, I started a frantic climb up to meet him. He had them alright (or vice versa), and he was trailing them behind him in an 'S' pattern like a kite

tail. They were Zekes on floats, and while they were over twice as maneuverable as our F6F's, they had only small guns.

"Buck brought them head-on toward me, and evidently I caught them by surprise. I knocked off two of them almost as fast as you can say 'one . . . two.' The third turned too quickly for a shot, but Buck got him on the way back. In the next furious half hour or so, the air seemed saturated with little float planes. Buck downed four of them, and I got one more in the air and one on the water when he tried to run for cover in a secluded inlet. The Jap flak knocked down one of their own aircraft as well—while Buck and I were chasing it.

"As the sun began to rise, the air cleared magically, and we thought we had them routed completely. We went about the business of charting the ships that were pouring from the harbor. While I was intent on this, a flash went by my canopy. I swung around to look, and there was a Jap not more than one hundred feet behind me filling me full of bullets. Before I could elude him in a

(USN)

ACES OF VF-9

When this photo was taken, these aces had the number of victories shown first in parentheses, the second figure showing number of kills at the end of the war: Lt. E. A. Valencia (7½—23); Lt. W. J. Bonneau (7—8); Lt. Armistead B. Smith (6—10½); Lt. M. J. Franger (6—9); Lt. H. McWhorter (10—12); Lt. Commander H. N. Houck (5—5); Lt. M. A. Hadden (8—8); Ensign J. M. Franks (5—7); Lt. A. E. Martin, Jr. (5—5); Lt. L. A. Menard (8—9).

vertical dive, he had shot out my hydraulic system, radio, gun chargers and had punctured my oil line.

"Sheer instinct told me how to get back to the fleet eighty miles away, but I got there. Because of the urgency of the situation, I had to land aboard the Yorktown — the only carrier in a position to land my staggering fighter immediately. Even that was none too soon. My engine froze from lack of oil the moment I hit the deck.

"Buck got nailed the same way, in an almost identical experience with another Jap fighter, and landed with a bullet in his shoulder."

The unusual experience of five kills in one mission—acedom at a stroke—came the way of Lieutenant Commander Kenneth J. Dahms of Winnebago, Minnesota. He ended the war with 7.5 victories but five all at once on what he called his 'Okinawa Turkey Shoot' could not fail to remain foremost in his combat memories. Dahms succinctly describes the action as 'twelve of us tangling with forty-seven Japs . . . we shot them all down.' An average of four kills per Navy pilot in one combat encounter is tops in any league.

Francis M. Fleming of Portland, Oregon, saw service in the Pacific with Air Group 16, and is credited with 7.5 aerial victories. Two of these kills were gained on Fleming's first combat mission, from which he vividly recalls the prowess of the Japanese pilots:

"In November of 1943 we were flying just north of the Gilberts in a position to intercept Jap planes coming down from the Marshall Islands. I was one of twelve Hellcats on CAP at 15,000 feet. We found our bogey in a perfect intercept with about 2,500 feet altitude to our advantage.

"The planes were Zeros, and there must have been between twenty and twenty-four of them. We made a coordinated attack and completed the pass before the Jap pilots knew there were any other planes near them. This was my first aerial combat!

"The first enemy I fired on just kept flying straight ahead, smoking heavily but not burning. I had to recover from my initial dive and was not able to follow him to see what happened to him. This plane was classified as a probable.

"After the first pass, the wildest dogfight you ever saw erupted. My wingman got separated from me after the first pass, and when I located him, he had a Zero hot on his tail, pouring the fire to him. I swung in behind the Zero and was just ready to open up when the Jap spotted me on his tail.

"He maneuvered violently and left my wingman's tail. I was real close to him, and in good firing position. I had hardly touched the triggers when the Zero disintegrated immediately in front of me. I had to dodge violently to avoid flying into the engine from his plane.

"Then I found I was not alone. A Zero was on my tail and closing fast. I took violent evasive action but he stuck with me, because the Zero was much more maneuverable than the Hellcat at speeds less than 200 knots. This cat-and-mouse maneuvering went on for what seemed like an eternity, with the Jap and me trying to second-guess each other. He was fighting to get into firing position on me, and hadn't fired a single round yet, with me trying to get the hell away from him.

"Slowly it dawned on me that these guys were not the easy prey that I had allowed myself to believe. The private dogfight was getting a little wearing, and my desire for self-preservation steadily mounted. I decided to pull a little maneuver that I had learned from an old World War I combat pilot, whose name escapes me now.

"Shoving everything forward to get as much speed as possible, I straightened out a little and went into a shallow dive to get speed quicker. When the Zero began to follow and close on me, I started a turn to the left and stayed in this turn, deliberately allowing the Zero to cut across the turn to where he figured he had me and was about to open fire.

"Then I made as tight a turn to the right as possible at this higher speed. The Zero could not follow the right turn because of the high control forces. Chopping the throttle and turning back to the left, I found myself neatly behind him.

"Closing in, I opened fire. He burned, lost first one wing and then the other, and went straight in from about 12,000 feet."

Two and a half years of combat with VF-11 and a strong will to win brought seventeen aerial victories to Lieutenant Commander Charles R. Stimpson of Salt Lake City, Utah. This pilot's aggressiveness was a legend among those who flew with him. His modestly-told story veils this all-important trait of the fighter ace. Writes Commander

THE NAVY VF-9 Squadron early in WWII

With six German planes and 118 Japanese planes confirmed early in the war, VF-9 pilots and crewmen proudly posed for this historic photo.

(USN)

Stimpson from Rancho Santa Fe, California, where he now lives:

"While on CAP over the Hornet on 14 October 1944, a large group of bogies were picked up on our radar and we were vectored to them. We were just completing our first carrier strikes on Formosa, and the Japs were really out in strength to get us.

"When my division leader's radio became inoperable, I assumed the lead of the two four-plane divisions. We intercepted the attacking Jap force of sixteen Zekes plus a number of bombers about seventy miles from Hornet. In that battle I destroyed five confirmed and three probables.

"The exciting and memorable part of it for me was that with only eight planes, we met and totally defeated a numerically superior force and prevented a full-scale attack on our carriers."

Hanging on tightly to an enemy's tail has always been a fundamental of the dogfighting type of aerial combat. This principle of classical aerial warfare was evidently emphasized strongly in the training of Lieutenant Commander Warren D. Skon of St. Paul, Minnesota, for in his first aerial battle it meant the difference between being shaken off by an agile foe and an aerial victory:

"My first victory was my first sighting of an enemy aircraft in June of 1944 off the coast of Guam. I followed the Jap Zero into a split-ess, which he had taken as an evasive maneuver. He was slippery and nimble, but I stayed right with him. Leveling off just above the waves he could never have believed I was still there. I let him have a burst and he burned, snap-rolled twice and plunged into the water."

Lieutenant Commander Skon is credited with seven aerial victories.

If an enemy in aerial combat makes a cardinal tactical blunder, it is tantamount under the dynamic conditions of war in the air to his giving an opponent in a street fight a free crack at his chin. A Japanese formation leader presented an incredulous Commander Samuel L. Silber with just such an opportunity:

"On 1 January 1944, my squadron escorted bombers and torpedo planes on an attack on Kavieng. As the bombers entered their final push-over I led my fighters over them. Just at this point we were attacked by numerous Zekes.

"As I turned into my section leader on a weave maneuver, the leader of a Jap flight turned away from me. I could hardly believe it. He exposed almost his entire flight to me and my wingman. I shot down three Zekes in the time it takes to make a tight 360-degree turn.

"My excellent wingman, Ensign Robert Beedle, also got one. Three days later on another attack on Kavieng, Beedle and I were again attacked by numerous Zekes, but without any free shooting gallery openings as on the previous occasion. I was wounded and Beedle was shot down. He was movie star William Holden's brother, and in real-life was very much like the character Holden played in The Bridges of Toko-Ri—something that came home strongly to me many years later when I saw that film."

Sam Silber is credited with seven aerial victories, and hails from Baltimore, Maryland.

A flight commander in Fighting Squadron 5 aboard the U.S.S. Yorktown, Lieutenant Commander Robert W. Duncan of Marion, Illinois, finished World War II with seven aerial victories. His combat report after an attack on Truk tells of a wild melee with the redoubtable Zeros:

"I spotted about ten Zekes coming at us out of the sun from about 20,000 feet. We began at 14,000. My section and Merrill's began to weave. One Zeke started an approach at me; he was coming in from about ten o'clock with a good position for a high-side run, but instead he elected to flip over on his back and approach upside down. Immediately I turned in and under him where he couldn't pull through me.

"He managed to hit Burnett's plane aft of the cockpit and shot away a piece of his elevator. As the Zeke passed over us I turned toward him and caught him as he recovered with a long burst at four o'clock low. He began to burn. Another Zeke recovered right then almost in front of me . . . I got off a tail shot, but missed.

"This Zeke then turned back toward me and as he passed, I turned, got on his tail with a short burst and set him on fire. Now a Zeke was trying to get on my tail from eight o'clock above, but I turned into him and we began several violent scissors maneuvers toward each other. He fired short bursts at me twice, but was behind each time. He then decided to break off and forget the whole thing, starting to glide towards some clouds at 4,000 feet.

"I caught him at 8,000, however, and closed

fast, firing as I came. He burst into flames as I overran. I blacked out when I pulled up, and then I climbed to 8,000 again, where yet another Zeke was coming head-on. He started firing when we were still well apart—a short burst. I opened up on him, and just as it appeared we might collide, he rolled over on his back and I pulled up. Banking sharply, I started swinging around to get at him again. I'd probably already killed the pilot, because the Zeke slowly began a gliding right-turn spiral and finally crashed."

Having a new pilot on his first combat operation for a wingman often caused experienced fighter leaders some anxiety. The capabilities of the neophyte were unknown, yet the leader would be depending on him to keep enemy fighters off his own neck. Good leaders had a natural tendency to keep an eye on the newcomer. This was not only to evaluate his potential, but also to help keep him alive so he could develop into a full-fledged and dependable combat pilot.

Captain John Blackburn, who is credited with eleven aerial victories in the Pacific Theater of World War II, found that he had no cause to worry about one particular neophyte wingman. He is unnamed in this account from Captain Blackburn, but the newcomer's combat awareness made a deep impression on his leader:

"We were flying high cover over a dive-bombing strike at Rabaul in February of 1944. I led a four-plane flight of Corsairs which got seven kills over Zekes and Hamps and broke up a significant part of the opposition to our bombing strike. The bombers were unharmed, and there was no damage to any of our fighters. My four kills were all seen by my wingman, a pilot on his first combat mission."

One of the hard-case pilots of the American Volunteer Group in China was Lieutenant Commander Edwin S. Conants. That is the name he assumed when he joined the Flying Tigers. Various strategems like name-changes were used to try and conceal the combat activity against Japan—prior to Pearl Harbor—of pilots who had been trained as professional aviators by the U.S. and who had been commissioned American officers. These officers "resigned" and enlisted, in some cases under pseudonyms to avoid breaking international law or exciting Japanese hostility.

Elaborate and amusing as these activities sometimes were, it is doubtful if anybody was

fooled—except perhaps and briefly the U.S. Navy in the case of Conants. He duly transferred back to the Navy after America entered the war. When his ace qualification was published, the Navy couldn't find "Conants" in its records. His real name was, and is, John Francis Perry, and he had been originally commissioned under that name. After straightening out the mess, the Navy decided in 1945 to let Perry stay in its books under his old Flying Tiger pseudonym. When the real Ed Conants stands up, it is with official credit for six aerial victories.

The invasion of Saipan by the U.S. in June of 1944 was a pivotal event in the Pacific war. The Japanese were in no doubt as to the crucial nature of this lodgement, and the urgent need to inflict a reverse on the U.S. Navy. If possible, the invasion had to be undone. This led the Japanese to commit their main battle fleet for the first time since the Battle of Midway two years previously—the historic carrier battle that had blocked Japan in the Central Pacific.

The six Japanese carriers that came with battleships and numerous other warships put aloft a veritable blizzard of fighters, bombers and torpedo bombers. More Japanese planes joined them from Guam. This sudden plethora of targets was made to order for the eager and now experienced and well-armed U.S. Navy fighter pilots. Backed by excellent radar control and unsurpassed communications, they blasted literally hundreds of Japanese planes out of the sky on 19 June 1944. History and legend now call this downing binge the "Marianas Turkey Shoot," and it was undoubtedly one of the finest days in the history of the U.S. Navy. Fighters and antiaircraft gunners brought down 346 Japanese aircraft!

Making history on that unforgettable day was Lieutenant (j.g.) Alexander Vraciu, originally from East Chicago, Illinois, and now (1978) a banker in Walnut Creek, California. Schooled in aerial combat by the redoubtable Lieutenant Edward "Butch" O'Hare, Vraciu ended the war as the Navy's fourth-ranking fighter ace with nineteen aerial victories. Combat at Rabaul and in two strikes at Truk, combined with his early O'Hare training, had made him an ace by the time the Marianas Turkey Shoot came along. He was fully equipped to benefit from the abundant Japanese targets:

"As part of the American task force protecting the Saipan operation, we were expecting an attack by over 400 Japanese carrier planes on the morning of 19 June 1944. Bogeys were picked up on radar approaching in several large groups and carrier fighter aircraft were scrambled to supplement the CAP already aloft. I was part of a standby group of twelve fighters launched from the Lexington.

"As we were climbing for altitude at full military power, I heard the Fighter Director Officer saying 'Vector 250, climb to 25,000 feet pronto.' VF-16 skipper Paul Buie was leading our three divisions of four planes each. I led the second division of F6F Hellcats.

"Contrails of fighters from other carriers could be seen converging overhead, all heading in the same direction. Shortly afterwards the skipper began to pull ahead steadily. He was riding behind a new engine and was soon out of sight. We had seen his wingman drop out—the full-power climb was too much for his engine and his propeller froze. Ditching in the ocean, he was picked up twelve hours later by a destroyer.

"My engine was throwing an increasing film of oil on my windshield, forcing me to ease back slightly on the throttle. My division stayed with me, and two other planes joined us. When I found that my tired engine would not go into high blower, our top altitude became 20,000 feet. This limitation was reported to the FDO.

"All the way up, my wingman, Brockmeyer, kept insistently pointing toward my wing. Thinking he had spotted an enemy, I attempted to turn over the lead to him, but he would only shake his head negatively. Not understanding what he meant, I finally shook him off to concentrate on the immediate task. I found out later that my wings weren't fully locked—the red, safety barrel locks were showing—hence Brock's frantic pointing.

"Despite our efforts, it was apparently all over before our group reached this particular attacking wave of enemy planes. I was ordered to return my group to orbit over the task force at 20,000 feet, but barely had we returned when the FDO directed us to Vector 265 degrees. There was something in his voice that indicated he had a good one on the string. The bogeys were 75 miles away when reported, and we headed out hoping to meet them halfway. I saw two other groups of Hellcats converging from the starboard side—four in one group

and three in the other.

"About 25 miles away, I tallyhoed three bogeys and closed towards them. I figured in the back of my mind that there had to be more than three planes, remembering the serious tone to the FDO's voice. There were more all right. Spot-gazing intently, I suddenly picked out a large, rambling mass of at least fifty planes 2,000 feet below on the port side. My adrenalin flow hit High C. They were about thirty-five miles from our ships and heading in fast. I could see our attack as a fighter pilot's dream.

"Then my combat acumen gave me a warning nudge. Puzzled and suspicious, I looked about for the fighter cover that normally would and should be overhead. None could be seen. By this time our position was perfect for a high-side run. Giving a slight rock of wings, I began a run on the nearest inboard straggler, a Judy dive-bomber.

"Peripherally I was conscious of another Hellcat having designs on that same Judy. He was too close for comfort, almost blindsided, so I aborted my run. There were enough cookies on the plate for everyone, I thought to myself. Streaking underneath the formation, I got a good look at them for the first time—Judys, Jills and Zeros. I radioed an amplified report.

"After pulling up and over, I picked out another Judy on the formation edge. The Jap was doing some mild maneuvering and the rear gunner was squirting away as I came down from the stern. Working in close, I gave him a burst and he caught fire, heading down to the sea with a trail of smoke.

"Pulling up again, I found two more Judys flying a loose wing. I came in from the rear, sending one down burning. Dipping the Hellcat's wing, I slid over on the one slightly ahead, blasting it on the same pass, and it caught fire. I could see the rear gunner still peppering away at me as he disappeared in a sharp arc downward. For a split second I almost felt sorry for the little bastard.

"That made three down. We were now getting close to the fleet. The enemy had been pretty well chopped down, but a substantial number still remained. We probably wouldn't score a grand slam. I reported this back to base.

"The sky was an incredible sight, full of smoke, tracer, debris and bits of planes. We were trying to ride herd on the remaining attackers so they wouldn't scatter. Another meatball broke formation up ahead, and I slid over onto his tail, again working in close because of my oil-smeared windshield. I gave him only a short burst. It was enough. The burst went into the sweet spot at the root of his wing tanks. Either the pilot or the control cables must have been hit as well, because the burning plane twisted out of control crazily.

"Despite our efforts, the Jills were now descending to begin their torpedo runs. The remaining Judys were about to peel off to go down with their bombs. I headed for a group of three Judys in a long column. As I reached the tail-ender we were almost over our outer destroyer screen, but still fairly high. The first Judy started nosing over into his dive. As he did so, I saw a black puff beside him—our 5-inchers were opening up.

"Foolishly I overtook the nearest one, disregarding the flak. Scarcely had I touched the gun trigger than his engine started flying to pieces. The Judy started smoking, then torching alternately on and off as it disappeared downward.

"The next one was about one-fifth of the way down in his dive on our warships. Trying

for one of our destroyers, he was intent on this as I caught up with him. A short burst produced astonishing results. He blew up with a sky-shaking explosion right in front of my face. The heat belched into my cockpit. I must have hit his bomb. I'd seen planes blow up before, but never like this.

"Yanking up sharply to avoid the scattered pieces and flying hot stuff. I radioed in: 'Splash number six; there's one more ahead diving on a BB (battleship—Aus.), but I don't think he'll make it.'

"Hardly had the words left my mouth than the Judy caught a direct hit that removed it as a factor in the war. He had flown into a solid curtain of steel and lead roaring up from the battle wagon below. With the Judy gone, I looked around. I could see only a sky full of Hellcats. Glancing backward along our route, there was a thirty-five-mile-long pattern of flaming oil slicks on the water."

The redoubtable Lieutenant Vraciu could have added that he used only 360 rounds of ammunition that morning, and required less than eight minutes to shoot down six dive bombers. The next day, he added a Zero to his total and for the ensuing three months was the

TWO PACIFIC ACES WITH INSIGNIA

Joe Foss of the Marines (right) and Gene Valencia of the Navy accounted for forty-nine Japanese planes in World War II between them. At a meeting of the American Fighter Pilots Association they hold the red shield "R" insignia of the Richthofen Wing of the new German Air Force, at that time commanded by the world's greatest fighter pilot, Colonel Erich Hartmann of Germany. Insignia itself dates from JG-2 Richthofen of World War I fame. In this case it was autographed to the American aces by Hartmann and his pilots.

(Toliver Collection)

top-scoring Navy ace.

In the same violent action—the Marianas Turkey Shoot—Lieutenant Commander Norman Berree also had a highly successful day. He emerged from the war with nine aerial victories. His recollection of 19 June 1944 packs a lot of action into a few telegraphic words:

"Eight of us in Hellcats intercepted mucho Jap aircraft. Made an overhead run on a Judy, exploding it at close range. Flew through the explosion. Was able to knock down two other Zekes before my ammo was expended."

Navy Captain Berree has retired and presently resides in Cantonment, Florida.

As the fighter pilots of the U.S. Navy, with the aces in the van, gradually rolled back the Japanese tide, the dimensions of the new era of naval air power had been fitted into the grand Pacific strategy. Decisive sea battles had been fought utilizing only aircraft, with battle wagons and their big guns never sighting each other. Aircraft carriers became the major determinants of sea power in the Pacific, instead of a source of theoretical controversy—as had been the case in the nineteen thirties.

The fighter aces of the Navy would be spearheading the Allied thrusts in the Pacific until the final day of the war. They faced a fanatical, incredibly brave foe who proved that he would undertake even suicide for his country. Every available retaliatory measure involving the air weapon would be hurled against the Americans. The Marianas Turkey Shoot had been a fighter pilots' picnic, but the road from there to the Japanese home islands was to call forth the best in the U.S. Navy and its fighter aces.

The U. S. Navy Aces of World War II

(USN-Nolan)

Captain Fred E. Bakutis, USN (11.00)
Brockton, Massachusetts.
Bakutis flew with VF-20. He rose in rank to admiral.

Lt. Benjamin C. Amsden, USN (5.00):
Boulder, Colorado. VF-22.

(USN)

(USN)

Lt. Bruce MacD. Barackman, USN (5.00): McLean, Virginia. VF-50.

(USN)

Lt. Hugh Nash Batten, USN (7.00): Tanneytown, Maryland. VF-83 aboard USS ESSEX (CV-9). 6 April 1945, Batten and his wingman, Lt. Sam Brocato, each got four Zeros, eight out of the nine encountered.

(USN)

Lt. James B. Cain, USN (8.50): Alexandria, Virginia. VF-45.

(USN)

Commander Marshall U. Beebe, USN (10.50): Corona del Mar, California. VC-39 and VF-17. On 18 March 1945 over Kanoya airfield, Kyushu, Japan. Beebe was credited with five aerial victories.

(USN)

Lt. Richard L. Bertelson, USN (5.00): Eden Prairie, Minnesota. VF-29. April 1945 near a small island north of Okinawa, Bertelson shot down three Zeros.

Lt. Samuel Joseph Brocato, USN (6.00): This Baltimore-born fighter pilot scored four of his six victories in one battle. Flying as wingman for Lt. Commander Hugh Batten, the two met nine Japanese Zekes and splashed eight of them on 6 April 1945. He flew with VF-83 off CV-9, the USS ESSEX.

(USN)

(USN)

Lt. Carland Edward Brunmier, USN (6.00): Bloomington, California. VF-44 USS LANGLEY. Shot down three Zeros on 24 October 1944.

(USN)

Commander Robert E. Clements, USN (5.0): Commander Clements, from Buena Vista, California and Daytona Beach, Florida, fought with VF-11 in the PTO in WWII, scoring five victories.

(USN)

Lt. Richard D. Cowger, USN (6.00): Oak View, California. VC-39 and VF-17.

(USN)

Lt. Commander Anthony J. Denman, USN (6.00): Greenwich, Connecticut. VF-18.

(USN)

Lt. Francis M. Fleming, USN (7.50): Sunland, California. VF-16.

(USN)

Seven Victories

Lt. Commander Frank E. Foltz, USN, is credited with seven Japanese planes during service with VF-30 and VF-18. Hometown: Detroit, Michigan.

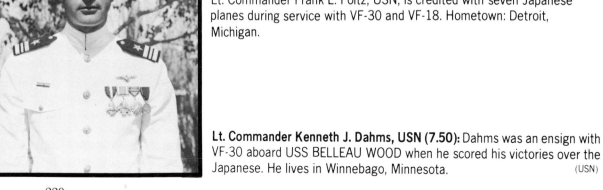

Lt. Commander Kenneth J. Dahms, USN (7.50): Dahms was an ensign with VF-30 aboard USS BELLEAU WOOD when he scored his victories over the Japanese. He lives in Winnebago, Minnesota. (USN)

Lt. Robert Wayne Duncan, USN (7.00): This product of Marion, Illinois, fought with VF-5 aboard USS YORKTOWN. (USN)

(USN)

(USN)

Commander John T. "Ted" Crosby, USN (6.00): Oakland, California. VF-18.

13.5 VICTORIES
America's Heroes are buried in Arlington, Virginia, but Commander George C. Duncan is a hero who was born there. He served with VF-15 in the Pacific.

Lt. James B. French, USN (11.00) Bakersfield, California. VF-9 aboard USS LEXINGTON and USS YORKTOWN. French was a member of the Valencia "Mowing Machine" Division. Today he is one of the owners of TBM, Inc., the largest Air Tanker company in the world.

(USN/French)

221

Commander David McCampbell, USN (34.00)
Lake Worth, Florida, VF-15.
Did not fly combat until late in the war.
First victory 11 June 1944. On June 19th shot down
five Japanese planes. On October 24th, McCampbell and
wingman Lt. Roy Rushing cornered over thirty Japanese
fighters who went into a large Lufbery circle for defense.
When they finally had to break out of the circle,
McCampbell got nine of them and Rushing got five.
McCampbell was awarded the CMH for this action.

(USN)

(USN)

Lt. Commander Roy F. Gillespie, USN (6.00):
Eugene, Oregon. VF-30.

Ensign Carl C. Foster, USN (8.50):
Utica, New York. VF-5.   (USN)

(USN)

Lt. Hayden A. "Buck" Gregory, USN (5.00):
Albuquerque, New Mexico. VF-82.

SUCCESSFUL TEXAN
Lt. Commander Arthur R. Hawkins of Lufkin, Texas shot down
fourteen Japanese aircraft in World War II. His service was
with VF-31.   (USN)

FLYING SAILOR FROM COLORADO

Captain Harold N. Funk, USN, was born and raised in Colorado, a state without a seacoast. He nevertheless became a flying ace with the Navy in WWII, gained six victories with VF-23 and VF-26. A Navy Cross winner, Funk also served as C.O. of Air Group 102 aboard the carrier BONHOMME RICHARD during the Korean War. He retired as a captain.

(USN)

(USN)

Admiral Leo Bob McCudden, USN (5.00)

McCudden is from Sioux City, Iowa, but now lives in Reno, Nevada. He flew with VF-20 and VF-11. "After combat over Formosa, I picked up the mike to call for a rendezvous and my mouth was too dry to talk!"

(USN)

Admiral Noel Gayler, USN (5.00): Philadelphia, Pennsylvania. Gayler flew with VF-3 and VF-12.

(USN)

Lt. Commander Elbert Scott Mc-Cuskey, USN (14.00): VF-42, VF-6 and VF-8. Clearwater, Florida.

(USN)

Lt. Thomas Gilbert McClelland, USN (7.00)

Born in Lethbridge, Alberta, Canada, McClelland moved to Albuquerque, New Mexico. Flying with VF-5 off USS YORKTOWN and USS FRANKLIN, against Truk (16-17 February 1944) and against Saipan, Woleai and Palau. Deceased 21 December 1948.

(USN)

Lt. Commander John C. C. Symmes, USN (10.50): Lyons, New York. As a lieutenant Symmes flew with VF-21, VGS-12, VC-12, and VF-15.

Nine Victories

Commander Louis A. Menard, Jr., USN, downed nine Japanese aircraft in WWII service with VF-9 and VF-12. (USN)

(USN)

Lt. Robert E. Murray, USN (10.33): From Muncie, Indiana, Murray flew with VF-29 aboard USS CABOT for his victories. "The Japanese pilot stood up in the cockpit and shook his fist at me!"

(Toliver Collection)

DOUBLE ACE — USN — PACIFIC

Lt. Richard E. Stambook, USN, is credited with eleven victories over the Japanese in WWII. His unit was VF-27. Stambook's home is in Solana Beach, California.

Lt. Carl Eugene Smith, USN (7.00): Lufkin, Texas, VF-14.
(USN)

(USN)

Commander Sam Leonard Silber, USN (7.0):
Baltimore, Maryland. VF-17, VF-18.

(USN)

Lt. Wilbur Butcher Webb, USN (7.00)
Ardmore, Oklahoma and Wichita Falls, Texas.
VF-2 aboard USS HORNET. Webb shot down
six confirmed plus a probable over Orote
Peninsula, Guam on 19 June 1944.

SUPERB TACTICIAN

Lt. Commander Eugene A. Valencia of VF-9 on the carrier YORKTOWN became famous throughout the Pacific Fleet for his "mowing machine" tactics. Two two-fighter sections alternately descended on enemy formations like mower blades. Valencia survived the war as leader of the most successful fighter division in the Navy, with twenty-three victories credited to his own account. A tireless official of the American Fighter Aces Association, he died of a heart attack in 1972. Commander Valencia was the Navy's third-ranked ace.   (USN)

(USN)

**Lt. Commander Charles R. Stimpson,
USN (17.00):** Rancho Santa Fe, California.
VF-11. Stimpson downed five confirmed and
three probables on 14 October 1944 near Formosa.

Lt. Commander Alexander Vraciu, USN (19.00):
Danville, California. VF-3, VF-6, VF-19, VF-20.

225

Heaving Up a Piece of the Past

(Lockheed Missiles and Space Company)

Divers position themselves to prepare this World War II vintage Grumman Hellcat fighter for final transfer into well of floating drydock during recovery operations. The F6F was lost in 1944 in 3,400 feet of water off San Diego, California, there to be located in 1970 by Lockheed's Deep Quest submersible.

7

U.S. NAVY ACES OF WORLD WAR II (2)

As 1943 drew to a close, the balance of the Pacific air war had tipped against Japan. The Americans now had superior aircraft, were steadily acquiring numerical superiority, and had become tactically habile since Pearl Harbor. U.S. shipyards were producing an unrivaled procession of new aircraft carriers. The Navy was handling them superbly— decisively aided in its operational dispositions by the code breakers' penetration of the enemy's most secret war communications.

The Japanese were everywhere checked. The war was being turned around. Although the Japanese pilots were aware of these changes, they fought on with fanatical bravery. The more pressure the U.S. Navy put on Japan, the more defiant and angry her pilots became. Legends have been woven around the unrelenting hostility of the Japanese flyers, but behind the legends lies an incredible reality. Lieutenant Commander Robert E. Murray ended the war with 10.33 aerial victories after a busy combat career. One Japanese pilot burned his defiant image into Murray's memory:

"On 16 October 1943, Task Force 38 was under a night attack by Japanese bombers from Formosa. The cruisers Houston and Canberra were both torpedoed and had to be taken under tow. Two carriers were dispatched from the task force to escort them away from Formosa, and I was on the U.S.S. Cabot with VF-29 flying F6F's.

"About 1200 the next day, we were still only 180 miles off the coast. There were eight of us up on CAP when CIC got a large bogey on the screen, coming in for the disabled ships to finish them off. There were between seventy-five and eighty Jap planes—fighters, twin-engined bombers and single-engined torpedo planes. We intercepted them about thirty-five miles from the force.

"Our eight F6F's shot down twenty-seven of these Jap planes, and fighters scrambling from our carriers got another five, for a total of

thirty-two. I shot down four myself, consisting of one Zeke, a twin-engined Francis and two Jill torpedo bombers.

"As I went by one of the Jills just before it hit the water, the Japanese pilot stood up in the cockpit and shook his fist at me. He was still shaking it when his aircraft went in."

Lieutenant Michele Mazzocco Jr., of Peekskill, New York, is credited with 6.5 aerial victories in the Pacific. His career also includes dropping a bomb on the giant Japanese battleship Yamato, and sinking a Japanese submarine with rocket fire. Mazzocco is another fighter ace with good cause to remember Japanese fighter pilot courage:

"During the Okinawa battle, swarms of Jap aircraft were dispatched from Kyushu on suicide missions against the U.S. fleet, then operating in support of the Okinawa invasion. Contacts of our CAP's with the enemy units were numerous, and in one such contact I engaged a Zeke in a dogfight at approximately 18,000 feet.

"My plane was an F6F Hellcat, and because of good radar interception, I was able to fire a short burst into the Zeke before being detected. He was smoking badly, and I expected him to go down at any moment, but instead he climbed sharply and opened fire on me.

"We both knew that he would not make it back to the home islands, that it was just a matter of time before he went in. He was nevertheless going to fight to the last. During the dogfight, some 15,000 feet of altitude was lost and somehow we ended up in a head-on run.

"I had the choice of either meeting him head-on or turning and offering him the best shot. I decided to trade shots. We were both scoring hits on one another. I saw he wasn't going to veer off—that a collision was not only inevitable, but deliberately planned by him.

"Waiting until the last possible moment, my heart in my throat, I pulled up hard and to *the right. His left wing came through the bottom arc of my prop and debris flew all over the sky. The concussion was tremendous. Jarred to the bone, I lost control of my plane for a moment that seemed like an eternity.*

"Recovering control, I could see him spinning slowly down toward the sea. The Jap plane was blazing and minus a large portion of the left wing. My wingman checked my plane and told me my belly tank had taken most of the punishment in the collision. I managed to jettison the tank and made an emergency landing on the carrier. Mr. Grumman surely built a tough one when he built that Hellcat. God bless him."

Commander Richard J. Griffin of New York City also encountered a memorable Japanese foe while flying with VF-2. Griffin is credited with eight victories, and resides today at Gladwyne, Pennsylvania. His encounter was an old-fashioned pilot-to-pilot test of strengths:

"I engaged in a dogfight with this Jap pilot at 800 feet and 200 knots airspeed. This boy really knew his business. After three or four scissors maneuvers, none of which gained any angular advantage for either of us, my airspeed was dropping rapidly. It was only a matter of time before my adversary would be in the saddle.

"We were so closely matched, however, that neither of us could gain the advantage, until another Hellcat made a pass at the Jap. Being alert, the Jap flicked to counter, and that gave me the opportunity to fire and get strikes. He bailed out at about 200 feet.

"I really appreciated that Jap pilot's professional ability. This was my sixth or seventh victory, and by that time I was concerned by the manner in which an enemy was downed, such as 'sloppy' or 'clear'."

Odd conduct on the part of a beaten Japanese fighter pilot stuck in the memory of Lieutenant Commander Thomas S. Harris of Tamaroa, Illinois, through nine aerial victories in the Pacific:

"Just north of Okinawa my wingman had damaged a Tony, and in the melee we had become separated from the flight. I got behind the Tony and poured some lead into him. Finally a small fire started under the engine nacelle, and then his engine froze.

"The Tony started down in a gentle glide toward Okinawa. I kept firing, trying to make the fire spread. To my amazement, the Jap

pilot climbed out on the left wing, but then held on with his head and shoulders still inside the cockpit.

"While watching this strange drama, I ceased firing. It was incredible. The pilot looked almost like a midget, and what his intentions were I'll never know. Perhaps he wanted to ride the plane down to a lower altitude before bailing out, for fear of being shot in his parachute.

"I intended to burn the plane for certain destruction. When I aimed and shot at the left wing tank, some of my tracers appeared to hit him. This is the way it appeared to me at the time. The Jap pilot let go and went hurtling past me like a bundle of rags, his chute streaming behind him. It never opened. The plane never burned very fiercely."

Tom Harris stayed in the Navy after the war, and served with the Navy's first carrier jet squadron in 1948. Later he was an Exchange Pilot with the Air Force's Air Defense Command 33rd Fighter Interceptor Wing. Resigning his Navy commission in 1954, he became a commercial test pilot, and now lives near Sandoval, Illinois.

Many pilots have speculated on what the Japanese might have accomplished in the Pacific war had their otherwise able Zero not been such a tinder box. The tough, durable Hellcat and Corsair could often absorb the Zero's best punch and still keep flying and fighting. Rarely could the Zero survive the accurate blast of six 50-caliber guns. There were occasions, some of which are recounted in this book, where one gun, or even one *bullet* was enough to score a flamer on a Zeke.

Such a one-gun encounter came the way of Navy ace Horace B. Moranville of Monmouth, Oregon. In Lieutenant Commander Moranville's view, for him it rolled aerial combat back to World War I for a few brief but memorable minutes:

"During a fighter battle over the Philippines, I had shot down two Jap fighters when my guns jammed. I left the flight to try and clear my guns. After several tries I was able to get one gun working, and just as I did so, I spotted a lone Jap plane racing low over the ground.

"I decided I'd better try and get him before he saw me, so I made a dive on to his tail. I opened up with my one gun. After just a few rounds he made a sharp turn, dug his wing into the ground and crashed instantly."

Moranville's luck did not always run quite as well. He was shot down himself in January of 1945 over Indo-China, and spent four months as a POW. He is credited with six aerial victories.

The Zero did not have self-sealing fuel tanks, and as a consequence a hit in the fighter's tanks—especially tracer—usually sent the Japanese pilot to join his ancestors. The violent flammability of the Zero certainly became legendary among Pacific pilots, but if you talk about "fragile Japanese aircraft" to Lieutenant Commander Marvin R. Novak, he will tell this surprising story:

"The most memorable combat experience for me was a fifty-mile chase of a Betty during the Marianas campaign. With a division of four Hellcats we caught and shot up a Betty cruising not more than ten feet above the water. We four Hellcat pilots loaded the Betty with 50-caliber slugs from highside, level, rear and frontal attacks. There was no opposition at all, and we could afford the time for careful aim. We poured a fantastic volume of lead into that one bomber, expending all our ammunition.

"Finally, there were only one or two guns still firing. Twenty minutes had passed. Then the Betty, almost as though from the sheer weight of the lead we had pumped into it, slammed into the water amid mountainous flames and debris."

Lieutenant Commander Novak hails from Manitowoc, Wisconsin, and spent his World War II career mainly with VF-14. He is credited with five aerial victories. His experience with the Betty shows that not all Japanese aircraft were easy flamers, nor were any of them a sure thing.

A wild battle over Bougainville has stuck in the memory of Commander Roger R. Hedrick of Hollywood, California, since it was a struggle in which more Japanese planes went down in flames than were claimed by his Corsairs:

"I led a flight of six Corsairs on station as high cover over Empress Augusta Bay on Bougainville, against thirty-six Jap fighters covering one hundred Jap bombers attacking our invasion forces. Our medium and low CAP fighters had intercepted the bombers as we took on the Jap high cover.

"The ensuing dogfight lasted thirty-five minutes. Pilots and observers aboard ship later reported seventeen *burning aircraft had* come plunging down through the overcast, but we claimed only five kills. This was due to so many of our damaged targets disappearing into the low deck clouds, most of them on fire. All the Jap planes were driven off, leaving our lower CAP flights free to hit and repulse the Japanese bomber attack."

Commander Hedrick was also aboard the U.S.S. *Bunker Hill* as C.O. of Air Group 84 when kamikazes attacked the carrier. He considers himself lucky to have survived this suicidal Japanese assault, which claimed the lives of 104 of his personnel. Hedrick came out of the war with twelve aerial victories.

For many aces, their first aerial combat is the most memorable, win, lose or draw. All study and experience confirms the importance to a fighter pilot's future development of his first encounter with a shooting foe. Captain Donald Gordon became an ace in World War II with seven aerial victories, but his first time in combat on 29 October 1942 has left the deepest impression. The Battle of Santa Cruz was the scene of his fledgling experience.

"I was launched at 0700 as part of an eight-plane CAP to defend the task force from aerial attack. My station, in company with Ensign Gerald Davis, was over the U.S.S. Enterprise.

"At approximately 0750 I was instructed to take a heading to intercept incoming bogies. Three Jap dive-bombers were soon sighted. Attacking them just before they commenced their bomb run on Hornet, *I closed in and fired, observing something fly off the first Jap machine. Shifting my sight to the right wingman and firing again, I saw a small fire start in the rear cockpit. This fire went out when I quit firing.*

"At this time I was in a vertical dive and the AA was heavy, so I pulled out and watched the dive-bombers continue their attack. No bombs were seen to drop. One of the dive-bombers plunged into the Hornet, *hitting the carrier forward of the island. The other two dive-bombers crashed into the nearby water. I did not claim either as a victory.*

"After clearing the AA area, three more Jap torpedo aircraft were sighted low over the water. Davis and I made a run. I fired too soon, but closed and one torpedo bomber crashed into the water, another jettisoned his 'fish' and the third one disappeared.

"A Zero was seen soon afterward making a run on one of our F4F's. I was in good shooting position and pulled the trigger. Four rounds

popped and then the guns quit. I was out of ammo and so was my wingman. My few shots and our presence had nevertheless forced the Jap off the F4F's tail.

"Returning to the Enterprise *to rearm, we were waved off because of a new Jap attack. Ensign W. Redding joined me and saw a torpedo-plane attack coming in on the task force. Although out of ammo, I made a head-on pass at one of the torpedo planes and in avoiding me he dug a wing in the water and crashed. I claimed two torpedo planes destroyed and one probable.*

"It was my most exciting mission, and I learned three vital things about air fighting:

1. Only fire when in range.

2. Conserve your ammunition.

3. Continue after your quarry until you are sure it is a kill."

The hundreds of fighter pilots who went through many missions as neophytes without ever even firing their guns, will agree that Don Gordon got a crash course in aerial combat on 29 October 1942.

From fighter ace to financial world is the pathway trodden by Lieutenant Commander Everett Hargreaves, who hailed originally from Saskatchewan, Canada. His years as a bank examiner in Milwaukee, Wisconsin, are fairly typical of many fighter aces. The war is a long way away. They are mostly modest men and their associates often do not know that they won through to the coveted title of "ace." Hargreaves downed 8.5 Japanese aircraft in World War II, and contributes this narrative of the tension and excitement of naval air operations in wartime:

"It is difficult to pick out any one flight and say it was the most exciting, especially after a lapse of years. They were all flights of duty, and we took the assignments as they came— such as the late-afternoon launch of eleven fighters, twelve dive-bombers and nine torpedo-bombers from the U.S.S. Hornet *west of Guam.*

"The strike group headed for the enemy fleet, which had been sighted for the first time since Midway. I was flying in the fighter escort, but we were all carrying 500-pound bombs for maximum striking power. The bombs could be dropped if enemy air action started, but we carried the bombs all the way in.

"Flying west into the sun, we passed the given point of sighting with no contact, and flew on for approximately one hundred miles before our strike group made contact. AA shells began to appear immediately, and by the time we reached our pushover point, you could see the flashes on the ships below. They were sending up the heaviest concentration of flak we'd seen up to that time.

"The attack was made just at sunset. I think that dive was about the longest I ever made—if not in altitude certainly in time— for the hail of enemy tracer lacing with your own was not a nerve-soothing sight.

"After dropping our bombs we grouped again in the greying dusk, heading for home, with every pilot thinking of the instructions we received when we were standing the night-fighter watch. 'If launched before midnight, bail out when you get low on fuel, for the admiral will not take a chance of putting the carriers into the wind long enough to land you aboard and give the Jap Bettys their chance at the fleet.'

"Certainly they were not going to carry that instruction through with so many planes in the air, not only from Hornet, *but all the other ships too, even though the old Navy men were probably the only pilots experienced in carrier landings at night.*

"The dusk gradually died, and darkness set in. Over water, with no reflection of city or ground lights on the horizon to help brighten the sky and give you a navigational checkpoint, a moonless night and the black sea below made a safe return to the carrier seem very remote. There was a tendency to feel lost.

"Adding to the tension, every one of us knew that the extra miles flown to the target had taken a lot of fuel. We were low on gas— very low. Soon came the first radio call. A buddy had no juice left and was being forced down to that black, fathomless depth below. Who would be next? Me?

"Automatically, I leaned my fuel mixture just a wee bit more, hoping that my old battle-worn plane was not quite such a gas eater. Every few minutes we heard some other pilot call the flight leader that he was going in. By the time we sighted the wakes of our own fleet below, the radio was so choked with distress calls that you couldn't hear the landing instructions given by the carriers.

"My fuel indicators gave me much more leeway than some of the pilots reporting in, so I stayed high above and circled, to try and give

some of the other pilots a chance to land first. The carrier decks were clear, but not for long.

"Inexperienced and harried pilots were crashing into the barriers, a grim and nerve-wracking sight. Then Admiral Mitscher gave his historic order. 'Turn on the lights,' he said, accepting the risk of Jap subs getting our fleet.

"Landings now speeded up. When it looked like I could join the traffic circle without ten others all at the same time, I started in and got a 'cut' on the first pass. I taxied forward and was spotted.

"Just as I was climbing out of the cockpit, I saw the plane captain drop everything and bolt. He had a good reason. What turned out to be the Air Group Commander making the last landing of the night came barreling through the only remaining barrier. Flames were shooting out of his ship, which came swerving to my side with the roll of the carrier. For a petrifying moment, I wondered if I'd come through the rest of the operation only to get it on Hornet's deck.

"The rampaging aircraft finally settled on top of the port gun mount—a few scant inches from going over the side. Hornet was a glum ship to come back to, for only a handful of her planes landed. Things brightened, however, as we sat relaxing over a cup of coffee, for the teletype started to give information on pilots who had landed on other ships.

"Before the day was out, all our squadron had been accounted for. No one who was in that operation will ever forget the lights going on during the landings."

What did the well-trained Navy fighter pilot do when his guns jammed? He kept firing. That is what another *Hornet* alumnus, Lieutenant Commander Willis E. Hardy, did when he was chasing kamikazes:

"Flying an F6F Hellcat off the *Hornet* on 6 April 1945 my wingman and I encountered a swarm of kamikaze-bent Japs north of Okinawa. Some very violent maneuvering on my part had jammed my ammo belts in the cans, and by the time I was on my fifth Jap of the afternoon, only one gun was firing—and that only one round at a time, each time I would kick the charger button.

"The fifth Jap was finally flamed after twenty minutes of 'line-up, get off one round-break-recharge' routine. My score for the mission was one Zeke, two radial-engined Judys and two Vals. My wingman got three more and stuck with me the whole time, giving mutual defense."

Originally hailing from Corning, California, Commander Hardy spent his World War II service with VF-17 on the U.S.S. *Hornet*. He is credited with seven victories, and holds the Navy Cross.

With twenty-four victories scored in the Pacific, Captain Cecil Elwood Harris of Cresbard, South Dakota, is the Navy's second-ranking fighter ace. He was a schoolteacher in sleepy Onaka, South Dakota, in 1941, and war clouds persuaded him to become an aviation cadet in the summer before Pearl Harbor. History records that it was a good decision for Harris and the U.S.A.

(USN)

FIFTY-EIGHT MEATBALLS!
Top U.S. Navy ace David Mc-Campbell (34) and the number two Navy ace Lieutenant Cecil E. Harris (24) display Japanese Victory symbols signifying their total of 58 aerial victories. On three separate occasions, Lieutenant Harris scored four kills.

He flew fighter cover for the North African invasion in 1942, and then went to the Pacific to serve with VC-18, VF-36 and VF-18. Captain Harris is an extremely modest man, and his own story of what he considers his most timely victory epitomizes his self-effacing character:

"My most timely mission was when I was assigned to a search mission one day. There were four planes in the group, each assigned to guard a different sector and escort a bomber. The weather was overcast as we took off, and while making a turn around the carrier just below the clouds, two enemy aircraft dropped down through the overcast just ahead of me—and very close to the fleet.

"They started their run immediately, and I closed on the leader. Shooting him to pieces, I then turned to get behind the second Jap. Luckily, I shot it down before it reached the bomb release line. Both planes fell harmlessly in the water amidst the ships, and I continued my assigned mission."

Only nine other U.S. aces in World War II downed more aircraft than Cecil Harris, and he shares tenth place in World War II scoring with the redoubtable John C. Meyer of the USAAF, who later added 2 Korean War victories to his 24 in WWII and eventually rose to four-star general rank. Harris had a stellar record for whirlwind engagements—downing four Japanese planes on each of three separate days.

Cecil Harris, the Navy's "quiet man," sought a quiet life after the war. He returned to teach school in his native South Dakota. Recalled to Navy duty in the Korean War, he remained on active service with the U.S. Navy after the "police action" ended, making the Navy his career.

Another Harris who made the Navy his career (Annapolis '39) is Commander LeRoy E. Harris of Brownwood, Texas. He wound up like most Texans being called "Tex," and flew with VF-2 and VF-10 with great distinction. He is credited with twelve aerial victories. His most vivid combat memory is of the first aircraft carrier attack on Manila on 24 September 1944:

"I led the fighter escort for the Hornet (CVA-12) group attack on shipping and installations about Manila Bay. We caught the Japs with their kimonos down, and had no opposition. After covering the bombers and the torpedo plane attacks, we strafed Jap auxiliary shipping that filled the bay.

"When we started home, several flights of Tonys jumped us. I led my division into them, instructing the others to stay with the bombers. I got one Tony and the others got two in the first pass. Tonys dove for the deck, and we followed.

"Caught another shortly afterward and destroyed him at one hundred feet, running out of ammo in the process. I broke off and commenced rendezvous. I found the second section, also without ammo, being attacked by three Tonys. I called them and told them to head for home while my wingman and I made a head-on pass at the Japs.

"Luckily, on our first pass the Japs broke and ran—but so did we! Just before landing I discovered that the last two feet of my left wing tip had been mangled by an explosive shell."

Lieutenant Charles H. Haverlund, Jr., returned from the Pacific with 6.5 aerial victories, after service on the *Enterprise* and *Lexington*. Although an ace himself with his full share of combat experiences, Haverlund's most vivid memory of aerial combat is of another ace—the late Lieutenant (j.g.) Douglas Baker, credited with sixteen aerial victories:

"The most exciting aerial victory I can recall was not one of my own, but the first victory of many by the late Lieutenant (j.g.) Douglas Baker. Doug had all the prime requisites of a fighter pilot, and combined his many outstanding abilities as an aviator with the uncanny ability to see and identify aircraft long before they were sighted by anyone else in the flight.

"These attributes were all coordinated beautifully by Doug around the first of October, 1944. I was flying on his wing, when, as happened so many times later, he sighted Jap fighters and initiated an attack. My own excitement over a first encounter was apparently not shared by Doug, as his perfectly executed run and short firing burst had his target spinning in flames almost instantly, while I chalked up a clean miss on my own target."

Rarities among America's fighter aces are *night aces.* Commander William E. Henry of Bakersfield, California, is one of these rare birds, having scored six of his ten victories at night. One of these night encounters he remembers well:

"My most exciting victory was my first

night intercept, which I completed on an Emily. I scored immediate hits, and after setting fire to his port engine, I pulled out to the port quarter to avoid debris if the Nip plane exploded. Then a port turn by the Jap pilot put me close abeam—with the Jap's engine fire dying out.

"The rear gunner immediately saw me, and cut loose at very close range, but did not score a hit before I retired beyond the limit of visibility. Keeping track of the enemy was easy. The fire had gone out, but a bright glow remained. As I pulled astern of the Jap to do the job right, the fire started up again before I could get in another burst. The Emily went into a starboard spiral and crashed into the water."

If you fly with Trans World Airlines, you may find yourself in the care of Navy fighter ace Kenneth G. Hippe of Peoria, Illinois. A Commander in the reserve, Ken flew with VC-13 in the Pacific and is credited with five victories. He is one of the distinguished few American fighter pilots to become an "instant ace" by scoring all five victories in one mission:

"On 24 October 1944, we took off on a CAP and intercepted a Lilly—a twin-engined Jap bomber—over Leyte Gulf. Luckily, I shot it down. I was then directed by radar to intercept a raid coming in, and got four of this big formation of Lillys. Only one of this complete formation of twenty-one bombers was unaccounted for by my division and the others who joined the scrap. All the action took place in ten minutes. I was flying an FM-2 and just happened to be in the right place at the right time."

When Lieutenant Charles W. Huffman of Rockville, Missouri, bounced some Zekes after a radar interception, he was hardly prepared for what ensued:

"On 15 October 1944, while attached to U.S.S. Wasp with VF-14, my division was flying a CAP over the task force. We received a vector and another division was assigned to follow, as numerous bogies were reported. I was a wingman on the division leader, but he was having radio trouble so he passed the lead to me.

"I took the next few vectors and radar placed me about 3,000 feet above and about nine o'clock from fifteen to twenty Zekes. I announced contact with the enemy to the ship, and proceeded to attack with the other seven

planes following.

"From close behind I set the lead aircraft on fire. I was about four hundred feet astern of him. Just as I stopped firing, the Jap plane seemed to stop in midair and exploded. As I flew through the flames and pieces of the aircraft, I could feel the fierce heat in the cockpit.

"After getting in the clear, and while checking my engine instruments and controls, I realized someone was shooting at me. Turning around I saw two Zekes sitting about five hundred feet behind me with all guns firing. I could see the muzzle flashes.

"Some hectic maneuvering followed. I finally got away from my pursuers, and with the fight over I returned to the ship. There were half a dozen holes in my right wing, but the major damage was to the flaps, ailerons, elevators and rudder. All of them had to be changed. The heat from the exploding Jap fighter had scorched the paint and left the fabric in ripples on the flaps.

"The controls were unfit for further service and I felt real lucky to have eluded the other two Japs in view of this. This was my most exciting and memorable combat flight."

Huffman survived the war, and is credited with six victories.

Wheat and cattle ranching at Moscow, Idaho, are a far cry from piloting a fighter in the Pacific War. Lieutenant Commander Elvin L. Lindsay made the transition successfully, and while he ranches quietly today, he has this memory of the violent times in which he became a Navy ace. He is credited with eight victories flying with VF-19:

"After completing a recce flight over Nielson Field near Manila, six of us in Hellcats headed north to look for targets. As we approached Clark Field, we spotted fifteen enemy planes making a rendezvous around their base.

"For one terrible instant my heart sank. We were only six against fifteen, and there were several new-type fighters among their planes. But we approached unseen—the decisive edge—and slashed into their flight with such sudden fury that three of their planes went down on the first pass.

"In defensive formation we continued picking off singles in a series of dogfights until thirteen Japs were down without loss to us. We were proud of ourselves, but back on our carrier our skippper demanded, 'What in hell do you mean letting two planes get away like

that?'.'"

Commander Charles Mallory is credited with eleven kills by the Navy, one more than he himself claims. This kind of anomaly occurs sometimes when the pilot cannot take time from combat to watch the actual crash of a wounded adversary, and someone else confirms his victory at a later date. Mallory flew off the U.S.S. *Intrepid* with VC-30, VF-36, VF-18 and VF-151. The big carrier was part of a task force providing fighter cover for bombers attacking Manila on 21 September 1944. Mallory had a memorable day:

"It was late afternoon, and the sky was clear except for scattered white cumulus clouds at 5,000 feet. I was assigned top cover for the group with six F6F's at 18,000 feet.

"The fighters began their nervous weave, and it seemed to intensify as they picked up speed approaching our target, Clark Field. The air had been full of Jap fighters all day, and we expected to be jumped at any moment. I played a hunch, and called for my top cover group to start climbing as we passed the last range of mountains and started across the green field of central Luzon. A few minutes later we were at 24,000 feet, as our dive-bombers and torpedo planes started their attack.

"Numerous enemy bogies were spotted simultaneously, and the lower fighter cover became engaged with Jap fighters which outnumbered them two to one. There were calls coming over the radio fast and furious. 'Look out, Frog, there are two Tonys behind you!' 'Break, Break!' and so on.

"At 24,000 feet, meanwhile, I started a circle around the field. Just when I felt we were missing the big fight below and was getting set to go down, my wingman, Lieutenant (j.g.) Beatley called 'Poncho!'—he'd spotted twenty-four Jap fighters, five miles away, ten o'clock low. They were in tight formation and flying towards us at about 20,000 feet.

"I called for the attack, but instructed my group not to lose our altitude advantage, and to be prepared for a defensive fight. Rolling into a dive with the other planes spread out in pairs, we hit the enemy before they had time to spread.

"Lining up a Tony in my gunsight on the first pass, I squeezed the trigger and saw tracers eating into the enemy cockpit. I pulled up just as he exploded in a ball of flame. The next few minutes were a free-for-all. My

planes kept their altitude and covered each other very well. My wingman had his guns shot out on the first pass, but he stayed with me and covered me just the same.

"Suddenly I looked down and saw one of our fighters about 5,000 feet below the rest of us, boxed in by five Tojos. He would be shot down in a matter of seconds. Calling for a break, I went into a dive.

"The Jap fighter shooting at the F6F was only about a hundred feet behind the American machine, and I placed the pip of my gunsight in front of the F6F to compensate for lead. As the range closed to firing distance, I squeezed the trigger and saw the Tojo buck and roll over, flames spurting out all along his side.

"In the pull-up my plane shuddered and my air speed dropped off to 180 knots. Looking to the rear, I saw a Tojo on my tail. My left elevator had been shot away, my wheels were hanging down, and big holes were being blown in my wings where the 20mm cannon shells were exploding.

"With what control I had left, I twisted into a dive, then pulled up as if I were going to split-ess, but instead flew on my back. The Tojo thought I was going to pull through the split-ess and rolled with me, but he pulled on through. Righting my plane I headed for the nearest cloud, and took a heading for the coast.

"Two of my group joined me at the coast, and all six had joined up when we reached the carrier. All six aircraft were badly damaged, and two pilots were wounded. All of us landed OK, but my plane never flew again. My plane captain counted sixty-seven holes, but my Grumman Hellcat had brought me safely home as it did so many other Navy pilots. It was quite a battle. I was credited with five kills for the day."

In the ranks of the "reluctant" aces—those who seem embarrassed by their distinction—is Lieutenant Commander Lee Paul Mankin of Mammoth Springs, Arkansas. Mankin claims only four aerial victories although the Navy credits him with five. He hesitates to take credit for the fifth kill because he literally chased the enemy plane into the water without firing a shot. The Navy view was that the downed Japanese aircraft wasn't going to come back up again, and so Mankin is an ace with five kills.

Among other famous ships of the Pacific

war, Mankin served aboard both the *Saratoga* and the *Enterprise*. He recalls best a battle over Guadalcanal, for which he had an appreciative audience.

"Above Guadalcanal with VF-5 I was confronted by two Zeros. Fortunately, one gave up and the other made a wrong turn, which put me behind him. With only one 50-caliber gun working, I centered his cockpit in my sight and let go. I followed him up a steep climbing right turn, and at the very top of the climb he exploded into flames.

"Five minutes later I landed at Henderson Field, and the reception I received from the Marines on the ground was more than adequate reward for the sweat I'd just experienced. Those Marines were an appreciative bunch of men. This victory stuck in my mind because it was a straight fighter-against-fighter battle, and I had often wondered how I would fare in such a situation."

Many of the Navy's top fighter pilots passed through VF-3 under the command of Lieutenant Commander Edward "Butch" O'Hare, a great combat tutor whose career has already been described. Among the aces who incubated with O'Hare is Lieutenant Commander Richard H. May, who ended the war credited with six victories. May carries a memory with him that gives the uninitiated the true flavor of aerial combat, and provides a pang in the solar plexus for the initiated:

"Eight Hellcats were catapulted from the U.S.S. Langley *early one morning during darkness to sweep the Truk area for enemy fighters, and to coordinate and protect our own bomber attacks. Truk was swarming with planes, as it was a highly fortified Jap base. Our task group had orders to neutralize Truk at all costs.*

"Our fighters were supposed to rendezvous with two hundred other task group flights from the other carriers in our group. Due to miserable weather conditions, our eight were unable to locate the main attack group. The eight of us under the leadership of the skipper headed for Truk alone—some 150 miles due east.

"The eight of us were split into four sections of two planes each. I led the second section behind the skipper. Lieutenant (j.g.) John Pond, a Tennessee boy, was flying my wing position. Approaching Truk at 16,000 feet, Lieutenant Hills—an RCAF veteran leading

the last section—suddenly tallyhoed a large gaggle of bogies at 8,000 feet. These bogies were flying southeasterly over the enemy group of islands. We counted forty-three Zekes and Tonys in the formation.

"The skipper signaled attack. We dove on the unsuspecting Japs below, and the element of surprise was with us. No doubt radar had alerted the enemy to our main general attack, and this was the first group of enemy fighters climbing for altitude.

"We were ten minutes ahead of the main flight of task group fighters, so these climbing enemy planes were taken by surprise. Diving at full power, we were on them before they spotted us. I picked out an enemy division leader, leading a flight of four Zekes in the middle of the formation, allowing plenty of mils in the gunsight for the deflection shot of about forty-five degrees. John Pond drew his bead on the enemy division leader's wingman.

"At a thousand yards we opened up with our six 50-caliber wing guns, blasting those two Japs into eternity. The entire enemy formation scattered as we tore into them. They broke up into sections and singles, climbing vertically in panic to gain precious altitude. My section bore down through swirling fragments of enemy aircraft at high speed. We recovered quickly, pulling as many G's as possible, heading straight back up—recovering altitude and at the same time rolling back toward the enemy.

"Diving, twisting, exploding and burning aircraft filled the sky. The fear that seized me most was of collision. Zeros were everywhere, milling, looping and blazing. John Pond was expertly handling his controls to stay with me in the gyrations and aerobatics necessary to get back to the enemy. We dove, twisted, rolled, split-essed, recovered, pulled into eye-popping, brain-blurring turns in an effort to get the necessary lead in our gunsights to drive our bullets home.

"Rolling out of a half-wing-over, I gave a Tony a long burst, smoked him, pulled back on the stick, and then headed down toward the sea to pick up more valuable flying speed. Not a moment too soon. A flaming enemy fighter went hurtling past my cockpit, missing me by but a few feet. He was the victim of one of my buddies, but he almost took me with him.

"By this time, the fight had become a sort of aerial alley brawl. Planes were blowing up,

burning and disintegrating all over the sky. Chutes were mushrooming. Tracer laced and zipped across the scene. The battle seemed to last an hour, but actually it lasted only a few minutes. Fiercely fought at high intensity, the battle ended as abruptly as it had begun. One minute the sky was crawling with Jap planes and the next minute it was empty. The enemy—those that were still healthy—had scattered.

"The record credited our lonely eight Hellcats with twenty-three confirmed kills and eleven probables. John Pond confirmed two aerial kills and one probable. The record credited me with three confirmed kills and two probables in this wild encounter over Truk, which was by far the most exciting action experienced by me in five hundred hours of combat flying time."

Commander May now lives (1978) in Scottsdale, Arizona.

Navy ace Hamilton McWhorter of Athens, Georgia, who now makes his home in El Cajon, California, came out of World War II as a Navy Commander, with twelve aerial victories. He took part in such historic actions as Tarawa, Saipan and the Marshall Islands landings. He earned five DFC's and seven Air Medals. His story tells how he earned one of these decorations:

"I was flying an F6F as section leader in escort for a bombing and torpedo strike on Truk on 16 February 1944. As the SBD dive-bombers were pushing over into their dives, I saw three fighter aircraft about two miles away turn towards us. At that distance, and head-on, they looked very much like friendly F6F's. My wingman and I nevertheless turned into them—just in case.

"I was not positive they were enemy aircraft until they were within three thousand feet or so, then I saw that they were painted orange and black. They were in loose left echelon, the leader apart from the other two. I rolled into them, turning on to the tail of the first of the two wingmen, my wingman lining up on the leader.

"My wingman, Lieutenant Bud Gehoe of Wilkinsburg Manor, Pennsylvania, shot the leader down just as I fired on the number two man. My target burst into flames, and I pulled over on to the third plane, who was still maintaining the most perfect formation possible.

"He exploded almost the moment I touched the trigger. The elapsed time between

shooting down the two planes was perhaps five seconds, and counting my wingman's kill, the combat had not lasted over ten seconds."

Every fighter ace has a warm place in his heart for the ground crews that service and arm his aircraft. They all know that without a dependable machine, their own skills and capabilities in aerial combat would be nullified. Lieutenant George Pigman, Jr., of New Orleans, Louisiana, ended the war with 8.5 victories. Pigman is an attorney today, and speaks for dozens of his fellow aces regarding the role of the men on the ground:

"Every plane you shoot down is a new and exciting experience. It is impossible to say which is really the greatest thrill, but the victory that I remember best occurred over Formosa, in 1944.

"We had heard about a new Japanese fighter called the Tojo, which looked like the P-47 Thunderbolt, carried 20mm cannons and heavy armor plate. Naturally, this machine was not as maneuverable as the Zero, but it was supposed to be quite a plane, and in this encounter I suddenly saw one coming at me head-on. Never will I forget those flashing guns blazing at me, although it only lasted a few seconds. Each flash was a bullet or shell aimed at me.

"I was firing too. I knew my guns were scoring, and so were his. As he went under the right wing, I pulled up and to the left. The Tojo was burning, and the pilot was bailing out. This encounter was just one of the many instances of the crucial contribution made by nonflying personnel.

"There had been no airmanship, tactics or maneuvering—nothing like that. All I had to do—all I could do—was sit still and pull the trigger. That Tojo went down because those on the ground had provided me with a reliable aircraft whose performance was perfect that day. There were other times when the skill and experience of the pilot meant the difference between defeat and victory, but on that occasion the credit should have gone to someone other than me—the nonflying personnel."

Lieutenant Commander Ralston Murphy Pound, Jr., of Charlotte, North Carolina, ran up six aerial victories while flying with VF-16 off the *Lexington*, and with VF-150 off the *Lake Champlain*. Like almost every other pilot who took part in that particular imbroglio, his best memory is of the Marianas Turkey

Shoot—the day the Japanese carriers came out of hiding:

"*While covering the Saipan landings we had a field day in one of the war's most colorful aerial battles. The Japs lost over three hundred planes that day to Navy aircraft and flak, with very slight loss to us.*

"*I had flown two four-hour CAP's, starting before daybreak, without making contact with the enemy. Our planes had been shuttling between our fleet and the enemy fleet all day, and late in the afternoon the air group commander, Commander Ernie Snowden, USN, asked for someone to fly wing on him to follow the action.*

"*After takeoff we joined up and headed where our planes were engaging the enemy. We flew an hour before we located the action, and as we flew around observing, a Jap plane made a pass at us. Commander Snowden took chase, and made his first kill. During the action I lost contact with him and found myself in the middle of several of our planes chasing a Judy bomber.*

"*I tried a side pass and the Judy started a half-spin. I followed his maneuver, and ended up looking straight at him from the right side about fifty feet away. I was so close that I could see the pilot and observer clearly. I opened up with all guns, and as I fired, a ball of flame belched out of his engine. Flying through the fireball, I broke off my run.*

"*As I rolled I saw the Judy's engines quit, and he started a gentle glide to the ocean about 4,000 feet below. All the planes around were now making passes on the sitting duck,*

but I had done the damage, and since neither pilot nor observer tried to get out—or fired a shot after my run—I was credited with the victory. The Judy didn't burn, but kept gliding until it hit the water.

"*Several boys from my squadron saw the action and confirmed the kill. Later I joined up with the group commander and we landed safely, with his first plane and my sixth to our credit. I flew a total of twelve hours that day. I was one tired guy, but very happy.*"

As the Navy task forces grew in power and skill they pressed the air war closer and closer to the Philippines, Formosa, Okinawa and then the home islands of Japan. The enemy's defense stiffened the closer the offensive came to Asian shores. Land-based bombers—the biggest threat to the carrier forces—could be used in increasing numbers, and more strikes could be initiated against the far-ranging U.S. Navy ships.

Operations against Formosa from the *Lexington* gave Lieutenant Commander Luther D. Prater—appropriately from Lexington, Kentucky—one of the most harrowing experiences that can come the way of a carrier pilot: landing without an arrester hook. Prater is credited with eight victories, three of which were followed by a hairy landing:

"*Sixteen of Lexington's fighters were launched before dawn for the first fighter sweep on southern Formosa. Upon arrival over the airfields in our assigned area, we were attacked by an estimated forty Jap fighter planes. Most of our planes were separated in the battle, and each time I spotted a Hellcat,*

U.S. NAVY PILOTS WITH 73½ VICTORIES BETWEEN THEM: In 1944, these aces of VF-19 posed aboard USS LEXINGTON. Back row: Lieutenants Robert A. Farnsworth (5); Luther Del Prater (8); William J. Masoner (12); Joseph J. Paskoski (6) and Bruce W. Williams (7). Front row: Lieutenants Paul O'Mara (7½); Albert Seckel (6); Herman J. Rossi (6); Elvin L. Lindsay (8); and Theodore Hugh Winters (8).

(USN/Lindsay)

two or three Zekes would be jumping him.

"Finally I got behind a Zeke that was firing at the squadron commander. Closing to about 600 feet, I opened fire. The Jap plane exploded with the first burst and crashed in flames. Thirty seconds later, I saw a Zero coming at me head-on. Pulling my plane up I opened fire, the second and third bursts slamming into his engine. He flamed and crashed.

"Shortly afterward, while the squadron commander and I were strafing parked planes on a small airstrip, he crashed and was killed. After three more strafing runs, I was able to contact three of our planes in that area and started climbing to rendezvous with them. Three Zekes jumped me at 6,000 feet, and I managed to duck into a cloud.

"Coming out of the cloud, I spotted one of these three Zekes and made an immediate attack. Chasing him down to treetop height, I finally hit his engine. His plane exploded and crashed. Now it was time to get back to the carrier. After joining up with three of our planes we all proceeded to the Lexington for a landing.

"During the landing approach, I discovered that my arresting hook had been damaged and would not extend. After circling the carrier for about ten minutes, I was given my choice: ditch in the drink or land on the carrier 'the hard way'—with no hook.

"On my first approach, I managed to land safely aboard without damaging the plane or myself, and without doubt was the happiest man in the Navy when I climbed out of that plane."

Almost everyone has seen wartime combat film of battered fighters landing on carrier decks without hooks, and the devastating pile-ups that often ensued. Commander Prater's relief at getting down safely can be readily understood by anyone who has viewed such Navy footage. Even with a hook, many didn't make it due to combat damage and component failure on landing.

In Denver, Colorado, there's a building contractor named Vincent A. Rieger. Building wasn't always his business. During World War II he served aboard the U.S.S. *Cabot*, and became an ace with five aerial victories. He well remembers 11 June 1944:

"Fighter Division 4, of which I was number two man, accompanied by Divisions 2 and 6 was assigned a sweep against fields on Saipan, Tinian and Rota—all islands of the Marianas group. We went in low to avoid radar detection, and forty miles out, eight of us started climbing to act as top cover.

"A 12,000-foot overcast kept us at 11,000 feet. Upon arrival we found the fields below us being well beaten up by waves of our carrier aircraft. We thought we'd caught the enemy by surprise. Then tracers spurted past in front of my eyes. We'd been surprised instead.

"Swiveling around, I saw several Zekes coming straight down through the overcast, making overhead runs on us. We dropped tanks, spread out to scissor and I saw a Zeke flatten out directly behind Lieutenant Turner, my division leader. Turner turned toward me, and I turned toward him, which gave me a head-on shot as the Zeke turned with Turner. This was a mistake for the Jap. My first burst exploded him in midair. I narrowly avoided the debris of his plane.

"A second Zeke, following my first kill, lost heart and started to bolt. He put himself in perfect position as I pushed over, gained speed and closed, opening fire. The Jap blazed immediately and the fight was now almost over, except for a Hellcat that was obviously in trouble with a Zeke sitting on his tail.

"I got over to him, knocked the Zeke down, and discovered the Hellcat was our number three man, Lieutenant Conant, who had his canopy shattered by Jap fire and was bleeding about the face and neck from cuts. I led him to our rendezvous point and we flew back to our carrier and landed OK."

Lieutenant Roy Warrick Rushing of McGehee, Arkansas, was one of the pilots who flew as top Navy ace David McCampbell's wingman in the fall of 1944. Rushing is credited with thirteen aerial victories and four probables during World War II, bad film in his gun camera and lack of full confirmation no doubt depriving him of the extra victory credits. His service with VF-15 is a cherished memory, as he goes about his peacetime work as an industrial engineer in McGehee, Arkansas. Flying as McCampbell's wingman during the celebrated nine kills in one mission scored by the Navy's top ace, left its mark on Rushing's memory:

"On the morning of 24 October 1944, our task force was off the coast of Luzon. Most of our Air Group were out on strikes, and six of us who had been on an earlier mission were on standby alert. Among us was Commander David McCampbell, our top ace. I was his

wingman.

"As the morning advanced, our radar picked up a large bogey coming from the Philippines and we were scrambled. They were Jap dive-bombers with several layers of fighter cover. Most of the fighter escorts were carrying bombs, too. McCampbell and I took advantage of clouds to get above the Japs, who were stacked up to 24,000, while the remainder of our flight was ordered to strike the dive-bombers coming in at 15,000 feet. McCampbell and I discovered that our quarry consisted of about forty fighters and twenty dive-bombers.

"Immediately we went to work. In the course of the next thirty to forty-five minutes we managed to break up their force and chase them back to Luzon. We turned back because we were running low on gas and ammo, but could not be taken back aboard because the deck was not clear.

"Lower on gas than most of us, McCampbell had to be taken aboard another carrier, the Langley. The rest of us sweated it out and then were taken aboard our own ship, the Essex. McCampbell destroyed nine on this mission—the most successful single-mission score by any U.S. fighter pilot—and I was credited with six."

Even enthusiastic advocates of air power in the prewar years had reservations about the value of naval aviation. The tendency was to regard the aircraft carrier as an untried, clumsy and vulnerable weapons system of unknown and dubious value. These cautious concepts were a far cry from the mighty sweeps of Navy fighters—1,200 at a time—that drummed in over Japan in the last days of World War II.

This setting provides the most vivid combat memory of Lieutenant Robert A. Clark of Hartford, Connecticut, who is credited with seven aerial victories against the Japanese. His story is a classic of its kind:

"At 0700 on 14 March 1945, I was flying wing on Lieutenant Charles Weiss as part of a twenty-plane Hellcat sweep over airfields in the vicinity of Kure, Japan. The sweep was only a small part of a vast attack on Kure Naval Base that day, with over 1,200 carrier-based aircraft involved. Our job was to keep enemy aircraft from rising against the dive-bombers and torpedo planes headed for the basins and anchorage to destroy what was left of the Jap fleet.

"The morning was bright and cold, and as we approached the Shikoku coast, we flew over snow-covered ground. Fuji was visible far away, and as we flew in close formation at 13,000 feet I took in the beauty of the scene. My thoughts were also of the hail of flak we would have to face in attacking the three airfields assigned to us as targets.

"The idea of vigorous aerial opposition didn't occur to us because of the repeatedly poor showing of the Japanese in meeting previous attacks. We figured that with the number of planes we had in the air this morning, they probably wouldn't even show a head. Not so.

"Just a few minutes later, crossing the Shikoku coastline with our tactical radio channels silent, two flights of about thirty-five planes each approached us on the same level from twelve o'clock. We paid them no special attention—until they pounced on us like hawks! Then Charlie himself yelled into the mike, 'Hey, fer cats' sakes! Those aren't sixes (F6F's), they're Japs! Everybody weave! Weave! . . . Weave!

The divisions broke off to meet the attack, and just as Charlie turned tightly in a dive to the right, two Japanese fighters came up in a sweeping turn to meet us head-on. They were flying in tight section, firing as they came.

"In a split second Charlie was gone from in front of me, and I bent around in a tight-G turn to the left, looking for the rest of the Jap planes. At that moment, a Zeke came right across my path from left to right in a climb, and I punched off a mad burst at him, twisting to hold the sight on him as he passed.

"His canopy shattered as he went by about a thousand feet away. He started to burn just behind the engine. He rolled off in a steep spiral, and I inverted to follow him down, but the whole plane was ablaze now. Just as I was completing my roll-out I heard a loud bang in the wing section of my own plane. I didn't bother to check what it was, but snapped into a split-ess and dove for the deck.

"Pulling up in a tight recovery and nearly blacking out from the high-G, I suddenly found myself at 13,000 feet again. I sneaked a quick look at the wing. There was a hole near the tip . . . not big enough to worry about.

"Just then I caught another Zeke maneuvering in lazy turns in front of me. As he zig-zagged past the sight I started firing on him. One of his landing wheels came down and he dropped his flaps on me. I had to chop my throttle practically to nothing to stay with him . . . firing all the time. Pieces flew off his plane and zipped past me. Just as I overran him, his whole plane was engulfed in a ball of fire.

"By now the radio was a scrambled jabber of pilots screeching for help and yelling advice and warnings to each other. About 3,000 feet above us a circle of Jap planes was apparently loafing through the fight, but I soon saw their game. They'd formed a Lufbery Circle, World War I style, and were waiting until a Hellcat got on some Jap's tail. Then they'd jump him in section and shoot him down, returning immediately to the upper circle for another crack at 'Glumman airplane.'

"This tactic worked. We lost eight of the twenty Hellcats in that fight. One Hellcat went screaming by me in a plunging dive—his belly tank on fire. Someone was yelling on the radio, 'Drop it! For God's sake drop it! Yer on fire!' The sky was a flaming kaleidoscope of burning airplanes, flashing insignia and lacing tracer. Four or five chutes floated down amid the smoke and debris.

"The entire Hellcat flight had been broken up by the Jap attack, and the fight had become a series of individual duels over a wide area of the sky. Out of ammo and without a wingman, I noticed a Tony trailing me. I lunged for the coast and the task force, knowing that the Tony was only good for 330 knots at best. I made a long, flat, running dash at near max speed and lost him after a few minutes.

"After getting back to the Hornet, we rendezvoused the survivors of our ill-fated sweep. We had lost eight. We had accounted for twenty-one Japanese aircraft, and also discovered that our dive-bombers and torpedo planes had excellent success at the Kure Base with minimum losses. Charlie had parachuted and was taken prisoner by the Japanese, as were several others."

The daily sweeps over Japan conducted by the pilots of the U.S. Navy provoked the sternest resistance by the Japanese, whose pride, as well as their homeland was being attacked. Commander Robert C. Coats won 9.5 aerial victories in the Pacific, but assault on the home skies of Japan left the deepest impression:

"My division was launched from the Hornet with a flight of about sixty F6F/F4U fighter-bombers to deliver 500-lb bombs and rockets against the Kanoye airfield complex in the Kagoshima Bay area. This was the final daylight launch of the day.

"The flight proceeded through broken clouds and below a 12,000 foot overcast for about 200 miles to the target area. There the lower overcast became solid under us, at around 8,000 feet, with clear air up to the next overcast base. The flight initiated attack on time estimate and despite heavy flak concentration.

"My division was composed of three F6F's, each loaded with six 50-caliber machine guns and one 500-lb general purpose bomb. My number four man aborted and did not accompany the flight. Just prior to following in the attack, my number three man tallyhoed a bogey, and we broke off to attack the airborne enemy. The number three man initiated the attack, obtaining strikes on the outer wing panel of the Jap machine and turning him into my section.

"It was a George. My wingman and I got strikes on fuselage and engine, starting him smoking and then burning as he dived into the overcast. We didn't follow, as the number three man tallyhoed a second Jap plane. We stayed in this clear area between the overcast layers and fired on about ten Jap planes—all singles.

"Undoubtedly, they had evacuated the lower area because of our heavy strike on the Kanoye complex. After exhausting the enemy above the overcast, we dived through to deliver our bombs. In the dive, we saw a flight of five Zekes in the traffic pattern around Kanoye West.

"We dived into them, but at the speed and angle of attack could not stay with them for other than short bursts. We regrouped and our number three man again spotted a bogey—a Tony this time—north of the field. He attacked and followed him down for a sure kill.

"Proceeding to Kanoye East and dropping our bombs, my wingman and section leader made this run without ammo. I ran out of ammo myself on the final part of the run. Despite two hits sustained on this run, my wingman was able to continue back with us, and at last light we turned back for a night landing aboard the Hornet. We had scored damaging hits on every enemy we fired on, and had all of them at least smoking. Because they dived into the overcast, we could not claim definite kills.

"What made this encounter memorable was the manner in which my wingman, then Lieutenant (j.g.) G. J. Foster, and my section leader, then Lieutenant (j.g.) W. T. Colvin, so completely and perfectly executed this mission. Rookies when launched from Hornet, they returned as veterans."

Tokyo seemed a long way away in December, 1941, but the power center of Japan was receiving regular visits from U.S. Navy fighters by the early months of 1945. The first fighter sweep over the Japanese capital was an epic moment for U.S. carrier aviation, an operation that etched itself in the memory of Lieutenant Henry Champion of VF-9 on the *Essex* and *Yorktown*:

"I was on the first fighter sweep over Tokyo at daybreak on 16 February 1945. We were the first fighters to invade Japan proper and our mission was to destroy enemy aircraft in support of the pending Iwo Jima landings.

"The sky in the sector to which I was assigned was jumping with Jap planes of all types. There were at least fifty of their machines and a similar number of Hellcats in this one little ball of sacred air over their capital—all locked in deadly combat. With my wingman I shot down the first Jap we came to, and later I exploded another in midair."

Henry Champion came out of the war a fighter ace with five kills. He was also a prolific destroyer of aircraft on the ground. These strikes he holds to have been far more dangerous than the air-to-air combat that made him an ace. There are dozens of aces who agree on the relative hazards of ground strafing and straight air-to-air combat, rating the former as by far the more dangerous to life and liberty.

An immaculately executed "bounce" of an enemy pilot is something of which every fighter pilot dreams. Such a bounce came the way of Navy ace Willard Ernest Eder of Buffalo, Wyoming, in the waning months of the war. Commander Eder finished his combat career with six aerial victories to his credit, including two that were the result of a classic bounce on 18 March 1945:

"I was leading the fighter cover for a strike by bombers on Omuta, Kyushu. My division of four planes was flying highest cover. About thirty miles short of the target we spotted a sixteen-plane gaggle of mixed Jap fighters lin-

ing up for a pass on our bombers below. We slid in behind the enemy planes and closed the gap, wondering whether we would get close enough to blast them before being spotted.

"We got into firing range unseen. We all opened fire simultaneously, and the tremendous hail of fire knocked down seven Japs and damaged another before they could scatter. I destroyed one Rufe and one Tojo, and also damaged another Tojo in this engagement that lasted approximately one minute."

Poetic justice was being meted out in the final days of the Pacific war. The U.S. Navy had taken the brunt of the first blow against America struck by the Axis, a devastating stroke against both naval forces and naval morale. Everything came full circle as the U.S. Navy, resurrected and now unconquerable, struck the final blow against Japanese air power on 15 August 1945. The last confirmed aerial victory of World War II is credited to Lieutenant Commander Thomas H. Reidy of North Field, Illinois. This historic victory is recounted here by Tom Reidy, who passed away on 23 February 1974 with ten aerial victories and two Navy Crosses to his credit:

"On the morning of 16 August 1945, I led a sixteen-plane fighter sweep to the Tokyo Bay area. Mission was to destroy airborne aircraft, and if none were sighted, to attack Atsugi airfield near Tokyo.

(USN)

TRUK, SAIPAN, GUAM, TINIAN, TOKYO

Lt. Henry K. Champion, USN, is credited with five victories in Navy's epic roll-back of Japanese power in World War II. He served with VF-9 aboard USS ESSEX.

"At 0540 hours and while about fifteen minutes offshore, I sighted a Jap reconnaissance bomber, a Myrt, headed toward the fleet. His mission was probably recon or kamikaze, or both. I told the boys I'd take him and dropped my bomb for the fight. One pass and I'd shot him down.

"I proceeded towards Tokyo, when at 0545 I received a coded message that the war was over. I had shot down the last Japanese plane of World War II for my tenth and final victory."

As the smoking skeleton of the last kamikaze was quenched under the waters of Tokyo Bay—sent there by a fighter ace of the U.S. Navy—the score of Pearl Harbor had been settled. Air power, and especially naval air power, had been the key to grand strategy in the Pacific, and had sealed the military doom of Japan. For the U.S. Navy it had been a righteous war. Both the Navy and the American nation would always look with pride upon the role played in Allied victory by the fighter aces of the U.S. Navy.

(USN)

Lt. Charles Henry Haverland, USN (6.50)
Haverland, from Grand Blanc, Minnesota, flew with VF-20 and VF-18 off ENTERPRISE and LEXINGTON. He pays great homage to his section leader, the late Lt. Doug Baker, who had the eyes of an eagle.

U. S. Navy Aces
of World War II (2)

Lt. Everett C. Hargreaves, USN (8.50): Canadian-born, Hargreaves flew with VF-2. When last contacted, he called Milwaukee, Wisconsin home. In WWII he flew with VF-2 off USS ENTERPRISE and the new USS HORNET. Also with VF-188 aboard USS BUNKER HILL and with VF-27 off USS INDEPENDENCE. (USN)

(USN)

Lt. Commander Cecil E. Harris, USN (24.00)
Harris was born in Faulkton, North Dakota, but resides
in Alexandria, Virginia. He flew with VF-18 and
VF-27, scoring four victories on one mission three
times. He is the number two ranking ace of the Navy.

(USN)

**Commander Robert Charles Coats, USN
(9:33):** VF-17 ace Coats operated off USS
BUNKER HILL and USS HORNET to score
his victories. Today he calls Jacksonville,
Florida his home.

Lt. Robert H. Davis, USN (6.50): Loomis, California, and Rio
Rico, Arizona. VF-18.

(USN)

Lt. Richard Hobbs May, USN (6.00): May, from Portland, Oregon but now calling Solana Beach, California his home, flew with VF-3 in Hawaii, VF-10 (ENTERPRISE) and VF-32 (LANGLEY) to score his six victories.

(MAY)

(USN)

Commander William E. Henry, USN (10.00)
VF-79, VF-41. One of the few night aces, Bill Henry had 6½ night kills and 3½ day. One night victory was at Clark Field, Philippines, when he caught a twin-engine Japanese head-on in the landing pattern. "I never got a close look at him, just fired into his landing lights!"

(USN)

Lt. Albert E. Martin, USN (5.00): Warwick, Rhode Island. VF-9.

BATTLESHIP BOMBER

Lt. Michele Mazzocco, Jr., of Peekskill, New York, downed 6.5 Japanese aircraft in the Pacific. He also scored a direct hit with a bomb on the giant Japanese battleship YAMATO, and sank a Japanese submarine with rocket fire. U.S. Navy VF-30.   (Toliver Collection)

Lt. Charles Mitchell Mallory, USN (11.00)
Mallory, from Dunbar, West Virginia, fought with VF-18 and VF-36. Biggest day was 21 September 1944 over Luzon when he shot down five Japanese planes and barely made it back to home base in his sieved F6F. On the back of this photo, which he sent home, he wrote, "Plenty tough! A rip-snorting fighting fool! Raring to go . . . (back home!)"

(Mallory)

(USN)

Lt. Commander Lee Paul Mankin, USN (5.00)
As a Navy lieutenant Mankin fought with VF-2 (SARATOGA), with VF-6 (ENTERPRISE), and VF-5 again at Guadalcanal. He claimed but four kills but was officially credited with a fifth that he chased into the water near Henderson Field. He is from Springfield, Missouri.

(USN)

TWELVES HAS THIRTEEN! Lt. Wendell V. Twelves, USN (13.00): Spanish Fork, Utah. VF-15.

Lt. Elvin Lester Lindsay, USN (8.00): Born in the unlikely place called Potlatch, Idaho, El Lindsay joined the Navy and fought with VF-19. Today he lives in Moscow, Idaho and is a kingpin in the VF-19 reunion association.   (USN)

(USN)

Captain Edward C. Outlaw, USN (6.00): Durham, North Carolina. Outlaw flew with VF-32. He retired in the rank of rear admiral.

(USN)

Commander Roger William Mehle, USN (13.33)
Now living at Virginia Beach, Virginia, Mehle was a young lieutenant when he flew with VF-6 and VF-28 in the Pacific.

(USN)

Commander Hamilton McWhorter III, USN (12.00)
From Athens, Georgia but now living in El Cajon, California, McWhorter flew with VF-9 off USS RANGER in the North African invasion. In the Pacific, he flew with VF-12 aboard USS RANDOLPH.

(USN)

Lt. Luther Delano Prater, USN (8.00)
Lexington, Kentucky and Los Angeles, California. VF-19 and VBF-19. In one sortie destroyed three Zeros, then landed back aboard USS LEXINGTON without his arresting hook. Made it safely on the first approach . . . "happily."

Lt. Ralston Murphy Pound, Jr., USN (6.00): Charlotte, North Carolina. Pound flew with VF-16 (LEXINGTON) and VF-150 (LAKE CHAMPLAIN). He was in on both Truk raids but recalls twelve hours of flying one day in the Saipan invasion as his happy day.

(USN)

(Toliver Collection)

TEN DOWN WITH THE USN

Lt. Russell L. Reiserer flew with VF-10 and VF-76 in the Pacific in WWII. The Los Altos, California man is credited with 10.5 victories.

(USN)

Admiral John S. Thach, USN (7.00): Coronado, California. VF-3. Retired in grade of admiral.

(USN)

Lt. Thomas J. Rennemo, USN (7.00): VF-18. Hometown Whitewater, Wisconsin.

THREE IN ONE DAY

Lt. Commander Carl Van Stone, U.S. Navy, had his best day on 21 March 1945, with two Betty bombers and one Zero fighter confirmed. Fighter Bomber Squadron 17 was his unit. Five victories in WWII.

(Toliver Collection)

ENTERPRISE ACE

Lt. Commander Joseph E. Reulet called the USS ENTERPRISE home for most of his USN service in WWII. He served with VF-10 and is credited with five aerial victories. Reulet also served in Korean waters during the police action, aboard USS PHILIPPINE SEA.

(Toliver Collection)

USMC Pilots at Guadalcanal

VMF-121 Pilots, Feb. 1943

Captain Joe Foss, standing on the wheel of a Wildcat, poses with other members of his fighting squadron.

8

FIGHTER ACES OF
THE U.S. MARINE CORPS

Piloted with the dash and elan that distinguish the U.S. Marine Corps, Marine fighter aircraft were a vital part of the American campaigns in the Pacific in World War II. While the primary mission of Marine aviation from its inception was to provide air support for Marine ground forces, the Pacific campaigns saw Marine fighters far more widely employed. They harried the Japanese in aerial combat on a grand scale, as well as backing up the "mud Marines" with energetic close-support flying.

The aggressive spirit and feisty morale that are essential to the making of any Marine found adequate outlet in aerial combat. The USMC claimed and was credited with 2,355 aircraft shot down in air-to-air combat*—a considerable achievement for a relatively small force. To this record must be added the untold hundreds of Japanese aircraft destroyed on the ground by Marine fighter pilots.

The spearhead tasks of the Marine Corps in the Pacific war ensured that Marine fighter pilots were in the van of the aerial action. These flyers wrote many glorious chapters into Marine history during the dark days of Guadacanal and the struggle for the Solomons. They added more after the turn of the tide. Marine aviation produced not only outstanding fighter pilots, but some fabulous characters as well.

One Marine who has passed into folklore as well as carved his niche in formal history is Colonel Gregory "Pappy" Boyington. Unsurpassed by any other American fighter ace for sheer color, flamboyance and fighting skill, Boyington ended the war with twenty-eight aerial victories to his credit. He was one of America's leading heroes of the entire conflict.

Boyington scored twenty-two of his victories while flying with Marine Corps units in the

Pacific. The remaining six kills he gained while flying with Chennault's Flying Tigers in China. He was one of the commissioned American professionals who signed on with the Flying Tigers after "resigning" from the USMC. This has created a perennial controversy as to who is the top-ranked Marine ace of World War II. Although all the details are known inside out, buffs will always argue this point of Marine distinction.

Boyington's rival is Joseph Jacob Foss, credited with twenty-six victories, all of them while in service with the Marine Corps. Few fighter pilots can match the career of Foss for either distinction or diversified service to his country. He entered public life after World War II, and was elected Governor of South Dakota. He also became a Brigadier-General in the Air National Guard.

Because of this career and background, Foss is regarded as the all-American boy of Marine Corps aviation. Most of the quasi-official material circulated about him refers to Foss as the Marines' top ace. Purists are correct that he is entitled to this honor.

Pappy Boyington, on the other hand, has always been something of a black sheep. He was many times an embarrassment to his superior officers. For a long time the Marine Corps did not seem able to make up its mind whether Boyington belonged to them or not. Pappy destroyed more enemy aircraft in combat than any other Marine pilot, and this distinction cannot be taken from him.

Suffice it to say of the Foss-Boyington statistical comparison that both were outstanding fighter pilots and leaders. Both provided the wartime press with morale-building feats. Both have become historical personalities through the war, and since. The Marine Corps was big enough for both of them.

Boyington immortalized himself and the gang of outcast, rambunctious pilots he led as the "Black Sheep" Squadron. Tough guys,

*The 124 USMC fighter aces accounted for nearly half the total number of enemy planes shot down—1011½ aircraft.

hard cases, roisterers and misfits, they were dumped on Pappy—the name they gave him because he was older than they were. He welded them into the most successful fighter squadron in the Pacific, and they would have flown into hell for him.

Boyington's prowess in downing Japanese aircraft set the real tone for his squadron. Only results mattered. Marine commanders who went by the book found Boyington brash, rude, and so frank that talking to him was like getting a punch in the nose. His roistering and insobriety totally obliterated the "officer and gentleman" image valued by the Marines as it is in the other services. In the Marine pantheon, however, the highest god is victory. Pappy and his Black Sheep served that god and no other.

Pappy came home a hero, a truly fabulous figure idolized by a grateful nation. The war was over, but Pappy had now to fight a civil war—his struggle with himself. "Show me a hero and I'll show you a bum" he bellowed at the world from the pages of his best-selling book *Baa Baa Black Sheep.* He obviously felt that way about himself, but it is clearly untrue of heroes generally—especially the many quiet heroes whose stories are told in this book.

Boyington's civil war frequently had him in the newspapers as the years rolled by. The struggle was as strenuous as any he had made against the Japanese, but victory was incomparably more elusive. In his evening, he found peace and fulfillment as a painter. Inside the war hero the soul of an artist had slept.

The hit television series *Black Sheep Squadron* has put Pappy Boyington back on the national map and back into the national heart. The success of the TV show has made him the best known American fighter ace of all time, since it is shown all over the world. He has brought the Marine Corps more publicity than a billion dollars could buy, adequate recompense for the high Marine feathers he ruffled in the Pacific.

Boyington's "Black Sheep," scattered now to dozens of different trades and towns, remember their old boss with a special, deep affection. His ups and downs in civil life were about what the Black Sheep expected of Pappy. His decision to run for Congress—a race in which he was defeated a decade ago—brought the following irreverent but typical Black Sheep comment:

"Well, old Pappy has tried everything else, and there he is right down at the bottom of the barrel—running for Congress!"

Thus did Boyington set the stamp of his personality on the men he led. They will never see him as anything other than the wild man he was in his Pacific days—a flying, shooting demon who more closely approximated the hell-for-leather fighter pilot of fiction than any other American ace.

Boyington was a superb pilot. A wrestler in his college days, he made good use of his powerful neck muscles in out-turning his Japanese foes, using this development as a built-in G-suit. Pappy was a crack shot and blessed with an almost psychic acumen in combat that saved his life often.

The enduring kinship between Black Sheep is well expressed by Major Robert W. McClurg of Coshocton, Ohio, when he says: "The fact that I was the wingman of Pappy Boyington means more to me than medals—by far." Bob McClurg is an ace with seven victories, and remembers what it was like to fly with Boyington's VMF-214:

"I was flying wing on Pappy when we took off from Vella Lavella on 18 October 1943, to escort SBD dive-bombers over Kahili Air Base on Bougainville. Our mission was to knock out new Jap fighter planes that were now ready for operation, and the fighters under Pappy were to protect the SBD's while they bombed the Jap fighter fields.

"When we got over the target area flying at 28,000 feet, my Corsair developed a magneto flash and the engine conked out. The prop windmilled and I lost considerable altitude. Just at that moment the dive-bombers were peeling off to lay their eggs on Kahili. The Jap Zeros jumped our fighters from about 30,000 feet from behind a huge thunderhead.

"At the same time, the new Jap fighters were taking off from Kahili field to intercept the SBD's as they came in on their bombing run. I was meanwhile fighting to start my engine again. Cutting on and off momentarily, it was running very rough when I got down to 2,500 feet. Figuring on a water landing, I was looking for an offshore area so I could be picked up by the Dumbo or Black Cat rescue PBY.

"Ahead and below I spotted two Zekes flying formation and climbing for altitude, and I quickly figured I had a good chance to take one of the slant-eyed boys with me. Closing in

Colonel Gregory "Pappy" Boyington, USMC (28.0): America's most famous fighter ace to come out of WWII. His popularity has been enhanced by a television series purporting to portray the escapades of his wartime squadron known as the "Black Sheep." Boyington left the Marine Corps to join the American Volunteer Group (AVG) in China where he unofficially is credited with six aerial victories. Rejoining the USMC, Boyington scored twenty-two victories to bring his total to 28.0. In the USMC he led VMF-214. He lives in Fresno, California. Fly on his left shoulder managed to survive clouds of DDT.

on the rear Jap of the two-plane formation, at 2,000 feet on a stern run I set him blazing.

"They'd been flying loose formation, and the rear plane was quite a bit behind, so I assumed the leader never saw me flame his wingman, who by this time was almost down to the drink and still blazing. As I pressed home my attack on the leader, he saw my tracer immediately, and pushed over to break away. Even though my engine was still running rough as hell, my guns still functioned OK. The leader now rolled over and burned all the way down to the water.

"By now I was down to five hundred feet and flying like crazy for friendly water. Nursing the plane away from the Jap-held island, I was about to attempt a water landing when my engine cut back in again and took me home to base. The kills on these Japs were confirmed by an Army flyer who was flying

low cover that day. He saw the whole thing and told the Intelligence Officer. I got the DFC for this action."

On the following day, 19 October 1943, Bob McClurg again went into action as Pappy Boyington's wingman and tells this story:

"It was a volunteer strafing raid on Kahili. I remember adding up the scores of our division members as we took off in pouring rain and darkness. There was Pappy with over twenty Jap kills and me with my seven in one section, and Chris Magee and Don Moore with nine and three kills respectively in the other. As a division, we had over thirty Jap planes to our credit.

"Pappy led us directly to the target. In our haste to get at it, Pappy separated from us. Chris Magee and I strafed nine Jap planes on the strip at dawn and beat up a couple of gun emplacements. They fired the shore battery guns at us, trying to have us fly into geysers of water because we were too low for AA fire.

"Pappy strafed Kara airfield by himself and a Jap sub as well. I was lucky I came back as I just missed flying into the signal tower on Kahili. I got the DFC for this operation also."

In scoring his twenty-six aerial victories, Joseph J. Foss had innumerable brushes with death. His most memorable encounter was his first, which he recalls in these words:

"My first encounter was probably the most stimulating I ever engaged in. I made several errors and the Good Lord let me get by with them. One was to concentrate on one opponent and not notice who he was with—target fixation. As a result, I got him, and his three buddies gave me the works!

"I made a dead-stick landing on Henderson Field as his friends chased me to the very ground. I came in a little hot and almost ran into the palm grove. There were more than 250 holes where their lead had pierced my aircraft and not me."

During the Guadalcanal battle in November 1942, Foss almost died by drowning as a sequel to an aerial battle with superior Japanese forces. Foss downed three aircraft but took some engine hits in his Wildcat that crippled the plane and forced him into the ocean.

The impact as his fighter went plunging into the sea slammed his canopy shut. As the Wildcat started sinking quickly, the Marine found that the canopy latch had jammed. Struggling with the latch, Foss became

(Toliver Collection)

ALL AMERICAN HERO

Seen here as a Marine Corps captain, Joseph J. Foss scored twenty-six victories in a spectacular combat career that made him one of the folk heroes of WWII. His twenty-six victories were all scored with the USMC. A trained sharpshooter from boyhood, Foss cut a swathe through the Japanese in the Guadalcanal area before being withdrawn from combat and sent back to the U.S. He later became governor of South Dakota, a brigadier general in the Air National Guard and commissioner of the American Football League. He was also first president of the American Fighter Aces Association.

desperate in the confined space as the sea poured in and began filling the cockpit. In water up to his chin, Foss finally got the latch to pop and forced his way clear of the doomed Wildcat.

Dragged to the surface by the combined pull of his parachute pack and his Mae West, which he inflated once clear of the sinking aircraft, Foss now faced a long swim. The nearest shore was the island of Malaita, dismayingly remote two miles away. Still floundering toward the island hours later in darkness, Foss was about to be devoured by a horde of sharks when an Australian sawmill operator in an outrigger canoe hauled him aboard to safety.

His outdoor boyhood in South Dakota served him well, for his shooting skill with rifle and shotgun made him a superlative aerial marksman. In his first two blistering combat

tours—totalling only sixty-three days—he became the first American ace to tie Eddie Rickenbacker's World War I score. Withdrawn from combat after Guadalcanal was secured in 1943, Joe Foss came back to the U.S.A. a national hero and received the Congressional Medal of Honor from President Franklin Roosevelt. Eddie Rickenbacker and Joe Foss were the two highest-scoring American pilots at that time, with twenty-six victories each.

His standing as an ace and hero, combined with his unrivaled combat record, was invaluable to the Marine Corps. Foss was put to work on training and morale-building duties. He did not get back to the Pacific for his second tour of duty until February 1944, and did not add to his score. Worth noting here is that if Foss were able to engage in combat activity for one full year, on the same basis as during the Guadalcanal struggle, his score projects to 156 victories. Enemy pilots were continuously employed in this fashion, and marksmen among them did indeed exceed the century mark.

The postwar years were kind to Joe Foss, and he responded with hard work and devotion to his opportunities. Successful in both politics and business, he is an esteemed figure among the fraternity of fighter aces. He was the first President of the American Fighter Aces Association, and now lives in Scottsdale, Arizona.

The seventh-ranking fighter ace of the Marine Corps is Lieutenant Colonel Marion E. Carl, who is credited with 18.5 victories. Carl is one of the heroic band of Marine pilots who helped turn the tables in the Battle of Midway Island. Serving at that time with Marine Air Group 22, Carl and his comrades sacrificially attacked the raiding Japanese Zeros with obsolescent Brewster Buffalo fighters and a handful of Wildcats.

Carl survived this epic battle, which forced the Japanese to mount a second air strike against Midway and opened the enemy force to attack by American carrier-borne dive-bombers. More than half of the twenty-five fighter pilots of Marine Air Group 22 failed to return.

Captain Marion Carl found himself not long afterward at "The Canal," site of much Marine glory. From his hectic and successful combat career, Carl best remembers this incident:

"In September of 1942, while lowering my landing gear in the pattern at Henderson Field on Guadalcanal, a Zero jumped me. I pulled up the gear and headed for an antiaircract battery. The Zero pulled away, so I took after him.

"Reversing very quickly, the Zero started to meet me head-on then pulled up very steeply. I stood my Wildcat on its tail, and caught him with a ninety-degree deflection shot. He exploded not far off the beach. I still have the oxygen bottle from that enemy plane—the only thing that floated in."

Colonel Carl's decorations include two Navy Crosses, five DFC's and fourteen air medals. He continued serving with the Marine Corps and in the postwar years added to his illustrious record as a fighter ace. Among the first Marine pilots to fly jets, he has held both the world's speed record and the world's altitude record at various times. As Major General Marion Carl he retired from the Marine Corps and lives near Triangle, Virginia.

A valiant Marine ace who did not survive World War II was the colorful First Lieutenant Robert M. "Butcher Bob" Hanson. This skillful aerial fighter entered the war with a perspective on life and the world that few Americans his age could equal. He knew what he was fighting for, and it made him a fierce and intrepid combatant.

Hanson was born in Lucknow, India, on 4 February 1920, the son of missionary parents. Educated by turns both in the U.S. and India, the husky young American at age 18 was heavyweight wrestling champion of the United Provinces in India. On his way back to America in 1938, Hanson included a bicycling trip through Europe in his plans, and was a spectator to history in Vienna during the *anschluss.* Four years later, Hanson was making history himself—as a fighter ace in the Pacific war and one of the Marine Corps' greatest air heroes.

Lieutenant Hanson is the third-ranked Marine ace behind Boyington and Foss. He is credited with twenty-five aerial victories. His feat in shooting down twenty of these machines in only six consecutive flying days is probably unequalled by any other American pilot. On 24 January 1944, Hanson brought down four Zeros after battling them alone over New Britain. Three weeks later, Hanson's meteoric career—reminiscent in its brilliant

brevity of World War I's Frank Luke—ended when his fighter crashed into the sea during an escort mission over Rabaul.

Hanson was awarded both the Navy Cross and the Medal of Honor for his feats in the air. His Medal of Honor citation says in part:

" . . . he was a master of individual air combat, accounting for a total of 25 Japanese aircraft in this theater of war. His great personal valor and invincible fighting spirit were in keeping with the highest traditions of the United States Naval Service."

The Navy made a more permanent memorial to Lieutenant Hanson in the form of a destroyer, named U.S.S. *Hanson* in honor of the Marine ace.

Guadalcanal was the supreme testing time in the life and career of Colonel John Lucian Smith, who wrote an indelible combat record during August and September of 1942 when the heat was really on. He was the 28-year-old C.O. of VMF-223 at this time, and his leadership was outstanding, being by the route of example. Between 21 August and 15 September 1942 he personally downed sixteen Japanese aircraft.

His aggressive and daring tactics inspired and heartened VMF-223 during what were probably the most challenging days Marine air power would know in World War II. VMF-223 responded by downing eighty-three aircraft in the same period. The then Major Smith was awarded the Congressional Medal of Honor and when he was withdrawn from combat shortly afterwards, he had nineteen victories. As the leading Marine ace of that time, he was the example that Joe Foss and others who followed would aim to excel. Smith proved that with the right pilot a Wildcat could knock down a Zero, and that was a major contribution to morale.

Annapolis-trained Harold W. Bauer was thirty-four years old in the dark days of 1942—another "old man" fighter pilot. In the Guadalcanal battles he proved that there's no age barrier for a true professional. On 3 October 1942 he shot down four Japanese fighters and sent another away smoking.

Two weeks later, Bauer led twenty-six planes on a 600-mile over-water ferry flight. Just as he was completing this important mission, Bauer saw a squadron of Japanese aircraft attacking U.S.S. *McFarland.* Alone and with his fuel almost exhausted, Bauer hurled himself on the attacking Japanese planes. His aggressive, lone-hand assault sent four of the enemy machines down and demoralized the remainder. He is credited with eleven victories in World War II, eight of them gained in the two actions described. Colonel Bauer was awarded the Congressional Medal of Honor posthumously, having been KIA on 14 November 1942.

The unquenchable Marine spirit is nowhere better epitomized than in the fourth-ranked Marine ace of all the wars, Lieutenant Colonel Kenneth A. Walsh. Credited with twenty-one aerial victories, he has the rare distinction among Marine aces of having received his pilot's wings while still a private.

Walsh enlisted in the Marine Corps as a private in 1933. By sheer ability and persistence he won assignment to flight school. The Marine Corps would never regret this assignment. Walsh flew as an enlisted man until 1942, when he was finally commissioned. A wild aerial melee in which he took part on 30 August 1943 was the most significant of several bold deeds that won him the Congressional Medal of Honor.

After taking off with his fellow pilots of VMF-124 to escort B-24 bombers raiding Kahili airfield on Bougainville, the supercharger on Walsh's Corsair failed. Cursing his bad luck in having to abort the mission, he spotted the newly operative American airstrip on Munda. Pushing his ailing Corsair over into a dive, Walsh made all speed for this sanctuary, a bold idea already forming in his mind.

Piling out of his plane, Walsh was met by Major Jim Neefus, C.O. of the advanced airstrip, an officer with whom Walsh had served previously. Neefus immediately granted his urgent request for another aircraft, and Walsh vaulted straight into the cockpit of a Corsair sitting on standby alert. Back in the air within ten minutes of landing, he went racing full throttle after the bombers it was his duty to protect.

With an ideal 30,000 feet of altitude, Walsh caught up with the bombers just as they were being bounced by a swarm of Zeros. Streaking in from astern at just the right angle and with perfect timing, the aggressive Marine threw the Japanese fighter attack on the bombers into confusion. Fierce fighting ensued with Walsh hacking down four Zeros before being shot into the sea himself by a concentration of the Japanese planes.

Plucked from the ocean by Seabees who had seen him crash, Walsh was back flying combat from Henderson Field within three days. For this spirited mission in protecting the B-24's and other kindred feats of arms in the air, Kenneth Walsh was awarded the Congressional Medal of Honor. Withdrawn from combat not long afterwards, he didn't get back at the Japanese until 1945, by which time targets were getting scarce for fighter pilots. He was able to add only one more confirmed kill for a lifetime score of twenty-one. Lieutenant Colonel Kenneth Walsh retired from active duty on 1 February 1962, and presently resides in Santa Ana, California.

NINE MARINE FIGHTER ACES WON THE CONGRESSIONAL MEDAL OF HONOR

Providing close-support for island invasions proved to be extremely hazardous missions for the U.S. Marines. The wonder is not that nine USMC fighter pilots received the highest of awards, it is to wonder why more of them did not receive the recognition. The top four, the 6th, 9th and 13th ranking aces all won the CMH. This is Captain Kenneth A. Walsh, 21-victory ace who comes from Washington, D.C. and now lives in Santa Ana, California. He fought with VMF-124 and VMF-223.

(USMC-Wilson)

The nightfighter ace is one of the rare birds among the 1,300 or so American fighter aces. This distinction belongs to Major Robert Baird of Los Angeles, California, a Marine fighter pilot who got his night eye in over Okinawa early in 1945. He shot down three Bettys, one Jake, one Frances and one Nell at night while flying with VMF(N)-533. Retired as a colonel, Baird now lives in Honolulu, Hawaii, and tells this story of night action:

"On night CAP I was vectored onto a bogey, a Frances, and splashed him. I was so close to him, however, that when he blew up the explosion covered my Hellcat with oil. In this condition I was vectored to another bogey—a Betty this time—and had to look out the side to see him because of the oil on my windshield.

"The pursuit of the Betty was a duel, lasting three minutes or so, and we exchanged numerous shots. Mine must finally have got to him because he started spinning and I saw him blow up in the darkness below me."

In Fresno, California, there lives a Marine fighter ace who made up his five confirmed kills with a mix of day and night fighting. Major Bruce Porter passed out of Pensacola in August 1941, and as an eager young Marine fighter pilot was moved out of the U.S. with his unit for the South Pacific in February 1942. Combat didn't come his way until 1943, when he was among the first pilots to pick up the new Vought Corsairs in the New Hebrides to fly them back to action on Guadalcanal.

Porter was mounted on this splendid machine the first time he saw a Zero, and was credited with a kill in this first action. Two more followed before the end of his first nineteen-month tour in the Pacific. After indoctrination into night fighting he was eventually assigned as C.O. of VMF(N)-542, flying out of Okinawa. His unit's main mission was to protect the fleet from the fanatical and lethal kamikaze attacks—fighters being employed around the clock to maintain this protection.

Major Porter recounts his successful action at night during this tense time:

"Besides the picket ship's radar, we had a small radar set in the F6F's. This airborne unit worked up to about five miles in range. The picket ship's job was to detect approaching bogeys, then vector us until the bogeys appeared on our airborne radar in the F6F.

"The picket ship would usually vector us by altitude and heading to make an approach from below and behind the bogey. When he got it on our cockpit screen, we had to make the approach and continue to close until we had the target visually. We were looking for identification by silhouette and exhaust fire. It was touchy. Usually we had only a couple of seconds to make identification and fire.

"On 15 June 1945, while on a routine patrol in the Ieshima sector—our farthest sector towards Japan—I received an alert on a bogey. The heading was west at Angels 13,000. Soon I saw the blip come on my screen at its extremity. I began adjusting my speed for a slow closure rate. The Ieshima controller wanted to know if I had contact and I gave him an affirmative.

"At about 2115 hours I made visual contact with the enemy and made it out as a twin-engined machine. I gave it a short burst with the 50-calibers and the 20mm. Tracers marked a true line to and into the enemy machine. A few seconds was all it took. The airplane broke right and nosed down, as if the pilot had fallen forward on the stick, bursting into flames as it went. The radar controller confirmed the kill a few minutes later.

"High excitement accompanied this victory, and hadn't worn off before the same operator at Ieshima was on the air again: 'Bogey at Angels 14,000, indicating 180 knots, vector 145 at 13,000.' He vectored me right in behind and below. I made a visual at 2225 hours, identifying it as a bomber. When close enough again, I opened up with everything I had. The tracers lit up the night as they exploded forward and into the enemy ship. As before, the plane burst into flames, peeled right and then nosed down to the sea. Radar also confirmed this kill.

"I was greatly excited by this action, a success that also boosted the radar controller's morale. He sat there night after night handing out vectors without too much effect. Then in one night, two kills. When someone asked me the next day how it felt to be the newest ace—the two night kills brought me to five—I stood there with my mouth hanging open."

Only seven American fighter pilots have become aces in each two wars involving the United States.* The Marine Corps has a

The first American fighter pilot to become an ace in two separate wars was probably Major Albert J. "Ajax" Baumler, who scored eight kills in the Spanish Civil War and is credited with five kills in WWII flying with the 10th Air Force in the Far East. Baumler died in 1973.

representative in this elite group, Lieutenant Colonel John F. Bolt. During World War II, Bolt served aboard the U.S.S. *Block Island* and was credited with six aerial victories. In Korea, Bolt became the only Marine Corps ace of that war, and the only Marine Corps jet ace, when he downed six MiG-15's. During his Korean duty, Lieutenant Colonel Bolt was attached to the USAF's 39th Interceptor Squadron and flew forty-two missions.

Lieutenant Dean Caswell hailed originally from Banning, California, but lives today in Edinburg, Texas, this memory of a violent aerial battle still with him:

"On 26 April 1945, in the Okinawa campaign, we were providing air cover 150 miles north of Okinawa for three radar picket destroyers. A vital part of Vice Admiral Marc A. Mitscher's famed Task Force 58, these destroyers had been having fits as a result of kamikaze attacks.

"Action began with my three F4U Corsairs vectored toward a bogey coming in high. Up we went for the enemy, clawing altitude at full throttle. There was a bad haze that got worse as we climbed, and we couldn't see a thing. We were high, on oxygen, and it was extremely cold up there.

" 'Many bogeys dead ahead, twelve miles,' rasped the controller's voice in our headphones. If we couldn't see any better than this, we were going to miss them. Everything was a dirty yellow haze. We heard a 'tallyho' from nearby friendly planes and almost immediately saw aircraft going down in flames about two miles to starboard. Quite a show.

"Suddenly my stomach tightened and I got an ominous feeling of hostile presence. We had run smack into twenty to twenty-five Jap fighters in the haze. We were no longer spectators enjoying someone else's flamers.

"Initially we tried to fly by the book, but things got screwed up awfully fast. The lead F4U did a split-ess after a Zeke and I was left with the third man of the flight, First Lieutenant John McManus, USMC. You might say we were left holding the bag—the bag being a sky full of Zekes and Tonys.

"Things happened fast. I was on their tail. Then they were on my tail. Some of those Japs were good pilots. Round and round, tight, high-G turns and milling confusion. Amid this melee I steadied on a meatball target and it exploded in orange flames as I pulled the trigger.

"This wasn't a new feeling. I'd done it before, but each time my exultation barely overcame the paralyzing fear that grips your guts when you are fighting overwhelming odds. There were plenty of targets. The Japs were going round and round and we were in the middle. The battle sorted itself out into that sort of thing.

"Mac got one, and I saw it flame out of the corner of my eye. I got another one. We began to weave, Mac and I, protecting each other, until I got caught between two fires—a Zeke in front and a Tony in back. Quicker than you can say it, my six 50's blew the Zeke apart and Mac got the Tony hugging my tail.

"Aggressiveness alone could save us, and we again pressed the attack. Confuse the enemy, upset him, demoralize him—that's what we were trying to do—and we were doing it. The Japs had lost seven aircraft in as many minutes and were in danger of shooting each other down in their efforts to get at us. All their losses had been huge, terrifying flamers, those colossal gouts of fire that so often ended the lives of Japanese pilots in grisly barbecue.

"These livid firebursts were heightened in effect by the haze. The balance probably tipped in our favor because they did not get us and yet the two Corsairs, full of fight, kept coming at them and scoring flamers. Mac and I continued to hustle and our shots were soon snap bursts at fleeing Japs. We actually turned the rest of them for home, with my Corsair riding herd on two Zekes. I put one of them in my sights and drew blank—no ammo. I signaled to Mac and he took over, sending yet another Jap down in flames."

Dean Caswell ended the war with seven aerial victories. Intense action like that described burns itself into the memory of a fighter pilot like a movie film, because concentration at such times is total. When facing overwhelming odds, as in Caswell's case, the experience is all the more intense.

In the case of Lieutenant Colonel James Norman Cupp of Red Oak, Iowa, he set down many of his experiences during the actual war years 1943-44. The thirteen-victory ace kindly provided the following passage from an unpublished manuscript of aerial combat with the Marine Corps. Cupp's unit was the famous Hellhawks Squadron, VMF-213. His story has a strong sense of immediacy like any contemporary account, and deals with events right after the first F4U Corsairs were delivered to VMF-213, in the Solomons in September 1943:

"We were on our way to patrol over Vella Lavella on 17 September when the news came from our ground controller that a large bogey was heading down our way. The sky was dotted with puff clouds that stretched up to 18,000 feet, and as leader of a four-plane division, I figured that the enemy aircraft would be riding just over the top of the clouds.

"We started climbing towards the southern tip of the island, dodging clouds all the way. Nosing through a hole we saw a massive formation of dive-bombers plowing in about five miles away from us at the same level. The same instant I looked up and saw a string of eight Zeros zigzagging across the sky and less than a hundred feet above my head! We turned over on our backs and headed for cover, radioing the Japs' position and course. The Zeros saw fit not to follow, and so after a few thousand feet we hauled up to try it again.

"The second section lost a little ground in this maneuver. As we headed along on a course parallel to the bombers, looking for another hole in the overcast to poke through, there was quite a lot of air between our first and second sections. Only a short time passed, however, before we saw our opening and headed through it.

"This time the string of Zeros were looking down their guns at us, and we quickly repeated our breakaway maneuver. This time we were followed. The mistake the Zeros made was to get in between our two sections. As my wingman and I headed for lower altitude, Avey and Stewart of the second section were blasting away merrily. The odds were quickly whittled down to even, and the remaining Zeros left my tail for safer places.

"The Jap bombers meanwhile were getting on their target. By the time we gained our altitude, we found most of them in their dive and only a few left for us upstairs. We had a speed advantage and as we came from behind, we chopped our throttles and sat there. We could almost reach out and touch them as our six guns on each plane opened up.

"The bomber I was on looked like a toy suddenly thrown to the floor. Pieces started flying from it and suddenly there was nothing there. Then I saw one in the distance, already in his dive, and was determined to get him at all costs. All that was possible at the moment was

to follow him down and avoid as much of our own AA fire as possible. I gladly noted that Stewart, my wingman, was still with me.

"We leveled off right over the water and began sidling over to our target. My eyes had been so focused on the one plane that I was surprised to see another bomber flying alongside the first, and another—and another. Looking around I found the whole area covered with enemy aircraft. We'd followed our man to the rendezvous where all planes completing their runs were assembling in formation for the return trip to Kahili airfield on Bougainville.

"I pulled back on the throttle to keep from overrunning them and started in. Their efforts to avoid destruction were almost pathetic. They were already less than ten feet off the water, and all they could do aside from firing the rear gun was to skid from side to side.

"One I came upon had a very earnest desire to live. He threw his plane around with all his might, and it was hard to keep my bullets going into him. First the gunner slumped over and next the engine started burning. Instantly the whole plane was a flaming torch skidding across the water.

"I pulled up and crossed over the top of Stewart and came down again. The bomber ahead of me was jerked around and I came closer without firing. The closer I came, the more violent he became until finally one wing dug the water and he crashed. I pulled up, crossed back over Stewart and continued on up the line.

"Their gas tanks were bulletproofed and flamers were rare. This was disheartening, but we did well in spite of it. Every time I turned to look back over the course, I could see a Jap plane hit the water. I was able to count three of Stewart's, though it was hard to keep track of him. Four of mine hit the water, but we passed over most of them so fast it was impossible to watch the effect.

"We were nearing the head of the column and had just finished off one together when my little world started falling apart. A 20mm shell came through the tail and exploded the CO2 bottle behind my seat. The noise scared the hell out of me. Another came over my head and hit the accessory section just back of the engine. Another shell punched a hole in my left wing, carrying away my flap.

"By this time I had gathered enough presence of mind to turn around and look for

the trouble. *Trouble there was, and plenty. Four Zeros were sitting a thousand feet above and behind me, getting set to take turns at me. When I saw their altitude advantage, the fire of hope dimmed. Stewart had pulled ahead and did not respond to my radio.*

"Undaunted, I pressed on the sending button, hurriedly gave my position and shouted for help from anybody. With those holes staring at me from my fuselage, I was sure that I couldn't stay in the air long. I would have ditched then and there, but didn't relish the prospect of being strafed while swimming around among the sharks.

"The alternative was to shove the throttle home, just on the offchance that something remained of the engine. It did. That beautiful, faithful greyhound of a plane leaped like a bat out of hell. I was on a rough heading for home at the time, and the Japs must have been too low on fuel to risk a chase away from their own base. They made no effort to follow.

"I landed at Munda without flaps or brakes. Only a trickle of oil was getting to the engine, and most of it had leaked out. The skin of the plane was sieved with small-caliber holes in addition to the gaping ones that sent me scampering home. My life was charmed that day."

Lieutenant Colonel Jack E. Conger, Marine ace from Havelock, N.C., and Orient, Iowa, not only picked on Japanese aircraft—shooting down ten of them—he also tackled Japanese destroyers. He sank two destroyers in concert with three other Marine pilots in the Solomons. In 1944, Conger sank another destroyer in the Palaus.

He emerged victorious from an unforgettable aerial battle in the Solomons by making highly unorthodox use of his aircraft. He tells the story here of what must surely be one of World War II's strangest aerial victories:

"In October of 1942 I was at Guadalcanal, and was involved in a dogfight with a Zero. I finally got myself into an advantageous position on his tail and pressed the trigger. Nothing! I was out of ammo. I didn't like the idea of breaking off and giving him the chance to get on my tail.

"I decided to ram this Jap and I used my propeller like a buzzsaw. It cut the Jap plane into two pieces! My aircraft went into a violent spin, and I was afraid to bail out for fear of being swiped by the tail section. My plane hit the drink and miraculously I was

able to get out. *After inflating my Mae West I saw the Jap pilot I had brought down floundering in the water about a hundred feet away.*

"A few minutes later a boat with Marines and Coast Guardsmen aboard came out to pick me up. We then tried to get the Jap pilot in the boat also, but he was completely unwilling. While trying to fish him out of the water with a grappling hook, the Jap pulled a pistol and tried to shoot at us. Luckily the pistol misfired, probably due to dampness. We clouted him unconscious with the boat hook and pulled him aboard."

Guadalcanal was the site of an aerial battle on 12 December 1942 involving a young Marine lieutenant a few weeks short of his twenty-second birthday. Jefferson J. DeBlanc of St. Martinsville, Louisiana* recalls this action:

"We dove from 5,000 feet to intercept Jap twin-engined Betty bombers making torpedo runs on the fleet off Henderson Field. We had to dive through our own AA fire, and two of our planes were shot down in the process. There were twenty-five Bettys. I managed to shoot down two before they reached the fleet and smoked a third, sending him veering off course. With all the friendly steel that was flying around, and by that time only fifty feet off the water, I was fortunate, through God, not to get any 'arrows' in the F4F-3"

This story is typical of the many modest men of high achievement in the ranks of America's fighter aces. A more vivid account of the kind of aerial warrior DeBlanc was appears in his Congressional Medal of Honor citation. This extract refers to an action undertaken by VMF-112 on 31 January 1943, when DeBlanc was still two weeks short of his twenty-second birthday:

"Taking off with his section as escort for a force of dive-bombers and torpedo planes ordered to attack Japanese surface vessels, First Lieutenant DeBlanc led his flight directly to the target area where, at 14,000 feet, our strike force encountered a large number of Zeros protecting the enemy's surface craft.

"In company with the other fighters, First Lieutenant DeBlanc instantly engaged the hostile planes, and aggressively countered their repeated efforts to drive off our bombers,

---

*As this is written, DeBlanc resides in Brunssum, the Netherlands.

persevering in his efforts to protect the diving planes and waging fierce combat until, picking up a call for assistance from the dive-bombers under attack by enemy float planes at 1,000 feet, he broke off his engagement with the Zeros, plunged into the formation of float planes and disrupted the savage attack . . . "

The dive-bombers were thus able to press home their attack and withdrew thereafter. DeBlanc's citation continues:

"Although his escort mission was fulfilled upon the safe retirement of the bombers, DeBlanc courageously remained on the scene despite a rapidly diminishing fuel supply and, boldly challenging the enemy's superior numbers of float planes, fought a valiant battle against terrific odds, seizing the tactical advantage and striking repeatedly to destroy three of the hostile aircraft and disperse the remainder.

"Prepared to maneuver his damaged plane back to base, he had climbed aloft and set his course when he discovered two Zeros closing in behind. Undaunted, he opened fire and blasted both Zeros from the sky in a short, bitterly fought action which resulted in such hopeless damage to his own plane that he was forced to bail out at a perilously low altitude atop the trees on enemy-held Kolombangara. A gallant officer, a superb airman and an indomitable fighter, First Lieutenant DeBlanc had rendered decisive assistance during a critical state of operations, and his unwavering fortitude in the face of overwhelming opposition reflects the highest credit upon himself and adds new luster to the traditions of the United States Naval Service."

He ended the war as Major Jefferson J. DeBlanc, with nine aerial victories to his credit. When the chips are down, the U.S.A. is always able to find such men.

The eleventh-ranking Marine Corps ace, with fourteen aerial victories to his credit is Archie G. Donahue of Texas City. Now in the Marine Reserves, the former Lieutenant Colonel Donahue sells real estate and insurance. He well remembers this incident from a distinguished combat career:

"I was credited with five kills in one battle at Okinawa, but my most exciting victory was my first Zeke off Guadalcanal. Lieutenant Hughes and I were escorting several bombers to attack a Jap battlewagon. A flight of nine or ten Zekes came down at us to break up our

formation. I blew up the lead Jap with a lucky short burst. The rest of them immediately quit and left us alone.

"There were no further attacks from the air, but this incident—and the subsequent storm of AA fire from the Jap battlewagon and its escort—made this the most exciting mission of my career."

Also in the Marine Reserves is former Lieutenant Frank Carl Drury, an ace who flew with VMF-212 and VMF-113 in the Pacific. He scored six kills, five of them during the Solomons campaign. He best remembers this encounter:

"We were on a predawn patrol and joined combat over Rekata Bay, San Isabel Island. Eight of our F4F's were dog-fighting float-equipped Zeros below 2,000 feet and in almost total darkness. They used running lights and we did not, but it was still pretty hairy. One Zero shot down another Zero in a case of mistaken identity. When I got into firing position on one of the Japs I found only one of my guns firing. It was enough. He flamed and plunged into the ocean.

Frank Drury was not done with combat flying when Japan surrendered. He flew again with VMF-331 in Korea for eight months before returning to civilian life as a citizen of Danby, Missouri.

Like Drury, Marine ace Bill Farrell of Gardena, California, flew in two wars with the USMC. In Korea, Bill flew in the ground attack role by day with VMF-311, and by night with VMF(N)-513. As has been pointed out earlier in this book, fighter pilots in the ground attack use of air power do a monumental and dangerous job, often completely missing out on opportunities for aerial combat because of their primary mission. Bill Farrell destroyed over fifty-two trucks in Korea, and strafing skills developed in World War II further aided in the dislocation and disruption of North Korean logistics.

Lieutenant Colonel Farrell is credited with five victories in World War II, and his most vivid recollection is of a thrilling pursuit while flying with VMF-312:

"In May of 1945, while attached to VMF-312 at Kadena on Okinawa, three squadron mates and I were on CAP thirty miles north of Okinawa. We were relieved on station, but before leaving for home base we took one more tour of our patrol area. Cloud cover was about nine-tenths, and a formation of thirty-five

Zekes, Tojos and Vals were spotted through breaks about a thousand feet above us and on a collision course.

"Their formation was a V of V's, and our formation of four pulled into rear position and started firing. In the ensuing ten minutes' dogfight, which passed from 10,000 feet down to water level, fourteen Japs were confirmed destroyed and three others probably destroyed.

"I witnessed the destruction of one of our Corsairs—the pilot was lost—but I personally accounted for the Zeke that exploded him. I followed this fellow for 4,000 feet to the water, in a dive in which every time I fired my guns he would pull out of range as my aircraft slowed. Finally I started him burning as we leveled out on the water.

"His sudden slow-down caused me to close to such a near wing position that I could see the frightened expression on his face as he spotted me. He was trying to climb out of the cockpit through the flames, but his aircraft hit the water and exploded violently.

"In this fight I shot down one Tojo, two Zekes and one Val and shared another Val. I also probably destroyed another Zeke for a total of 4.5 destroyed and one probable. My grand total for World War II was five destroyed and one probable, as I had shared the destruction of another Val a few weeks previously."

Dewey F. Durnford, Jr., of Columbus, Ohio, flew with VMF-323 in World War II and scored 6.33 aerial victories. Like Frank Drury and Bill Farrell he also flew in Korea. Forty-nine missions in World War II were followed by seventy-six missions with VMF-311 in the Korean War, and sixty more missions as an exchange pilot with the USAF in F-86 Sabrejets. While flying Sabres, Durnford was credited with a shared kill of a MiG-15, bringing his total victory credits to 6.83. Major Durnford's outstanding combat memory is of an action in World War II:

"While flying number three in a flight of Corsairs covering the invasion of IeShima, our flight was vectored to a picket ship that was under attack. I first spotted this DD smoking badly from a direct hit near the bridge. As we approached, I saw a Jap Lily bomber commencing another run.

"Firing from six o'clock high, I flamed him and he crashed about 800 yards short of the DD. Ten minutes later we spotted another

bomber and our flight was now down to the leader and myself, the remainder having returned to Kadena for various reasons. Finding his guns jammed, the leader made feinting runs while I closed in to fire. On the first pass I smoked the port engine, and as I pulled away my own cockpit began to fill with smoke.

"The Jap tail gunner had been pouring it to me, and I immediately figured he had hit my aircraft. When I opened the canopy to bail out, the smoke cleared instantly and I suddenly realized that it was the bomber's smoke. I strapped back in and started back toward the burning bomber when the Helen released a Baka.

"This was the first of these new weapons to be observed in this area, and I was properly amazed. The Baka spun into the sea, and I closed on the Helen, this time blowing off the port engine. Then the wing came off and he plunged down to the sea in flames."

Lieutenant Colonel Kenneth DeForrest Frazier of Burlington, New Jersey, ran up 12.5 kills in World War II. The lively sky above Guadalcanal was the setting for the combat experience that Frazier now recollects—involving two illustrious Marine aces, Marion Carl and Harold Bauer:

"On 3 October 1942, while flying over northern Guadalcanal with a flight of F4F's led by Captain Marion Carl, we engaged a superior number of Zeros. In a brief engagement, I shot down two Zeros before my plane was struck by 20mm cannon fire from a Zero that slipped in behind me while I was occupied with one of my victims.

"My engine stopped and fire broke out in the forward section of the aircraft. I dove through a large cloud to shake my attacker and then bailed out. Floating down in my parachute, I was shaken out of my skin by the sight and sound of tracer bullets whizzing past within inches of my head. My attacker had followed me down and was strafing me in my parachute.

"After a few seconds of this—a terrifying eternity amid that lethal hail—a lone F4F piloted by Lieutenant Colonel H.W. Bauer (now deceased) closed in on this strafing Zero. Bauer's fire drove the enemy plane off, trailing black smoke, despite Bauer's only having one or two guns operating.

"I made a successful landing in the ocean several miles from the northeastern tip of

Guadalcanal. Two hours later, I was picked up by an American destroyer and returned to Henderson Field none the worse for wear."

Colonel Frazier's deliverance by the redoubtable Harold Bauer was paralleled in the combat career of Colonel Julius W. Ireland of Baltimore, Maryland. Colonel Ireland had a distinguished career with the Marine Corps, which included 5.33 aerial victories in World War II. He does not forget the reason that he survived the war:

"In January of 1944 while over Rabaul, I became separated from my wingman and found myself in the unenviable plight of having a Zero firmly positioned on my tail. Unable to shake him, he just about had me boresighted when a lone Navy F6F appeared from nowhere and blew the Jap out of the sky.

"I am positive that had he not appeared at that exact moment, I would not be here today, taking this opportunity to thank that unknown Navy pilot for saving my life."

Lieutenant Colonel Kenneth M. Ford of Whittier, California, shot down five aircraft in the Pacific to become a Marine ace. Like many other aces he returned to the fray in Korea in 1952-53, this time as a helicopter pilot. He had this combat experience over the Russell Islands in World War II:

"As wingman I followed my section leader from the main formation toward the Jap Zero horde over the Russell Islands. A Zero turned into my section leader's tail, and I shot him down in flames. The section leader continued on by the Jap force flying in the opposite direction, and as I was then right next to the Zeros with no chance to escape, I turned into the center of their force.

"This probably saved my skin. Confusion ensued. There was such a rush of Jap planes trying to get on my tail for the kill that they got in each other's way. This let me get some good shots into the rest of them before the rest of the Corsairs joined the battle."

Major Thomas Mann, Jr., of Sullivan and Graysville, Indiana, is credited with ten aerial victories, four of them achieved on his last air operation out of Guadalcanal. On 11 November 1942, fighters from VMF-121 were scrambled at 0900 to intercept bogies:

"The bogies turned out to be ten AICHI-99 dive-dombers with Zeros as escort. We followed the dive-dombers and I shot down my first at 5,000 feet, my second one as it released its bomb in the dive, my third in retirement

and the fourth in retirement about five miles northeast of Savo Island. My luck then ran out.

"My next target, another AICHI-99 assisted by a flock of Zeros, made a target out of me. I was hit and shot down. The next ten hours I spent in the drink, swimming for the shore. For the ensuing six days I lived with natives on the northernmost island of the Florida group. They returned me to Tulagi in their war canoe on 18 November 1942."

What better way to transport a warrior than in a war canoe?

Another of the professional Marine Corps pilots who resigned his commission in 1941 to join the Flying Tigers is the late Lt. Col. Edmund F. Overend of Coronado, California. Like many other aces who entered World War II this way, he cut his combat teeth in the skies over Rangoon. His first victory came on his first combat mission, and has stayed ever since uppermost in his memory:

"My first mission was by far the most exciting, and took place on 23 December 1941. That day was my first day off in quite a while, and dressed in civvies with a shirt and tie, I was on my way to town with my good friend, Charlie Older.

"When the alarm went off we ran to the field and took off in two P-40's, primarily to get them off the field and avert their destruction. As we climbed away we looked up and saw two formations of about fifty Bettys with fighters escorting them and decided to attack. I aimed a long distance ahead of them to pick up altitude, and finally made a poor head-on run, being a little off course.

"Their turret gunners were no better than I was, and no damage resulted to either Charlie Older or me, so I dove deep and came up underneath the formation. I closed in to about fifty feet, firing all the way. Finally the right engine started to burn on the plane I was working on. The machine drifted out of the formation and started to go down.

"Being green, I followed it to make the kill sure instead of letting it go and getting some more of the Bettys. I finally struck the turret gunner and he went down over his guns. The bomber now went into a steep dive, and in excitement and elation at having splashed it, I dived steeper and steeper with the doomed enemy. The P-40 being a good deal more streamlined than the Betty, I finally found myself passing the bomber!

I pulled away sharply, Oscars hard after me. Evading them, I returned to base. Although I saw plenty of action that day and my technique improved considerably, it was never matched for sheer excitement and that dry feeling that reaches from the throat to the navel."

Overend is credited with nine victories in World War II, and among his memorabilia preserved a contemporary letter from this same period. Written on 10 January 1942, less than three weeks after his first aerial battle, the letter conveys in the classic style of such contemporary writings, the atmosphere of the times. Ed Overend was attempting to outline to his fiancee something of the conditions encountered in Rangoon when the Japanese were riding high:

"The raid on the city that we intercepted had not been severe, but they had sent fighters down and machine gunned people in the streets. The Indians and Burmese were naturally curious anyway, and while they stood out in the streets watching the fight the planes swooped down and killed literally killed hundreds of them. It was really a ghastly business and I was glad that at least I had seen the clean side of it all—if it can be said there is a clean side. The next day evacuation started, following a broadcast from Bangkok by the Japs to the effect that they would be over with "gifts" for the Americans on Christmas Day. We had knocked down thirteen of them the first day and we knew that when they came again it would be in force.

"It was really a sight to see the hundreds of trucks in the convoys going up the road and thousands of people walking, riding on wheelbarrows, carts, baby buggies, bicycles and everything they could put a wheel on. I noticed particularly the things they considered to be their most valuable possessions. One fellow was carrying an umbrella and a lantern. Another woman was dragging a tiny baby and had the cloth they usually carry the baby in filled with wood. My native bearer had given the job to a friend, and said to tell me that he would be back after the war to take care of me.

"Things were a little rough, but on the

(USAF)

AMERICAN FIGHTER ACES ASSO. INSIGNIA

Colonel Jack T. Bradley, USAF, and Brigadier General Joe Foss (USMC) hold Aces Asso. insignia at early meeting of the group. In background at left is Colonel Walker M. Mahurin, USAF, and in foreground at left, profile, is Commander Eugene A. Valencia, USN.

twenty-fifth we were ready for them although there were only twelve of us. We took off at 11 o'clock on Christmas morning, and got the word that they were on their way. Climbing to 20,000 feet, I was cold to the marrow. After about twenty minutes I noticed the number four man in the formation—there were six of us together—wag his wings violently and my heart jumped. I saw them at once. There was one formation of thirty and another behind them, and still another behind that. Above were the Jap fighters. I couldn't stop to count. We were already setting course to intercept the first group.

"I felt a lot more confident than on the twenty-third. As I look back I felt eager, because I knew I was part of a group and we had all met the enemy before. We knew they feared us. One of them who had parachuted down had said that they didn't like the Americans because we came at them from so many angles.

"We were not orthodox in our attacks and he accused us of being, of all things, pugnacious! Well, I was more confident, as I have said, and I had found that deep friendship and fellowship that I told you was one of my reasons for coming. It is greater and warmer than I had ever anticipated. I hope you do not think I am trying to make you think that I am a hotshot fighter pilot, for that is farthest from my intention. I just thought you might like to know how an average fellow thought and acted when he really played for keeps . . . .

"We were the only ones that were able to intercept the bombers because they are very fast for medium bombers, and the other six of our boys were tangling with the fighters. We strung out in a line and swooped very deep to come up under the bombers. I aimed at the leader so that as they moved by I would be in a good position for one of the rear wingmen.

"We were moving in to about two hundred yards before we opened fire, and then, still firing, we would close to about 70-100 yards, after which, all we had to do was get away. The Japs opened fire on us at about 500 yards and waiting while you got into effective range was really an eternity. After my first burst one of the bomber's engines caught fire and he pulled out directly in front of me.

"I turned to follow him and his wing sheared off and gasoline sprayed a sheet of flame behind him. Climbing back I could see two other bombers dropping out and going down in dives. On one of them the rudder was hanging grotesquely like a great tail skid. After three more attacks I pulled up to one bomber, and as I closed I got a little too flat, that is, I fell behind him too much and they have a machine gun in the very tip of the tail. He nosed down and started out of the formation, but as I tried to pull away, I couldn't. My controls were jammed by the shots that had gone into the ailerons.

"My engine stopped, and I started down with the bomber ahead of me and going down too. I looked at my altimeter. 20,000 feet. I decided that was too high. One of my buddies had jumped on the first day and they machine gunned him all the way down. I decided that if I could not turn, at least I could glide straight. I trimmed it up and prepared to look around.

"I'd had a thousand practices at forced landings, but this was the real McCoy. I could only go straight, but I didn't know whether the wing would stall when I got slow or not, so I prepared to shoot over the rice paddies and drop my flaps when I saw something good. The bomber went in about 5,000 feet below and I continued going straight. Finally, I was sliding over the rice paddies at 140 mph with natives bolting in all directions.

"I hit and was thrown against the belt pretty hard, bruising my left arm, but she finally skidded to a stop. My propeller looked like the leaves on a lotus blossom, but other than that it was OK. My wheels had been up, so it was a belly landing and the "Tommyhawk" is a good plane for that. The rice paddies have two-foot ridges in them about every hundred and fifty feet or so. These jar you a good deal but it isn't as bad as it may sound.

"I hadn't the haziest idea of where I was. When I waved to some natives, they ran away. I waved at some more and they came at me brandishing horn-handled sickles. When they saw that I didn't have slant eyes they all smiled. Through pidgin and gestures I got them to get me some paper, and sent a message by boy runner telling them where I was down. The runner would return in two turns of my watch . . . but three hours passed.

"The head man invited me to his house, and brought out a large ceremonial mat for me to sit on, and then came a big pot of tea and some raw eggs. I took the tea. Natives came running from all directions. The head man's front porch collapsed from the weight of them.

Everyone laughed and asked me to put on my flight gear, so I wore my oxygen mask, goggles and helmet and they got a big kick out of that.

"Soon one of the richer ones offered me a bicycle, and said I could ride to the nearest town in just two hours. I started over the rice paddies on a bicycle. I can just barely sit down yet and it was three weeks ago. After ten miles of this I came to a town of 600—all natives. They had a Jap parachutist in jail there with a broken leg. They furnished me with a Ford V-8, four soldiers, two drivers and a bottle of rum. Squeezing into this Ford we proceeded for another jolting twenty miles over the rice paddies. About four miles south we came on the bomber I'd shot down. The plane had not burned and the pilot was dead at the controls. One gunner was dead inside, and the bombardier had jumped from 300 feet with a knapsack and without a parachute.

"They were the first men I had ever seen dead, and yet, as I looked at them, I had absolutely no emotion! Even though I had been instrumental in it all, it just didn't seem real. I took the camera out of the plane after looking it over thoroughly and continued my return to my unit. The final leg home was via a steam launch for about twenty miles. I was the last to return. One other pilot had been shot down, but landed safely. We destroyed thirteen bombers and thirteen fighters—a good day's work although I had missed lunch and dinner both."

The final paragraph of Ed Overend's letter home sums up the high motivation of the officers the U.S.A. trained as fighter pilots in the nineteen thirties to win America's wars wherever and whenever they might come:

"I heard the President's message to Congress today, via my shortwave radio. His statement as to the necessity of putting the tools into the hands of the men who were fighting, was indeed heartening. To those of us who are as far from home as we can get, it gives a new lease on life to know that there is such tremendous effort being made at home, to make our work effective. Time is indeed the essence,

Semper fidelis,
Love,
Ed"

The "Charlie Older" mentioned by Overend in his first account of combat over Rangoon is Colonel Charles H. Older of Los Angeles,

California, another Marine Corps pilot who volunteered for the Flying Tigers after resigning his commission. Older shot down 10.00 aircraft with the AVG, then downed 8½ more after transferring to the 23rd Fighter Group in the 14th Air Force. His total is 18.50 victories in World War II. The official USAF list credits Older with 7.0, however.

Older was trained as a pilot as a Marine Aviation Cadet at Pensacola, Florida, in 1939-1940. He served with the First Marine Corps Fighter Group in 1940-1941 prior to signing up with the AVG. Older survived the war and took up a legal career. Tops in aerial combat, he proved equally adept in his new field and is now a distinguished judge in Los Angeles.* He also handles the legal affairs of the American Fighter Aces Association.

Assuming that a fighter pilot is top quality material and has been intensively and thoroughly trained, he must still have opportunity to fight in the air. Many highly trained and eager fighter pilots had to fly numerous missions without even getting one shot at the enemy. Captain Robert B. See of the Marine Corps had the rare experience of finding both combat and a kill on his first mission, and with Pappy Boyington his unforeseen, temporary C.O.

"On a fighter sweep over Rabaul in New Britain, I was flying tail-end Charlie in another squadron, as three planes in my division had to turn back. I just joined up with the first three-plane division I found.

"Sixty F4U Corsairs led by Pappy Boyington encountered approximately 140 Zeros and Tonys over Simpson Harbor. That melee was the wildest of all dogfights. I had all I could do to stay with it, and I didn't get a single good shot until I spotted a lone Zero pulling a tight chandelle to evade a pursuing Corsair.

"He was going slow and a set-up, so I dove on him. When I fired, I expected six 50-calibers to blaze out, but only one gun fired intermittently. Now I could visualize an unhappy ending to this otherwise perfect bounce, with the Zero turning on my tail and gunning me. Despite this potential threat, I kept boring in on him and suddenly the left wing of the Zero ignited into a ball of flame.

---

*Colonel Older is currently a judge in the Superior Court of Los Angeles County. He vaulted into the limelight in the mid-70's, albeit reluctantly, when he served as judge for the Manson trials in Los Angeles.

"I was astounded to see the Zero fall off in a steep spiral into the sea. As he went in, the impact set off a phosphorous wing bomb he was carrying, which produced a dense white cloud of billowing smoke. That kill was well marked."

Captain See flew with VMF-321 and is credited with five aerial victories.

Considerable contrast exists between flying fighter combat with the Marines and owning a chain of haberdashery stores, but Harold E. Segal of Chicago, Illinois, and more latterly of Alhambra, California, is an ace who has survived the hazards of both. Harold Segal rose to the rank of major in the USMC and shot down twelve Japanese aircraft. He will never forget 11 July 1943:

"I was flying wing on Jim Swett on an eight-plane patrol mission over Kolobangara. This mission was near completion, two planes had returned to base with engine trouble and Swett sent the other four planes back. He and I were to stay only a few minutes longer.

"Just as we turned to start back to base, Swett spotted bogies, forty bombers and a horde of escort Zeros both high and low. Swett headed directly for them, and although my engine was acting up, I followed. As we headed for the bombers, Zeros attacked us and one came between Swett and me. A fast three-second burst and there was one less Zero.

"Following Swett, I tried to hit one of the bombers, without success, using about one hundred rounds of ammo. Diving away, I almost escaped, but one Zero had me wired and riddled my plane with holes from nose to tail. I managed to climb away toward some clouds, but saw ten Zeros below and dove on them. In one run I managed to flame two of them.

"Then all hell broke loose. I was shot at from every angle by the Japs, finally going down into the water, where the Japs strafed me as I swam and ducked under the water during each of their firing passes. I waited until they ran out of ammo or got low enough on fuel to pull out, and then I climbed into my liferaft. Thirty-six hours later a destroyer picked me up."

Harold Segal's leader on this mission, Jim Swett, is another distinguished Marine ace. As Lieutenant Colonel James Elms Swett with 15.5 victories over Japanese aircraft to his credit, he is among the most highly regarded aces within that elite fraternity.

Colonel Swett's Congressional Medal of Honor Citation gives a compressed and accurate account of this officer's finest hour, on 7 April 1943. At that time, Swett was a 22-year-old 1st lieutenant flying as a division leader with VMF-221 in the Solomon Islands:

"In a daring flight to intercept a wave of 150 Japanese planes, First Lieutenant Swett unhesitatingly hurled his four-plane division into action against a formation of 15 enemy bombers and personally exploded three hostile planes in midair with deadly and accurate fire during his dive. Although separated from his division while clearing the heavy concentration of antiaircraft fire, he boldly attacked six enemy bombers, engaged the first four in turn, and unaided, shot down all in flames.

"Exhausting his ammunition as he closed the fifth Japanese bomber, he relentlessly drove his attack against terrific opposition which partially disabled his engine, shattered the windscreen and slashed his face. In spite of this, he brought his shattered plane down with skillful precision in the water off Tulagi without further injury. The superb airmanship and tenacious fighting spirit which enabled First Lieutenant Swett to destroy seven enemy bombers in a single flight were in keeping with the highest traditions of the United States Naval Service."

The Seattle-born Swett stands right behind the U.S. Navy's David McCampbell for the largest number of victories in a single mission. Swett's feat remained the high-water mark for naval and marine pilots—indeed for all U.S. fighter aces—until McCampbell brought off his epic nine kills in one mission a year and a half later.

Although the archetypal Marine has perhaps been overdrawn by Hollywood, the Corps has produced innumerable rugged, dashing and fearless heroes. Alongside these men, who resemble the Hollywood image without being duplicates, stands a long line of quiet, modest heroes to whom their own valor in combat seems to be a lifelong embarrassment. Among them is Major Franklin C. Thomas, Jr.

Credited with nine aerial victories in World War II, Thomas bears a high reputation among his fellow Marine pilots as a combat flyer. You may be sure that if other aces say that one of their fraternity was exceptional, no further endorsement or elaboration is necessary. Details couldn't in any event be extracted from Frank Thomas, whose response to a request for his most memorable combat experience typifies this ace:

"Most exciting experience? All my combat experiences were exciting. Hell—I was scared to death the whole time."

More than this Thomas would not say about his combat career, which extended from December of 1942 until March 1944. The records nevertheless reveal that he was shot down and so badly wounded in his final battle that he required nine months in a hospital to recuperate.

Colonel Donald K. Yost of Princeton, New Jersey, is credited with eight aerial victories as part of a distinguished career that includes command of VMF-111 at Samoa in 1942, and of VMF-121 in the Solomons from December 1942 through February 1943. Later in the war, as Air Group Commander of MCVEG-4 aboard the *Cape Gloucester* he ran up his own eight victories. His first victory, which he never claimed, made the deepest impression on him.

"This was on the afternoon strike of 23 December 1942, while my squadron was providing close fighter support for eleven SBD's bombing Munda Airport, New Georgia, from Henderson Field on Guadalcanal. As the bombers approached their push-over point to dive on the airfield, Zeros appeared at all altitudes as the eight P-39's between 15,000 and 20,000 feet, the eight F4F's below 18,000 feet and the eleven SBD's were all jumped simultaneously by about fifty Zeros.

"The four P-38's flying high cover at 30,000 feet were unaware of the presence of the Zeros. Communications were bad between planes of our own squadron, and practically nonexistent with the Army Air Force units. Hence, it was pretty much a free-for-all.

"As my flight started down with the SBD's my wingman spotted a Zero off to the side and went after it. My radio call to him to stay with me was unanswered, and he was not heard from again. I continued down with the SBD's believing my other planes were following, but as I attacked six Zeros making a pass at the SBD's I found I was alone.

"After one pass, I found the six Zeros above me and in a position to make runs on me. They took it in turns. While five stayed in position above me, one Zero would make a pass, fire, do a slow roll and pull up to the tail end of the other five. Then another would

make his firing pass. It was just like we used to practice gunnery runs, and the way it was set up they were likely to get their target drogue eventually—me.

"While the Japs were making their runs, I maneuvered to cause full-deflection shots— then as they pulled out and started up, I would fire on them. I was rewarded by having two in succession burst into flames and disappear. The Jap leader maintained position but did not make runs, thereby keeping me set up for the other Jap pilots. I was at such a disadvantage that if two Japs made simultaneous passes they would probably get me, so I looked around for friendly planes or a cloud to jump into.

"There were no friendly planes, but there was a cloud about a mile away and above me. Figuring that the Jap leader was waiting for a good straightaway shot and that he would be on me immediately if I tried to climb for the cloud, I set myself in a position whereby he could come down on me from behind—but I never took my eyes off him.

"He started his Zero down, and when he was well committed and closing fast, I turned into him and fired, with which he immediately broke off, and I bolted for the cloud. Just before I reached the safety of the cloud, tracers went smoking past me to the right and left and slightly above my wings. I snapped over quickly to evade this fire and apparently ducked under the engine of a Zero, for I saw it pass above me and to my left just before I got up into my cloud.

"In the cloud I climbed to 10,000 and when I came out of it I turned back towards Munda, looking for friendly planes. I stayed close to the clouds that usually hang over the center of the islands in the South Pacific in the afternoons. I saw plenty of milling planes, but could not recognize any friendly ones. I was about to turn back toward the Canal when far below me I spotted eleven SBD's heading for home. Behind the last SBD was a Zero, closing in with another Zero to the right and above the first.

"Figuring I didn't have time to hit the wingman and get to the lead Zero before he shot up the SBD's, I passed by the top Zero and squeezed the trigger as I closed on the tail of the lead Zero. The thin, futile sound of only one outboard gun firing followed my trigger squeeze.

"As I fired, the Jap pulled up in a steep

wingover, with me following part-way, but I broke off and ducked into the bottom of a cloud. I figured his wingman would be on me. When I came out of the cloud I charged all my guns and found them all functioning perfectly. Again I could see no friendly aircraft, so headed for home alone.

"I was the last plane on the whole mission to get back to base. My wingman was never found, and from the story pieced together it appears that he shot down a Zero but was shot down by another Zero while doing so. Several days later, when they got time, the pilot and gunner of the tail SBD came over to the squadron to thank the pilot who shot the Zero off their tail. According to their story, the Zero completed his wingover burning, and plunged into the sea. I had not reported that plane and did not later report it, as it seemed unimportant at the time."

The Marine Corps made a tremendous contribution to Pacific victory, both in the land battles and in the skies. The Marine Corps uniform was worn by 124 aces, who among them shot down 1011¼ of the 2,355 enemy aircraft accredited to the Marines in aerial combat. These aces again demonstrated that single statistical fact about their own fraternity: aces account for a disproportionate number of all aerial victories by all pilots. In the case of the Marines in World War II, their aces were responsible for more than forty percent of all aerial combat kills.

The Marine aces more than proved themselves statistically. They added a new dimension to the illustrious combat traditions of the USMC. Air power had come to stay, and the Marines had learned how to use this new weapon. Two Marine aces, Boyington and Foss, became legends in their own lifetime, enriching American folklore and burnishing anew the record of Marine heroism.

(USMC)

Captain Donald N. Aldrich, USMC (20.0)
Aldrich, from Chicago, Illinois, was the 5th-ranking Marine ace. He flew with VMF-215. In 1947 Aldrich was killed in an accident while flying a fighter.

(USMC)

Lt. Stuart C. Alley, Jr. (5.0): Marine Lt. Alley scored three kills on one mission over the East China Sea. He hailed from North Muskegon, Michigan and Grand Prairie, Texas.

(USMC)

Captain Frank B. Baldwin, USMC (5.0): This Philadelphia Marine fighter pilot posed for this photo in the Russell Islands on 3 July 1943.

(USMC)

Lt. Harold W. Bauer, USMC (11.0) CMH
Bauer, from North Platte, Nebraska flew with VMF-212 based at Guadalcanal. He was killed in action on 14 November 1942, and was a lieutenant colonel at the time of his death.

(USMC)

Major George C. Axtell, USMC (6.00): Arlington, Virginia. VMF-323. Retired as a lieutenant general.

Major John F. Bolt, USMC (6 WWII + 6 Korea = 12.0: Bolt, from Sanford and New Smyrna Beach, Florida, was the Marine Corps' first jet ace in Korea. In WWII he fought with VMF-214 off the carrier USS BLOCK ISLAND. There he shot down six Zeros. In Korea, Bolt flew 92 missions with VMF-115, then flew another 42 missions as an exchange officer with the 39th Squadron of the USAF 51st Fighter Group. His six MiG victories all came while flying with the USAF. (USMC)

268

(USMC)

Major Marion Eugene Carl, USMC (18.50): Carl's biography reads like Superman. This Hubbard, Oregon fighter pilot was at Midway, the Solomon Islands, Guadalcanal, Vella LaVella, Bougainville, Emirau . . . He scored one at Midway, 15½ at Guadalcanal, two over Rabaul. Carl held the world's speed record of 650.6 mph set in August 1947 and the world's altitude record of 83.235 feet in August 1953. One memory: "When caught with my gear down in the pattern at Henderson Field, I managed to hit a Zero with a 90 degree deflection shot. BOOM! I still have the Zero's oxygen bottle, the only thing that floated in."

Major Robert M. Baker, USMC (7.0)
The Marine Corps identifies this photo as being of Robert M. Baker, VMF-23 and VMF-121. If so, Baker is wearing the leather flight jacket of one E. W. Russell while posing for this portrait.

(USMC)

(USMC-D. Q. White)
Captain Richard L. Braun, USMC (5.0): Braun, from Santa Monica, California and Cherry Point, North Carolina, flew two tours of combat with VMF-15. This photo taken at Vella LaVella 14 November 1943.

(USMC)
Captain Robert Baird, USMC (6.00 at night)
Honolulu, Hawaii. VMF-533 (N). Baird was the only USMC night fighter ace of WWII. He shot down three Betty bombers, a Frances, a Nell and a Jake in slightly over 30 days. Three USMC night fighter pilots had 4 night kills.

269

Captain William E. Crowe, USMC (7.0)
This photo was made at Miramar NAS near San Diego on
15 October 1943. Crowe, from Norfolk, Virginia, fought
with VMF-124.

(USMC)

(USMC)

Captain Dean Caswell, USMC (7.0)
Operating off USS BUNKER HILL with VMF 221,
Caswell shot down seven Japanese planes to
qualify as "ace." He was born at Banning,
California but calls Edinburg, Texas "home."

**Captain William Northrop Case,
USMC (8.0):** An ace of the famous
"Black Sheep" squadron, this photo
of Captain Case was made in the
Russell Islands on 5 October 1943
by SSgt. Hart.

(USMC)

(USMC)

Major William A. Carlton, USMC (5.0): T/Sgt. D. Q. White took
this photo of Carlton at Vella LaVella on 24 November 1943.
Carlton was from Allen Park, Michigan.

Lt. William Perry Brown, USMC (7.0): April 1945 on Okinawa, this picture of Brown was taken by Sgt. Charles Corkran.   (USMC)

(USMC)

Major James Norman Cupp, USMC (13.00)

Cupp, a Navy Cross winner, flew his combat with VMF-213, the HELLHAWKS. He was born in Corning, Iowa but calls Red Oak his hometown. He says, of a patrol over Vella LaVella on 17 September 1943, "My life was charmed that day!" His F-4U Corsair, sieved by Japanese bullets, faithfully took him to Munda and a hairy but safe landing.

(USMC)

Captain Jack E. Conger, USMC (10.00): Havelock, North Carolina. VMF-212. Over Guadalcanal, Conger shot down a Zero and collided with another, parachuted to safety.

(Toliver Collection)

SIX RISING SUNS

Captain A. Roger Conant of the Marines looks pensive prior to takeoff with VMF-215. He had six victories credited at the time of the photograph, and did not add to that score before the fight was stopped.

(USMC)

Lt. Colonel Hugh M. Elwood, USMC (5.17): Falls Church, Virginia. C.O. of VMF-212, 1 January 1944—23 April 1944.

(USMC)

Major Jefferson D. Dorroh, USMC (6.00)
Ontario, Oregon. VMF-323. April 22,
1945, shot down six Japanese planes
in a twenty minute battle. Ace in a day!

(USMC)

Captain Jefferson Joseph DeBlanc, USMC CMH (9.00)
DeBlanc, from Saint Martinville, Louisiana, fought with
VMF-112 in the PTO. 12 December 1942 over Guadal-
canal his division tangled with twenty-five Japanese
Betty bombers. "I was fortunate, through God,
not to get any arrows, in my F4F-3." He won the
CMH for action over Kolobangara on 31 January 1943.

(USMC)

Lt. Eugene Dillow, USMC (6.0): Dillow,
from Cobden, Illinois, lost his life in aerial
combat. This photo taken at the Russell Islands
4 July 1943.

Major Loran D. Everton, USMC (12.0): This photo
taken 29 April 1943 at El Toro Marine Corps Air
Station, California.   (USMC)

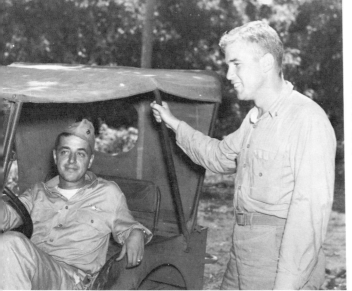

(USMC)

Major Leonard K. Davis and Lt. Thomas H. Mann, Jr., USMC (5.0 and 10.0): These two VMF-121 pilots accounted for fifteen Japanese planes between them. Photo by J. F. Murphy at Upolu.

(USMC)

Brigadier General John F. Dobbin, USMC (8.00) Brighton, Massachusetts. As a lieutenant colonel Dobbin fought with VMF-224 over Guadalcanal, qualifying as "ace" in October 1942. Later in the war he commanded Marine Carrier Group 1 flying off USS BLOCK ISLAND with VMF-511.

(USMC)

Major Archie G. Donahue, USMC (14.00) Major Donahue, from Casper, Wyoming and Texas City, Texas, served through the Guadalcanal campaign with VMF-112, scoring nine of his kills. Late in the war he fought the Iwo Jima, Okinawa battles with VMF-451 scoring five more victories. He wears the Navy Cross.

Major Dewey Foster Durnford, USMC (6.83): Durnford scored 6.33 victories in WWII flying with VMF-323 in the PTO. During the Korean War, he flew with the USAF 335th Squadron of the 4th Fighter Wing as an exchange pilot and was credited with a shared kill, half victory, over a MiG 15, bringing his total to 6.83. He is from Columbus, Ohio, but now lives aboard a yacht with Melbourne, Florida as his home port.

(USMC)

(USMC)

Captain Howard J. Finn, USMC (6.0)
Finn scored five victories in the Solomons in 1943 and claimed his sixth during a follow-on combat tour over Tokyo.

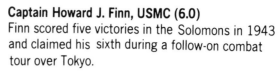

(USMC)

Captain Kenneth Murray Ford, USMC (5.0): Born in Smyrna, Turkey, Ford flew with VMF-121 in WWII. In the Korean fracas, Ford flew 35 missions as a helicopter pilot.

(USMC)

Captain Joseph J. Foss, USMC CMH (26.00)
Rightfully, Foss should be titled as the top ace of the USMC, since he scored all 26 kills with them. (Boyington with 28 had scored six with the AVGs and only 22 with the USMC). Foss was born in Sioux Falls, South Dakota, but called Pierre, South Dakota his hometown. He now lives in Scottsdale, Arizona as a retired brigadier general.

(USMC)

Lt. Kenneth DeForrest Frazier, USMC (12.5): From Burlington, New Jersey, Frazier flew in the PTO with VMF-223.

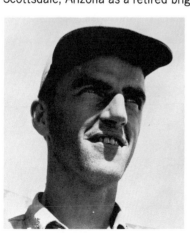

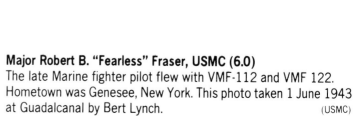

Major Robert B. "Fearless" Fraser, USMC (6.0)
The late Marine fighter pilot flew with VMF-112 and VMF 122. Hometown was Genesee, New York. This photo taken 1 June 1943 at Guadalcanal by Bert Lynch.

(USMC)

(USMC)

Brigadier General Paul John Fontana, USMC (5.00)
New Bern, North Carolina. Five Japanese planes shot down in four days over Guadalcanal brought Fontana his acedom. He was then commander of VMF-112. Fontana has now retired with the rank of major general.

(USMC-Mankan)

Lt. William B. Freeman, USMC (6.0): Freeman survived being shot into the sea by the Japanese near Guadalcanal and went on to score six victories himself.

(USMC)

Lt. Don Homs Fisher, USMC (6.0)
Another "Black Sheep" squadron ace, Fisher shot down two Japanese aircraft the first time he contacted an airborne enemy. Sergeant E. M. Hart made this picture on 15 October 1943 in the Russell Islands.

(USMC-MacArdle)

Colonel Robert E. Galer, USMC, CMH (13.00): Colonel Galer, from Dallas, Texas, flew his combat in the PTO with the Marines' VMF-224. He retired as a brigadier general.

(USMC)

Captain Fred E. Gutt, USMC (8.0):
Gutt, shown here as a second lieutenant at Miami, Florida on 28 April 1942, flew with VMF-223.

Captain Albert Edward Hacking, USMC (5.0)
This VMF-221 pilot from Boston and Pawtucket, Rhode Island got his five down in less than two weeks near Bougainville.

(USMC-S/Sgt. E. H. Hart)

(Toliver Collection)

EIGHT DOWN AT THE CANAL
Between August and November 1942, Major George L. Hollowell, USMC, shot down eight Japanese aircraft over Guadalcanal. He flew with VMF-224.

(USMC-Douglas White)

First Lt. Robert Murray Hanson, USMC, CMH (25.00)
Born in India, the son of Methodist missionaries, Lt. Hanson flew combat with VMF-214 and VMF-215. Over Rabaul, Hanson scored twenty kills in seven days! Six days later Hanson met his own fate and was awarded the CMH posthumously. He was from Newtonville, Massachusetts.

Lt. Roger A. Haberman, USMC (7.0)
Photographer Stotz caught Haberman in this pose at San Diego on 19 April 1943.

(USMC)

276

(USMC)

Major Herman "Hap" Hansen, Jr., USMC (5.50)
Santa Barbara, California. In October 1942, flew first close reconnaissance flights over Guadalcanal. Later, C.O. of VMF-112 aboard USS BENNINGTON. Shot down three kamikaze planes, celebrated his 25th birthday and became an ace on 12 April 1945.

(USMC)

Lt. Alvin J. Jensen, USMC (7.0)
Jensen, in this picture by Sergeant D. White made at Vella LaVella 14 November 1943, had just finished his third combat tour.

(USMC)

Lt. Charles David Jones, USMC (6.0): This VMF-222 pilot was awarded the Silver Star for gallantry in combat. Photo at El Toro MCAS in 1945.

(USMC)

Captain Edward James Hernan, USMC (8.0)
Captain Hernan hails from Dallas, Texas. Sergeant D. White took this photo at Vella LaVella 14 November 1943.

277

(USMC)

Lt. Charles Kendrick, USMC (5.0): Photo made 7 May 1942 at Miami, Florida.

(USMC)

Captain Gregory K. Loesch, USMC (8.5): This photo made at Guadalcanal while Loesch was flying with VMF 121. Deceased.

Captain C. H. "Link" Laughlin, USMC/AVG (5.20)
Coral Gables, Florida. Link scored all his victories in the CBI with Chennault's original Flying Tigers. "I credit survival in my first encounter to a series of short circuits in the cerebral apparatus. One set of neurons said 'Go right!' and another set yelled 'LEFT!' so I breezed through the swarm of Zeros with crossed controls. Now the Japs had seldom seen a P-40 flying sideways. A helluva hard target to properly lead."

(Toliver Collection)

(USMC)

MARINE ACE
Lt. Colonel Floyd C. Kirkpatrick, USMC, is credited with 5.5 victories in the Pacific over the Japanese. His unit was VMF-441, and his home is in Redding, California.

AT GUADALCANAL, 1943
First Lt. Joseph P. Lynch of the Marines in his fighter on Guadalcanal. He ended the war as Captain Lynch with 5.5 victories gained with VMF-224.

(Toliver Collection)

(USMC)

Major Herbert H. Long, USMC (10.00):
Maitland, Florida. VMF-121 and VMF-122.

(USMC)

Captain John B. Maas, USMC (5.5): Photo taken
at San Diego in 1945.

(USMC

Major Charles Murphy Kunz, USMC (8.0)
Kunz flew with VMF-224 at Guadalcanal, VMF-221
at Midway and commanded VMF-311 at Okinawa.
He is from Springfield, Missouri, but now
lives in Costa Mesa, California.

(USMC)

Captain William M. Lundin, USMC (5.50): El Toro,
California. VMF-121. This photo taken at
Guadalcanal 24 June 1943.

279

(USMC/Sgt. W. G. Wilson)

(USMC)

Captain Paul A. Mullen, USMC (6.5): This photo taken at Guadalcanal 25 June 1943.

Captain Christopher Lyman Magee, USMC (9.0)
Magee scored his victories with VMF-214, but this photo was taken in June 1945 when he was flying F7F aircraft with VMF-911.

(USMC)

Captain John L. Morgan, USMC (8.5)
Morgan scored his first seven kills within the span of three weeks over the Solomon Islands. Photo made 18 July 1943 at Guadalcanal by Sgt. W. Wilson.

(USMC)

Lt. Jeremiah J. O'Keefe, USMC (7.0): O'Keefe, from Ocean Springs and Biloxi, Mississippi, shot down five Kamikaze's on 22 April 1945.

VMF121 FIGHTER PILOTS AT GUADALCANAL:
These pilots helped VMF121 score a total of 110 victories in just two months over Guadalcanal. Left to right: Lt. Roger A. Haberman (7.0), Lt. Cecil J. Doyle (5.0), Capt. Joseph J. Foss (26.0), Lt. William P. Marontate (13.0), and Lt. Roy M. Ruddell (4.0).

(USMC)

(USMC)

Lt. John McManus, USMC (6.0): With VMF-213 during the Iwo Jima operation and with VMF-221 (BUNKER HILL) at Okinawa and Japan. McManus was a member of the USMC Phantom stunt team in 1949.

Lt. Selva E. McGinty, USMC (5.0)
(USMC)

(USMC)
Captain Robert Wesley McClurg, USMC (7.00)
McClurg, from New Castle, Pennsylvania and Syracuse, New York, flew with VMF-214.
"The fact that I was the wingman of Pappy Boyington means more to me than medals . . . by far!"

(AVG)

Major Edmund F. Overend, USMC (9.00): Coronado, California. An AVG ace with six victories, Overend returned to the USMC and commanded VMF-321 from 1 October '43 until 28 October 1944. He scored 3 more, bringing his total to 9.00.

281

(USMC)

Lt. Zenneth A. Pond, USMC (6.0):
"Z for Zenneth" Pond flew with VMF-223. This photo taken at San Diego on 29 April 1942.

(Toliver Collection)

NIGHT FIGHTER ACE
Colonel R. Bruce Porter of the Marine Corps smiles as he returns from a mission in the Far East with VMF(N)-542. Night fighter aces are the rare birds among America's aerial elite. Porter downed five Japanese aircraft through his aptitude for night action.

Lt. Colonel Gilbert Percy, USMC (6.0)
Percy scored his victories while a lieutenant and captain with VMF-112. This photo made 28 August 1956.   (USMC Cpl. Joyal)

(USMC)

(USMC)

Major Robert G. Owens, Jr., USMC (7.0):
This photo taken at Vella LaVella on 14 November 1943 by Sgt. D. Q. White.

Lt. Colonel Nathan T. Post, USMC (8.0):
USNA graduate Post flew with VMF-122 and 221. Born in Kansas City, Missouri, he calls San Francisco his hometown. Photo made 28 April 1943 by Sgt. Edwin Hart.

(USMC)

(USMC)

(USMC)

Major Hyde Phillips, USMC (5.0)
Fought at Midway and Guadalcanal. Hails from Shelbyville,
Illinois, New York City and New Rochelle, New York.

Lt. Jack Pittman, USMC (7.0)
Pittman scored his first victories as a T/Sgt. This photo
taken 4 July 1943 in the Russell Islands by Sgt. Edwin Hart.

Lt. Colonel Frederick R. Payne, USMC (7.5)
Payne flew with VMF-212.

Major Francis E. Pierce, USMC (6.0)
(USMC Sgt. Edwin Hart)

283

(USMC)

Major Donald H. Sapp, USMC (11.0)
Sgt. Edwin Hart took this photo in the
Russell Islands on 15 September 1943.

(USMC/Sgt. W. G. Wilson)

Captain Hartwell V. Scarborough, USMC (5.0)
15 August 1943 in the Russell Islands.

(USMC)

**Captain Robert Bryon See, USMC
(5.00):** San Francisco, California.
VMF-321.

(USMC)

**Captain Edward O. Shaw, USMC
(13.00):** Spokane, Washington.
VMF-213. KIA 1944.

(USMC)

Captain Orvin H. Ramlo, USMC (5.0)
Photo taken 24 April 1942 at San Diego, California.

(USMC)

Major Joseph Hunter Reinburg, USMC 7.0
Photographer Bert Lynch shot this picture of Reinburg at Guadalcanal on 4 July 1943 shortly after the pilot made ace by shooting down two enemy planes bringing his total to five at the time. Reinburg now lives at Wabasso, Florida.

(USMC)

Major Harold Edward Segal, USMC (12.00): Alhambra, California. VMF-221.

(USMC)

Captain Frank H. Presley, USMC (6.0)
Presley, from Norfolk, Virginia and Encinitas, California, flew with VMF-121. This photo taken by a Major Onenken at Guadalcanal.

Major Perry L. Shuman, USMC (6.0)
Shuman hails from Lakeland, Florida and Falls Church, Virginia. Photo 9 May 1943 by Sgt. Edwin Hart at Guadalcanal.

(USMC)

(USMC)

Major James E. Swett, USMC (15.50) CMH
Belmont, California. Swett flew with VMF-221 and on 7 April 1943 shot down seven Japanese dive bombers plus a probable to win the CMH.

(USMC/Sgt. E. M. Hart)
Lt. Stanley T. Synar, USMC (5.0)
Wellston, Warner and Muskogee, Oklahoma. Photo taken 19 July 1943 in the Russell Islands.

(Toliver Collection)
SIGHT OF HOME
Dawning grin on the face of Captain William N. Snider, USMCR, is due to his seeing behind the photographer the American coastline near Bremerton, Washington. Snider was arriving home from Pacific service in June 1945, with 11.5 aerial victories to his credit scored with VMF-221.

Major Franklin C. Thomas, Jr., USMC (9.0)
"All my combats were exciting! I was scared to death the whole time!" This fighter pilot from Martinsburg, West Virginia is an Amherst graduate. He scored all nine victories during January 1944, all of them over Rabaul. Photo taken 10 January 1944 most at Bougainville by Sgt. Wm. Wilson.

(USMC)

(USMC)

Lt. Francis A. Terrill, USMC (6.08): Terrill scored his victories over Okinawa.

(USMC)

Captain Harold L. Spears, USMC (15.00)
Ironton and Newark, Ohio. VMF-215.
Ranked No. 10 among the USMC aces.

(USMC)

Lt. Robert F. Stout, USMC (6.0): 24 October 1941 at San Diego, California.

(USMC)

HERO OF THE DARK DAYS

Lt. Colonel John L. Smith, USMC, ran up an impressive string of victories over Japanese fighters while with VMF-223 in the struggle for Guadalcanal. A professional Marine fighter pilot and older than the men he led, Smith's repeated triumphs were an inspiration during the lowest ebb of American fortunes. He won the Congressional Medal of Honor and is credited with 19 aerial victories.

(USMC)

Captain Wallace E. Sigler, USMC (5.33): Orange, Connecticut. VMF-112.

287

(USMC/Bert Lynch)

Captain Wilbur J. Thomas, CMH, USMC (18.5)
Thomas, from El Dorado, Kansas and Los Angeles, California, is tied with Marine Marion E. Carl for honors as the seventh ranking Marine ace. This photo made 18 July 1943 at Guadalcanal when Thomas had seven kills to his credit.

(USMC/G. Lynch)

Lt. Milton N. Vedder, USMC (6.0): At Guadalcanal 15 July 1943.

(USMC)

MEDAL OF HONOR MARINE ACE
Lt. Colonel Kenneth A. Walsh, USMC — seen here in a wartime portrait as a captain — was recognized by fellow pilots as one of the most aggressive and indomitable aces produced by the Marines. With 21 aerial victories, he is one of the few American pilots to exceed 20 victories, and he won the Medal of Honor. Walsh survived WWII and retired as a lieutenant colonel.

(USMC)

Major Eugene A. Trowbridge, USMC (12.0): Photo made at San Diego 30 April 1942.

Major Robert Wade, USMC (8.0)
Wade, from Philadelphia and now living in Santa Ana, California, scored seven kills in WWII and shot down a MiG-15 in the Korean War while flying as an exchange pilot with the USAF 51st Fighter Group. Photo taken in Korea 24 July 1952.

(USMC/SSgt. L. G. Oliver)

(USMC)

Lt. Colonel Donald K. Yost, USMC (8.00)
C.O. of VMF-121 from 1 January to 12 March 1943.
24 December 1942 shot down 4 Zeros in a
scrap at Munda.

(USMC/San Diego 1945)
Lt. Gerard M. H. Williams, USMC (7.0)

Captain Herbert J. Valentine, USMC (6.00)
Seattle, Washington. VMF-312. Scored 5½ kills
on 25 May 1945 off Okinawa.

(USMC)

(USMC)

**Major Michael R. Yunck,
USMC (5.00):** Washington,
D.C. Last wartime C.O. of
VMF-311.

Lt. Colonel Gregory J. Weissenberger, USMC (5.0)
From La Crosse, Wisconsin and Galveston, Texas. This photo
was made by Sgt. C. L. Smith at Guadalcanal on 15 June 1943.

THE NEW EPOCH AND THE OLD — KOREA

A Sabrejet fighter of the USAF returns to base in Korea after a mission to the north, but the Korean woman field worker with her basket seems unperturbed. The jets will one day disappear, but the fields will always be there to till, regardless of who dies in the skies above.

(Toliver Collection)

9

ACES OF
THE KOREAN WAR

When North Korea planned and launched its invasion of South Korea, Uncle Sam was taken by surprise. A remote and impoverished Oriental country about the size of the State of Florida, was ready and willing to risk war with the U.S.A. in its determination to communize South Korea. Events moved rapidly as America reacted. Behind the euphemism of a United Nations "police action," war between America and North Korea was soon a bloody reality. When the fighting began, America's air strength was barely equal to the sudden challenge.

The deplorable unpreparedness of the United States for both great world wars was reproduced in 1950. All the deadly procrastinations and omissions of the nineteen-twenties and thirties were repeated in compressed fashion between 1945 and 1950. The fresh memory of America's awesome World War II strength became a substitute for power in being. Politicians responsible for appropriations were deluded into thinking that modern weapons could be conjured into being at the drop of a vote. When the invasion of South Korea struck, the impact was like Pearl Harbor all over again, and American air power was a shadow of its former self.

The Air Force that had grown by 1945 to an invincible two hundred combat wings was reduced by drastic disarmament to forth-three wings. The formations and aces who had made America supreme in the skies had gone back to selling insurance and teaching school. The battle-tested fighter squadrons were disbanded. Their aircraft were either scrapped or parked to await slow decay in America's southwestern desert—the sun bleaching out the rows of meatballs and swastikas on their fuselages that told of victory in the air.

Americans had gone abroad to fight World War II so that they could go back to peaceful life at home. American disarmament made this clear. These peaceful actions and intentions were misconstrued, and then exploited by Red planners. The U.S.A. was resolute for peace. Low defense budgets underlined the peaceful intentions of the American nation, even as these same budgets undermined the rapid introduction of the jet age.

The American approach to the jet epoch became as slow and awkward as the original approach to the air age prior to World War I. The Germans had been the first to make jet fighters operational in World War II, and had even used rocket-powered fighters. America reacted to this threat by launching a jet program of its own. When the Axis collapsed in 1945, removing the actual challenge and stimulus of war, jet fighter development began to dwindle.

By 1946, the Lockheed F-80 jet was being produced only slowly. The first tactical unit to receive this machine was the 412th Fighter Group at March Field, California. The complete conversion of this unit to jets was not accomplished until late in 1946. This tardiness was but one symptom of a larger defense pattern that featured massive reductions in strength.

The Air Force began to undergo a complete transformation in equipment, personnel and command. Reserves were released from active duty, and the USAF was reduced almost to skeleton status. The continual reduction of American air strength led the Department of Defense to lodge some of the strongest protests ever presented to the Congress and the President. Despite the clear lessons of the past, the American body politic proved almost impervious to warnings that dwindling American air power was an invitation to aggressors. The Korean War finally got the message across, but at a high price in blood and treasure.

Asia had always been the poor relation of Europe in American military and political thought. The "Germany first" policy of World War II reinforced this concept. Following that struggle, military planners continued to concentrate mainly on the possibility of a European war with the Soviet Union. This was considered to be the most likely and probable area of conflict.

Russia was nevertheless an Asiatic power as well, and universally recognized as such. Emphasis and attention were focused mainly on Russia's activities in Europe, because the main thrust of Soviet policy was toward communizing Eastern Europe and subverting governments in Western Europe where power could not be seized. The armed irruption of North Korea into South Korea forced a complete overhaul of American thinking and dispositions.

At the time of the invasion of South Korea in June 1950, Air Force units in the Far East were being converted slowly to jet aircraft. Tachikawa AFB and the battle-scarred Clark AFB in the Philippines became the junkyards for the once superb P-51 Mustang. As the jets flowed out slowly to the squadrons, the Mustangs came back to be scrapped.

Forsaken, neglected and growing in numbers in these junkyards, the Mustangs suddenly became worth their weight in gold for Korean employment. The P-51 had few equals for the important ground-support role. They were rushed back into top condition and were used to punish the thousands of ground targets offered by the North Korean forces.

At the controls of a Mustang, Major Louis B. Sebille became the USAF's forty-third winner of the Congressional Medal of Honor. Leading a squadron of P-51's of the 18th Fighter Bomber Wing, Major Sebille was hit by ground fire directed at his formation by an armored car or tank. Sebille's wingman could see that the major was wounded, as his Mustang was weaving and Sebille could be seen struggling to sit upright. His cockpit canopy was covered in blood.

Sebille knew he was mortally wounded. His voice came crackling over the radio, "I'm going back to get that bastard!" He turned his Mustang around and drove it at full throttle, all guns roaring, into a concentration of Red troops and vehicles. Sebille's last act caused heavy enemy casualties and was as brave a thing as an American pilot has ever done. The Japanese of World War II called this "jibaku,"* but the American way was always for the warrior to preserve his life.

Korea became primarily a theater of air-to-ground combat, the fighter-bomber pilots flying innumerable missions against ground targets. The Reds initially showed little comprehension of the decisive influence of airpower on ground operations such as theirs, and had little tactical airpower of their own. Their supply columns and convoys were frequently hacked to pieces from the air.

Anguished appeals went up from Red ground commanders over this slaughter, and the North Kore 1 high command promptly passed on the pressure. Russian-built jets duly appeared over Korea in response. Dogfights were the order of the day once more, this time at near sonic speeds. Aerial combat and its heroes were soon again filling the pages of America's newspapers and magazines. The Korean ground war, like World War I in whose crucible the fighter ace had been born, was dirty and cruel.

The straightforward glory-type stories of aerial combat between the Soviet-built MiG-15 and the American Sabrejet, concealed the wider importance and true purpose of these battles. Without the American jets to protect them, the slower, older Mustangs and other ground-support aircraft would have been at the mercy of the Communist jets. For the infantryman facing swarming hordes of North Korean and then Chinese soldiers, the "police action" would have assumed a different character in the absence of close air support. The ground war would have become impossibly costly for the U.S.

First Lieutenant William G. Hudson shot down the first Communist aircraft in aerial combat. Flying a P-82, Hudson* overtook a propeller-driven YAK-11—another product of the Soviet aircraft industry—and downed it on 27 June 1950 with some accurate gunnery. The ubiquitous Mustang could be considered present on this historic occasion, since the P-82, later to be designated F-82, consisted of two Mustangs joined together by a stubby ten-foot midwing.

The first Communist jet fighter was shot down by Lieutenant Russell J. Brown, on 8 November 1950. Brown was mounted on an F-80, and his victory over the Russian-built MiG-15 is believed to be the first confirmed

*Jibaku, translated literally, means "self-blast." It is not to be confused with seppuku or hara-kiri, which means suicide by self disembowelment, generally used to save face or avoid disgrace. Jibaku was a highly honorable death in the Japanese viewpoint.

*Flying in the other cockpit of the North American P-82 on this mission was Captain Carl S. Fraser.

victory in an all-jet aerial dogfight.

America's first jet fighter ace was Major James Jabara, of Wichita, Kansas. Jabara scored his first MiG-15 kill on 3 April 1951, following it up with two more kills on 10 and 12 April 1951. Ten days later the fourth MiG went down under Jabara's guns. Two more kills on 20 May 1951 made him an historic ace—America's first in the jet age.

Returned to the United States for special duty and many accolades, Jabara was anxious to return to combat. At his own request he was back in Korea in January 1953, and ran up another nine kills against the MiG-15's. A short, dark, nuggety and vigorous man, Jabara ended the Korean conflict as the second-ranking jet ace of the United States. His all-time total is 16.5 enemy aircraft destroyed in aerial combat.

Jabara was a triple ace in Korea, and like many Korean War pilots he had flown fighters in the ETO in World War II. He was credited with 1.5 victories in Europe. Two other German aircraft were not confirmed. This experience of combat undoubtedly contributed to his outstanding abilities as a Sabre pilot. Honored and esteemed in the American fighter pilot fraternity, the modest Jabara met an untimely end in 1967. The ace who had survived all the hazards of combat flying died in the crash of a Volkswagen.

The politically-established "sanctuary" for the enemy beyond the Yalu River, the often incomprehensible political factors swirling around the Korean conflict, and the remoteness of the country from the U.S. created special problems for American fighter pilots that their forebears of the two world wars had never had to face. Their new tools of trade— the jets—sent aerial warfare into yet another phase, as different from World War II as that conflict had been from World War I.

These differences are well described by a participant, Colonel Robert P. Baldwin of Los Angeles, California, in a contemporary letter written to Colonel Toliver, co-author of this book. Colonel Baldwin was C.O. of the 51st Fighter Interceptor Group in Korea in 1953. He summed up the new mode of aerial combat in these terms:

"Air-to-air combat at 45,000 feet is something entirely new to WWII vets. The old razzle-dazzle, ham-fisted fighter pilot is out. Now it's accurate, precision, feather-touch flying. If you get clumsy it costs you valuable speed, altitude, position—maybe your fanny! The MiGs have a tremendous weight advantage, being at least 3,000 pounds lighter than our F-86's. The only way we can overcome that advantage is to fly at speeds where the drag ratio is the deciding factor.

"The F-86 matches the MiG-15 on the power-drag scale anywhere above the .8 mach reading. So the unwritten law is 'If you don't have .8 or better, don't look for a fight.' That, plus taking advantage of the very few bad characteristics of the MiG, accounts for most of our success.

"The MiG is prone to snap in a right-hand turn, and it loses considerable maneuverability around .95 mach. Flying our F-86 is no snap either, and staying in formation is rough.

THE LOCKHEED P-80 JET!

Too late to get into WWII, this little gem of a plane would have given the ME-262, which the Luftwaffe had in combat for a year before the end of the war, a better-than-even tussle. In 1946, however, the USAF was cutting back radically because another war would not come along for a score of years ... hopefully. A few of the P-80's, later called F-80's, went into fighter units but most of them were flown directly from the Lockheed/Van Nuys facility to San Bernardino Air Depot in California and put into storage! In 1950, when Kisarazu Airbase in Japan deteriorated, USAF decided not to equip Far East Air Force units with jets, but a last minute change of plans allowed the jets to be assembled in the Philippines. Co-author Toliver is the pilot of this F-80 over Luzon, early 1951.

(Toliver Collection)

You maintain position by playing turns and altitude and you never reduce power."

From Colonel Baldwin's description, it is clear that in Korea as in the other great conflicts, the skill and ingenuity of a fighter pilot in exploiting enemy weaknesses bulked large in the achievement of acedom. Colonel Baldwin became an ace in Korea and is credited with five aerial victories. He now lives in Yuma, Arizona.

When the opposition became too rough for the Communist pilots, there was always the haven beyond the Yalu River, to which the Red airmen bolted with the Americans in hot pursuit. There were some spectacular races, because the idea was to knock the fleeing Red pilot down before he reached the river and thereby gained "sanctuary." In the history of aerial warfare there had never been anything like these weird, politically-imposed rules that protected enemy men and material from destruction at the hands of pilots specially trained by the U.S. to destroy its enemies.

The story of such a chase to the Yalu is told by Major Frederick C. Blesse of Richmond, Virginia, who destroyed ten aircraft in combat over Korea:

"Leading a flight of two F-86's, I spotted several MiG-15's. They split up when we pressed our attack, and we finally singled out one and got him. We made a wide circle and started home, but another single MiG bounced us. The next four or five minutes we looped, rolled and finally got a snap at him from about thirty-five degrees angle off at 1,500 feet distance.

"He began to smoke, and pulled up vertically, ruddering into a spin. He spun, with my wingman and me following around the outside, from 15,000 feet down to 4,000 feet, where he began firing his cannon to reduce his nose weight. I was ready for him, when at 1,800 feet he neatly recovered in a direct heading for the Yalu River.

"I moved in, taking the regular high side approach shot. Pieces of his fuselage and tail flew off, followed by his canopy. Fire began to trail the MiG, but he still wouldn't bail and kept driving for the Yalu. I dropped back to the six o'clock position and gave him another burst. Out of cockpit he came, so close I had to turn hard left to avoid him.

"I didn't realize that my two kills this day made me the leading ace with six MiG victories and an LA-9 kill. I then ran the string to

ten kills, which held the lead until February 1953, when Colonel Royal Baker got his eleventh kill."

Major Blesse flew the F-86 in scoring all his victories, although he flew 67 missions in Mustangs between November 1950 and February 1951. This action was with the 18th Fighter Bomber Group. Blesse thus had his share of the low-level strafing work, and he also flew 35 missions in the F-80 jet as well as his 121 missions in the Sabrejet. As Major General Blesse he retired from the USAF in 1975.

The Colonel Royal Baker mentioned by Blesse was Brigadier General Royal N. Baker, USAF, a distinguished Texan who flew fighters in both World War II and Korea. Baker's career included 160 combat missions in British Spitfires during World War II with the 31st Fighter Group. He is credited with 3.5 victories in that conflict, and as with many other aces of the Korean War, put this earlier experience to good use after transitioning to jets.

Brigadier General Baker shot down his fifth enemy aircraft in Korea in November of 1952, thereby becoming the USAF's twenty-first jet ace. Another eight enemy aircraft fell to his guns in Korea, including one LA-9. His lifetime score was 16.5 victories for both the wars in which he flew. The decorations of this distinguished ace, who died in 1973, included the Silver Star, Legion of Merit, *forty* Air Medals and the French Croix de Guerre. Only one other pilot has been awarded more than the forty Air Medals won by Baker. He is Lieutenant Colonel Clyde B. East of Chatham, Virginia, a twelve victory World War II ace, who garnered forty-two Air Medals. Bracketing Baker on the low side is four-star General James E. Hill,* with thirty-nine Air Medals, and five victories won with the Ninth Air Force in the ETO.

The same shooting skill that made outstanding aces in both the world wars was also required in Korea. For all their speed, the jets did not alter this fundamental of aerial warfare, and heat-seeking missiles had yet to come. Most pilots of the Korean War speak in awe and admiration of the marksmanship of one particular pilot—Captain Manuel Fernandez of Key West, Florida.

---

*Currently commander of North American Air Defense Command (NORAD) at Colorado Springs, Colorado.

As the third-ranking jet ace with 14.5 victories over MiG's to his credit, Fernandez ran up this score between September 1952, and May 1953, in 125 missions. Significant indeed is Fernandez's prior appointment as gunnery instructor at Nellis AFB in Nevada, his last duty prior to going to Korea. There is an old saying that the best way to learn a subject thoroughly is to teach that subject. Fernandez's long study and practice of the mechanics and art of gunnery paid off handsomely in combat. Now America's top living jet ace, Fernandez well remembers this combat incident:

"I was approaching the Yalu River with a flight of four when the radar people warned us of bandits in the area. My squadron commander was leading the second element and was forced by aircraft malfunction to return to home base. I was also unable to jettison my left tank. I was trying to shake it off when I found my element was underneath forty-odd MiGs.

"Two enemy aircraft were approaching from my left, and I turned in behind them. They started a high-speed turning dive, pulling away, so I tried a burst on the leader—and saw strikes on his fuselage. He began smoking and slowing down. His wingman turned up and into the sun and disappeared. I gave the wounded MiG two more short bursts and saw good strikes.

"Then the enemy wingman came slicing down out of the sun and joined formation on his smoking leader. I banked slightly and fired a short burst at the wingman. The bullets hit his nose section and exploded his ammunition.

"The wingman broke sharply to the right, and then reversed. His canopy came off and the pilot bailed out. I was still close to the original MiG and I closed in to 200 feet and fired a long burst. This caught the MiG in the bottom of the fuselage. Flame came whipping back from him, and I was forced to break to the right. The pilot was slumped over the controls, and I broke off the attack to return home."

Captain Harold E. Fischer of Lone Rock, Iowa, flew 105 missions with the 8th Fighter Bomber Wing between March of 1951 and December 1951. After a short rest in Japan, he returned to Korea for 70 missions in Sabres. With ten victories he became a double MiG ace, but his second tour of duty was destined

(USAF via June Cooper)

FIRST CASUALTY IN KOREA

The top fighter ace of the USAAF 20th Fighter Group in WWII with 9.0 aerial victories, Ernest C. "Red" Fiebelkorn, shown here as a captain in WWII, was the first American pilot to lose his life in combat over North Korea.

to last until 31 May 1955. Shot down during a rhubarb with the MiG's, Fischer was captured by enemy ground troops and hustled north of the Yalu to captivity.

Fischer was held as a POW long after the majority of captured Americans were released. He finally regained his freedom two years after the end of the Korean "police action." Fischer's most vivid combat memory is of his fifth aerial victory, the one that made him an ace:

"Radar vectored my flight into four MiGs. The number two man of the MiG flight panicked when we bounced them, and his three fellow pilots zoomed for altitude. I went after the number two MiG, who nearly stalled and then began a long dive.

"I latched on at great distance. Intermittent bursts from my guns started finally to hit him, stopping his engine and setting him on fire. Gradually I closed at low altitude, and pulled alongside to see why he did not bail out. The pilot was struggling with his canopy, which was jammed, and he could not eject. Finally, he tried to ram me, and then crashed with his aircraft. This victory made me an ace."

The hitting power of the Sabrejet's armament was often the cause of much criticism. Many World War II fighters had a heavier punch than the Sabrejet, one of them being the first operational jet fighter, the German Me-262. Some variants of the Me-262 carried four 30mm cannons, accurate fire from which simply tore enemy aircraft to pieces. While much of the criticism of the Sabre's armament seems justified, Captain Cecil G. Foster of San Antonio, Texas, tells a story of the Sabre's guns in his most memorable combat experience. Foster was flying as element leader on 26 September 1952, in a flight of four Sabrejets when the incident occurred:

"My flight leader initiated a bounce on two MiG-15's, and I turned to protect him. I was bounced by six MiG's. We entered a scissors maneuver, and everyone was firing at everyone else at ninety-degree angles. With my first burst I scored lucky hits on both the MiG leader and his wingman. The leader exploded instantly. This was a real surprise, as we were at 40,000 feet and MiG's seldom burned or blew up at this extreme altitude.

"The wingman was also hit and smoking, and fire began to show. The pilot ejected as I was positioning for my next pass. To my knowledge, this is the only time that two MiG ve been shot down with a single burst from a _ bre—a burst of only one second's duration."

Captain Foster's experience is reminiscent of Colonel "Hub" Zemke's immortal recollection of his aerial battles—*"They were all easy—once I hit them."* Cecil Foster is the twenty-third American jet ace, with nine victories to his credit.

To be nicknamed "Hoot" is the inevitable fate of most fighter pilots named Gibson, a throwback to the old hell-for-leather cowboy of early Western movies. Captain Ralph Duane Gibson of Mt. Carmel, Illinois, is no exception. Five aerial victories over MiG fighters put this "Hoot" Gibson into the fraternity of aces. His account of combat action with the 4th Fighter Group tells of fleeting opportunity seized in lightning fashion:

"On 18 June 1951, a bright summer day, I was flying my thirty-fifth Sabre mission to the Yalu. The mission was routine, flying cover for F-80's and F-84's on a fighter bomber sweep. I was leading an element on my squadron commander's right.

"We were forty miles out of the Yalu when contrails were sighted ahead, moving toward us. We counted at least thirty-six MiG's. We were eight in number. Dropping tanks, we

made a 270-degree turn to the left. During the turn, I flew high cover for the flight, where I met a flight of the MiG's—one of them passing within ten feet of my aircraft. At 600 mph ten feet is a paper-thin margin!

"As we completed the turn, my CO was on a MiG's tail, and the MiG's wingman was maneuvering to get behind the CO. I called and said that my wingman and I would get the second MiG. We turned in to the attack.

"Leading the turn, my wingman fired two long bursts into the MiG. The enemy jet burst into flames before I could fire on him, and spun off burning to crash a few seconds later. When my wingman and I rolled out on a southerly heading, I saw a MiG drop into position behind my friend. I shouted to him to 'break left!' as I came in on the MiG's tail, firing bursts as I came.

"On the first burst, the enemy reversed his turn, but I easily out-turned him, closed to about five hundred feet and opened up on him again. He made evasive turns, and I fired again, getting numerous hits around the wing root and cockpit. Flames streamed from his speed brakes and he crashed to the ground.

"Rolling out of this fight, my wingman and I ran into yet another MiG. He was higher and in front of us, coming in from our ten o'clock position. We made a hard turn into his attack and closed to five hundred feet. I fired one burst into his right wing root, and the whole right wing flew off his aircraft. He went in immediately.

"Hoot" Gibson stayed with the USAF through to his retirement as a colonel. For a considerable time he was leader of the Thunderbirds, the USAF aerobatic team flying out of Nellis AFB, Nevada. He makes his home as this is written in Tucson, Arizona.

One of the best-liked members of the fraternity of American aces is Colonel James K. Johnson, of Phoenix, Arizona. Johnson typifies the compact, quick, super-alert stamp of individual that makes up a large proportion of the ace fraternity. Greying now, but still dark and dapper, Johnson is a remarkably handsome man with an impish sense of humor. "James K." as he is often called, is as brilliant socially as he has been in aerial combat.

Johnson shot down the only German aircraft he tangled with in World War II, and became a double ace against the MiGs with ten aerial victories in Korea. The citation to his Distinguished Service Cross is a fitting testimony to his qualities and skill:

"Colonel James K. Johnson distinguished himself by extraordinary heroism in connection with military operations against an armed enemy of the United Nations as pilot of an F-86 type aircraft, 4th Fighter-Interceptor Wing, 5th Air Force, on 30 June 1953. On that date, Colonel Johnson was leading a flight of four F-86 aircraft deep within enemy territory when a flight of twelve enemy MiG aircraft were sighted at 35,000 feet.

"Colonel Johnson immediately initiated a forceful attack, and concentrated on destroying one of the enemy aircraft. Closing on the single MiG, Colonel Johnson held his fire until he was within 1,200 feet, at which time he scored numerous hits on the wing and fuselage of the enemy aircraft. To assure that he did not lose his tactical advantage, and with full knowledge of the potential danger from other MiG's in the enemy flight, Colonel Johnson continued the attack.

"With unswerving singleness of purpose,

Colonel Johnson began firing from a range of 600 feet, continuing his devastating barrage until he was only about fifty feet from the enemy aircraft, at which time it began to burn and disintegrate. Only then did Colonel Johnson turn to face the fire of the other MiGs. While expertly maneuvering to escape the attacking enemy aircraft, Colonel Johnson experienced a loss of engine power, which later proved to be the result of damage caused by debris from the destroyed enemy aircraft. In spite of this handicap, Colonel Johnson valiantly turned to attack the enemy MiGs, and by superb airmanship and aggressiveness, outmaneuvered them until they withdrew from the area. Colonel Johnson then brought his disabled aircraft back to base.

"Through his intrepidity in the face of the enemy, and by his high personal courage, outstanding professional skill and devotion to duty, Colonel Johnson reflected great credit upon himself, the Far East Air Forces and the USAF."

There have been some notable examples of

F-80 STRAFING ATTACK — KOREA
A 5th Air Force F-80 fighter made things hot for a small village housing North Korean vehicles and troops. A tank and a smoking jeep can be seen on the road. Photograph was made by a USAF RF-80 photo reconnaissance plane accompanying strafing strike in North Korea.

(USAF Photo)

deflection shooting mentioned in this book. Generally forbidden to fighter pilots are successful snap shots at a hundred degrees deflection. The spirit of the fighter pilot is nevertheless by nature that of a gambler. Academicians in recent years have concluded that all the great aces were limit-testers and rulebenders. Sometimes when presented with such temptations as the ninety-degree deflection shot, the pilot is unable to resist. Off goes a ninety-degree deflection shot, sent on its way with a heavy charge of wishful thinking. If Lady Luck lends her caress to the affair, spectacular results may ensue.

A classic instance forms the outstanding combat memory of Major Clifford D. Jolley of Cleveland, Ohio. He flew with the 4th Group in Korea, and writes of his rolling the dice aloft in these terms:

"On 8 August 1952, while flying top cover for two groups of F-80s in the area of Anju, my wingman and I were bounced by two MiGs from six o'clock. I called for my wingman to break hard left so I could clear his tail. The MiGs pulled up hard. I called a fast reverse and fired broadside at one as he flashed past me—and my shots set him afire! The pilot bailed out. This gave me my fifth victory and made me the USAF's eighteenth jet ace."

Team work was indispensable to survival over Korea. The advent of the jet, the high-altitude combat, flashing speeds and radar assistance from the ground eliminated the lone wolf fighter pilot. The lone wolf was no more than a historical curiosity, while the commander of jet formations had to be more than ever a thoughtful and alert aerial general. Science and technology demanded high intelligence in the air.

Throwing firsthand light on these matters is Colonel George L. Jones of Vero Beach, Florida, commanding officer of the 334th Squadron of the 4th Fighter Group from July to October 1951, and of the 51st Fighter Group from November 1951 to March 1952.

Colonel Jones is credited with 6.5 aerial victories in Korea, and his story vividly illustrates the planning required for a successful jet fighter mission:

"During one phase of the Korean conflict, it was noticed that the Communists were able to identify our Sabrejets approaching the target area early enough to get set for the attack. By the time we arrived in 'MiG Alley,' the enemy pilots usually had a five to ten thousand foot

altitude advantage.

"On 29 March 1953, our group was committed to make a fighter sweep through North Korea to the Yalu River. On this particular day, seeking to surprise the enemy pilots on their initial climb out, I obtained permission from the group commander to take off with a flight of four aircraft ten minutes before the main mission. Strict radio silence was maintained as we taxied out and took off. Shortly after we became airborne, my number four man had to abort the mission. I signaled the number three man to escort him back to base. With my wingman, Major Wendel Brady, I continued on as planned.

"As the lead element of MiGs swept in front of us, I turned in behind them and started my attack. As I began coming up behind the nearest MiG my wingman called out, "There's a MiG above you and to your left who looks as though he's going to attack." I told Brady to keep an eye on this MiG and call out if the MiG got into firing position on me.

"I was now slowly overtaking the MiG I had picked out to attack, and since I was gradually closing on him, I decided to hold my fire until within point-blank range. The MiG wingman now became extremely aggressive, and two or three times started to turn in to make an attack. Each time he would start in, Brady would turn into him in such a way that if the MiG wingman continued his attack, Brady would end up right behind him. The MiG would therefore withdraw from that particular attack. All the while, I continued to close in on the lead MiG.

"When I got 1,400 feet behind the MiG and 500 feet below him, I pulled back on the stick and closed to a position directly behind him at a range of 800 feet. We were now at 42,000 feet. As soon as my sight pipper settled into position, I squeezed the trigger and saw a heavy concentration of hits on the MiG. Debris flew off his aircraft and he decelerated rapidly.

"My aircraft was closing in on the slowing MiG so fast that I was afraid of running into him. As soon as I lifted my finger from the trigger, I discovered a loss of engine power, due to compressor stall. Smoke, oil and hydraulic fluid entering my air intake aggravated this condition. When the compressor stalled, I was in the middle of the smoke left by the blown-up MiG. I couldn't see where I was going and was concerned with running into debris. I threw the stick over to the left

side of the cockpit, retarded the throttle and started a steep dive to break the compressor stall and regain power.

"Usually stalls like this can be broken quickly. But at 25,000 feet my engine had not regained power, and I began debating whether to pull out of the dive and begin gliding to the coast. I decided to take it down to 20,000 feet, and if the engine didn't catch by then, to pull up and join the local gliding club.

"At 20,000 feet the engine regained power. What a reassuring feeling it was. I started to climb back up, but now the engine appeared to be running rough and my airspeed was much less than it should have been. Running a quick check, I found my speed brakes were extended. I had automatically put them out to slow down when collision with the MiG was imminent. I'd put them out with such force that I'd stripped the plastic button from the speed brake control switch. With some difficulty, I could still actuate the control, and immediately the aircraft began to accelerate.

"My canopy was coated with hydraulic fluid and oil from the exploded MiG, but on looking through some clear spots I could see that my wingman had stayed with me all this time. Brady told me that during the entire fight the MiG wingman had made many attempts to turn in on me, but that he had kept him off while I made the kill. When his leader was blown up and I was groping around with my stalled engine, the MiG wingman tried again, but was once more forced to pull up by Brady and was lost from the fight entirely.

"Later, as we headed back for home base, I kept thinking to myself, 'Teamwork is the answer—teamwork and confidence.'"

The intelligent use of radio silence, backed up with this kind of teamwork, put the aerial warfare of Korea in a different category to that engaged in by the pioneers of World War I. Nevertheless, the Germans in particular in that conflict studied meticulously the tactics and habits of their enemies on each section of the front, even studying the backgrounds of the Allied squadron and wing commanders. As with the incident described by Colonel Jones, they shaped their tactics to entrap and disadvantage the incoming Allied aircraft.

A tradition that threaded its way through aerial warfare was the so-called "victory roll." A slow roll or barrel roll performed over the pilot's own airfield at low altitude, it came to signify success in aerial combat. The tradition eventually came to demand one roll for each enemy aircraft downed.

The tradition originated in World War I, but was by no means a universal practice. The more daring and exuberant pilots introduced the victory-roll idea, and occasionally performed it in World War I, usually on special occasions. The majority of World War I pilots took a different view of things. They were so glad to see their home airfields, and get safely down on them, that they had neither the

GOING HUNTING
Sabre-jets of the 51st Fighter Interceptor Wing takeoff for a hunt over Northern Korea. The North American F-86 Sabre, successor of World War II's North American P-51 Mustang, gave the USA a total of 39 Korean War Aces.

(USAF)

energy nor the taste for risky, low-altitude maneuvers. Their flimsy, "ground-hungry" machines no doubt induced a healthy aversion to too much victory rolling.

The maneuver was nevertheless the kind of dramatic highlight in which fiction writers have always reveled. The victory roll became a special favorite of screen writers because of its breathtaking visual appeal, and was featured in numerous flying films in the grand era of such swashbucklers between the world wars. World War II's pilots were thus extensively exposed to the victory roll during their boyhood years through these movies. Many came to regard the victory roll as a hallowed tradition of combat flying.

These pilots naturally carried the tradition of the victory roll to a much more general application in World War II than it had ever enjoyed in World War I. The vastly improved performance and design of World War II fighters also made the maneuver more feasible, assuming that superior aerobatic skill was being employed. Tragedy permeated the tradition at this point.

Many fine combat pilots of World War II were possessed of indifferent aerobatic ability, frequently owing their combat success more to marksmanship than flying skills. The execution of a victory roll, at altitudes from ten to one hundred feet above the runway, called for considerable aerobatic ability—especially when multiple kills demanded multiple rolls. The tragic truth is that many American fighter pilots plunged to their doom attempting victory rolls. Pilot error frequently found a potent partner in unsuspected battle damage in victory-roll crashes.

In Korea, the victory roll appeared less frequently than in World War II. F-86 Sabrejets returning from combat at the Yalu were usually extremely low on fuel on reaching home base, and victorious pilots seldom took the hazardous chance in making the roll. Korean War pilots were also a more seasoned breed, frequently with a World War II career behind them. Getting combat film to the lab took precedence with them over emulating Errol Flynn and Richard Barthelmess, and the memory of World War II victory-roll crashes was also hardly something that would fade.

In the classic pattern of the pursuit pilot is the most memorable combat experience of Captain James H. Kasler of Indianapolis, Indiana. Captain Kasler's fourth and fifth aerial victories came together on 15 May 1952:

"I was leading a two-ship element near the Yalu River when I spotted three MiG's at about 1,000 feet altitude. I split-essed on the lead aircraft and opened fire at 1,200 feet, closing to about 100 feet and pulling up on the MiG's wing. I could see the pilot sitting in a ball of flame. The MiG banked to the right and struck the ground, leaving a wide trail of fire.

"I looked out to the right and saw another MiG firing, with Albert Smiley,* my wingman, as his target. I bent around after the MiG and called Smiley to break. Smiley had been so intent on watching the MiG I'd downed that he had failed to see the MiG getting on his tail. The MiG overshot Smiley and dove for the treetops. The Red flak was terrific at this time, the gunners apparently not giving a hoot whether they hit their own MiG or not.

"I chased the MiG about fifty miles on the deck until we reached the sea. He pulled sharply in an Immelmann, and as he started down again, I scored a burst. By this time, I'd closed in to about five hundred feet, and as we came down out of the loops we were over the mud flats.

"With the haze over the coast, it was impossible to distinguish ground from sky. I didn't realize I was in any danger until the MiG splashed into the mud. We were both doing between 550 and 600 mph, and were still in a sixty degree dive when the MiG hit.

"As the fountain of mud and water shot up where he went in, I dropped my dive brakes, chopped the power and grabbed the stick with both hands. For a few seconds that seemed like years, I thought I was going to join my opponent in the mud. Then I saw the nose come back over the hazy horizon. I don't know how close I came to the mud, but I would estimate at ten feet or less—not much of a safety margin at 600 mph."

Captain Kasler is credited with six aerial victories. He flew with the 4th Fighter Group, the stellar outfit in Korea.

Serving with the 4th at the same time as Kasler was another jet ace, Major Thomas Latshaw of Amarillo, Texas. Latshaw was flying his second-to-last combat mission in Korea when he became the fourteenth jet ace on 4 May 1952. His story reveals how easy it is

*First Lieutenant Albert Smiley was credited with three victories over MiG-15s while flying with the 335th Squadron in Korea.

even for an ace to be downed in aerial combat if his wingman goes astray:

"It was my ninety-ninth mission at a time when only one hundred missions were allotted to an individual. I had four kills at the time, and was determined to make the most of any chance I might get to have a fifth kill.

"We entered the combat area at an altitude that placed us just under the contrail level, about 35,000 feet. Maintaining radio silence and punching off the drop tanks when they were dry, we continued to search for a likely bounce. We spotted a flight of four MiGs at 25,000 feet. To the rear of the flight of MiGs and stacked up approximately 4,000 feet were four more MiGs. More flights of MiGs were stacked up above these, in and above the contrail level.

"My element leader also had four MiGs at this time, and was eager to enter the fray. Diving to the attack on the MiGs in the van of the formation, we dropped dive brakes so as not to overshoot them, and I selected the number two man flying on the left side of the MiG formation.

"I opened fire at approximately 2,500 feet range, and hoped to score an easy and rapid kill before the MiGs behind and above us could dive to the attack. The MiG I was firing on, however, broke down and to the left at the same time that my element leader overshot the MiG he had selected.

"I followed the MiG down, firing and scoring successive strikes until we were approximately 2,000 feet above the ground. He pulled up and I immediately began to lose out. Realizing I had my dive brakes still out, I closed them and began closing in on the MiG. At this time, my wingman disappeared, and I prepared to pour some more fire into the MiG, I spotted tracers arcing across my canopy. I looked up. A MiG and his wingman went flashing over me. They were so close I could still hear their cannons firing.

"Since they'd dived on me from above and had high airspeed, while mine was low, they overshot and slid almost a mile to the outside of my flight path. Taking advantage of their error, I began firing at the MiG once again. Just as my tracers sped towards the MiG, I noticed additional tracers intermingling with mine. I made a rapid check. A MiG was firing at me from seven o'clock.

"Things were getting hot, so I rapidly got back on the gunsight and fired at the MiG in

(USAF)

GUN-CAMERA FILM CONFIRMS KILL
This series of photographs taken from a gun camera mounted in an F-86 Sabre, graphically shows MiG-15 being hit and beginning to flame. Claim for a victory was allowed.

front of me, lighting him up this time. The pilot ejected. In the meantime, the MiG at seven o'clock had found the range and put a cannon shell through my left wing tank. I had to take violent evasive action to get rid of him."

Captain Leonard William Lilley of Washington, D.C., shot down his fifth MiG-15 on 18 November 1952 to become America's twenty-second jet ace. A West Point graduate, Captain Lilley accounted for seven MiG-15's before being returned to the United States in February 1953, for reassignment. He was yet another of the luminaries of the 4th Fighter Group, and his story of jet combat over Korea, to quote him, will "hold up any bar in the Air Force."

"On 4 September 1952 I was flying close support on fighter bombers, who were bombing the main supply route leading south from Sinuiju, North Korea. First Lieutenant Drury Callahan was my wingman. While heading north at 18,000 feet, just under an overcast, we passed eight MiGs in a staggered-V formation, heading south.

"We immediately swung south and fell in trail with this formation. The MiGs started to turn right, and this enabled us to close in to effective firing range. Still unobserved, we closed to within 1,500 feet of the lead MiG. I opened fire, and the MiG burst into flames and started to dive straight ahead. We pursued, firing all the while.

"As we dove, four MiGs chandelled to the left, and three pulled up to the right. In short order, we were nicely boxed in. The four from the left came whipping in just as the flaming MiG pilot ejected. We broke hard into them. This set us up for the three MiGs on the right, who then came in firing.

"We continued our turn to the left, managing to keep this turn tight enough for the MiGs to fire out and never hit us. The original four, however, now repositioned themselves and took up a firing position right where their three pals left off. Our turn carried us right to the deck. By this time, the MiGs were firing at us from head-on ninety degree angle-off, and from our six o'clock position.

"Just as our fuel reached the point of no return, the seven MiGs all broke off and pulled up into the overcast. With a new lease on life, we headed for our home base, 160 miles to the south. Minutes later we arrived, limp and exhausted, but with a story that would hold up any bar in the Air Force."

To illustrate the background of a remarkable fighter ace, whose successful career he predicted, co-author Colonel Raymond F. Toliver takes over in the first person for a few paragraphs.

"At San Bernardino, California, in 1946 and 1947 I had many opportunities to bounce and be bounced in mock aerial combat by a National Guard pilot who really appeared to be a 'hot rock.' This ANG pilot was the best and most aggressive I have ever encountered, and eventually a meeting on the ground was held in order to let me meet this character face-to-face.

"He was Major Robert John Love, Canadian-born and close to my idea of what a fighter pilot should be. He turned out to be just as good in real combat as these previews indicated, and it came as no surprise to me to learn that in four months and fifty-two missions with the 4th Fighter Group in Korea in 1952, Bob shot down six MiG-15's to become the eleventh USAF jet ace.

"The two stories of Bob Love's Korean experiences in this book are to my mind classics of fighter pilots' talk and jargon. You can almost see him banking his jet, palms of his hands down, and sadly needing yet another pair of hands to show how the enemy pilots flew."

Major Bob Love now speaks for himself:

"This was one of those 'max effort' days when we managed six aircraft up out of the squadron on a cover mission. These birds, F-86A and F-86E, were tired 'A' models up through the middle of the 'E' series. Our flight of four was to cover west to east, south of the 'creek' from the Yellow Sea and meet my two-ship element working east to west from the Mizu area.

"I was flying a tired 'A' with another on my wing, flown by a pilot who always aborted opposite Cho-do Island on the way in, and today was no exception. Lieutenant Ted Campbell was spare, and filled in on my wing with an 'E' when my first boy dropped out. We held radio silence, driving to Mizu and turning west at 27,000 feet, just south of the creek. We were under an overcast, in haze, with about two miles' visibility.

"I punched off the tanks and watched Ted clean up. I checked Ted's area to the south and east (left wing) and then checked my own five o'clock position just in time to find seven MiG's breaking hard on us from the north and level. Had we been five seconds later, they would have passed in front of us ninety degrees off, north to south.

"Their drops (tanks) were already fluttering down, so I called a hard right break into them,

and once I saw the lead MiG driver, an instructor type, was washing through badly in his turn, I called a hard reverse back into him. We met about ten degrees off. I am sure Ted didn't hear the reverse call, as his reverse was delayed just long enough for the MiG to latch on behind him.

"At this time, I noted the MiG instructor type's students were still in their turn to west, and rather wide in 'flock' formation. I reversed the third time and followed the MiG on Ted, turning my six o'clock to the students. I spent the next four minutes and several thousand feet of altitude trying to catch that full-power 'E' Sabre and the MiG in some real rough crossed-needle 360-degree turns. At times, I felt Ted would have to shake the MiG without my help, as when I managed to trim on the inside, Ted would reverse and leave me again on the outside, running out of breath and strength.

"I fired short bursts of tracer, trying to scare the MiG off, but the range was letting the tracers burn out. Each few seconds we would meet The Students, in string, head-on, around these five- and six-G turns. We'd worked down to around 15,000 feet when Ted could no longer read me due to plugged ears, and pulled up to the west in a climbing turn. Ted at this time was convinced he'd lost the MiG, but broke down and to the east when he heard my call.

"During the entire rat race the MiG fired at Ted, but failed to score a single hit. Once I could fly the tired 'A' under the first line, I caught the MiG in close range with two bursts after his climbing turn. The canopy and engine doors left the MiG and the driver continued a slow turn from south to east.

"In his hard, fast break to the east, Ted received only part of my call to 'reverse and pick us up at three o'clock.' He reversed and disappeared under me to the south—toward 'Long Dong.' The MiG reversed in these few seconds, and with no canopy, engine doors gone, dumping fuel and belching smoke, he stuck the nose down and headed east. He fired the rest of his ammo, and simply pulled hard over the top.

"Following him, I was once again on the first line (no elevator deflection) and lost him as he pulled up into the sun. I managed to trim around somewhat of a pullup. I climbed into the sun until reading 170 knots, and being once again in the middle of The Students, I

went out the bottom, joined with Ted farther south and back to home plate.

"I never saw the lame MiG after his break upward. A photo Joe with an 86-escort flight from 334th Fighter Interceptor Squadron witnessed the scrap and confirmed the MiG as splashed. I felt this MiG driver was one of the better types, and mach-wise, his MiG could give an 'A' model Sabrejet trouble. This was one of those scraps at low altitude and working downhill, where a few muscles, a G-suit and those hours of rat-racing with your buddies pays off."

The ebullient Bob Love also writes of another encounter with the MiG's:

"Once airborne and on combat frequency we picked up the first flights calling MiG's out and shooting in general. Being off late, and to catch the MiG's before they turned north again, we maintained a flat, fast climb up the west coast, turning right (east) and paralleling The Creek on the south side. It sounded a little quiet over the horn, and it appeared the MiG's were about to leave the scraps east of us and go home.

"We dropped tanks. At about 30,000 feet we met the first two 'early returns' almost head-on. These boys were going slightly more down and in a westerly direction. We broke left on to their tails, when we were bounced by two more from about three o'clock high. These latter two fired and broke up hard from west to south. Continuing on up, our element three and four latched on to these second two MiG's and chased them all the way up to where only a MiG would operate. Both these MiG's were damaged.

"'Jumpin' Bob' (Second Lieutenant Bob Straub) and I continued on a NNW heading after the first element of MiG's. We couldn't close enough to fire until the MiG's started a slow turn to the south. I threw in two short bursts and the wingman bailed, almost hitting Jumpin' Bob's bird. The element leader had broken hard up and to the north as we continued to turn south. Incidentally, the MiG wingman's hot seat functioned perfectly, as he separated from the seat on slipstream contact and his chute blossomed at once.

"'Junior Bob' (Lieutenant Bob Campbell) of our element three and four had moved to the inside of our turn south and called, 'Break left and cover me, I've got one cold.' We broke hard left, and three MiG's in an uneven string had passed under us to the east, ninety *degrees off. As we completed the hard turn, I was able to tell Campbell he was covered and detect which of the string he intended to chop up.*

"Campbell made a four o'clock pass on the number two MiG, cutting the enemy bird in half. Number three MiG slid on to Campbell's tail. I shook this MiG with a short burst and called a hard up and right break to Campbell. The number three MiG I'd hit finished in true Hollywood fashion, looping east to west at 8,000 feet. I flew slot man on this boy, hitting well through the first half of the loop, firing out inverted. Dumping fuel, parts and debris, and smoking badly, the MiG continued on through the first half of a Cuban eight, but neglected to pull out.

"During this acro show, Jumpin' Bob was in element, and as I completed firing he yelled, 'Break left!' I had just rolled right side up. One MiG came in from four o'clock and almost rammed the element. Bob didn't waste time calling this left break again, as he had a flight of four MiG's firing from seven o'clock at him. He could hear the cannons in the pit.

"We continued our hard left break to the south, and were clear of MiG's in twenty seconds. Their top cover almost worked—almost got us. Low over the water we checked our birds for hits. There were none. Our damage was one jammed gun on each side of my aircraft due to G's and heat. We had knocked off three MiG's in less than two minutes."

On this mission, all three pilots with Bob Love were also named Bob. They had to work out a call sign appropriate to each pilot. Bob Love for radio purposes became "Old Bob." His wingman Bob Straub, who was credited with two MiG's destroyed in Korea, was "Jumpin' Bob," while the number three man, Lieutenant Bob Ferber became "Ferb." The number four pilot, Lieutenant Bob Campbell went by just plain "Bob" or "Junior Bob." Novel names were used, to quote Bob Love, "because with ears plugged and 5-G's on the man talking, Able, Yellow and Purple all sounded the same. But a name like Jumpin' Bob could be understood under all but the roughest conditions."

For readers who might be wondering if Bob Love was using some strange foreign language in these unexpurgated combat accounts, this is "fighter talk." Strange terms unfamiliar to the ground-bound layman will be found in the Glossary of Fighter Slang in the Appendix. With the aid of this list, Bob Love's classic accounts can be readily translated. After his Korean War service Bob Love flew for many years with the California Air National Guard, and in more recent times has been quenching his passion for flying as a notable air race pilot.

There appeared from time to time in the ranks of the "MiG Drivers," as Bob Love would call them, combat pilots of formidable skill and tenacity. Their identity to this day remains a mystery. An encounter with such a

"BREAK LEFT!....."
Sabrejets of the 51st Fighter Interceptor Wing turn into enemy territory in their never-ending search for the elusive MiG-15 fighters of the North Koreans. The enemy has not yet been sighted, or these fighters would have dropped their wing tanks.

(Toliver Collection)

top quality pilot forms the outstanding combat memory of Lieutenant James F. Low of Sausalito, California. Jim Low was the only Second Lieutenant to become a jet ace in the Korean War. He ended the conflict with nine kills over the Red jets, one of which he recounts here:

"We were on a fighter sweep over North Korea in the vicinity of Siuho Reservoir on 18 December 1952. My wingman and I were cruising around 30,000 feet when two MiG's appeared at two o'clock level about five miles away. We closed in on them, and they split, one going high, the other low. They were camouflaged with brown and green spots. It looked best to jump the MiG that had gone low, since the other one had turned away and seemed to care nothing for his buddy's fate.

"My wingman was in a better position for a bounce, so I told him to take the MiG. Little did we know that we had tangled with a honcho (A topnotch fighter pilot — Aus.) We closed in, my wingman getting to within five hundred feet of the MiG, but he was unable to pull any lead on his target. The MiG was constantly pulling a high-G load, and my wingman's bullets fell uselessly behind the enemy machine.

"I told him to quit firing until he had lead, but he had target fixation and soon fired off all his ammunition. All this time I was flying his wing and keeping his tail clear. Finally he screamed, 'Yellow three, you better take him. I'm out of ammo!' I slid down on the MiG's tail while my wingman slid high.

"I tried pulling lead on this MiG, squeezed off a couple of bursts, but I also underled him. I concentrated now on getting the necessary lead before firing again. The enemy pilot continued his evasive maneuvers, and could that guy fly? First rolling under and split-essing, we ended up 'on the mach' about a hundred feet off the deck. He wound around hills and mountains reversing and trying to shake me. With no success at this, he started a chandelle, trying to outzoom me, but I cut him off in the turn and stuck with him.

"Finally he relaxed a little and I caught him with a short burst in the tail section. He continued to turn, but I hit him with another good burst in the engine and wing root. He blew his canopy and I thought he would bail out, but I waited and waited, fighting to stay above and behind him. He had a dead engine and was decelerating, so this was difficult to do.

"Then he pulled straight up, firing, hoping to catch me overshooting. He didn't. As he rolled over I caught him dead center with a long burst. He never pulled out of the dive, and crashed thunderously about ten miles east of the reservoir."

While it is true that the modern jet pilot flies in far greater comfort than his predecessors of the two world wars, with less physical effort necessary to maneuver his aircraft, all this depends upon the aircraft remaining free of battle damage. Combat conditions suddenly sometimes returned Korean jet pilots to the era of helmet-and-goggles. Colonel Winton W. "Bones" Marshall vividly remembers his own unwelcome return to open cockpit and tearing slipstream:

"The 4th Fighter Wing was intercepting a large formation of Red TU-2 bombers, escorted by LA-9 and MiG-15 fighters. Their mission was to wipe out our United Nations island holdings which were supporting radar installations and rescue operations. They were going to bomb and strafe these installations into oblivion. Led by Colonel Benjamin Preston* and Colonel Harrison Thyng, our attack completely broke up their formation and caused them to abort the mission.

"I was lucky enough to get one LA-9 and one TU-2 and damage another of the bombers. Following one pass, I was hit head-on by the cannon fire of an LA-9, which made a large hole in my wing and shot off my canopy. The shell that hit the canopy went on to hit and demolish my headrest, throwing my head up against the instrument panel and cracking my helmet.

"I usually lean far forward when I fly, or I would have probably had my head blown off. Shrapnel from the shell damaged the cockpit interior and sieved my parachute, which was a package of tatters. My wingman, Lieutenant Honaker—one of the finest fighter pilots I have ever flown with—shot down the LA-9 immediately, and then escorted me for a cold trip home. It was forty below zero at that altitude in the middle of a bitter Korean winter.

"I was not sure whether the aircraft was going to continue to run, but the F-86 is one of the best aircraft I have ever flown and it brought me safely home."

Colonel Marshall hails from Beverly Hills,

**Colonel Preston shot down three MiG's and an LA-9 in the Korean War.*

FIGHTER ACES OF THE U.S.A.

California, and for the action described was awarded the Silver Star and Purple Heart. In Korea he destroyed 4.5 MiG's, one LA-9 and one TU-2 for a total of 6.5 confirmed victories. Today, he is a Lieutenant General, Retired, and lives in Honolulu, Hawaii.

The political considerations that provided sanctuary for enemy aircraft beyond The Creek—the term used by fighter pilots for the demarcation line of the Yalu River—were despised by the men who were asked to put their lives on the line in aerial combat. Pursuits that certainly would have ended in a MiG downing had to be broken off at The Creek, and the Americans suffered the frustrating experience of watching beaten enemy pilots land safely. The scenario could not have been more enraging had the enemy pilots thumbed their noses after dismounting from their MiG's on their protected fields.

The World War II fighter aces among the Americans found it all especially incomprehensible. Those who had flown in Europe had known what it was to pursue and hunt and shoot down the enemy wherever he could be found—in the air, on the ground, or taking off or landing. "Sanctuary" for the enemy in Korea was like a gangster hiding in a church. Colonel Harrison Reed Thyng of Barnstead, New Hampshire, was one of the illustrious "inner seven" who made acedom in both World War II and Korea. His nine World War II kills included German, French, Italian and Japanese aircraft. To these he added five of the Soviet-built MiG's in Korea.

Harry Thyng got great satisfaction from one particular victory in Korea. Given the "sanctuary" situation, Colonel Thyng's most memorable combat experience could hardly be other than an indelible recollection:

"I was flying an F-86E up over northern Korea early in the spring of 1952. I was flying top flight at 45,000 feet up and down the Yalu, covering a fighter-bomber strike in the Sinuiju area.

"MiG-15's started taking off from Antung, and as they came across the Yalu, they were immediately engaged by other flights of my group—the 4th. The battle had just started when I saw six MiG's cornering one of my F-86E's. With my wingman, I dove down to eight hundred feet and gave the MiG leader a short burst after getting on his tail.

"Naturally, as he had just taken off, his tanks were loaded with fuel and my burst hit

him in the tank located just behind the cockpit. The low altitude was very conducive to explosion and burning, and the MiG partially exploded and headed quickly for Antung—back to sanctuary. He made a fiery crash in the middle of his own airfield, and disrupted all further action from that field for the next few hours. I believe the morale of the Reds must have been severely shaken when this pilot went in under their very noses, as he was the leader of the attacking MiG formation."

Harry Thyng retired as a Brigadier General and now lives in Pittsfield, New Hampshire.

Lieutenant Colonel George A. Davis made ace in World War II with seven victories gained during service with the Fifth Air Force. A Texan from Lubbock, Davis was possessed of an unquenchably aggressive spirit to go with his piloting and marksmanship. In the Korean War, Davis became the first double jet ace with his tenth kill on 13 December 1951. He lost his life engaging a superior force of MiG's on 10 February 1952. Davis downed two of the enemy aircraft before hits sent him crashing into a mountainside. He was the top scoring jet ace of the Korean War at the time of his death, with fourteen aerial victories in that conflict. Only thirty-five American aces since the inception of aerial combat have downed more than twenty aircraft, and Davis is one of them.*

The top jet ace of the United States is Captain Joseph McConnell, Jr., of Dover, New Hampshire, who is credited with sixteen MiG-15's. His baptism of fire had also been in World War II, but not as a pilot—he was a navigator on B-24's. After pilot training he showed much promise and was sent to the Far East Air Force in August of 1952. Assigned to the 51st Fighter Interceptor Wing in Korea, he had a long running-in period. He did not bring down a MiG until 14 January 1953.

From that point on, in fighter pilots' parlance, McConnell was "hot." He proved to have a nose for the enemy and the marksmanship to make it count. By 18 May

*Lieutenant Colonel Davis was awarded the Congressional Medal of Honor, posthumously for "conspicuous gallantry and intrepidity." On 10 February 1942, then Major Davis and his wingman attacked approximately twelve enemy MiG-15's and in the ensuing battle against such odds, shot down two and damaged a third MiG before he himself was shot down. Davis crashed to his death thirty miles south of the Yalu River.

(W. W. Marshall Collection)

SABREJETS LINE UP
U. S. F-86 Sabrejet fighters line up for takeoff at an airfield in South Korea.

1953, four months after his first victory, Mc-Connell had sixteen victories and was the top scoring jet ace of the Korean War. He had flown 106 missions and as a dashingly handsome, dark-haired jet pilot, had become a national hero. He was in the classic mold of the fighter ace.

Returned to the U.S. in May 1953, McConnell had survived the war and numerous, deliberate attempts by heavily armed enemies to take his life. Like Richard Bong, John Herbst, Buzz Wagner and numerous other fighter pilots who survived aerial combat, the radiant McConnell was killed in an aircraft accident. He was testing a new and more powerful model of the Sabrejet that had carried him to glory when he crashed and was killed on 25 August 1954.

The only other pilot in the history of aerial combat to score sixteen confirmed kills while flying a jet is the late Lieutenant Colonel Heinz Bär of the World War II Luftwaffe. He and Captain McConnell might be considered tied for world primacy as jet aces. Like McConnell, Bär was killed in a postwar aircraft accident. We will meet him among the enemy aces in an ensuing chapter.

The U.S. Navy found history repeating itself in the Korean War, when it produced only one ace in the conflict. Naval air power from carriers made a mighty contribution to the UN struggle in Korea, the mobile offshore bases providing unanswerable flexibility in the use of air power. Navy fighter pilots simply did not have the opportunities to grapple with the enemy air force that came the way of

USAF units. Just as David Sinton Ingalls was the U.S. Navy's only World War I ace, Lieutenant Guy Bordelon bears the same distinction in the Korean struggle.

The past repeated itself in another way in Bordelon's rise to acedom. Just as "Washing Machine Charley"—a noisy, slow-flying Japanese aircraft—was a feature of the nights on Guadalcanal, so did a similar type of visitation disturb the nocturnal peace of Seoul in 1953. The Reds used single, propeller-driven aircraft to disrupt the rest of Seoul by droning about and dropping bombs at odd intervals randomly into various parts of the city. No crucial damage was done, but the nuisance value of these intruders was high.

Lieutenant Bordelon was part of the effort made by the UN command to strangle the nocturnal noise merchants from the north. In another echo of World War II, he was flying an F4U Corsair, and in a stellar night flying performance clawed down five intruders between 29 June and 16 July 1953. His victims were four YAK-18's and one LA-2. He had become the Navy's only Korean War ace.

The U.S. Marine Corps also produced only one ace in the Korean conflict, Lieutenant Colonel John F. Bolt, who was attached to the USAF's 39th Interceptor Squadron. Marine aviation in Korea was held more to the classic, doctrinal role of close-support flying, with little opportunity offered the pilots to tangle with the MiG's. Lieutenant Colonel Bolt is the Marines' only jet ace, and the only Marine to become an ace in both World War II and Korea. He is credited with six victories in each conflict for a lifetime total of twelve.

The final victory of the Korean air war is credited to Captain Ralph Sherman Parr, America's thirty-fourth jet ace. Parr saw plenty of Korea's abundant close-support flying during 165 missions in F-80's, prior to his transfer to the 4th Fighter Group. In forty-seven missions in the Sabrejet, he downed ten enemy aircraft—nine MiG's and one IL-2. His most memorable aerial encounter reveals how poor enemy marksmanship can deliver a fighter pilot from the jaws of death:

"While on a combat patrol in North Korea and flying at 42,000 feet, I spotted a flight of MiG's at extremely low altitude. I made a vertical diving attack, in which I lost the remainder of my flight. At 3,000 feet I selected the leader of a sixteen-ship formation of MiG's. They spotted me.

"As the fight began, right on the deck, my gunsight failed. By using extreme close range firing, I was able to destroy two MiG's and damage a third. My aircraft sustained no damage—an incredible thing. No fewer than seven MiG's fired themselves out of ammo at my aircraft, at ranges from five to six hundred feet *during this battle. The remainder of my flight intervened, and the MiG's bolted for the Yalu."*

Ralph Parr joined the USAAF as a flying cadet in 1942 and made the USAF his career. Only ten other fighter pilots besides Parr ended the Korean War with ten or more aerial victories. He shot down an IL-2 near Hoha-dong less than twelve hours before the Armistice on 27 July 1953. America's airmen thus closed their account in the Korean War with Ralph Parr's becoming a double jet ace.

Forty new aces had been created by the Korean War, consisting of thirty-eight Air Force aces, one Navy ace and one Marine Corps ace. Numerous other pilots became aces as a result of combining their Korean scores with World War II credits. There were World War II aces who added to their scores in Korea without managing a second "five down."

In this latter category were some of the top guns from the ETO in World War II. They included John C. Meyer (24 World War II, 2 Korea), Glenn T. Eagleston (18.5 World War II, 2 Korea), and Walker M. "Bud" Mahurin (20.75 World War II, 3.5 Korea). Less than 10 percent of the USAF pilots credited with aerial victories in Korea became aces, which again illustrates the elite nature of acedom.

Enemy losses in aerial combat totaled 893 aircraft, which serves to illustrate the smaller scale of aerial combat in Korea compared with the two world wars. Both in and out of military circles, but usually in quarters where so-called "cost effectiveness" is a favored idea, there has been a tendency to deprecate the role of fighter aircraft in the Korean War. The "cost" of the Yalu patrols by jet fighters has been estimated more in terms of dollars then in the realities of tactical and strategic needs. By no means uncommon in some military quarters is the statement that U.S. jets shot down only 841 MiG's, and that this cost so many millions of dollars or so much per aircraft and it was therefore "expensive."

There are people in high places today who actually still believe that modern wars can be paid for, in the sense that individuals pay for cars and houses and refrigerators. Aside from the manifest truth that all war is expensive

MiG-15 UNDER TEST
Five top U.S. test pilots checked out this captured MiG-15 on Okinawa, seen here being taxied for takeoff.
MiG-15 had its share of virtues but was generally evaluated as inferior to the American F-86 Sabrejet. Tests were conducted in October of 1953.

(Official USAF Photo)

THE USAF TESTS A MiG-15 FIGHTER

A captured MiG-15 fighter from Korea takes off from a USAF airfield on Okinawa during evaluation tests of the nimble Russian-built fighter. Chief aerial antagonist of the American Sabrejets, the MiG-15 was flown on this occasion by Captain Tom Collins of the Wright Air Development Center. The jet tagging along behind is an F-86 Sabrejet, for tests of the MiG-15 in simulated aerial combat. Among the other famous pilots who flew the MiG-15 was Major Charles E. "Chuck" Yeager, with 11.5 victories as a fighter pilot in WWII and the first man to fly faster than sound. The MiG-15 was thoroughly "wrung out" by U.S. experts.

(Toliver Collection)

folly, from which only an all-around improvement in human nature can deliver the world, there is danger in financial intellectualizing about fighters in Korea. Their contribution can only be evaluated in terms of the overall struggle and their influence upon events.

What would have been the consequences for the UN and the USA of having 841 MiG-15's wade into the obsolescent close-support aircraft employed by the UN to aid and protect our ground forces? What would *that* have cost? The fearful devastation of enemy supply systems wrought by the UN command's World War II aircraft governed the whole unfoldment of the ground war. The Sabre umbrella kept the Red jets in check. This allowed the UN forces to utilize the residue of Allied airpower from World War II in a manner out of all proportion to its age.

Korean War pilots had the benefit of well-controlled policies governing rotation, rest and recuperation. Combat missions were normally limited to 100. USAF personnel serving in Korea were entitled each six weeks to three days' temporary duty in Japan. They could also choose the station in Japan at which they would spend the three days.

This procedure was sometimes modified, but was fairly standard throughout the conflict. Korea in this respect was quite a contrast to World War II conditions, where the primary factor governing the rotation of fighter pilots was the number of missions flown. Each air force in World War II set its own requirements for the number of missions. These requirements were then varied to suit the dynamics of the particular theater of operations, those dynamics including the availability of replacement pilots.

The calibre of enemy opposition in World War II, the terrain over which the fighter war was conducted, the number of missions actually involving combat and similar factors all entered into rotational and rest policies. Depending on the air force with which he was serving, a World War II fighter pilot could count on flying from thirty-five to 150 missions before being sent back to the U.S.A. or to the rear areas.

Korean War pilots could frequently get a few fast days in Japan by ferrying tired F-86 Sabres back to the repair depot in Japan. After their rest period, they ferried restored Sabres back to their combat station. They were thus able to get all-important breaks from combat duty, together with a complete change of scene and the charm of Japanese life.

Outstanding combat pilots might occasionally have their tours extended from 100 to perhaps 120 or 125 missions. Even these extensions were frequently curtailed before completion. There were just too many fighter pilots in the USAF who needed the combat experience. This resulted in fairly strict adherence to rotation policies.

Many pilots in the Korean fracas never completed 100 missions before returning to Japan to complete their overseas tour, or before returning to the States. Numbers of other pilots could not adapt themselves to the highly taxing requirements of jet combat and tactics. These men were weeded out as rapidly as possible, to make way for more capable pilots.

The Korean War also provided an opportunity for many pilots senior in age and grade to take part in a limited number of missions.

These tours were usually limited to thirty-five missions. Officers whose specific assignments in the USAF would benefit from such familiarization were given this opportunity. The average Korean War jet pilot flew fewer than 100 missions.

After the Korean War, Uncle Sam did not repeat the one-sided and profligate disarmament that had followed World War II and laid the basis for Red military adventure in Korea. Sufficient physical force had now to be kept in being, and new military technology had to be driven forward. Few rational persons now doubted that a poorly-armed and ill-prepared Uncle Sam would result in Red subversion of western civilization.

Aerial warfare had become involved in some strange new principles like "sanctuary," not fighting to win, limited war and deliberately prolonged indecision. All this had chafed on and enraged the Korean War aces, because it was alien to the fundamental American idea of fighting to win. The aces of the Korean War were forced to live with these new realities, but their guts were committed to knocking the other guy down, and nothing would ever change their conviction that this was how the enemy was beaten.

Fighter plane development continued after Korea. Missiles were clearly going to play a large role in future aerial combat. New young men would fly the new jets. Fantastically complex aerial technology would be at their fingertips in Asia, and politics would be eternally at their elbows. What Korea had introduced in the jet epoch, Vietnam would bring forth in much fuller measure.

(Toliver Collection)

FIVE OF AMERICA'S BEST

These pilots are all jet aces, gathered in a historic group during the Korean War. From left, they are Captain Lonnie R. MOORE with 10 kills; Colonel Vermont GARRISON with 10 kills in Korea, and 7.33 kills while flying with the USAF in WWII; Colonel James K. JOHNSON, 1 kill over the WWII Luftwaffe and 10 MiGs in Korea; Captain Ralph S. PARR, 10 kills in Korea; and Major James JABARA, 1.5 victories in Europe in WWII and 15 MiG-15s shot down in Korea. Captain Moore was killed in an F-101 crash in 1956, and Major Jabara in a Volkswagen wreck in 1967.

Major Donald E. Adams, 6.5 Korea
Adams, from Caton, Painted Post and Naples, New York, scored four victories in the ETO in WWII, then in the Korean War was the 13th pilot to shoot down five MiG jets. He shot down 6.5 MiGs before failing to return from a mission in mid-1952. Total score: 10.5 victories.

(USAF)

Aces of the Korean War

(USAF/M. Constant)

Colonel Robert P. Baldwin, USAF (5.0 Korea)
Baldwin flew with 1st Group in Italy in WWII. In Korean War he commanded the 51st Fighter Group and became an ace when he scored his fifth MiG-15 kill on 11 June 1953. Currently living in Yuma, Arizona, Baldwin is considered by many to be one of the finest pilots in America.

311

(USAF/M. Constant)
Captain Richard S. Becker, USAF (5.00 Korea) Fleetwood, Pennsylvania. Becker flew with the 4th Fighter Group.

(USAF/M. Constant)
Colonel Royal N. Baker, USAF (13 Korea) McKinney, Texas. As a 1st Lt. and Captain, Baker scored 3.50 victories in WWII in the MTO with the 31st Fighter Group. In the Korean War, as a Colonel, he shot down 12 MiG-15s and a Russian LA-9, bringing his total to 16.50 for both wars. Baker rose to Major General, died in 1975.

Major John F. Bolt, USMC (6.00 Korea) New Smyrna Beach, Florida. Marine Corps Major Bolt is one of the "Inner-seven" aces who qualified as an ace in two wars. In WWII he flew with VMF-214 (USS BLOCK ISLAND) in the Solomon Islands and scored six victories. In Korea, Bolt flew with VMF-115 for 92 missions, then was assigned to the USAF 39th squadron, 51st Fighter Group as an exchange pilot. In less than two months he had six confirmed MiG-15s to his credit, bringing his total to 12.00 for both wars.

(USAF)

(USAF/M. Constant)

Major Stephen L. Bettinger, USAF (5.00 Korea)
Kirkland, Washington. Bettinger scored 1.0 victory in WWII
in the MTO with the 66th Fighter Squadron. In the Korean
War, with the 4th Fighter Group, he added five MiG-15s to
bring his total to 6.00 victories.

Captain Henry Buttelmann, USAF (7.00 Korea)
Bayside, New York.
51st Fighter Wing.
All seven were MiG-15 jets.

(USAF/M. Constant)

DOUBLE ACE IN KOREA
Major Frederick C. Blesse, Tantallon, Maryland,
downed nine MiG fighters and one LA-9 to become
a double ace with ten victories in Korea. He was
top scorer in Korea until overtaken by Royal Baker
in February 1953. Blesse later saw Vietnam service, retired as a Major General in 1975.

(USAF/M. Constant)

(Toliver Collection)

313

DOUBLE ACE AND P.O.W.
Iowan Harold E. Fischer, Jr. ran up 10 victories in Korea
during 70 missions with the 51st Fighter Interceptor Wing
to become a double ace. Shot down in a battle with MiGs
7 April 1953, Captain Fischer was captured by Red ground forces,
held captive for 22 months after the end of the Korean War.

(Toliver Collection)

Major Manuel J. Fernandez, Jr. USAF (14.50 Korea)
Key West, Florida. 334 squadron of the
4th Fighter Wing. All victories were
against MiG-15s.

(USAF/M. Constant)

(USAF/M. Constant)

Colonel Francis S. Gabreski USAF (6.50 Korea)
Dix Hills, New York. America's top
living fighter ace, Gabreski was top
scorer in the ETO in WWII with 28
victories with the 56th Fighter Group.
In the Korean War, Gabreski added 6.5
MiG-15s to his total, bringing it to 34.5.

Captain Manuel J. Fernandez, Jr. USAF (14.50)
Key West, Florida. Fernandez was the 26th USAF
ace of the Korean War and ranked third in number
of kills behind McConnell (16) and Jabara (15).
He flew with 334 squadron, 4th Group.

(USAF)

(USAF)

Major James P. Hagerstrom, USAF (8.50 Korea)
Waterloo, Iowa. Hagerstrom is one of the "Inner-seven," a pilot who made ace in two wars! In WWII with the 8th Fighter Squadron in the SWPA, he scored six victories over the Japanese. In the Korean War, flying with the 334th and 67th squadrons, he added 8.5 MiG-15s to bring his total to 14.50.

(USAF/M. Constant)

Major Clyde A. Curtin Portland, Oregon. 4th Fighter Wing. Curtin got a double on 19 July 1953 to qualify him as an ace with 5.0.

Lt. Cecil G. Foster, USAF (9.00)
Midland, Michigan and San Antonio, Texas 16th squadron, 51st Fighter Group. Foster was promoted to Captain after his 6th victory 22 November 1952. He returned to combat in January 1953 and scored three more victories in three days.

(USAF/M. Constant)

315

(USAF/M. Constant)

(Toliver Collection)

AMERICA'S FIRST JET ACE

Major James Jabara got his combat initiation in Europe in WWII, and went on in Korea to become America's first jet ace. His ETO kill tally was 1.5 victories, his Korean score 15 MiGs for a lifetime total of 16.5 victories. Flew with the 334 Squadron, 4th Wing in Korea. He was killed in an automobile accident in 1967.

(USAF/K-14)

Captain Leonard W. Lilley, USAF (7.00)
Alexandria, Virginia 4th Fighter Group. Born in the Panama Canal Zone, Lilley went to West Point before learning to fly.

(USAF)

Captain Clifford Dale Jolley, USAF (7.00 Korea)
Cleveland, Ohio. The 18th fighter pilot to make ace in Korea, Jolley flew with the 4th Wing, 335th Squadron.

(USAF/M. Constant)

(USAF)

Colonel George L. Jones, USAF (6.50 Korea): Vero Beach, Florida. Jones flew with the 413th Fighter Group from Ie Shima, near Okinawa, in WWII but did not score any victories. In Korea his first 1.5 MiG-15 kills were with the 4th Wing. The next two were with the 51st Wing and the last three with the 335th Squadron, 4th Wing.

(USAF/Constant)

Captain Ralph D. "Hoot" Gibson, USAF (5.00 Korea): Tucson, Arizona. Erstwhile leader of the Thunderbird Acrobatic Team, Gibson scored his acedom flying with the 4th Fighter Wing's 335th Squadron.

(USAF)

(USAF/M. Constant)

HE CAUGHT A "HONCHO"
Captain James F. Low USAF ran into a
brilliant Communist fighter pilot in Korea
in a thrilling chase he describes in the text.
Low won the battle, and shot down eight other
MiGs during the Korean War. He served
with the 335th Squadron, 4th Fighter
Interceptor Wing.

(USAF/M. Constant)

Colonel Vermont Garrison, USAF (10.00 Korea)
Mountain Home, Idaho. Garrison, as an instructor in
Mustangs flew with the RAF early in WWII. After transfer-
ring to the USAF, he scored 7.33 kills with the 4th Fighter
Group in the ETO. In the Korean War he shot down ten MiG-
15s to bring his total to 17.33 aerial victories!

(USAF)

**Captain Lonnie R. Moore, USAF
(10.00 Korea):** Fort Walton, Florida.
335th Squadron, 4th Fighter Wing.

Captain Iven C. Kincheloe, Jr. USAF (5.00 Korea)
Cassapolis, Michigan. Scored five MiG-15 kills flying with
the 25th Squadron, 51st Fighter Wing and destroyed four more
enemy aircraft on the ground. Kincheloe set the world's
altitude record 126,200 feet on 7 Sept. 1956. Died in
the crash of an F-104 at Edwards Air Force Base, California
on 26 July 1958.

(USAF/M. Constant)

318

Major Winton W. "Bones" Marshall, USAF (6.50 Korea): With a nickname of "Bones" and a serial number like "9999A" one might suspect this wry-humored, sharpshooter would go places, and he did. In 3 months in the 4th Group, Bones flew 100 missions and scored 6.5 victories. An extremely capable officer, he rose to Lt. General and has now retired to live in Honolulu.

(USAF)

(USAF/M. Constant)

Major Leonard William Lilley, USAF (7.00 Korea)
Alexandria, Virginia
334 Squadron, 4th Fighter Wing.
Lilley is a 1945
graduate of the U.S. Military Academy

THE REAL FIGHTER TYPE
Major Robert J. Love scored six victories in Korea over Mig-15s, and was firm believer in plenty of practice at Air Combat Maneuvering. Canadian-born Love enlisted in the RCAF in 1941, transferred to the USAF in 1942 but saw no combat in WWII. He made up for that in Korea. Love has become a successful air race pilot in recent years.

(Toliver Collection)

(USAF)

Captain Robert H. Moore, USAF (5.00 Korea):
Austin, Texas. Moore flew with the 336th
Squadron, 4th Fighter Wing. This photo taken in
1960 at Air Defense Command, Colorado
Springs. Author Toliver is at right.

(USAF/M. Constant)

Captain James H. Kasler, USAF (6.00 Korea):
Momence, Illinois. In WWII, Kasler was tail gunner
on a B-29 of the 5th Squadron, 9th Bombardment
Group stationed in the Marianas Islands (20th AF).
He was the 15th USAF fighter pilot to make ace in
the Korean War. He flew F-86s with the 335th
Squadron, 4th Wing. In his third war, Jimmy Kasler
was shot down and captured by the North Vietnamese and was one of the few lucky ones who
survived years of torture and returned home after
the war.

TOP ACE, KOREAN WAR
Captain Joseph McConnell, Jr., downed 16 enemy aircraft
in the Korean War to become top ace of that conflict.
He was the first American ace to down 15 enemy aircraft at
the controls of a jet fighter. McConnell saw WWII aerial
combat, but as a navigator on B-24 bombers. He survived
two wars only to die in a test-flying accident
on 25 August 1954.

(Toliver Collection)

(USAF/M. Constant)　　　　　　　　　　　　　　(USAF)

Colonel Harrison R. "Harry" Thyng, USAF (5 Korea + 5 WWII): Pittsfield, New Hampshire. Thyng is one of the "Inner-seven" aces who made ace in two wars. The seven are USMC Major Bolt; USAF G. A. Davis, F. S. Gabreski, V. Garrison, Thyng, and W. T. Whisner. A WWII ace with five victories while flying in the MTO with the 309th Fighter Squadron, Thyng added five MiG-15s in Korea with the 4th Fighter Wing. Retired as a Brigadier General.

Captain Robert Thomas Latshaw, USAF (5.00 Korea): Amarillo, Texas. Latshaw was a navigator on B-29s in the Pacific in WWII. Trained as a pilot between wars, he fought with the 335th Squadron, 4th Fighter Wing in Korea.

(USAF)

Major William T. Whisner, USAF (5.50 Korea): Tampa, Florida and Shreveport, Louisiana. One of the "Inner-seven" aces who were aces in both WWII and in Korea. Whisner scored 15.5 aerial victories fighting with the 487th squadron, 352nd Fighter Group, 8th AF, ETO in WWII. In Korea he scored 5.5 more, all MiG-15s, two with the 334th squadron, 4th Wing and 3.5 with 25 Squadron, 51st Wing. 21.00 total aerial victories.

(USAF/M. Constant)

(USAF/M. Constant)

Major Robinson Risner, USAF (8.00 Korea)
Risner flew with the 336th Squadron, 4th Fighter
group for his eight kills of MiG-15s. He was shot
down in the Vietnam War, captured by the Viet Cong
and held prisoner for several years. He is one of the
bravest of all military men. Retired as a Brigadier General.

(USAF)

**Captain Dolphin D. Overton III, USAF (5.0
Korea):** Smithfield, North Carolina. 16th
Squadron, 51st Fighter Group.

(USAF/M. Constant)

Major Ralph Sherman Parr, Jr. USAF (10.00 Korea)
Fort Walton Beach, Florida
Saw WWII service in the SWPA with the
49th Fighter Group, 5 Air Force. No victories. In Korea,
Parr destroyed nine MiG-15s and one IL-2 for a total of 10.00
while flying with the 335th Squadron, 4th Fighter Group.

Major William H. Wescott, USAF (5.0 Korea)
Rancho Palos Verdes, California. Flew with the
25th Squadron, 51st Fighter Group.

(USAF)

(USAF)

Colonel James K. Johnson, USAF (10.00 Korea): Las
Vegas, Nevada. Johnson shot down the only Me-109
he got a shot at in WWII flying with the 404th Fighter
Group, ETO. In Korea, with the 4th Fighter Wing,
Johnson added ten MiG-15s to bring his overall total
to 11.00. He was born in Phoenix, Arizona.

Colonel George I. Ruddell, USAF (8.00 Korea)
Riverside, California. 2.5 victories in WWII with the 514th
Fighter Squadron in the ETO, Ruddell scored eight victories
over MiG-15s in Korea, bringing his total to 10.5.

(USAF/M. Constant)

TOO LATE FOR KOREA, TOO EARLY FOR VIETNAM!

(USAF)

TOO LATE FOR KOREA, TOO EARLY FOR VIETNAM!

The NAA F-100 Super Sabre. American pilots in Korea discovered the NAA F-86 was too evenly matched with the MiG-15, so NAA came up with the F-100. The Korean War ended before it could be deployed. By the time America became involved in the Vietnam War, the Super Sabre was obsolete, yet many were used throughout the war. This one, nicknamed "Triple Zilch" for obvious reasons, was the 20th Fighter Wing Commander's plane in England in 1957-1960: Co-author Toliver's plane. When last heard from, Triple Zilch was stripped of it's classy paint job and was being flown by the Texas Air National Guard.

10

FIGHTER ACES OF VIETNAM

After the Korean War, Uncle Sam did not again trustingly disarm in a repetition of events following World War II. Illegal confinement of POW's—including fighter aces and pilots—long after the end of hostilities in Korea, reminded Uncle Sam to keep his guard up. America had a world-wide enemy. A political system compulsively inimical to the U.S.A. was bringing more and more nations under its sway, not only through subversion, but also through armed force in the case of Hungary. An enduring peace could not be realistically anticipated after the Korean War because of these aggressive acts. Vietnam was part of the pattern of Communist expansion and takeover.

The radical changes brought about in aerial combat through the advent of the jet fighter had hardly been assimilated before a new technical epoch was opened. Development of the transistor triggered immense advances in electronics technology, and especially in radar and computers, that were staggering in their portent. Unprecedented "thinking power" could be compressed into a small, lightweight chassis, and its product made available instantly at the press of a button. Air-to-air missiles came of age, and America's heat-seeking *Sidewinder* missile was designed to home on the tail-pipe of an enemy aircraft.

Nationalist Chinese fighter pilots flying U.S.-built Sabres had been first to put the Sidewinder missile to the acid test of actual combat. On 24 September 1958, in a savage and updated version of Korean War combat, fourteen Sabres tangled with twenty Red Chinese MiG's. Six of the Sabres carried Sidewinders. They cut a swathe through the MiG's. Four Sidewinder kills were claimed in this one engagement by the Nationalist pilots. The heat-seeking missile had proved its worth.

Jet aircraft capable of twice the speed of sound were a concomitant development in this new epoch of missiles and sophisticated electronics. Capable of carrying huge loads of ordinance, these aircraft were putting a new face on fighter aviation. Multi-mission aircraft became the vogue. War planners saw aerial combat in the old formats simply fading into history. Aircraft would now fight at long distance, with guided missiles or heat-seeking missiles. The idea gained currency that fighter pilots might not even see each other. Guns were no longer necessary. The Red Baron was dead.

These theories and ideas surrounding the new technology had two main consequences for American fighter aviation. First, a pure *air superiority fighter* was not developed after the Korean War. Secondly, there was a marked decline in the training of fighter pilots in ACM—air combat maneuvering. The tried and true essentials of aerial combat were de-emphasized in the presence of the incredible think-boxes with which fighter planes were now equipped.

Vietnam forced a revision of this thinking. The human element was restored to pride of place—riding on top of the new technology rather than subdued to these devices. The man in the cockpit turned out yet again to be all-important. The modern fighter aircraft was a means of extending his powers as a warrior—like any weapon from a club on up—and the more capable, knowledgeable and skilled the pilot the more efficient the weapon. Vietnam proved once more the cardinal value of a superlative human element in aerial warfare.

When the U.S. began its major involvement in Vietnam in 1965, the leading American fighter aircraft was the McDonnell Douglas F-4 Phantom. Developed originally by the U.S. Navy as a fleet air defense interceptor, the Phantom was armed with missiles designed to down bombers attacking the fleet, and not suited to air-to-air fighter combat. Because dogfighting was considered to be unlikely in the age of supersonic aircraft and missiles, the

Phantom was not armed with a gun. The 54,000-pound aircraft was a versatile, powerful, multi-mission machine, capable of exceeding Mach 2 and of hauling an awesome load of ordnance at lesser speeds.

As the USAF and USN began attacking targets in North Vietnam in February 1965, the Red response was a Soviet announcement that Russian-built antiaircraft weapons and surface-to-air missiles (SAM's), would be installed to protect Hanoi and Haiphong. The Russians would direct construction of these installations. This was the beginning of the most sophisticated aerial defense system yet devised for a relatively small geographical area. The system would claim the lives of many U.S. fighter crews, and the liberty of many more who would become POW's.

Russian-built fighters were soon defending North Vietnam. The MiG-17's that initially appeared were the last of the first-line, dogfighting subsonic aircraft of the major powers. Dubbed the *Fresco,* the MiG-17 was an aerial hot rod less than one third the weight of the Phantom, whose bulk positively dwarfed the Russian machine. The MiG-17 carried three cannons. Designed to operate close to their own bases in the air superiority role, these Russian fighters were well-suited to the defense of North Vietnam. MiG's downed three F-105 Thunderchiefs on 4 April 1965. By 17 June 1965, the first MiG downings were claimed by U.S. Navy Phantoms. Dogfighting wasn't dead after all.

MiG-17's and the later MiG-21 *Fishbed* were the main antagonists of U.S. fighter pilots in Vietnam. American fighters were mainly employed in bombing missions against targets in North Vietnam. These assignments were made possible by the tremendous payload, fighting power and high speed of the Phantoms on the one hand, and by the USAF's trusty aerial tankers on the other. Phantoms took off from Thailand bases fully loaded and refueled on their way in to the targets in North Vietnam. They refueled again on the way out to make it back to their bases. Tactical aircraft were thus used on strategic missions, chiefly aimed at paralyzing enemy industrial potential and the flow of supplies to

(Koku-Fan)

UNHOLY ENEMY PAIR
SAM missile poised in launch position and MiG-17 were integral parts of well-integrated and closely concentrated air defense system set up to protect Hanoi and environs. Missiles, fighters and radar made bombing attacks on North Vietnam highly hazardous to USAF and USN.

southern Vietnam.

Strategic bombers meanwhile undertook essentially tactical missions in one of aerial history's most surprising reversals of role. With highly sophisticated radar and ground control, B-52's from Guam were able to drop thirty tons of ordnance apiece on Red positions and concentrations in South Vietnam. Untroubled by fighter opposition, guided by advanced radar at high altitude and out of sight and sound of the invaders below, B-52's at the electronically computed point unloaded on the unseen enemy miles below. The Viet Cong would suddenly find themselves under a cataract of explosive and steel, seemingly arriving out of thin air.

As the bombing missions against the north by American fighter aircraft were kept up, the opposition stiffened—both the MiG's and the developing ground defense system. Automatic flak, missiles and fighters began working in a well-coordinated defense network. Soon it became necessary to mount MiG CAP's (MiG Combat Air Patrols) to intercept the enemy interceptors. Other American fighters were used as flak suppressors. Sometimes two protective fighters had to be provided for each fighter bomber going in to bomb targets in North Vietnam. Fighter operations had never been more complex or demanding on fighter crews.

America's fighter pilots in Vietnam eagerly sought combat with the MiG's. Downing a MiG in fighter-to-fighter combat was a high distinction for a fighter pilot. The Russian-built machines were elusive and well-directed from the ground on intercept. Excellent pilots developed among the MiG drivers. Like the Germans and Japanese of World War II, they had plenty of targets provided by the eternally-pressing Americans, and the North Vietnamese pilots were operating close to their own bases.

By the end of May 1966, Captain Nguyen Van Bay of the North Vietnam Air Force had become the first ace of the war—on either side. His seven kills were widely publicized, including releases in popular European magazines. The 32-year-old Van Bay was reputed to have knocked down four Thunderchiefs, one Super Sabre and two Phantoms. The U.S. had yet to produce an ace in Vietnam, despite a high level of operational activity. There were brilliant individual victories credited against the MiG's, but nobody

had been able to achieve the magic "five down."

At this period a veteran in the art of ACM, and also an ace from World War II, came upon the scene and galvanized U.S. fighter pilots with an inspiring and stellar performance. Forty-five-year-old Colonel Robin Olds, late of the 479th Fighter Group in the ETO in World War II, became commander of the 8th Tactical Fighter Wing at Ubon, Thailand, on 30 September 1966. He was credited with twelve aerial victories over the Luftwaffe.

When Olds took over the 8th TFW, he had a long and distinguished career behind him. Young fighter pilots could not fail to be impressed with their new old man. Olds had entered West Point in 1940, captained the Point's football team and flown P-38's and P-51's with the 8th Air Force against the Germans. He had named his first fighter plane in World War II *Scat I*. By war's end he was mounted on *Scat VIII* and had survived 107 combat missions.

Before climbing into *Scat XXVII*, his Phantom II jet in Thailand, Olds had also admirably filled in the years between World War II and Vietnam. He had co-founded the USAF's first jet acrobatic team. Flying a P-80, he had placed second in the Thompson Trophy Race in Cleveland. Olds flew the RAF's first operational jet fighter—the Gloster Meteor—in 1948, and he also became the first non-Britisher to command a regular Royal Air Force squadron.

This was a high honor with strong links to the successful past. Olds was put in command of a hallowed unit, the famous Number One Squadron at Tangmere, wartime base of the legless ace Douglas Bader—the immortal "Stationmaster" of Tangmere. Varied flying commands in the U.S., West Germany and Libya ensued, then some years at the Pentagon followed by command of the 81st Tactical Fighter Wing in England. Olds had also lived in real life one of the young fighter pilot's fantasies—he had married a movie star. Mrs. Olds is the former Ella Raines. When Robin Olds took over command of the 8th TFW he brought with him an aura of achievement, leadership and professional competence that could not fail to inspire.

Between 2 January 1967 and 20 May 1967, Olds downed four MiG's to add to the twelve Luftwaffe aircraft he had shot down in World War II. He was rotated back to the U.S. after

100 missions, and thus came "within an ace" of becoming an ace in each of two separate wars—something achieved by only seven other Americans flying in American units. As Brigadier General Olds he became an inspiring Commandant of Cadets at the Air Force Academy in Colorado Spr+ings.

An authoritative contemporary account of aerial warfare in Vietnam by General Olds appeared in *Horizons* in 1968, published by Grumman Aircraft Engineering Corporation of Bethpage, Long Island, New York. This publication was kindly and thoughtfully supplied to the authors by none other than Francis "Gabby" Gabreski, top-scoring living U.S. ace and a public relations executive with Grumman. A rare perspective on aerial fighting is provided by General Olds, and the clarity of his presentation shows why he was able to go from P-38 Lightning to Phantom jet—and leave Vietnam as a top-scoring MiG killer among men young enough to be his sons.

A complete spectrum of problems and principles in the Vietnam fighter game are covered in his account, entitled *The Lessons of Clobber College.* Here are the relevant excerpts, with the kind permission of Grumman Aircraft:

"It isn't until 11 August 1967 that HQ Seventh Air Force at Tan Son Nhut, near Saigon, orders us to bomb the Paul Doumier Bridge.

"The Doumier Bridge carries highway and railroad traffic across the Red River in the northeast section of Hanoi, vital to the movement of war materiel from Communist China to the North Vietnamese and Viet Cong forces in South Vietnam. The only Red River span within 30 miles of Hanoi, it and its approaches are guarded by SAM (Surface-to-Air Missile) sites, automatic weapons sites, and more than 100 37mm, 57mm and 85mm antiaircraft cannon sites. And the entire MiG force is well within range of the target area.

"If we don't knock out the bridge on the first try, the defenses probably will get even tighter. It will take pinpoint precision to hit the 38-foot width of the mile-long span and not damage the nearby civilian areas.

"My 'Wolfpack' F-4C's join KC-135 tankers from the Strategic Air Command and F-105's from Takhli's 355th Tactical Fighter Wing, and Korat's 388th Tactical Fighter Wing. Colonel Bob White, former X-15 pilot and

astronaut, leads the first group, the 355th. Each Thud (F-105) is heavily loaded with one 3,000-pound bomb under each wing and a centerline drop tank. . . . From Ubon to Hanoi the weather is clear with visibility unlimited all the way.

"Ahead of us are EB-66's, whose job is to identify and jam enemy radar, along with F-105's which will go after the antiaircraft sites. Behind are RF-101's and RF-4C's of the 11th and 432nd Tactical Reconnaissance Squadrons. After we've pulled off the target, but while the enemy is fully alerted and throwing everything he's got, they'll fly over the bridge and photograph the results.

"As we fly down the Red River toward Hanoi—about thirty miles from the target— seven SAM's are fired at our F-4's. But we evade them, as well as the heavy antiaircraft fire. Twenty miles from the target, four MiG's pass 200 feet below the flak suppression force of F-105's but, strangely, don't engage them. We and the 105's keep formation and refuse to jettison our bombs, contrary to the MiG's wishes. We're frequently glancing over our shoulders at the trailing MiG's wondering whether we'll have to cut in our afterburners to outrun them.

"Now the flak is even heavier and, as one pilot remarks, 'we're trying to run several blocks in a rainstorm without letting a drop hit us.' We're engulfed in the black smoke of 85mm bursts. More SAM's but there's little point in evasive action against one site only to be hit by another. As the force starts down the bomb run, hundreds of 37mm and 57mm open up on us. Aircraft are hit but not downed.

"The first group of F-105's is jinking hard off the target and pulling away. We can see their 3,000-pounders walking across the bridge. The center span falls into the Red River. Now we go in and blast the 85mm sites. Lieutenant Colonel Harry Schurr, leading the third group—the 388th Thuds—sees their 3,000-pounders 'popping like big orange balls' as they hit the bridge. Another span has been dropped.

"More SAM's narrowly miss the force as we turn hard right, reassemble at Thud Ridge, the best-known checkpoint in the air war, and head for the waiting tankers. Every aircraft is recovered safely, although several have taken serious hits.

"The Doumier raid illustrates one of the most unique features of the air war—that ful-

ly half of our pilots' concern is with what's coming up from the ground. When you're up in the barrel around Hanoi, it's like flying through the Ruhr in World War II.

"In that war, you caught hell from the ground if you blundered over a few major, heavily defended target areas. But, generally, the fighter pilot could weave around and not get shot at by the heavy stuff. You got down low, and there were lots of countrysides you could fly over and lots of lucrative targets that were lightly defended.

"Not that I am one who holds with the contention that the flak in North Vietnam is thicker than that encountered in Germany. I don't think there's any way to equate the two ground-fire situations.

"In Germany, the 88mm guns protecting such places as Berlin, Mersburg, Magdeburg, Osnabruck and Hamburg were concentrated in great mass. They used to fling up against every slow-moving bomber formation a barrage of flak that blackened the sky for as long as a mile and perhaps a half-mile deep and a half-mile wide.

"It was an absolutely incredible sight. The bombers were moving at something like 200-225 mph ground speed, depending on the wind. The ground gunners had plenty of time

to shoot—almost at their leisure. That flak certainly was thicker than anything seen near Hanoi.

"In this war, you don't float around within 50 miles or so of Hanoi. Even with external bombs our F-4's are traveling very near the speed of sound. When we roll in on the target, the North Vietnamese have to shoot quickly. The flak up north is said to be worse than Germany's because it is about ten times as accurate. The 85mm is much more numerous and accurate than the German 88's. For the exposure time, we get a much greater density of flak. Also, all targets are in a relatively condensed area. The enemy can afford the luxury of concentrating its defenses in known target areas because, geographically, he's small and doesn't have many major targets.

"Although North Vietnamese ground fire is not as thick as World War II's, it's worse in the sense that it's far more accurate and deadly. You get more thrown at you in a shorter span of time and it's thrown at you on every mission up around Hanoi—very impressive, indeed.

"The only way you can go into these heavily defended areas today and get out again is by executing a carefully prepared, well-coordinated plan that every man follows to the letter. You can deviate, but this takes ex-

NORTH VIETNAMESE FIGHTER PILOTS

Four North Vietnamese fighter pilots discuss tactics on an airfield near Hanoi. Flying Russian-built aircraft, the North Vietnamese pilots were uneven in piloting skill, but their top ace shot down thirteen American aircraft.

(Koku-Fan)

perience. Even if you were allowed to, you would not go in and make an armed reconnaissance on a road north of Hanoi or between Hanoi and Haiphong. This would be sheer stupidity. If you go in and strafe, you'd better be prepared for some pretty high losses. We lost many fighters doing just that in World War II. In North Vietnam, we don't operate that way.

"You see a MiG coming at you, so you want to ram full power and pull five G's in a turn away from him. But you don't do that because you could get zapped by a SAM. If you see a SAM and sort of split-S down to the grass, you're out of your ever-lovin' mind because the small arms fire can get you down there—where the SAM's are trying to force you. The SAM's are a terrible menace, but not a deadly menace and we have ways of evading them. If you get busted out of formation, you're terribly vulnerable. Two of our F-4's were shot down that way. But even if you do get broken off, your ECM (Electronic Countermeasures) gear will help you against the opposition, such as enemy gun-laying radars on the ground.

"In an area smaller than many of our states, the enemy has concentrated innumerable automatic weapons, more than 5,000 anti-aircraft guns, more than 200 SAM sites which have fired more than 5,000 SAM's, and a sizable MiG force. The bombing of the north forced him to develop a sophisticated and reasonably well-integrated air-defense system. We can jam his radar, which sights his guns and SAM's and tells his MiG's where we are at all times. But the less time we spend in his heavily defended areas, the less chance we take of getting clobbered. The problem is to achieve a balance between our capability to do the job and an acceptable survivability rate."

From first hand experience with both German and North Vietnamese pilots, General Olds makes the following comparison:

"The MiG pilots are a lot better than the average German pilot toward the end of World War II. They know their airplanes well and fly them well. When they're turned loose, they're very fierce competitors. More than competitors, they're downright dangerous. Sometimes, when they've forced us to jettison our bombs before reaching the target, we've had to go in and teach them a lesson or chase them out. But our basic job over there is to bomb targets, not chase MiG's. If they happen

to get in the way, so much the worse for them.

"The last dogfight score I recall was 110 MiG's downed to 48 U.S. airplanes. As of May 1967, when I shot down my third and fourth MiG's, 603 U.S. planes had gone down in North Vietnam. As of 24 September 1968, the total stood at 899.

"I could go up today in a P-51 and wrestle with those MiG's and they'd never touch me. But I might not touch them, either. So I get something much better than a MiG-17, like the F-4. But now I have to touch the 17 very carefully. If I try to fight this kind of fight, I'm in deep trouble. He's going to zap me."

On armament, General Olds has cogent comment:

"Air-to-air missiles gave our fighters a tremendous capability relative to the MiG-17, which carried only cannons and rockets. But fighting a MIG with a gunless F-4 is like fighting a guy with a dagger when he's got a sword, or maybe vice versa. A fighter without a gun, which is the most versatile air-to-air weapon, is like an airplane without a wing. Five or six times, when I had fired all my missiles, I might have been able to hit a MiG if I'd had cannon, because I was so close his motion was stopped in my gunsight.

"When we got the General Electric Vulcan M-61, which fires 6,000 20mm shells a minute, it turned out to be the greatest gun ever built for a fighter. It jammed very little. One of our exceptional pilots, Captain Darrel Simmons, shot down two MiG's with this Gatling in one day. He got them where he wanted them and just tapped the trigger twice for a total of 494 rounds. Of my 18 or more MiG scraps, the longest one was just 14 minutes. You have only a few seconds to fire in any MiG engagement, so I found our single Gatling's 6000 rounds per minute more than adequate. . . ."

The summation of General Olds' experience is probably the most pointed of all his comments in the remarkable *Horizons* article he wrote with editor Burnham Lewis:

"Perhaps the biggest lesson Clobber College over there taught us is that dogfighting today is surprisingly like our experiences in World War II and Korea. We found ourselves doing the things that people in the services swore would never be done again. Squadron formation, Colonel Olds? You're a romanticist. You're thinking in the past. You have to think in the future. As a matter of fact, you'll never dogfight again. You don't need a gun because you have missiles.

"These predictions, and some others, proved to be tactically unsound. We and the enemy advance along parallel lines. Basically, little has changed."

One thing that did change in Vietnam was the victory credits system. Since it took two men to fly the F-4 Phantom, a pilot and a RIO (Radar Intercept Officer), the decision was made by higher headquarters to credit both members of each crew with a victory when a downing was confirmed. Thus, an ace who had five victories, also had a RIO with five victories. This was a radical departure from the traditional "pilots only" qualifications for acedom.* Although not concerning himself in these comments with the business of scores and kill credits, Brigadier General Olds had this to say in *Horizons* regarding the GIBS (Guy in the Back Seat):

"When I first arrived in Thailand, I heard that some pilots flying F-4's down south wished they could do away with the guy in the

---

*The authors do not, however, classify the radar operator (or gunners, in WWI and WWII cases) as *fighter aces.* The RIO's and GIB's are credited with *assists, similar to the method used by the German Luftwaffe in WWII for the radar/gunners in the night fighters. The present USAF method would seemingly make thousands of B-17 and B-24 gunners "aces," if applied to that war.*

back seat and substitute extra fuel. But up north, in the enemy's backyard, that won't work. You need the backseater's extra eyes and total attention for operating your radar system. A one-place fighter is fine in your own backyard where our Air Defense Command F-106 interceptor pilots usually operate.

"In this permissive environment, they can make the interception, with that big square building on the ground doing a lot of the radar work for them. If an F-4 driver puts his head down in the cockpit to operate radar during an air-to-air scrap deep in enemy territory—he's dead.

"But for all around air superiority, permissive and non-permissive, I prefer a one-man crew. Microminiaturization of avionics should enable the lone pilot to manage all the controls and flip all the switches. Without a second crewman, he should be able to see much more behind him. The major fault of the F-4 is that it's a neckbreaker."

Combat following the general lines described by Brigadier General Olds did not produce a too-impressive overall kill ratio in favor of the U.S.A. The highly educated and thoroughly trained American pilots were not doing much better than three to one in a kill ratio over the MiG drivers. By April of 1968 the U.S. could claim only 110 MiG's downed.

(Koku-Fan)

TOP ENEMY ACE'S FIGHTER

MiG-17 fighter bearing number 3020 is believed to be the aircraft of Colonel Tomb, top-scoring enemy ace of the Vietnam War, with 13 kills over U.S. planes. Tomb flew both the MiG-17 and the MiG-21. Tomb is believed to have died in combat in the MiG-17 after an epic maneuvering battle with the U.S. Navy's Randy "Duke" Cunningham.

There still was no U.S. pilot ace.

Unhappy with this overall scene, the U.S. Navy took action. Captain Frank W. Ault was put in charge of an extensive analysis of Southeast Asian aerial combat through Naval Air Systems Command. The "Ault Report" as it became known, recommended several improvements. Chief of these was the need for expanded and intensified training in ACM (Air Combat Maneuvering). This was to be a post-graduate course in what Korean War ace Bob Love called "rat racing with your buddies" back in Chapter Nine. The Navy acted promptly on the Ault Report. The U.S. Navy Fighter Weapons School, soon known to the pilots as TOP GUN, was organized at Miramar Naval Air Station near San Diego, California. Training in ACM for qualified fighter crews was commenced.*

The Ault Report and the Navy had correctly understood the situation. Dogfighting wasn't dead. With the new missiles, the art of getting kills was the art of maneuver. Nobody could hope to get good at it without a great deal of practice against experts. The Navy insisted also that ACM training be beefed up in fleet fighter squadrons. The best crews emerging from this enhanced fleet ACM activity were sent to TOP GUN at Miramar NAS.

TOP GUN put these premier fighter crews through 75 hours of classroom work and 25 combat training flights, eventually extending the course to five weeks. The T-38 was used to simulate the MiG-21 and the A-4E simulated the MiG-17. The crews that passed through TOP GUN became in turn the resident experts in ACM with their own fleet fighter squadrons.

When aerial combat was renewed early in 1972, the effects of TOP GUN soon became obvious. The pre-bombing halt kill ratio for Navy fighters against the MiG's had been 3.7 to 1. After TOP GUN, the ratio ballooned to 13 to 1. Out of TOP GUN came the first pilot ace of the Vietnam War and the U.S. Navy's only pilot ace of the conflict—Lieutenant Randall "Duke" Cunningham.

Born in Los Angeles on the day after Pearl Harbor, Randy Cunningham is a strongly-motivated man of outstanding character, who exemplifies the new breed of supersonic

*The USAF also had an Air Combat Maneuvering training course but was forced to curtail it primarily because they were having so many accidents with the unstable F-4 Phantom.

fighter pilot. He was a highly-educated and broadly experienced young man before entering the Navy in 1967, holding a Master's Degree in Education from the University of Missouri. His searching, analytical mentality sent him plunging into every book available on combat flying—all the way back to World War I. When he departed the U.S.S. *Constellation* after his historic "five down" tour, he left behind a tall stack of such books and a well-thumbed NATROPS manual. He knew combat and he knew his weapons system.

With Lieutenant (j.g.) Willie Driscoll as his RIO, Cunningham brought down a MiG-21 on 19 January 1972. This was his first kill and the first Navy victory over the MiG's in about a year and a half. There was great jubilation when Cunningham returned to the *Constellation* with this particular kill. The drought was over.

Cunningham's second victory came right after the big North Vietnamese invasion of the south in May of 1972. Navy fighters were working around besieged An Loc, and Cunningham and Driscoll were flying MiG-CAP

(USN/Billy Mason)

FIRST AMERICAN ACE OF VIETNAM WAR:
US Navy Lt. Randall "Duke" Cunningham, left, and his radar intercept officer (RIO), Lt. William P. Driscoll, made up the first fighter crew to score five victories in the air over Vietnam. Here they are shown looking over an F-14 "Tomcat" model in the office of the Secretary of the Navy.

(Koku-Fan)

THIRTEEN AMERICAN KILLS

The thirteen victory stars on the nose of this MiG-21PF bespeak thirteen U.S.-flown aircraft downed by its pilot. Colonel Tomb, North Vietnamese ace was top ace of entire war before being shot down by the U.S. Navy's Randy Cunningham with Bill Driscoll as Weapons Systems Operator. This MiG-21 variant was capable of Mach 2 above 30,000 feet and carried Atoll Air-to-air missiles. Launch rails for the Atoll can be seen underwing.

for a strike against a training area for Red truck drivers. He nailed a MiG-17 with a Sidewinder missile and came very close to being nailed by the MiG driver's buddies. Cunningham and Driscoll had the always chilling experience of seeing tracer whizz past their canopy.

A great day came for Cunningham on 10 May 1972, with three confirmed MiG-17's during a strike on the railyards southeast of Hanoi. He not only made ace—America's and the Navy's first with this fifth kill—but put an end to the career of North Vietnam's top ace, Colonel Tomb. Randy Cunningham's own account of his fifth victory is presented here from Lou Drendel's book ". . . And Kill MiGS," published by Squadron Signal Publications, Inc. of Warren, Michigan 48091.

Aviation history enthusiasts anxious to know more detail of the Vietnam war as regards American aircraft and pilots can do no better than obtain Mr. Drendel's brilliantly illustrated books. His aviation war art is among the finest ever presented. From ". . . And Kill MiGS," here is Cunningham's account of the battle that made him an ace:

"I bored in on the 17 . . . head on. Suddenly his whole nose lit up like a Christmas tree! I had forgotten that the A-4's didn't shoot at you, but this guy was really spitting out the 23mm and 37mm! I pulled hard, up in the vertical, figuring that the MiG would keep right on going for home. I looked back and . . . there

was the MiG . . . canopy to canopy with me! He couldn't have been more than thirty feet away . . . I could see the pilot clearly . . . leather helmet, goggles, scarf . . . we were both going straight up, but I was outzooming him. He fell behind, and as I came over the top, he started shooting. I had given him a predictable flight path and he had taken advantage of it. The tracers were missing me, but not by much! I rolled out, and he pulled in right behind me.

"Now I don't know if its ego . . . you know, you don't like to admit that the other guy beat you . . . or what, but I said: 'That SOB is really lucky!' Anyway, I told Willie, 'Alright, we'll get this guy now!' I pulled down, and I was holding top rudder, trying to knuckle at the nose. As soon as I committed my nose, he pulled right into me! I thought, 'Oh-Oh, maybe this guy isn't just lucky after all!' I waited for his nose to commit, then I pulled up into him . . . that's a rolling scissors. Well, here's where my training came into play again. In training, I had fought against Dave Frost in the same situation, and I had learned that if he had his nose too high, I could snap down, using the one G of gravity to advantage, and run out to his six o'clock. I would be a mile, a mile and a half out of range before he could get turned around. This is just what happened. We separated, turned around, and engaged again. Same thing. Up into a rolling scissors . . . advantage, disadvantage . . . ad-

333

vantage. . . disadvantage. . . disadvantage. . . disengaged, came back, engaged again, and went up in the vertical again. This is one of the very few MiG's that ever fought in the vertical. They like to fight in the horizontal. We kept engaging, and I never could get enough advantage on him to get a shot . . . everything my airplane did, he reacted to instinctively.

"He was flying damn good airplane! Well he kept at it, with me outzooming him in the vertical, and him shooting every time I got out in front. I thought, 'He's going to get lucky one of these times!'

"The next time we started up in the vertical, an idea came to me . . . I don't know why . . . your mind just works overtime in a situation like that . . . anyway, as we're going up, I went to idle and speed brakes . . . and he shot out in front of me! I think it really surprised him . . . being out in front for the first time. Anyway, we're both going straight up and losing speed fast. I was down to 150 knots and I knew I was going to have to go to full burner to hold it. I did, and we both pitched over the top. As he came over, I used rudder to get the airplane to turn to his belly side. He lost lift coming over the top and, I think, departed the airplane a little bit. I thought, 'This is no place to be with a MiG-17 . . . at 150 knots . . . that slow . . . he can take it right away from you.' But he had stayed too long. He was low on fuel, and I think he decided to run. He

pitched over the top and started straight down. I went after him and, though I didn't think the Sidewinder would guide straight down with all the heat of the ground to look at, I squeezed one off anyway.

"The missile came off the rail and went to his airplane. There was just a little flash, and I thought, 'God, it missed him!' I started to fire my last Sidewinder and suddenly . . . a big flash of flame and black smoke erupted from his airplane. He didn't seem to go out of control, but he flew straight down into the ground. He didn't get out."

This marked the demise of Colonel Tomb, top-scoring ace of the whole Vietnam War. Intelligence sources knew it was Tomb, but the precise means by which this knowledge was obtained remains classified—as does so much else about the Vietnam air war. On the way back to the carrier, America's first pilot ace since Korea ran afoul of a SAM, and he and Driscoll ditched in the Gulf of Tonkin. Marine helicopters plucked the triumphant pair—drenched but delighted—from the water and upon their return to the *Constellation* there was great rejoicing.

A firm believer in the team concept while yet an outstanding individual, Cunningham later became a TOP GUN instructor—along with his RIO Willie Driscoll. He is the kind of man who will continue to studiously research everything he can about aerial com-

DEATH OF A MOST CAPABLE ENEMY: MiG-21 believed to have been piloted by the top North Vietnamese fighter ace, Colonel Tomb, takes fatal hits.

(USN)

bat. An ace and an accomplished teacher, Cunningham will now be finding himself in all those revised ace books he will study, perhaps to guide a new generation of ace fighter pilots serving the U.S.A.

In the classic mold of an American hero is the first USAF pilot ace of the Vietnam war, Captain Richard S. (Steve) Ritchie. He made his "five down" on 28 August 1972, and is the only other pilot ace besides Cunningham since Korea. His career has another parallel to Cunningham's. Ritchie was the youngest-ever instructor at the USAF Fighter Weapons School in 1969—something that gave him a background similar to that bestowed by TOP GUN training.

A graduate of the Air Force Academy (Class of '64), Ritchie was born in Reidsville, North Carolina, on 25 June 1942. His fifth victory involved some tense moments in a closing situation head-on with two elusive MiG's. All five of Ritchie's kills were against the MiG-21, and he was the only pilot in Vietnam to down five of these aircraft. On this occasion, the MiG driver zigged when he should have zagged, with disastrous consequences.

Ritchie was flying MiG-CAP when a radar picket ship off the coast reported two bandits airborne, obviously attempting to intercept the strike force. Turning west in response, Ritchie was appalled by the most massive thunderhead he'd ever seen—dead ahead. Skirting the monster brought the flight over a heavy SAM and flak area, but the Red gunners stayed mercifully silent.

The picket ship then reported that the bandits had turned back towards Hanoi, two flights of Phantoms hounding them far astern. This meant they would be coming straight at Ritchie—40 miles distant and closing fast.

At a rate of 1200 mph the distance was rapidly devoured, and after a radar lock-on by the man in the back seat, Ritchie knew he had to get a visual fix quickly or miss his chance. With four kills and two tours of duty as a fighter pilot, he knew the blinding swiftness of opportunity in jet combat. Now you have it— gone in a flash.

Ritchie's eagle vision scanned the sky. His Phantom in full afterburner, the young American climbed and turned toward the blip on his back seat man's scope. "3½, 3, 2½ miles . . ." The RIO tolled them off. Ritchie caught sight of the enemy bird, and tightened his left turn as far as it would go. G forces

sucked savagely on the body of the man who would be an ace.

Ritchie fired two Sparrow missiles, and almost as they left the rails came the shout of his back-seat man "Out of range . . ." Firing was one of those split-second calculated risks. If the MiG had turned into him, he would have had a kill. Overtaking in the 6 o'clock position now, the range was right. Off went the last two Sparrows. The now-distant MiG slid into a thin overcast as the seconds ticked away. Then the MiG emerged from the haze, and as the enemy plane did so, one Sparrow whooshed past him to his left. The MiG driver hauled hard right, and flew directly into the other Sparrow. A surging fireball consumed the MiG. The man from North Carolina had become the USAF's first Vietnam ace.

Ritchie resigned from the USAF in order to pursue a career in public life. He made an unsuccessful run for Congress, but will undoubtedly be heard from again politically in due course. His natural patriotism got a massive boost during his service in Southeast Asia. He never forgot how his own glories depended upon the host of dedicated people who supported him as a combat pilot. As he told Walt Hern in a 1976 interview for *Talon*, the Cadet Magazine of the Air Force Academy:

"The downing of five MiG-21 aircraft was the result of the efforts of many, many, brave and dedicated people. I was in the right place at the right time. I survived, everything worked—and I am very proud to have received much of the credit which belongs to so many others. There are many fighter pilots who could have done the same thing I did, but I had a unique opportunity in the combat arena. And there were three keys to our success when given that opportunity.

"These were preparation, teamwork and discipline. The average MiG battle over Hanoi took place in sixty seconds or less. In an instant of time everything a fighter pilot had worked for, trained for, studied and learned for over a period of five, ten, fifteen or twenty years, had to come together, and work—in an instant of time. He had to be prepared.

"Teamwork was essential to that mission and it was a tremendous team effort—front and back seat in the airplane, the eight guys in the flight of four, the two-hundred men in the strike force, the refuelling tankers and all the rest. Some two hundred people were directly

involved in the launch and recovery of a flight of F-4's, and there were hundreds more who were indirectly involved. Had it not been for these people who were proud of their work and performed it in a professional and outstanding manner, I would not be a Fighter Ace. I probably wouldn't be alive, and I am very grateful."

Steve Ritchie left his mark in history, but he may yet make a larger one. A dedicated advocate of the free enterprise system, he has stumped the U.S.A., impressing on his fellow Americans how much they have to lose if they do not awaken to trends of decadence already far advanced in the land of the free and the brave. He is President of the Combat Pilots' Association, and wears the mantle of ace and hero with great dignity and pride.

The top scoring RIO of Vietnam was a Radar Intercept Officer, Captain Charles DeBellevue, who was Steve Ritchie's GIBS. DeBellevue was GIBS on six MiG kills, thereby topping in the credits both Duke Cun-

ningham and Steve Ritchie, the only two pilots to make ace in Vietnam.

Much about weapons, tactics and technical apparatus used in the Vietnam conflict remains under military security. This is likely to hold true for many years to come. The world remains unsettled, with armed conflict breaking out periodically and always holding the possibility of widening hostilities. As to what was learned in fighter aviation for the price that was paid, history would teach us only that we learn but little from history. Hardly a cost-effective arrangement.

The services did learn how to improve the capabilities of trained fighter pilots. TOP GUN was worth every dime of its cost, and it appears to be a permanent part of the Navy's approach. That the USAF's only ace, Steve Ritchie, was the youngest instructor at the USAF's Fighter Weapons School and learned his business by teaching others and through endless practice, was not lost on the USAF. Vietnam also taught the theorists that the Red Baron wasn't dead after all—just dozing.

JAPAN'S AIR SELF DEFENSE FORCE (JASDF):
A few years after WWII ended, Japan was allowed to build up a self defense military force. They revived their aircraft manufacturing capabilities by contracting with American industry and building American war items. This photo shows some of hundred-plus Lockheed F-104 Starfighters now being flown by Japanese pilots. F-104s were used in the Vietnam War whenever the MiG-21s began to oppose the USAF F-105s and F-4s during the early days of the war.   (Japan Self Defence Force photo)

Fighter Aces of Vietnam

(USAF)

(USAF)

THE FIRST TEAM!
28 August 1972, pilot Steve Ritchie and WSO Chuck DeBellevue flank their F4 crew Chief Sgt. Reggie Taylor Reason for the big smiles....the fifth victory for the team.

THE THRILL OF VICTORY....
Winners of a duel where the loser most likely will lose his life, the relief and smile of success beam from the faces of WSO Captain Chuck DeBellevue and pilot Captain Richard Steve Ritchie.

(USAF)

337

Captain Richard Stephen Ritchie, USAF (5.0) Vietnam
The USA produced but two fighter pilot aces in the Vietnam War, Duke Cunningham of the Navy and Steve Ritchie of the USAF. Ritchie, from Reidsville, North Carolina but now living in Golden, Colorado, flew with the 366th Tactical Fighter Wing in Vietnam in 1968 and after a stint at Nellis AFB as an instructor in the Fighter Weapons School, returned to Vietnam with the 555th T.F. Wing and shot down five MiG-21 aircraft in the span of three and one-half months.

(USAF)

(USAF)
Captain Steve Ritchie on 28 August 1972

(USAF via J. R. Beaman, Jr.)

NEW FIGHTER ACE!
Captain Steve Ritchief, USAF, front cockpit, and Captain Chuck DeBellevue (WSO emerging from the rear cockpit) smile flushed with success after scoring their fifth team-work aerial victory over North Vietnam. Holding Ritchie's helmet while standing on the ladder, is that all-important third man of the modern fighter team, crew chief Sgt. Reginald Taylor.

555TH FIGHTER SQUADRON PLANES IN ARMING AREA:
USAF photographer Sgt. C.F. Stutts shot this picture showing five F4 Phantoms having their weapons armed just before takeoff in Vietnam. Ace Steve Ritchie's combat flight was known as "Buick Flight" and included some of the best of the USAF fighter pilots and WSOs, such as Don Binkley, Bill Graham, Mike Francisco, Gary Shoulders, John Madden, Chuck DeBellvue and Larry Petit. (USAF)

338

(McDonnell Douglas Photo)

(USN)

FIRST AMERICAN ACE OF THE VIETNAM WAR

Lieutenant Randy "Duke" Cunningham (right) of the U.S. Navy was the first American pilot ace of the Vietnam conflict. With Lieutenant (j.g.) Willie Driscoll as his Weapons Systems Officer — seen here in the back seat of their Phantom jet — Cunningham shot down North Vietnam's top ace on 10 May 1972 to become an ace himself. Cunningham and Driscoll are both credited with five aerial victories.

TWO FIGHTER TEAMS POSE AFTER THEIR FIRST VICTORIES:

Photographer Stutts made this photo showing Captain S.L. Eaves, weapons system operator, and his pilot, Lt. J.D. Markle, with Captain Charles D. DeBellevue, weapons system operator, and his pilot, Captain Steve Ritchie, on 10 May 1972 shortly after both teams had scored their first aerial victories.

(USAF)

Combat Over the English Channel

A Messerschmitt 109 of the Luftwaffe has just shot down an RAF Spitfire, whose wingtip can be seen digging into the water. Engrossed in observing the crash, the Luftwaffe pilot forgot about the victim's wingman, whose bullets can be seen striking in the 109's wingroots. In background, the cliffs of Dover.

(Drawing by George Lucas, Nunda, N.Y.)

11

THE
ENEMY ACES

America's fighter aces won their laurels against skilled and determined foes. The Americans were made to fly and fight hard for their glories. An overview of American acedom would be incomplete without some record of the men they flew against, especially in World War II, the period of greatest engagement in aerial warfare.

Famous German aces of World War I have been well described in scores of books. Their names are etched in history. Suffice it to say of them here that when the Americans finally got into action in their own units in 1918, they faced an experienced and highly capable foe mounted on better aircraft than their own. The raw Americans did remarkably well against this seasoned opposition.

Still improving at war's end, the Americans had rolled up a solid ratio of victories to losses. Experience had added its weight to good training and natural ability. History has written the record, including the famous German names against whom the Americans flew. Perhaps the most famous German ace was Hermann Goering—later to become founder of the World War II Luftwaffe. Only the "Red Baron," Manfred von Richthofen, was better known after WWI.

World War I's open history book was not repeated in World War II, due to wartime security and propaganda policies. Little mention appeared in wartime of the Germans or Japanese in any human context. The Japanese were depicted as being almost sub-human. This dehumanization was characteristic of World War II, and resulted in an astounding lack of historical information about enemy combat pilots.

American aces hardly ever knew the name of an enemy ace during World War II. Propaganda policies resulted in the fighter aces of the warring powers knowing little or nothing about each other, even decades after the shooting stopped. There were a few notable exceptions, such as the wartime reputation of Germany's Adolf Galland, but otherwise America's aces fought against faceless enemies.

Japanese military custom reinforced this anonymity. Japanese tradition could allow only dead heroes. Death was more cherished than life. Dying well was heavily emphasized, with medals awarded only at the close of wars or episodes of armed conflict, or upon the death of the warrior. Exemplifying the Japanese exaltation of death was their promotion of dead pilots one rank poshumously. Distinguished pilots and kamikaze drivers were promoted two ranks.

Publicity for the aerial victories of their leading aces was unthinkable to the Japanese military caste of the World War II epoch, and so was any special recognition within the service. Only on the eve of Japan's collapse in 1945 was a special citation announced for two air fighters, Soichi Sugita with eighty victories, and Saburo Sakai with sixty-four. Sakai is today the most successful living Japanese fighter pilot.

Japan's rigid system saw the Japanese pilots fight through most of the war in non-commissioned rank. The commissioning of Saburo Sakai—after sixty aerial victories and eleven years as a combat pilot—set a record for rapid promotion! Such combat achievements in the U.S. Navy would have assured a pilot of rapid advancement.

These Japanese restrictions united with the wartime Allied propaganda policies to leave the Japanese fighter pilots in almost total obscurity. They were as little known in their own country as they were in Allied lands. History now lifts the veil of the past.

The Japanese were flying aerial combat over the Asian mainland for a decade before World War II. Scant attention was paid in Western countries to these aerial battles or their lessons. Fierce border battles were conducted with Soviet forces in the nineteen thirties that were rehearsals for World War II.

Between May and September of 1939, a full-scale war raged along the border of Manchukuo and Mongolia. Hundreds of aircraft milled in combat above infantry and armored divisions of the new epoch. This aerial warfare eclipsed World War I in scope and ferocity. Between 22 and 26 June 1939, the Japanese Army Air Force (JAAF) claimed 88 Russian planes downed. The Russians on 27 June 1939 hurled more than 200 aircraft at the Japanese in an effort at aerial mastery. Approximately 150 Japanese aircraft met the onslaught. In the greatest aerial battle in history up to that time, the JAAF claimed more than 90 victories.

Japanese aces of this hidden war quicky excelled the new generation of German pilots who had fought in Spain. Sergeant-Major Hiromichi Shinohara scored over 50 kills against the Russians. He was nicknamed the "Richthofen of the Orient," and exemplified the invaluable cadre of high quality fighter pilots produced by these border wars. They were unrivalled in their experience of modern aerial warfare. No wonder they stunned the Americans with their expertise in the first days after Pearl Harbor. They had become experts in practicing on the Russians!

Veteran Japanese aces of Manchukuo in some cases became aces a second time in World War II, battling the Americans. Among the JAAF aces who are credited with this feat are:

Lieutenant Colonel Tateo Kato
Major Saburo Togo
Warrant Officer Katsuaki Kira
Second Lieutenant Chiyoji Saito

The Imperial Japanese Navy (IJN) also produced aces before World War II who repeated the feat against American pilots. Among them was Sub-Lieutenant Tetsuzo Iwamoto, with 14 kills the top-ranked Japanese Navy ace of the prewar period. He became Japan's greatest ace in World War II. Other IJN aces from China were:

Ensign Kaneyoshi Muto (5 kills China, 28 kills in WWII)
Sub-Lieutenant Sadaaki Akamatsu (11 kills China, 27 in WWII)
Petty Officer 1/C Masayuki Nakase (9 kills China, 18 in WWII)
Ensign Kuniyoshi Tanaka (12 kills China, 17 in WWII)

The obscurity of the Japanese aces has been also due to non-availability of authoritative records. The Japanese themselves destroyed many of these documents in the final days of the war. Their expectation was that the avenging Americans would declare any pilot who had shot down an American aircraft a war criminal.

Orders were issued two days before the surrender by HQ to all units, directing them to destroy all military records. Pilots were advised to destroy their flight logbooks, uniforms, photographs and any other "incriminating" material. There was general obedience to this order. The consequent lack of documentation has greatly complicated the work of Japanese and American historians.

Since less than ten percent of Japanese fighter pilots survived the war, there are gaps in documentation that have no counterpart elsewhere in fighter aviation history. Possibly half of the fighter pilots who survived went underground. Disgraced by surrender after losing the war, their ancestry blighted under the codes of *bushido*, they disappeared into new identities.

Surfacing now after some thirty years, some of these men have returned to their homes and families. Among them are pilots who buried their records and souvenirs rather than destroy them, and this priceless material has been exhumed and examined. A void in aviation history is now being filled.

The order to destroy all records has complicated the Japanese victory credits system, which was inconsistently applied during the war. After keeping records on each fighter pilot in 1941 and 1942, higher headquarters decided in 1943 to block decisively any search for personal glory and aggrandizement. Individual credits for downings were thereafter prohibited, and victories were credited to squadrons and groups.

Pilots accepted this ruling, but secretly kept records and diaries. Some maintained secret logbooks. Much of this clandestine record is now becoming available, fleshing out the stories of the most successful fighter aces of the Pacific war.

The top fighter ace of Japan does not enjoy the certain, solid status of America's Dick Bong. For more than thirty years, Warrant Officer Hiroshi Nishizawa of the Japanese Naval Air Arm was generally recognized as the top Japanese ace. He has been credited with 103 victories, but as more diaries and records appear—together with eyewitness accounts—there is doubt that Nishizawa is Japan's top fighter hero.

Sharing honors with Nishizawa nowadays is Sub-Lieutenant Tetsuzo Iwamoto, also of the IJN. His diary records 202 victories, a compilation that has been partially documented and calculated at both 102 and 86. These figures have just as much statistical and historical validity—at the present time—as the 150 kills attributed to Nishizawa in wartime newspapers, the 147 kills Nishizawa claimed in a letter to his parents, or the 86 kills Nishizawa claimed in a conversation with his C.O., Lieutenant Commander H. Okamoto, just three days before his death.

Whatever the final statistical record may be, the current evidence supports Iwamoto's claims more soundly than those of Nishizawa. Supporting reports show that Iwamoto scored 142 victories over Rabaul alone. Iwamoto's C.O. at Rabaul and elsewhere after the beginning of 1944 was Navy Captain Takeo Shibata, who now lives in Matsuda City, Chiba Prefecture, Japan. He believes that

(Izawa collection)

JAPAN'S NO. 1 ACE, NAVY LT. TETSUZO IWAMOTO (94 to 188)

In eight years of combat (China and WWII) Iwamoto claimed 216 victories and another 22 probables. However, his 202 claimed in WWII included shared kills and historians have been unable to document several claims made dropping aerial-burst bombs on American formations. It appears likely that Iwamoto scored 188 victories in WWII plus 14 in China for a total of 202.

(Izawa collection)

JAPAN'S NO. 2 ACE, WARRANT OFFICER HIROSHI NISHIZAWA

Nishizawa claimed 200 WWII victories plus another 20 probables. A review of his claims for July 15, 1943 over Rubiana Islands, for July 25 and August 4, 1943 over Rendova Islands, and for October 24, 1943 over Rabaul cannot be documented at this time. It appears Nishizawa had approximately 190 total victories and since these were all during WWII he would be Japan's top ace of that war, but Iwamoto appears to be Japan's top ace of all wars.

Iwamoto claimed 142 in the Rabaul period, plus 60 while flying off the carrier Zuikaku in the Indian Ocean, the Coral Sea and in Japan, Okinawa and Formosa. Combined with his 14 prewar kills in China, Iwamoto's potential total reached 216 victories.

Japanese historians today, and Captain Shibata, conservatively divide their fighter pilots' scores by two, crediting Iwamoto with 101 in World War II and 115 in his lifetime. Captain Shibata remembers Iwamoto well, since he had a certain affinity for the gifted sharpshooter. A graduate of the Japanese Naval Academy (1924), Captain Shibata contributes these reminiscences of Iwamoto:

"He was an excellent pilot, in general flight as well as in combat. He was a loner to some extent, but an unusually fine combat leader. He was trustworthy, a man of his word, but intolerant of others' mistakes in combat situations. In other situations he was more tolerant, and thoughtful of everyone.

"He was a proud and impulsive man, yet reserved and not cocky at all. Many of the other pilots did not like him, but that was because he was a disciplinarian and harsh in his criticism of others' mistakes.

"Iwamoto was just, and insisted his men be treated fairly. He liked to drink, too, and usually when drinking would fall asleep meekly. He was a man of firm character and strong convictions, and therefore contrasted sharply with the careerist types who unquestioningly do the bidding of superior officers."

Tetsuzo Iwamoto was born on 14 June 1916, and enlisted in the IJN, which trained him as a pilot. Iwamoto graduated with the 34th Training Program in December 1936. Assigned to Number 12 Fighter Group in China in February 1938, Iwamoto demonstrated his gifts by downing four Chinese-flown Russian aircraft on his first encounter in the air. A fifth probable victory in this battle was never confirmed. Iwamoto's self-confidence soared, and supported all his successes in the next seven and a half years of war.

The Americans who fought this remarkable combat pilot were battling one of the world's best. His destruction of over 100 American-flown aircraft is a feat that only he and Nishizawa could claim. Iwamoto survived the war, but died 20 May 1955 from septicemia at the age of 38. Ill health had plagued him for years, a legacy from wartime bouts with dysentery and malaria, and an American bullet in his back caused him misery until it was surgically removed. Iwamoto's full biography will appear shortly from the pen of co-author Raymond Toliver, under the title *Fighter Ace of Japan—Iwamoto.*

Until the discovery of the Iwamoto diaries, Hiroshi Nishizawa was thought to be the top ace of Japan. Born in 1920 in Nagano Prefecture, he enlisted in the IJN in 1936, graduating from flight training school in October 1941. Nishizawa's first victory was near Rabaul on 3 February 1942. Transferred to the Tainan Air Corps in April 1942, he fought in New Guinea and the Solomons until November, amassing 30 victories over the Americans. Six months were spent back in Japan training with a new unit, after which Nishizawa was back in Rabaul with the 253rd Fighter Group. His American foes over Guadalcanal and surrounding areas included U.S. Navy and Marine Corps aces whose stories are told earlier in this book.

Nicknamed "The Devil" by his fellow pilots, Nishizawa had a demonic style of flying and fighting. He could make the Zero do his bidding in the air as could no other Japanese combat pilot. His fierce will seemed to infuse itself through the whole aircraft, so that in his hands the machine could transcend its design limits. Hardened Zero pilots found themselves enthralled to the point of rapture by the unmatched vigor of his aerobatic flying.

Nishizawa was riddled with tropical diseases and often racked with dysentery. Big for a Japanese at five feet eight inches, the cadaverous-looking Nishizawa was a withdrawn, aloof and reserved man, who avoided the society of his fellow pilots. His constant sickness enhanced these introversions. The ailing Nishizawa was nevertheless galvanized by the call to scramble. His infirmities fell from him like a cloak as he sprang into his Zero, and once aloft his legendary vision and fighting skill showed no evidence of his sickness. On two occasions, Nishizawa was credited with 15 victories, the first time on 15 July 1943 over Rubiana Island and the second on 4 August 1943 over Rendova Island.

He wasn't mounted on a Zero on 26 October 1944. Nishizawa was flying a lumbering twin-engined transport, loaded with fighter pilots, to pick up some Zeros at Clark Field in the Philippines. U.S. Navy Hellcats intercepted the transport, and even the invincible Nishizawa's skills were useless. The life of

"The Devil" ended in a fiery crash.

Contemporary historians of eminence in Japan are Ikuhiko Hata and Yasuho Izawa, who have been researching the Japanese fighter aces for years. They are considered to be the most knowledgeable historians on the subject. Feeling that large claims of Japanese aces would be deemed exaggerated when compared with U.S. claims of Japanese downings in the same war theater, they instituted a drastic statistical formula. Hata and Izawa *divide Japanese claims by two!* In the absence of firm substantiation they simply regard aces' claims as being inflated by a whopping fifty percent.

The reasons for the relatively low scores of the American aces in the Pacific may be summarized thus:

1. Relative rarity of available targets. Many American pilots flew over 50 missions without ever seeing a Japanese aircraft.

2. American aces were rotated out of combat almost as soon as their scores became noteworthy, Bong and Foss being two examples.

3. The Japanese were presented with hordes of targets. As American superiority mounted, Japanese opportunities increased.

4. Japanese aces flew many more combat missions than their American counterparts, stayed in action longer and were not rotated out of combat for morale or similar purposes.

Large scores in acedom have always been linked to abundant opportunities. Had the Japanese put as many aircraft into the Rabaul area as the Americans, for example, there would undoubtedly have been many U.S. aces with more than 60 victories, had some of the more brilliant Americans been permitted to continue in combat by their higher commanders. American leaders appreciated that as the exposure rate of a fighter pilot increased, so did his chances of being downed, and they wanted to keep their aces alive. History endorses their wisdom: 90 percent of the Japanese aces were killed, and 90 percent of America's aces survived. The high scores of the Japanese were paid for by ceaseless operational activity, and with the ultimate coin—the ace's life.

Ranked third among Japan's aces was Petty

(Izawa collection)

JAPAN'S NO. 3 ACE, SHOICHI SUGITA (70-140) Navy Petty Officer First Class (PO/1c) Sugita claimed first victory 1 Dec 1942 when he rammed a B-17 over Buin. KIA on takeoff from Kanoya, Kyushu on 15 April 1945 by US Navy fighters.

Officer First Class Shoichi Sugita, credited with at least 70 victories under the ultra-conservative Hata/Izawa statistics. Sugita fought right through to the final months, and his commanders say that he had at least 140 confirmed victories. He was taking off in his Shiden (Lightning) fighter from an airfield at Kanoya, attempting to intercept an American fighter sweep, when he was strafed on the runway. His aircraft became his funeral pyre.

The greatest living Japanese ace is Saburo Sakai, a lieutenant at war's end and one of the bravest men who ever flew under any flag. Sakai started in China with two victories, and fought to the end in 1945, with 64 kills credited. His war career contains episodes that border on the incredible, and include a 600-mile fight from Guadalcanal to Rabaul after running afoul American SBD's. Sakai was nearly blind and half paralyzed, but he got home.

Recovering from his wounds, and minus his right eye, he returned to the shambles aloft. On the eve of Japan's surrender, he took up a Zero *at night* and shot down a U.S. B-29. He attributes his survival to the poor air-to-air

NAVY LT(JG) SABURO SAKAI (64)
Sakai, best known of the few Japanese aces still living, claims 64 aerial victories. Japanese historians, applying the "divided-by-two" rule, credit him with 32 to 64. Sakai scored two kills in China in 1938. This photo made of Sakai in Hankow, China in 1938. (Izawa collection)

shooting of a number of American pilots, each of whom had him cold during his four combat years in the Pacific. Sakai's story has been vividly told in *Samurai*, the book he wrote with Fred Saito and the distinguished American aviation historian, Martin Caidin.

Lieutenant Naoshi Kanno of the IJN was a fighter ace who specialized in attacking the B-17, an aircraft whose defensive firepower terrified many Japanese pilots. Kanno's score is variously estimated at from 25 to 52 victories, and includes twelve B-17's. Kanno perfected early in the South Pacific the same diving and rolling attack from dead ahead later employed by the Germans against the B-17. He was shot down and killed on 1 August 1945 in the final defense of Japan.

Japanese fighter aces had at least one surpassing character in their ranks, Sub-Lieutenant Sadaaki Akamatsu of the IJN. His superiors regarded him as incorrigible. The young ladies of Japan adored him as a hero.

His fellow pilots found Akamatsu a flying enigma—a rule breaker and risk taker who nevertheless amassed between 38 and 65 victories in his career. Akamatsu disregarded regulations in an outrageous affront to the rigidity of the IJN. He declined to attend pilot briefings. Orders were sent to him by runner or telephone to the joy house of his choice. At takeoff time he would come steaming on the airfield in an ancient car, waving a sake bottle and yelling like a banshee. Akamatsu was repeatedly broken in rank, and still was a sub-lieutenant ten years after he was commissioned.

His combat achievements won him latitude from his superiors. Aloft he was superb, even downing Mustangs and Hellcats while flying the tricky Raiden fighter that could easily be out-turned by the American machines. The 400 mph Raiden was developed to tackle the B-29, and was not considered a match for the nimble Mustang. Akamatsu is known to have

NAVY LT(JG) SADAAKI AKAMATSU, (27 to 54): Akamatsu at left, cut his combat teeth over China in 1938, scoring 11 victories. An old head of 31 when WWII started, Akamatsu fought in the Philippines, East Indies, Calcutta and over Japan. He was one of the most successful Raiden pilots.

(Shigema Tokutomi via Izawa)

downed at least ten Mustangs and Hellcats.

Akamatsu went all the way from China to 1945. A double ace in China with 11 kills, he also survived the big war through skill and luck. He is one of the few Japanese aces to survive and stay above ground, as a restaurateur in Kochi, Japan.

The daring and aggressive Warrant Officer Kinsuke Muto of the IJN hacked down at least four of the massive B-29 bombers. Another ace from the China period, Muto was one of the few Japanese pilots to gain multiple kills over the American giant. Credited with well over 20 kills by 1945, Muto had also reached the rank of Ensign, almost six years after he became an ace.

Twelve F6F Hellcats winging in to strafe Tokyo in February of 1945 were challenged by the lone Muto in an obsolescent Zero. He gave the Americans a flying and shooting lesson. Four Hellcats went down despite the odds in this blistering engagement, and Navy records show that these were the only losses over Tokyo that day. The remaining American pilots knew they had run into a honcho.

The Zero in its later variants was outclassed by the American fighters pressing in on Japan. Muto kept flying the Zero until June, and managed to keep getting kills. He lost his life attacking a Liberator on 24 July 1945, failing to survive the war by a few weeks. His score is set between 28 and 60 victories, including his first five kills in China.

Japanese confirmation rules for aerial victories were similar to the Allies, but were loosely applied and subject to inconsistent policies. To minimize weight, they did not carry gun cameras in their Zeros. There is nevertheless little evidence of false claiming. Since no medals or promotions were given for fighter pilot prowess, there was no motive for inflating totals.

The Japanese had many successful aces whose names are virtually unknown even in their homeland. Some typical JAAF aces are:

Warrant Officer Hiromichi Shinohara—58
Master Sergeant Satoshi Anabuki—39
Lieutenant Mitsuyoshi Tarui—38
Warrant Officer Isamu Sasaki—38
Major Yasuhiko Kuroe—30

The Japanese Navy produced the three top fighter aces of Japan—Iwamoto, Nishizawa and Sugita—as well as a host of lesser-scoring pilots, as typified by:

Warrant Officer Takeo Okumura—50 plus 4 in China
Warrant Officer Toshio Ohta—34
Warrant Officer Shizuo Ishii—29 plus 3 in China
Lt. Commander Jun-ichi Sasai—27
Petty Officer First Class Masajiro Kawato —18

(Izawa Collection)

TOP ACE OF NOMOHAN INCIDENT IN CHINA: 2nd Lt. Hiromichi Shinohara, Japanese Army Air Force, scored 58 victories in Manchuria between 27 May 1939 and his death in combat on 27 August 1939.

M/SGT. SATOSHI ANABUKI (39-78)
Army M/Sgt. Anabuki survived WWII and served in the new Self Defense Force until retirement recently.

(Izawa collection)

347

(Y. Abe collection)

The last-mentioned Japanese ace made a new life for himself as an immigrant to the U.S.A. Now "Mike" Kawato, he flew a Bicentennial Memorial Flight between 10 August and 7 September 1976—a solo journey from Seattle to Tokyo via Honolulu and Wake Island. He then flew non-stop from Tokyo to Crescent City, California in 35 hours and 15 minutes—a new world record for non-stop flight by light planes.

Kawato dedicated his solo, single-engined odyssey to the "aviators from the U.S.A. and Japan who served in the Pacific during World

TOP JAPANESE ACE DURING TRAINING DAYS:
Cadet Tetsuzo Iwamoto, seated right front and grinning broadly, loved all phases of flying and developed into the finest combat pilot in the Japanese Navy. This photo taken in 1936. Aircraft is a Type 90 fighter, quite similar to the USAF Boeing P-12.

(Ryoji Ohhara collection)

JAPANESE NAVY ACES IN THE SOLOMONS
Six Navy pilots pose late in 1942. In the center of the back row is NCO Shoichi Sugita (70 to 140 victories). Front row: NCO Ryoji Ohhara (16-32), Munichi Ohshoya, and NCO Yoshio Nakamura (9-18).

War II, with special thanks to the aviation pioneers from both nations who tried in the past to conquer the Tokyo-U.S.A. route. Their courage and spiritual guidance helped me to succeed."

The scores and this overview should give an idea of the redoubtable foe faced by the American aces in the Pacific. The Japanese fighter aces emerge now from the shadows of history, and stand without shame or dishonor beside their counterparts in all nations who fought for the skies.

EARLY DAYS OF WWII ON TAINAN:
Ensign Susumu Ishihara, center, a flight leader in the Navy stationed at Tainan, poses with fellow fighter pilots shortly after the war began in 1941. Ishihara survived the war, scored a total of 16 to 32 aerial victories and was killed in an aircraft accident several years after the war.

(Ishihara via Izawa

(Izawa collection)

TUNING UP FOR WORLD WAR II
First Squadron of the 11th Sentai in Manchuria, 1939. Capt. Bunji Shimada, seated, poses with pilots of his unit. Shimada scored 27 victories before crashing on 15 September 1939. WO Bunji Yoshiyama, center holding pistol, scored 20. Capt. Tomoari Hasegawa, fourth from right, had 19 in Manchuria plus three in WWII, and Lt. Hiromichi Shinohara, far right, was top scorer in the Nomohan Incident with 58.

Most American pilots who flew both in Europe and in the Pacific in World War II consider the Germans to have been superior to the Japanese. Some who flew longest over Europe consider the Luftwaffe fighter aces the best pilots of World War II—bar none. The statistical record supports this estimate.

The top ten Luftwaffe aces between them destroyed 2,588 Allied aircraft, a staggering figure unhappily received on the Allied side. The sheer magnitude of this achievement—viewed against the scores of the Allied aces—certainly invites skepticism. Objective investigation of German scoring procedures by the authors, however, leaves no doubt that the Germans were rigid in their procedures and strict in their kill confirmation rules. "No witness—no kill" was the unwavering Luftwaffe requirement.

The names of Germany's great World War II aces, with perhaps a few exceptions like Adolf Galland and Werner Moelders, were unknown outside Germany even a decade after World War II. Germany's leading ace of the conflict, Colonel Erich Hartmann, downed 352 enemy aircraft, or more than four times as many as von Richthofen in the First World War. Until the authors presented Hartmann's official biography, *The Blond Knight of Germany,* in 1970, he was virtually unknown outside Germany. The German translation of this book entitled *Holt Hartmann vom Himmel!* has even been the major source of information on Hartmann within his own country.

The authors were also the first historians in the English-speaking world to provide a comprehensive review of the Luftwaffe fighter force and its leading personalities. Their currently available book, *Fighter Aces of the Luftwaffe* (Aero Publishers, Inc., Fallbrook, California, 1977), provides the interested reader with in-depth studies of the pilots and leaders who gave the Luftwaffe fighter arm its characteristic spirit and vigor. Only the merest outline is therefore necessary here, since the World War II German aces are now completely out of the historical shadows.

The Germans had to do far less hunting for their quarry than Allied pilots. The unfoldment of the war ensured that most of the time the targets of the German aces came to them, both in Russia and on the Western Front, including the Mediterranean. The combination of such lavish opportunities with the practice

WORLD'S NO. 1 FIGHTER ACE, ERICH HARTMANN (352.0)
Lt. Hartmann, shown here a few months after his 22nd birthday led a charmed life at the controls of a Messerschmitt 109. He was not once wounded though he entered combat over 800 times.

(Toliver collection)

NUMBER 2 ACE OF ALL TIME, MAJOR GERHARD BARKHORN: (301.0)
One of the finest gentlemen of Europe is also one of the best fighter pilots. In the post-war Luftwaffe, Barkhorn rose to the rank of Major General.

of making pilots fly until they were killed, resulted in enormous scores for those aces who survived this intense and continuous operational activity.

The Russian Front air war was by far the biggest air war of all. The Russians themselves admit to having lost at least 75,000 aircraft, while historians and analysts set this figure near 95,000 aircraft.* *Somebody* shot down all those Russians. Most of them were downed by Luftwaffe fighter pilots, many of whom flew between 1,000 and 2,000 missions!

Pilots flying these enormous numbers of missions were involved in literally *hundreds of actual aerial battles.* Erich Hartmann flew 1400 missions and engaged in over 800 battles in gaining his 352 victories. On the Allied side, by contrast, the most active fighter pilots flew between 250 and 400 missions. One American pilot with 254 missions actually fired his guns at an airborne target only 83 times, and this may well be the best record of any American pilot.

From 1942 onward, Russian air power made a continuous comeback from initial reverses, and it was quite commonplace for German pilots in a *schwarm* of four fighters to take off and attempt to intercept one hundred, two hundred or three hundred Russian aircraft.

*Approximately twice the combined losses of the RAF and USAAF.

Some German aces in these incredible, milling struggles shot down as many as thirteen Russian machines in a single mission. Those who survived the attrition piled up scores that dwarfed those of the best Allied aces.

The concept of the Red Air Force as being little more than target drogues for these habile Germans is not historically supportable. The top-scoring fourteen Allied fighter aces of World War II were all Russians. Russian pilot quality in general was not as good as the Luftwaffe, but in the elite Guards regiments were aces as good as any in the world. Kozhedub and Pokryshkin, the two top Russian aces, had scores of 60 and 59 victories respectively.

When the Americans got into action in their own units in Europe, they found veterans of this intense, prolonged aerial fighting in the formations they opposed. The abilities of these habile Germans stood out in the memorable encounters top American aces had with these Luftwaffe honchos. Gabreski, Mahurin, Blakeslee and Zemke all had days of phenomenal scoring against mediocre opponents. Three, four or five German fighters could be downed on a single mission.

These same top Americans on other days would meet the identical type of German aircraft that they had knocked down readily in previous battles. To their dismay and chagrin they would find a master of aerial combat at the controls of the enemy machine. With everything in their favor bouncing the other aircraft, they would get only a draw. Sometimes they were lucky to get a draw.

Captain Robert S. Johnson was as tough, quick and sharp as any ace in the USAAF, and he was lucky to get a draw. He owed his life to the armor plate behind his cockpit. After running afoul of a particularly expert German pilot, Johnson's Thunderbolt was so full of holes it could hardly fly. The German pilot had exhausted his ammunition, and he flew alongside Johnson and gave him a friendly wave.

The German flew away and landed, requesting confirmation of a kill because he did not believe that Johnson's soggy and weaving P-47 could possibly fly more than a few miles. Johnson survived and got home, but his P-47 was scrapped. Postwar investigation has strongly suggested that it was Major Georg-Peter Eder who so thoroughly sieved Johnson's fighter. If so, Johnson could hardly have found a more worthy foe.

Eder ended the war with 78 victories. He is one of the bravest fighter pilots of all time. Eder was one of the German aces who developed the head-on method of attacking the B-17 Fortress. He downed 36 of the American heavies, but U.S. gunners nailed Eder nine times. In all, he was shot down 17 times and wounded 14 times before he called it a war in 1945. When he encountered Bob Johnson, Eder had been flying since Battle of Britain days. A chivalrous pilot, he frequently spared his foes and thus has "only" 78 confirmed kills.

Erich Hartmann's career began in gliders well before World War II. He had the benefit of a full and detailed training before going into action on the Russian front in August 1942. A man with outstanding analytical ability, he noticed that dogfighters on the Eastern Front were being regularly shot down—even the top-scoring ones. Hartmann developed a distinctive style of his own and avoided dogfighting—the turning battle that so often ended badly for his fellow Germans.

His method was to get as close as possible to the enemy aircraft before firing. He would press his attack until the bulk of the other machine filled his windshield. Every bullet and shell went into the enemy machine at full velocity. The effect was devastating. When Hartmann hit them this way, he found that

they didn't come back up again the next day.

Hartmann also thoughtfully devised self-protective escape maneuvers, utilizing negative-G to make it impossible for a pursuing pilot either to hit him or to follow him until he was out of danger. His carefully conceived attack and defense tactics took him to the summit of acedom, and not once in more than 800 aerial battles was Hartmann wounded.

He won the Diamonds to his Knight's Cross of the Iron Cross, and his combat career included several clashes with USAAF Mustangs in Rumania and Czechoslovakia. He downed seven American fighters in these battles but was lucky to escape with his hide in the last Rumanian battle. Ammunition exhausted and fuel low, he found himself barely ahead of a horde of Mustangs intent on his demise.

Fuel gone, he bailed out, and was relieved when the leader of the American formation flew past and gave him a friendly wave. The knightly traditions of aerial combat had survived, and it is to the credit of all who fought in the air that sportsmanship had not completely disappeared from combat. The Germans maintained this tradition as a Luftwaffe policy.

Hartmann surrendered to U.S. units in Czechoslovakia in 1945, and was turned over to the Red Army under high level Allied agreements. He was ten and a half years in illegal confinement in Russia, stripped of every right extended to prisoners of war. Hartmann did not return to Germany until 1955, at which time one third of his life had been spent in prison.

Hartmann rebuilt his life with his wife Ursula, who had waited loyally and lovingly for him throughout his imprisonment. He had a good career in the new German Air Force, raising and training its first jet wing, and upon his retirement became headmaster of a flying school. He is alive as this is written, a man deeply respected by America's aces.

The only other pilot besides Hartmann to exceed 300 victories is Gerhard Barkhorn, who retired from the German Air Force as a Major General. He downed 301 planes in World War II, and earned a reputation for decency, fairness and chivalry without peer in the Luftwaffe. A typical Barkhorn trait was never to argue over a victory with another participating pilot. He would not even toss a coin in such instances, but just gallantly conceded the kill to the other man.

He took 120 missions, including the battle of Britain, to score his first victory on 2 July 1941 in Russia. He will tell you what it was like in Russia in the good weather months. A fighter pilot took off, flew and fought until out of fuel or ammunition, then landed to refuel and rearm. He immediately took off again and repeated the cycle. The airfields were right behind the front, the enemy usually numerous. Barkhorn once flew eight missions in one day. His war career included more than 1800 combat missions and 1104 actual aerial battles. He ended the war in the hospital after an Me-262 crash. American aces who have met him are unanimous in their warm reaction to his noble character and humanity.

American aces are familiar as well with the third-ranked fighter ace of all time, Guenther Rall. For many years he was F-104 Project Officer for the Luftwaffe at Palmdale, California, and met socially many of the American aces he had fought against in the ETO. Rall rose to become *Inspekteur* of the GAF, the title that force accords its chief, before his 1976 retirement.

Rall gained his 275 aerial victories in World War II in a spectacular career that saw him engage Americans, British, French and Russians aloft. He flew in the Battle of France, the Battle of Britain, Greece, Crete, Russia and in the final defense of Germany against the Western Allies. A squadron leader at 22, he had run up 36 victories before a Russian fighter clobbered him at dusk and sent him down to a body-breaking crash. With a broken back and partial paralysis, Rall was sentenced to "no more flying" by the doctors, one of whom he married.

Rall now brought off a triumph of the will. He overcame his broken back, and literally forced his way into aerial combat, incensed at being left behind in the scoring race. Guenther Rall is widely considered to have been the greatest angle-off gunner in the Luftwaffe, able to hit other aircraft from incredible distances and angles.

Rall was hit himself by an American P-47 over Berlin. His left thumb was sliced off and his fighter riddled. Bailing out, Rall descended with his spurting stump to find a German farmer mistaking him for an American. His career nearly ended on the wrong end of a pitchfork. He survived the war and his wounds, a rough passage in postwar Germany when "militarists" were dis-

NUMBER 3, MAJOR GUNTHER RALL (275)
Indomitable, Rall flew throughout the war in spite of a broken back and several tours in various hospitals. He is the third ranking ace of all time, rose in rank in the post-war Luftwaffe to Lt. General and commanded the Luftwaffe in the mid-1970's.

(Rall collection)

criminated against, and rose to command the GAF. He is still married to his wartime doctor, and will hold up his thumb to American friends and say, "A souvenir of your Air Force!"

There were many German aces with over 100 victories, most of them on the Russian Front. As a means of equalizing fighting achievements for the award of decorations, the Luftwaffe instituted a "points" system for fighter pilots. This points arrangement put single and multi-engined aircraft into a numerical coding so that tackling the American bomber boxes, for example, brought more points than facing single-engined fighters in Russia. This system resulted in pilots always having more "points" than actual kills, and was one element in the Western Allies discounting high German scores. The whole matter is described in detail in the authors' book on the Luftwaffe.*

American pilots in the ETO were flying against Luftwaffe opponents in some cases who had over 100 victories against the Western Allies. Among the most formidable was Lieutenant Colonel Heinz "Pritzl" Baer, who ended the war with 220 victories, 124 of them scored over Western-flown aircraft. Some idea of Baer's operational activity can be gained from his 1,000 missions, in the course of which he was *shot down himself eighteen times.* He survived the war, only to be killed in front of his family on 28 April 1957, while demonstrating an aircraft designed for safe sport flying. Only the legendary Star of Africa, Hans-Joachim Marseille downed more Western aircraft (158) than Baer, but his victories were over the RAF.

Other Luftwaffe luminaries facing the Americans were Lieutenant Colonel Kurt Buehligen with 112 victories over the RAF and USAAF, Colonel Josef "Pips" Priller with 101 victories, and the unforgttable Lieutenant General Adolf Galland, with 104 victories. Not even a fleeting account of America's aerial foes in Europe dare omit Galland, whose own book, *The First and the Last*, is required reading for anyone seeking insight into the World War II Luftwaffe.

The vast majority of Galland's 104 victories were over single-engined fighters. Successful in the Battle of Britain, he caught Hitler's eye and Goering's fancy, and was promptly

(Baer collection)

NUMBER 8 TOP JET ACE WWII
Colonel Heinz Baer was the top jet ace of WWII with 16 confirmed victories in the Me-262 jet fighter. He flew from 1939 to 1945 and was credited with 220 aerial victories.

promoted to wing commander. He became General of the Fighter Arm in 1941 upon the accidental death of his friend and rival, Werner Moelders—the first fighter ace to down 100 enemy aircraft.

Galland hated being taken off operations and flew fighters whenever the opportunity came his way. He stayed in close touch with the realities of the air war by living them in this fashion. His perspective remained uniquely accurate because of this top-to-bottom grasp of his responsibilities.

Galland's "ground war" against the irrational and sometimes downright destructive edicts of Goering is a testament to his strong character, invincible firmness of mind and strategic genius. The Allies were fortunate that Galland's efforts to abort the air assault on Germany were throttled or misdirected by Goering. When Galland was able to put his tactical and strategic measures into effect, the Allies always suffered.

*The "points system" was used only on the Western front.

A fighter and hunter to his marrow, Galland spent his final days as a Luftwaffe ace fighting in the air. He was the only Lieutenant General in German history to command a squadron—JV-44. He knew once more the thrill of air superiority, piloting the Me-262 against the Allied aerial hordes.

Posting Galland to command JV-44 had been a coordinated effort of Hitler, Goering and Himmler. He was to prove the Me-262 as a fighter or die in the attempt. Galland proved that the jet fighter was all he had claimed, but he didn't quite die doing this. He ended his combat career in a foxhole with cannon fragments in his knee. Galland survived the war and is today a successful businessman in Germany, respected and admired by the American aces who flew against him.

There is now no longer any of the old apprehensions and prejudices that once prevented fair depiction of enemy fighter pilots. The years ahead will see the publication of much information on the Japanese fighter aces. The Luftwaffe aces are now far better known than they were in the aftermath of World War II.

(Galland collection)

ADOLF GALLAND, COMMANDER OF THE DAY FIGHTERS, (104)

Galland, shown here wearing the "Diamonds" award at his throat, flew 280 sorties in the Spanish War as a dive-bomber, and 425 sorties on the Western front in WWII. Galland rose to Lt. General before war's end. He so strongly supported his fighter pilots against the jealous headquarters types who advised Reichsmarschal Goring concerning their moral intrepidity in the face of the thousands of allied aircraft attacking Germany, that he was relieved as General der Jagdflieger and assigned as a squadron commander in the Me-262 jets.

Captain Hans-Joachim Marseille, (158)
Germany's most popular fighter pilot during his short life. An exuberant, gregarious personality Marseille developed into an exceptionally capable fighter pilot and unsurpassed master of the difficult art of shooting at a moving target from a moving platform. Killed 30 September 1942 in Africa when his Messerschmitt 109 engine failed and his baleout was unsuccessful.

(Obermaier collection)

355

STELLAR INVESTITURE 1943   (Grasser Collection)

Four of Germany's leading fighter aces came together at this Berlin investiture. From left they are: Major Prince Heinrich zu Sayn-Wittgenstein, one of the Luftwaffe's top night fighters with 83 night kills; Major Hartmann Grasser, 103 victories won on all fronts; Major Walter Nowotny 258 aerial victories, sixth ranking ace of the world, and one of only nine fighter pilots to win the coveted Diamonds to his Knights Cross; and Major Guenther Rall, whose 275 victories made him the third ranking ace of all time.

(Toliver collection)

The Enemy Aces

NUMBER 4 ACE, LT. OTTO KITTEL (267):
Slow to get started, Kittel soon learned the art of aerial gunnery under the tutelage of Philipp and Nowotny, Goetz and Eckerle. He lost his life on 14 February 1945 over the Russian front when a direct hit by flak disintegrated his aircraft.

(Batz Collection)

NUMBER 6 ACE, MAJOR WILHELM BATZ, (237)

Batz was an instructor in the Luftwaffe from 1937 until 1942 and had thousands of lying hours when he finally got into fighters on the Eastern front. He fired hundreds of thousands of bullets into thin air before hitting his first enemy plane.

After seven months he still had only one victory and was a squadron commander of no distinction. A year later he found his shooting eye and in the next thirteen months brought his total to 237. He survived the war.

(Toliver collection)

NUMBER 7 ACE, MAJOR ERICH RUDORFFER, (222).

Nine parachute jumps allowed Rudorffer to survive six years of war, from the Battle of Britain to the jets. He scored 222 kills fighting on the channel front, in Africa and on the Soviet front. He holds the record for the most kills scored on a single mission — thirteen during a single sortie on 6 November 1943 in Russia.

Obermaier collection)

NUMBER 10 ACE
MAJOR HEINRICH EHRLER, (209)

Kommodore of JG-5 fighting in Northern Norway and Finland, Ehrler was the leading ace of the north. He lost his life in combat on 4 April 1945 while flying the Me-262 jet.

(Obermaier collection)

NUMBER 9 ACE, MAJOR HERMANN GRAF, (212).

Graf rose from Sergeant pilot to Colonel and commanded Fighter Wing 52 (JG 52). He won the four highest German decorations in the span of just eight months.

NUMBER 14 ACE, LT. ANTON HAFNER (204)

"Tony" Hafner scored all his kills with JG-51, 20 of them in Africa and the remainder on the Soviet front. He was the top ace of JG-51, but lost his life when he flew into a tree while pursuing a Yak-9 on 17 October 1944.

(Obermaier collection)

NUMBER 12 ACE, HANS PHILIPP (206)

Some sources credit Philipp with 213 victories. "To fight against 20 Russians or 20 Spitfires is a joy . . .but to curve into 70 Fortresses lets all the sins of one's life pass before one's eyes!" Philipp lost his life in a battle with Thunderbolts on 4 October 1943 over Nordhorn.

(Boehm collection)

(Obermaier collection)

NUMBER 15 ACE, CAPTAIN HELMUT LIPFERT, (203).

Fifteen times Lipfert was shot down (thirteen by flak) but he was never wounded. Scored his first 100 victories in fifteen months and the next 100 in twelve months. Survived the war.

(Boehm collection)

NUMBER 11 ACE, MAJOR THEODOR WEIS-SENBERGER, (208)

Including eight victories with the Me-262, Weissenberger tallied 208 or more before war's end. He lost his life racing cars in Nurburgring in 1950.

(Boehm Collection)

NUMBER 13 ACE, LT. WALTER SCHUCK (206): Schuck flew most of his combat with JG-5 EISMEER in the far North, but later scored eight victories with the Me-262 jet. He survived the war.

(Krupinski collection)

CAPTAIN WALTER KRUPINSKI, (197)
"Graf Punski" ranks 16th among Luftwaffe aces.
He rose to the rank of Lt. General in the post-war Luftwaffe.

(Galland collection)

ACE OF TWO WARS—25 YEARS APART
Generalleutnant Theo Osterkamp scored 32 victories in WWI and six more in WWII before he was grounded by his headquarters. Osterkamp died in 1975 at the age of 83.

(Boehm Collection)

NUMBER 17 LUFTWAFFE ACE
Major Anton Hackl won the Swords to his Knight's Cross in WWII, for 190 aerial victories, equally divided between the Russian and Western fronts. Major Hackl flew with JG-11, JG-26 and JG-300.

359

(Obermaier Collection)

Major Joachim "Jochen" Muncheberg. (135)
Muncheberg's combat career included tours on all fronts with 102 victories over the western allies and 33 over the Soviets. This photo made on 9 September 1942. Killed during combat on 23 March 1943 when the wings separated from his fighter.

Colonel Walter "Gulle" Oesau, (125)
Oesau scored eight victories during the Spanish Revolution and was the third WWII fighter pilot to score 100 kills. Killed in a combat against American P-38s on 11 May 1944.

(Obermaier Collection)

QUIETLY ONE OF THE MOST IMPORTANT LUFTWAFFE ACES:
Major General Gordon M. Gollob replaced Adolf Galland as General der Jagdfliegers (General of the fighters) on 31 January 1945. Dive-bomber, test pilot, first man to rack up 150 aerial victories, Gollob was a most talented military officer from his earliest days (1936) in the Luftwaffe. He was the third winner of Germany's most coveted decoration, the Eichenlaub mit Schwertern and Brillanten zum Ritterkreuz des Eisernen Kreuzes (in short, the "Diamonds").

(Boehm Collection)

Lt. Colonel Johannes Steinhoff (176)
One of the most brilliant of all Luftwaffe officers, "Macki" Steinhoff survived a near-fatal Me-262 jet crash and, in the post-war Luftwaffe, rose to Lt. General and commanded the Air Force. He is well-known in American circles having served a tour in the USA and in NATO. (Steinhoff Collection)

(Boehm Collection)

TOP SCORING NIGHT FIGHTER ACE OF ALL TIME
Major Heinz-Wolfgang Schnaufer scored 121 victories against the Allies in WWII, all of them at night. He won Germany's highest decoration, the Diamonds to his Knight's Cross, and also survived the war. He was killed in an automobile accident in 1950

(Galland Collection)

"WHAT SHALL WE DO ABOUT THOSE PESKY SPITFIRES?"
Top level meeting at LeTouquet, France during the Battle of Britain brought Galland, Lutzow, Maltzahn, Osterkamp, Molders and Viek together, as shown here. Spitfires were out-turning the Me-109s but the Messerschmitts had a speed advantage. Decision was to change from dogfighting tactics to the high speed hit-and-run maneuver which proved to be a very intelligent move.

(Obermaier Collection)

NUMBER TWO NIGHT FIGHTER ACE:
Lt. Colonel Helmut Lent scored 102 night victories and eight day fighter victories for a total of 110 kills. Lent lost his life in a crash at Paderborn on 5 October 1944.

JG-26 Staff Meeting—January 1945:
This photo made during the Battle of the Bulge. A few days later Major Franz Gotz, left, became Kommodore of JG-26 as Colonel Josef "Pips" Priller (center) moved up to become General of the Fighters-West. Major Walter Krupinski (right) became Kommandeur of the 3rd squadron of JG-26. Gotz had 63 victories, Priller 101 and Krupinski 197.

(Krupinski Collection)

(Izawa Collection)

OUT ON THE TOWN!
Two Navy aces sightsee in a nearby village between alerts in 1944. W.O. Kazuo Sugino (left) scored between 32 and 64 victories and survived the war. W.O. Kiyoshi Itoh (sometimes spelled Ito) scored between 17 and 34.

(K. Takahashi Collection)

HAPPILY HOMEWARD BOUND IN 1944!
These five NCOs of the Japanese Navy may not look happy but they are. They were happy to be leaving Truk Islands but the U.S. Navy attack on Guam and Saipan bollixed the trip considerably. They were shot down 19 June 1944 trying to land at Orote Point on Guam and they returned to Japan aboard a submarine. Extreme left is Ken-ichi "Kanji" Takahashi (14 to 28), and the tallest and most gentlemanly of all Japanese fighter pilots, Warrant Officer Sadamu Komachi (18 to 36 victories) far right. Both survived the war. Other pilots are unidentified.

(Izawa Collection)

PILOTS OF THE THIRD FIGHTER GROUP
This photo, taken at Takao, Taiwan in December 1941 just before the war in the Pacific began, shows in the rear row second from right NAP/1c Kaneyoshi Muto (28 to 56 victories including five over China). In the front row, left to right: unknown, Masayuki Nakase (18 to 36, including nine in China); Sadaaki Akamatsu (27 to 54, including eleven in China); T. Kurosawa; Sadao Yamaguchi (12 to 24); and an unidentified pilot.

(Izawa Collection)

FOUR HAPPY FIGHTERS:
Pilot upper right is Lt. Yasuhiko Kuroe, Japanese Army Air Force, who scored between 30 and 60 aerial victories, including two during the Nomohan Incident, Kuroe survived the war but lost his life while fishing in November 1965.

Navy W.O. Kaneyoshi Muto (28-56)
Scored five victories in China in late 1937 and 1938. Brought his total to somewhere between 28 and 56 in WWII before being shot down and killed on 24 July 1945 over Bungo Strait. In February 1945 over Atsugi, near Tokyo, he single-handedly attacked twelve F6F Hellcats, shooting down four and escaping unhurt.

(Ryogi Ohhara Collection)

(Izawa Collection)

Army Lt. Goro Furugori. (30 to 50)
Furogori scored 20 victories in the Nomohan Incident war, then added another 10 to 30 in WWII with the 22nd Sentai. KIA at Tacloban on 3 November 1944 in a battle with P-38s. NCO at right is unidentified.

Dashing Fighter Pilot, Navy NA/1c Takeo Tanimizu (18-36)
This photo made aboard JUNYO in June of 1942. Tanimizu wears a Hachimaki with Hinomaru under his helmet and a Nanbu automatic pistol at his waist.

(T. Tanimizu Collection)

12

ACES OF
THE FUTURE

Technology moves forward in seven-league boots. Few men can predict accurately what vehicles will be devised for powered flight in the coming decades. No one knows what new scientific and technical principles are to be unlocked. Aircraft capable of Mach 3, three times the speed of sound, criss-cross the U.S.A. daily. Spy satellites, manned spacecraft and space laboratories are in the here-now, already woven in various ways into modern life.

Americans have landed on the moon, and American probes have gone to the planets. A Russian exploratory vehicle crawled around the moon's surface for months under control from earth. The Americans, Russians, French and British have developed new fighter aircraft that are capable of exploiting the entire spectrum of atmospheric space—from low altitudes to the upper stratosphere.

Other Buck Rogers-type wonders are vertical-rising fighters capable of supersonic speeds; rigid-rotor helicopters that can hover and yet accelerate to over 300 mph; missiles guided by radar, by heat-seeking devices and even by wire; laser beams for guidance and even destruction. These things are either technical realities or under active experimental development. Things have come a long way since Eddie Rickenbacker strapped on a Nieuport.

Tomorrow the human element will continue to occupy a crucial place in the whole technical unfoldment. If the history of aerial combat has one clear message for the future, it must surely be that a superlative human element maximizes the value of the machine. The new battles of space exploration and dis-covery require the best that is in mankind. The fighter ace has always been the military epitome of courage, daring, ingenuity, skill, swiftness of mind, steadfastness and devotion to duty. Such qualities will always be needed, no matter how different the machines of tomorrow.

America's 1416 knights of the air have passed into history. One hundred eight Americans became aces in World War I. Twenty Americans fighting with the RAF in World War II shot down five or more enemy airplanes. The USAAF in World War II, *not* including the American Volunteer Group in China, added 697 more aces while the Marine Corps provided an additional 124, the U.S. Navy 386. The Korean War produced forty more fighter aces and the Vietnam engagement another two. The AVGs had twenty-six fighter aces, the Spanish Civil War had two Americans who made ace, and seven Americans qualified while flying with the Royal Canadian Air Force. In addition, four more fighter pilots made ace by scoring victories in WWII and followed with additional scores in Korea, making the five or more necessary to become ace. All told, there are approximately 1416 U.S. aces from all wars.

If all aerial combat as we have known it is to vanish in due course, at least America's military glories have been enhanced by the fighter ace. He gave his country a new kind of folk hero, born in and native to the technological era of the twentieth century. His exploits and individualistic traits have brightened the military records of our age, and kept alive the last vestiges of knightly chivalry.

ACE LISTS

** TOPS AND FIRSTS **

FIRST AMERICAN TO SHOOT DOWN FIVE ENEMY AIRCRAFT IN WWI
  Capt. Frederick Libby (Shot down 10 as an observer in RFC)
FIRST AMERICAN ACE OF WWI
  Capt. Alan M. Wilkinson (19 victories with RFC)
FIRST AMERICAN ACE TO SERVE WITH THE AEF
  Capt. Raoul G. Lufbery (17 victories)
FIRST AMERICAN AEF ACE OF WWI
  Lt. Paul F. Baer (8 May 1918)
TOP AMERICAN ACE OF WWI
  Capt. Edward V. Rickenbacker (26 victories)
TOP AMERICAN ACE WITH FOREIGN GOVERNMENT(WWI)
  Capt. Stanley C. Rosevear, RFC (23 victories)
FIRST AMERICAN ACE OF WWII
  Pilot Officer William R. Dunn (27 August 1941) with RAF 71 Eagle Squadron
FIRST AMERICAN USAF ACE OF WWII
  Lt. Boyd D. "Buzz" Wagner (16 December 1941)
TOP AMERICAN ACE OF WWII
  Maj. Richard Bong, USAF (40 victories)
TOP NAVY ACE WWII
  Capt. David McCampbell (34 victories)
TOP U. S. MARINE CORPS ACE WWII
  Lt. Col. Gregory Boyington (28 victories incuding six scored with the AVG in China)
  Col. Joseph J. Foss (26 victories, all with USMC)
TOP AMERICAN ACE WITH FOREIGN GOVERNMENT WWII
  Wg. Cdr. Lance Wade (RAF) (25 victories)
MOST KILLS IN A SINGLE MISSION
  Capt. David McCampbell, USN (9 confirmed, 2 probables)
TOP AMERICAN ACE OF PACIFIC THEATER OF OPERATIONS WWII
  Maj. Richard Bong (40 victories)
TOP AMERICAN ACE OF EUROPEAN THEATER OF OPERATIONS WWII
  Maj. Francis S. Gabreski, USAF (28.0)
FIRST AMERICAN ACE OF KOREAN WAR (1950-1953)
  Capt. James Jabara (20 May 1951) (15.0 victories)
TOP AMERICAN JET-ACE OF KOREAN WAR
  Capt. Joseph McConnell (16.0 victories)
FIRST AMERICAN TO SCORE AN AERIAL KILL IN KOREA
  1st Lt. William G. Hudson (F-82 pilot shot down a YAK-11, 17 June 1950)
FIRST JET-TO-JET KILL OF KOREAN WAR AND FIRST JET-TO-JET KILL IN HISTORY:
  1st Lt. Russell J. Brown (F-80 over MiG-15, 8 November 1950)
TOP LIVING AMERICAN ACE (1977)
  Col. Francis S. Gabreski

WWII	28.0
Korea	6.5
Total	34.5

FIRST AMERICAN ACE OF TWO WARS
  Maj. A. J. "Ajax" Baumler

Spanish Civil War	8.0
WWII	5.0
Total	13.0

FIRST AMERICAN ACE OF VIETNAM WAR
  Lt. Randy "Duke" Cunningham, USN
FIRST USAF ACE OF VIETNAM WAR
  Capt. Richard "Steve" Ritchie, USAF

WORLD WAR I ACES: 1914-1918

AEF   American Expeditionary Force
FFC   French Flying Corps
*   Lafayette Escadrille of the FFC
RFC   Royal Flying Corps (British)
Note: AEF pilots did not split or share victory credits. If more than one pilot was in on an aerial victory, each pilot claimed a full credit of one victory. In 1969, the Historical Research Division at the Air University, Maxwell Air Force Base Alabama, issued USAF Historical Study No. 133, which was a thorough review of AEF victory claims, and revised the victory credit authorizations to bring them in line with WWII accreditation methods and procedures. The USAFHS 133 tabulations are listed in the column at the far right of these lists.

NAME	HOME TOWN	RANK	UNIT	CLAIMED	USAFHS 133
Baer, Paul F.	Ft. Wayne IN	1st. Lt	FFC*	9.00	7.75
Bair, Hilbert L.	New York NY	1st Lt.	AEF 103 Sq RFC	5.00	3.88
Baylies, Frank L.	New Bedford MA	Lt	FFC*	12.00	
Beane, James D.	Concord MA	1st Lt	22 Sq AEF	6.00	3.83
Bennett, Louis B.	Weston WV	1st Lt	40 Sq RFC	12.00	
Biddle, Charles J.	Andalusia PA	Major	FFC* 13 Sq AEF	7.00	3.16
Bissell, Clayton L.	Kane PA	Capt	148 Sq AEF	5.00	5.00
Brooks, Arthur R.	Short Hills NJ	2nd Lt.	139/22 Sq AEF	6.00	2.66
Buckley, Harold R.	Aqawam MA	Capt	95 Sq AEF	5.00	2.36
Burdick, Howard	Brooklyn NY	1st Lt	17 Sq AEF	7.00	6.00
Calahan, Lawrence K.	Chicago IL	1st Lt	85 Sq RFC 148 Sq AEF	5.00	2.00
Campbell, Douglas	Mt. Hamilton CA	Capt	94 Sq AEF	6.00	5.50
Cassady, Thomas G.	Spencer IN	Capt	FFC* 28 Sq AEF	9.00	6.63
Chambers, Reed M.	Memphis TN	Major	94 Sq AEF	7.00	6.00
Clay, Henry R., Jr.	Ft. Worth TX	1st Lt	148 Sq AEF	8.00	7.00
Connelly, James A.	Philadelphia PA	Lt	FFC*	8.00	
Cook, Everett Richard	Germantown TN	Capt	91 Sq AEF	5.00	1.23
Cook, Harvey Weir	Indianapolis IN	Capt	94 Sq AEF	7.00	5.66
Coolidge, Hamilton	Boston MA	Capt	94 Sq AEF	8.00	5.58
Creech, Jesse O.	Washington DC	1st Lt	148 Sq AEF	8.00	6.00
Curtis, Edward P.	Rochester NY	Capt	95 Sq AEF	6.00	2.91
D'Olive, Charles R.	Cedar Falls IA	Lt	93 Sq AEF	5.00	4.00
Donaldson, John Owen	Washington DC	Capt	85 Sq RFC	8.00	8.00
Erwin, William P.	Chicago IL	1st Lt	1 Sq AEF	8.00	3.75
Furlow, George W.	Rochester MN	1st Lt	103 Sq AEF	5.00	2.66
George, Harold	Niagara Falls NY	1st Lt	139 Sq AEF	5.00	2.49
Gillette, Frederick H.	Baltimore MD	Capt	RFC	20.00	
Grey, Charles G.	Chicago IL	Capt	213 Sq AEF	5.00	2.80
Griffith, John S.	Seattle WA	Capt	60 Sq RFC	9.00	
Guthrie, Murray K.	Mobile AL	1st Lt	13 Sq AEF	6.00	3.66
Haight, Edward M.	Astoria NY	1st Lt	139 Sq AEF	5.00	2.49
Hale, Frank L.	Fayetteville AR	Capt	85 Sq RFC	18.00	
Hall, James Norman	Colfax IA	Capt	FFC 103/94 AEF	6.00	1.83
Hamilton, Lloyd A.	Burlington VT	1st Lt	RFC & 17 AEF	9.00	6.83
Hays, Frank Kerr	Chicago IL	1st Lt	13 Sq AEF	6.00	3.10
Healy, James A.	Jersey City NJ	Capt	147 Sq AEF	5.00	2.90
Holden, Lansing C.	New York NY	1st Lt	95 Sq AEF	7.00	6.50
Hudson, Donald	Kansas City MO	Capt	27 Sq AEF	6.00	2.48
Huffer, John W.F.M.	(Born) Paris, France	1st Lt	FFC	7.00	
Hunter, Frank O'D.	Savannah GA	1st Lt	103 Sq AEF	8.00	6.50
Iaccaci, Paul T.	New York NY	Capt	20 Sq RFC	18.00	
Iaccaci, Thayer A.	New York NY	Lt	22 Sq RFC	11.00	
Ingalls, David Sinton	Chagrin Falls OH	Lt USN	213 Sq AEF	5.00	
Jones, Clinton	San Francisco CA	2nd Lt	22 Sq AEF	8.00	6.16
Keating, James A.		Major	49 Sq RFC	6.00	2.50
Kindley, Field E.	Gravette AR	Capt	RFC & 148 AEF	12.00	11.00
Knotts, Howard C.	Carlinville IL	2nd Lt	17 Sq AEF	6.00	5.50
Knowles, James Jr.	Cambridge MA	1st Lt	95 Sq AEF	5.00	4.20
Kullberg, Harold A.	West Somerville MA	Lt	1 Sq RFC	16.00	
Lamb, Dean I.		Lt	4 Sq RFC	5.00	

NAME	HOME TOWN	RANK	UNIT	CLAIMED	USAFHS 133
Lambert, Wm. Carpenter	Ironton OH	Capt	24 Sq RFC	22.00	
Landis, Reed G.	Chicago IL	Capt	RFC	10.00	10.00
Larner, G. DeFreest	New York NY	Capt	FFC* 103 Sq AEF	8.00	3.33
Libby, Frederick	Sterling CO	Capt	25 Sq RFC	14.00	
Lindsay, Robert O.	Madison NC	1st Lt	139 Sq AEF	6.00	2.44
Lufbery, Raoul G.	Boston MA	Major	N-124 FFC*	17.00	
Luff, Frederick E.	Cleveland OH	1st Lt	RFC	5.00	5.00
Luke, Frank Jr.	Phoenix AZ	2nd Lt	27 Sq AEF	18.00	15.83
Magoun, Francis P.		Lt	1 Sq RFC	5.00	
Malone, John J.	Regina, Canada	Capt	Royal Navy	20.00	
Matthews, Alexandre	Louisburg WV	Lt	84 Sq RFC	5.00	
MacArthur, John K.	Everett WA	2nd Lt	27 Sq AEF	6.00	3.15
McClure, David M.	Pittsburgh PA	1st Lt	213 Sq AEF	6.00	3.00
Meissner, James A.	Brooklyn NY	Major	94 Sq AEF	8.00	5.66
			147 Sq AEF		
Miller, Ewart S.	E. Palestine OH	1st Lt	139 Sq AEF	5.00	0.00
Miller, Zenos R.	Evanston IL	1st Lt	27 Sq AEF	5.00	4.00
O'Neill, Ralph A.	Nogales AZ	2nd Lt	147 Sq AEF	5.00	1.39
Owens, J. Sidney	Baltimore MD	2nd Lt	139 Sq AEF	5.00	1.10
Pace, W. J.		Capt	RFC	5.00	
Parsons, Edwin C.	Springfield MA	Lt	N-124 FFC*	8.00	
Peterson, David McKelvy	Honesdale PA	Major	FFC* (1.0)	5.00	4.00
			94/95 Sq AEF		
Ponder, William T.	Mangum OK	1st Lt	FFC* (3.0)	5.00	5.00
			103 Sq AEF (2)		
Porter, Kenneth L.	Dowagiac MI	2nd Lt	147 Sq AEF	6.00	2.15
Prince, Norman	Prides Crossing MA	2nd Lt	N-124 FFC*	5.00	
Putnam, David E.	Brookline MA	1st Lt	FFC* (2.0)	6.00	6.00
			139 Sq AEF (4.0)		
Ralston, Orville A.	Lincoln NE	1st Lt	RFC & 148 AEF	5.00	4.25
Rickenbacker, Ed. V.	Columbus OH	Capt	94 Sq AEF	26.00	24.33
Roberts, E.M.	Duluth MN	Lt	60 Sq RFC	7.00	
Robertson, Frank A.	Oakland CA	Lt	29 Sq RFC	6.00	
Robertson, Wendel A.	Fort Smith AR	Lt	139 Sq AEF	7.00	2.94
Rogers, Bogart		Capt	32 Sq RFC	5.00	
Rose, Oren J.	Kansas City MO	Capt	92 Sq RFC	16.00	
Rosevear, S. C.		Capt	201 Sq RFC	23.00	
Rummel, Leslie J.	Newark NJ	1st Lt	93 Sq AEF	7.00	5.16
Schoen, Karl J.	Indianapolis IN	1st Lt	139 Sq AEF	7.00	1.92
Seerley, John J.	Chicago IL	1st Lt	13 Sq AEF	5.00	1.10
Sewall, Sumner	Bath ME	Capt	95 Sq AEF	7.00	4.53
Springs, Elliott White	Lancaster SC	Capt	RFC & 148 AEF	12.00	10.75
Stenseth, Martinus	Twin Valley MN	1st Lt	28 Sq AEF	6.00	6.47
Stovall, William H.	Stovall MS	1st Lt	13 Sq AEF	7.00	3.83
Strahm, Victor H.	Bowling Green KY	Capt	91 Sq AEF	5.00	2.00
Swaab, Jacques M.	Philadelphia PA	1st Lt	22 Sq AEF	10.00	8.50
Thaw, William	Pittsburgh PA	Lt Col	FFC* (4.0)	5.83	1.83
			103 Sq AEF		
Tipton, William D.	Tarretsville MD	1st Lt	33 Sq RFC	5.00	3.00
			17 Sq AEF		
Tobin, Edgar G.	San Antonio TX	1st Lt	103 Sq AEF	6.00	4.83
Todd, Robert M.	Cincinnati OH	2nd Lt	17 Sq AEF	5.00	3.83
Vasconcells, Jerry C.	Denver CO	1st Lt	27 Sq AEF	6.00	4.66
Vaughn, George A.	Dongan Hills NY	1st Lt	17 Sq AEF	13.00	9.50
			84 Sq RFC		
Veil, Chas. Herbert	Big Run PA	Capt	N-150 FFC*	5.00	
Vernam, Remington DeB.	New York NY	1st Lt	22 Sq AEF	6.00	4.50
Warman, C. T.	Philadelphia PA	Lt	RFC	15.00	
Wehner, Joseph F.	Everett MA	1st Lt	27 Sq AEF	5.00	3.50
Westing, F.	Philadelphia PA	Lt	RFC	5.00	
White, Wilbert Wallace	New York NY	1st Lt	147 Sq AEF	8.00	6.66
Wilkenson, Alan M.		Major	48 Sq RFC	19.00	
Williams, Rodney D.	Waukesha WI	1st Lt	17 Sq AEF	5.00	3.50
Wright, Chester E.	Cambridge MA	1st Lt	93 Sq AEF	9.00	6.33
Zistell, Errol H.	Bay Village OH	Lt	42RFC/148AEF	6.00	3.00

15 OR MORE VICTORIES

	CLAIMED	OFFICIAL
Rickenbacker, Edward V.	26.00	24.33
Rosevear, S. C.	23.00	
Lambert, William Carpenter	22.00	
Gillette, Frederick W.	20.00	
Malone, John J.	20.00	
Wilkenson, Alan M.	19.00	
Hale, Frank L.	18.00	
Iaccaci, Paul T.	18.00	
Luke, Frank	18.00	15.83
Lufbery, Raoul G.	17.00	
Kullberg, Harold A.	16.00	
Rose, Oren J.	16.00	
Warman, C. T.	15.00	

AMERICAN ACES OF WORLD WAR II

CMH	- Congressional Medal of Honor	USN	- United States Navy
*	- Ace added to score in Korean War	USMC	- United States Marine Corps
**	- Ace added to score in Vietnam War	AVG	- American Volunteer Group (China)
USAF	- United States Air Force or	RAF	- Royal Air Force
	United States Army Air Forces	RCAF	- Royal Canadian Air Force
		CACW	- China American Composite Wg.

Grades (ranks) shown are rank held at time of last combat victory.

NAME	HOME TOWN	RANK	UNIT	CLAIMED	USAFHS 85
Abernathy, Robert W.	Pulaski TN	Capt	USAF 353 Gp.	5.00	5.00
Ackerman, Fred F.		Ens.	USN VF80	5.00	
Adams, Burnell W.	Chester IL	Capt.	USAF 8 Gp.	7.00	7.00
Adams, Charles E. Jr.	Denver CO	1st Lt	USAF 82 Gp.	6.00	6.00
Adams, Fletcher E.	Ida LA	Capt.	USAF 357 Gp.	9.00	9.00
Adams, Robert H.	Pomeroy WA	1st Lt	USAF 8 Gp.	5.00	5.00
Ainlay, John M.	Santa Monica CA	1st Lt	USAF 31 Gp.	8.00	8.00
Aldrich, Donald N.	Chicago IL	Capt	USMC VMF215	20.00	
Alexander, Richard L.	Piper City IL	F.O. Capt	RAF(2)USAF(3)	5.00	3.00
Alison, John R.	Gainesville FL	Lt.Col.	AVG/AF 23 Gp.	6.00	6.00
Allen, Calvin D. Jr.	Hufford Woods IL	1st Lt	USAF 52 Gp.	7.00	7.00
Allen, David W.	Belvedere CA	1st Lt	USAF 475 Gp.	8.00	8.00
Allen, William H.	Oklahoma City OK	1st Lt	USAF 55 Gp.	5.00	5.00
Alley, Stuart C. Jr.	North Muskegon MI	2nd Lt	USMC VMF	5.00	
Ambort, Ernest J.	Little Rock AR	2nd Lt	USAF 49 Gp.	5.00	5.00
Ammon, Robert H.	Sinking Springs FL	1st Lt	USAF 339 Gp.	5.00	5.00
Amoss, Dudley M	Greenwich CT	1st Lt	USAF 55 Gp.	5.50	5.50
Amsden, Benjamin C.	Boulder CO	Lt	USN VF22	5.00	
Anderson, Alexander L.	New York NY	Lt	USN VF80	6.00	
Anderson, Charles F. Jr.	Gary IN	1st Lt	USAF 4 Gp.	10.00	10.00
Anderson, Clarence E.	Lancaster CA	Capt	USAF 357 Gp.	16.25	16.25
Andersen, Leslie E.	Cheverly MD	1st Lt	USAF 82 Gp.	5.00	5.00
Anderson, Richard H.	King of Prussia PA	1st Lt	USAF 318 Gp.	5.00	5.00
Anderson, Robert H.	Eau Claire WI	Lt	USN VF80	10.00	
Anderson, William Y.	Crystal Lake IL	1st Lt	USAF 354 Gp.	7.00	7.00
Anderson, Wyman D.	Cashton WI	1st Lt	USAF 79 Gp.	6.00	6.00
Andrew, Stephen W.	Dallas TX	Maj	USAF 49/352 Gp.	9.00	9.00
Andrews, Stanley O.	St. Petersburg FL	1st Lt	USAF 35 Gp.	6.00	6.00
Arasmith, Lester L.	Omaha NE	1st Lt	USAF 311 Gp.	5.00	5.00
Aron, William E.	Oaklyn NJ	1st Lt	USAF 325 Gp.	5.00	5.00
Aschenbrenner, Robert W.	Chatsworth CA	Capt	USAF 49 Gp.	10.00	10.00
Aust, Abner M. Jr.	Barstow FL	Capt	USAF 506 Gp.	5.00	5.00
Axtell, Eugene D.		1st Lt	USAF 422 Sq.(N)	5.00	5.00
Axtell, George C.	Arlington VA	Maj	USMC VMF 323	6.00	
Baccus, Donald A.	Carmichael CA	Lt.Col.	USAF 356 Gp.	5.00	5.00
Bade, Jack A.	Elk MN	1st Lt	USAF 18 Gp.	5.00	5.00

NAME	HOME TOWN	RANK	UNIT	CLAIMED	USAFHS 85
Bailey, Oscar C.	Rockport TX	LCDR	USN VF28	5.00	
Baird, Robert	Honolulu HI	Capt	USMC VMF533(N)	6.00	
Baker, Douglas	Lindsay OK	LT	USN VF20	16.00	
Baker, Ellis C. Jr.	Stillwater OK	1st Lt	USAF 35 Gp.	6.00	6.00
Baker, Robert M.	Acton CA	Maj	USMC VMF121	7.00	
Bakutis, Fred E.	Brockton MA	CDR	USN VF20	11.00	
Balch, Donald Luther	San Francisco CA	Maj	USMC VMF	5.00	
Baldwin, Frank B.	Philadelphia PA	Capt	USMC VMF	5.00	
Balsinger, Henry W.	LT	USN VF29	6.00		
Bank, Raymond W.	Chicago IL	1st Lt	USAF 357Gp.	5.00	5.00
Bankey, Ernest E. Jr.	Woodland Hills CA	Capt	USAF 364 Gp.	9.50	9.50
Banks, John L.	Webster Groves MO	LT	USN VF2	8.50	
Banks, William M.	Lewisburg WV	Maj	USAF 348 Gp.	9.00	9.00
Barackman, Bruce MacD.	McLean VA	LT	USN VF50	5.00	
Barber, Rex T.	Culver OR	1st Lt	USAF 18 Gp.	5.00	5.00
Bardshar, Frederic A.	LaJolla CA	CDR	USN VF27	8.00	
Bare, James D.	Wetumka OK	LT	USN VF15	6.00	
Barkey, Robert M.	South Field MI	1st Lt	USAF 326 Gp.	5.00	5.00
Barnard, Lloyd Glynn	Jacksonville FL	LT	USN VF2	8.00	
Barnes, James M.	Binghamton, NY	LT	USN VF83	6.00	
Barnes, Truman S.	San Francisco CA	1st Lt	USAF 18/347 Gp.	5.00	5.00
Barrick, John F.	TX	Sgt	RCAF 17 Sq.	5.00	
Bartelt, Percy R.		Capt	AVG	7.00	
Bartling, W. E.	Studio City CA	Capt	AVG	7.25	
Baseler, Robert L.	Westminster CA	LTC	USAF 325 Gp.	6.00	6.00
Bassett, Edgar R.	Scarsdale NY	ENS	USN VF42	9.00	
Batten, Hugh N.	Tanneytown MD	LT	USN VF83	7.00	
Bauer, Harold W. (CMH)	North Platte NE	Lt Col	USMC VMF212	11.00	
Baumler, Albert J.	Denison TX	Capt	Span. Civil War (8) USAF 23 Gp. (5)	13.00	5.00
Bearden, Aaron L.	Houston TX	2nd Lt	USAF 80 Gp.	5.00	5.00
Beatley, Rodman C.	Washington DC	LT	USN VF	6.00	
Beaudry, Paul H.N.	Springfield MA	ENS	USN VF80	6.00	
Beavers, Edward H. Jr.	Scranton PA	Capt	USAF 339 Gp.	5.00	5.00
Becker, Robert H.	Shattuck OK	Capt	USAF 357 Gp.	7.00	7.00
Beckham, Walter C.	Albuquerque NM	Maj	USAF 353 Gp.	18.00	18.00
Beebe, Marshall U.	Corona del Mar CA	CDR	USN VF17	10.50	
Beerbower, Donald M.	Hill City MN	Capt	USAF 354 Gp.	15.50	15.50
Beeson, Duane W.	Boise ID	Capt	USAF 4 Gp.	19.33	17.33
Benne, Louis	Phoenix AZ	1st Lt	USAF 14 Gp.	5.00	5.00
Bennett, Joseph H.	Morton TX	Capt	USAF 56, 4 Gp.	8.50	8.50
Benz, Walter G. Jr.	New Braunfels TX	Maj	USAF 348 Gp.	8.00	8.00
Berkheimer, Jack S.	Temperance MI	ENS	USN VF41(N)	5.00	
Berree, Norman R.	Cantonement FL	LT	USN VF15	9.00	
Bertelson, Richard L.	Eden Prairie MN	LT	USN VF29	5.00	
Beyer, William R.	Danville PA	Capt	USAF 361 Gp.	9.00	9.00
Bickel, Carl G.	El Monte CA	1st Lt	USAF 354 Gp.	5.50	5.50
Biel, Hipolitus T.	St. Paul MN	1st Lt	USAF 4 Gp.	5.33	5.33
Bille, Henry S.	Paradise CA	Maj	USAF 355 Gp.	6.00	6.00
Billo, James D.	Gold Beach OR	LCDR	USN VF10/18	5.00	
Bishop, Lewis S.	Pensacola FL	Capt	AVG	5.20	
Bishop, Walter D.	Kansas City KS	LT	USN VF29	5.00	
Blackburn, John T.	La Jolla CA	CDR	USN VF17	11.00	
Blair, Foster J.	Stroudsburg PA	LCDR	USN VF5/17	5.00	
Blair, Samuel V.	Rancho Mirage CA	Capt	USAF 348 Gp.	7.00	7.00
Blair, William K.	Solana Beach CA	LT	USN VF2	5.00	
Blakeslee, Donald J.M.	Fairport Harbor OH	Col	RAF/AF 4 Gp. (4)	15.50	11.50
Blaydes, Richard B.	Houston TX	LT	USN VF2	5.00	
Blickenstaff, Wayne K.	Chino CA	Lt Col	USAF 353 Gp.	10.00	10.00
Blumer, Laurence E.	Walcott ND	Capt	USAF 367 Gp.	6.00	6.00
Blyth, Robert L.	Charleston SC	LT	USN VF27	6.00	
Bochkay, Donald H.	Highland CA	Maj	USAF 357 Gp.	14.83	13.83
Boggs, Hampton E.	Oklahoma City OK	Capt	USAF 80 Gp.	6.00	9.00
Bolt, John F. Jr.	New Smyrna Beach FL	Maj	USMC VMF	6.00 +6 Korea	
Bolyard, John W.	Panama City FL	Capt	USAF 23 Gp.	5.00	5.00
Bond, Charles R.	Richardson TX	Capt	AVG	9.25	
Bong, Richard I. (CMH)	Poplar WI	Maj	USAF 35/49 Gp.	40.00	40.00
Bonneau, William J.	Oakland CA	LCDR	USN VF9	8.00	
Bonner, Stephen J. Jr.	Urbana IL	1st Lt	USAF 23 Gp.	5.00	5.00

NAME	HOME TOWN	RANK	UNIT	CLAIMED	USAFHS 85
Booth, Robert J.	Visalia CA	1st Lt	USAF 359 Gp.	8.00	8.00
Borley, Clarence A.	Yakima WA	LT	USN VF15	5.00	
Bostrom, Ernest O.	East Orange NJ	1st Lt	USAF 352 Gp.	5.00	5.00
Bostwick, George E.	Ft. Worth TX	Maj	USAF 56 Gp.	9.00	8.00
Boyington, Gregory (CMH)	Fresno CA	LTC	AVG(6)USMC VMF214	28.00	
Bradley, Jack T.	Falls Church VA	LTC	USAF 354 Gp.	15.00	15.00
Bradley, John L.	Shreveport LA	Maj	USAF 33 Gp.	5.00	5.00
Brassfield, Arthur J.	Browning MO	LT	USN VF42	7.00	
Braun, Richard Lane	Cherry Point NC	Capt	USMC VMF215	5.00	
Brewer, Charles W.	Tulsa OK	LCDR	USN VF15	6.50	
Brezas, Michael	Bloomfield NJ	1st Lt	USAF 14 Gp.	12.00	12.00
Bridges, Johnnie J.	Shelby NC	LT	USN VF3/7	6.25	
Bright, John G.	Reading PA	Maj	AVG/AF23 Gp.	7.00	
Bright, Mark Kenneth	Anderson IN	LT	USN VF5/46	9.00	
Broadhead, Joseph E.	Rupert ID	Maj	USAF 357 Gp.	10.00	8.00
Brocato, Samuel J. Jr.	Baltimore MD	LT	USN VF83	6.00	
Brooks, James L.	Los Angeles CA	1st Lt	USAF 31 Gp.	13.00	13.00
Brown, Carl A. Jr.	Texarkana TX	LT	USN VF27	10.00	
Brown, Gerald A.	Phoenix AZ	Capt	USAF 55 Gp.	5.00	5.00
Brown, Harley L.	Wichita KS	1st Lt	USAF 20 Gp.	6.00	6.00
Brown, Harry Winston	Alamo CA	Capt	USAF 475/49 Gp.	5.00	6.00
Brown, Henry William	Sumter SC	Capt	USAF 355 Gp.	17.20	14.20
Brown, J. Danforth	Tampa FL	Sq Ldr	RCAF	5.00	
Brown, Meade M.	Louisville KY	Capt	USAF 348 Gp.	6.00	6.00
Brown, Quince L.	Bristow OK	Maj	USAF 78 Gp.	12.33	12.33
Brown, Robert Harold	Medfield MA	2nd Lt	USAF 325 Gp.	7.00	7.00
Brown, Samuel J.	Tulsa OK	Maj	USAF 31 Gp.	15.00	15.50
Brown, William Perry Jr.	Santa Ana CA	LT	USMC VMF311	7.00	
Browning, James W.	Syracuse KS	Capt	USAF 357 Gp.	7.00	7.00
Brueland, Lowell K.	Callender IA	Maj	USAF 354 Gp.	12.50	12.50
				+2 Korea	
Bruneau, Paul J.	San Diego CA	CDR	USN VF	5.00	
Brunmier, Carland E.	Bloomington CA	LT	USN VF44	6.00	
Bryan, Donald S.	Paicines CA	Capt	USAF 352 Gp.	13.33	13.33
Bryan, William E. Jr.	Ocean Springs MS	Maj	USAF 339 Gp.	8.50	7.50
Bryce, James A.	Altus OK	LT	USN VF22	5.25	
Buchanan, Robert L.	North Baltimore OH	ENS	USN VF29	5.00	
Buck, George T. Jr.	Tchula MS	Capt	USAF 31 Gp.	6.00	6.00
Buie, Paul D.	Nashville GA	CDR	USN VF16	9.00	
Burckhalter, William E.	Great Neck LI NY	LT	USN VF16	6.00	
Burdick, Clinton D.	Brooklyn NY	1st Lt	USAF 356 Gp.	5.50	5.50
Burgard, George T.	Salinsgrove PA	Capt	AVG	10.75	
Burley, Franklin N.	Monterey LA	LT	USN VF18	7.00	
Burnett, Roy O. Jr.	Oswego OR	LT	USN VF5	8.00	
Burriss, Howard M.	Granville OH	LT	USN VF17	7.50	
Bushner, Francis X.	Miami FL	LCDR	USN VC33	6.00	
Buttke, Robert L.	Sacramento CA	Capt	USAF 55 Gp.	5.50	5.50
Byrne, Robert J.	St. Louis MO	1st Lt	USAF 57 Gp.	6.00	5.00
Byrnes, Matthew S. Jr.	Hamilton, Ontario, Can.	LT	USN VF9	6.00	
Byrnes, Robert C.	Winfield LA	Capt	USAF 18 Gp.	5.00	5.00
Cain, James B.	Alexandria VA	LT	USN VF45	8.50	
Callaway, Raymond H.	Grove City MN	Maj	USAF 3CACW	6.00	6.00
Campbell, Richard A.	Ferriday LA	1st Lt	USAF 14 Gp.	6.00	6.00
Candelaria, Richard G.	Las Vegas NV	1st Lt	USAF 479 Gp.	6.00	6.00
Carder, John B.	Red Oak IA	1st Lt	USAF 357 Gp.	5.00	7.00
Care, Raymond C.	San Antonio TX	Capt	USAF 4 Gp.	6.00	6.00
Carey, Henry A. Jr.		LT	USN VF	9.00	
Carl, Marion Eugene	Triangle VA	Maj	USMC VMF221/223	18.50	
Carlson, Kendall E.	Red Bluff CA	Capt	USAF 4 Gp.	6.00	6.00
Carlton, William A.	Allen Park MI	Maj	USMC VMF	5.00	
Carmichael, Daniel A. Jr.	Bexley OH	LT	USN VF6/28	13.00	
Carpenter, George	Paris TN	Maj	USAF 4 Gp.	13.33	13.33
Carr, Bruce W.	Satellite Beach FL	1st Lt	USAF 354 Gp.	14.00	14.00
Carr, George R.	Bogalusa LA	LT	USN VF15	11.50	
Carroll, Charles H.	Philadelphia PA	LT	USN VF2	6.00	
Carroll, Walter J. Jr.	New York NY	1st Lt	USAF 82 Gp.	8.00	8.00
Carson, Leonard K.	Clear Lake, Iowa	Capt	USAF 357 Gp.	18.50	18.50
Carter, James R.	Las Cruces NM	Capt	USAF 56 Gp.	6.00	6.00
Case, William Northrop	Vancouver WA	Capt	USMC VMF	8.00	

NAME	HOME TOWN	RANK	UNIT	CLAIMED	USAFHS 85
Castle, Nial K.	Lemon Grove CA	2nd Lt	USAF 49 Gp.	5.00	5.00
Caswell, Dean	Edinburg TX	LT	USMC VMF221	7.00	
Cesky, Charles J.	Baltimore MD	Capt	USAF 352 Gp.	8.50	8.50
Ceuleers, George F.	Georgetown CO	LTC	USAF 364 Gp.	10.50	10.50
Champion, Henry K.	Greenville MS	LT	USN VF9/8	5.00	
Champlin, Fredric F.	West Palm Beach FL	Capt	USAF 475 Gp.	9.00	9.00
Chandler, Creighton	New Orleans LA	Capt	USMC VMF215	6.00	
Chandler, George T.	Wichita KS	Capt	USAF 18/347 Gp.	5.00	5.00
Chandler, Van E.	Greeley CO	1st Lt	USAF 4 Gp.	5.00* +3 Korea	5.00
Chapman, Philip G.	Fort Smith AK	Maj	USAF 23 Gp.	7.00	7.00
Chase, Levi R.	Cortland NY	LTC	AF 33/2CDO	10.00	12.00
Check, Leonard J.		LCDR	USN	9.50	
Chen, Arthur (Chinese)	Portland OR	1st Lt	AVG	5.00	
Chennault, Claire	Commerce TX	Gen.	AVG/USAF	Unk.	
Chenoweth, Oscar I.	Miami FL	LT	USN VF17	8.50	
Chick, Lewis W. Jr.	Blanco TX	LTC	USAF 325 Gp.	6.00	6.00
Christensen, Fred J.	Watertown MA	Capt	USAF 56 Gp.	21.50	21.50
Clark, James Averell Jr.	Westbury LI NY	LTC	USAF 4 Gp.	11.50	10.50
Clark, Lawrence A.	Huntington Park CA	LT	USN VF83	7.00	
Clark, Robert A.	Hartford CT	LT	USN VF17	7.00	
Clark, Walter E.		LCDR	USN VF5/10	6.00	
Clements, Donald C.		LT	USN VF	5.00	
Clements, Robert E.	Buena Vista GA	CDR	USN VF11	5.00	
Cleaveland, Arthur B.	Springfield OH	2nd Lt	USAF 57 Gp.	5.00	5.00
Clinger, Dallas A.	Alpine WY	Capt	USAF 23 Gp.	5.00	5.00
Cloud, Vivian A.	Baltimore MD	Capt	USAF 475 Gp.	5.00	5.00
Coats, Robert C.	Jacksonville FL	LCDR	USN VF17	9.33	
Cochran, Paul R.	Hutchinson KS	2nd Lt	USAF 82 Gp.	5.00	5.00
Coen, Oscar H.	Wallum ND	F/Lt	RAF(3)USAF 4 Gp.(2.5)	5.50	2.50
Coffey, Robert L. Jr.	Johnstown PA	LTC	USAF 365 Gp.	6.00	6.00
Coleman, Thaddeus T.	Jacksonville, FL	LCDR	USN VF6/23	10.00	
Coleman, Wilson M.	Tallahassee FL	LCDR	USN VF13	6.00	
Collins, Frank J.	Tampa FL	Maj	USAF 325 Gp.	9.00	9.00
Collins, William M. Jr.	Chevy Chase MD	CDR	USN VF8	9.00	
Collinsworth, J. D.	Phoenix AZ	Capt	USAF 31 Gp.	6.00	6.00
Colman, Philip E.	Augusta GA	1st Lt	USAF 5CACW	5.00* +4 Korea	5.00
Compton, Gordon B.	Wichita KS	Capt	USAF 353 Gp.	5.50	5.50
Comstock, Harold E.	Fresno CA	Maj	USAF 56 Gp.	5.00	5.00
Conant, Arthur Roger	Newport Beach CA	Capt	USMC VMF215	6.00	
Conants, Edwin Stanley	Lakeside CA	LT	USN VF17	6.00	
Condon, Henry L. II	Opelika AL	Capt	USAF 475 Gp.	5.00	5.00
Conger, Jack E.	Havelock NC	Capt	USMC VMF212	10.00	
Conger, Paul A.	Sherman Oaks CA	Maj	USAF 56 Gp.	11.50	11.50
Conroy, Thomas J.	Kingsville TX	LT	USN VF27	7.00	
Cook, Walter V.	Universal City TX	Capt	USAF 56 Gp.	6.00	6.00
Coons, Merle M.	Fountain Valley CA	Capt	USAF 55 Gp.	5.00	5.00
Copeland, William E.	Arlington Heights IL	LT	USN VF19	6.00	
Cordray, Paul	Dallas TX	LT	USN VF17	7.00	
Cormier, Richard L. (Zeke)	Rancho Santa Fe CA	LT	USN VF80	10.00	
Cornell, Leland B.	Newport RI	LT	USN VF	5.00	
Cowger, Richard D.	Oak View CA	LT	USN VC39/VF17	6.00	
Cox, Ralph L.	Pasadena CA	Capt	USAF 359 Gp.	5.00	5.00
Cozzens, Melvin	Powell WY	LT	USN VF29	6.50	
Cragg, Edward	Cos Cob CT	Maj	USAF 8 Gp.	15.00	15.00
Craig, Clement M.	Washington DC	LCDR	USN VF22	12.00	
Cramer, Darrell S.	Ogden UT	Maj	USAF 55 Gp.	7.50	7.00
Cranfill, Niven K.	Temple TX	Maj	USAF 359 Gp.	5.00	5.00
Crawford, Ray	Alhambra CA	2nd Lt	USAF 82 Gp.	6.00	6.00
Crenshaw, Claude J.	Monroe LA	1st Lt	USAF 359 Gp.	7.00	7.00
Crim, Harry C. Jr.	Atlanta GA	Maj	USAF 21 Gp.	6.00	6.00
Cronin, Donald F.	Towson MD	LT	USN VF10/8	6.00	
Crosby, John T.	Oakland CA	LT	USN VF18	6.00	
Crowe, William E.	Norfolk VA	Capt	USMC VMF124	7.00	
Cruikshank, Arthur W.	Eglin AFB FL	Maj	USAF 23 Gp.	8.00	8.00
Cullerton, William J.	Elmhurst IL	1st Lt	USAF 355 Gp.	6.00	5.00
Cummings, Donald M.	San Bernardino CA	Capt	USAF 55 Gp.	6.50	6.50
Cundy, Arthur C.	Tallahassee FL	1st Lt	USAF 353 Gp.	5.00	6.00

NAME	HOME TOWN	RANK	UNIT	CLAIMED	USAFHS 85
Cunningham, Daniel G.	Chicago IL	LT	USN VF17	7.00	
Cupp, James N.	Red Oak IA	Maj	USMC VMF213	13.00	
Curdes, Louis E.	Fort Wayne, IN	1st Lt	USAF 82 Gp.	9.00	9.00
Curry, John Harvey	Dallas TX	F/O	RAF 601 Sq.	6.33	
Curtis, Robert C.	Washington DC	Maj	USAF 52 Gp.	14.00	14.00
Curton, Warren D.	Spring City TN	1st Lt	USAF 49 Gp.	5.00	5.00
Cutler, Frank A.	Cleveland OH	Capt	USAF 352 Gp.	8.50	7.50
Czarnecki, Edward J.	Wilmington DE	1st Lt	USAF 475 Gp.	6.00	6.00
Dahl, Perry J.	Colorado Springs CO	Capt	USAF 475 Gp.	9.00	9.00
Dahlberg, Kenneth H.	Wayzata WI	Capt	USAF 354 Gp.	14.00	14.00
Dahms, Kenneth J.	Winnebago MN	ENS	USN VF30	7.50	
Dalglish, James B.	Rome NY	Maj	USAF 354 Gp.	9.00	9.00
Damstrom, Fernley H.	Oliva TX	1st Lt	USAF 49 Gp.	8.00	8.00
Daniell, Jack S.	Birmingham AL	1st Lt	USAF 339 Gp.	5.00	5.00
Daniel, William A.	Alexandria LA	Col	USAF 31 Gp.	5.00	5.00
Davenport, Merl W.	Detroit MI	LT	USN VF17	6.00	
Davidson, George H.	Lake Como FL	LT	USN VC27	7.00	
Davies, C. E.		LT	USN VF	5.00	
Davis, Barrie S.	Zebulon NC	1st Lt	USAF 325 Gp.	6.00	6.00
Davis, Clayton E.	Shalimar FL	Capt	USAF 352 Gp.	5.00	5.00
Davis, George A. Jr. (CMH)	Lubbock TX	1st Lt	USAF 348 Gp.	7.00* +14 Korea	7.00
Davis, Glendon V.	Parma ID	Capt	USAF 357 Gp.	7.50	7.50
Davis, Leonard K.	Chicago IL	LTC	USMC VMF121	5.00	
Davis, Ralph H.	Lexington MA	LT	USN VF	7.50	
Davis, Robert H.	Rio Rico AZ	LT	USN VF18	6.50	
Dawkins, George E. Jr.	Rancho Santa Fe CA	Capt	USMC VMF	5.00	
Day, William C. Jr.	Red Lion PA	1st Lt	USAF 49 Gp.	5.00	5.00
Daymond, Gregory A. (Gus)	Burbank CA	SqLdr	RAF/USAF 71 Sq.	7.00	
Deakins, Richard S.	Jonesboro TN	1st Lt	USAF 325 Gp.	5.00	5.00
Dean, Cecil O.	Salina KS	2nd Lt	USAF 325 Gp.	6.00	6.00
Dean, William A. Jr.	Jourdanton TX	CDR	USN VF2	11.00	
Dean, Zach W.	Altoona KS	1st Lt	USAF 475 Gp.	7.00	7.00
Dear, John W. Jr.	Meridian MS	LT	USN VF2	7.00	
DeBlanc, Jefferson J. (CMH)	St. Martinville LA	Capt	USMC VMF112	9.00	
Decew, Leslie	Bakersfield CA	LT	USN VF9	6.00	
Degraffenreid, Edwin L.	Lakeview OR	2nd Lt	USAF 8 Gp.	6.00	6.00
Dehaven, Robert M.	Encino CA	Capt	USAF 49 Gp.	14.00	14.00
Della, George	Strathmore CA	1st Lt	USAF 348 Gp.	5.00	5.00
Delong, Philip Cunliffe	Treasure Island FL	Capt	USMC VMF212	11.17* +2 Korea	
Denman, Anthony J.	Greenwich CT	LCDR	USN VF18	6.00	
Denoff, Reuben H.	Kennewick WA	LCDR	USN VF9	5.00	
Dent, Elliott E. Jr.	Birmingham AL	Capt	USAF 49 Gp.	6.00	6.00
Devine, Richard O.		LT	USN VF10	6.00	
Dewing, Lawrence A.	San Diego CA	LT	USN VF14	5.50	
Dibb, Robert A. M.	Los Angeles CA	LT	USN VF6	8.50	
Dick, Frederick E.	Barrington RI	Capt	USAF 49 Gp.	5.00	5.00
Dikovitsky, Michael	Cleveland OH	1st Lt	USAF 348 Gp.	5.00	5.00
Dillard, Joseph V.	Downey CA	Lt	USMC VMF323	6.33	
Dillard, William J.	Longview TX	Capt	USAF 31 Gp.	6.00	6.00
Dillow, Eugene	Cobden IL	Capt	USMC VMF221	6.00	
Dobbin, John Francis	Brighton MA	LTC	USMC VMF224	8.00	
Doersch, George A.	Thousand Oaks CA	Capt	USAF 359 Gp.	10.50	10.50
Donahue, Archie Glenn	Texas City TX	Maj	USMC VMF112	14.00	
Donaldson, I. B. Jack	Kiefer OK	2nd Lt	USAF 49 Gp.	5.00	5.00
Doner, Landis E.	Plymouth WI	LT	USN VF2	8.00	
Dorris, Harry W.	Harrisburg IL	Maj	USAF 31 Gp.	5.25	5.25
Dorroh, Jefferson D.	Ontario OR	Maj	USMC VMF323	6.00	
Dorsch, Frederick J. Jr.	Pittsburgh PA	Capt	USAF 31 Gp.	8.00	8.50
Douglas, Paul P. Jr.	Conway AR	LTC	USAF 368 Gp.	7.00	7.00
Doyle, Cecil J.	Marshall MN	2nd Lt	USMC VMF121	5.00	
Drake, Charles W.	Martinsville NJ	2nd Lt	USMC VMF	5.00	
Dregne, Irwin H.	Viroqua WI	LTC	USAF 357 Gp.	7.00	5.00
Drew, Urban L.	Datchet Slough, Eng.	1st Lt	USAF 361 Gp.	6.00	6.00
Drier, William C.	St. Louis MO	Capt	USAF 49 Gp.	6.00	6.00
Driscoll, Daniel B.	Westport CT	LT	USN VF31	5.00	
Drury, Frank C.	Danby MO	Maj	USMC VMF212	6.00	
Drury, Paul E.	Wynnewood PA	LT	USN VF27	6.00	
Dubisher, Francis E.	Williamsburg IA	Maj	USAF 35 Gp.	5.00	5.00

NAME	HOME TOWN	RANK	UNIT	CLAIMED	USAFHS 85
Dubois, Charles H.	Chesterfield MO	1st Lt	USAF 23 Gp.	5.00	5.00
Duffy, James E.	Gardena CA	LT	USN VF15	5.00	
Duffy, James E. Jr.	N. Caldwell NJ	Capt	USAF 355 Gp.	5.20	5.20
Duffy, Richard E.	Walled Lake MI	2nd Lt	USAF 57 Gp.	5.00	5.00
Duke, Walter F.	Leonardtown MD	Capt	USAF 80 Gp.	8.00	7.00
Dunaway, John S.	Hilt CA	1st Lt	USAF 8 Gp.	7.00	7.00
Duncan, George C.	Arlington VA	LT	USN VF15	13.50	
Duncan, Glenn E.	Houston TX	Col	USAF 353 Gp.	19.00	19.50
Duncan, Robert W.	Marion IL	LT	USN VF5	7.00	
Dungan, Fred L.	Yonkers NY	LT	USN VF2	7.00	
Dunham, William D.	Spokane WA	LTC	USAF 348 Gp.	16.00	16.00
Dunkin, Richard W.	Anderson IN	Capt	USAF 325 Gp.	9.00	9.00
Dunn, Bernard	Smackover AR	LT	USN VF29	5.33	
Dunn, William R.	Arlington TX	P/O	RAF (5)	6.00	1.00
			USAF 406 Gp. (1)		
Dupouy, Parker	Seekonk MA	Capt	AVG(6.5)	6.50	
			USAF(0)		
Durnford, Dewey F.	Melbourne FL	Capt	USMC VMF323	6.33	
				+.5 Korea	
Eagleston, Glenn T.	Davis Creek CA	Maj	USAF 354 Gp.	18.50	18.50
				+2 Korea	
Eason, Hoyt A.	Eclectic AL	1st Lt	USAF 35 Gp.	6.00	6.00
East, Clyde B.	Agoura CA	Capt	USAF 10 Gp.	12.00	12.00
Eastmond, Richard T.	American Fork UT	LT	USN VF1	9.00	
Eberts, Byron A.	Liberty MO	LT	USN VF	6.00	
Eccles, William G.	Los Angeles CA	LT	USN VF11	6.00	
Eckard, Herbert	Huntington Park CA	LT	USN VF9	7.00	
Edens, Billy C.	Tyronza AR	2nd Lt	USAF 56 Gp.	8.00	7.00
Eder, Willard E.	Buffalo WY	LT	USN VF3/29	6.00	
Edner, Selden R.	San Jose CA	Fl/Lt	RAF 121 Sq.	5.00	
Edwards, Edward B. Jr.	Lansdale PA	1st Lt	USAF 373 Gp.	5.50	5.50
Edwards, William C. Jr.	Waipahu HI	LT	USN VF80	6.00	
Egan, Joseph L. Jr.	New York NY	1st Lt	USAF 56 Gp.	5.00	5.00
Elder, John L.	Ebensburg PA	Maj	USAF 355 Gp.	8.00	8.00
Elder, Robert A.	Hernando MI	Maj	USAF 353 Gp.	5.00	5.00
Elliott, Ralph E.	Jacksonville FL	LT	USN VC27	9.50	
Elliott, Vincent T.	Burbank CA	1st Lt	USAF 475 Gp.	7.00	7.00
Elwood, Hugh McJ.	Falls Church VA	LTC	USMC VMF212	5.17	
Emerson, Warren S.	Palestine TX	Capt	USAF 354 Gp.	6.00	6.00
Emmer, Wallace N.	St. Louis MO	Capt	USAF 354 Gp.	14.00	14.00
Emmert, Benjamin H. Jr.	Tempe AZ	1st Lt	USAF 325 Gp.	6.00	6.00
				+1 Korea	
Emmons, Eugene H.	Lawrenceville IL	1st Lt	USAF 325 Gp.	9.00	9.00
Empey, James W.	Bath NY	1st Lt	USAF 52 Gp.	5.00	5.00
England, James J.	Jackson TN	Maj	USAF 311 Gp.	10.00	10.00
England, John B.	Caruthersville MO	Maj	USAF 357 Gp.	17.50	17.50
Ernst, Herman E.		1st Lt	USAF 422 (N)	5.00	5.00
Evans, Andrew J.	Montgomery AL	LTC	USAF 357 Gp.	6.00	6.00
Evans, Roy W.	San Bernardino CA	Maj	USAF 359 Gp.	6.00	6.00
Evenson, Eric A.	Wichita KS	LT	USN VF30	8.00	
Everhart, Lee R.	Petersburg IL	Capt	USAF 8 Gp.	6.00	6.00
Everton, Loran D.	Crofton NE	Maj	USMC VMF212	12.00	
Fairbanks, David C.	New York NY	Sqd Ldr	RCAF 274 Sq.	12.50	
Fair, John W.	Orange Park FL	LT	USN VF80	6.00	
Fanning, Grover E.	Kansas City MO	1st Lt	USAF 49 Gp.	9.00	9.00
Farmer, Charles D.		LT	USN VF10	5.00	
Farnsworth, Robert A. Jr.	Jackson MS	LT	USN VF19	5.00	
Farrell, William	Gardena CA	LT	USMC VMF312	5.00	
Fash, Robert P.	Northbrook IL	LT	USN VF50/15	6.50	
Faxon, Richard D.	Great Barrington MA	1st Lt	USAF 31 Gp.	5.00	5.00
Fecke, Alfred J.	Duxbury MA	LT	USN VF29	7.00	
Feightner, Edward L.	Washington DC	LT	USN VF10/8	9.00	
Feld, Sylvan	Lynn MA	1st Lt	USAF 52 Gp.	9.00	9.00
Felts, Marion C.	Roberta GA	1st Lt	USAF 49 Gp.	5.00	5.00
Fenex, James E. Jr.	West Lake PA	Capt	USAF 324 Gp.	5.00	5.00
Fiebelkorn, Ernest C.	Lake Orion MI	1st Lt	USAF 20 Gp.	9.50	9.00
Fiedler, Arthur C. Jr.	Oak Park IL	Capt	USAF 325 Gp.	8.00	8.00
Fiedler, William F. Jr.	Akron OH	1st Lt	USAF 347/18 Gp.	5.00	5.00
Fields, Virgil C. Jr.	Jay OK	Capt	USAF 31 Gp.	5.00	5.00
Finn, Howard J.	Belmond IA	Capt	USMC VMF124	6.00	

NAME	HOME TOWN	RANK	UNIT	CLAIMED	USAFHS 85
Fischette, Charles R.	Clyde NY	1st Lt	USAF 31 Gp.	5.00	5.00
Fisher, Don Homs	Beaufort SC	Capt	USMC VMF214	6.00	
Fisher, Edwin O.	Portland OR	Capt	USAF 362 Gp.	7.00	7.00
Fisher, Rodney W.	San Francisco CA	1st Lt	USAF 1 Gp.	5.00	5.00
Fisk, Harry E.	Colorado Springs CO	Capt	USAF 354 Gp.	5.00	5.00
Fisk, Jack A.	Peoria IL	Capt	USAF 475 Gp.	7.00	7.00
Flack, Nelson D. Jr.	Hatboro PA	Capt	USAF 49 Gp.	5.00	5.00
Flatley, James H. Jr.	Green Bay WI	LCDR	USN VF42/10/5	6.50	
Fleischer, Richard H.	Altadena CA	Capt	USAF 348 Gp.	6.00	6.00
Fleming, Francis M.	Sunland CA	LT	USN VF16	7.50	
Fleming, Patrick D.	Jamestown RI	LCDR	USN VF80	19.00	
Flinn, Kenneth A.	Walnut Creek CA	LT	USN VF15	5.00	
Foltz, Frank E.	Detroit MI	LT	USN VF18	7.00	
Foltz, Ralph E.	Pleasant Hills CA	LT	USN VF15	5.00	
Fontana, Paul John	New Bern NC	LTC	USMC VMF112	5.00	
Ford, Claude E.	Sarasota FL	Maj	USAF 82 Gp.	5.00	5.00
Ford, Kenneth M.	Whittier CA	Capt	USMC VMF121	5.00	
Formanek, George Jr.		LT	USN VF	5.00	
Forrer, Samuel W.	Fitzpatrick AL	LT	USN VF71	5.50	
Forster, Joseph M.	Tempe AZ	1st Lt	USAF475 Gp.	9.00	9.00
Fortier, Norman J.	Barrington NH	Capt	USAF 355 Gp.	5.83	5.83
Foss, Joseph Jacob (CMH)	Scottsdale AZ	Maj	USMC VMF121	26.00	
Foster, Carl C.	Utica MI	ENS	USN VF5	8.50	
Foulis, William B. Jr.	Houston TX	Capt	USAF 348 Gp.	6.00	6.00
Fowle, James M.	Miami FL	1st Lt	USAF 364 Gp.	8.00	8.00
Fowler, Richard E. Jr.	Sweeney TX	LT	USN VF15	6.50	
Foy, Robert W.	Oswego NY	Maj	USAF 357 Gp.	17.00	15.00
Franger, Marvin J.	Alexandria VA	LT	USN VF9	9.00	
Franklin, Dwaine R.	Deming, NM	1st Lt	USAF 52 Gp.	7.00	7.00
Franks, John M.	Easton PA	LT	USN VF9	7.00	
Frantz, Carl M.	Brownsville PA	1st Lt	USAF 354 Gp.	11.00	11.00
Fraser, Robert B.	Genesee NY	Maj	USMC VMF112	6.00	
Frazier, Kenneth D.	Burlington NJ	Maj	USMC VMF223	12.50	
Freeman, Doris C.		LT	USN VF	9.00	
Freeman, William B.		LT	USMC VMF121	6.00	
French, James B.	Bakersfield CA	LT	USN VF9	11.00	
Frendberg, Alfred L.	Hillsboro ND	LT	USN VF16	6.00	
Froning, Alfred C.	LaParte City IA	1st Lt	USAF 57 Gp.	6.00	6.00
Fryer, Earl R.	Boyertown PA	Capt	USAF 55 Gp.	7.00	4.00
Funk, Harold N.	LaHabra CA	LCDR	USN VF23/26	7.00	
Gabreski, Francis S.	Dix Hills NY	LTC	USAF 56 Gp.	28.00 +6.5 Korea	28.00
Gabriel, Franklin T.	Evanston IL	LT	USN VF2	8.25	
Gailer, Frank L. Jr.	San Antonio TX	1st Lt	USAF 357 Gp.	5.50	5.50
Galer, Robert E. (CMH)	Dallas TX	Col	USMC VMF224	13.00	
Gallup, Charles S.	Chicago IL	Capt	USAF 35 Gp.	6.00	6.00
Gallup, Kenneth W.	Clint TX	LTC	USAF 353 Gp.	9.00	9.00
Galt, Dwight B.	Hyattsville MD	LT	USN VF31	5.00	
Galvin, John R.	Coronado CA	LT	USN VF8	7.00	
Gardner, Warner F.	Cazenovia NY	Maj	USAF 82 Gp.	5.00	5.00
Gardner, William A.	Concord NH	Capt	USAF 8 Gp.	8.00	8.00
Garrison, Vermont	Mountain Home ID	1st Lt	RAF/USAF 4 Gp.	7.33 +10 Korea	7.33
Gaunt, Frank L.	North Platte NE	Capt	USAF18 Gp.	8.00	8.00
Gayler, Noel	Philadelphia PA	CDR	USN VF3/12	5.00	
Gentile, Donald S.	Piqua OH	Capt	USAF 4 Gp.	19.83	19.83
Gerard, Francis R.	Sea Girt NJ	Capt	USAF 339 Gp.	8.00	8.00
Gerick, Steven	Pittsburgh PA	2nd Lt	USAF 56 Gp.	5.00	5.00
Gholson, Grover D.	Oxford NC	Capt	USAF 475 Gp.	5.00	5.00
Gibb, Robert D.	Lansing MI	1st Lt	USAF 348 Gp.	5.00	5.00
Gile, Clement D.	Rye NY	LT	USN VF17	8.00	
Gillespie, Roy F.	Eugene OR	LT	USN VF30	6.00	
Gimbel, Edward L.		Fl/Lt	RAF 401 Sq	5.00	
Giroux, William K.	Kankakee IL	Capt	USAF 8 Gp.	10.00	10.00
Gladen, Cyrus R.	Salem OR	1st Lt	USAF 18 Gp.	5.00	5.00
Gladych, Michael	Poland	Sq.Ldr	att USAF 56 Gp.	10.00	10.00
Gleason, George W.	Montrose CO	Capt	USAF 479 Gp.	12.00	12.00
Glenn, Maxwell H.	Winnfield LA	Maj	USAF 80 Gp.	8.00	7.50
Glover, Fred W.	Asheville NC	Maj	USAF 4 Gp.	10.33	10.33
Godfrey, John T.	Woonsocket RI	Capt	USAF 4 Gp.	16.33	16.33

NAME	HOME TOWN	RANK	UNIT	CLAIMED	85
Godson, Lindley W.	Colonia NJ	LT	USN VF23	5.00	
Goebel, Robert J.	Torrance CA	Capt	USAF 31 Gp.	11.00	11.00
Goehausen, Walter J. Jr.	Issaquah WA	Capt	USAF 31 Gp.	10.00	10.00
Goodnight, Robert E.	Portland OR	1st Lt	USAF 354 Gp.	7.25	7.25
Goodson, James A.	Brussels, Belgium	Maj	USAF 4 Gp.	15.00	14.00
Gordon, Donald	Fort Scott KS	LT	USN VF10	7.00	
Gordon, Mathew M. Jr.		Capt	USAF 23 Gp.	4.00	5.00
Goss, Edmund R.	Arlington VA	Maj	USAF 23 Gp.	6.00	6.00
Gould, Norman D.	San Jose CA	1st Lt	USAF 56 Gp.	5.00	4.00
Graham, Gordon M.	Taft CA	LTC	USAF 355 Gp.	7.00	7.00
Graham, Lindol F.	Ridgewood NJ	Capt	USAF 20 Gp.	5.50	5.50
Graham, Robert F.		2nd Lt	USAF 422 NFR	5.00	5.00
				(assists-R)	
Graham, Vernon E.	St. Augustine FL	LT	USN VF82	5.00	
Grant, Marvin E.	Aurora CO	1st Lt	USAF 348 Gp.	7.00	7.00
Gray, James S.	Washington DC	LCDR	USN VF6/78	5.50	
Gray, John Floyd	Champaign IL	LT	USN VF5	8.25	
Gray, Rockford V.	Cincinnati OH	Maj	USAF 365/371 Gp.	6.50	6.50
Green, Herschel H.	Palos Verdes CA	Maj	USAF 325 Gp.	18.00	18.00
Gregg, Lee O.		1st Lt	USAF 449 Sq.	6.00	7.00
Gregory, Hayden A.	Albuquerque NM	LT	USN VF82	5.00	
Gresham, Billy M.	Lake Charles LA	1st Lt	USAF 475 Gp.	6.00	6.00
Griffin, Joseph Henry	Oklahoma City OK	Maj	USAF 23/367 Gp.	7.00	7.00
Griffin, Richard J.	Gladwyne PA	LT	USN VF2	8.00	
Griffis, James W.	Heidelberg, Germany	Capt	USAF 1/14 Gp.	6.00	4.00
Griffith, Robert C.	Austin TX	1st Lt	USAF 82 Gp.	5.00	5.00
Gross, Clayton K.	Portland OR	Capt	USAF 354 Gp.	6.00	5.00
Grosshuesch, LeRoy V.	Ogden UT	Capt	USAF 35 Gp.	8.00	8.00
Grosvenor, William Jr.	N. Kingstown RI	Capt	USAF 23 Gp.	5.00	5.00
Gumm, Charles F.	Spokane WA	1st Lt	USAF 354 Gp.	6.00	6.00
Gupton, Cheatham W.	Durham NC	1st Lt	USAF 49 Gp.	5.00	5.00
Gustafson, Harlan I.	Norristown PA	LT	USN VF8	6.00	
Gutt, Fred E.	Madison WI	Capt	USMC VMF223	8.00	
Haas, Walter A.	McLean VA	LT	USN VF42/3	6.00	
Haberman, Roger A.	Long Beach CA	Capt	USMC VMF121	7.00	
Hacking, Albert C. Jr.	Boston MA	Capt	USMC VMF221	5.00	
Hadden, Mayo A. Jr.	Cocoa Beach FL	LT	USN VF9	8.00	
Hagerstrom, James P.	Waterloo IA	1st Lt	USAF 49 Gp.	6.00*	6.00
				+8.5 Korea	
Hall, George F.	West Palm Beach FL	1st Lt	USAF56 Gp.	6.00	6.00
Hall, Sheldon O.	Pandoro OH	Capt	USMC VMF	6.00	
Halton, William T.	Brooklyn NY	Maj	USAF 352 Gp.	11.50	10.50
Hamblin, Louis R.	Ft. Bridger WY	LT	USN VF80	6.00	
Hamilton, Henry B.	Larue TX	WO	USMC VMF212	7.00 assists	
				as gunner	
Hamilton, Robert M.	Baldwin LI NY	LT	USN VF83	6.00	
Hammer, Samuel E.	Neal KS	1st Lt	USAF 80 Gp.	5.00	5.00
Hampshire, John F.	Grants Pass OR	Capt	USAF 23 Gp.	13.00	13.00
Hanes, William F. Jr.	Ft. Walton Beach FL	1st Lt	USAF 52 Gp.	6.00	6.00
Hanks, Eugene R.	Albuquerque NM	LT	USN VF16	6.00	
Hanna, Harry T.	Westfield IN	1st Lt	USAF 14 Gp.	5.00	5.00
Hanseman, Chris J.	Mendovi WI	1st Lt	USAF 339 Gp.	5.00	5.00
Hansen, Herman Jr.	Santa Barbara CA	Maj	USMC VMF122	5.50	
Hanson, Robert Murray (CMH)	Newtonville MA	1st Lt	USMC VMF214	25.00	
Hardy, Willis E.	San Juan Capistrano CA	LT	USN VF17	7.00	
Hargreaves, Everett C.	Milwaukee WI	LT	USN VF2	8.50	
Harman, Walter R.	Escondido CA	LT	USN VF10	5.00	
Harmeyer, Raymond F.	New Orleans LA	1st Lt	USAF 31 Gp.	6.00	6.00
Harrington, A. A.	Fairfield CA	Flt Lt	RAF 410 Sq.	7.00	
Harris, Bill (NMI)	Springville CA	LtCol	USAF 18 Gp.	16.00	16.00
Harris, Cecil E.	Alexandria VA	LCDR	USN VF18/27	24.00	
Harris, Ernest A.	Morristown TN	Capt	USAF 49 Gp.	10.00	10.00
Harris, Frederick A.	Glendale AZ	Capt	USAF 475 Gp.	8.00	8.00
Harris, Leroy E.	Brownwood TX	LT	USN VF10/2	12.00	
Harris, Thomas L.	Santa Paula CA	Capt	USAF 357 Gp.	5.00	5.00
Harris, Thomas S.	Sandoval IL	LT	USN VF18/17	9.00	
Hart, Cameron M.	Westfield NJ	Capt	USAF 56 Gp.	6.00	6.00
Hart, Kenneth F.	Martinez CA	1st Lt	USAF 475 Gp.	8.00	8.00
Hartley, Raymond E. Jr.	Kansas City MO	Capt	USAF 325/353	5.00	5.00
Hatala, Paul R.	Cleveland OH	Capt	USAF 357 Gp.	5.50	5.50

NAME	HOME TOWN	RANK	UNIT	CLAIMED	USAFHS 85
Hatch, Herbert B.	Birmingham MI	2nd Lt	USAF 357 Gp	5.00	5.00
Hauver, Charles D.	Poughkeepsie NY	1st Lt	USAF 357 Gp.	5.00	5.00
Haverland, Charles H. Jr.	Grand Blanc MN	LT	USN VF20	6.50	
Haviland, Fred R. Jr.	Chicago IL	Capt	USAF 355 Gp.	9.00	6.00
Hawkins, Arthur R.	Lufkin TX	LT	USN VF31	14.00	
Haworth, Russell C.	Cedar Hill TX	1st Lt	USAF 55 Gp.	5.00	5.00
Hayde, Frank R.	Kansas City MO	LT	USN VF31	5.00	
Hayes, Thomas L. Jr.	Annandale VA	Lt Col	USAF 357 Gp.	8.50	8.50
Haywood, Thomas C.	Playa del Rey CA	Capt	AVG	5.25	
Head, Cotesworth B. Jr.	San Francisco CA	Capt	USAF 18 Gp.	12.00	13.00
Hearrell, Frank C.	Corpus Christi TX	LCDR	USN VF18	5.00	
Heath, Frank C.		LT	USN VF10	7.00	
Hedman, Robert (Duke)	Las Vegas NV	Capt	AVG	5.00	
Hedrick, Roger R.	Hollywood CA	LCDR	USN VF17/84	12.00	
Heinzen, Lloyd P.	Colorado Springs CO	LT	USN VF8	6.00	
Heller, Edwin L.	Philadelphia PA	Capt	USAF 352 Gp.	5.50*	5.50
				+3.5 Korea	
Henderson, Paul M. Jr.	Lakeland FL	LT	USN VF1	5.00	
Hendricks, Randall W.	Youngstown OH	Maj	USAF 368 Gp.	5.00	5.00
Hennon, William J.	Mound MN	Capt	USAF 49 Gp.	7.00	7.00
Henry, William E.	Bakersfield CA	LCDR	USN VF79/41	12.00	
Herbst, John C.	Pala CA	LTC	USAF 23 Gp.	18.00	18.00
Hernan, Edwin James Jr.	Dallas TX	Capt	USMC VMF214	8.00	
Hibbard, Samuel B.	Harvard MA	LCDR	USN VF47	7.33	
Hill, Allen E.	Sterling IL	Capt	USAF 8 Gp.	9.00	9.00
Hill, David L.	San Antonio TX	Col.	AVG(11.25)USAF 23 Gp. 17.25		6.00
Hill, Frank A.	Pompton Plains NJ	Maj	USAF 31 Gp.	7.00	7.00
Hill, Harry E.	Mitchell VA	LT	USN VF5	7.00	
Hill, James E.	Stillwater OK	Maj	USAF 365 Gp.	5.00	5.00
Hippe, Kenneth G.	Huntington LI NY	LT	USN VF3	5.00	
Hiro, Edwin W.	Chisolm MN	Maj	USAF 357 Gp.	5.00	5.00
Hively, Howard D.	Athens OH	Maj	USAF 4 Gp.	12.00	12.00
Hnatio, Myron M.	Dearborn MI	1st Lt	USAF 348 Gp.	5.00	5.00
Hoag, John B.	Los Angeles CA	ENS	USN VF82	5.00	
Hockery, John J.	Independence MO	Capt	USAF 78 Gp.	*7.00	7.00
				+1 Korea	
Hodges, William R.	Winston Salem NC	Capt	USAF 325 Gp.	5.00	5.00
Hoefker, John H.	Taylor Mill KY	Capt	USAF 10 Gp.	8.50	8.50
Hoel, Ronald W.	Virginia Beach VA	LT	USN VF8	6.00	
Hofer, Ralph K.	Salem MO	2nd Lt	USAF 4 Gp.	16.50	15.00
Hoffman, Cullen J.	Atlanta GA	1st Lt	USAF 325 Gp.	5.00	5.00
Hoffman, James E. Jr.	Cleveland OH	1st Lt	USAF 52 Gp.	6.50	6.50
Hogg, Roy B.	Springfield VA	Capt	USAF 325 Gp.	6.00	6.00
Holloway, Bruce K.	Knoxville TN	COL	USAF 23 Gp.	13.00	13.00
Holloway, James D.	Columbus NC	1st Lt	USAF 82 Gp.	6.00	6.00
Hollowell, George L.	Laguna Beach CA	Major	USMC VMF224	8.00	
Holmes, Besby F.	San Francisco CA	1st Lt	USAF 18 Gp.	5.00	5.50
Homer, Cyril F.	Sacramento CA	Capt	USAF 8 Gp.	15.00	15.00
Hood, William L.	Benton Harbor MI	1st Lt	USMC VMF	5.50	
Hopkins, Wallace E.	Waco TX	Lt	USAF 361 Gp.	6.00	4.00
Horne, Francis W.	Aucilla FL	1st Lt	USAF 352 Gp.	5.50	5.50
Houck, Herbert N.	Cromwell MN	LCDR	USN VF9	5.00	
Hovde, William J.	San Antonio TX	Major	USAF 355 Gp.	*10.50	10.50
				+1 Korea	
Howard, James H. (CMH)	Clearwater FL	Col	AVG (7.33)		
			USAF 354 Gp. (6)	13.33	6.00
Howard, Robert L.	Oakland CA	1st Lt	USAF 49 Gp.	6.00	6.00
Howe, David W.	East Hickory PA	1st Lt	USAF 4 Gp.	6.00	6.00
Howes, Bernard H.	Staughton PA	1st Lt	USAF 55 Gp.	6.00	6.00
Hoyt, Edward R.	Denver CO	Capt	USAF 35 Gp.	5.00	5.00
Hubbard, Mark E.	Wausau WI	LTC	USAF 20 Gp.	6.50	6.50
Hudson, Howard R.		LT	USN VF9	5.00	
Huffman, Charles W.	Rockville MO	LT	USN VF	6.00	
Humphrey, Robert J.		LT	USN VF	5.33	
Hundley, John C.	Fort Stockton TX	Capt	USMC VMF	6.00	
Hunt, Edward E.	Los Angeles CA	1st Lt	USAF 354 Gp.	7.50	6.50
Hunter, Alvaro J.	Winter Park FL	Capt	USAF 33 Gp.	5.00	5.00
Hurd, Richard F.	Dobbs Ferry NY	1st Lt	USAF 31 Gp.	6.00	6.00
Hurlbut, Frank D.	Salt Lake City UT	FO	USAF 82 Gp.	9.00	9.00

NAME	HOME TOWN	RANK	UNIT	CLAIMED	85
Hurst, Robert	Grand Junction CO	LT	USN VF	6.00	
Icard, Joe W.	Granite Falls NC	2nd Lt	USAF 56 Gp.	5.00	5.00
Ilfrey, Jack M.	Houston TX	Capt	USAF 1 Gp.	8.00	8.00
Ince, James C.	Boulder CO	1st Lt	USAF 475 Gp.	6.00	6.00
Ireland, Julius W.	Baltimore MD	Maj	USMC VMF223	5.33	
Isaacson, Clayton M.	Grand Forks ND	Capt	USAF 82 Gp.	5.00	4.00
Jackson, Michael J.	Edison NJ	Maj	USAF 56 Gp.	8.00	8.00
Jackson, Willie O. Jr.	Converse LA	LTC	USAF 352 Gp.	7.00	7.00
Jamison, Gilbert L.	Olympia WA	Capt	USAF 364 Gp.	7.00	7.00
Jasper, Clarence M.	Long Beach CA	Flt Lt	RAF 418 Sq.	5.00	
Jeffrey, Arthur F.	San Jose CA	LTC	USAF 479 Gp.	14.00	14.00
Jenkins, Otto D.	Kermit TX	2nd Lt	USAF 357 Gp.	8.50	8.50
Jennings, R. H.		LT	USN VF82	7.00	
Jensen, Alvin J.	Memphis TN	1st Lt	USMC VMF214	7.00	
Jensen, Hayden M.	St. Paul MN	LT	USN VF5	5.00	
Jernstedt, Kenneth A.	Hood River OR	Capt	AVG	10.50	
Jett, Verl E.	Twain Harte CA	Capt	USAF 475 Gp.	7.00	7.00
Johnson, Arthur G. Jr.	Litchfield MN	1st Lt	USAF 52 Gp.	8.50	8.50
Johnson, Byron M.	Lincoln NE	LT	USN VF2	8.00	
Johnson, Clarence O.	Ada MN	Capt	USAF 82 Gp.	7.00	7.00
Johnson, Evan M.	Carlisle PA	Capt	USAF 339 Gp.	5.00	5.00
Johnson, Gerald R.	Eugene OR	LTC	USAF 49 Gp.	22.00	22.00
Johnson, Gerald W.	Little Rock AR	Maj	USAF 56 Gp.	17.00	16.50
Johnson, Robert S.	Woodbury NY	Capt	USAF 56 Gp.	28.00	27.00
Johnson, Wallace R.	Overland Park KS	LT	USN VF15	5.00	
Johnston, John M.	Portland OR	LT	USN VF17	8.00	
Johnston, Robert D.		LTC	USAF 81 Sq.	6.00	6.00
Jones, Charles David	Mineola NY	Lt	USMC VMF222	6.00	
Jones, Curran L.	Salado TX	Capt	USAF 35 Gp.	5.00	5.00
Jones, Cyril W. Jr.	Athens TN	1st Lt	USAF 359 Gp.	6.00	6.00
Jones, Frank C.	Montclair NJ	Capt	USAF 4 Gp.	5.00	5.00
Jones, James M.	Epps LA	LT	USN VF3	7.00	
Jones, John L.	Paterson NJ	Capt	USAF 8 Gp.	8.00	8.00
Jones, Lynn F.	Mercedes TX	Capt	USAF 23 Gp.	5.00	5.00
Jones, Warren L.	Live Oak CA	2nd Lt	USAF 14 Gp.	5.00	5.00
Jorda, J. Wayne	New Orleans LA	Maj	USAF 82 Gp.	5.00	4.00
Jordan, Wallace R.	Long Beach CA	Maj	USAF 49 Gp.	6.00	6.00
Jucheim, Alwin M.	Grenada MS	Capt	USAF 78 Gp.	10.00	9.00
Julian, William H.	Dallas TX	Maj	USAF 78 Gp.	5.00	5.00
Karger, Dale E.	McKees Rock, PA	1st Lt	USAF 357 Gp.	7.50	7.50
Kane, William R.		CDR	USN VF10	7.00	
Karr, Robert A.	Waterloo IA	Capt	USAF 52 Gp.	6.00	6.00
Kearby, Neel E. (CMH)	San Antonio TX	Col	USAF 348 Gp.	22.00	22.00
Keen, Robert J.	Jacksonville FL	1st Lt	USAF 56 Gp.	6.00	6.00
Keith, LeRoy W.	St. Louis MO	LT	USN VF80	6.00	
Kemp, William T.	East Peoria IL	2nd Lt	USAF 361 Gp.	6.00	6.00
Kendrick, Charles	San Francisco CA	1st Lt	USMC VMF223	5.00	
Kennedy, Daniel	Joliet IL	1st Lt	USAF 1/33 Gp.	5.00	5.00
Kepford, Ira C.	Greenwich CT	LT	USN VF17	17.00	
Kerr, Leslie H. Jr.	Evanston IL	LT	USN VF23	6.75	
Kidwell, Robert H.		LT	USN VF45	5.00	
Kienholz, Donald David	Spokane WA	1st Lt	USAF 1 Gp.	6.00	6.00
Kincaid, John R.		LT	USN VF10	5.00	
Kincaid, R. A.	Oakland CA	CDR	USN VF1	5.00	
King, Benjamin H.	Oklahoma City OK	Capt	USAF 359 Gp.	7.00	7.00
King, Charles W.	Green Bay WI	Maj	USAF 35 Gp.	5.00	5.00
King, David L.	Johnsville CA	1st Lt	USAF 373 Gp.	5.00	5.00
King, William B.	Langley AFB VA	1st Lt	USAF 354 Gp.	5.50	5.50
Kingston, William J. Jr.	Kissimee FL	LT	USN VF83	6.00	
Kinnard, Claiborne H. Jr.	Franklin TN	LTC	USAF 355 Gp.	8.00	8.00
Kinsey, Claude R.	Aurora IL	2nd Lt	USAF 82 Gp.	7.00	7.00
Kirby, Marion F.	Lampasas TX	1st Lt	USAF 475 Gp.	5.00	5.00
Kirk, George N.	Milan IL	LT	USN VF10	7.00	
Kirkland, Lenton F. Jr.	Cairo GA	1st Lt	USAF 474 Gp.	5.00	5.00
Kirkpatrick, Floyd C.	Redding CA	Capt	USMC VMF441	5.50	
Kirkwood, Phillip L.	Washington DC	LT	USN VF10	11.00	
Kirla, John A.	Port Chester NY	1st Lt	USAF 357 Gp.	11.50	11.50
Kiser, George E.	Somerset KY	Capt	USAF 49 Gp.	9.00	9.00
Klibbe, Frank W.	Aurora CO	2nd Lt	USAF 56 Gp.	7.00	7.00

NAME	HOME TOWN	RANK	UNIT	CLAIMED	USAFHS 85
Knapp, Robert H.	Des Moines IA	Capt	USAF 348 Gp.	5.00	5.00
Knight, William M.	Sioux City IA	LT	USN VF14	7.50	
Knott, Carroll S.	Bakersfield CA	1st Lt	USAF 14 Gp.	5.00	5.00
Koenig, Charles W.	Oakland CA	1st Lt	USAF 354 Gp.	6.50	6.50
Kopsel, Edward H.		1st Lt	USAF 422NFR Sq. (radar assists)	5.00	5.00
Koraleski, Walter J. Jr.	Detroit MI	Capt	USAF 355 Gp.	5.53	5.53
Kostick, William J.	Memphis TN	ENS	USN VF17	5.00	
Kruzel, Joseph J.	Shalimar FL	LTC	USAF 49/361 Gp	5.50	6.50
Kuentzel, Ward A.	Delano CA	2nd Lt	USAF 82 Gp.	7.00	7.00
Kunz, Charles Murphy	Costa Mesa CA	Maj	USMC VMF221	8.00	
Ladd, Kenneth G.	Salt Lake City UT	Capt	USAF 8 Gp.	12.00	12.00
Laird, Dean S. "Diz"		LT	USN VF	6.00	
Laird, Wayne W.	Merced CA	1st Lt	USMC VMF112	5.00	
Lake, Kenneth B.	Memphis TN	ENS	USN VF2	6.00	
Lamb, George M.	Eugene OR	Maj	USAF 354 Gp.	7.50	7.50
Lamb, Robert A.	Waldwick NJ	Capt	USAF 56 Gp.	7.00	7.00
Lamb, William E.	Washington DC	LT	USN VF27	*6.00 +1 Korea	
Lamoreaux, William E.	Dallas TX	LT	USN VF8	5.00	
Lampe, Richard C.	Globe AZ	1st Lt	USAF 52 Gp.	5.00	5.50
Landers, John D.	Joshua TX	LTC	USAF 49/357/78 Gp.	14.50	14.50
Lane, John H.	Phoenix AZ	1st Lt	USAF 35 Gp.	6.00	6.00
Laney, Willis G.		LT	USN VF84	5.00	
Lang, Joseph L.	Hyde Park MA	Capt	USAF 4 Gp.	7.83	7.83
Langdon, Ned W.		LT	USN VF18/17	5.00	
Larson, Donald A.	Yakima WA	Maj	USAF 339 Gp.	6.00	6.00
Lanphier, Thomas G.	La Jolla CA	Maj	USAF 18 Gp.	5.00	5.50
Larson, Leland A.	Gladwin MI	2nd Lt	USAF 10 Gp.	6.00	6.00
Lasko, Charles W.	Nemacolins PA	Capt	USAF 354 Gp.	7.50	7.50
Lathrope, Franklin C.	Blue Island IL	2nd Lt	USAF 1 Gp.	5.00	5.00
Laughlin, C. H. "Link"	Coral Gables FL	Capt	AVG	5.20	
Lawler, Frank	Coronado CA	Capt	AVG	8.50	
Lawler, John B.	New Cumberland PA	Capt	USAF 52 Gp.	11.00	11.00
Lazear, Earl R. Jr.	Bluefield WV	1st Lt	USAF 352 Gp.	5.00	5.00
Lee, Richard J.	Affton MO	1st Lt	USAF 1 Gp.	5.00	5.00
Leikness, Marlow J.	Danville IL	Capt	USAF 14 Gp.	5.00	5.00
Lenfest, Charles W.	Monument CO	Capt	USAF 355 Gp.	5.00	5.50
Lenox, Jack Jr.	Rockledge PA	2nd Lt	USAF 14 Gp.	5.00	5.00
Lent, Francis J.	Minneapolis MN	1st Lt	USAF 475 Gp.	11.00	11.00
Leonard, William N.	Norfolk VA	LT	USN VF42	8.00	
Leppla, John A.	Lima OH	LT	USN VF10	5.00	
Lerch, Alfred		ENS	USN VF10	7.00	
Lesicka, Joseph J.	Westmoreland CA	1st Lt	USAF 18 Gp.	9.00	9.00
Leverette, William L.	Lykesland SC	LTC	USAF 14 Gp.	11.00	11.00
Lewis, Warren R.	Superior IA	Maj	USAF 475 Gp.	7.00	7.00
Lewis, William H.	Oxnard CA	Capt	USAF 55 Gp.	8.00	7.00
Liebers, Lawrence P.	Glendale CA	2nd Lt	USAF 82 Gp.	7.00	7.00
Liles, Robert L.	St. Louis MO	Maj	USAF 23 Gp.	6.00	5.00
Lillie, Hugh D.	Grand Rapids MI	LT	USN VF10	5.00	
Lindsay, Elvin L.	Moscow ID	LT	USN VF19	8.00	
Lines, Ted E.	Mesa AZ	1st Lt	USAF 4 Gp.	10.00	10.00
Littge, Raymond H.	Altenburg MO	Capt	USAF 352 Gp.	10.50	10.50
Little, James W.	Lexington KY	1st Lt	USAF 23 Gp.	*5.00 +1 Korea	7.00
Little, Robert L.	Spokane WA	Capt	AVG	10.50	
Loesch, Gregory K.	Baltimore MD	Capt	USMC VMF121	8.50	
Loisel, John S.	Richardson TX	Maj	USAF 475 Gp.	11.00	11.00
Lombard, John D.	Ionia MI	Maj	USAF 51 Gp.	6.00	7.00
London, Charles P.	Huntington Beach CA	Capt	USAF 78 Gp.	5.00	5.00
Long, Herbert H.	Maitland FL	Maj	USMC VMF121/122	10.00	
Long, Maurice G.	Apple Valley CA	Capt	USAF 354 Gp.	5.50	5.50
Lopez, Donald S.	Alexandria VA	1st Lt	USAF 23 Gp.	5.00	3.00
Louie, Clifford	Seattle WA (Chin/Amer)	Capt	AVG	5.00	
Loving, George G. Jr.	Lynchburg VA	Capt	USAF 31 Gp.	5.00	5.00
Lowell, John H.	Golden CO	LTC	USAF 364 Gp.	7.50	7.50
Lowry, Wayne L.	Mason City NE	1st Lt	USAF 325 Gp.	11.00	11.00
Lubner, Marvin W.	Brussels, Belgium	Capt	USAF 23 Gp.	6.00	6.00
Lucas, Paul W.	Boone IA	Capt	USAF 475 Gp.	6.00	6.00
Luksic, Carl J.	Joliet IL	1st Lt	USAF 352 Gp.	8.50	8.50

NAME	HOME TOWN	RANK	UNIT	CLAIMED	USAFHS 85
Luma, John F.	Helena MT	Flt Off	RCAF 418 Sq.	5.00	
Lundin, Walter A.	Yonkers NY	LT	USN VF15	6.50	
Lundin, William M.	El Toro CA	Capt	USMC VMF121	5.50	
Lustic, Stanley J.	Elbert WV	1st Lt	USAF 318 Gp.	6.00	6.00
Lutton, Lowell C.	Kankakee IL	1st Lt	USAF 475 Gp.	5.00	5.00
Lynch, John J.	Alhambra CA	Sqd Ldr	RAF 71 Sq.	13.00	
Lynch, Joseph P.	Canton MA	Capt	USMC VMF224	5.50	
Lynch, Thomas J.	Catasaugua PA	LTC	USAF 35 Gp.	20.00	20.00
Maberry, L. A.		LT	USN VF84	5.00	
MacDonald, Charles H.	Dubois PA	Col	USAF 475 Gp.	27.00	27.00
Maas, John B. Jr.	Quantico VA	Maj	USMC VMF112	5.50	
MacKay, John A.	St. Albans VT	2nd Lt	USAF 1 Gp.	5.00	5.00
Magee, Christopher Lyman	Chicago IL	Capt	USMC VMF214	9.00	
Magoffin, Morton D.	Pleasanton CA	Col	USAF 362 Gp.	5.00	5.00
Maguire, William J.	Boston MA	Capt	USAF 353 Gp.	7.00	7.00
Mahon, Jackson B.		P/O	RAF 121 Sq.	5.00	
Mahon, Keith	Oklahoma City OK	Capt	USAF 51 Gp.	5.00	5.00
Mahoney, Grant M.		LTC	USAF 23/1 AC	6.00	5.00
Mahurin, Walker M.	Newport Beach CA	Maj	USAF 56/3AC	*20.75 +3.5 Korea	20.75
Malcahy, Douglas W.		LT	USN VF31	8.00	
Mallory, Charles M.	Dunbar WV	LT	USN VF18	11.00	
Maloney, Thomas E.	Cushing OK	Capt	USAF 1 Gp.	8.00	8.00
Mankin, Jack C.	Kansas City MO	Capt	USAF 475 Gp.	5.00	5.00
Mankin, Lee P.	Springfield MO	LT	USN VF5/6	5.00	
Mann, Thomas H. Jr.	Graysville IN	Capt	USMC VMF121	10.00	
Manson, Armand G.	Buffalo NY	LT	USN VF18/82	7.00	
March, Harry A. Jr.	Washington DC	LT	USN VF6/17	5.00	
Markham, Gene E.		Capt	USAF 353 Gp.	5.00	5.00
Marontate, William P.	Seattle WA	1st Lt	USMC VMF121	13.00	
Marsh, Lester C.	Los Angeles CA	1st Lt	USAF 339 Gp.	5.00	5.00
Marshall, Bert W. Jr.	Dallas TX	Maj	USAF 355 Gp.	7.00	7.00
Martin, Albert E. Jr.	Warwick RI	LT	USN VF9	5.00	
Martin, Kenneth R.	Leawood KS	Col	USAF 354 Gp.	5.00	5.00
Mason, Joe L.	Columbus OH	Col	USAF 352 Gp.	5.00	5.00
Masoner, William J. Jr.	Chicago IL	LT	USN VF19	12.00	
Mathis, William H.	Nashville GA	1st Lt	USAF 318 Gp.	5.00	5.00
Mathre, Milden E.	Cedar Falls IA	2nd Lt	USAF 49 Gp.	5.00	5.00
Matte, Joseph Z.	San Antonio TX	1st Lt	USAF 362 Gp.	5.00	5.00
Maxwell, Chester K.	Alva OK	Capt	USAF 357 Gp.	5.00	5.00
Maxwell, W. Robert	Columbia SC	LT	USN VF17	8.00	
May, Earl	Milwaukee WI	LT	USN VF17	8.00	
May, Richard Hobbs	Solana Beach CA	LT	USN VF32	6.00	
Mayo, Ben I. Jr.	Little Rock AR	Maj	USAF 78 Gp.	5.00	4.00
Mazzocco, Michele A.	Peekskill NY	ENS	USN VF30	6.50	
McArthur, Paul G.	Reform AL	1st Lt	USAF 79 Gp.	5.00	5.00
McArthur, T. H.	Caradan TX	Capt	USAF 82 Gp.	5.00	5.00
McCampbell, David (CMH)	Lake Worth FL	CDR	USN VF15	34.00	
McCartney, H. Allen Jr.	Watertown NY	Capt	USMC VMF	5.00	
McCauley, Frank E.	Hicksville OH	1st Lt	USAF 56 Gp.	5.50	5.50
McClelland, Thomas G.	Albuquerque NM	LT	USN VF5	7.00	
McClurg, Robert W.	New Castle PA	Capt	USMC VMF214	7.00	
McColpin, Carroll W.	Novato CA	SLDR/Col	RAF(3)USAF 404 Gp	8.00	
McComas, Ed O.	Winfield KS	LTC	USAF 118 RCN	14.00	14.00
McCorkle, Charles M.	Honolulu HI	Col	USAF 31 Gp.	11.00	11.00
McCormick, William A. Jr.	Somerset NJ	LT	USN VF8	6.00	
McCuddin, Leo B.	Reno NV	LT	USN VF20	5.00	
McCuskey, Elbert S.	Clearwater FL	LCDR	USN VF42/6	14.00	
McDaniel, Gordon H.	Sweetwater TN	1st Lt	USAF 325 Gp.	6.00	6.00
McDonald, Norman L.	West Palm Beach FL	Maj	USAF 52/325	11.00	11.50
McDonald, R. "Red"		ENS	USN VF	5.00	
McDonough, William F.	Temple City CA	Maj	USAF 35 Gp.	5.00	5.00
McDowell, Donald	Los Angeles CA	1st Lt	USAF 354 Gp.	8.50	8.50
McElroy, James N.	Orlando FL	Capt	USAF 355 Gp.	5.00	5.00
McGarry, William D.	Los Angeles CA	Capt	AVG	10.25	
McGee, Donald C.	Mansfield OH	Capt	USAF 8 Gp.	6.00	6.00
McGinty, Selva E.	Stilwell OK	1st Lt	USMC VMF441	5.00	
McGinn, John L.	Los Angeles CA	LTC	USAF347/55 Gp	5.00	5.00
McGowan, Edward C.	Columbus OH	LT	USN VF9	6.50	
McGrattan, Bernard L.	Utica NY	Capt	USAF 4 Gp.	8.50	8.50

NAME	HOME TOWN	RANK	UNIT	CLAIMED	USAFHS 85
McGuire, Thomas B. Jr. (CMH)	Patterson NJ	Maj	USAF 475 Gp.	38.00	38.00
McGuyrt, John W.	Steamboat Springs CO	1st Lt	USAF 14 Gp.	5.00	5.00
McKennon, Pierce W.	Fort Smith AR	Maj	USAF 4 Gp.	12.00	11.00
McKeon, Joseph T.	Redlands CA	Capt	USAF 475 Gp.	6.00	6.00
McKinley, Donald J.	St. Ansgar IA	LT	USN VF25	5.00	
McLachlin, William W.	Louisville KY	LT	USN VF5	5.50	
McLaughlin, Murry D.	Basin WY	Capt	USAF 31 Gp.	7.00	7.00
McManus, John	El Toro CA	Lt	USMC VMF212	6.00	
McMillan, George B.	Winter Garden FL	LTC	AVG(4.25)USAF51Gp.	8.25	4.00
McMinn, Evan D.	Pittsburgh PA	FO	USAF 56 Gp.	5.00	5.00
McPherson, Donald M.	Adams NE	ENS	USN VF83	5.00	
McWhorter, Hamilton III	El Cajon CA	LCDR	USN VF9/12	12.00	
Megura, Nicholas	Bridgeport CT	Capt	USAF 4 Gp.	11.83	11.83
Mehle, Roger W.	Virginia Beach VA	LT	USN VF6/28	13.33	
Meigs, Henry II	New York City NY	1st Lt	USAF 18/6NFS	6.00	6.00
Menard, Louis A.	Jacksonville FL	LCDR	USN VF9/12	9.00	
Mencin, Adolph	Rogers AR	LT	USN VF31	6.00	
Meroney, Virgil K.	Pine Bluff AR	Capt	USAF 352 Gp.	9.00	9.00
Merritt, George L. Jr.	Cumming GA	Maj	USAF 361 Gp.	5.00	5.00
Meuten, Donald W.	Oakland CA	1st Lt	USAF 49 Gp.	6.00	6.00
Meyer, John C.	Forest Hills NY	LTC	USAF 352 Gp.	*24.00 +2 Korea	24.00
Michaelis, F. H.	Washington DC	LCDR	USN VF12	5.00	
Miklajcyk, Henry J.	Syracuse NY	Capt	USAF 352 Gp.	7.50	7.50
Miller, Armour C.	Cleverlock NY	Capt	USAF 1 Gp.	6.00	6.00
Miller, Everett	Pomona CA	1st Lt	USAF 1 Gp.	5.00	5.00
Miller, Johnnie G.	Arlington TX	LT	USN VF30	8.00	
Miller, Joseph E. Jr.	Los Angeles CA	Capt	USAF 474 Gp.	5.00	5.00
Miller, Thomas F.	Portland OR	2nd Lt	USAF 354 Gp.	5.25	5.25
Millikan, Willard W.	Alexandria VA	Capt	USAF 4 Gp.	13.00	13.00
Milliken, Robert C.	Hanna WY	1st Lt	USAF 474 Gp.	5.00	5.00
Mills, Henry L.	Leonia NY	Maj	USAF 4 Gp.	6.00	6.00
Milton, Charles B.	Jasper FL	LT	USN VF15	5.00	
Mims, Robert	Dallas TX	LT	USN VF17	6.00	
Minchew, Leslie D.	Montgomery AL	Capt	USAF 355/359	5.50	5.50
Mitchell, Harris E.	Hutchison KS	LT	USN VF9	10.00	
Mitchell, Henry E.	Vancouver WA	LT	USN VF6	6.00	
Mitchell, John W.	San Anselmo CA	LTC	USAF 347/15 Gp.	*11.00 +4 Korea	11.00
Moats, Sanford K.	Mission KS	1st Lt	USAF 352 Gp.	8.50	8.50
Molland, Leland P.	So. Fargo ND	Capt	USAF 31 Gp.	11.00	11.00
Mollard, Norman W.		LT	USN VF45	6.00	
Mollenhauer, Arthur P.	Redwood City CA	ENS	USN VF18	5.00	
Momyer, William W.	Seattle WA	Col	USAF 33 Gp.	8.00	8.00
Monk, Franklin H.	Peoria IL	1st Lt	USAF 475 Gp.	5.00	5.00
Montapert, John R.	Van Nuys CA	LT	USN VF44	6.00	
Moore, John T.	Montgomery AL	Maj	USAF 348 Gp.	7.00	7.00
Moore, Robert W.	St. Matthews KY	Maj	USAF 15 Gp.	12.00	12.00
Moran, Glennon T.	St. Louis MO	1st Lt	USAF 352 Gp.	13.00	13.00
Moranville, Horace B.	Monmouth OR	LT	USN VF11	6.00	
Morehead, James B.	Petaluma CA	1st Lt	USAF 49 Gp.	7.00	7.00
Morgan, John L. Jr.	Arlington TX	Capt	USMC VMF213	8.50	
Morrill, Stanley B.	Willimantic CT	1st Lt	USAF 56 Gp.	9.00	9.00
Morris, Bert D. Jr. (Wayne)	Fallbrook CA	LT	USN VF15	7.00	
Morris, James M.	Tampa FL	Capt	USAF 20 Gp.	7.33	7.33
Morriss, Paul V.	Norcross GA	Capt	USAF 475 Gp.	5.00	5.00
Moseley, Mark L.	Atlanta GA	Capt	USAF 56 Gp.	6.50	6.50
Moss, Robert C.	Doerun GA	Capt	AVG/USAF 23 Gp.	7.00	
Moseley, William C.		LT	USN VF1	6.00	
Mugavero, James D.	Port Huron MI	1st Lt	USAF 35 Gp.	6.00	6.00
Mulcahy, Douglas W.	Yonkers NY	LT	USN VF31	8.00	
Mulhollen, Robert F.	Chicago IL	1st Lt	USAF 311 Gp.	6.00	5.00
Mullen, Paul A.	Pittsburgh PA	Capt	USMC VMF214	6.50	
Munson, Arthur H.	Utica NY	LT	USN VF27	5.00	
Murphey, Paul C. Jr.	Meridian TX	Capt	USAF 8 Gp.	6.00	6.00
Murphy, Alva C.	Knoxville TN	Capt	USAF 357 Gp.	8.00	6.00
Murphy, John B.	Darlington SC	LTC	USAF 359/357 Gp.	6.75	6.75
Murray, Robert E.	Muncie IN	LT	USN VF29	10.33	
Myers, Jennings L.	Ahoskie NC	1st Lt	USAF 8 Gp.	5.00	5.00
Myers, Raymond B.	Dundee MS	LTC	USAF 355 Gp.	5.50	5.50

NAME	HOME TOWN	RANK	UNIT	CLAIMED	USAFHS 85
Narr, Joseph L.		Lt	USMC VMF121	8.00	
Neale, Robert H.	Camano Island WA	Capt	AVG	15.50	
Nelson, H. A.		ENS	USN VF20	5.20	
Nelson, Robert J.	Sioux City IA	LT	USN VF5	5.00	
Nelson, Robert K.		ENS	USN VF20	6.70	
Newkirk, John V.	Scarsdale NY	Capt	AVG	10.50	
Nichols, Franklin A.	El Paso TX	Maj	USAF 49/475	5.00	5.00
Noble, Myrvin E.	Smithfield UT	LT	USN VF2	7.50	
Nollmeyer, Edward M.		Maj	USAF 51 Gp.	5.00	5.00
Nooy, Cornelius N.	Smithtown LI NY	LT	USN VF31	19.00	
Norley, Louis H.	Conrad MT	Maj	USAF 4 Gp.	11.33	11.33
Novak, Marvin R.	Manitowac WI	LT	USN VF14	5.00	
Novotny, George P.	Allenpark MI	1st Lt	USAF 325 Gp.	8.00	8.00
Oberhansly, Jack J.	Palmdale CA	Maj	USAF 78 Gp.	5.00	5.00
O'Brien, Gilbert M.	Charleston SC	1st Lt	USAF 357 Gp.	7.00	7.00
O'Brien, William R.	Houston TX	Capt	USAF 357 Gp.	5.50	5.50
O'Connor, Frank Q.	Oregon City OR	Capt	USAF 354 Gp.	10.75	10.75
Odenbrett, Harvey		LT	USN VF6	7.00	
O'Hare, Edward H. (CMH)	Chicago IL	LCDR	USN VF3/2	12.00	
Ohr, Fred F.	Caldwell ID	Capt	USAF 52 Gp.	6.00	6.00
O'Keefe, Jeremiah J.	Biloxi MS	1st Lt	USMC VMF323	7.00	
Olander, Edwin L.	Northampton MA	Capt	USMC VMF	5.00	
Older, Charles H.	Los Angeles CA	S/Ldr/LTC	AVG(10)	18.50	7.00
			USAF 23 Gp (8.50)		(USAF)
Olds, Robin	Steamboat Springs CO	Maj	USAF 479 Gp.	**12.00	12.00
				+4 Vietnam	
Olsen, Austin LeRoy	Seattle WA	ENS	USN VF30	5.00	
Olson, Norman E.	Fargo ND	Capt	USAF 355 Gp.	6.00	6.00
O'Mara, Paul Jr.	San Leandro CA	LT	USN VF19	7.50	
O'Neill, Eugene W.	Coral Gables FL	Capt	USAF 56 Gp.	5.00	4.50
O'Neill, Danny (Hugh D.)		LT	USN VF	7.00	
O'Neill, John G.	Gasport NY	1st Lt	USAF 49 Gp.	8.00	8.00
O'Neill, Lawrence F.	Baldwin MO	1st Lt	USAF 348 Gp.	5.00	5.00
Orth, John	Romeo MI	LT	USN VF1	6.00	
Osher, Ernest K.	Maitland FL	Capt	USAF 82 Gp.	5.00	5.00
Ostrom, Charles H.	Miami FL	LT	USN VF21	7.00	
Outlaw, Edward C.	Durham NC	LCDR	USN VF32	6.00	
Overcash, Robert J.	Mooresville NC	1st Lt	USAF 57 Gp.	5.00	5.00
Overend, Edmund F.	Coronado CA	Maj	AVG(6)USMC(3)	9.00	3.00
Overfield, Lloyd J.	Leavenworth KS	1st Lt	USAF 354 Gp.	9.00	9.00
Overton, Edward W. Jr.	Arlington VA	LT	USN VF15	5.00	
Owen, Donald C.		Capt	USMC	5.00	
Owen, Edward M.	Arlington VA	LT	USN VF5	8.00	
Owens, Joel A.	Skiatook OK	Maj	USAF 1 Gp.	5.00	5.00
Owens, Robert G. Jr.	Newport Beach CA	Maj	USMC VMF215	7.00	
Paisley, Melvyn R.	Kent WA	1st Lt	USAF 366 Gp.	5.00	5.00
Parham, Forrest F.	Kensington MN	Capt	USAF 23 Gp.	5.00	5.00
Paris, Joel B. III	Roswell GA	Capt	USAF 49 Gp.	9.00	9.00
Parker, Harry A.	Milford NH	Capt	USAF 325 Gp.	13.00	13.00
Parrish, Elbert W.	Orlando FL	ENS	USN VF80	7.00	
Pascoe, James J.	Poughkeepsie NY	1st Lt	USAF 357 Gp.	6.00	5.50
Paskoski, Joseph J.	Millville NJ	LT	USN VF19	6.00	
Paulk, Edsel	Vernon TX	2nd Lt	USAF 325 Gp.	5.00	5.00
Payne, Carl W.	Columbus OH	Capt	USAF 31 Gp.	7.00	5.00
Payne, Frederick R.	Rancho Mirage CA	LTC	USMC VMF212	7.50	
Pearce, James L.	Palos Verdes Estates CA	LT	USN VF18/17	6.00	
Peck, James Eldridge	Berkeley CA	FltLt	RAF(5)USAF52 Gp(1)	6.00	1.00
Percy, Gilbert	Chico CA	Capt	USMC VMF112	6.00	
Perdomo, Oscar F.	San Gabriel CA	1st Lt	USAF 507 Gp.	5.00	5.00
Petach, John E.	Perth Amboy NJ	Capt	AVG(4)USAF23Gp	5.25	
Peterson, Chesley G.	Santaquin UT	SqdLdr	RAF(6)USAF4Gp(1)	7.00	7.00
Peterson, Richard A.	Alexandria MN	Capt	USAF 357 Gp.	15.50	15.50
Philips, David P.	Troy MI	LT	USN VF30	5.00	
Phillips, Edward A.	Blacksville WV	LT	USN VF	5.00	
Phillips, Hyde	Shelbyville IL	Maj	USMC VMF223	5.00	
Picken, Harvey P.	Minot ND	LT	USN VF18	9.00	
Pierce, Francis E. Jr.	Coronado CA	Maj	USMC VMF121	6.00	
Pierce, Joseph F.	Duncan OK	1st Lt	USAF 357 Gp.	7.00	7.00
Pierce, Sammy A.	Ayden NC	1st Lt	USAF 49 Gp.	7.00	7.00
Pietz, John Jr.	Valley Stream NY	1st Lt	USAF 475 Gp.	6.00	6.00

383

NAME	HOME TOWN	RANK	UNIT	CLAIMED	USAFHS 85
Pigman, George W. Jr.	New Orleans LA	LT	USN VF15	8.50	
Pisanos, Spiros N. "Steve"	Plainfield NJ	1st Lt	USAF 4 Gp.	7.00	6.00
Pittman, Jack Jr.	Amarillo TX	1st Lt	USMC VMF221	7.00	
Plant, Claude W.	Portland OR	LT	USN VF15	8.50	
Poindexter, James N.	Milville NJ	Capt	USAF 353 Gp.	7.00	7.00
Pompetti, Peter E.	Ft. Worth TX	1st Lt	USAF 78 Gp.	5.50	5.50
Pond, Zenneth A.	Jackson MI	Lt	USMC VMF223	6.00	
Pool, Kenneth R.	Igloo SD	1st Lt	USAF 8 Gp.	5.00	5.00
Pool, Tilman E.	Houston TX	LT	USN VF17	6.00	
Pope, Albert J.	Atlanta GA	LT	USN VF13	7.25	
Popek, Edward S.	Tacoma WA	Maj	USAF 348 Gp.	7.00	7.00
Porter, Philip B.		1st Lt	USAF 418 NFR	5.00	5.00
			(Radar assists)		
Porter, Robert Bruce	Fresno CA	1st Lt	USMC VMF(N)542	7.00	
Poske, George H.	Los Angeles CA	Maj	USMC VMF	5.00	
Post, Nathan T.	San Francisco CA	LTC	USMC VMF221	8.00	
Pound, Ralston M. Jr.	Charlotte NC	LT	USN VF16	6.00	
Powell, Ernest A.	New Rochelle NY	Capt	USMC VMF	5.00	
Powers, Joe H. Jr.	Tulsa OK	Capt	USAF 56 Gp.	14.50	14.50
Powers, MacArthur	Inwood LI NY	2nd Lt	USAF 324 Gp.	7.50	5.00
Prater, Luther D. Jr.	Lexington KY	LT	USN VF19	8.00	
Preddy, George E. Jr.	Greensboro NC	Maj	USAF 352 Gp.	26.83	26.83
Prescott, Robert W.	Fort Worth TX	Capt	AVG	5.25	
Presley, Frank H.	Norfolk VA	Capt	USMC VMF121	6.00	
Price, Jack C.	Grand Junction OH	Maj	USAF 20 Gp.	5.00	5.00
Prichard, Melvin M.	Atlanta MI	LT	USN VF20	7.25	
Priest, Royce W.	Dallas TX	1st Lt	USAF 355 Gp.	5.00	5.00
Pryor, Roger C.	Gulfport MS	Capt	USAF 23 Gp.	5.00	5.00
Pugh, John Forrest	Brogan OR	Capt	USAF 357 Gp.	6.00	6.00
Purdy, John E.	Kettering OH	1st Lt	USAF 475 Gp.	7.00	7.00
Quiel, Norval R.		LT	USN VF10	6.00	
Quigley, Donald L.	Marion OH	Maj	USAF 23 Gp.	5.00	5.00
Quirk, Michael J.	Gulf Breeze FL	Capt	USAF 56 Gp.	12.00	11.00
Rader, Valentine S.		1st Lt	USAF 111RCN	6.50	6.50
Ramlo, Orvin H.	Decorah IA	Capt	USMC VMF223	5.00	
Rankin, Robert J.	Petersburg VA	1st Lt	USAF 56 Gp.	10.00	10.00
Ray, C. B.	Bakersfield CA	1st Lt	USAF 8 Gp.	5.00	5.00
Reber, James V. Jr.	Reading PA	LTJG	USN VF30	11.00	
Rector, Edward F.	Alexandria VA	Capt	AVG(6.5)USAF23Gp.(3)	9.50	9.50
Redmond, Eugene D.	Los Angeles CA	LT	USN VF2/10	9.00	
Reed, William N.	Marion IA	LTC	AVG(11.5)USAF3Gp.	17.50	6.00
Reese, William C.	Bear River UT	1st Lt	USAF 357 Gp.	5.00	5.00
Reeves, Horace B.		1st Lt	USAF 475 Gp.	6.00	6.00
Reeves, Leonard R.	Lancaster TX	1st Lt	USAF 311 Gp.	6.00	6.00
Register, Francis R.	Bismarck ND	LT	USN VF5/6	7.00	
Rehm, Dan R. Jr.	Houston TX	LT	USN VF50/8	13.00	
Reidy, T. Hamil	Northfield IL	LT	USN VF83	10.00	
Reinburg, J. Hunter	Wabasso FL	Maj	USMC VMF121	7.00	
Reiserer, Russell L.	Los Altos CA	LT	USN VF10/76	10.50	
Rennemo, Thomas J.	Whitewater WI	LT	USN VF18	7.00	
Reulet, Joseph E.	Vacherie LA	LT	USN VF10	5.00	
Revel, Glenn M.	Chase KS	LT	USN VF14	5.50	
Reynolds, Andrew J.	Seminole OK	1st Lt	USAF 49 Gp.	10.00	10.00
Reynolds, Robert	Orlando FL	1st Lt	USAF 354 Gp.	7.00	7.00
Rhodes, Thomas W.	Washington DC	LT	USN VF6	5.00	
Richardson, Elmer W.	Ft. Worth TX	Maj	USAF 23 Gp.	8.00	8.00
Riddle, Robert H.	Chicago IL	1st Lt	USAF 31 Gp.	11.00	11.00
Rieger, Vincent A.	Denver CO	LT	USN VF2	5.00	
Rigg, James F.	Saginaw MI	LCDR	USN VF15	11.00	
Righetti, Elwyn G.	San Antonio TX	LTC	USAF 55 Gp.	7.50	7.50
Riley, Paul S.	York PA	1st Lt	USAF 4 Gp.	6.50	6.50
Rimerman, Ben	Omaha NE	1st Lt	USAF 353 Gp.	7.00	4.50
Ritchey, Andrew J.	Arlington VA	1st Lt	USAF 354 Gp.	5.00	5.00
Robbins, Jay T.	Cooledge TX	Maj	USAF 8 Gp.	22.00	22.00
Robbins, Joe D.	Escondido CA	LT	USN VF6/85	5.00	
Roberson, Arval J.	White Stone VA	1st Lt	USAF 357 Gp.	6.00	6.00
Roberts, Daniel T. Jr.	Los Angeles CA	Capt	USAF 475 Gp.	14.00	14.00
Roberts, Eugene Paul	Spokane WA	LTC	USAF 78/364	9.00	9.00
Roberts, Newell O.	Anderson IN	Capt	USAF 1 Gp.	5.00	5.00
Robinson, Leroy W.	Hopeville GA	ENS	USN VF2	5.00	

NAME	HOME TOWN	RANK	UNIT	CLAIMED	USAFHS 85
Robinson, Ross F.	St. Paul MN	ENS	USN VF2	5.00	
Roddy, Edward F.	Fresno CA	Capt	USAF 348 Gp.	8.00	8.00
Rogers, Felix Michael	Bel Air CA	Capt	USAF 354 Gp.	7.00	7.00
Rose, Franklin Jr.	Springfield VA	1st Lt	USAF 354 Gp.	5.00	5.00
Rosen, Ralph J.	Laconia NH	LT	USN VF8	6.00	
Ross, Herbert E.	Fresno CA	Maj	USAF 14 Gp.	7.00	7.00
Ross, Robert P.	Lillington NC	LT	USN VF	5.50	
Rossi, Herman J. Jr.	Wallace ID	LT	USN VF19	6.00	
Rossi, John R.	Fallbrook CA	Capt	AVG	6.25	
Rounds, Gerald L.	Fontana CA	1st Lt	USAF 82 Gp.	5.00	5.00
Rowland, Robert R.	Virginia Beach VA	Col	USAF 348 Gp.	8.00	8.00
Ruder, LeRoy A.	Mekossa WI	1st Lt	USAF 357 Gp.	5.50	5.50
Rudolph, Henry S.	Howe IN	1st Lt	USAF 354 Gp.	5.00	5.00
Ruhsam, John W.	Sarasota FL	Maj	USMC VMF323	7.00	
Runyon, Donald E.	Smithtown NY	LT	USN VF6/18	11.00	
Rushing, Roy W.	McGehee AR	LT	USN VF15	13.00	
Rynne, William A.	New Rochelle NY	Capt	USAF 325 Gp.	5.00	5.00
Sandell, Robert J.	San Antonio TX	Capt	AVG	5.25	
Sangermano, Philip	Petersborough NH	1st Lt	USAF 325 Gp.	8.00	8.00
Sapp, Donald H.	Miami FL	Capt	USMC VMF222	11.00	
Sargent, John J.		LT	USN VF18/84	6.00	
Savage, Jimmie E.	Dorchester TX	LT	USN VF11	7.00	
Sawyer, Charles W.	Emmett ID	Maj	AVG(4.25) USAF 23 Gp.	5.25	1.00
Scales, Harrell H.	La Verne CA	LT	USN VF31	6.00	
Scarborough, Hartwell V. Jr.		Capt	USMC VMF	5.00	
Schank, Thomas D.	Greeley CO	1st Lt	USAF 55 Gp.	5.00	5.00
Schecter, Gordon E.		LT	USN VF45	5.00	
Schell, J. L.	Weston CT	LT	USN VF3	5.00	
Scheible, Wilbur R.	Sarasota CA	Capt	USAF 356 Gp.	6.00	6.00
Schiel, Frank	Prescott AZ	Capt	AVG/USAF 23	7.00	
Schildt, William J.	San Diego CA	1st Lt	USAF 82 Gp.	6.00	6.00
Schilling, David C.	Kansas City MO	Col	USAF 56 Gp.	22.50	22.50
Schiltz, Glenn D. Jr.	No. Canton OH	1st Lt	USAF 56 Gp.	8.00	8.00
Schimanski, Robert G.	Spokane WA	Capt	USAF 357 Gp.	6.00	6.00
Schlegel, Albert L.	Cleveland OH	Capt	USAF 4 Gp.	8.50	8.50
Schreiber, LeRoy A.	Plymouth MA	Maj	USAF 56 Gp.	12.00	12.00
Schriber, Louis	Oshkosh WI	Capt	USAF 8 Gp.	5.00	5.00
Schuh, Duerr H.	Douglas WY	1st Lt	USAF 352 Gp.	5.00	5.00
Scott, Robert L.	Sun City AZ	Col	USAF 23 Gp.	10.00	10.00
Sears, Alexander F.	Abilene TX	1st Lt	USAF 352 Gp.	5.00	5.00
Sears, Meldrum L.	Paris IL	1st Lt	USAF 1 Gp.	7.00	7.00
Seckel, Albert Jr.	Oak Park IL	LT	USN VF19	6.00	
See, Robert Byron	San Francisco CA	Capt	USMC VMF321	5.00	
Segal, Harold E.	Alhambra CA	Capt	USMC VMF221	12.00	
Seidman, Robert K.	Pittsburgh PA	1st Lt	USAF 14 Gp.	5.00	5.00
Self, Larry R.	Dallas TX	LT	USN VF15	8.50	
Shackford, Robert W.	Coronado CA	LT	USN VF2	6.00	
Shafer, Dale E.	Waynesville OH	LTC	USAF 339 Gp.	8.00	7.00
Shands, Courtney	Washington DC	CDR	USN VF71	6.00	
Shaw, Edward O.	Spokane WA	Capt	USMC VMF213	13.00	
Shaw, Robert M.	Pittsburgh PA	1st Lt	USAF 357 Gp.	8.00	8.00
Sherrill, Hugh V.		LT	USN VF81	6.00	
Shields, Charles A.	Metairie LA	LT	USN VF41	5.00	
Shipman, Ernest	Mahway LI NY	1st Lt	USAF 31 Gp.	7.00	7.00
Shirley, James A.	Seneca SC	LT	USN VF27/22	12.00	
Shoals, Robert Bruce	Pasadena CA	Capt	USAF 51 Gp.	5.00	5.00
Shomo, William A. (CMH)	Pittsburgh PA	Capt	USAF 82 Gp.	8.00	8.00
Shoup, Robert L.	Port Arthur TX	1st Lt	USAF 354 Gp.	5.50	5.50
Shubin, Murray Jr.	Dormont PA	Lt	USAF 347 Gp.	11.00	11.00
Shuler, Lucien B.	Griffin GA	1st Lt	USAF 18 Gp.	7.00	7.00
Shuman, Perry L.	Falls Church VA	Maj	USMC VMF121	6.00	
Sigler, Wallace E.	Orange CT	Capt	USMC VMF112	5.33	
Silber, Sam L.	Baltimore MD	LCDR	USN VF27/18	7.00	
Simmons, John M.	Gadsden AL	1st Lt	USAF 325 Gp.	7.00	7.00
Simmons, William J.	Los Angeles CA	1st Lt	USAF 354 Gp.	6.00	6.00
Singer, Arthur Jr.	El Cajon CA	LT	USN VF15	10.00	
Sipes, Lester H.	Albuquerque NM	LT	USN VF2	5.00	
Sistrunk, Frank	Phoenix AZ	LT	USN VF17	5.00	
Skogstad, Norman C.	Barron WI	1st Lt	USAF 31 Gp.	12.00	12.00
Skon, Warren A.	St. Paul MN	LT	USN VF2	7.00	

NAME	HOME TOWN	RANK	UNIT	CLAIMED	USAFHS 85
Slack, Albert C.	Lufkin TX	LT	USN VF15	6.50	
Sloan, William J.	Richmond VA	1st Lt	USAF 82 Gp.	12.00	12.00
Smith, Armistead B. Jr.	La Jolla CA	LT	USN VF9	10.50	
Smith, Carroll C.		Maj	USAF 418 NFS	8.00	8.00
Smith, Carl Eugene	Chula Vista CA	LT	USN VF14	7.00	
Smith, Clinton L.	Jackson MS	LT	USN VF9	6.00	
Smith, Cornelius M. Jr.	Tavares FL	Capt	USAF 8 Gp.	11.00	11.00
Smith, Daniel F. Jr.		LT	USN VF20	6.00	
Smith, Donovan F.	Niles MI	1st Lt	USAF 56 Gp.	5.50	5.50
Smith, Jack R.	San Simon AZ	Capt	USAF 31 Gp.	5.00	5.00
Smith, John C.	Portsmouth OH	1st Lt	USAF 475 Gp.	6.00	6.00
Smith, John L. (CMH)	Lexington OK	LTC	USMC VMF223	19.00	
Smith, John Malcolm	Owatonna MN	LT	USN VF	10.00	
Smith, Kenneth G.	Watsontown PA	Capt	USAF 4 Gp.	5.00	5.00
Smith, Kenneth D.	Port Arthur TX	LT	USN VF90	5.00	
Smith, Leslie C.	Caruthers CA	Maj	USAF 56 Gp.	7.00	7.00
Smith, Meryl M.	North East PA	LTC	USAF 475 Gp.	9.00	9.00
Smith, Nicholas J. III	Lynchburg VA	LT	USN VF13	6.00	
Smith, Paul A.		1st Lt	USAF 422 NFS	5.00	5.00
Smith, Richard E.	Evansville IN	1st Lt	USAF 35 Gp.	7.00	7.00
Smith, Robert H. "Snuffy"	Eagle River WI	Capt	AVG(5.25)USAF18Gp.	5.25	
Smith, Robert T.	Sherman Oaks CA	Capt	AVG	8.67	
Smith, Virgil H.	McAllen TX	1st Lt	USAF 14 Gp.	5.00	5.00
Snider, William N.	Vicksburg MS	Capt	USMC VMF221	11.50	
Sonner, Irl V. Jr.	El Monte CA	LT	USN VF29	5.00	
Southerland, James J.	Jacksonville FL	LCDR	USN VF8/72/10	5.00	
Sparks, Kenneth C.	Blackwell OK	1st Lt	USAF 35 Gp.	11.00	11.00
Spears, Harold L.	Newark OH	Capt	USMC VMF215	15.00	
Spencer, Dale F.	Clymer NY	1st Lt	USAF 361 Gp.	9.50	9.50
Spitler, Clyde P.	Oak Park MI	LT	USN VF2	5.00	
Stambook, Richard E.	Solana Beach CA	LT	USN VF27	11.00	
Stanch, Paul M.	Audubon NJ	Capt	USAF 35 Gp.	10.00	10.00
Stangel, William J.	Waubun MN	Capt	USAF 352 Gp.	5.00	5.00
Stanley, Gordon A.	Coronado CA	LT	USN VF3	8.00	
Stanley, Morris A.	Alvin TX	1st Lt	USAF 357 Gp.	5.00	5.00
Stanton, Arland	New Milford CT	Maj	USAF 49 Gp.	8.00	8.00
Starck, Walter E.	Milwaukee WI	Capt	USAF 352 Gp.	6.00	6.00
Starkes, Carlton B.	Moffett Field CA	LT	USN VF5	6.00	
Starnes, James R.	Wilmington NC	Capt	USAF 339 Gp.	6.00	6.00
Stebbins, Edgar E.	Austin TX	LT	USN VF5	5.00	
Stephens, Robert W.	St. Louis MO	Maj	USAF 354 Gp.	13.00	13.00
Stewart, Everett W.	Dallas TX	LTC	USAF 355/4 Gp.	7.83	7.83
Stewart, James C.	Sacramento CA	Maj	USAF 56 Gp.	12.50	11.50
Stewart, James S.	Beverly Hills CA	LT	USN VF31	9.00	
Stewart, John S.	Monument CO	Capt	USAF 23 Gp.	9.00	9.00
Stimpson, Charles R.	Rancho Santa Fe CA	LT	USN VF11	17.00	
Stokes, John D.	Maplewood LA	LT	USN VF14	6.50	
Stone, Carl Van	Raleigh NC	LT	USN VF	5.00	
Stone, Robert J.	Tracey MN	Lt	USAF 318 Gp.	7.00	4.00
Storch, John A.	Long Beach CA	LTC	USAF 357 Gp.	10.50	10.50
Stout, Robert F.	Laramie WY	Maj	USMC VMF121	6.00	
Strait, Donald J.	Shalimar FL	Maj	USAF 356 Gp.	13.50	13.50
Strand, William H.	Pasadena CA	Capt	USAF 35 Gp.	7.00	7.00
Strane, John R.	Alexandria VA	LT	USN VF15	13.00	
Strange, Johnnie C.	Meridian MS	LT	USN VF50	5.00	
Streig, Frederick J.	Pensacola FL	LT	USN VF17	5.50	
Sturdevant, Harvey W.	Pasco WA	LT	USN VF72/10	6.00	
Sublett, John L.	Midland TX	Capt	USAF 357 Gp.	8.00	8.00
Suehr, Richard C.	Fayetteville NC	1st Lt	USAF 35 Gp.	5.00	5.00
Sullivan, Charles P.	Roanoke IL	Capt	USAF 35 Gp.	5.00	5.00
Summer, Elliott	Providence RI	Capt	USAF 475 Gp.	10.00	10.00
Sutcliffe, Robert C.	Trenton NJ	1st Lt	USAF 348 Gp.	5.00	5.00
Sutherland, John F.	Clayton MO	LCDR	USN VF8/72	5.00	
Swett, James E. (CMH)	Belmont CA	Maj	USMC VMF221	15.50	
Swinburne, Harry W.	Delhi IA	LT	USN VF45	5.00	
Swope, James S.	Dallas TX	LT	USN VF11	10.00	
Sykes, William J.	Atlantic City NJ	1st Lt	USAF 361 Gp.	5.00	5.00
Symmes, John C. C.	Lyons NY	LT	USN VF21	10.50	
Synar, Stanley T.	Muskogee OK	Capt	USMC VMF112	5.00	
Talbot, Gilbert F.	Olakmas OR	Maj	USAF	5.00	5.00

NAME	HOME TOWN	RANK	UNIT	CLAIMED	USAFHS 85
Tanner, William F.	San Antonio TX	Capt	USAF 353 Gp.	5.50	5.50
Tapp, James B.	Lompoc CA	Maj	USAF 15 Gp.	8.00	8.00
Taylor, Oliver B.	Sausalito CA	Col	USAF 14 Gp.	5.00	5.00
Taylor, Ralph G. Jr.	Las Vegas NV	Capt	USAF 325 Gp.	6.00	6.00
Taylor, Ray A. Jr.	Quanah TX	LT	USN VF14	6.50	
Taylor, Will W.	Marion FL	LT	USN VF41	5.00	
Terrill, Francis A.	Tacoma WA	1st Lt	USMC VMF	6.08	
Thach, John S.	Coronado CA	CDR	USN VF3	7.00	
Thayer, William Paul	Dallas TX	LT	USN VF26	5.50	
Thelen, Robert H.	Omaha NE	LT	USN VF	6.50	
Thomas, Franklin C. Jr.	Martinsburg WV	Capt	USMC VMF112	9.00	
Thomas, Robert F.	Setauket NY	LT	USN VF21	5.00	
Thomas, Wilbur J.	Los Angeles CA	Capt	USMC VMF213	18.50	
Thompson, Robert D.	Hubbard TX	1st Lt	USAF 31 Gp.	5.25	5.25
Thornell, John F. Jr.	Highland CA	1st Lt	USAF 352 Gp.	17.25	17.25
Thwaites, David F.	Annapolis MD	Capt	USAF 356 Gp.	6.00	6.00
Thyng, Harrison R.	Pittsfield NH	LTC	USAF 31/413 Gp.	*5.00 +5 Korea	5.00
Tierney, Robert E.	Los Altos CA	1st Lt	USAF 422 NFS	5.00 (Radar assists)	5.00
Tilley, John A.	Homestead FL	1st Lt	USAF 475 Gp.	5.00	5.00
Tilley, Reade Franklin	Colorado Springs CO	Pilot Off	RAF 126 Sq.	7.00	
Tinker, Frank G.	Little Rock AR	Spanish Civil War		8.00	8.00
Toaspern, Edward W.	Barryville NY	LT	USN VF31	5.00	
Topliff, John W.	Warrington FL	LT	USN VF8	5.00	
Tordoff, Harrison B.	Mechanicsville NY	Capt	USAF 353 Gp.	5.00	5.00
Torkelson, Ross E.	Everest KS	LT	USN VF21	5.00	
Tovrea, Philip E. Jr.	Phoenix AZ	1st Lt	USAF 1 Gp.	8.00	8.00
Townsend, Eugene P.	South Gate CA	LT	USN VF27	5.00	
Tracy, F. W.	Kinston NC	LT	USN VF18	6.00	
Trafton, Frederick O. Jr.	Austell GA	1st Lt	USAF 31 Gp.	5.50	5.00
Troup, Franklin W.	Decatur AL	LT	USN VF29	7.00	
Trowbridge, Eugene A.	Bloomington MN	Maj	USMC VMF224	12.00	
Troxell, Clifton H.	Ravenna OH	Capt	USAF 8 Gp.	5.00	5.00
Truax, Myron M.	Sullivan City TX	LT	USN VF83	7.00	
Truluck, John H.	Walterboro SC	1st Lt	USAF 56 Gp.	7.00	7.00
Turley, Grant M.	Aripine AZ	2nd Lt	USAF 78 Gp.	6.00	6.00
Turner, Charles H.	Jacksonville FL	LT	USN VF15	6.50	
Turner, Edward B.	Spartanburg SC	LT	USN VF14	7.00	
Turner, Richard E.	Scottsdale AZ	Maj	USAF 354 Gp.	11.00	11.00
Turner, William L.	Idalou TX	LTC	USAF 3CACW	10.50	7.00
Twelves, Wendell V.	Spanish Fork UT	LT	USN VF15	13.00	
Tyler, Gerald E.	Sarasota FL	1st Lt	USAF 357 Gp.	7.00	7.00
Tyler, James O.	Ashland VA	Maj	USAF 52 Gp.	8.00	8.00
Umphres, Donald E.	Philips TX	LT	USN VF83	6.00	
Valencia, Eugene A.	San Francisco CA	LCDR	USN VF9	23.00	
Valentine, Herbert J.	Seattle WA	Capt	USMC VMF312	6.00	
Vanden Heuval, George R.	London, England	1st Lt	USAF 49 Gp.	5.50	5.50
Van der Linden, Peter J.	Joliet IL	LT	USN VF8	5.00	
Van Dyke, Rudolph Daniel	Dayton OH	LT	USN VF	5.00	
Van Haren, Arthur Jr.	Phoenix AZ	LT	USN VF2	9.00	
Varnell, James S. Jr.	Charleston TN	Capt	USAF 52 Gp.	17.00	17.00
Vaughn, Harley C.	Corpus Christi TX	Maj	USAF 82 Gp.	7.00	7.00
Vaught, Robert H.	Los Angeles CA	Capt	USAF 49 Gp.	5.00	5.00
Vedder, Milton N.	Los Angeles CA	1st Lt	USMC VMF213	6.00	
Vejtasa, Stanley W.	Circle MT	LT	USN VF5/10	11.00	
Vincent, Clinton D.	Natchez MS	Col	USAF 23 Gp.	6.00	6.00
Vineyard, Merriwell W.	Whitewright TX	LCDR	USN VF2	6.00	
Vinson, Arnold E.	Monticello MA	Capt	USAF 82 Gp.	7.00	5.33
Visscher, Herman W.	Portage MI	1st Lt	USAF 82 Gp.	*5.00 +1 Korea	5.00
Vita, Harold E.	Solana Beach CA	LT	USN VF9/12	6.00	
Vogt, John E.	Oklahoma City OK	Capt	USAF 318 Gp.	5.00	5.00
Vogt, John W. Jr.	Annapolis MD	Maj	USAF 356/56	8.00	8.00
Voll, John J.	Goshen OH	Capt	USAF 31 Gp.	21.00	21.00
Voris, Roy M.	Santa Cruz CA	LT	USN VF2	7.00	
Vorse, Albert O.	Woodside CA	LT	USN VF3/6	10.50	
Vraciu, Alexander	Danville CA	LCDR	USN VF6/16	19.00	
Wade, Lance C.	San Augustine TX	WgCdr	RAF 145 Sq.	25.00	

NAME	HOME TOWN	RANK	UNIT	CLAIMED	USAFHS 85
Wade, Robert	Santa Ana CA	LT	USMC VMF323	*7.00 +1 Korea	
Waggoner, Horace Q.	Waggoner IL	1st Lt	USAF 353 Gp.	5.00	5.00
Wagner, Boyd D.	Johnstown PA	LTC	USAF 49/8 Gp.	8.00	8.00
Waits, Joe W.		1st Lt	USAF 162RCN	5.50	5.50
Walker, Thomas H.	Mound MN	1st Lt	USAF 347 Gp.	6.00	6.00
Walker, Walter B. Jr.	Stamford CT	1st Lt	USAF 325 Gp.	5.00	5.00
Walsh, Kenneth A. (CMH)	Santa Ana CA	Capt	USMC VMF124	21.00	
Wandrey, Ralph H.	Cottonwood AZ	Capt	USAF 49 Gp.	6.00	6.00
Ward, Lyttleton T.		LT	USN VF83	5.00	
Wang, Kuan Fu		1st Lt	USAF 3CACW	5.50	5.50
Warford, Victor E.	Chickasha OK	Maj	USAF 31 Gp.	8.00	8.00
Warner, Arthur T.	Chatham NJ	Maj	USMC VMF215	8.00	
Warren, Jack R.	San Jacinto CA	Capt	USAF 357 Gp.	5.00	5.00
Waters, Edward T.	Highland Park MI	1st Lt	USAF 82 Gp.	7.00	7.00
Watkins, James A.	Arlington TX	Capt	USAF 49 Gp.	12.00	12.00
Watson, Ralph J.	Washington DC	Maj	USAF14/52 Gp.	5.00	5.00
Watts, Charles E.	Van TX	LT	USN VF18/17	8.75	
Watts, Oran S.	Tulare CA	Capt	USAF 23 Gp.	5.00	5.00
Weatherford, Sidney W.	San Marcos TX	1st Lt	USAF 14 Gp.	5.00	5.00
Weaver, Charles E.	Atlanta GA	Capt	USAF 357 Gp.	8.00	8.00
Weaver, Claude III	Oklahoma City OK	Pilot Off	RAF 403 Sq.	13.50	
Webb, Wilbur B.	Ardmore OK	LT	USN VF2	7.00	
Webb, Willard J.	Alton IL	Maj	USAF 80 Gp.	5.00	5.00
Weigel, George	San Francisco CA	Capt	AVG	5.00	
Weissenberger, Gregory J.	Galveston TX	LTC	USMC VMF213	5.00	
Welch, Darrell G.	San Antonio TX	Capt	USAF 1 Gp.	5.00	5.00
Welch, George S.	Wilmington DE	Capt	USAF 8 Gp.	16.00	16.00
Welch, Robert E.	Brown City MI	Capt	USAF 55 Gp.	6.00	6.00
Welden, Robert D.	Aspen CO	1st Lt	USAF 354 Gp.	6.25	6.25
Wells, Albert P.	Long Beach CA	1st Lt	USMC VMF	5.00	
Wendorf, Edward G.	La Jolla CA	LT	USN VF16	6.00	
Wenige, Arthur E.	Ashville NC	1st Lt	USAF 49/475 Gp.	6.00	6.00
Wesolowski, John M.	Detroit MI	LT	USN VF5	7.00	
Wesson, Warren M.	Brooklyn NY	1st Lt	USAF 78 Gp.	6.00	5.00
West, Richard L.	Chillicothe MO	Capt	USAF 8 Gp.	12.00	14.00
West, Robert G.	Parkersburg IA	LT	USN VF14	5.00	
Westbrook, Robert B.	Hollywood CA	LTC	USAF 347/18 Gp.	20.00	20.00
Wetmore, Ray S.	Kerman CA	Capt	USAF 359 Gp.	22.59	21.25
Whalen, William E.	Hamilton NY	1st Lt	USAF 4 Gp.	6.00	6.00
Wheadon, Elmer M.	Studio City CA	Capt	USAF 18 Gp.	7.00	7.00
Whisner, William T.	Tampa FL	Capt	USAF 352 Gp.	*15.50 +5.5 Korea	15.50
White, Henry S.	Los Angeles CA	LT	USN VF11	5.00	
White, John H.	Kensett AR	1st Lt	USAF 31 Gp.	5.00	5.00
White, Robert H.	Kansas City MO	Capt	USAF 49 Gp.	9.00	9.00
White, Thomas A.	Kelso WA	2nd Lt	USAF 82 Gp.	6.00	6.00
Whittaker, Roy E.	Knoxville TN	Capt	USAF 57 Gp	7.00	7.00
Wicker, Samuel J.	Sanford NC	Maj	USAF 364 Gp.	7.00	7.00
Wilhelm, David C.	Chicago IL	Capt	USAF 31 Gp.	5.00	5.00
Wilkins, Paul H.	Billings MT	2nd Lt	USAF 14 Gp.	5.00	5.00
Wilkinson, James W.	Austin TX	Capt	USAF 78 Gp.	7.00	7.00
Williams, Bruce W.	Salem OR	LT	USN VF19	7.00	
Williams, Gerard M. H.	Berkeley Heights NJ	Lt	USMC VMF	7.00	
Williams, James M.	Austin TX	1st Lt	USAF 23 Gp.	6.00	6.00
Williams, Russel D.	Hamden CT	1st Lt	USAF 23 Gp.	5.00	5.00
Williamson, Felix D.	Cordela GA	Capt	USAF 56 Gp.	13.00	13.00
Wilson, Robert C.	Jackson WY	LT	USN VF31	6.00	
Wilson, William F.	Strong City KS	Capt	USAF 355 Gp.	5.00	5.00
Winfield, Murray	Dearborn MI	LT	USN VF	5.50	
Winks, Robert P.	Richardson TX	1st Lt	USAF 357 Gp.	5.50	5.50
Winston, Robert A.	Washington IN	LCDR	USN VF31	5.00	
Winters, Theodore Hugh Jr.	Virginia Beach VA	LT	USN VF19	8.00	
Wire, Calvin C.	Wilmar CA	1st Lt	USAF 475 Gp.	7.00	7.00
Wire, Ralph L.	Ada OK	Maj	USAF 51/49 Gp.	5.00	5.00
Wirth, John L.	Gary IN	LT	USN VF31	14.00	
Wiseman, Lee V.	Llano TX	Capt	USAF 1 Gp.	5.00	5.00
Witt, Lynn E. Jr.	Bowden GA	Capt	USAF 8 Gp.	6.00	6.00
Wolf, John T.	Garden Grove CA	LT	USN VF2	7.00	
Wolfe, Judge E.	Flint MI	Capt	USAF 318 Gp.	9.00	9.00

NAME	HOME TOWN	RANK	UNIT	CLAIMED	USAFHS 85
Wolford, John L.	Cumberland MD	1st Lt	USAF 1 Gp.	5.00	5.00
Wood, Walter A.		ENS	USN VF20	5.25	
Woods, Sidney S.	Yuma AZ	LTC	USAF49/479/4 Gp.	7.00	7.00
Woody, Robert E.	Roanoke VA	Capt	USAF 355 Gp.	7.00	7.00
Wooley, Millard Jr.	Castro Valley CA	LT	USN VF17/18	5.25	
Woolverton, Robert C.		LT	USN VF45	6.00	
Wordell, Malcolm T.	New Bedford MA	CDR	USN VF41/44	7.50	
Wrenn, George L.	Charlotte NC	LT	USN VF72	5.00	
Wright, Ellis Wm. Jr.	Mesa AZ	Capt	USAF 49 Gp.	6.00	6.00
Wright, Max J.	Chappell NE	Capt	USAF 14 Gp.	5.00	5.00
Yaeger, Robert R. Jr.	Hebbronville TX	Capt	USAF 35 Gp.	5.00	5.00
Yeager, Charles E.	Cedar Ridge CA	Capt	USAF 357 Gp.	11.50	11.50
Yeremain, Harold	Fallon NV	ENS	USN VF17	6.00	
York, Robert M.	Old Orchard Beach ME	1st Lt	USAF 359 Gp.	5.00	5.00
Yost, Donald K.	Maitland FL	LTC	USMC VMF121	8.00	
Young, Owen Dewitt	Tenafly NJ	LT	USN VF	5.00	
Yunck, Michael R.	Washington DC	Maj	USMC VMF311	5.00	
Zaeske, Earling W.	Highland Park IL	LT	USN VF2	5.50	
Zemke, Hubert	Oroville CA	Col	USAF 56/479 Gp.	17.75	17.75
Zink, John A.	Saint Mary OH	LT	USN VF11	5.00	
Zoerb, Daniel J.	Kingsport TN	Capt	USAF 52 Gp.	7.00	7.00
Zubarik, Charles J.	W. Allis WI	1st Lt	USAF 82 Gp.	6.00	6.00

ACES OF THE AMERICAN VOLUNTEER GROUP (AVG)

Neale, Robert H.	15.50
Reed, William N.	11.50
	(+6 USAF=17.50)
Hill, David L. "Tex"	11.25
	(+6 USAF=17.25)
Burgard, George T.	10.75
Jernstedt, Kenneth A.	10.50
Little, Robert L.	10.50
Newkirk, John V.	10.50
McGarry, William D.	10.25
Older, Charles H.	10.00
	(+7 USAF=17.00)
Bond, Charles R.	9.25
Smith, Robert T.	8.67
Lawler, Frank	8.50
Overend, Edmund F.	8.00
Howard, James H.	7.33
	(+6 USAF=13.33)
Bartling, William E.	7.25
Bartelt, Percy R.	7.00
Bright, John G.	7.00
Moss, Robert C.	7.00
Schiel, Frank	7.00
Rector, Edward F.	6.50
	(+3 USAF=9.50)
Rossi, John Richard	6.25
Boyington, Gregory A.	6.00
	(+22 USMC=28.00)
Haywood, Thomas C.	5.25
Petach, John E.	5.25
Prescott, Robert W.	5.25
Sandell, Robert J.	5.25
Smith, Robert H. "Snuffy"	5.25
Bishop, Lewis S.	5.20
Laughlin, C. H. "Link"	5.20
Hedman, Robert "Duke"	5.00
Raines, Robert J.	5.00
Sawyer, Charles W.	4.00
	(+1 USAF=5.00)

AMERICANS WHO BECAME ACES WHILE FLYING WITH THE RAF IN WWII

Wade, Lance C.	WgCo	33, 145 Sq.	25
Weaver, Claude III	F/O	185, 403 Sq.	13.5
Lynch, John J.	S/Ldr	71, 249 Sq.	13
Fairbanks, David C.	S/Ldr	501, 273, 3 Sq.	12.5
McColpin, Carroll W.	S/Ldr	71, 121 Sq.	8
Curry, John H	S/Ldr	601, 80 Sq.	7
Daymond, Gregory A.	S/Ldr	71 Sq.	7
Harrington, A. A.	Lt.	410 Sq.	7(night)
Jones, Ripley O.	F/Lt	126 Sq.	7
Tilley, Reade F.	F/O	121, 601, 126 Sq.	7
Peterson, Chesley G.	S/Ldr	71 Sq.	6+1USAAF
Barrick, John F.	F/Lt.	17 Sq.	5
Campbell, John A.	P/O	258 Sq.	5
Dunn, William R.	P/O	71 Sq.	5+1USAAF
Edner, Selden R.	F/Lt	121 Sq.	5
Gimbel, Edward L.	F/Lt	401, 403, 421 Sq.	5
Jasper, Clarence M.	F/Lt	418 Sq.	5
Luma, John F.	Lt.	418 Sq.	5
Mahon, Jackson B.	F/Lt	121 Sq.	5
Peck, James E.	F/Lt	126 Sq.	5+1USAAF

and one who came close but didn't quite score five:

Thorne, James N.	P/O	64,122,504,401 Sqs.	4-5/6

ACES OF THE KOREAN WAR
(All USAF except as noted)

Name		Rank	Wing	Score
Adams, Donald E.	Painted Post, New York	Maj	51	6.5
Baker, Royal N.	McKinney, Texas	Col	4	13.0
Baldwin, Robert P.	Yuma, Arizona	Col	51	5.0
Becker, Richard S.	Fleetwood, Pennsylvania	Capt	4	5.0
Bettinger, Stephen L.	Kirkland, Washington	Maj	4	5.0
Blesse, Frederick C.	Tantallon, Maryland	Maj	4	10.0
Bolt, John F. (USMC)	New Smyrna Beach, Florida	Maj	51	6.0
Bordelon, Guy P. (USN)	Virginia Beach, Virginia	CDR	VC-3	5.0
Buttelmann, Henry	Bayside, New York	1st Lt	51	7.0
Creighton, Richard D.	Houston, Texas	Maj	4	5.0
Curtin, Clyde A.	Portland, Oregon	Capt	4	5.0
Davis, George A. Jr. CMH	Lubbock, Texas	Maj	4	14.0
Fernandez, Manuel J.	Miami, Florida	Capt	4	14.5
Fischer, Harold E.	Swea City, Iowa	Capt	51	10.0
Foster, Cecil G.	San Antonio, Texas	Capt	51	9.0
Gabreski, Francis S.	Dix Hills, New York	Col	4/51	6.5
Garrison, Vermont	Mountain Home, Idaho	Lt Col	4	10.0
Gibson, Ralph D.	Tucson, Arizona	Capt	4	5.0
Hagerstrom, James P.	Waterloo, Iowa	Maj	18	8.5
Jabara, James	Wichita, Kansas	Maj	4	15.0
Johnson, James K.	Las Vegas, Nevada	Col	4	10.0
Jolley, Clifford D.		Capt	4	7.0
Jones, George L.	Vero Beach, Florida	Lt Col	4	6.5
Kasler, James H.	Momence, Illinois	1st Lt	4	6.0
Kincheloe, Iven C. Jr.	Cassopolis, Michigan	Capt	51	5.0
Latshaw, Robert T. Jr.	Amarillo, Texas	Capt	4	5.0
Lilley, Leonard W.	Alexandria, Virginia	Capt	4	7.0
Love, Robert J.	San Bernardino, California	Capt	4	6.0
Low, James F.	Altamonte Springs, Florida	1st Lt	4	9.0
Marshall, Winton W.	Honolulu, Hawaii	Maj	4	6.5
McConnell, Joseph Jr.	Apple Valley, California	Capt	51	16.0
Moore, Lonnie R.	Ft. Walton, Florida	Capt	4	10.0
Moore, Robert H.	Austin, Texas	Capt	51	5.0
Overton, Dolphin D. III	Smithfield, N.C.	Capt	51	5.0
Parr, Ralph S. Jr.	Ft. Walton, Florida	Capt	4	10.0
Risner, Robinson	Austin, Texas	Majj	4	8.0
Ruddell, George I.	Riverside, California	Lt Col	51	8.0
Thyng, Harrison R.	Pittsfield, N.H.	Col	4	5.0
Westcott, William H.	Rancho Palos Verdes, Calif.	Maj	51	5.0
Whisner, William T.	Tampa, Florida	Maj	51	5.5

TEN OR MORE VICTORIES

Name	Score
McConnell, Joseph Jr.	16.0
Jabara, James	15.0
Fernandez, Manuel J.	14.5
Davis, George A. Jr.	14.0
Baker, Royal N.	13.0
Blesse, Frederick C.	10.0
Fischer, Harold E.	10.0
Garrison, Vermont	10.0
Johnson, James K.	10.0
Moore, Lonnie R.	10.0
Parr, Ralph S. Jr.	10.0

ACES IN TWO WARS
ACES OF WORLD WAR II AND KOREA

NOTE: All officers are assigned to U. S. Air Force except as indicated.

Bolt, John F. (USMC)	6.00	6.00	12.00
Davis, George A. Jr.	7.00	14.00	21.00
Gabreski, Francis S.	28.00	6.50	34.50
Garrison, Vermont	7.33	10.00	17.33
Hagerstrom, James P.	6.00	8.50	14.50
Thyng, Harrison R.	5.00	5.00	10.00
Whisner, William T.	15.50	5.50	21.00

OTHER ACES WITH VICTORIES IN TWO WARS

NOTE: All officers are assigned to U. S. Air Force except as indicated.

Adams, Donald E.	4.00	6.50	10.50
Andre, John W. (USMC)	4.00	1.00	5.00
		(night)	
Baker, Royal N.	3.50	13.00	16.50
Bettinger, Stephen L.	1.00	5.00	6.00
Brueland, Lowell K.	12.50	2.00	14.50
Chandler, Van E.	5.00	3.00	8.00
Colman, Philip E.	5.00	4.00	9.00
Creighton, Richard D.	2.00	5.00	7.00
Delong, Philip C. (USMC)	11.17	2.00	13.17
Durnford, Dewey F. (USMC)	6.33	0.50	6.83
Eagleston, Glenn T.	18.50	2.00	20.50
Emmert, Benjamin H. Jr.	6.00	1.00	7.00
Heller, Edwin L.	5.50	3.50	9.00
Hockery, John J.	7.00	1.00	8.00
Hovde, William J.	10.50	1.00	11.50
Jabara, James	1.50	15.00	16.50
Johnson, James K.	1.00	10.00	11.00
Lamb, Wm. E. (USN)	6.00	1.00	7.00
Liles, Brooks J.	1.00	4.00	5.00
Little, James W.	7.00	1.00	8.00
Mahurin, Walker M.	20.75	3.50	24.25
Mattson, Conrad E.	1.00	4.00	5.00
Meyer, John C.	24.00	2.00	26.00
Mitchell, John W.	11.00	4.00	15.00
Olds, Robin	13.00	4.00	17.00
Price, Howard J.	4.00	2.00	6.00
Ruddell, George I.	2.50	8.00	10.50
Visscher, Herman W.	5.00	1.00	6.00
Wade, Robert (USMC)	7.00	1.00	8.00

ACES OF THE WAR IN VIETNAM

Cunningham, Randall "Duke"	Los Angeles CA	Lt	USN	5.00
Ritchie, Richard S.	Reidsville NC	Capt	USAF	5.00

NOTE: These two pilots were the only fighter pilots to score five aerial victories in the Vietnam war. Three Weapon System Officers, WSO, were credited with 5 or more "radar assists" however.

DeBellevue, Chas. B.	WSO for Ritchie and Madden	Capt	USAF	6.00
Feinstein, Jeffrey S.	WSO for Baily, Westphal and Leonard	Capt	USAF	5.00
Driscoll, W.	WSO for Cunningham	LT	USN	5.00

AMERICAN ACES WITH TWENTY OR MORE VICTORIES—ALL WARS

			WWI	*WWII*	*Korea*	*TOTAL*
Bong, Richard	Maj	USAF	-	40.00	-	40.00
McGuire, Thomas B.	Maj	USAF	-	38.00	-	38.00
Gabreski, Francis N.	Col	USAF	-	28.00	6.50	34.50
McCampbell, David	Capt	USN	-	34.00	-	34.00
Johnson, Robert S.	LtCol	USAF	-	28.00	-	28.00
Boyington, Gregory	LtCol	USMC	-	28.00	-	28.00
MacDonald, Charles H.	Col	USAF		27.00		27.00
Preddy, George E.	Maj	USAF	-	26.83	-	26.83
Foss, Joseph Jacob	Maj	USMC	-	26.00	-	26.00
Meyer, John C.	Col	USAF	-	24.00	2.00	26.00
Rickenbacker, Edward	Capt	AEF	26.00	-	-	26.00
Hanson, Robert M	1st Lt	USMC	-	25.00	-	25.00
Wade, Lance C.	Wg Co	RAF	-	25.00	-	25.00
Mahurin, Walker M.	LtCol	USAF	-	20.75	3.50	24.25
Harris, Cecil E.	Lt	USN	-	24.00	-	24.00
Rosevear, S. C.	Capt	RFC	23.00	-	-	23.00
Valencia, Eugene A.	Cdr	USN	-	23.00	-	23.00
Wetmore, Ray S.	Capt	USAF	-	22.59	-	22.59
Schilling, David C.	Col	USAF	-	22.50	-	22.50
Johnson, Gerald R.	LtCol	USAF	-	22.00	-	22.00
Kearby, Neel E.	Maj	USAF	-	22.00	-	22.00
Lambert, William C.	Capt	RFC	22.00	-	-	22.00
Robbins, Jay T.	LtCol	USAF	-	22.00	-	22.00
Christensen, Fred J.	Capt	USAF	-	21.50	-	21.50
Davis, George A. Jr.	Maj	USAF	-	7.00	14.00	21.00
Voll, John J.	Maj	USAF	-	21.00	-	21.00
Walsh, Kenneth A.	Maj	USMC	-	21.00	-	21.00
Whisner, William T.	Maj	USAF	-	15.50	5.50	21.00
Eagleston, Glenn T.	Col	USAF	-	18.50	2.00	20.50
Aldrich, Donald M.	Capt	USMC	-	20.00	-	20.00
Gillette, Frederick W.	Capt	RFC	20.00	-	-	20.00
Lynch, Thomas J.	Lt Col	USAF	-	20.00	-	20.00
Malone, John J.	Capt	R.N.*	20.00	-	-	20.00
Westbrook, Robert B.	Lt Col	USAF	-	20.00	-	20.00

*Royal Navy

THE TOP FIGHTR ACES OF OTHER NATIONS
WWI (1914-1918)

BELGIUM

Lieut. Willy Coppens de Houthulst	37
Adjutant Andre de Meulemeester	11
Lieut. Edmond Thieffry	10
Capitaine Fernand Jacquet	7
Lieut. Jan Olieslagers	6

FRANCE

Capt. Rene Paul Fonck	75
Capt. Georges Guynemer	54
Lieut. Charles Nungesser	45

Capt. Georges F. Madon	41
Lieut. Mautice Boyau	35
Lieut. Michael Coiffard	34
Lieut. Jean Pierre Bourjade	28
Capt. Armand Pinsard	27

GERMANY

Rittm. Manfred Frhr. v. Richthofen	80
1st Lt. Ernst Udet	62
1st Lt. Erich Lowenhardt	53
Lt. Werner Voss	48
Lt. Fritz Rumey	45

Capt. Rudolph Berthold	44	Lt.Col. William A. Bishop (Canada)	72
Lt. Paul Baumer	43	Lt. Col. Raymond Collishaw (Canada)	62
Lt. Josef Jacobs	41	Maj. J.T.B.McCudden(England)	57
Capt. Bruno Loerzer	41	Capt. A.W. Beauchamp-Proctor(SAAF)	54
Capt. Oswald Boelcke	40	Capt. D.R. MacLaren (Canada)	54
Lt. Franz Buchner	40	Major W.G. Barker (Canada)	53
		Capt. P.F. Fullard (England)	52
		Major R.S. Dallas (Australia)	51

ITALY

Major Francesco Baracca	34
Lt. Silvio Scaroni	26
Lt. Col. Pier Ruggiero Piccio	24
Lt. Flavio T. Baracchini	21
Capt. Fulco R. di Calabria	20

RUSSIA

Major A.A. Kazakov	17
Capt. P.V. d'Argeyev	15
Lt.Cdr. A.P. de Seversky	13
Lt. I.W. Smirnoff	12
Lt. M. Safonov	11
Capt. Boris Sergievsky	11
Ensign Eduard Thomson	11

GREAT BRITAIN
(UNITED KINGDOM)

Major E.C. Mannock (England)	73

SPANISH CIVIL WAR (1936-1939)

Nationalist Forces

		Republican Forces	
Major Joaquin Garcia Morato	40	Colonel Andres Garcia Lacalle	11
Major Julio Salvador Diaz	23	Capt. Jose Bravo Fernandez	10
Major Angel Salas Larrazabal	22	Capt. Zarauza Manuel Clavier	10
Capt. Manuel Vasquez Sagaztizobal	22	Capt. Miguel Zamudio Martinez	10

WORLD WAR II (1939-1945)

BELGIUM

Lt. Count Rodolphe de Hemricourt de Grunne	13
Major Count Ivan Du Monceau de Bergandal	8
Lt. Jean H.M. Offenberg	7

W/O Nils Katajainen	36.0
Lieut. Kauko Puro	35.0
Lieut. Lauri Nissinen	32.5
Major Jorma Karhunen	31.0

CZECHOSLAVAKIA

Sgt. Joseph Frantisek	28
Lt. Karel Kuttelwascher	18
Capt. Alois Vasatko	12.33
Lt. Francois de Perina	11
Lt. Rotnik Rezny	32

FRANCE

Capt. Marcel Albert (Russia)	23
Wingco. Jean Demozay (RAF)	21
Lieut. Pierre LeGloan	18
Major Edmond Marin la Meslee	16

CHINA

Note: Names marked * show scores which include victories gained during the Chinese-Japanese War between 1937 and 1941

Col. Liu Chi-Sun*	11.50
Lt. Wang Kuang-Fu	8.50
Major Kao Yu-Hsin	8.00
Major Kuan Tan	8.00
Capt. Yuan Pao-Kang*	8.00
Lt.Col. Chow Che-Kai	6.00
Lt. Chow Ting-Fong	6.00
Lt. Chen Chi-Wei*	5.00
Capt. Tsang	5.00

GERMANY

Major Erich Hartmann	352
Major Gerhard Barkhorn	301
Major Gunther Rall	275
1st Lt. Otto Kittel	267
Major Walter Nowotny	258
Major Wilhelm Batz	237
Major Erich Rudorffer	222
Lt. Col. Heinz Bar	220
Col. Herrmann Graf	220
Major Heinrich Ehrler	209
Major Theodor Weissenberger	208
Lt. Col. Hans Philipp	206
1st Lt. Walter Schuck	206
1st Lt. Anton Hafner	204
Capt. Helmut Lipfert	203
Major Walter Krupinski	197
Major Anton Hackl	192
Capt. Joachim Brendel	189
Capt. Max Stotz	189
Capt. Joachim Kirschner	188
Major Kurt Brandle	180
Lt. Gunther Josten	178

FINLAND

W/O Eino Ilmari Juutilainen	94.0
Capt. Hans Wind	78.0
Major Eino Luukkanen	54.0
W/O Urho Lehtovaara	44.0
Capt. Risto Olli Puhakka	43.0
W/O Oiva Tuominen	43.0

Col. Johannes Steinhoff 176

Note: 106 Luftwaffe pilots are credited with 100 or more aerial victories. 24 Night-fighter pilots are credited with 50 or more night victories. 22 Luftwaffe pilots have 5 or more victories while flying jet or rocket-propelled fighters.

GREAT BRITAIN (UNITED KINGDOM

Pattle, Marmaduke T. St. J. (So. Africa)	41.00
Johnson, James E. (British)	38.00
Malan, Adolf G. (So. Africa)	35.00
Clostermann, Pierre H. (France)	33.00
Finucane, Brendan (Ireland)	32.00
Beurling, George F. (Canada)	31.33
Braham, John R. D. (British)	29.00
Tuck, Robert R. S. (British)	29.00
Duke, Neville F. (British)	28.83
Caldwell, Clive R. (Australian)	28.50
Carey, Frank R. (British)	28.33
Lacey, James H. (British)	28.00
Gray, Colin F. (New Zealand)	27.50
Lock, Eric S. (British)	26.00
Wade, Lance C. (American)	25.00

HUNGARY

Lieut. Dezso Szentgyorgyi	34
Capt. Gyorgy Dbbrody	26
Lieut. Laszlo Molnar	25
Lieut. Lajos Toth	24

JAPAN

Note: JNAF = Japanese Navy Air Force.
JAAF = Japanese Army Air Force.
* = some or perhaps all victories were scored in the war over China and Manchuria in 1938, 1939 time period.

W/O Hiroyoshi Nishizawa JNAF	87 to 174
Lt. Tetsuzo Iwamoto JNAF*	80 to 182
P/O Shoichi Sugita JNAF	70 to 140
Lt. Saburo Sakai JNAF*	32 to 64
W/O Hiromichi Shinohara JAAF*	58
P/O Takeo Okumura JNAF*	54 to 98
M/Sgt Satoshi Anabuki JAAF	51 to 96
Lt. Mitsuyoshi Tarui JAAF*	38 to 76
W/O Isamu Sasaki JAAF	38 to 75
P/O Toshio Ohta JNAF	34 to 68
W/O Kazuo Sugino JNAF	32 to 64
Major Yasuhiko Kuroe JAAF*	30 to 60

Author's note:
There is a wide disparity in the scores of the Japanese aces because records have been unavailable. However, the higher scores are based upon claims made by the pilots and reports made by fellow pilots, whereas the lower scores are arbitrarily arrived at by current historians who have taken the claims, divided them by two and used that figure as a base point for future studies as heretofore hidden historical records become available.

NORWAY

Capt. Svein Heglund	14.50
Lt. Col. Werner Christie	11.00
Capt. Helmer G. Grundt-Spang	10.33
Major Martin Y. Gran	9.50
Capt. Marius Eriksen	9.00

POLAND

S/Ldr/Maj. B. Michael Gladych	22.00
	(10 with USAF)
Wingco Stanislav F. Skalski	21.00
Wingco Witold Urbanowisz	20.00
S/Ldr Eugeniusz Horbaczewski	16.50
Wingco Marion Pisarek	12.50
S/Ldr Jan E. L. Zumbach	12.33
S/Ldr Anthoni Glowacki	11.33
P/O Michael K. Maciejowski	10.50
Wingco Henryk Szczesny	10.33

RUMANIA

Capt. Prince Constantine Cantacuzene	60
Capt. Alexandre Serbanescu	50
Lieut. Florian Budu	42
Lieut. Jon Milu	18

RUSSIA—USSR

Major Ivan Nikitich Kozhedub	62
GrdsCol Aleksandr Ivanovich Pokryshkin	59
GrdsCpt Dimitriy Borisovich Glinka	56
GrdsCpt Nikolai Gulayev	56
GrdsCpt Grigoriy Andrianovich Rechkalov	53
Capt. Kirill A. Yevstigneyev	52
Lt. Arsenii V. Vorozheikin	52
GrdsCpt Alekandri F. Klubov	50
Lt. Ivan M. Pilipenko	48
Lt. Vasili N. Kubarev	46
Capt. Nikolai M. Skomorokhov	46
Lt. Vladimir Bobrov (incl. 13 in Spain)	43
Capt. Pavel N. Kamozhin	46
Lt. Alexandri I. Koldunov	46
GrdsMaj Vitaliy Ivanovich Popkov	40
Capt. Kostilev	40
Capt. Lapanskii	40

Author's note:
It has been impossible to confirm exact scores of Soviet pilots due to the policies of the political regime of the USSR. This list is, therefor, made up from the best sources available which include, among many others: The Institute for the Study of the USSR in Munchen, Germany; eminent historians and authors including Christopher Shores, Hans Otto Boehm, Hans Ring, Henry Sakaida, and many otjers. It is understood that some Soviet fighter pilots with substantial scores became political "untouchables" after the war and therefor had their names removed from the documents that have found their way into Western civilization.

YUGOSLAVIA

Note: All listed except Petrovic are Croats, an ethnic group of Yugoslavs.

Lt. Cvitan Galic	36
1st Lt. Mato Dubovac	34
1st Lt. Jan Gerthofer	33
Sgt. Isidor Kovaric	28
Sgt. Jan Reznak	26
1st Lt. Mato Culinovic	18
Lt. Dragutin Ivanic	18
Lt. Bosko Petrovic (Jugoslav, Spanish War)	7

INDEX

W

Y

Z